MIND
THROUGH THE AGES

THE BIRTH OF INTELLIGENT CO-OPERATION

Almost certainly man's most remote prehuman ancestors practiced herd co-operation, just as many animals do—but exchange of intelligent ideas had to await the invention of language. Probably the two achievements—ideas and language—grew up together by firesides of an evening, as men prepared for the morrow and learned to exchange ideas while practicing their arts.

MIND
THROUGH THE AGES

A HISTORY OF HUMAN INTELLIGENCE

By Martin Stevers

ILLUSTRATED WITH LINE DRAWINGS
BY HAL AND JEAN ARBO AND THE AUTHOR

Doubleday, Doran & Company, Inc.
GARDEN CITY 1941 NEW YORK

PRINTED AT THE *Country Life Press*, GARDEN CITY, N. Y., U. S. A.

The Author's Reason for Writing This Book

As THE FIRST CHAPTER SUGGESTS, the primary reason for writing this book was a belief that today science offers all of us a new and immensely illuminating understanding of human nature. Since I realize full well that to those who know the work of recent decades in this field the claim of novelty at this time may seem strange or even naïve, I beg leave here to explain the basis for my belief.

Let me say at once that to me the heart of our new light upon man lies, not so much in new *facts,* as in new *understandability*. Our understandings of man seem to me to be about where the physical sciences stood during the opening decades of this century. Also I believe I have had benefit of experience with understandability in each field when I say this.

In physics I had the privilege, some thirty years ago, of a year's training with Robert Andrews Millikan at the University of Chicago. No one who has studied with this truly great *teacher* (as well as scientist) need be told how he could impart crystal-clear understandings of baffling subjects almost without effort. My experience, however, was particularly memorable because no year could have been more propitious for exercise of this inestimable gift.

At that time the so-called "new physics" was being born out of discoveries concerning X rays, radioactivity, Einstein's new ideas about measuring time and Max Planck's upsetting quantum concepts of black-body radiation. All these matters, however, were in the higher flights of professional pondering; they lacked the "down-to-earth" underpinning of basic theory which everyone could understand. Now in that year Dr Millikan was making his notable contribution toward such an underpinning with his Nobel-prize feat of measuring the

v

electronic charge. Needless to say, we badgered him mercilessly for information about his work; and never could anyone have been more generous with mere fledglings. In many a demonstration and informal talk he opened up all the new intellectual possibilities then in the making and science's hopes for replacing baffling mystery with clean-cut understanding.

Today these hopes have been more than fulfilled. The possibilities which Dr Millikan envisaged for us then have become the very foundations of instruction. They are the stock in trade of all popular explanations of radio, atom smashing, artificial radioactivity and such seemingly weird concepts as the exploding universe.

Meanwhile, during these thirty years of change in the physical sciences, my lot has fallen largely in dealing with "understandability" concerning mankind itself. For much of this time I have been writing and editing juvenile encyclopedic material to serve the modern educational policy of placing social understandings first in training the next generation. Now this work, strange as the fact may seem to some who have not grappled with this specific task, calls above all else for exactly the sort of fundamental clarity which has come into the physical sciences.

The young mind does not care for abstractions, generalities and refinements of terminology. It wants to know above all else, "how it works," "why it happens this way." Unfortunately, this was just the sort of demand which could not be met for many a year concerning many of the most important fundamentals.

Inquiries about why men get angry could be met with the pros and cons of the James-Lange theory of emotions—a thorny and debatable abstraction, full of gaps in its portrayal of the mechanisms involved. Why did the Greeks fail in the end after their brilliant beginning? This was hard to answer when history itself was more than half at sea on this question. Hence a large part of the task in devising material for this field has consisted of constant watch for new developments in knowledge, both to keep all background material correct, even if the new knowledge itself was not presented, and to seize every chance for offering satisfying answers in place of glossing over or even evading questions.

Today, happily, the worst of these gaps seem closed well enough to permit at least outlining man's nature in plain terms of "how it works." Mendel's laws are no longer a statistical summation of un-explained results; we can say, just as we can tell why a watch ticks, how heredity works. Psychoanalysis no longer rests upon little better than thin air in physiological theory, with its only justification in principle being results achieved, nobody knew exactly how. Today its subject matter and workings are rapidly becoming as understandable as the etiology and treatment of pneumonia or toothache. So it is with many another former gap—and so the time seems ripe for trying to draw together all this new knowledge into a "down-to-earth" understanding of man.

How well- or ill-advised the attempt and the execution may have been, the text itself must say. Here I would like only to add explanations of a few choices I made in trying to accomplish this purpose. First among these is the matter of completeness.

Obviously no single volume could do more than scratch the surface in even one division of all that enters into a rounded understanding of man. Completeness, or even adequate recognition of all important highlights, would be an impossible ideal. I could at best try to select illuminating facets of the subject and hope that they would suggest a reasonably satisfying outline of the story.

I must enter a similar plea of "confession and avoidance," as the lawyer says, in the matters of sources and authority. This book, after all, is not a treatise intended for scholarly consideration; it is simply an attempt to place before the general reader a simple reflection of the new understandings now available. I have felt free, therefore, to suggest authorities on a basis, most of all, of readability, and to omit even mention of first-rank original sources when they seemed to me either abstruse or not readily available in even a fairly stocked library.

In closing I would like to express my appreciation, first of all, to my long-time friend Burton Rascoe for his share in encouraging me to undertake the task. I owe appreciation also to my publishers for sympathetic understanding of the many difficulties involved and the time required, as well as for most cordial willingness to give everything possible to presentation of the subject within the necessary limitations of a single volume addressed to the general reader.

MARTIN D. STEVERS.

August 5, 1940.

Contents

Part I BEGINNINGS

    I Our New Hope for Understanding Man 3
   II The Nature of Intelligence 10
  III How Life Originated and Evolved 17
  IV The Physical Relations between Brain and Thought 29
    V The Birth of the Manlike Mind 41

Part II THE MAKING OF TRUE MAN

  VI Meet "the First Man"! 59
 VII The Conquest of Nature Begins 67
VIII The Nature of Early Thought 80
  IX Man's First Failure in Europe 88

Part III THE DAWN OF CIVILIZED LIVING

    X The Cradles of Civilization 105
  XI Sumerian Contributions to Civilization 117
 XII The Controlling Force of Ideas 129
XIII History Begins in Egypt 137
XIV 3000 B.C.—A Milestone Date in Man's Career . . . 148
 XV The Nomad Energizers of Early Ancient Life . . 161

Part IV ANCIENT HISTORY—
The Warrior-Religious States

  XVI Slaves, Kings and Priests in Sumer 171
 XVII The Indestructible Culture of Egypt 179
XVIII Preparations for a New Day in Thought . . . 192
 XIX First Stirrings of New Viewpoints 202

Part V ANCIENT HISTORY—
The Greco-Roman Climax

XX The Dawn of Free Thought among the Greeks . . 215
XXI Beginnings of Philosophy and of Democracy . . . 225
XXII Greek Thought Comes to Flower in Athens . . . 235
XXIII Athenian Philosophy and the Alexandrine Age . . 248
XXIV Rome Rises to World Mastery 270
XXV The Collapse of Rome and of Ancient Life . . . 285

Part VI MEDIEVAL HISTORY—
The Forerunner of Modern Life

XXVI The Dawn of the Middle Ages 303
XXVII The First Shaping of Medieval Life 314
XXVIII The Crusades Transform Europe 330
XXIX Beginnings of the Struggle for Free Thought . . . 346
XXX The Medieval Climax 357
XXXI The Medieval Dissolves into the Modern . . . 368

Part VII MODERN HISTORY
The Rule of Reason

XXXII First Fruits of the Modern Period 385
XXXIII Freedom of Thought Hits Its Stride 399
XXXIV Commerce and the Common Man 418
XXXV Mental and Political Revolutions in the Eighteenth
Century 429
XXXVI The Mechanistic Spirit of the Nineteenth Century 4 2
XXXVII The Twentieth Century and Its Outlook . . . 456
Appendix A
Current Theories Concerning Modern Human Races . . 468
Appendix B
Fixing Time (Chronology) for Prehistory and for Ancient
Times 477
Appendix C
Development and Spread of the Alphabet 487
Appendix D
The Prehistoric Settlement of Europe in Neolithic Times . 493
Index 497

Illustrations

The Birth of Intelligent Co-Operation . . . . . *Frontispiece*

FACING PAGE

A Baby's Disjointed Idea of Its World 13
Mendel's Laws and the Gene Theory 20
Nervous Action and Nervous Systems 31
Milestones in Brain Development 34
The First Rise Above Ape Mentality 45
How a Growing Brain Changed the Head 50
How Ice Age Glaciation Changed the World's Climate . . 75
How Stone Tools Reveal Growing Mental Power . . . 78
How the Fourth Ice Age Gripped Europe 93
Art Among the Ice Age Cave Men 96
Cradles of Civilization 106
Glimpses of Life in Busy Sumer 127
Modern and Ancient Ideas of the Heavens 154
Patient Toil in Ancient Egypt 180
The First Clue to the Original Alphabet 187
How Greek Astronomers Probed the Heavens 223
Was the Sun or the Earth the Center of the Universe? . . 256
The Puzzling Motions of the Planets 258
The Wonder City of the Hellenistic World 265
Slot Machines and Steam Engines in Alexandria 266

                                                    FACING PAGE

"The Nerves of Rome"—Fast Travel on Superb Roads .   .   . 281

At Sea with "The Terrors of the North" 320

The Topmost Experiment in Dark Age Education   .   .   . 325

The Problem of Circumnavigating Africa   362

Astronomers and the Longitude Problem   398

A Mathematical Key to Modern Science 409

Simpson's Four Bottles for Explaining the Ice Age 476

The End of the Ice Age in Scandinavia   479

Development of the Alphabet   489

PART I
BEGINNINGS

CHAPTER I

Our New Hope for Understanding Man

WHEN ADVERSITY or calamity strike, men are willing to think as at no other time and to ask themselves, "Why must this be? Cannot something be done to spare us this affliction?" So it was, certainly, when the calamity of widespread war struck the world on September 1, 1939, only some twenty years after mankind had been scourged by the struggle of 1914–18. So it was at an earlier date, when the economic catastrophe of the early 1930s swept through every civilized land—and so it will be for years to come, as men struggle to repair the ravages of the latest conflict.

Pessimists may point also to the folly of 1939, coming while the crippled and the bereaved of 1919 still lived to testify to the waste of war, and ask what the race really learned from the earlier affliction. For once, however, the pessimist is wrong. We have follies and woes enough oppressing us, it is true; but we also have something else, something which no generation before us has possessed in like measure. We have, for the first time in the history of thought, the true key to better ways to use if we will. We have the remedy for the greatest handicap among all the drags which have worked throughout the ages to stultify man's struggle for better ways.

This handicap is not hard to identify. We can name it readily as an inveterate tendency in handling social ills to deal feebly with symptoms, instead of grappling boldly with causes. Century after century men have been plagued with wars, and they have looked to peace treaties for an end to their trials. Almost never have they sought to cut at the root of war itself. They have revolted against oppressive rulers, laws and governments—and rarely have their remedies gone

3

beyond a new ruler, a change in some details of the laws and perhaps changes in some detailed workings of government. History offers not a baker's dozen of earnest, well-conceived attempts to adjust our government and social ways to those deep-running forces in human nature which in the end override all opposing practices.

Behind all this pettiness of remedies stands, of course, a most ample reason. Before men could rise above details to grappling with fundamentals they had to *understand* the fundamentals, and in all problems of human conduct the most important fundamental has been man himself and the reactions of human nature to life's problems. Always man's greatest need has been to *know himself,* to understand his own conduct—and through all ages man has found himself to be an utterly baffling mystery.

The barest mention of mysteries in connection with man will show how little most of us know what we really are and why we act as we do. For one illuminating example we need only consider the mystery of our nature as thinking beings.

At the very core of man's being lie those distinctive attributes, man's intelligence and what many believe to be his soul. These attributes set man off from everything else in the universe—yet, try as man will, he can neither understand nor explain these attributes as he can explain a rainbow, the steam engine or the workings of modern medicine and surgery upon the body.

Almost equal mystery enshrouds many aspects of man's *social* being, his ways of trying to live on satisfactory terms with others of his own kind.

In his studies of Nature man can say why a hungry animal does one thing while a satisfied animal does another. Fires burn, crops grow and machines work just as expected, once the controlling laws have been discovered and applied correctly. But where are law and reason to be found in human conduct, when the very same situation prompts some men to respond like saints while others prove to be sinners? What understandings and rules can explain why some men, even though under no pressure of need, insist upon grabbing like so many hungry wolves while others respond to even dire need with unselfish nobility? Such questions need answers if man is to understand himself aright, and yet as late as the dawn of the twentieth century ability to answer was pitifully low. The state of our ignorance at the time was described almost bitterly in 1891 by William James.

James was world famous then for his contributions to psychology, the science which is supposed to explain the workings of man's mind.

He was appraising all that had been accomplished in this science, down to that time—and his opinion was bleak enough:

A string of raw facts; . . . a little classification and generalization on the mere descriptive level; . . . but not a single law in the sense in which physics shows us laws, not a single proposition from which consequences can causally be deduced. . . . This is no science, it is only the hope of a science. (Quoted from the last chapter of *Psychology: Briefer Course*.)

These words were written in 1891, but they could have been written almost as fairly in 1921 about any science concerned with the mental and social nature of man. But then a turn came and the dawn of a new light appeared—a new light which now shines more brightly than ever before. Man need only see it and follow it to find the true remedies for his age-old political and social ills.

This new light came into being, as do most great truths, out of approaches from many angles.

One angle was through the physical nature of man. Up to that time biologists and physiologists had earmarked many a question about physical life as likely to remain unanswered forever. Among these seemingly unsolvable mysteries were the problems of how life came to be upon the earth, why different species appeared and how heredity works to develop single fertilized cells into living beings as diverse as a mouse and a whale, a primrose and an oak.

At about this time, however, these stubborn problems began to yield up their secrets. Progress grew apace, and today the outlook stands transformed. An example of the new prospects is afforded by the attitudes revealed at a symposium on heredity held by the British Association for the Advancement of Science in 1938. The weekly journal *Nature* of September 17, 1938, commented as follows:

The discussion . . . marks the end of that long period during which biologists in general had lost interest in the subject, because it seemed incapable of investigation by quantitative or experimental methods. . . . Recent developments . . . have made it possible to discuss the whole subject anew and even to design experiments intended to solve problems now for the first time capable of being posed in definite terms.

Knowledge of how man came to be—and particularly white man—likewise became reasonably clear. One slight example of the new confidence which fills workers in this field of knowledge is a statement made to the Royal College of Surgeons on February 14, 1938, by Sir Arthur Keith, dean of British anthropological anatomists. He had this to say about certain key discoveries which had been made at Mount Carmel in Palestine:

The early Palestinians are of profound interest, because, if not our actual ancestors, they are certainly near akin to the human stock which . . . gave the world its Caucasian or white inhabitants. . . . Everyone is familiar with the place held by Palestine in our conception of human life at the dawn of history; the excavations made at Mount Carmel by Miss Garrod are destined to give that small country . . . an equally important place in our picture of man's prehistoric world.

In the field of prehistory the thin guesses of the early 1920s as to when, where, how and why civilization originated have been replaced by a reasonably complete understanding. The understanding includes a fair idea of when and how Noah's flood occurred and it adds a reasonable dating for the Tower of Babel. Thereafter the brilliant start and the later stagnation of Egyptian civilization stand explained, as do the later rise and fall of both Greece and Rome.

In psychology the new understandings are all but revolutionary—so much so that psychologists can look back, almost as they would upon the efforts of children, toward the stumbling block which had wrecked all earlier attempts to understand human nature. The nature of the mistake is set forth clearly enough in Professor Ross Stagner's *Psychology of Personality* (1937). Professor Stagner starts his statement with a quotation from Roman wisdom:

"Wipe out imagination: check desire: extinguish appetite: keep the ruling faculty in its own power," wrote the Roman sage, Marcus Aurelius. Thus do we find in epigram a maxim which has guided psychology for over 1600 years. . . .
Long after the intellectual Renaissance, philosophers still believed that the proper study of psychology was the rational life of man. To the modern psychologist this attitude seems rather like . . . "wishful thinking"; because [the philosophers] *wanted* to consider man a rational animal, they neglected consideration of his irrational, appetitive side.

And there, in this question of whether man is essentially an intelligent creature, is where biology, prehistory, history, psychology and sociology have flowed together and given us a bright new light upon human nature. They have shown us where our trouble has been all the time. It has lain exactly where Professor Stagner says, in our self-flattering assumption that we live by the light of reason and intelligence, whereas the truth is almost exactly the other way around.
Far from being in control, intelligence never has been more than a

frail bark afloat upon a sea of brute nature. It could function, and even win advances, when the sea remained calm; but always the sea and its storms have shaped man's career much more than did his intelligence. This is the real truth about man and the true road to an understanding of man's nature.

On its face this viewpoint may seem nothing more than the age-old reproach which preachers and philosophers have always hurled at sinful man. But actually the old reproach and our new knowledge are as far apart as are night and day.

The older preachments rested upon appeal to ethics, divine authority and hope of reward or punishment hereafter. They did untold good, but they have always been subject to one glaring weakness. They were most effective with the good, the sensitive and the idealistic among mankind—the very ones who need no setting aright.

In the summer of 1939 most nations and most peoples needed no persuasion about the folly of war. The person who needed persuading was Adolf Hitler. The law-abiding citizen needs no restraint by criminal statutes and police; the problem is how to control the thief and the murderer. And here, in this problem of controlling the brutal and the lawless among mankind, is where the older system of social controls has scored mankind's most lamentable failure.

For a measure of this failure, we need only remember that men have been struggling with this problem for perhaps ten thousand centuries since thought began and for some fifty centuries since civilized living began.

Now remember that not five centuries have run since Columbus discovered America; not two centuries have passed since Watt invented the first practical steam engine; and we are not yet through the first century of our ability to interchange mechanical and electrical power. Yet can anyone claim for a moment that our present methods of shaping and controlling the conduct of man even deserve mention, in comparison with our ability to control electricity and to match the birds by traveling through the air?

The questions answer themselves. We need no further test of how we have fallen short in mastering our most important task. But this failure only emphasizes the importance of understanding our new light upon the nature of man. It offers us the same sort of insight upon the problem which Columbus and others gave to geography in their time. It can accomplish for man's social problems the kind of advance which Watt, Fulton and Stephenson gave to manufacturing and transportation and the Wrights gave to aviation. And it can do this by showing us exactly where our trouble has lain and what to do about it.

We realize now that through all the ages of man's struggle to master Nature, Nature was countering by confronting man with the problem of mastering himself; and in proportion as man's troubles with physical Nature became less, his troubles with human nature became more vexing and complex. He learned to his sorrow that by winning freedom to do as he liked he had won opportunity *to go wrong* as well as to be right. Every new power he won could be used for ill as well as for good—and all too often, in making his choice, man listened to the wrong adviser.

He thought always that he was heeding the promptings of intelligence. Actually, all too often he was obeying promptings from the brute, and he was utterly unable to discriminate accurately between these advisers because he did not even realize that the brute still lived in his intelligence, with ample power to color and even control his decisions. He was dealing with an enemy, but he did not even know what the enemy was. The situation was foursquare with man's tragically futile attempts to suppress yellow fever in the days before the mosquito's share in spreading the disease was understood.

Now, in contrast, we know what our difficulty has been. Just as knowledge of the mosquito's responsibility for spreading yellow fever enabled Gorgas and Goethals to change Panama from the world's prize pesthole to a veritable health resort and drive through the Panama Canal in scarcely more than ten years, so are we equipped to deal intelligently with the fundamentals of human nature. We can attack with clear understanding the forces which produce depressions, political maladministrations, Hitlers, Mussolinis, the futilities and the fumblings of the world's Chamberlains and kindred ills. In short, we can do for society what Galileo, Newton, Kepler, Pasteur and their kind did for science, or what eighteenth- and nineteenth-century inventors did for industry. We can, if we like, build a really workable social and political world.

Naturally such a statement requires backing up before it can command attention from thoughtful men; it gains life and force only as the evidence which supports it is set forth. Hence the evidence should be paraded forthwith—and the parading of it leads us over a long road.

First must come the foundation of our new understanding, the linkage between the brute and the power of reasoning in the mind of man. This requires examining intelligence itself, sufficiently to set it apart from all other mental attributes and powers. Then comes the story of how this power struggled into being out of brute mentality, and also how the age-old animal heritage clings to this power and drags upon it. Next this interrelation needs tracing through the ages, to provide profitable examples of how it has betrayed man's efforts to improve his lot. Lastly will come the bearing of all this upon modern life and the question of what can best be done to curb the brute and to use intelligence most fruitfully.

Such a road obviously is long, but a long road merely calls for an early start. Shall we start, then—beginning with the heart and core of the entire story, the attribute of intelligence which led Linnaeus some two centuries ago to use the term *sapiens,* meaning "knowing," in his scientific name *Homo sapiens* for man?

CHAPTER II

The Nature of Intelligence

To see why man should be called *sapiens,* or "knowing," we cannot do better than follow the procedure used by Charles Spearman, professor emeritus of psychology at the University of London, in his penetrating survey, *Psychology Down the Ages* (1937). His approach is the eminently sensible one of tracing intelligence upward from its dawning as seen today in babies.

Unfortunately for nonprofessional readers, Spearman's treatment of this problem is highly technical—but it can be restated simply by drawing upon medical knowledge for a necessary clue.

According to medical experience the mind works upon various levels of efficiency, from the primitive to the most highly sophisticated. Anesthetic drugs paralyze these levels progressively from top to bottom; ether or chloroform can blot out even sheer animal sensitivity to pain. This obviously takes the mind as close as it can come to death's door without passing through, and the dawn of consciousness after such an experience, as reported by many a scientific-minded patient, should yield a close parallel to how intelligence dawned originally in the minds of the earth's first thinkers.

The first awareness is a bare realization of being alive. Physical surroundings are not perceived; the patient floats in a void, which may stand still or may sway sickeningly. Then the nose reports that this void is permeated with a faint "hospital smell." The skin reports contact with cool, starched sheets and a stiffly level, firm bed. These impressions come and go; patients say that one instant they are in bed, next instant they are disembodied again and floating in space.

An experience which often comes next is hearing spirit voices speaking perhaps fifty miles away, but during the span of a sentence they come hurtling through space, like a talking express train. Then

10

the patient recognizes the speakers as doctors, internes and nurses. A cautious peep from one eye may disclose a nose, a chin or some portion of a garment, seemingly floating in space without attachment to a body. Patients may recognize one of these detached features and murmur a greeting, but the effort often sets the whole world swaying, like tree limbs in a gale, and the patient gladly sinks as deeply into sleep as his condition permits.

Now this experience shows clearly enough how intelligence dawned in the world long ages ago and how it dawns in the minds of babies today.

The experience starts with coming awake, or realization of being alive. How and why human beings have the ability to do this is one of the most profound mysteries in all Nature, but this mystery need not detain us now. Our interest is in what this self-awareness or self-consciousness *does,* after it comes awake, to conduct thought.

Obviously the mind thinks by organizing its material—sense impressions from without and ideas from within—into *patterns of understanding.* We form such a pattern when we combine the sight of a black flapping object in the air with the sound of a "caw" and decide, "There goes a crow!"

Normally we do not notice this putting together; we heed only the end product, such as our decision about the crow. But recovery from anesthesia reveals the process, because the ability to think comes back in fragments rather than as a smoothly working whole. Patients hear a voice before they can judge its location and distance; they glimpse a nose or an eye but do not shift the glance to other features and so see the entire person. Only after the effects of the anesthetic have cleared away more completely do impressions click together into complete understandings.

Just so, according to Spearman, did intelligence first come into the minds of men—and just so does it come awake in every baby's mind. Spearman states this theory formally in three *laws of neogenesis:*

1. A person tends to know himself and items of his own experience.
2. On the presentation of two items, a person tends to know relations between them.
3. On the presentation of an item, together with a relation, a person tends to conceive the correlative item.

The first law covers the self-awareness and the perception of scattered impressions which come in the first stages of recovery from anesthesia. The second law covers simple judgments, such as the one about the crow. The third law states the heart of all higher thinking, of the sort which we call intelligent.

Fine examples of this thinking appear in a source which Spearman used, Millicent Shinn's *Biography of a Baby* (1900). Although out of date in theory, this work gives the *facts* of infant thinking as well as any modern psychologist could, and the writing is as charming and clear as the usual psychological text is obscure and technical.

The subject of the book is the baby daughter of Miss Shinn's sister, during the infant's first year of life.

The author observed that the baby was aware of light but seemed to pay no attention to the blurs of darkness that moved through it; that she felt motions and the actions of her own muscles and seemed to react to shocks of sound; she seemed to feel touches on her body but without any sense of the place of the touch.

The baby also seemed to have no ego, or self-consciousness, for the first few months. This endowment seemingly had to wait until after the eyes, ears and other sense organs had become functional and some degree of muscular co-ordination had been acquired. Then ego seemed to dawn, and promptly the baby embarked upon incessant attempts to become acquainted with itself and its little world.

Its stand-by for doing this was testing everything possible with its mouth. The resulting actions suggest strongly that it built up understandings, just as we have said, by putting scattered impressions together into larger understandings.

As one instance, the young experimenter had no idea at first that her fingers were attached to her arms. Often while sucking a thumb she flourished the arm, and she was amazed to have this action whisk away the tasty thumb. Bumps on the back of her head astonished her; apparently she had not realized that anything existed "in back" to be bumped.

A final instance of noticing scattered impressions and organizing them into patterns was Miss Shinn's report that the first person who won recognition as an individual was grandfather. Apparently he was put together in the baby's mind from scattered impressions of gleaming eyeglasses, a shiny bald pate, a playful manner and a formidable but highly clutchable beard.

In themselves such perceptions do not set man apart from the brutes. A dog knows its master; a hawk can perceive shape, movement and location. The distinctly human quality in thought enters when the thinker begins to perceive *relations* that underlie and ex-

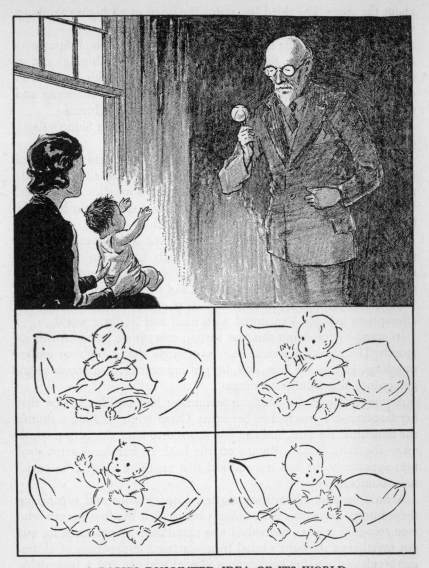

A BABY'S DISJOINTED IDEA OF ITS WORLD

These pictures suggest how a baby's first disjointed impressions gradually became organized into patterns that have meaning. At the top, as explained in the text, the baby is learning that glittering eyeglasses, a shiny bald head and a beard mean "grandfather." Below, by flourishing its arm while sucking a thumb, the baby learns that the thumb is attached to the arm.

plain separate impressions. Revealing examples of how this is done can be found in modern studies made of chimpanzees, by Wolfgang Köhler in Germany and by Professor R. M. Yerkes of Yale. A typical experiment, summarized from Yerkes's book *Almost Human* (1926), runs thus:

A banana was hung in the ape's cage out of reach by climbing, and boxes were placed in the cage. At first the chimpanzee tried leaping, then striking with a box. No use; the banana could not be reached thus. At last the chimpanzee seemed to realize the uselessness of these direct methods, and apparently it "took time out" to look the situation over. Then it piled box upon box, mounted the improvised platform and seized the banana!

Now—what must have happened in the chimpanzee's mind to bring this about?

Obviously a considerable degree of constructive imagination had been used. The chimpanzee saw the banana out of reach and the boxes lying helter-skelter. It saw also how the boxes when rearranged would bridge the gap between itself and the banana.

Thus the chimpanzee seems able to think in terms of a simple pattern, the pattern of arrangement in *space,* of seeing one thing here and another there. Moreover, it can rearrange the pattern of things-as-they-are to a mental image of things-as-they-should-be. Similarly, human youngsters develop ability to use the same pattern when only a few months old. We can see babies of this age eying everything and learning locations and distances in their little worlds.

Chimpanzee and baby thinking also match each other in possessing the next higher pattern in order of complexity—arrangement in *time*. This pattern amounts to keeping a sequence of events in mind, as happening one after another; and it is the root of memory. A chimpanzee undoubtedly has ability to remember. If it has used a stick to poke at something, then laid the stick away, it may fetch the stick next day if a need for poking arises.

But here is also the place at which man rises definitely above the chimpanzee level. The example given of chimpanzee memory seems to be the summit of the ape's mental powers. It never remembers ideas of any complexity whatever. Also chimpanzees never pass on what they learn to their children and thereby help the youngsters get along more easily in life. When we see remembering, applying and teaching, human mentality is at work—and well-developed memory is only one of man's three higher patterns of understanding.

The next higher one is the pattern of *causality,* the realization that one phenomenon happens or exists because something else has happened or existed. Apparently this realization dawns in a baby's mind when it changes the character of its play.

At first play consists merely of throwing objects about, apparently from sheer delight in having the ability to throw. This urge to throw applies to father's watch, if the baby can get hold of it. Sooner or later, however, the baby perceives something more important about a watch. It comes to realize, after much listening to a watch held to the ear, that this shiny thing is the *source* of the fascinating "tick tick" sound.

Once the baby realizes this it has grasped the idea of *causality,* the understanding that certain phenomena are linked together as cause and effect. This understanding is the indispensable foundation for all constructive planning above the rudest rearrangements such as a chimpanzee can accomplish. It is the mainspring of *invention,* of toolmaking and of the manipulations which man applies to material objects and natural forces to improve upon raw Nature.

The capstone of human ability to form and apply patterns of understanding is the ability to conceive *abstract principle.* This ability can be explained by comparing the average man's reactions to a symphony concert with those of a trained musician.

The average man can enjoy the march of lilting melody, sonorous tone and the play of "voices" among the instruments—but there his understanding stops. He "hears with the ear," so to speak. The musician does this too, but he does not stop with this. While he is "hearing with his ears," in his mind he traces the march of musical keys, changes in musical time, the play of counterpoint and the harmonic texture of the music. He can draw out, or *abstract,* an array of *principles* which give organization and structure to the composition.

This ability to conceive abstract principle is the root of all the highest types of thinking done by man. Within this process lies the power to produce the philosophical subtleties of a Platonian philosophy and the superb lines of a Parthenon or a Gothic cathedral. It yields the scientific insight which builds skyscrapers, conquers germ plagues, forecasts weather and even traces out the inner nature of man. Fertile imagination, strong emotion and other elements enter into thought, but the organizing power of abstract thinking provides the framework which holds all else together.

This much gives us a sufficient sketch of the distinctive hallmark of humanity, the ability to think, as this ability is explained by our new modern understandings. We are ready, then, to consider the other aspect of human nature, the sea of *brute* nature upon which this bark of intelligence floats with more or less ability to steer its course, as circumstances may dictate.

Our approach to this subject should be far different from the method we used for uncovering the nature of intelligence.

To start dealing with intelligence we assumed the existence of man's self-awareness, or consciousness. Nothing else could be done, because nobody can say how or why we have this attribute. We can only say that it is a sort of capstone placed somehow upon our other mental abilities and go on to see how it conducts thought.

Brute nature, however, does not offer such a mystery. It seems to be completely mechanistic, a living machine made of flesh and blood instead of metal—and the logical approach to the brute, therefore, is just the one which serves best for explaining any other machine. The first thing is to see how the machine is put together.

To do this for the brute in man requires going back a long way, to the very appearance on the earth of the brute's most fundamental endowment, the attribute of sheer physical *life*.

CHAPTER III

How Life Originated and Evolved

THE STORY of life's beginnings starts, chasteningly enough for man's pride of knowledge, with a mystery. Man still cannot tell how his home, the earth, came into being.

It is true that students of such matters have a theory, called the *tidal hypothesis,* of how the earth was born. The story starts, not less than two billion years ago and not more than five billion years ago, when a huge comet or, more accurately, a fast-traveling sun, passed near our own sun. By force of gravitational attraction the visitor drew huge spurts of fiery gas from our sun, but even as these spurts flew out the aberrant visitor receded far enough to cease attracting this material. The attractive force of the sun was not strong enough to pull the gaseous masses back home from the distance they had reached. Thereupon these masses fell into orbits, began coursing around the sun, and became the planets of the solar system.

Our own particular blob of gas soon cooled into a pear-shaped mass that spun on its axis every four hours instead of once in every twenty-four hours, as it does today. This rapid spinning, and the drag of the tides, put more strain on the spinning mass than it could withstand. The pear-shaped tip broke off, spiraled outward and fell into an orbit around the earth, as the moon.

This is science's best word on this subject at the moment—and the theory has many yawning gaps. It fails to tell how our own sun and the visiting sun came to be. It does not even stand up under thorough mathematical analysis. It is simply the nearest to a good guess which has appeared as yet.

Once the beginning is passed, however, science can do far better! In particular, it can give reasonably good dating to every phase of the earth's story, from the first cooling right down to our own time. This can be done by studying the *radioactive decay of matter,* and particularly the decay of the heaviest substance of all, the element uranium.

The basis of this dating method is the fact that uranium, like all radioactive substances, continually shoots off atoms of the light gas helium; and whenever this happens the atom of uranium becomes a lighter substance. Each lighter substance "decays" in its turn by shooting off helium, through a whole chain of substances, including radium, until the atoms finally become lead. Moreover, the rates of decay never change, whatever the state of the physical surroundings; and the rates are extremely slow. Five billion years is required for one half of any given bit of uranium to change into other substances.

Obviously, then, if a bit of uranium and accompanying "decay substances" are found in some geologic deposit, the relative amounts of all these substances tells *how long* the uranium has been there decaying; and in 1917 Barrell published the first comprehensive datings of geologic eras, periods and epochs by use of this method. He found that the oldest stratified rocks—that is, rocks laid down when the earth was cool enough to permit deposits of material in strata or beds—were between 1¼ and 2¾ billion years old. Later studies give an age of about 1.8 billion years for the oldest-known rock. Life probably could not have existed much before then.

Two billion years or so is the total time span, then, for life upon the earth—obviously, because life as we know it could not have existed until the surface of the earth had cooled to somewhere near its present temperature. The next question is, when within this time span, and how, did life come to be?

The "when" has been answered reasonably well for many years. Fossils of once-living forms are found from the early Paleozoic times of perhaps seven hundred million years ago, and even at that time the forms were highly organized. The simplest life must have begun, then, at least a billion years ago and perhaps earlier. But the "how" of life's beginnings still seemed an impenetrable mystery when Henry Fairfield Osborn published his masterly work, *The Origin and Evolution of Life,* in 1917.

In that book Osborn strove to combine the fruits of all investigations to date into an intelligent guess as to how life came to be. He pointed out why water, made of oxygen and hydrogen, inevitably became the principal fluid in life. It was everywhere; it was neutral, neither acid nor alkaline; and it had high specific heat, or ability to hold a relatively even temperature when the heat in the surroundings changed. As living organisms developed they could not help using water as their principal fluid.

Oxygen would certainly be the energizing element, or "fire of life," because of its avidity for combining with almost all other elements. Carbon and nitrogen, with their peculiar abilities to form complex compounds, would be the "scaffolding" or "framework" elements that hold together the proteins, carbohydrates, fats and so on of living tissues. But how were all these substances drawn together into living organisms, and how did heredity transmit all these complex physicochemical arrangements from generation to generation? Osborn could only write the heading "Pure Speculation" over his vague and tentative treatment of these subjects.

Even as he wrote, however, the desired answers were taking shape.

The noted chemist Emil Fischer (1852–1919) was closing a lifetime of brilliant work which included discovering how to combine lifeless chemicals into proteinlike substances. Not long afterward E. C. Baly of Liverpool began to uncover the nature of primitive photosynthesis—that is, combination of carbon dioxide and water into carbohydrates such as simple sugars, without aid from any force or substance other than the energy in sunlight. These researches did not cover the problem by any means, because even if these pioneers had produced such "life subtances" complete, they would not have explained how the substances were combined to form living organisms; but they were laying splendid foundations for later successes in dealing with this larger problem.

Meantime Thomas Hunt Morgan and others were learning how the processes of *heredity* pass on inherited characteristics from generation to generation—a question which had baffled biologists from the days of Darwin down to their time.

During all these decades of discouragement biologists had contented themselves with supposing that inherited characteristics must be carried somehow by some sort of units or mechanisms within the reproductive germ cells. Gregor Mendel's laws of heredity, shown in diagrams on the next page, strengthened this supposition, because they worked just as chance combinations of such units should occur. Finally biologists suspected that "heredity units" were carried somehow in tiny threads of material called *chromosomes,* which exist in germ cells.

Hunt and others followed up this reasoning with amazingly patient and ingenious experiments upon the fruit or vinegar fly, *Drosophila*

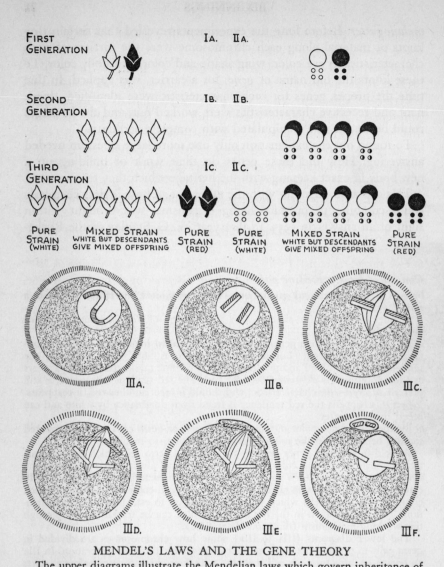

FIRST GENERATION   IA.   IIA.

SECOND GENERATION   IB.   IIB.

THIRD GENERATION   IC.   IIC.

PURE STRAIN (WHITE) | MIXED STRAIN WHITE BUT DESCENDANTS GIVE MIXED OFFSPRING | PURE STRAIN (RED) | PURE STRAIN (WHITE) | MIXED STRAIN WHITE BUT DESCENDANTS GIVE MIXED OFFSPRING | PURE STRAIN (RED)

IIIA.   IIIB.   IIIC.

IIID.   IIIE.   IIIF.

MENDEL'S LAWS AND THE GENE THEORY

The upper diagrams illustrate the Mendelian laws which govern inheritance of many characteristics. The name is for the Austrian monk Gregor Mendel (1822–84), who worked out these laws by experimenting with sweet peas in a monastery garden at Brünn (Brno) in Bohemia.

The basis of the laws can be illustrated by inheritance of blossom color from two parents, one with white blossoms and the other with red (the first generation, IA). The blossoms of the second generation (IB) will be all white, but in the third generation (IC) one fourth of the blossoms will be red. This color will breed true as a *pure strain* thereafter. One third of the whites—that is, one fourth of the entire generation—also will breed true, but the remaining whites will

Continued at bottom of the next page

melanogaster. Before long the experiments revealed that certain tiny knots of material along each chromosome were the carriers of such characteristics as eye color, wing shape and color, and body color. To these knots the old name of *gene,* for a carrier, was applied. In due time the proper genes for each characteristic were identified, dominant and recessive characteristics were worked out, and the heritages could be traced and manipulated with complete certainty.

To round out the explanation only one more large question needed answering. How did these genes do their work of building up a new body in exact keeping with the heritage which they transmitted?

This question, together with the other one of how lifeless chemicals could combine to produce living organisms, was brought within sight of an answer in 1935. In that year W. G. Stanley of the Rocke-

Continued from preceding page

behave as did the second generation. These last whites, therefore, constitute a *mixed strain.*

Mendel accounted for all this with his doctrine of *dominant* and *recessive* characteristics.

He assumed that each generation receives an equal inheritance of color tendency from each parent. But if this inheritance is both white and red, the tendencies do not blend and produce pink. The white masks the red and appears as though pure; it is *dominant* over the red. The red tendency, however, is still present as a *recessive* characteristic; and should it meet another red, it reappears. When this happens the red tendency is freed from dominance by white and can breed true thereafter.

Mendel could not point out anything in seed or germ cells which accounted for this behavior; but the modern gene theory does so readily.

As told in the text, genes are tiny portions of a germ cell which carry characteristics such as blossom color; and every individual always has two genes, one from each parent, for each and every inherited characteristic. This fact is indicated in diagram IIA, with circles to indicate blossom color and dots under each circle for the germ cells which the plant passes on to establish the next generation. The result shown in the left-hand diagrams can be traced readily through this working mechanism (diagrams IIB and IIc).

The lower diagrams (IIIA to IIIF) show how chromosomes are divided in germ cells to provide the right number of genes for the next generation. In IIIA an oöcyte or immature egg cell is shown with four chromosomes before it starts to ripen into a mature egg or ovum. In IIIB the chromosomes have arranged themselves in pairs, and in IIIc a spindle mechanism is preparing for the splitting action shown in IIID. Half these chromosomes pass to a polar body (IIIE and IIIF) which degenerates. The remainder of the cell now has only half the correct number of chromosomes—and this is the proper state of the mature cell.

Meanwhile male cells called spermatazoa have undergone a similar chromosome reduction. When a sperm cell and an egg unite in the fertilization process the union restores the full number of chromosomes. Thus the germ of the new individual has its proper heritage, half from each parent and mixed according to Mendel's laws.

feller Institute for Medical Research announced successful isolation of a substance which seemed to meet every requirement suggested by this earlier work for a primordial form of life.

This substance was a *virus,* a form of life which was supposed to be organized in droplets too small to be seen by the finest microscope and hence much smaller than any disease germ. Bacteriologists suspected that some unidentified substances of this type were responsible for such diseases as smallpox and infantile paralysis in man and other diseases in plants and animals, but for many years nobody had managed to isolate one of these elusive substances in a form sufficiently pure to permit positive identification and study.

In 1935, however, Stanley achieved this with either the virus itself, which causes mosaic disease in tobacco plants, or an exact analogue of it. This substance proved to be a protein, and his drastic treatments of it would certainly have destroyed even as lowly an organism as a bacterium; yet this substance retained its ability to eat, to grow, and, in time, to reproduce.

Here, then, was life organized on the physicochemical level—that is, without the fine structure that is found in bacteria and amoebae; and almost immediately biologists saw how such substances might well have been gathered together with Baly's carbohydrates to create life.

In the beginning various viruses might have taken shape in the sea, according to the physicochemical principles employed by workers such as Fischer, while carbohydrates were forming separately. Then at some time in those primordial days some particular virus took up a carbohydrate, and the union gave greatly increased efficiency, by enabling the protein to use "energy food"—that is, carbohydrate—for maintaining its activities. Rapid growth of the mass would follow, until it split into parts, and the parts then would repeat the process of growing and splitting.

But this notion of the virus suggested immediately how Morgan's tiny genes could have worked their way into living structures.

If various chemical compounds could come together to form a virus, several viruses could come together to form an organism. The organism could grow and acquire an organized structure, such as we see in single-celled plants and animals; and in time a portion might break off, carrying with it a proper array of viruses, and start building up a new individual. The new individual would, of course, be "true to type," because it consisted of exactly the same viruses which had built the parent mass.

Organisms such as yeasts reproduce in just this way, by throwing off a portion called a spore. By an extension of this process more highly organized plants and animals could develop organs for producing these special reproductive portions as germ cells. If within these cells the essential viruses are organized into groups, these would be Morgan's genes.

Within a few months after Stanley's achievement Dr Oscar Riddle of the Carnegie Institution suggested this possibility to the American Association for the Advancement of Science in the following terms:

There exists scarcely a doubt that during long periods of earth history, preceding the appearance of living matter, many localized areas of the earth's surface provided suitable conditions for the synthesis of sugar and some amino acids. . . . These syntheses of organic matter wholly apart from life are facts which must now be utilized in dealing with the question of the origin of life.

There is a new word to add. . . . For some years it has been fairly evident that these substances or units known as viruses . . . show the one property which is characteristic of life—that of reproduction. They have seemed part of a bridge between those smaller but lifeless organic molecules . . . which . . . form spontaneously . . . and those larger molecular aggregates which are . . . cells endowed with all the properties of life. . . . These early indices have been strengthened and extended by Stanley's successful preparation and study of "A Crystalline Protein Possessing the Properties of Tobacco-Mosaic Virus." . . .

Here we seem to have beautiful facts concerning . . . a protein which will indefinitely build itself anew when given contact with a suitable bit of living tissue. . . . When these properties . . . are compared with the known and probable properties of the gene we find parallels which can hardly be fortuitous—and possibly we here encounter other planks for that bridge leading from spontaneously formed organic molecules to those molecular aggregates (protoplasm) which are fully endowed with life. . . .

Does . . . "liveness" issue from the *aggregation* (and organization) of several chemically different genes? . . . If this should prove true, or partly true, it would mean that the bridge of which we have spoken has less length than we have imagined. The longest single missing span may be that reaching from spontaneously formed sugars and amino acids to a protein molecule like that of a virus.

Here, then, is science's latest word concerning the origin of life, and it sweeps away most of the uncertainties which have befogged and bewildered discussions about the physical nature of man throughout the history of scientific thought.

First and foremost it shows how to dispose of the century-old argument between so-called mechanists and vitalists—that is, between those who insisted that ultimately everything in life could be explained in physicochemical terms and those who insisted that physical and chemical forces must be supplemented by a guiding "vital spirit," a "form-giving essence" or, in the currently fashionable term, an *entelechy*. The new view suggests that each of these positions is partly wrong and partly right.

The mechanists will win and the vitalists will lose, in all probability, as knowledge grows along the line suggested by Dr Riddle, through ability to explain such supposedly vitalistic processes as heredity. So also, as will appear in a later detailed exploration of the subject, the simpler forms of mental life may well be explainable in purely physicochemical terms. Indeed, the mechanistic viewpoint may in time push itself successfully into levels as high as the mentality of the chimpanzee.

But even if all this be accomplished, everything we know suggests that one aspect of human nature will still defy mechanistic explanation. This aspect was pointed out in our examination of intelligence as the mystery of self-awareness, or self-consciousness, and the situation has been summed up with striking pithiness by Sir J. Arthur Thomson and Patrick Geddes in their *Life: Outlines of General Biology* (1931), when they said that "a machine cannot have a theory that it is a machine."

That is the point always to remember—"A machine cannot have a theory that it is a machine." So far as anyone can see now, even with aid from all our new understandings, the self-awareness of man promises to transcend understanding by science; it continues to defy explanation by mechanistic principles. A mystery remains enthroned at the very core of man's life, and as long as this is so a tremendously important segment of life remains as the legitimate domain of the spiritual and the moral in our thinking and in our philosophies.

Another fruit of the new viewpoint is the prospect for early liquidation of a most vexing problem about heredity. This was the question of why, if heredity runs true to type, do variations occur, and even those sudden changes called *mutations* which seem responsible for new species. The answer still lies beyond the frontier of established knowledge; but science nevertheless has learned enough, by following the gene theory, to indicate what the answer will be.

H. J. Müller and many other experimenters have found that treating the germ cells of many easily changed animals such as fruit flies with X rays results in striking bodily changes. Apparently the X rays batter down the delicate gene structures, then the disordered fragments reunite during the fertilization of the egg cell. If a new individual can emerge at all from such a start, it will have an altered heritage; and if enough individuals have the same alteration, they could well establish a new species.

This procedure is obviously unnatural, because no X-ray machines exist in Nature. Hence in Nature something must take their place, and what might that something be?

Cosmic rays? Perhaps; widespread tests and experiments are being conducted the world over to test out this idea. Drastic changes in the chemical conditions of the surroundings is another possibility; this also is being studied intensively. But this final question is technical, after all. The important fact is that many forces capable of causing mutations exist; the rest of the developmental mechanism amounts to no more than the old Darwinian principle of *natural selection* by *survival of the fittest*.

According to this doctrine living creatures respond to forces which constantly produce small variations and mutations in form and function. These variations are cast upon the world to survive or perish, according to their fitness. Those best fitted to survive do so; and in time, by passing on their variations, these survivors establish new species.

Still another important gain from the new understanding is a real test—in principle, at least—for settling the old argument about which characteristics, both physical and mental, are inherited and which are acquired through impact from surroundings and pressure from life experiences.

In times past we heard constantly, on the one hand, that inherited traits of character are all but as fixed as "his father's chin and his mother's nose." Others asserted that practically all traits of character could be molded by training and circumstance; and the actual truth could never be learned until men knew just how much heredity did and did not carry from generation to generation. Neither could they hope to learn, as long as they did not know what the mechanisms might be. Today these mechanisms are known, and progress can be expected from now on toward settling this old problem.

The last aspect of this mixed biological and geologic record which needs notice now is the march of events which provided a large-scale calendar for the development of life, including the rise of man.

These developments are datable in mixed geological and biological terms because of the fact, already mentioned, that new forms and types arise when the genes are subjected to transforming forces from without. Some measure of this goes on constantly, but the larger strides in evolutionary development have occurred at several distinct times when cataclysmic changes amounting to revolutions have swept over the face of the earth. These revolutions were pointed out clearly by the Austrian geologist Eduard Suess (1831–1914) in his five-volume book *Das Antlitz der Erde* (The Face of the Earth), published in separate volumes between 1883 and 1909.

Suess treated the march of earth history as akin to what happens to the skin of an apple when it dries. That is, he pictured the core of the earth as continually shrinking, probably because of cooling, and every once in so often the skin or crust had to collapse into a new set of wrinkles, which we call mountain ranges, in order to remain fitted onto the core. These readjustments constituted "revolutions," and Suess named each one for mountains which it produced.*

The importance of these revolutions in man's story lies in what they did to life.

Usually before each upheaval the earth's mountains had been planed down by erosion nearly to sea level, and widespread oceans prevented extremes of heat and cold. Old forms of plants and animals flourished and produced many fantastic variations and specialized forms. Then would come the revolution, with a great outburst of volcanic action. New mountain ranges blocked the sweep of rain-bearing winds and spread drought over wide areas; high regions often acquired glaciers. Under such conditions only the sturdiest of the old life survived, and new forms that had special suitability for the new conditions took over the partially depopulated lands and seas. Thereby the various revolutions brought in the vertebrate structure, air breathing, warm blood, the birth of living young and all the other major features which mark physical man.

---

*This theory has been challenged in almost every detail, and the worst weakness in it was Suess's inability to explain the shrinking of the earth's core. Geologists still cannot do this, although modern knowledge of radioactivity is helping mightily. A good example of modern thought is the view advanced by John Joly (*The Surface History of the Earth*, 1925) that revolutions were caused by constant generation of heat through radioactivity. For a long time the earth's crust could withstand the pressure and slow internal melting caused by this heat, then it cracked, relieved the strain and fell into a new surface configuration.

This idea does not withstand detailed criticism any more than did Suess's explanation; but in spite of such failures in explaining the central mechanism, the general idea of revolutions, whatever the cause, has been strengthened rather than weakened since Suess's time.

THE OUTSTANDING ERAS OF EARTH HISTORY

ARCHEOZOIC—"Beginning Life"

Began two billion years or more ago; end uncertain. Strong crustal movements and intense volcanic activity.

LIFE.—Viruslike beginnings, giving rise to unicellular plants (bacteria, algae) and animals.

PROTEROZOIC—"Earlier Life"

From uncertain beginning until between 700 and 550 million years ago. At least two periods of mountain building.

LIFE. —All major types of animals except perhaps vertebrates developed in the sea. Prominent types—corals, sponges, saclike coelenterates (jellyfish, etc.), worms, mollusks and crustacea.

PALEOZOIC—"Ancient Life"

From between 700 and 550 million years ago until between 240 and 190 million years ago. An early *Acadian-Caledonian* revolution produced the roots of the Green and Cascade mountains in North America and the Scottish Highlands. A later *Hercynian-Appalachian* revolution occurring largely in the Carboniferous Age produced the old mountains of Eurasia, Africa and the roots of the Appalachians and the Ozarks in North America.

LIFE.—Development of fishes with internal skeletons of skull, vertebrate backbone and ribs. Small and giant mosses and ferns led establishment of plant life on land; crustaceans gave rise to air-breathing insects. Midway in the era the vertebrates established themselves on land as amphibians (newts, frogs, etc.)

MESOZOIC—"Middle Life"

From between 240 and 190 million years ago until between 115 and 95 years ago. A relatively quiet time; mountains and continents were eroded (peneplenated) almost to sea level.

LIFE.—The Age of Reptiles and of the rise of flowering plants. The reptiles included the monster dinosaurs, flying types and sea dwellers. They were cold-blooded and reproduced almost entirely by egg-laying.

CENOZOIC—"Recent Life"

The era from the end of the Mesozoic to the present. Formation of the present continents and high mountain ranges such as the Rockies, the Coastal Ranges, the Andes, the Alps and the Himalayas. Marked toward the end by a great Ice Age lasting from 1 to 1½ million years.

LIFE.—The Age of Mammals, warm-blooded, hair-covered animals that bear living young, and of feathered birds, which retain reproduction by means of eggs. The Ice Age saw the rise of man.

Indeed, this vital relation was seen dimly long before Suess's day and gave rise to the system of names which links life with geologic age. As early as 1833 Charles Lyell started this by proposing new names for the last two of the original divisions used by geologists—Primary (oldest), Secondary, Tertiary and Quaternary. Lyell proposed instead to divide the last two into three parts, with names ending in "cene," for the Greek *kainos,* recent. For the first parts of the names he proposed "eo" from *eos,* dawn; "mio" from *meion,* less; and "plio" from *pleion,* more. Thus he achieved the names Eocene, Miocene and Pliocene.

In 1840 and 1841 Phillips carried the idea farther by proposing the names Paleozoic, Mesozoic and Cenozoic for the old Primary, Secondary and Lyell's combination of the Tertiary and the Quaternary. (They meant ancient, middle and recent life respectively, from *zoe,* life.) Lyell's scheme also was enlarged by inserting the Oligocene (from *oligos,* scant) between the first two divisions and subdividing the end portion of Lyell's Pliocene into the Pleistocene (from *pleistos,* most) and the Holocene (from *holos,* entire). This was done because geologists had discovered that the Pliocene did not flow smoothly into modern times; a formidable Ice Age intervened. The name Pleistocene was coined for this age, while the name Holocene applies to the few thousand years of modern conditions which have followed the Ice Age. These two names together equal the old Quaternary. As we shall see later, the Pleistocene saw the rise of man.

Thus geology gives us a timetable of events for checking man's story, and radioactivity dating enables us to assign time spans in broad terms to these events. We are well equipped, therefore, to keep a firm control in terms of time and circumstance upon the entire story of how the brute nature of man arose from primordial life on the virus level.

CHAPTER IV

The Physical Relations between Brain and Thought

"MULTUM IN PARVO," says a Latin maxim—"much in little"—and nothing illustrates the maxim better than does the debt of even the loftiest thought to that relatively simple structure, the nerve cell. Everything in thought, even to the most intricate mental feats of the mathematician, the poet or the philosopher, is worked out by only one physical process, the passage of nerve impulses through nerve fibers. The relation between this physical process and the accompanying mental phenomena covers the entire working connection between the brain and human thought.

Of course the moment we start to trace this relation we find that science is not even within hailing distance as yet of ability to explain the entire process. Nothing is known yet, to mention one lack, about how nerves rose out of viruslike beginnings. Enough *is* known, however, to inspire confidence that the story will be worked out in due time and in physicochemical terms. Certainly the outlines of how nervous impulses act are plain today, and this gives all the foundation needed for tracing the step-by-step development of the brain, up to the complex structure found in man.

We see that the simplest example of nervous action is a certain sensitivity of tissue to stimuli, as shown in the *receptor-effector* hookup. Such hookups appeared in the ancestors of that lowly animal the sea anemone, or "sea flower," during Proterozoic times, a billion years or more ago; and human beings still retain some receptor-effector tissue in the iris of the eyeball. These structures can contract or relax the iris, according to the amount of light striking the eye, without intervention of any nervous action.

Anemones also possess the next higher development, a nerve net, an interconnection of nerves which carries stimuli throughout the

29

body. This net enables the creature to respond with much or all of its body to stimuli. Touch the animal with acid anywhere and the mouth shrinks down; place food near one tentacle and all near-by tentacles are stirred into activity.

The next higher scheme of organization is seen in the jellyfish. This creature has a nerve net, like the anemone, but it also has an arrangement of localized trigger mechanisms or *reflex arcs*. This arrangement is simple, yet beautiful in its service to the jellyfish.

When something touches the receiving or *afferent* end of a fiber nervous force is released and shoots along the fiber to the central cell of the arc. There a reinforcing charge is triggered off and shoots along a delivery or *efferent* fiber to a muscle. In the muscle the nervous discharge sets up a chemical reaction which causes contraction, and the contraction draws together whatever structures are attached to the muscle at its ends.

That is all; yet this simple mechanism serves the animal well enough. Let food touch the receiving end of a reflex arc and the trigger action stirs the muscle in a near-by tentacle; the tentacle sweeps the food into the creature's mouth. Similarly the animal swims away from dangerous contacts, and it can lash out at prey or enemies with poisoned dartlike structures.

Such activities, of course, are completely automatic; the jellyfish has no more "awareness" than does a telephone instrument. This is true also in the next higher level, in which reflex arcs are tied together into a *central nervous system*. How such a system works can be seen in the balancing of reflexes which determines whether a catfish will or will not eat when an object touches its mouth.

Suppose the object contacted is soft and wriggly, about like a worm. Immediately the proper nerves send reports of sensations to the medulla oblongata, at the base of the brain. The medulla returns them to the mouth muscles according to their character. Reports which indicate a foodlike character tend to make the muscles contract; unfavorable reports cause relaxation. Whether the catfish eats or not will depend upon how these stimulations add up.

For most situations in catfish life this equipment serves well enough. But to realize how primitive it really is we need only confront the catfish with a slightly different kind of morsel. This morsel feels like a worm, tastes like a worm and in fact *is* a perfectly eatable worm, save for one fact. It conceals a fisherman's hook!

Alas for the catfish—its nervous equipment is not competent to deal with this situation! To the catfish mind stuff that feels like food

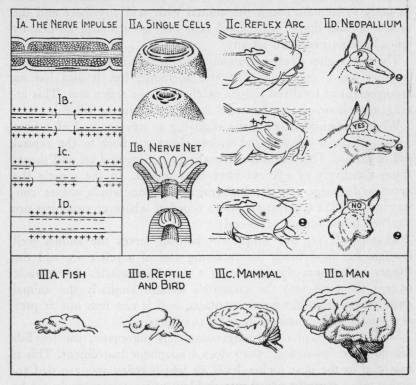

| IA. THE NERVE IMPULSE | IIA. SINGLE CELLS | IIc. REFLEX ARC | IID. NEOPALLIUM |

IB.

Ic.

ID.

IIB. NERVE NET

| IIIA. FISH | IIIB. REPTILE AND BIRD | IIIc. MAMMAL | IIID. MAN |

NERVOUS ACTION AND NERVOUS SYSTEMS

Transmission of the nervous impulse is shown at the upper left, commencing with a nerve in cross section and the actual nerve fiber in the center. Around it are a *myelin* or fatty sheath and an outer sheath, the *neurilemma.*

According to the modern *polarized-membrane* theory, this structure transmits nervous impulses with electrified particles or ions of opposite charge on the two surfaces of the neurilemma. In a resting nerve the neurilemma is an insulator and keeps the two kinds of ions apart. Excitation breaks down the insulating power, and the ions flow around the edges of the break (IB), spreading the break each way along the fiber (Ic). This constitutes "passage of the nervous impulse." Meanwhile the neurilemma at the site of excitation soon recovers insulating power (ID). To account for the fact that nerves actually transmit impulses one way only, the theory holds that two-way travel occurs along all the fibers attached to one nerve cell; but only one fiber, called the *axon,* has the chemical apparatus needed to pass the impulse across a "joint" or synapse to receiving fibers or *dendrites* from other cells.

Diagrams IIA, B, c and D show the types of nervous system discussed in the text, while diagrams IIIA, B, c, D show brain growth from fish to man.

31

and tastes like food *is* food, and a hungry catfish acts accordingly. Presence of a hook means nothing—not even if the catfish escapes and encounters the same baited hook again. It will grab again, because it must, just as a steel trap must close when sprung.

Usually this type of automatic, invariable response appears in human conduct only in such elementary activities as coughing, sneezing and winking; but man can revert to the catfish level of uncontrollable responses in actions which usually are controlled by conscious choice. A striking example is afforded by the *dipsomaniac*.

When we say "dipsomaniac" we do not mean the perverse fellow who drinks because he enjoys the exhilaration of intoxication or the one who becomes besotted to drown his sorrows. We mean the true dipsomaniac, the so-called confirmed drunkard, the one who may say, and mean what he says, that he "would give anything to straighten up, but can't."

Most of us misunderstand him just as we do the catfish if we call it stupid or greedy. We seek to reform him by prayer, exhortation and by showing him the ruin which lies ahead unless he mends his ways, and we overlook the fact that in his case the homely saying, "He drinks like a fish," is literally true.

Some congenital defect, some psychic aberration or some impairment caused by continued drinking has cut off his human birthright of ability to control drinking intoxicants. He is as helpless as the catfish. Let him see or smell liquor, and nothing short of physical restraint can keep him from drinking it.

This "fish type of thinking" marks the height of Paleozoic development up to the time when certain fish, the Crossopterygians, crawled forth upon the land and became amphibians.

This newer, freer and more varied life gave high "survival value" to more flexible nervous responses—and so, when the Appalachian (or Hercynian) revolution remade the face of the earth, higher responses appeared in the new reptiles and the primitive birds of the Mesozoic era. These reactions were of the type formerly called *instincts*.

The old word "instinct" meant an invariable and perhaps complicated response with which an animal could meet a situation new to it. A yearling bird was said to hatch her brood, without previous training or experience, "by instinct." Today physiologists prefer to divide these "instinctive" responses into *simple reflexes* and *chain reflexes*.

A simple reflex consists of one stimulation and one response, like the catfish's grabbing at food. A chain reflex is a series of responses which are touched off one after another, like firecrackers exploding in a lighted pack. Completion of each step in the chain touches off the next step—and the standard example of this is the yearling bird's first nesting and brooding. She can do so because the necessary sequence of responses has been built into her nervous structure by ages of natural selection, and they are touched off in proper order by her physiological responses to spring and mating.

But while reptiles and birds were acquiring these elaborate resources Mesozoic life also was producing the fourth and highest type of nervous organization. This type, seen almost exclusively in mammals, has a by-pass or accessory structure which lets nervous impulses follow their usual courses through the lower channels but stores up the results in pleasure or pain. Neurologists give this comparatively new structure the appropriate name *neopallium* or "new mantle"—and obviously its ability to store up experience is the physical foundation of ability to learn. The neopallium therefore deserves attention in keeping with its importance.

The first feature to notice about the neopallium is the value of its situation as a sort of covering for all the older structures of the brain.

If the neopallium had been "hooked in" with the older structures, it would have become enmeshed in their workings and it would be all but as automatic in its responses; but it is not hooked in. It lies blanketlike above and apart from the older structures and in admirable position to act like a monitor or supervisor in a telephone exchange. As long as all is going well it can "let well enough alone," but the moment trouble threatens it can cut in and become active.

The second feature which helps make learning possible is *plasticity*.

This term is the formal name for the tendency the neopallium shows to become functionally grooved like wet clay by everything that courses through it. Since our knowledge of how the process affects life owes much to notable experiments made upon dogs by the Russian physiologist Ivan Pavlov (1849–1936), modern psychology uses his term *conditioning* for the working process. The heart of it is the fact that the neopallium keeps a record of how pleasure or pain results from actions such as the catfish's automatic grabs at a baited hook. This record saves animals which are blessed with a neopallium from repeating such mistakes.

The first experience of the sort grooves in a "memory of pain." Thereafter any start upon the same sequence stirs this "pain

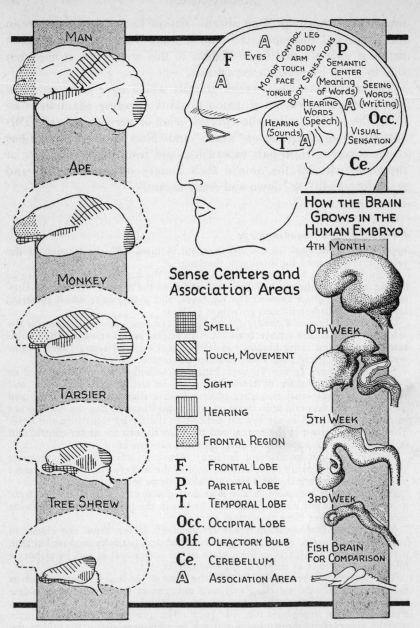

MAN

APE

MONKEY

TARSIER

TREE SHREW

Sense Centers and Association Areas

▦ SMELL

▨ TOUCH, MOVEMENT

☰ SIGHT

▥ HEARING

▦ FRONTAL REGION

F. FRONTAL LOBE
P. PARIETAL LOBE
T. TEMPORAL LOBE
Occ. OCCIPITAL LOBE
Olf. OLFACTORY BULB
Ce. CEREBELLUM
A ASSOCIATION AREA

F A A LEG
BODY
Eyes ARM
MOTOR CONTROL
TOUCH
FACE
TONGUE BODY SENSATIONS
P SEMANTIC CENTER (Meaning of Words)
SEEING WORDS (Writing)
HEARING WORDS (Speech) A Occ.
HEARING (Sounds) VISUAL SENSATION
T A Ce.

HOW THE BRAIN GROWS IN THE HUMAN EMBRYO

4TH MONTH

10TH WEEK

5TH WEEK

3RD WEEK

FISH BRAIN FOR COMPARISON

MILESTONES IN BRAIN DEVELOPMENT

The diagrams at the left show the remarkable growth of the "seat of thought," the *neopallium,* in the most intelligent strain of creatures, the *primates.* At the

Continued at bottom of the next page

memory." A warning "Pain ahead!" flashes to the motor centers in the brain, and thereupon the animal stops the sequence of action *before* it suffers actual hurt! Thanks to the neopallium, it has been able to profit by previous experience.

The neopallium also enables animals which have it to *choose a course of action* when a situation presents opposing possibilities by using the process called the *effective level of nervous tension*. This amounts to an adding up of "Yesses" and "Noes" from the sensations of the moment, from past experiences and from the bodily state at the time—whether the animal feels hungry or satisfied, "up and ready for a fight" or "down and ready to run."

Continued from preceding page

upper right is the peak of this development in man, with the location of the principal centers used for intelligent thinking.

Brain history can be traced as shown, because the earlier steps still survive in "living fossils," creatures which have survived from the times when their development was the highest known. The creatures, and higher ones which illustrate later stages, contributed brain growth as follows:

TREE SHREW (genus *Tupaia*). A squirrellike creature with beady eyes on the sides of the head; the change from claws to fingers is just starting. These creatures creep or run along branches instead of making bold swings; their brains are but little different from those of other mammals.

SPECTRAL TARSIER (genus *Tarsier*). Huge spectaclelike eyes in the front of its head give some measure of binocular vision, or seeing with both eyes, and stereoscopic effect—that is, seeing objects from a slightly different angle and thereby gaining accurate indications of depth and distance. But the eyes do not turn in their sockets; to see toward either side the tarsier must turn the head. The brain has grown in the frontal and rearmost regions for motor control and in association areas for co-ordinating sight and movement.

MONKEY (various genera and families). Monkeys achieved perfect primate vision, both eyes looking front and movable in the sockets. All association areas in the brain are enlarged, and a separate lobe appears for hearing.

APE (order *Anthropoidea,* family *Simiidae*). Brain somewhat developed from monkey level toward human; chief lack now is in the height needed to provide manlike capacity for huge association areas.

MAN (order *Anthropoidea,* family *Hominidae*). Differs from ape chiefly in huge association areas. These areas are accommodated, partly by increased height, partly by deep folds (gyri) in the surface of the cortex and in part by elaborate folding of the brain, as shown at the lower right.

The early embryo brain, like the primitive brain of the low vertebrates, such as fishes, is substantially just the spinal cord enlarged at the top end, with a few swellings to serve important functions. In the third week of life the human embryonic brain resembles the fish brain. The primitive brain can remain straight, however, as shown, because it can be accommodated easily within the skull. The mammalian brain, however, and most of all, the human brain, must be folded, accordion fashion; and this folding proceeds as shown until the bends are almost pushed together. Thereafter the cerebral swellings find additional room by pushing back *over* the folded lower part of the brain.

The process is worth noting carefully, because even when consciousness and patterns of understanding appear in man they do not supersede this effective-level mechanism. They stand upon its shoulders, and indeed they are largely controlled by it. The effective level which obtains at any moment determines whether reason can control mental activity and bodily conduct or must give way to brute impulse and passion. It determines whether we are clear eyed, fresh minded and awake or confused, tired or asleep. And most important of all, it links the brute to the intelligent in the mind of man.

This kind of reaction obviously lies just below the highest endowments of all—man's self-consciousness and ability to form complex patterns of understanding. Concerning the former endowment nothing physical can be pointed out, but the seats of the latter ability commenced appearing in the brain perhaps a hundred million years ago in early Eocene times, in the line of *primate* animals—that is, creatures having toes (or fingers) equipped with nails, instead of claws or hoofs, at the ends of their limbs.

The course of primate brain development is shown in the accompanying illustration. The driving forces behind it seem to have been first, *hands,* and second, *tree life.*

Hands were vitally important because they combine to a greater or less degree every ability possessed by any other type of limb extremity. A hand can clutch and tear—not as well as clawed or taloned feet, but still reasonably well. It can crush to some extent, and it can twist and pull. While a hand cannot match a flipper for swimming, it serves nicely. Beyond this a hand, when well developed, can manipulate, take apart and, even more important, at its highest level of development it can put together again. Thus a creature which is endowed with hands can profit indefinitely from growth in mental power, while others are limited by their specialized extremities.

The second shaping force, tree life, was emphasized by Sir Grafton Elliot Smith (1871–1937). According to him in his *Essays on the Evolution of Man* (1924) and earlier works, tree life stimulated development of the brain toward higher levels because it forced a shift from *smell* to *sight* as the most important guiding sense.

Until this shift to tree life occurred the first mammals had relied largely upon smell for detecting food and receiving warning of enemies, as well as for guidance while moving about. This served well enough on the ground. But smell is a diffuse and lingering sense and too inaccurate to serve well in tree life. Therefore the higher primates turned to the much sharper sense of sight and also developed needed correlating centers called *association areas*. One example will show what these centers do.

Consider a monkey which has just caught a glint of yellow in a distant tree—a glint which might or might not come from a banana. This is a sensation from sight, but the monkey would have a sorry time if it swung off in response to such a hint alone.

It needs ability to compare the glint with memories of false hints from yellow flowers and from birds that wear a spot of "banana yellow." It must size up the task of leaping and swinging from branch to branch by consulting motor memories of how much effort will be required to cross each gap. Lastly, if some dark sinuous object several feet long is seen on one of the intervening branches, the monkey will profit mightily if its mental data can suggest whether this object is a vine or a boa constrictor. Such needs can only be met by brain centers which co-ordinate these data—and these co-ordinating centers are the association areas.

Since addition of these areas brings the brain practically to the human level, human mentality will soon be due for consideration. Hence a few preliminary considerations seem in order here.

First comes final consideration of the central mystery of man's mentality—*self-consciousness* or, as many would say, man's *soul*.

To explain this endowment in the same mechanistic terms which have served thus far, amounts to explaining how a telephone exchange not only can handle all its messages but also can stand apart from its work and say to itself, "All this is happening to me! I am the center of all this activity!" This task has baffled each and every mechanist who has grappled with it.

Perhaps the most daring attempt—or foolish, according to viewpoint—to deal with the question mechanistically was made by the founder of *behaviorism*, John B. Watson. In broad terms behaviorism asserts that thought and behavior must be considered as mere complicated psychophysical responses to stimuli, and such terms as "consciousness" and "will" are mere unscientific folklore. Watson stated this position bluntly in 1919 in his *Psychology from the Standpoint of a Behaviorist*:

The reader will find no discussion of consciousness and no reference to such terms as sensation, perception, attention, will and the like. These terms are in good repute, but I have found that I can get along without them. . . . I frankly do not know what they mean, nor do I believe that anyone else can use them consistently.

This doctrine has been assailed as everything from unproven to ridiculous. Perhaps the simplest objection to it is that Watson denied his own position when he used the word "I." If he could speak of himself and set himself apart from others, he knew very well one most important meaning of the word consciousness. He acknowledged the meaning of being aware of himself and of his separateness from others.

Other psychologists who attempted to explain consciousness by something more satisfactory than a denial that it exists have done no better. Indeed, they have all but given up. Present-day writings reveal only one note of hope that a mechanistic explanation of self-awareness will be achieved. This note was sounded clearly enough by C. Judson Herrick, professor of neurology at the University of Chicago, in his book *The Thinking Machine* (1929):

We look forward in the hope and confident expectation that the problems of mind and the problems of matter are not insoluble questions, that they must be solved together not separately, and that the scientific method will in due course open up the right road to travel toward this consummation.

This is sheer faith, of exactly the same quality as faith in religion. Here then, we could say, science and religion flow together into one attitude toward the supreme mystery of man's nature—and this is the sum and substance of the wisdom of the ages concerning the soul of man, as this wisdom stands today. We may hold with Herrick that someday, somehow, science will read the riddle, or we may hold with religion that here is a mystery which reminds man that after all he is man and not God. But whatever our choice, it must rest upon faith and faith alone.

One last word remains to be said about this problem of self-consciousness. Even if science cannot explain its fundamental nature, tremendous strides have been made in recent years in explaining *how it works* within the brain by studying so-called *Berger rhythms* or *electric brain waves,* dating from the first description given of the method by Hans Berger of Jena in 1931.

To detect these waves, electrodes are placed on the head and a delicate current is turned on. This current passes through the cortex or outer layer of the brain between the electrodes and also through a delicate recording instrument; and the heart of the method is the fact that the current *varies in strength* with the march of thought.

The delicacy of the method may be judged from the electrical tension of the changes which occur. The strongest have an electrical pressure of between 100 and 200 microvolts—and a microvolt is one millionth of one volt! For all their delicacy, however, these changes open up astonishing vistas of new understanding concerning human mental activity.

The first fact revealed is that throughout life the brain is in a state of electrical activity. The cells seem to charge themselves up to the "spilling over" point and then discharge, regularly and unfailingly, in several different rhythms or time cycles, according to the state of mental life and activity.

Sleep is marked by a state of low electrical tension. The brain cells do not accumulate the "discharge level" of tension, and the tension they do create cannot support conscious thought. But when the cells begin to "hang on" longer and accumulate higher charges before they discharge, consciousness returns. We face life "with full power turned on," so to speak, in the brain; and this power seems to be needed for mental activity. Whenever concentrated mental activity occurs the waves disappear from the part of the brain concerned. The energy seems to be consumed and does not build up to the discharge level.

Other significant correlations between the waves and mentality are seen in children and abnormal mentalities. Young children do not show the strong regular discharge which marks the conscious state in adults; this type of discharge develops only as the child approaches adult powers of thought. The waves become slowed down or irregular in cases of insanity and are broken up in the vicinity of brain tumors—a fact which surgeons are beginning to use for making diagnoses. Epilepsy is accompanied by an "electrical brain storm"— and the building up toward this chaotic discharge can often be detected eighteen hours before the seizure!

Another powerful new means for studying correlations between the brain and thought is application of *thermocoagulation* or electrocoagulation to the brains of animals. The process coagulates or "cooks" one level of brain cells at a time and thus in effect "peels" the brain in layers only one microscopic cell thick. Experiments to date show that many layers can be peeled off without doing noticeable harm, but the technique can be pushed to the extent of doing damage. The resultant impairment of mental processes in animals should reveal many a connection between brain and mentality which can be applied to man.

All this work naturally is in its infancy as yet; but, even so, it gives psychology its chance to match its studies of psychic or mental phenomena with the corresponding physical activities of the brain and thus create a complete rounded science.

Now, with this said, we have traced present knowledge of how life began and then how the nervous system and the brain took shape, right up to the human level. We are ready, then, to consider the culmination of all these developments in the event which interests us most—the production of the first man, or at least the first creature endowed with intelligence which could be called human.

CHAPTER V

The Birth of the Manlike Mind

Aʟʟ the developmental processes traced thus far have been building toward man, but obviously something extremely special in character will be needed to pick out this utterly unique creature and set him apart from all the others in the dominating position he holds.* When biologists are asked what this highly selective force could have been the favorite answer is, "a peculiar twist of *biological specialization.*"

By specialization they mean a co-ordinated refinement of both body and brain to give maximum efficiency when the animal finds itself in almost ideal surroundings. Then it may develop some feature such as a monkey's tail, which gives perfect adjustment to environment. Thereafter the urge for improvement ceases.

Now specialization may occur at a low level, as it did with the tree shrews, or circumstances may let general development proceed to a higher level before specialization sets in. This happened with the higher primates—lemurs, gibbons, monkeys and apes. One and all of them developed along general lines much above the tree-shrew level before they became specialized for tree life. But somehow at this period in primate history occurred one turn of Fortune's wheel which produced man.

Elliot Smith describes this turn by suggesting that one strain of the primate stock—shall we say a poor relation, a not-too-strong cousin?—found no good chance to become specialized. This cousin was buffeted about, probably in poor grasslands, instead of being able

---

*Biologists are not this flattering in the position they give man. They set him apart, but only to the extent of giving him and his supposed cousins of the past ages a separate family—the *Hominidae*—within the order *Anthropoidea* of the class Primates. The original name is from the Greek *anthropos* for man, and the name means "man-like." The higher apes and the gibbons (family *Simiidae*) are included.

to live in a rich forest; and this experience led to a seemingly miraculous result.

When he arrived in this habitat this abused primate probably had all four limbs equipped with hands, the time-honored heritage of the primate stock. The terrain would have trees enough to keep this heritage exercised but not enough to make tree climbing the principal activity. Hence any tendency to specialize would come in walking and in running, not in climbing.

This might have produced complete specialization, as it did with horses, had it started early in the history of the stock. But in this primate stock the urge toward specialization for walking came *after* adaptations to tree life had been grained deeply into the stock at perhaps the tree-shrew level. Therefore another principle of inheritance came into play, the rule that Nature *never reverses developmental trends*. Once a specialization has been established the genes become adjusted to passing on *that particular development* and they *must* pass this development on. Any further changes must accept older ones and build upon them as a foundation.

Our poor primate cousin on the grasslands was caught, then, in just such a situation. He needed specialization for efficiency in walking and running, but specializations for tree life had been ingrained beyond possibility of reversal. What would happen then? What could happen? The only solution lay in compromise. Development did not disturb the climbing element from the waist up. It merely changed the lower extremities into legs with feet—and, of course, changed the spine and the poise of the head to make the erect walking posture mechanically efficient.

Now this compromise was the making of man, not only in figure and posture but in mentality—and it did so by virtue of the fact that it *was* a compromise!

An all-around, four-limb specialization would have been a whole-hog affair and would have produced the usual narrowing of faculties. But here two specialties were present—the old one, climbing, and the new one, walking—and the two were, so to speak, at war with each other. Would not brain development therefore be kept hanging in the balance as well, with the association areas receiving most of whatever growth occurred because they provided the most valuable help in such a situation? And in time would not this trend produce mental power enough to begin conscious thought?

So runs Elliot Smith's reasoning—and it has been lent powerful support in recent years by discovery of certain fossils in South Africa which fit perfectly into such a scheme of development. The full significance of these fossils will become apparent instantly, once they are placed against the background of how and why the general contours and details of head form provide a good clue to the degree of development attained.

The developmental principles which govern shape of the head may be illustrated with some aid from a simple experiment.

Lay a ruler or a long pencil alongside the nose, to touch the chin and the eyebrow. Next note that this marker is substantially upright when the head is held in a normally level position. Now this verticality or uprightness of the face, as tested apart from the nose, is one of the most important of the features that mark a man; and the two localities which make this verticality important are the forehead above the eyebrow and the tip of the jaw.

The forehead may slope back a little from the upright line, but the divergence will not be great. This means that the front part of the skull has ample room inside—and room here is essential, because the frontal lobes of the brain are the seat of memory, imagination and the ability to plan.

The tip of the jaw is important because here is where a most important and distinctive readjustment was forced by the combination of a growing brain with feeding requirements.

Obviously the coarser and the poorer a creature's food is, the more it must eat to get the nourishment it needs; and a great aid in eating more is a large mouth. Thus in early days large mouths were needed —and since brains and skulls were small, only one design was possible. The mouth had to protrude, as a sort of apelike muzzle. If it carried fighting canine tusks, as it does today in male apes, the *prognathism,* or forward projection, was more pronounced.

But increasing intelligence required larger brains and larger skulls to contain them, and as this development proceeded the skull came in time to overhang the mouth. More than this, the mouth could become relatively smaller as growing intelligence aided in the food hunt; and naturally creatures which got rid of useless burdens were favored in Nature's ceaseless winnowing out of the less efficient stocks. Hence in this ratio between brain and mouth we have a handy rough test of relative mental and physical development.

The test amounts to setting off the ability to think against the ability to chew; and as Sir Arthur Keith pointed out in his book *The Antiquity of Man* (1924), the test is applied by comparing the cubic volume of the brain chamber with the area of the palate, or roof of the mouth. On this basis an ape's capacity for thinking is only from five to six times as great as its ability to chew. In modern man the ratio is better than fifty to one. Truly a great gain was made there!

At one point, however, the mouth did not shrink.

Inside the jawbone, or mandible, are the areas where the muscles of the tongue are attached. The tip of the jaw must be well forward, and the space between the sides must be generous, if the muscles are to have the freedom of action which is needed to produce speech. Hence, if the jaw space is limited, the possessor of the cramped jaw is limited in vocal utterance to grunts, howls and cries.

But how could this space be preserved as a matter of mechanical design if the original muzzlelike mouth was continually retreating beneath the ever larger brain case or skull? Only one solution was possible. The tip of the jaw had to remain where it was. Thus in time man acquired a *chin*—a feature which is as unique to man as is his huge brain.

The third development area which figures importantly can be judged best from the front or top view of the head. By testing with the fingers and watching in a mirror, anybody can convince himself that the broadest part of the skull lies above and a bit behind the ears. Beneath these bulges on each side lie the parietal association areas. They touch upon the motor and sensory centers to the front which deal with bodily movement, the visual centers in the back of the head and the hearing centers inside the ear, as shown in the diagram herewith. Imbedded in them also are the *semantic* centers, those which store up and apply the *meanings* of words. In view of the role played by language, both spoken and printed, high development in these parietal areas was indispensable.

These principles may sound theoretical, but every important step can be illustrated with fossils, commencing with the South African finds already mentioned.

The outstanding features of these finds are shown in the accompanying picture, and both the discoverers and others, such as Franz Weidenreich and W. K. Gregory, agree in placing them in or near the ancestral line of the hominids. Although lower than any true hominid in brain development, they were superior to any living ape. Their teeth were definitely human. The poise of the head suggests that they were manlike in posture and build of leg, and the development of the brain areas which controlled the hands seems ahead of anything seen in apes.

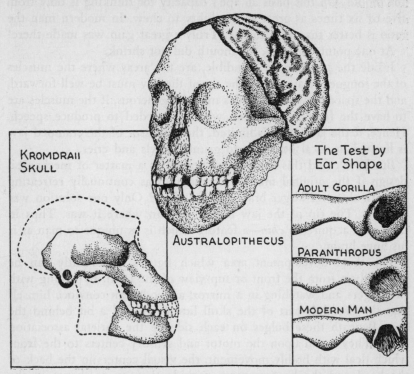

KROMDRAII SKULL

AUSTRALOPITHECUS

The Test by Ear Shape

ADULT GORILLA

PARANTHROPUS

MODERN MAN

THE FIRST RISE ABOVE APE MENTALITY

Two South African fossils which help greatly to show how the manlike or hominid strain developed above the ape level are *Australopithecus,* found in 1924, and the Kromdraii skull, or *Paranthropus robustus,* found in 1938. The first fossil consists of the face, part of the lower jaw and a brain cast which formed inside the cranium before the bone was destroyed. Prof. Raymond Dart's study of the specimen found the face of a young ape combined with markedly human development of teeth; and the brain, although far from grown, matched an adult gorilla brain in size. A well-developed parietal region suggested considerable use of the hands for manipulating.

The Kromdraii specimen consists of the shaded parts shown in the diagram; and the right-hand diagram shows one reason why many paleontologists place this fossil in the direct line of human ancestry. In these diagrams the ear parts are shown to be midway in shape between those of the gorilla and the same parts in modern man. The gorilla's earhole is surrounded by a swelling, or bulla. Man has a bony ring. *Paranthropus* is halfway between. In the gorilla the notch for the "joint" of the jawbone (to the left of the earhole) is shallow. In man it is deep; and again *Paranthropus* is midway between the two extremes.

The rise from this level to a low-grade prehuman level is seen in two other groups of finds—one dating from little more than the dawn of modern knowledge about man's physical ancestry and the second from our own days of rapidly unfolding knowledge. The first group is the type known as the Java ape man, or *Pithecanthropus erectus*. The second is Peking man, or *Sinanthropus Pekinensis*.

The Java ape man, also called "the Missing Link," is noteworthy in the history of discovery for the bombshell effect it had upon scientific opinion in the last decade of the nineteenth century.

At the time, scientific opinion was in a ferment about the origin of man, and the fires of argument had been kept hot by discoveries in Europe of fossilized skeletal remains of creatures which had been manlike but did not seem to have been men. Some scholars hailed these relics as proof that man had not been a unique type from the beginning; others sought to explain them as diseased-warped men.

While scientific opinion was in this state a young surgeon, Eugene Dubois, in the Dutch Colonial service in Java, made his momentous find in a gravel bed along the Solo River near Trinil, Java, during the winter of 1891–92. From the character of the bed and the type of animal fossils found in it Dubois placed the age as on the border line between the Pliocene and the Pleistocene.

The find itself consisted of a skullcap, two molar teeth and a femur, or thigh bone, recovered from somewhat separate locations; and when considered together, these finds suggested a creature which made a fine "Missing Link" between ape and man.

The skullcap was apelike in general contour. It had no forehead; the creature had rugged, overhanging eyebrows, and the vault or top was extremely low. But two features proved that no ape could have worn it in life. The volume of the brain was about twice the volume found in any living ape. Second, the association areas in the frontal lobe behind the forehead and in the temporal lobe behind the ear were developed far more than they are in apes.

All this might suggest, of course, that *Pithecanthropus* was merely an ape which had surpassed all others, living or dead, in brain development. The femur, however, overruled any such idea. Its features proved that the creature was accustomed to the erect posture. *Pithecanthropus* had passed, then, through the one specialization, aside from brain development, which marks the human stock. The teeth likewise were more human than simian. The creature undoubtedly was more man than ape.

Many of these conclusions have been challenged or even upset since 1892, and Dubois himself has changed his mind several times. But arguments about *Pithecanthropus* are largely unnecessary now. The whole question has been solved by the discovery of Peking man.

The story of this find begins late in 1927, when the city of Peking, as Peiping was then called, was ringed about by bandits. A young Swedish scientist, Dr Birger Bohlin, tried to enter the city after months of digging in a cave formation at Choukoutein, thirty-five miles to the southwest, and was robbed of all he had. But the bandits overlooked a fossilized "dragon's tooth," sole reward of all the digging; and since Bohlin had saved that he did not mind losing everything else.

He laid his precious find before Dr Davidson Black, professor of anatomy at the Union Medical College. Dr Black considered the teeth human but not from any hominid then known, so he created a classification, *Sinanthropus Pekinensis,* for the onetime possessor of the tooth. The age of the find seemed early Pleistocene.

The next task was digging out the Choukoutein cave in search of more relics, and rarely has any scientific effort been more richly rewarded. During the following years skulls and parts of skulls belonging to more than a score of individuals have been recovered, and they give us not merely a glimpse of an early type but a remarkable understanding of these early manlike creatures.

Peking man could use fire, as stands proved by charred bones, roasted hackberries and the charcoal from his hearths. His lower jaw, while still apelike in general shape, was well along in development of the structures needed for speech; and thinking power is further proved by the reason, unpleasant as it may be, why skulls predominated among the bones. From various scars on the skulls we know that Peking man had detached the heads from their bodies with stone knives and then carried them into the cave for some cannibalistic or ritualistic purpose. There was proof of thinking power, even though gruesome in nature—and proof also of ability to make tools and use them with considerable skill!

Thus the hint given by *Pithecanthropus* stands amply confirmed; and to this fact may be added one of the ironies of science. For practically a generation Dubois's find had stood alone, a lonely outpost of evidence, in spite of most intensive search for more specimens. The discovery of Peking man cleared up the subject—and since then, after more specimens of *Pithecanthropus* were no longer so badly needed, practically a dozen skullcaps and several more nearly complete specimens have turned up.

These specimens prove the primitive hominid nature of the Java ape man beyond question, and also the skullcaps attest the same gruesome custom which characterized Peking man. The caps had been detached from the lower skull just as modern Dyak headhunters perform the operation, and probably they were used as ritualistic drinking cups to give the strength and the wisdom, or both, of the vanquished to the conqueror, by magic.

Clearly such creatures are entitled to admission within the human family under any test of ability to think—and between them all, human mentality can be considered as established upon the earth. The story may be rounded out by noting only three important questions about all these men.

One question is *origin,* the place where these thinking types first emerged out of the parent primate stock. The second question is the problem of *dating,* or determining when these creatures lived. The third problem is the question of *race* or *strain*—that is, which of these types, if any, were ancestors of modern man and which ones belonged to divergent strains now extinct.

The first problem, that of origin, is narrowed down greatly at the very start by the fact that most portions of the earth could *not* have given birth to man.

Science cancels off both Americas and Australia at once. All the evidence suggests that manlike creatures did not live in them until comparatively recent times. All islands are out; they could not offer the range of experiences required to produce man. Finally no lands which had severe winters at the time need be considered.

Europe is a possibility but a remote one. The continent is a mere peninsula of the main Eurasian land mass; man would hardly have originated in such a side alley. The past spread of plants and animals supports this view. Always they appeared in Europe after having been developed in larger areas; never did they spring up in Europe itself. Similar reasoning casts doubt upon South Africa, even though primitive hominids have been found there. They *might* have originated there, but more probably they migrated there.

This leaves a broad belt which extends from China across central and southwestern Asia to central Africa, with Malaya and India added. From this belt science cancels out the Himalayas and the western China highlands as too high and therefore too cold, but

Arabia and the Sahara Desert are retained. These regions did not become arid until comparatively recent times.

Finally the possibilities are narrowed still farther if the ancestor of man was indeed produced by specialized adaptation for walking and running on flat grasslands.

Larger creatures such as man do not become adapted to flat land unless the region where their ancestors lived in formative days *was* flat. Prairie country, for example, would tend to produce such a development. But in the past ages, just as now, the only areas of flat, open land in the warmer parts of Asia lay north and west of the Himalayas and the Pamirs. South and west of these ranges lay forest or jungle, except in the gravelly Punjab south of the Himalayas.

This Central Asian location has been favored, therefore, by many scholars as the probable first home of the hominids—especially since W. D. Matthew presented a strong case for the idea in 1910 in his *Climate and Evolution*. The broad zone of southwestern Asia and northern Africa also has won consideration as a first home of the hominids. The region was suitable in every way; it adjoined the Egyptian site where anthropoid primates flourished during the Oligocene, and important finds made in East and South Africa can be accounted for as having wandered here from North Africa.

Thus science has two possibilities and no evidence as yet for choosing between them. For a general understanding of man, however, this scarcely matters.

The two centers were in land communication with each other during the times that figure importantly, and creatures which originated in one region could and would find their way to the other. Since many later events in the human record seem to come naturally from a Central Asian center, southwestern Turkestan will serve well enough, until more definite knowledge appears, as the original home of the *Hominidae*.

The second problem, that of *dating* the origin of man, is narrowed down, as was the problem of origin, by one important guiding fact.

The fossil record of manlike creatures runs back well through the Pleistocene, with the specimens constantly becoming more primitive and less manlike. Hence a Pliocene beginning is suggested. But an *earlier* beginning seems highly improbable, because no remains of this sort have been found which date *from* the Pliocene, let alone from earlier ages. The same is true of *artifacts* or man-made objects. The record runs back, with the artifacts becoming more and more primitive in form, to the Pliocene—and there it ends. A beginning of

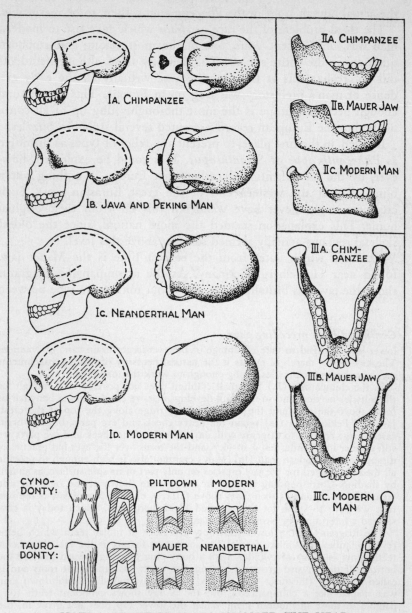

IA. CHIMPANZEE

IB. JAVA AND PEKING MAN

IC. NEANDERTHAL MAN

ID. MODERN MAN

IIA. CHIMPANZEE

IIB. MAUER JAW

IIC. MODERN MAN

IIIA. CHIMPANZEE

IIIB. MAUER JAW

IIIC. MODERN MAN

CYNODONTY:

PILTDOWN   MODERN

TAURODONTY:

MAUER   NEANDERTHAL

HOW A GROWING BRAIN CHANGED THE HEAD

The outstanding changes in head shape, from ape to modern man, are shown at the upper left, with the ever-larger brain indicated by a broken line. These diagrams show, too, how the bony parts of the upper face and the *mandible,* or

Continued at bottom of the next page

the actual human story in the Pliocene seems, then, to be reasonable.

The third problem of the *race* or *strain* which gave rise to modern man was, until recent years, one of the most vexing and stubborn questions in the entire subject. The difficulty arose, although students did not realize this at the time, because virtually all the early evidence of man's prehistory was dug up in Europe. This was natural enough because Europe is the most thoroughly dug up of all continents; but the European record presented several stubborn puzzles.

It failed, in the first place, to present any relics of types as primitive as *Pithecanthropus* or *Sinanthropus*. This could be explained, however, by the fact, mentioned earlier, that Europe is nothing but a blind alley at the western end of the great Eurasian mass. Such creatures might never have wandered this far from their original home. This explanation seemed the more natural, since the oldest skeletal remains actually seemed scarcely above this level.

The relic which dates from the earliest time is the Mauer jaw, found near Heidelberg, Germany. As the accompanying diagrams show, the jaw was brutally heavy and about midway in type between

Continued from preceding page

lower jaw, changed to take advantage of the ever-larger brain case, or *cranium*. The key to this march of events is the natural necessity of finding attachments on the cranium for muscles strong enough to work the mandible.

In the chimpanzee (IA) the small cranium does not provide area enough for the muscles needed, and so the skull develops massive cheekbones, a bony bar or *torus* above the eyes and the beginning of a ridge along the top of the crest. Java and Peking men (IB) retain the heavy cheek and eye parts, but the brain case is large enough to dispense with any top ridge. The cheek and eye parts are still smaller in Neanderthal man (IC), and the torus over the eyes has practically disappeared in modern man (ID). Man's cranium also is high enough to provide all the area needed for the jaw muscles on only part of its side surface, as shown by shading. Corresponding changes in the jaw are shown at the right, in side view (IIA, B, C), and as seen from above (IIIA, B, C). The Mauer jaw is the one relic we have to show for the so-called Heidelberg man, which today is considered a forerunner of Neanderthal man.

The diagrams at the lower left show a feature of molar teeth which helps reveal affinities of manlike fossils. The important feature is the fact that molar teeth grow as a sort of cylinder, with a bony plug growing inward to close the bottom. If this inward growth is strong, the tooth has prominent roots and is called *cynodont* (meaning "dog-toothed"). The jaw found with Piltdown man was shaped like a chimpanzee's, but the X ray shows cynodont teeth comparable to those in modern man. When the lower cap does not grow in, the tooth is almost flat-bottomed or *taurodont* (meaning "bull-toothed," since cattle and other herbivorous mammals show this tendency). The X ray and the teeth themselves of the Mauer jaw and of Neanderthal man show taurodonty. This feature sets the Heidelberg and Neanderthal men apart from moderns as a separate strain.

chimpanzee and modern man. It could have belonged well enough to a somewhat advanced descendant of the earliest known hominids.

Next after this relic in point of age came a rich array of finds, all belonging to the one general type, called *Homo neanderthalensis* or Neanderthal man. This type had a large brain but, contrary to the usual relation between brain and mouth, the jaws remained large. Massive cheekbones were supported, and the head was further strengthened, by a crosswise *torus,* or bony bar, above the eyes. Strong nasal bones transmitted shocks from the teeth to the torus and thereby guarded other facial bones from injury. Also they masked the nostrils and gave the face an apelike appearance. The jaw had only a bare suggestion of a chin. The structure of the knees hampered standing fully upright, while the backbone lacked the full S curve which makes the erect position practicable for modern humans.

These men occupied Europe until perhaps fifteen thousand years ago—and then suddenly modern man burst full blown into the continent. Such an entry raised an immensely puzzling question. Development from the Neanderthaloid stage hardly seemed possible, because Neanderthal man's ingrained gorillalike structure could hardly disappear from any direct descendants. But if Neanderthal man was not the ancestor of modern man, who was?

Curiously enough, science had possessed the answer ever since 1888, in a find made at Galley Hill on the Thames River in England! The evidence consisted of skull fragments and enough of the other parts, including leg bones, to give a good idea of development. The deposit in which the bones lay was hundreds of thousands of years old—and yet this individual could well have passed for a lowly specimen of modern man! The leg bones indicated fully erect posture; the face had none of the gorilloid features which marked Neanderthal man, and the brain was fully modern in size.

The evidence was plain enough, but the scientists could not bring themselves to believe it. Every scientific instinct of those full-blown Darwinian times said that creatures of this antiquity should have been much nearer the ape than was this specimen. (In 1888, it must be remembered, *Pithecanthropus* had not been discovered, to say nothing of *Sinanthropus.*) The scientists of the day felt sure, therefore, that this modern type of skeleton must have been buried in comparatively recent times in this ancient deposit, and they more or less dismissed Galley Hill man from further consideration.

Another shock of the same sort came, however, in 1912, with announcement of a new discovery—Piltdown man.

The so-called Piltdown man, which many anatomists think was really a woman, bears the scientific name *Eoanthropus dawsoni* ("dawn man," from *eos* for dawn and *anthropos* for man. The second name honors the discoverer, Mr Charles Dawson). The pieces of it were uncovered at various times between 1908 and the spring of 1912 near Piltdown, England, in a middle Pleistocene deposit.

The relics consist of scattered skull fragments, teeth and part of a lower jawbone, or mandible. The scattering created tremendously challenging puzzles. The skull parts are thoroughly human, but the jawbone, if found alone, would have been put down without question as that of a chimpanzee. Did these relics come, then, from one creature or two? From 1912 until now scientists have generated more heat and headaches than they have agreements over this problem.

Other arguments arose over attempts to reconstruct a complete skull from the fragments. The trouble here is that nowhere do the fragments join up unmistakably. An anatomist could allow a generous space between them and produce a large human type of skull. A niggardly allowance would yield an apelike specimen; and eminent anatomists argued endlessly over this problem.

These arguments were important as long as the Piltdown skull was the only known specimen, other than the forgotten Galley Hill man, of an early hominid with relatively high brain development. The available evidence was enriched in 1925 by discovery of the *London* or *Lloyd's* skull under one of the busiest spots in the modern world, the corner of Leadenhall and Lime streets, London, near the Bank of England. The relic was exposed forty-two feet down in excavations being made for a new Lloyd's Insurance Exchange building. Only the rear portion of the skull was discovered, but as far as the fragment went it fitted the high-mentality version of the Piltdown skull.

Finally the problem was practically settled in 1936 by discovery of the *Swanscombe skull*. This find consists of two fragments found in 1935 and 1936, respectively, by Alvan T. Marston in a gravel pit at Swanscombe, England. Marston had expert geologists and paleontologists examine the second find before it was dug out, to determine the geologic age. Then the anatomists appraised the relics as follows:

The relics consist of the occipital bone—that is, the rear and rearward base of the skull—and the left parietal, from above the ear. These pieces fit together and block out enough of the skull to reveal a shape and size of brain that could pass for modern. Moreover, such developmental trends as can be deduced agree with the high-mentality version of the Piltdown skull. Unquestionably, then, a high mental type comparable to modern man lived even in those remote times.

This finding disposed most effectively of the problems raised by Neanderthal man. The plain truth is that each type—the Neanderthal and the modern—had emerged from more primitive stock in remote Pleistocene times and had occupied portions of the earth ever since. The modern type had appeared in Europe in remote time, then moved out again. Neanderthal man appeared in his turn—then modern man came back and has occupied Europe ever since.

This finding runs counter to the earlier view that men of the modern type did not appear on the earth until comparatively recent times. The evidence, however, is indisputable, and the finding can only be accepted. The story of our own race—not of primitive forerunners or divergent cousins, but of our very own kind—begins in these remote times, and we are ready to see how man began using his ability to think for improving his lot in life.

Before undertaking this, however, we can well afford to notice certain new viewpoints about man's early career.

Until recent years scientists and laymen alike assumed that this career was a smooth progression. Man started with nothing, gradually added new ideas and inventions to his endowment, and thereby plodded forward steadily even if slowly toward better ways. This viewpoint served well enough as long as only a few fragments of the story were known; but as knowledge became more nearly complete this viewpoint proved to be utterly contrary to fact. The very existence just mentioned of a modern type of man half a million years or so ago is a good instance of why it will not do.

Obviously if such men existed in those days they had mental ability enough to progress within a few centuries, or a few millenia at most, from mere food grubbing to skilled hunting, domestication of useful animals and manufacture of clothing. Written language could be expected to grow out of speech and sign language together—and civilization would have been fairly born.

What a prospect this opens to the mind—civilization born one or two hundred thousand years ago instead of a mere five or seven thousand years ago, and ourselves in a position to enjoy a correspondingly richer heritage! Inevitably we ask, then, why this did not happen, since in all probability man was psychologically able to invent civilization at the close of the Mindel-Riss. What happened to cheat us, in the twentieth century after Christ, of the enormously rich heritage that could have been ours had these early men lived up to their opportunity?

A few years ago the best answers that could be given were such vague and inane generalities as "Progress had to be slow at first" and "It took time to make the first inventions." Today such answers are recognized as sheer evasions and contrary to fact as well.

Progress did not "have to be slow"; the later record shows that mankind invented all the essentials of civilized living in two or three thousand years at most. Plainly, then, something must have happened to *prevent* progress for hundreds of thousands of years, and the all-important question is what that "something" could have been.

Another requirement of the theory that man achieved smooth if slow progress is that he should have discarded his mistakes from age to age. But we of all peoples in any period of history know all too well how mankind stubbornly refuses to do this. Here we are, heirs to a historic record which has proved for thousands of years that empires built with force of arms do not endure. Yet today the world is being tortured once again by Adolf Hitler's attempt to make this age-old folly work.

Once again, therefore, something other than smooth progression is at work. Human nature must have traits which make men susceptible to folly in spite of experience. But if this is so, these traits are fully as important as the forces which produce progress.

Now with these considerations in mind we are ready to start seeing how man's mentality took shape. This can hardly be done profitably, however, by trying to begin with the actual oldest humans we know, Galley Hill man, Piltdown man and Swanscombe man. Finds in other localities prove that the men of these English days already had considerable skill as toolmakers. Beginnings then must be sought in an earlier age. So likewise the English setting is unsuitable for the story of mental beginnings. Europe almost certainly was a side alley, and these creatures represented backwash or "terminal migration" from the main center of development. For these reasons the story of beginnings should be placed in the grasslands of Central Asia, and the time should be the end of the Pliocene.

No setting could have been more propitious, because those days enjoyed one of the halcyon times in the history of the earth.

In almost any part of the earth we could select we should have beheld a generally smiling scene. The landscapes of mountain and plain, of forest, meadow and grassland, appeared much as they do now, but they were warmer, softer, more genial. Palms flourished throughout Europe; in them chattered groups of monkeys, while semitropical birds lent flashing color to the scene. The arctic regions probably had the climate of modern Canada. Where today grim desert is master of vast regions in northern Africa, in Mexico and in Arabia, smiling grasslands lay rolling to wide horizons.

The world of animals contained strange beasts but not many. Saber-toothed tigers roamed many of the lands, and various species of rhinoceros and elephant could be seen as far north as England; but the earth-shaking dinosaurs and grotesque flying reptiles of earlier ages had been extinct for perhaps a hundred million years. Horses, cattle and sheep roamed the grasslands of Asia; the more wooded regions of Asia, Africa and Europe harbored apes. In all the world-wide scene the only elements which we would miss were the works of man; such men as we might see would be living as rudely as any ape.

But in spite of rudeness the germs of higher intelligence were in the creatures—and to see how these germs produced the beginnings of human progress we can do nothing better than set ourselves back in imagination into these times and watch these early thinkers struggling slowly toward better ways.

PART II

THE MAKING OF TRUE MAN

CHAPTER VI

Meet "the First Man"!

A GENIAL SUN wheels overhead—a sun beaming with the same soft heat that draws snow-beset Northerners of our day to Florida and California every winter. Beneath its warm rays lies an open, almost barren landscape, a match for the present-day Great Plains in Kansas and Nebraska; the flatness is relieved on the horizon by a mountain range, with snow-capped peaks that gleam whitely against the blue sky. Before us is a brook, running swiftly with its burden of melted snow from these mountains; all else about us is a sea of grass, dotted with bushes and small trees.

Of human habitations or activity we see not a trace. No road, no cultivated patch of ground, not even a wisp of smoke from a camp-fire, greets the eye. No creak of wagon wheel, blow of ax or hoof-beat on a road falls upon the ear; we hear only the purl of the brook, the rustle of a dry, warm breeze in the grass, the buzz and the hum of insects. As we continue to note the true emptiness of our sur-roundings we begin to feel lonely beyond power of words to de-scribe. How lonely, we realize more fully when a few reflections drive home to us the full extent of our isolation!

We have said that in order to visit one of the first men we are seeking him in Central Asia, on the far-flung slope which descends northwestward from the Pamirs, the so-called roof of the world. We of today call the region Russian Turkestan. This would seem isolated enough even in our twentieth-century time; how much more so it is when we remember that we are separated by a million years or more from present-day civilization!

If food runs short, can we send back to our base of supplies for more, as modern explorers might do? Silly thought—no such thing as a base of supplies is in existence! And whom could we send, when the entire world does not contain a single soul, aside from ourselves, who could even understand us if we asked him to fetch food? In fact, barring ourselves, nobody exists who can talk at all, who even imagines that ideas can be exchanged by means of uttered sounds. Language is among the many arts which remain to be invented—at least all language beyond grunts, howls and cries which indicate satisfaction, fear, rage and pain.

No; by placing ourselves back in the days of humanity's beginnings we have stripped ourselves of practically every help which might be called human. We must get along precisely as do our wolf or tiger neighbors. If our own resources fail us, that is just too bad. Death under the nearest bush or at the first pounce of some predatory beast will be our portion the moment we weaken or falter in the slightest. Should drought or insects cut down our food supply, we can only stagger on, growing weaker and more desperate, until we collapse and perish.

Does the stark grimness of this situation seem appalling? It should, for then we may begin to see what human thought has done for us between such days and now——

Ha, what's that? We must be getting the spirit of the wilderness ourselves; we have been startled by a mere rustle near by, a rustle scarcely stronger than the perpetual swish born of the wind in the grass. As we look a small rabbitlike creature bursts from cover into the open stream bed. Immediately after comes a stone, hurled by some hand which we cannot see. The stone bowls the small animal over into a quivering ball of fur. A moment passes, then the thrower appears, creeping furtively from his grassy cover. We have our first glimpse of the manlike creature we have come to see.

Save for keen eyes set beneath heavy brows and a strong jaw, we see but little of his face. It is covered, like his body, with a lifetime growth of hair. But his lithe movements, and his wariness amounting almost to eyes in the back of his head, let us know that he is competent to care for himself in most emergencies.

Well for him that this is so! As he draws near his prey the grass rustles again. In a twinkling he is scrambling up a near-by tree. A huge hyena appears and favors our early man with a snarl and a show of teeth. Then it makes off with the little animal down the stream bed. Now we may get a really good look at the individual whom, for convenience, we shall call Og.

Why Og? Because later, when he and his fellows learn to talk, they will do so in monosyllables, short or drawn out into howls and cries, as may be. Modern babies say mama and dada long before they can say mother and father; undoubtedly the same rule held true during the mental babyhood of the human tribe. So Og let our man be; the question now is, what will he do?

For a time he just sits apelike on a tree limb, glancing nervously about and gibbering resentment over his lost meal. He is not an ape, of course, any more than a horse is a zebra or a tiger is a lion. But since he has no more clothes than an ape wears and lives exactly as an ape does, his appearance and manner are naturally quite apelike.

And what is he thinking about as he sits there while his fright dies down and his chattering anger fades?

We have foreshadowed the answer with our examples of recovery from anesthesia and the probable mental state of a baby, but these examples need refinement now.

They served well enough for a first survey, but obviously Og would not last a moment in this savage world if his mental state were no keener than either of these others. Instead of being weak and fumbling he has keen senses, fine precision of instant action and abundant energy. Indeed, he has every endowment that we do save one: he lacks the full light of intelligent understanding.

But can we imagine an adult manlike creature in full possession of all his mental faculties save this one? Yes, we can do this very readily. We need only take our own thoughts of a day, an hour, and strip from them every idea obtained from books, from newspapers, in school, at work or in conversation with our fellow men. Then we must take away all use of words—even so simple a thought as, "I believe I'd better climb that tree." What have we left? Not much; but whatever it is, it constitutes Og's mental life.

Will it amount to anything at all? Yes, it will be a definite mental life, and we can sense the quality of it readily by recalling the pleasant "think-of-nothing" mood which comes occasionally when we laze upon a pleasant ocean beach or in a hammock beneath fragrant, blossoming apple trees. There we have the pleasant side of Og's mental life—the side which comes uppermost when all is going well.

Next recall the feeling of "blind rush" which sends us scurrying should a sudden shower break over us. Just so did Og feel when he scrambled to safety from the hyena. Again remember our occasional "blind rages." Such battle moods will come to Og quite often. Now fill up a lifetime with a succession of such moods, pleasant and unpleasant. That succession will constitute mental life for Og.

He "thinks," just as he lives, for the moment only. What is to come, aside from desire for the next meal, is a blank. Og never bothers his head about tomorrow; he has no idea of what "tomorrow" means. Perhaps he feels a certain wariness when a tiger's roar stirs instinctive caution; otherwise past events are as blank as though they had never happened. The present concern, the warmth of the moment's sun or the chill of the moment's wind—the gnawing of hunger or the warm, lazy joy of a full stomach—such feelings probably make up mental life for Og and for all manlike creatures like him.

At first glance such a blank state may seem unlikely enough as a source for the genius of a Michelangelo or a Newton, the conquest of the air, or harnessing Niagara to run factories and light homes. Yet every step in this immense advance can be traced without undue trouble, as can also the ways in which man came to betray himself with his own follies. Indeed, the first stirrings of the advance can be detected just by watching for a few moments.

We have said that Og's mental life consists of moods which change with the moments, and presently we see the "now" wiping out feelings of the "has been" in his mind. He has ceased gibbering in resentment over the hyena's act of robbery, and he seems alert again for signs of food. Soon something stirs in the vicinity and attracts him; he drops from his perch and starts prowling, a wraithlike, hairy figure, along the dusty green, sun-flecked wall of grass which borders the stream bed.

After going a few hundred feet he pauses, listens for enemies, then climbs into a tree for fruit. With hunger appeased he comes down from the tree and edges across a bed of bare gravel toward the stream for a drink. After getting his drink he rises—then jumps, growls and examines his foot. Something has pricked or cut it. He picks up the offending article, a flint nodule broken in two and having a sharp edge. Anyone who has broken flint knows that such an edge can be sharp as broken glass; small wonder that not even the toughened sole of Og's foot could resist it!

Now, as we watch, Og turns the offending stone in his hand and stares at it. As he does so he feels a swish from a tree branch that overhangs the stream and raises his hands to brush it away, as he would a buzzing insect. In one hand he holds the flint; its sharp edge cuts several leaves.

Og examines them, looks again at the flint and his foot, then cuts once more at the branch as it sways past. More leaf fragments fall. Og grabs the branch, hacks at the woody stem; it comes apart. Og has discovered the flint knife—one of the first feats of this sort in all human history!

Now this plainly seems to be an act of reasoning, and so we might say that the light of intelligence is at least aglow in Og's mind; but we must not go too fast. This feat, significant as it is, still contains many elements of animal mentality. Indeed, two aspects of animal mentality explain almost the entire action. These aspects are *curiosity* and *playfulness*.

Most higher animals, as we know, have curiosity. Who of us has not seen horses, dogs and birds stare at strange objects, particularly if the objects flicker or move? We often see animals paw or nuzzle tin cans, bright cloths and the like. They do so because their senses have been challenged by some appearance which warns of possible danger, but a moment's attention has detected no threat. Therefore, since the appearance continues to attract, it draws the animal closer; and this drawing is curiosity.

Now mere animal curiosity, coupled with Og's ability to manipulate instead of merely pawing or nuzzling, will account for his examining the foot and the flint, then the leaves which he cut by accident. If we doubt this, we need only recollect that modern infants begin their activities with just such responses to the attractions offered by glittering objects, by a "tick tock" or anything that moves.

Similarly, playfulness will explain his hacking at the stem, provided we understand what the term means in this connection. Play is typically a youngster's activity, not an adult's; and it arises in youngsters because growing strength, untaxed as yet by the work of earning a living, creates urges toward exuberant actions, actions that follow the pattern of inherited life habits. Puppies tumble over each other and bite with toothless gums; kittens stalk inanimate moving objects if no living game is available; young humans love to handle bright objects, and when they become old enough they play make-believe games such as Tarzan and Cops and Robbers. In adult life individuals usually spend their energies earning a living, but occasionally even adults will play if they feel particularly good and have some idle time. Hence Og's hacking at the stem might well be set down to mere playfulness, save for two hints that some germ of intelligent thought was at work.

First, he *transferred* the idea of cutting from what had happened to his foot and the leaves to what he might be able to *make* happen to the branch. This amounted to use of constructive imagination. Second, his actions seem clearly purposive. He *wanted* to cut the branch or at least to see whether the flint would cut it.

When we say this we must be doubly careful, lest we assume without further ado that we have uncovered the true starting point of human thinking, the type of mental activity which gave birth to progress. So far we have not seen this, because modern findings about ape mentality tell us that Og has done nothing which a chimpanzee cannot do. As pointed out in Chapter II, this ape can apply as much constructive imagination as Og has used thus far, and it might conceivably cut at the branch just as Og has done. Before Og proves himself clearly superior to the ape he must remember, apply and teach. He should also demonstrate that he has perceived some elements of causality, of the "reasons why" which connect the sharp edge of the flint with the severing of the branch.

So, too, we can afford to keep in mind a great difference between older and present-day viewpoints about such incidents. The older view held that once Og acquired a development of brain which gave him superior mental powers he would commence using them. Therefore in this instance he would lose no time, according to the older view, after discovering the flint knife, in making good use of it for improving his mastery over Nature.

But such a notion arises from applying *our* viewpoint, our knowledge of how useful this knife can be; and this is utterly invalid. What counts is *Og's* viewpoint, if indeed he has any as yet—and what right have we to expect that he will make good use of this discovery? Why should he *want* to do anything useful? As long as water remains in the brook, roots and berries hold out, and predatory beasts do not steal too many of his kills, what more does he ask of life?

We see little or no reason to suppose that he would ask anything at all. Since he lived for the moment only, he had no incentive to learn or invent anything—and since he lacked incentive, in all probability he would not invent. At least this is the conclusion which can be fairly drawn from all that we know about primitive peoples and from the testimony of past ages. All this evidence suggests that man is not the inherently progressive creature we once naïvely assumed him to be. History says rather that clean-cut *desire* for progress has appeared only twice in the human record—once in ancient Greek times, and again in comparatively modern days, commencing at the period of the Crusades. At all other times man achieved advances only when something drove him to the task.

We must expect, then, to see some special incentive at work before Og will start thinking to good effect, save for one highly probable exception. He might well have achieved a limited *mastery of fire*. This would come naturally enough through the play impulse and Og's occasional contacts with this dread phenomenon, through seeing lightning-riven trees ablaze or perhaps vegetation set on fire by hot lava from a volcano.

We can imagine that Og would be terrified at first, as animals always are; then his human endowment of self-awareness, with its knack of noticing how happenings affect his interests, will come to his rescue. He will realize that as long as he is not touched by this dread monster he is not hurt. Rather, on chilly days, nearness to fire gives comfort; and this realization, like curiosity, will draw him nearer. Eventually playfulness will prompt him to light a brand by poking a stick into the fire.

What a moment that must have been for Og—a Promethean moment, when he must have felt godlike in his ability to flourish this dread, red, consuming thing about! Thereafter, by playing with fire, Og would learn that it kept wild animals away; he might also learn to like cooked food. Such accomplishments do not conflict with our earlier assertion that no campfire was to be seen anywhere on the landscape. Og might try to keep one burning whenever Nature provided the initial flame, but one rainstorm would quench it. Then he would have to wait for another natural flame, because as yet he has not learned how to *make* a fire.

This did not matter much, however, in mild Pliocene times. Og could well afford to let such an advance wait—and therefore, according to modern ideas, he *would* let it wait until some driving need suggested otherwise.

Thus we arrive fairly at the most important question of all concerning these early days. What happened to rouse up man's dormant abilities and set them working to good effect?

We need be in no doubt about the answer. Biology tells us that whenever life proves too easy for any creature, plant or animal, for a few generations, Nature applies the prod of *overpopulation*.

Any species of plant or animal, if left unchecked for long or allowed to live in undue prosperity, soon produces more of its kind than can hope to find food. This is as true of humans in a state of Nature as it is of any living creature, and even what seems a small increase to us was quite enough to constitute overpopulation in Og's day. With us, one more family added to every fifty square miles of land is not much; but for natural man, who lives on roots, berries and birds' eggs, fifty square miles or even more may be the minimum needed, according to the usual estimates, for one family. Then the addition of another family in such an area could scarcely be endured.

In a lush season both families might get along, but once food became scarce quarreling would start. Whoever lost in the inevitable fight would have to move on. Thereby the weaker folk would constantly be pushed out from good lands into poorer ones, until eventually the species would occupy every habitable portion of the globe by a conquering march which really was an unending flight of the weak.

Thus, paradoxically enough, in weakness would lie the germ of humanity's ultimate strength—for this situation would force the early thinkers into doing what no animal can do. When overpopulation drives animals onward they can only go as far as suitable climates and environments may extend. Then the weaker ones must perish, and the total population remains fixed at whatever number can find food within the range occupied. The early manlike creatures, however, had one trick left before they had to accept limitation of their numbers by starvation. They could use their previously neglected inventive abilities to improve upon unfavorable conditions, whenever forced in poor surroundings. In this way they could avoid overpopulation troubles for countless generations, and they would gain constantly in use of mental powers through doing so.

This may be considered, then, as explaining how and why dawning intelligence managed to achieve the beginnings of progress—and to visualize the record in vivid detail we need only assume that Og bowed to defeat in several ancient battles for feeding grounds and was forced to move on or perish. The moment he did so, all-powerful forces would compel useful thought on his part; and so he will exemplify for us how progress got its start.

Let us assume, then, that Og was pushed on and see what must have happened as he marched onward, naked as he was both physically and mentally, in search of a new home.

CHAPTER VII

The Conquest of Nature Begins

MAN STARTING OUT NAKED, with only his hands and his powers of thought, to conquer the world—surely here was an epic adventure if ever there was one! All of us respond to the thrill of it, for we all inherit traits and quirks of character from our remote ancestors who fought and won in this struggle. How else can we explain the undying appeal of the Robinson Crusoe story and of tales about explorers, cow hands and others who come to grips with savage Nature and equally savage men?

Well—here we are, ready to trace this story, not in fictionized form but in sober fact; and to start, let us ask what science can tell us about the directions in which Og could have marched. This will depend, naturally, upon the geography of Pliocene times.

The continental coast lines were somewhat different but not enough to concern us here, save for one item. The present Aral, Caspian and Black seas were united, or nearly so, into one great sea which also extended north over the flatlands of western Siberia, well toward the Arctic Ocean. The Himalayas and related ranges were not as high then as they are now; they were, just as they still are, being elevated. Otherwise the principal difference between Pliocene times and ours was in climate.

During Pliocene days the climate was genial—warm temperate or subtropical—over most of Europe and Central Asia. Thus man could live in a state of nature throughout a wide range; only when he wandered or was forced into high mountain ranges or onto elevated plateaus would he encounter disagreeable cold and scarcity of food due to cold. Water supply—wet and dry areas—are harder to estimate; but since the climate was more equable the world over than it is now, we may assume the existence of a reasonable water supply in every region that concerns us. In particular, Central Asia would have more rain than it does now, because the region did not have to get along, as it does now, with the last remnants of moisture brought by the westerly winds from the faraway Atlantic and Baltic seas. The winds undoubtedly recharged themselves with moisture from the huge Aralo-Caspian Sea.

So much for geography; we come now to asking whither, in this Pliocene array of lands around Central Asia, Og might have marched when he was forced to move on.

We see at once that he can hardly go far toward the east or the south. High mountains existed there even in Pliocene times, and their climates were much too cold for naked men. In particularly warm periods movement northeastward into Mongolia was possible, but let us ignore this, since it would not lead to the history of West Asian and European man which underlies ours. The Aralo-Caspian Sea bars movement to the westward. The only remaining direction is southwestward into the mountainous plateau we call Persia or Iran.

Here in this higher, cooler land Og would be forced to rouse up his dormant ability to invent and put it to work. To withstand cold nights he would need fire, and even more he would need ability to *make* fire; dependence upon chance flames lit by Nature no longer would do. He would need clothing, at least in winter, and he would need increased ability to hunt animals as fruit and nuts became scarce.

Such discoveries, however, would be made without particular difficulty, once Og had gained the all-important idea that he could invent, from his playing with fire or some similar experience. In fact, simple memory of chance discoveries, worked over with aid from a mere dash of constructive imagination, would serve well enough throughout the entire initial march not only into Iran but over the entire habitable earth. In this way, for example, the previously neglected discovery of the flint knife could come into use now both for help in killing animals and for trimming branches into clubs. The idea of trimming a club will be so simple, so obvious, that even Og can follow it through once the need arises. And once he does so, certain other applications also would be obvious. If his flint knife has helped him produce a club, why not use it to produce other objects, by cutting, whittling and trimming them into shape?

The invention of clothing would be one fruit of this idea. Even great apes know the comfort to be had from coverings; we can see them in zoos covering themselves with any fabric given them and enjoying the result. Naturally Og would have this understanding, and once he started hunting in earnest, the idea of using an animal's hide for covering himself would appeal to him. He has a knife which can skin off the pelt, and once he has the hide, thorns will do well enough for fastenings.

In similar fashion Og would learn to meet his greatest need of all— the need for a tool with which he could make fire at will. He could accomplish this by noting that when sticks are rubbed together long enough and hard enough they take fire. An even easier road to this discovery would be noticing, during some of his tinkerings with stones, that a flint gives off a spark when struck on a piece of pyrites or stone containing iron. Let the spark fall upon dry leaves or dry moss, and he could blow it into a flame.

In some such ways the invention of practical devices got a start; and behind all these detailed achievements stood one general gain, of paramount importance in the development of thought. As we know, thinking consists of applying patterns of understanding to data furnished by the senses, by memory and by understanding. One of the most important of these patterns is realization of *ability to invent, the knowledge* that something useful can be done to conquer difficulties. This comes in time from success with random inventions such as Og has been making. After making a number of them more or less by chance he will come to abstract from his memories of these feats the realization that he can devise ways and means to improve his lot whenever he likes. Thus one of man's most highly useful concepts would be added to his mental endowment.

Much the same random start undoubtedly was made in dealing with other problems which Og raised up for himself by his very achievement of applying thought to the conquest of Nature.

Once he has started using thought in this way, he will apply it inevitably in other directions as well. In place of brutelike indifference to his fellows, or at best a dumb animallike fidelity to his family, Og will begin to feel glimmerings of a notion that he can get along with his companions on some basis above brute competition. He will begin to wonder, just as young modern children do, about whys and wherefores in Nature, about his own future and a possible life after death. In short, he will find himself at grips with social and spiritual problems.

What he will think and do about them can be judged readily enough by considering the contrast between his feelings upon encountering a stranger and ours.

Today, should we be approached by a fellow man in a wilderness, we would welcome the stranger as a friend, unless we had reason to think otherwise. If we were eating primitive fashion in a berry patch, we might suggest, "We're nearly through here. Just watch out a moment for tigers, like a good fellow—then we'll watch while you eat." But would Og dare—or would he be able—to suggest any such co-operation?

Notice how much experience, how much capacity for understanding, is involved in our suggestion! We and our stranger can reach an agreement because each party understands that gains can be won by co-operation. But can Og and his fellows be expected to have this much wisdom? Hardly, when history proves abundantly that such lessons were only learned painfully step by step through the centuries, while current events prove that they are learned all too imperfectly even today!

Again we have conveyed an idea and reached an understanding by using language. But could Og do this? We have no valid reason for supposing so. No, on all counts, in Og's day, the arrival of a stranger while Og is feeding in the berry patch leaves only one safe course open. Og must assume that the other will try to push him aside and take his place. Since he is crouching while the stranger is standing, he will do well to correct this disadvantage immediately.

Of course the chances are good that he will provoke a fight by this very act. But this cannot be helped; the law of the jungle runs here, just as it does between animals. Such needless fighting is one of the penalties inflicted by lack of ability to think and apply common sense in solving life's problems.

How, then, we may fairly ask, did men ever learn to co-operate with each other instead of always fighting each other?

Sociologists are practically unanimous in replying that men learned this lesson, even in spite of themselves, through being placed in a situation where they could not do otherwise. They learned, while still mere children, to co-operate with their parents, their brothers and their sisters and their uncles, aunts, nephews and nieces in group undertakings.

By the time they became old enough to go along on their own they were accustomed to living with and co-operating with certain individuals whom they recognized. Therefore, hostility and suspicion were reserved for those whom they did not recognize; and that trait has persisted from Og's day to ours. Let anyone who thinks otherwise simply note the callous delight children take in tormenting strange children, or the contemptuous indifference which most grown-up Americans exhibit toward the woes and troubles of the folks commonly called "furriners," "wops," "hunkies," "chinks" and "dagoes"!

Indeed, sociologists go even farther back than the first human families for the origin of this so-called "gregarious instinct" or "herd instinct." In this they follow the doctrine which was brilliantly advanced in 1902 by Prince Peter Kropotkin in his book *Mutual Aid, A Factor in Evolution*. In this book we find unanswerable evidence that an "instinct"—or a "conditioning," if we prefer the more modern term—toward co-operation with familiar companions is well established among many species of animals; so we have no mystery here as concerns man. This so-called instinct was part of his inheritance when he became man.

Sociologists are equally emphatic that from the start man's primary social unit was the family; they regard the once-fashionable idea of "herd organization" with extreme suspicion, to say the least. We may feel sure, then, that Og and his kind had the germs of social organization in them when they first began to think, and unquestionably these germs would blossom when any such group was pushed into new, forbidding land. When our imaginary group reached Iran the members would be harassed by new troubles and tormented by cold. Wild beasts in this land of scarce food would be as ravenous as they and hence would be more than ever dangerous. Amidst all these perils would not Og and his fellows act as humans always do in such situations? Would they not draw closer together mentally and even huddle physically to find warmth and the reassurance of fellowship when the chill blasts of a winter night howled about them and the green eyes of wolves and leopards shone on them through the darkness?

We can hardly doubt this or doubt that an intense group feeling, the so-called social instinct, would cement them together. Moreover, this feeling would be strengthened by a powerful new factor. Heretofore their chief concern has been food, and, as we have seen, the food hunt can breed strife and discord. But now they need warmth as much as food. They will rally to the campfire—and campfires build fellowship just as strongly as limited berry patches breed fights.

Driving others away from one's own scanty supply of food is understandable enough, but wherein does a man benefit himself by driving others away from a fire which he is enjoying? Nay, he helps himself by letting them draw near. They like to play with fire as well as he. From time to time they will go to hunt firewood, and every stick that anybody brings benefits everybody in the group.

Here would be a practical object lesson in co-operation which even the dullest mind could not miss. We know how modern campers can growl at each other all through a rainy day, then mellow into renewed friendship while sitting around a cheery fire at night. Can we doubt that in the brutish minds behind the shrewd, habitually suspicious eyes which gleamed from beneath bushy brows around these ancient campfires new attitudes of fellowship, new understandings of co-operation, would be astir?

Another tendency, equally powerful for human good, would arise from the campfire. The period of evening rest beside the campfire has been man's time-honored hour for thinking of the morrow and making needed preparations. What time, then, could be better for comparing notes concerning toolmaking and all the other inventions which heretofore we have pictured as being made by one man alone? We may be sure that our little bands of prehistoric thinkers did "put their heads together" around campfires of an evening, and we can even imagine the course of events in such "conferences."

Little or nothing might be said; perhaps language still was in a formative state. Those present probably would act largely as though they were playing. Some of them might peck at a flint tool or whittle at a wooden one, half seriously, half idly. Others would content themselves with watching the workers; and ever and anon some worker would achieve a happy result—a new shape for a flint knife or a new, helpful quirk in fire-making tools. He would emit a murmur of pleasure. The others would crowd about and exclaim in their turn, then perhaps try to produce the same result themselves. Thereby the group would gain a new idea, and the gain would join the stock of ideas which the children would inherit.

Such activities also would help language forward mightily, but we cannot say more because no problem vexes science more than does this question of how language actually originated. Linguists have all but lost interest in the problem, since they have realized that there are no truly primitive languages in the psychological sense to serve as a basis of study and that their knowledge of psychology is not

sound or broad enough to help with the problem. For further understanding about the origins of language it will be necessary to wait
upon new studies of the behavior of children and of the higher apes.

We have seen that the root of the power to invent and contrive is
having a mental pattern or picture of being *able* to contrive. But
even as men learned to abstract meanings and relations from their
daily experiences, so would they come to associate certain spoken
sounds with these abstractions. How this association came about and
how sounds were chosen is the scientific puzzle. That it *did* come
about we cannot doubt. And once it did language, the exchange of
ideas by uttered sounds or speech, would have been born.

These are some of the ways in which newly kindled inventiveness
could make life easier for Og and his kind—and the temptation is
to assume that this ability would work constantly to achieve improvements. But already we have been put on our warning that such
an assumption is an application of our viewpoint, not of primitive
thinking. We may feel sure that our first thinkers would progress
this far because they had to—but would they go beyond this?

Nothing save the actual record is entitled to answer. Hence the
time seems at hand to turn from speculation and see what actually
happened, as far as we know the course of events. Also, since we
are fairly at grips now with man's story, we need some timetable,
some means for checking the pace of progress, which has more
accuracy to it than the vague terms "late Pliocene," "early Pleistocene"
and "Ice Age," which have served well enough thus far. Happily we
have just such a timetable in modern knowledge of what happened
during the Ice Age.

This age saw four major periods of glaciation, with three warm
interglacial periods between the cold stages; and the standard exposi-
tion of these events is the monumental study *Die Alpen im Eiszeitlter*
(The Alps in the Ice Age, 1909), by Albrecht Penck and Eduard
Brückner.

These authors named the four glaciations they had detected after
four Alpine rivers, the Günz, the Mindel, the Riss and the Würm.
They chose these rivers, along which the glaciations are exemplified,
rather than others because the names came in alphabetic order, corresponding to the glaciations—G for the first, M for the second, R
for the third and W for the fourth. Interglacial periods are named
for the glaciations which bracket them. The first, between the first
and second glaciations, is the Günz-Mindel; the second is the Mindel-

Riss; and the third is the Riss-Würm. We of today live in post-Würmian times; the term is equivalent to "Holocene."

The dating of these glaciations is based upon the time span of from one to one and one half million years usually allowed for the entire Pleistocene, as explained earlier on page 27. Within this time span the different glacial periods are dated largely by studies of *moraines,* the heaps of material which glaciers deposit at their outer edges. The age of a moraine can be estimated by measuring how deeply the material in it has been weathered.

Such estimates suggest that the glaciations came in two groups. The Günz and Mindel glaciations came relatively closely together and were followed by an enormously long interglacial period, the Mindel-Riss; it may have lasted from one quarter million to one half million years. The Riss and the Würm again came close together, and geologists believe that the Würmian glaciers began melting away some twenty-five thousand years ago. They were reduced to substantially their present extent of covering Greenland, Antarctica and the higher mountain ranges about 6800 B.C., or 8700 years ago.

Thus a rough timetable is provided for dating the early career of man; but our knowledge of these events provides even more. It tells us that man was whipsawed and prodded during this time, not only by pressure from overpopulation but by drastic changes in *climate.*

As worked out by C. E. P. Brooks in his *Evolution of Climate* (2nd ed., 1924) and by many others, the effects produced by the Ice Age may be compared to conditions today around the North Pole.

Over much of the Arctic region the air is continually being chilled and made heavier. Hence it sinks and flows along the surface toward the equator, producing cold winds which blow upon northern Scandinavia, Russia, Siberia and Canada. Occasionally these polar winds force their way well down into the temperate zone. Then in summer this zone has fine, bracing weather, while the usual result in winter is a bitter cold snap or perhaps a blizzard.

In each period of glaciation this polar icecap crept far southward—into or beyond the Great Lakes region in North America and correspondingly far elsewhere. Then its cold breath blew, not upon the far north but upon central France, central Germany and the whole northern half of Russia. Deep icecaps covered the Alps, the Pyrenees, the Carpathians and the ranges of Asia; and down the flanks of these miniature polar regions sank currents of cold air which blew out as strong, freezing winds over the surrounding regions.

HOW ICE AGE GLACIATION CHANGED THE WORLD'S CLIMATE

The upper view of Africa and Eurasia shows the small existing polar ice zone and the present planetary climate zones. The westerly winds bring cyclonic storms to the north temperate zone, and the parching trade winds blow over the subtropics. The lower picture shows how this wind and climate system was jammed southward, as explained further in the text, by Ice Age glaciers.

These blasts not only chilled the land; they broke up the normal circulation of wind and moisture over the temperate zone. For reasons too complex to be explained here the temperate-zone air circulation consists of westerly winds which blow more or less continuously from west to east around the earth. As these winds pass over oceans they pick up moisture; when they pass over land they drop this moisture as rain or snow. But when this circulation was broken up by the glacial blasts the inland regions no longer received much moisture, and the scene became desolation itself.

Dust blew about in great clouds to settle here and there, but most of all around the fringes of the icecaps. Wherever it settled in sufficient quantity it became compacted into the fine-grained soil we call *loess*. Today we find huge deposits of this sort in Nebraska, northern China, parts of the Danube basin and in northern Germany.

Under such conditions only mosses and lichens could grow; the landscape was a *tundra,* or treeless Arctic plain. During glacial times in Europe this tundra reached south to the Alps and also into the Balkans and Asia Minor. South of these limits came the zone of westerly winds, pushed far south of their normal courses by the glacial blasts; they gave the Mediterranean region, northern Africa and southwestern Asia the cool, moist climate we find in northern Europe today. Thanks to this fact the present-day deserts in Arabia and the Sahara were pleasant grasslands, or perhaps savannas—that is, regions dotted with thickets and trees.

Life, of course, had to shift south and north as these conditions came and went, or else adapt itself to the changes; and in the record of the actual adaptations made we have a good measure of how early man both used and failed to use his inventive abilities.

These adaptations are traced, naturally, through the *artifacts*— i.e., man-made objects—which these first thinkers used in their attempts to cope with raw Nature.

The oldest artifacts—or, more precisely, the oldest objects which might have been artifacts—bespeak a mentality barely a cut above the chimpanzee in thinking power. They are rudely shaped stones with a cutting edge—mere chips, for the most part. Indeed, they look like chips or flakes which had been broken naturally from nodules of flint and other fracturable stone; man simply knocked off a few chips here and there, to shape the flakes into a knife or other tool. So crude is the workmanship, many archaeologists deny that these objects were man made. Those who believe they were artifacts call them *eoliths* (from *eos,* dawn, and *lithos,* stone), to mark their supposed place in the human story.

After eoliths, however, come various tools of early Pleistocene age, which are sufficiently unlike anything found in Nature to qualify beyond question as deliberately made. Probably the cleverest is the hand ax, or *coup de poing,* as French archaeologists call this artifact. This tool is a piece of flint several inches long and chipped at one end into the semblance of a broad knife or chopper. It was used undoubtedly for cutting wood or meat and for digging up roots.

Many archaeologists also believe that by the time men had reached even this crude level of attainment they also began adjusting their tools to the environments where they found themselves. According to Oswald Menghin of Vienna, in the book *Early Man* (1937), these adjustments produced four outstanding types of tools.

Wood tools, of course, were used wherever wood could be had, but the perishable nature of wood tools insures that we cannot hope to learn much about them. The simplest stone tools were *flakes,* or small pieces of shaped stone. Flake tools were especially useful for life upon open grasslands or polar tundras. In such environments trees and vegetable food alike would be practically nonexistent, and men would want sharp, relatively light weapons and tools for killing and dressing game and hides.

The *hand axes* made of chipped stone grew up in moist climates which favored growth of trees, nutritious roots and other vegetable food. Under such conditions flakes would serve for light work, but something heavier would be needed for shaping wood and grubbing up roots. The hand ax served admirably, and this view about the tool fits in well with its geographic distribution from a probable origin in the forests of Africa. Two contributors to the book *Early Man* point out that an African origin is the only theory which will explain the spread of this tool south to the Cape of Good Hope, east to India and north in western Europe to the British Isles, together with a complete *lack* of hand axes in eastern Europe and in Asia north of India. These are precisely the regions which would be blocked to immigrants from Africa, even during interglacial times, by forbidding conditions on the Alps, the Balkans, the Caucasus, the Pamirs and the Himalayas.

The *bone industry* was relied upon by those unfortunates who lived right against the edges of the polar and mountain icecaps, as the Eskimos do today. Here no woodworking or digging tools would be needed. Good stone would be hard to find beneath the ever-

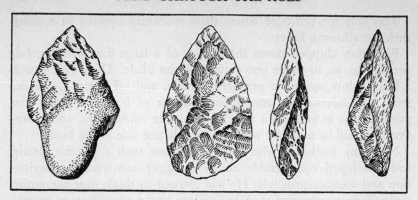

HOW STONE TOOLS REVEAL GROWING MENTAL POWER

These three specimens show growth of inventive ingenuity from a level barely a cut above the chimpanzee's rude thinking to a degree comparable to the modern level of thought. At the left a pre-Chellean hand ax shows a flint nodule, rudely chipped to provide a cutting tool and with much of the crust left on to provide a handhold. In the middle an Acheulean specimen shows careful chipping all over and the peculiar corkscrew edge often found in this type. The array concludes at the right with a Levalloisean knife which reveals high thinking power, as explained in the text.

present snow. Bone would be the only readily available material which could be worked into tools and weapons.

All these techniques had taken shape early in the tremendously long Mindel-Riss interglacial time which cut the fourfold Ice Age in two; the Galley Hill, Piltdown and Swanscombe precursors of modern man seemed to have been the workmen. They made advances too, even though unbelievably slowly, down to the chef-d'œuvre of the development, the Levalloisean knife. This implement, so named from finds made in the Paris suburb of Levallois-Perret, appeared toward the close of Mindel-Riss times, and it was a real triumph of inventive thinking. To appreciate why requires consideration of one fact about flintworking.

When a flint is struck a sharp blow a chip or flake flies off, and the plane of separation is smooth, like fractured glass, just as the edges have glasslike sharpness. The fractured surface will also have a roundish swelling, called a *bulb of percussion,* under the center of the impact; and the direction and strength of the blow determine the size and shape of the flake. Light blows knock off fine chips; a heavy, smashing blow, delivered with a hard stone, knocks off a huge flake.

This was the principle which these workmen applied in making their Levalloisean knives.

First they chipped down the surface of a large flint with careful, pecking blows to shape one surface of the blade. Then they struck a heavy blow upon the prepared surface, and off came the blade, with the underside as smooth as a surface of fractured glass. The product was as good as a man of that time could want, and moreover, it could be made by working up only one side of the blade.

Now any workman who could think out such a process clearly had developed considerable ability to apply constructive imagination and abstract principle. He had learned to think over the entire toolmaking process and then, at one step in the procedure, to *reverse* the working order by dressing a flake first and then knocking it loose. A man who could figure out such a change was no mental tyro. He had the level of ability which fits the modern-type skulls of the time.

Thereby the archaeological record bears out the conclusion, already drawn in Chapter V from the skeletal evidence, that the men of this day had all the mental endowment needed to pass from rude, savage living to civilized ways. We come once more, then, to the same momentous question. Why did they not do so?

Only a few years ago this question would have baffled even speculative thought. Today the answer is clear enough. We have come now to one of the many places in the human record where man chose the wrong road instead of the right one. He built into his ways of thinking a mistaken line of attack upon his problems; and the error deserves the most careful consideration, not only because it clogged progress for hundreds of thousands of years, but because it persists with all-too-woeful effect, even into modern days.

To uncover the error we need only follow one hint which is given us by a parallel between primitive thinking and the thinking done by modern children.

CHAPTER VIII

The Nature of Early Thought

A ONCE-POPULAR DOCTRINE of biology said that the embryo rehearses the history of the race—and regardless of whether this dictum fits all the facts in physical life, it certainly provides a handy key for understanding early human thought. To see why early thinking operated to block progress, rather than helping it, nobody need look farther than the thinking done by the modern child of two or three.

We all know well enough how such a childish mind explains its little world in terms of fairies, animals and plants that talk with each other, and similar personalized forces. The actual concepts are supplied, of course, by the child's elders, but the cast of mind which makes such material acceptable is the child's own. Impersonal forces and abstract principles are beyond its grasp; it must cast its explanations in terms of active, talking beings like the people it knows.

So it was with early man. He, like the child, was only beginning to use his ability to think, and sophisticated, abstract concepts were beyond his ken. Inevitably he turned, therefore, to personalized explanations of his world. The result was creation of faith in *magic*— that is, in ability to shape lives and control Nature by means of spells, charms and incantations.

This we know well enough, because we can trace this type of thinking even today, through all the primitive cultures in the world. An amazingly rich mine of such beliefs is available in Sir James George Frazer's *The Golden Bough* (12 vols., 1907–15) and shorter popular versions of the larger work. We also have plenty of interpretations which give organization and working principles to this sort of thinking. One of the simplest is the theory of *animism,* as developed in the seventies of the last century by Sir Edward Tylor (1832–1917) in his *Primitive Culture.*

Briefly, animism is the belief that everything, including sticks and stones, has a soul. If we consider the universe from the primitive point of view, would this not explain Nature's perverse moods, her genial moods of sunshine and plenty, her angry ones of thunder and lightning, tempest, blizzard and drought? The soul or souls in Nature were exhibiting exactly the changes in mood which man could see in himself!

Equally obvious, too, would be the way to deal with all these spirits in Nature. Why not propitiate them and persuade them to act in man's favor?

This gave rise to magic, or the art of manipulating, swerving or controlling Nature by means of charms, rites and incantations. Such arts were practiced for man's good by *shamans,* "medicine men" or "witch doctors." These men (and women) were members of the primitive group who seemed to be effective in such work. Shamans also were expected to circumvent the machinations of *witches* who misused magic or who used black magic to summon evil spirits for malign purposes.

Today this view is considered too simple to explain all that we know about the workings of the primitive mind. A typical criticism of this sort is given by A. A. Goldenweiser in his *Early Civilization* (1922). For a view which comes nearer to explaining all the known facts we have the interpretation offered by Lucien Lévy-Bruhl in several works, the latest being *Primitives and the Supernatural* (1935).

Lévy-Bruhl holds that the primitive mind makes two errors in its attitude toward the world. First, it runs the natural and its concepts of the supernatural all together into one, in the same naïve, confused way that a child mixes fairies with actual Nature. Second, because the primitive fears to offend the unseen powers, it dares not try to sort out the mixture into supernatural and controllable physical Nature. An unusually fine epitome of the resulting mentality is the following from a review of Lévy-Bruhl's book by the psychologist Joseph Jastrow, in *Science* of October 4, 1935:

The contours of Lévy-Bruhl's primitive mentality make a recognizable portrait. The decisive cast of the composition is emotional. The native is affectively tense; his thinking is in the service of his feeling; and the greatest of these powerful affects that stir the savage breast is not soothing music but exciting fear. He lives in a reign of terror with an annex of a homemade inferno. Sky, storm, floods, thunder, lightning, plagues, are real enough, but the punishing, avenging forces back of them, the evil spirits, even more so—and always there is the mystic calamity, death.

The idea of a natural death is beyond him; if a man dies somebody has bewitched him. . . .

His answer is an elaboration of luck ceremonials, charms, amulets, talismans, rituals of appeasement and superstitious wardings-off innumerable. . . . Every article of clothing, every act of sustenance from hunting and trapping to planting and reaping, from gathering to cooking and eating, is set in a ceremonial of fear, the avoidance of bad luck, the propitiation of good luck. . . .

There is a further clue to primitive mentality which Lévy-Bruhl calls *dispositions*. How are things, times, localities, operations, events disposed toward you? For everything is disposed to make or mar. . . .

Disposition sets the plot of a hundred dramas of a constantly dramatic primitive life. Ceremonials and dances are elaborate rituals for creating dispositions; ancestor worship is based upon the same principles, making the dispositions of the dead vital for the living—lest their ghosts haunt.

But be careful as you will, disaster stalks night and day; the fear world casts spells. The cause of causes is bewitchment. Sorcerers abound; unsuspected, another or you yourself carry the Evil Eye. Punishing witches, devising counter witchcraft, becomes the great primitive practice. Moreover, try as you will not to, you will transgress, violate a taboo, and then must be applied the purification ceremonies—a Bible in their wealth of prescriptions. Between fearing, avoiding and purifying, the primitive man spent his days, entangled in the web of his own psychology.

This is gripping and grim indeed—and while Goldenweiser and others have criticized many features of it, the chief objection is to Lévy-Bruhl's imputation of naïveté and "a-logical" or confused thinking. The primitive thinker is not "confused," the objectors say, about such matters as the sharp line between life and death. He simply sees the states of "before birth," birth, life, death and after death as a continuous chain. No confusion exists in his idea that a baby is not "officially born" until it has been ceremoniously accepted by the tribe. This seems to him no more than proper and natural recognition of a link in the chain. The idea is mistaken but it is not "confused." It flows logically enough from the mistaken premise.

So speaks sociology on the place of magic in primitive life. The destructive vice in the belief is, of course, obvious.

The man who believes in magic does not attempt to master his problems and his difficulties by using his own powers of thought. He relies upon useless spells and charms. Even when these devices fail his faith is not shaken. Either his magic was not strong enough to move the spirit he was addressing or it had been circumvented, either by some other spirit or by some person who was using evil magic to thwart him. The remedy for either one of these troubles was equally simple. One need only obtain more potent magic from the shaman or, if he can offer none, from some new shaman or wonder-worker.

Now, as the later record will show, such stultifying, paralyzing beliefs were held in the early days of thought, just as all primitives hold them today—and as long as such beliefs were entertained progress automatically stood blocked. Neither was this the full extent of the mischief! Behind the actual error itself stood potent mental forces which insured that man *never could escape this error* once it had become fastened upon him by any power of his own. He was like the drug addict of today, who can only be cured if some superior power places him forcibly under treatment which breaks up the addiction.

These stultifying forces therefore explain, even more than did faith in magic itself, the lack of progress during all this long period. Correspondingly, a sound understanding of man's career calls for examining these forces now, when they are beginning to be potent factors in human affairs. This will be easy, because these forces are nothing more than the same interworkings of brain and mind which we examined in Chapter IV at work in this matter of faith in magic. To pick up the thread we need only turn back to the reflexes which we saw at work in the catfish.

The first point to note here is how Nature adjusts these reflexes somewhat to every creature's needs from hour to hour and from day to day.

Suppose the fish's reflexes were arranged to keep the creature eating whenever it encountered food. What would happen if the fish found itself in a superabundance of food? Would it not gorge itself and then *keep on eating* to the point of disaster because its reflexes would not let it stop?

Of course it would if it had no other controls over its conduct. Actually it is saved from this by a sort of superreflex which tones or *keys* the other reflexes.

When the animal needs food the keying process creates a state of tension called *hunger*. The reflex responses to contact with food become acutely sensitive, and the animal acts vigorously when it encounters eatable material. Once it has enough, however, the keying process "turns off the current," so to speak. The feeding reflexes lose their sensitivity, and a feeling of repletion makes the animal indifferent to food.

Keying also serves in emergencies, such as awareness that an attack is impending from, say, a wolf.

This awareness comes from a group of reports—a rustle in the grass near by, a glimpse of grayish fur and perhaps a "wolfish" smell —to the animal's brain. Instantly the reflexes set to work.

At the first hint of danger hair or feathers are ruffed up over vulnerable parts such as the neck, to help confuse or baffle the attack. Blood is withdrawn from the skin and digestive organs; the animal "goes cold" or "freezes" into wariness. This withdrawal also concentrates blood for the next response.

Blood surges to the muscles and the brain; teeth and claws, if any, are bared for action. Caution, and even sensitivity to ordinary pain, are swept away; breathing speeds up. In every way possible the animal is keyed to make the fight *of* its life *for* its life.

So runs the keying process, in men as well as in animals. In men, however, one big difference exists, a difference which lies at the heart of the trouble caused by such errors as faith in magic. The basis of this difference is man's self-awareness or consciousness.

Obviously, this attribute is going to notice these states produced by keying, just as it notices heat and cold, or moisture and dryness. These recognitions constitute the *emotions,* those states of feeling good or bad, glad or sad, which lend rich color to life and also make life unbearable at times.

Our very speech shows how we have recognized, at least dimly, the physical basis of our emotional states.

Who of us has not felt the chill shrinking and "freezing" which we call fear or has not "seen red" when something particularly infuriating has happened? Neither are these terms mere figures of speech. They describe accurately what is happening inside us. We "freeze" and turn pale from fear because blood has been withdrawn from the skin. In rages we "see red" and our eyes and brains feel gorged with blood because they are so gorged—with "hot" or "fighting" blood, as we say.

Moreover, thanks to brilliant modern researches by Loewi, Dale, Cannon and others, we know the most important of the physical processes which Nature uses to produce emotional states.

When we "see red" in a rage the keying center has not sent separate messages to every muscle and fiber concerned with an order for appropriate action. It does send some messages of this sort, but the principal action is an order to the adrenal glands, perched on the top of the kidneys, to pour an extra shot of the *adrenalin* or *epinephrin* which they secrete into the blood. This is enough to produce all the action needed.

Epinephrin is "biological dynamite" in its effects. So powerful is it that physicians occasionally stir a "dead" heart into renewed action simply by injecting a bit of epinephrin into the heart muscle. Just a few traces of it in the blood keep the entire body keyed to normal tension. Naturally, then, an extra dose of this potent stuff keys the body almost instantly to fighting pitch.

To produce the opposite states of calmness and contentment the keying process uses another chemical, *acetylcholine*.

When the internal and external state of the body suggest that rest and calm are in order certain nerve endings release this substance at appropriate points in the body. Then heart and lung action slow down. Blood is made available for the digestive organs, and a sense of physical and mental peace is the result.

These processes can work, of course, with varying degrees of intensity.

Mild states of discomfort and well-being pass unnoticed, save that a pale reflection of them may appear in whatever conscious thinking we are doing. We "feel dull," as we say, or "keen," in the mind. But this indifference disappears rapidly enough when a feeling of colic or a burning sensation on the skin warns that something is wrong! So likewise, on the side of pleasant reactions, a state of well-being may be so strong, so charged with energy, that it bubbles up into the conscious level. Then we tell ourselves, "Say, I feel good!"

Still stronger emotions, such as fear and rage, may strike with force enough to swamp conscious judgment and decision. We are swept away by them; and all the ego can do is to note what is happening, almost as though seeing events in a dream, while we whirl into flight, fight or some similar intense response.

With this said we come to the grim fact which insured that man's faith in magic would be all but unshakable once it had become established in his mind. The fact itself is simple enough. Once man had gained the ability to imagine perils these imagined dangers *could be as effective* as actual ones to rouse up reason-swamping emotional reactions. Particularly would this be so whenever magic was concerned.

Since magic could control life itself, a threat against a man's magic, say by way of affront to the controlling agencies, was the same as a threat against his life—and it would create the same emotional states. Many a traveler has described the heartsick wail which swept through a tribe when some intrepid white man assailed the idol or the shaman—and why not? The sight of a natural flood or consuming fire bearing down upon the village could not create more dread than did fear of the punishment which the tribe expected for such impiety. So also does history tell of the frenzied rage with which mobs have assaulted impious challengers of the gods—and again, why not? The mob—so it thought—was defending its very source of life, its hopes for the future and its means for warding off unbelievable calamity and affliction. And all this would be done in a frenzy of terror, utterly beyond correction by the voice of reason. Those who knew better might as well have tried to argue with famished wolves as to attempt reasoning with men in such a state.

Neither, for that matter, need we look to primitive or to bygone ages for instances of this reason-swamping force at work! We still can see plenty of them in our own supposedly sophisticated day.

Let a professor or public speaker even suggest that we give some critical examination to the philosophy of our economic and governmental structure, and we know well enough what happens. Editorial columns fulminate the country over; the halls of Congress resound with demands that the speaker "go to Russia, where he belongs"; and not one of the outraged protestants thinks even for a moment of asking whether the rebel could possibly have any merit in what he says.

Should we be foolish enough to start expounding evolution to a fundamentalist, we would lose our audience almost immediately. The very word "evolution" creates an emotional charge of resentment or even rage in his mind, and all capacity to think reasonably is swamped. The narrow minded among scientists, those who know the techniques of science but have not mastered the philosophy of the scientific discipline, are equally irrational on their side of the argument. They call their opponents "hidebound bigots" and "intellectual cowards," and they refuse to see that religious beliefs, hopes and fears have any valid place in human thought.

In countless ways such as this, passion and prejudice, the reactions of emotion rather than of reason and right, are all too likely to rule the mind whenever situations and problems reach deeply enough to stir the old "instincts" of self-preservation, sex interests and the tendency to fight for one's possessions against raids by beast or man. All this is, therefore, more than enough to explain why progress should have remained at a standstill, caught in the paralyzing grip of faith in magic for hundreds or thousands of years.

To deal properly with this all-important subject naturally calls, first of all, for the record of its earlier influence and how the spell finally was lifted momentarily, with an almost immediate blossoming of civilization as a reward. Happily, the record of magic at work in early times is clear enough. We can find all we need in the career of the high-mentality type of men who displaced Neanderthal man in Europe at the close of the Ice Age.

CHAPTER IX

Man's First Failure in Europe

IF THE FIRST TRUE MEN IN EUROPE are to furnish prehistory's most ancient example of how man can be his own worst enemy, they deserve introduction as to who they were and how they came to be. Especially is this necessary as an assurance that the men were fully competent and not dullards who failed through lack of physical or mental ability. A few words, therefore, are in order concerning the race or strain of these men and about human races in general.

First the statement should be made that the subject of race is one of the most vexing of any topic concerned with man. Not much can be said about it with scientific certainty, and what little can be said ·is shot through with technicalities of biology and physiology. A résumé of this technical material, therefore, is given as Appendix A after the main text; here only a summary sufficient for organizing the story of man's career seems needed.

The first division of the human race is threefold: 1. Caucasian (white), 2. Mongoloid (yellow) and 3. Negroid (black).* The skin color associated with each type is mentioned, but, as explained in the Appendix, this test is considered childish and absurd by scientists

---

*This division not only describes what seems to be three definite racial strains; it reflects a moot question about human origins. This question is whether these types represent variations from a single human strain that emerged out of the primate stock (the monogenetic theory) or strains which emerged separately (the polygenetic theory). As an example of the evidence which must be considered, the Caucasian strain shows affinities as far back as we can trace with the Galley-Hill-Piltdown-Swanscombe type of man, while the Mongoloid has certain features reminiscent of the *Pithecanthropus-Sinanthropus-Heidelberg* line. The Negroid is a type by itself, with distinctive features not traceable to either of the other two lines; but in general the Negroid type is more akin to the white than it is to the Mongoloid. Further details about this problem are given in the Appendix.

88

because skin color can change even in one individual during his lifetime. Far better tests are hair type and skeletal features. Most people are familiar with the difference between the wavy hair of the white, the straight hair of the Mongoloid and the woolly or kinky hair of the Negro—and these types of hair do run with blood. If they change in response to climate, the change is slow. Among diagnostic skeletal features are the narrow nose of the white as opposed to the flat noses of Mongoloids and Negroes, the tendency to a slight curve in the shinbones of Negroes and the high squarish cheekbones of the Mongoloid.

Within each strain several subdivisions are recognized. The ones most commonly used for the white strain were formulated in their present meaning by Professor W. Z. Ripley in his *Races of Europe* (1900). First and perhaps oldest of these strains is the Mediterranean race, a type proved to be a separate strain by Sergi. These whites are long headed, oval faced, dark eyed and from sallow to dark in complexion. They have occupied the lands around the Mediterranean as far back as we know, and they show but little change from the high mental type of the Mindel-Riss as exemplified by the specimens from Galley Hill, Piltdown and Swanscombe.

The second white type is the *Teutonic, Baltic* or *Nordic*. These people are tall, blond and long headed. The present evidence suggests that they came from somewhere in Central Asia and worked across Russia and along the Baltic coast to Scandinavia, the British Isles and northern France. They are closely akin to the Mediterranean type in skeletal features.

The third race is the *Alpine,* so called because it is found in greatest numbers along the mountainous line of the highlands in Asia Minor, the Balkans, the Carpathians (plus the Danube basin) and the Alps. Thus the Alpine race holds the mid-region between the Mediterranean folk and the Nordics. Its members are typically medium or short, stocky and round headed. Both hair and eyes tend to be dark or at least not blond. An extreme type is the *Armenian, Anatolian* or *Armenoid;* it is marked by a skull flattened in back instead of bulging, and a peak instead of a dome on top.

To this array of types should be added the people we are about to consider, the men who replaced the Neanderthal folk in Europe during the close of the Ice Age. They deserve particular attention for several reasons. In point of physical type they are the oldest folk we know who are clearly linked to the white race, instead of being merely men of indefinite racial strain. They serve also to clear up many an older puzzle about the physical development of mankind. Finally, with them the curtain really rises upon the story of human intelligence at work.

We have caught glimpses of earlier thinking, as revealed in handiwork; but these glimpses tell us only how the workers coped with the rawest aspects of life, food getting, protection against savage beasts and the like. Here in these Ice Age Europeans we can actually see faith in magic at work and see what it did to them. We can see the artistic impulse kindling and even rising to glorious heights. By the time their story runs its course mankind will be embarked upon ways of living which ran without a break into our own.

Let us turn now to these folk, starting with the story of how their racial origin was discovered not so many years ago!

This discovery was achieved by remarkably fruitful excavations made at Mount Carmel in Palestine, during the early 1930s, by Miss Dorothy Garrod and associated workers. The job was one of the most thorough, as well as fruitful, in all the history of paleontology.

The caves were dug down to the undisturbed bottom, to obtain a complete record of occupancy—and this was done even though much of the material was cemented together and had to be hoisted out in one-ton blocks for laboratory disentanglement. The record of industry runs from a primitive flake culture, the Tayacian, down into the latest prehistoric times; but the crowning feature of the finds was two types of skeleton which, as Sir Arthur Keith said in the quotation given in Chapter I, are tremendously valuable for throwing light upon the origins of the white race.

One type is represented by a fairly complete female skeleton and other fragments found in the cave called The Oven (*et-Tabun*). The other is represented by the remains of ten individuals, men, women and children, found in the Cave of the Kids (*Mugharet-es-Skhul*).

The female is Neanderthaloid, although she differed in many ways from the European type. But the Skhul type fits admirably into the modern human line. It is far from being fully modern, but it was well on the way, Sir Arthur Keith believes. He suggests in particular that it was ancestral, or nearly so, to the later Cro-Magnon type of *Homo sapiens,* because of the long leg bones. The skull had a torus and a prognathous mouth; but the top was doming up toward truly human shape, while the lower jaw had a well-developed chin.

Associated with these skeletons were relics of handiwork which give a strong clue to the racial heritage of these people.

The clue starts with the dating of the different layers of the deposit. The level immediately below the skeletons contains tools exactly like the Acheulean type made in Europe during Riss-Würmian times— that is, in the interglacial times before the last glaciation—and hence the makers presumably were of high mental type. Now this technique persisted into the layer which contained the skeletons, thereby suggesting that the Skhul people were descendants of the earlier Acheulean workers. But the tools also show many Mousterian traits, characteristic of Neanderthal workmanship—and the implication from this is plain. The Skhul people were *hybrids,* crossbred from both the high mental type and from the Neanderthal!

The skeletal evidence, with its mixture of Galley Hill and Neanderthal characters, lends strong support to this implication; and scientists now are accepting this explanation as at least a tentatively established fact. This explains many an otherwise puzzling feature about the Cro-Magnon people who descended from the Skhul folk, and particularly the magnificent Cro-Magnon physique.

These people first became known from skeletons found in 1868 near the village of Cro-Magnon on the Vézère River in southwestern France. Among these skeletons was the giant frame of the famed Old Man of Cro-Magnon and the remains of the woman who gave cave men their reputation for rough manners. Her skull showed a gaping wound from a heavy club or other blunt instrument. The evidences of healing, however, showed that the stock was rugged as well as rough. She had survived the blow about a fortnight.

These people were as fine physical specimens as the race has ever produced. Some of the males stood six feet five inches high; the shape of the face suggests keen intelligence, and in size of brain they equaled or even surpassed modern man. Moreover, the stock had fine lasting qualities, because anthropologists think they can detect a scattering of descendants from it even today in southwestern France. They believe this because both these modern and the Cro-Magnons show the same strange *disharmonic* head—that is, a skull which is long from front to back, but has a short, squarish face and wide cheekbones instead of the oval shape which usually goes with a long head.

Such features, as well as the huge size of the males and the rugged strength of the stock, are exactly what might be expected of a successful hybrid or crossbreed—and this again supports the idea that these people were a cross between the high mental and the Neanderthaloid. And so it was that the re-entry of true man into Europe was led

by the most magnificently developed folk the race has ever produced.*

Knowing the truth about the physical origin of these peoples enables us to trace their career with hardly a break from the start.

The first locale is fixed by the fact that soon after the stock appeared the fourth or Würmian glaciation set in. This narrowed the
habitable land open to the Cro-Magnons to a region that extended
from lower parts of Iran in southwestern Asia, across the Isthmus of
Suez and through northern Africa, to the Atlantic. At the same time
the northern glaciation forced temperate climate, rain-bearing winds
southward and made this region a smiling grassland instead of the
desert that it is today.

During all this time the Cro-Magnons remained food *gatherers,* as
sociologists say, and developed no ability to be food *producers.* They
ate such fruit, berries, roots and birds' eggs as they could find and
hunted game; they made no effort to produce food by agriculture or
by herding animals. They invented no home comforts because as
hunters they had to follow the game and travel light; weapons were
all the baggage they could take. Hunt, eat and die—that was the
sum total of life for those Cro-Magnon men, and they did not dream
of anything easier or better.

Then, some twenty thousand years or so ago, the peak of the
Würmian glaciation passed, and the Cro-Magnons began filtering
into Europe from Africa. Entry undoubtedly was easy, because a
tremendous amount of water was frozen in the glacial ice, and the
ocean level was lowered hundreds of feet. This lowering extended
the seashores until in all probability only short passages over water,
easily made on rafts or skin floats, enabled men to migrate via Sicily
to Italy and thence along the Italian seashore to southern France.

Probably Neanderthal man opposed these immigrants bitterly, but
the fact that deposition of Mousterian relics ceased abruptly wherever
the Cro-Magnons and Aurignacians appeared in western Europe is

*The use of Cro-Magnons to exemplify early human history in Europe is thoroughly
justified, since they were the leading race. But a correct record should mention that
other strains were entering Europe at the same time. Among these were folk with
smaller bones and long harmonic heads; they might have been representatives of the
original Mediterranean Galley Hill type. The best examples of the type are probably
the skeletons found at Combe Capelle in France, and the physical type is often called
Aurignacian, even though the term applies more properly to a type of culture. Another type was the Grimaldi; some scholars consider this type Negroid. Still another
possible race was the Chancelade, allied to the modern Eskimo.

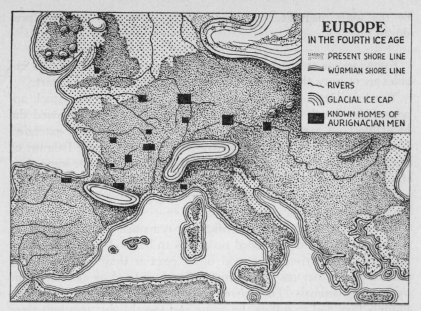

HOW THE FOURTH ICE AGE GRIPPED EUROPE

During any period of intense glaciation the icecaps take water enough to lower the oceans markedly. In 1922 Nansen estimated that the Fourth Glaciation lowered the ocean level 93 meters (305 feet); and this estimate is considered conservative. To show this amount of lowering, the former shore line is drawn at the present 50-fathom line (300 feet). The changes in ocean level turned the region around the British Isles into dry land.

testimony enough to the short shrift given these earlier folk. The newcomers found the battle against raw Nature somewhat harder, because cold was an ever more implacable enemy as they moved northward. At night they needed good shelter from piercing glacial winds; whenever they left their fires to go hunting reasonably wind-proof clothing was needed. But the relics left by these men prove that they were more than equal to meeting the challenge. They steadily improved their stone tools—knives, scrapers, burins or gravers, and awls—to meet their needs, and for hunting they developed bone points with a split base, called *points d'Aurignac*. Probably these points were bound to a light shaft and used as javelins.

Another improvement was *pressure flaking* of stone tools. The oldest method of shaping flint was by striking blows to break off pieces (*percussion flaking*), as described in Chapter VII. The pressure technique was far more precise and delicate. To use it the workers placed a piece of bone, wood or stone at the proper angle against the portion he wished to remove. Then he pressed smartly but smoothly upon the tool, and off popped the chip. The size of the chip and the direction of the fracture could be regulated with exquisite precision, and some pressure-flaked tools are all but as smooth as if they had been polished.

The problem of shelter all but solved itself; western Europe was dotted with caves and undercuts at the feet of cliffs. The rocky walls of such nooks provided windbreaks, except in one or two directions. Fires on the exposed side or sides not only provided warmth but kept off wild animals. Of course true man was not the first to appreciate the advantages of caves. Not only did he have to drive out Neanderthal men from them; often he had to oust cave bears, cave hyenas and perhaps cave lions. But such challenges merely gave good workouts to his powers.

Indeed, these Cro-Magnons had mental power enough, given a little time, to have developed fully civilized ways of life, if we may judge from their development of art—first sculpture in the round, then engraving and painting on flat surfaces.

This oldest art began, psychologists tell us, with crude sculpture because such art is largely suggested by Nature. A man finds a stone, a root or a gnarled branch which strikes him as being almost the figure of a man or an animal. He gives it a few finishing touches, and he has a satisfactory image.

From these beginnings art progressed to working "on the flat"— that is, scratching pictures on the sides of bones and horn implements and on the flat, rocky walls of caves. Psychologists consider this a more difficult feat than working in the round, because few natural objects are flat, and the artist must project roundness into the image from his own mind. That is, he must imagine the object shown to be round.

The fact that modern children usually begin to draw before they attempt modeling does not contradict this view. The modern child sees adults using pens and pencils on paper, and simple imitation gives him the knack of it, while admiring parents help him to interpret his childish scrawls. Hence drawing comes easier than modeling to the modern child. The reverse, however, would be true with early man. He lacked aid from sophisticated adults, and he had no materials which made drawing easy.

Trade by barter also was practiced; many burials far in the interior have yielded ornamental shells of animals which grew only in the

Mediterranean. Payment may have been made in flint, since a good quality was abundant in central and north Europe but rare in the south, where less satisfactory stone was largely used. Such trade not only enriched life but could promote exchange of ideas and hence speed progress, if these men cared for progress.

But unfortunately for prospects of progress, these people were obsessed with faith in magic as their means for dealing with life! Abundant evidence proves this obsession, beginning with a sort of signature which many artists left with their paintings.

To make this signature the artist placed one hand flat against the wall, then blew ocher around the hand with a blowpipe. This left a silhouette of the hand on the rock, and the silhouettes show that often one or more finger joints had been chopped off. Often the fingers were mere stumps!

Why should such mutilation have been practiced? Primitive peoples in modern times often cut off a finger joint as a sign of mourning or as part of a charm. Either practice would explain the mutilated hands of these artists.

Further evidence of belief in magic is the very location of the pictures. They were painted, not conveniently near the mouth of caves, but in the deepest, most inaccessible portions. This suggests to most students of prehistory, such as Abbé Breuil, that the pictures formed a part of secret ceremonies to which only medicine men, hunters and other initiates were admitted. And the animals are often shown pierced with darts or javelins, just as modern primitives often slay an animal image as a charm before a hunt.

True, objections can be raised to this view. An eminent student of ancient man, Marcellin Boule, has pointed out that magic does not require *fine* art. The crudest doll, the merest scrawl, will do. Yet these people produced fine art; hence, Boule argues, love of art must have been stirring in them, even if their art was used in magic ceremonies. Sociologists and archaeologists who hold to the magic interpretation can admit this, however, without backing down from their theory. They only regret that this fine art was being tangled up with magic.

Still further evidence for faith in magic is presented by the so-called *batons de commandement,* or "staffs of office," which became common at this time.

These staffs were carved from mammoth tusks, deer antlers or similar material. They were elaborately ornamented with animal figures and were pierced with one or more holes from side to side.

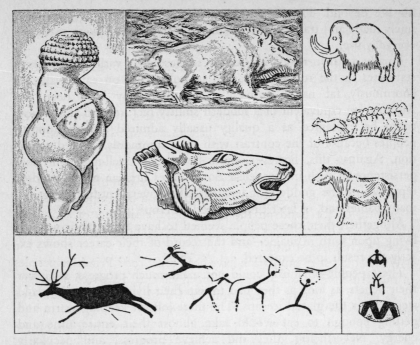

ART AMONG THE ICE AGE CAVE MEN

Many a modern sculptor would despair of matching the fine execution achieved by Cro-Magnon and other Ice Age artists if he had to work with their tools and under the conditions of their days. The "Venus of Willendorf" at the left—probably a fertility goddess—was carved in limestone with chipped stone tools. The bison (upper center) was modeled in clay, with illumination from the rudest of lamps, in the depths of the Tuc d'Audoubert, a cave in southwestern France. The spirited horse's head (lower center) was carved on a reindeer antler with stone tools—and so likewise were the engraved figures (right). A few of the rude but dashing figures in Capsian art are shown below the Magdalenian specimens. At the lower right the origin of the famous pebbles of Mas d'Azil is shown, as worked out by Obermaier. A squatting human figure became conventionalized into the M-like symbol.

Modern Eskimos use similar instruments for straightening arrows by drawing the arrow shafts through the holes, and some scholars accept this as the use of the baton. Others think that these instruments were javelin throwers.

But such proponents of the magic theory as MacAlister (*Textbook of European Archaeology,* 1921) urge that many of these staffs are fragile and often are not well designed for their work. The only possible use for such staffs was as a staff of office or magic wand— unless indeed they served as funeral gifts to serve the departed in his life beyond. Throughout history funeral gifts have often been finely made and fragile, while plain, stout implements were made for everyday use.

Finally, faith in magic is strongly suggested by various *Venuses*— statuettes in the round, or carved in bold relief on cave walls, of enormously fat naked women. Now these may have been the Aurignacian equivalent of a modern smutty picture, and the fatness could be explained as a quality usually admired among hunting peoples because of the contrast with their commonly half-fed condition. Against this, however, must be set the well-nigh universal persistence of such images, clear down into Christian times, as idols representing the goddess of fertility, who gave plentiful, fat game, many babies and, in later times, abundant crops.

Altogether, then, these people seemed to have based their ways of living upon faith in magic—and the record of their career shows exactly the result to be expected.

These people obviously could not make much progress, whatever their beliefs, as long as they had to win their living from a dry, cold steppe near the glacial icecaps. The mere jobs of keeping warm and getting enough to eat would take almost their entire time and energy. Nevertheless, they did achieve progress, and peculiarly enough, they did so in matters of spiritual interest rather than in dealing with everyday problems of winning a living. This progress produced the superb artistic ability which characterizes the *Magdalenian* culture at the very end of Ice Age times.

The ivory and bone carving in Magdalenian times would rouse envy in many a modern sculptor of the vivid effect and the fine detail; some of the horses fairly seem to snort before one's eyes. An even finer achievement, however, were engraved and painted pictures of animals, left in the remote depths of many caverns, and images modeled in clay on the floors.

With just a few deft lines these ancient artists pictured animals fighting or retreating. They caught the angry glare of an embattled bison's eye and made other eyes duller or more placid. So true to life were these pictures that a paleontologist can easily distinguish a heavy steppe horse, ancestor of many modern farm and work animals, from the light, graceful, desert or Celtic type, ancestor of modern racing and saddle mounts. These pictures were in polychrome, a strangely skillful and beautiful blend of different flat colors.

No such skill in picturing living animals appeared again until the days of the ancient Greeks, perhaps twelve thousand years later; and the Greeks had comfort and a wealth of materials for their work. These paleolithic artists achieved their effects with tools made of chipped flint, and they worked, half naked and shivering, with light from a lamp made by floating a moss wick upon melted fat in a hollowed-out stone! To a race which could do that, invention of the devices needed for founding civilization would have been simple had they possessed the incentive and the desire.

They looked, however, to magic for success, and they never thought of applying their fine mental powers to improving their ways in life. Indeed, they made the record even worse by missing a splendid chance for rescue from stagnation which came toward the end of their career. Occasionally a people in their situation is prodded into progress by forces from without, just as the Japanese were in the nineteenth century—and just as the Ice Age was coming to an end the Cro-Magnons were given this chance by arrival of a new, thought-stimulating culture in southwestern Europe.

This culture is called the Late Capsian; it embodied gains which had been made somehow in northern Africa while the Cro-Magnons and Aurignacians had been pursuing their career in Europe. The culture entered Europe in two more or less clearly defined streams.

One was Azilian. It came via Gibraltar, Spain, and the Pyrenees to France; and the type station for the culture is in a great cave along an underground river near the village of Mas d'Azil in the French Pyrenees. The other came from Italy through the Riviera into France; the type station is at Fère-en-Tardenois, somewhat east and north of Paris. Since the two cultures are strikingly similar, they are usually lumped into one and called the *Azilian-Tardenoisian.*

This culture was marked pre-eminently by *microliths,* or tiny chipped stones often no larger than a fingernail or even of needle-like size. These flints of course served many purposes, but the use which shows the greatest advance in thinking power consisted of flints set along a shaft and used like a saw for cutting. Here was development indeed! Such a tool could not have sprung from imitating any common natural object; these men clearly were attaining a masterly grasp upon the principles of toolmaking.

The most significant advance, however, was possession of bows and arrows. We need not dwell upon the importance to men of being able to kill at a distance; his mastery over even the most formidable of brutes now would be practically complete. How this momentous invention came about nobody knows. We do not even know that these people made it; they are just the first ones we know who had this aid.

Some of these people also had domesticated dogs. How they acquired "man's oldest friend" is not known, but the modern inclination is to guess that the alliance grew out of allowing wild dogs to eat scraps from the tribal meals. Puppies may have become attached to man in this way and proved willing to hunt in man's interest rather than their own. They had become *conditioned,* in the pyschological phrase, while still young to accepting man as the provider of food and campfire warmth on cold nights and to obeying his voice and gestures while on the hunt.

The original breed also is unknown, but some opinion exists that it resembled a Javanese chow. Interbreeding with wolves and other closely allied species is supposed to have produced the various modern breeds of domesticated dog.

These advances in practical living were matched by definite advances in more purely mental interests.

In art these people achieved a style which stood in striking contrast with Magdalenian art. The Magdalenians had always put down exactly what they saw; they were realists and almost never symbolized by suggesting objects with a few strokes or a dash of color. Only rarely did they attempt to show movement or to arrange figures in a composition that would suggest group action.

The Late Capsian art was almost an exact opposite in these characteristics. The figures were symbolic little silhouettes, sketchily done as to detail, and usually they were massed in groups which were engaged in the most lively action—hunting, dancing or warring upon their neighbors. In the sweep and the intense speed of motion shown we sense a high elation, an exuberant joy of power and a determination to use power to the full in getting what they wanted from life. Here was change indeed from the somber, careful presentations of Magdalenian art; and while we cannot say certainly what brought this change about, we can fairly think of the world-conquering power given by the bow and arrow. If we ourselves had recently acquired such an addition to our powers, might we not feel a godlike elation, a new and tradition-shattering sense of our relations with the world— and might we not show this in our art?

Still another significant item in this culture is the famous collection of painted pebbles which was recovered in the type station of Mas d'Azil.

These pebbles are painted with red ocher in geometric designs which are *symbols,* not pictures. Hence Azilian men clearly had included, in their use of ability to think, the representation of ideas by means of symbols. Obermaier proved this when he traced the development of these symbols from earlier conventionalized pictures in his *Fossil Man in Spain* (1924) and other publications.

The use made of these pebbles is unknown, but sociologists compare them to similar *churingas,* used by primitive Australians of today as charms or totem pieces for individuals in the tribe. If the Azilians had the same idea, we have a curious flash of insight into one probably disastrous episode in their career, because one deposit consisted of pebbles carefully broken into pieces. Could some enemies of the owners have done this to break the magic charm which protected each man? That would be abstract reasoning indeed—cursing a man by breaking a painted pebble!

Plainly, then, far-reaching advances were abroad in the land and the men of the Magdalenian culture certainly could have been roused up to new ideas and new ways by this example. But the archaeological record shows that they were not roused up. Their culture declined and either died or was absorbed without discernible trace into other cultures. As a people they faded from the human record, leaving only a few strains of Cro-Magnon physique to be detected here and there in the present-day population of southwestern France.

Thus in the very beginnings of man's career we have an excellent example of magic holding back progress. And if one example seems scarcely enough, the moral is clinched by the fact that the Azilian-Tardenoisians did no better! Indeed, they did not do so well.

The earlier men, after all, had been hampered by the tundra surroundings. The later comers occupied western Europe during the time in which the climate changed from boreal to modern. Yet instead of helping them this very change seems to have reduced them to a state of all but complete degradation.

The new warm and moist climate brought a dense growth of forest —and primitive man never has been able to get along well with his feeble tools in any dense forest growth. But if the Azilian-Tardenoisians had been progressive minded, they had ample time while the forests were developing to devise tools and ways of living which would turn the change to their advantage. Instead of progressing, however, they eked out a rather miserable existence by gathering shellfish, spearing fish with staghorn harpoons and killing small game with bows and arrows. As Peake and Fleure say in their volume *Hunters and Artists* (1927) of the series Corridors of Time:

Thus from a free and open hunting life the peoples of northwestern Europe had been reduced to the status of the poorest food collectors ... and it seems likely that our predecessors would have remained forever in this backward state, had not movements from the east brought a fresh impetus into their lives.

This sterile and backward period is called the Mesolithic or Epipaleolithic, and it is generally considered to be the logical end of modern man's first occupation of Europe.

A final sardonic comment upon this tragedy of missed opportunity is afforded by the view, ably urged by Ellsworth Huntington, that the modern climate of Europe ranks among the best known for sustaining health and promoting effort among white men.

The climate provides sunlight enough to produce vitamin D in the skin, but is not abundant enough to produce overstimulation or debilitation. The air is moist enough for health, but not too moist for easy breathing through the white man's typically narrow nose. The climate also is highly stimulating mentally. It is neither so lush that it provides a living without effort, as is true in many tropical lands, nor so harsh as to keep men on the verge of starvation, regardless of what they try to accomplish. It pitches the need for effort at exactly the right level. Men must work and contrive, in order to live; but once they do this, they are rewarded, first with an ample living, and then with a surplus of food sufficient to support many non-food producers who can devote their time, if they will, to making inventions, producing useful tools and structures, advancing knowledge, and otherwise improving mankind's richness and ease of life.

As a crowning aspect of desirability, the climate of Europe has the feature which Huntington finds to be most stimulating of all to effort —variability. Season follows season, confronting man with a steady march of problems to be solved throughout the year. From day to day and from week to week, storm follows fair weather, then gives way to good days again. Only rarely are the changes harsh enough to create emergencies; usually they simply keep men mentally alert enough to cope with conditions of the day. Thus these Mesolithic folk could not have found a better site for progressive living, had they been willing to live up to their opportunity.

But if faith in magic had this baleful influence in Europe and presumably everywhere else in those days, an obvious question asserts itself. If these men had no impulse toward progress, how did they ever make the start toward achieving civilization? What happened to prod, tempt or drive them into devising better ways of life?

The answer, as we shall now see, explains how men came to invent civilized ways of living.

PART III

THE DAWN OF CIVILIZED LIVING

CHAPTER X

The Cradles of Civilization

IF OUR ANALYSIS of man's beginnings has been correct, the key to progress will be the whip of special circumstances—an array of conditions powerful enough to break down man's obsession with primitive thinking and whip him into getting ahead. Now where may we expect to find such conditions in the days when the chill grip of the Ice Age was fading to a geologic memory?

Europe is out of the running because of the strangling forest growth. Central Asia is becoming a grassland that is rich with browsing animals, cattle, horses and sheep; man can win a good living here, but only by following the animals as a hunter would. The highest development to be expected is the life of a wandering herdsman or nomad. Central and South Africa we can ignore because we know as a matter of history that they did not contribute to the main stream of progress. Parts of China and of India met the requirements, and these regions did develop some of the earliest civilizations known; but these civilizations stood apart from the stream of progress which interests us.

What lands have we left to consider? Only the region around the Mediterranean and its outlier, Iran, to the northeast; and we need look no farther. As matters fell out, these lands offered exactly the combinations of special circumstance which were needed to whip man into progress. Indeed, circumstances went even farther in the beauty of their conformity to principle! They presented a striking instance of forcing man to learn through hardship and calamity, because the driving force was the scourge of utterly devastating drought throughout the entire original Afro-Asian cradle of true man.

The cause of this drought is not hard to identify. It was the same

105

shift of climate from glacial to postglacial conditions which transformed Europe from a polar tundra to a smiling land of western
forests and eastern grasslands. Formerly the Afro-Asian zone had
been blessed with westerly winds which brought rain-bearing cyclonic
storms. Now these winds were following the retreating icecaps northward, and the first home of man was coming under the breath of the
trade winds, which blow steadily toward the equator from either side
the year around.

These winds are beloved by sailors for their steadiness, but landsmen have good reason to curse them. As the air in them moves
equatorward it becomes warmer, and the warmer the air becomes,
the more moisture it tends to absorb. This action dries out any land
over which the trade winds blow, and this drying out was the calamity which began afflicting the Afro-Asian home of the first true men.
Lakes were drying up and rivers were running dry; the grass parched,
shriveled and then gave way to naked earth, hot glowing sand and
bare rock that radiated scorching heat. Men could do nothing but
flee in any direction that was open.

Whither could they flee? One possibility was across the Mediterranean, into Europe. The northern shores of this sea offered refuge
because they suffered only a partial drying out; they acquired the
so-called *Mediterranean climate* of moist winters and hot, dry summers. This happened because the parching winds just reached this
shore when they moved northward with the sun in summer; in
winter they retreated southward, and the westerlies brought rain.

In later times, when men knew more, this amelioration made agriculture possible; but as yet the north shore of the Mediterranean was
fit only for hunting life, and the men who fled in this direction, the
men of the Azilian and Tardenoisian cultures, simply carried on as
they had in their older Saharan homes. Farther north the forest would
do its work, as we have seen. Hence no special circumstances that
promised progress existed in this direction.

A very special combination of circumstances was to be found, however, in Egypt!

Most of Egypt was drying out, like the Sahara, but to the south lay
the highlands of Ethiopia and the east end of the tropical rain forest.
Rainfall on these two areas drained to the northward and kept the
Nile flowing all the year; and heavy monsoon rains over Ethiopia
from January to April, with heavy tropical rains thereafter farther
west, caused the Nile to flood every year during late summer and
the autumn. Then it deposited rich mud on either side of its course

throughout the length of Egypt. Thus, while North Africa as a whole did not receive rainfall enough to support life, life was possible and could even be rich upon a narrow strip along the Nile.

Here, then, was the driving force of special circumstance which would compel man to devise new ways. The hunters who sought refuge in the Nile Valley would think, because they had to. Their old ways were destroyed, and new ones had to be invented if they were to survive.

A somewhat similar state of affairs developed at this time east of Arabia.

Here, in glacial times, the parent of the present Persian Gulf had covered the site of modern Mesopotamia or Irak. The Tigris and the Euphrates were mere stubs of rivers; they ended at a rocky shore which can still be traced near Hit. During glacial times, however, gravel, sand and silt poured down these rivers and began to build out the land; and now the swampy Mesopotamian plain was creeping south into the gulf.

This plain, like Egypt, had good soil and abundant river water, but it received little rain, and forests could not grow. Here, then, was another region suited to be a cradle of civilization; and near by was the last region we need consider—the Mediterranean coast of Palestine, Syria and Asia Minor. The climate here was Mediterranean in type—rainy in winter and hot and dry in summer; but the mountains behind the coast received considerable snow in the winter and gave rise to many short rivers which relieved dryness in summer. Thus natural conditions here would force development of new ways.

In such fashion, then, Nature appointed the places in which civilization could be born, even while the hunters in Europe were sinking into their decline. Now of all these places where progress would be forced by Nature, which deserves first attention? One fundamental requirement for civilized living gives the answer. The land or lands which led the march would be those lands in which *agriculture* was first invented and practiced.

This follows because the fundamental requirements for progress are some amount of *leisure,* some slight feeling of *security* against the morrow and a slight degree of *freedom* to be original; and the key to achieving these advances was an *assured food supply* through agriculture.

Until man escaped the necessity of wondering every morning whether he was going to make a kill and eat that day, he had neither time nor energy for other matters. Even if the meat eater advanced from hunting to herding, he still had to let his animals seek new pasturage when they cropped off the grass where they were. This kept him on the move, and like the hunter he could not accumulate any burdensome possessions. Hence no wandering herdsman or nomad could achieve civilization.

But the man who practices agriculture can stay—nay, he *must* stay —in one place while he gathers his crop; and from this all else comes in due time. He can afford to build a house, for he may expect to remain where he is to enjoy this fruit of his labors. He can afford to invent labor-saving tools which give him leisure time. With a good harvest stored away in a house which he can defend against beast or man he has the beginning of security in hand. Thus he will be the first among all men to rise above the brute level of struggling for physical existence and to begin achieving the higher levels of living.

All this is elementary sociology—but the very simplicity of the analysis is an advantage. These simple considerations, coupled with what was happening around the Mediterranean at the time, strip all mystery from the birth of civilization. We can see that it was a natural and all but inevitable response to the needs of the time. So, too, can we see why it did not happen earlier. Only now were circumstances conspiring to force this advance.

It is equally plain that from now on the story will have two aspects. One, purely material in nature, is the record of the actual inventions and advances which brought civilized living into being. The other is mental in character. It traces how man's ways of thinking had to change in response to the new ways, until he formed viewpoints and mental habits which have endured with but little change down to our times. Thus we shall see ourselves in the making. And so to the story, beginning with the invention of agriculture!

The question of where agriculture first appeared still is unsettled in many a detail.

Of all the favorable regions named, Mesopotamia alone is absolutely out of the reckoning. Dry land was only in the making there at the time when agriculture almost certainly was invented. The case for Egypt has been urged by W. J. Perry in his *Growth of Civilization* (1924), using a practice which was common among the seminomadic Hadendoa of the Sudan as late as a century ago. Every season after the Nile flood these people came in from the surrounding territory and scattered millet seeds on the mud. Then, after an interval, they returned to reap the harvest; and if the first Egyptians did the same, the argument runs, they had only to learn the value of *cultivating* the land to complete the beginnings of agriculture. The whole process is so simple and so natural as to suggest that almost inevitably this was how agriculture came into existence.

Moreover, the wheat commonly grown in Egypt throughout ancient times was *emmer* or *Triticum dicoccum,* a variety with two grains to the spikelet; and Vaviloff has urged that the wild ancestor of emmer was a grass native to Ethiopia. He argues this from his studies of the spread of wheats through the world and also from studies of the chromosomes in the germ cells. But if the Egyptians turned a wild grass into emmer, this would seem to make them the inventors of agriculture.

Unfortunately for easy choice, the cases for Palestine, Syria, Iran and the Mediterranean borders of Asia Minor are equally convincing. The most common wheat today is bread wheat, or *Triticum vulgare;* and although no direct ancestor for this wheat is known, Vaviloff argues that its probable prototypes were native to southwestern Asia and possibly Afghanistan. H. J. E. Peake, in the issues of *Man* for March and April 1939, selects Palestine as the first home of agriculture, with emmer as the first crop.

A weakness of the case for southwestern Asia is the lack of a broad natural hint, comparable to the Nile floods, which would suggest sowing and cultivating; but men could easily have caught the idea otherwise. Some scholars have suggested noticing the superior growth of food grains scattered as offerings on graves. Others suggest noting the good effect upon ground of grubbing for edible roots.

We need not bother overmuch with such speculations; plenty of incidents in daily life would suggest the idea. Neither is the choice between these regions particularly important. Once either Egypt or western Asia generated the idea, it would spread to the other region across the Sinai Peninsula.

The most important aspect of the invention is what came of it, above and beyond an assured food supply from crops.

One inevitable gain was the art of *domesticating food animals.*

This would start when the first crop growers saved themselves trouble by rounding up herds of browsing animals and confining them in some small valley where the animals could eat their fill without roaming. If necessary, the captors could add grain. Thus men won a fine supply of meat, milk and hides or wool.

Leisure and security gained from improved food supply also gave both opportunity and incentive to develop labor-saving tools—particularly of the type which gives this entire phase of man's career its name of the Neolithic or New Stone Age. The name was coined by Sir John Lubbock (Baron Avebury) in 1865, in his book *Prehistoric Times*. He set off this age or, rather, this stage in human progress from the older Paleolithic or Old Stone Age of chipped and flaked implements, because neolithic workmen followed the initial flaking by grinding with sand, water and some hard stone until the implement became smooth and more or less polished.

With an ax of polished stone a man could cut down a tree and shape beams and planks—feats which no paleolithic man was able to perform. Another useful implement was the wedge-shaped *celt,* made by sharpening a large pebble or stone on one end and to some extent along the sides. It could be mounted on a handle to serve as an ax, an adze or a hoe. The hoe was particularly important because early agriculture undoubtedly took the form of *hoe culture* or *garden culture*. Men, or more usually women, undoubtedly prepared the soil for crops by hoeing up small patches of ground for long ages before plows were invented or used.

Settled life and good tools together made possible good shelter in weather-tight, permanent *houses.*

A house was no new idea, in principle; shelters had been constructed certainly since early paleolithic times. But the early shelters made by wandering hunter folk had been rude windbreaks of hides and branches. The hunters would have been foolish to waste effort upon anything better. These farmers, however, were set in one place; they could, and before long did, begin to build substantial homes.

One method that did not require heavy tools was *wattle-and-daub* construction—a method still to be seen in some modern primitive cultures. For framework the family erected the equivalent of a giant basket, using branches, rushes or both. Next they sealed the structure by daubing it inside and out with clay. Finally they capped off the house with a roof or thatch laid on branches trimmed to poles or even wove the materials used in the walls into a conical cap.

Logs, more or less trimmed to shape, also came into use in well-timbered regions. They were laid, as in American pioneer days, on top of each other to form sides and dovetailed at the corners. Construction of a log-house door might seem to have offered a challenge to these early architects, but archaeologists suggest that they solved the problem easily enough by scooping a passage through the dirt under one side. This would be a natural expedient in view of another common practice—the construction of *pit houses*.

In those days of working with rude tools all construction aboveground was extremely laborious and time consuming. Men therefore sank as much of the house as possible into the ground, by digging a pit deep enough to provide headroom under the contemplated roof. In the center the pit was deep and had a stone or clay hearth for the fire. The earth was left higher on the sides and finished off as benches. Once these were equipped with rushes, straw and coverings of hide or rude textiles the family had beds.

Finally, settled life prompted use of many raw materials which necessarily had not interested hunter folk.

Hunters had learned to use hides, hair, bones and horns as well as stone, but from all these only a limited array of products could be made by primitive workers. Settled food growers could afford to notice the tangles of rushes along river edges, tough grasses and other fibrous plants and to think of plaiting such materials into fabrics. Here would be the germ of matmaking and basketry.

Even nomads had learned to use the felting property of wool, the tendency shown by the fibers, with their rough scales, to cling together and form a thick warm fabric. Once a folk mastered basketry it could transfer the idea of interweaving from rushes and grasses to skeins of wool which had been twisted to make them strong and fine. Where flax was available the beaten-out fibers could be used. Here was the germ of spinning and weaving.

Next comes the supremely important art of pottery.

Archaeologists cannot say precisely where or how pottery came to be invented. A considerable body of opinion inclines, however, to consider it a development from basketry. Once people had learned to plait tough grasses, reeds or rushes into baskets, they would seek to make some of these containers waterproof by daubing them inside and out with clay. Some of these clayed baskets would be exposed, accidentally or in some rude cooking operation, to fire. The basketry would burn away, and the residue would be a rudely baked pot.

Other possible parental objects are gourds and leather bottles; and this diversity of parents is far from being a mere detail or guess. Often the effect upon shape and decoration enables an archaeologist to tell pretty well how a type of pottery originated. People who learned from basketmaking decorated their pots with scratched or incised lines that suggested basket texture. People who made gourd-like pots tended to use "free-field" decoration with spirals, meanders and even animals. The gourd type was especially characteristic of the early farmers in Asia Minor, since they and the gourd came from the same homeland. Thus the humble pot, far from being a mere pot, contained a lot of its maker's history in its very style.

A final valuable feature of pottery was its use by all classes; everyone could afford dishes and pots made of baked clay. Again, it was easily broken accidentally, and once broken it was utterly valueless; people promptly tossed it out upon the nearest rubbish heap. Thus a splendid record which did not decay grew generation after generation, and century after century, in the rubbish heaps of every early civilized community; and changes in style often betokened imports or even conquest by a new people. Altogether, then, potsherds and shards, broken as they are, provide one of the finest "books" we have on prehistoric times. To turn the pages, archaeologists need only dig down through layer after layer in prehistoric rubbish heaps and check the story told by the pottery fragments.

These achievements cover the important *material* advances which provided the foundations of civilization. To complete the record of this period we should turn now to mental aspects, to the ways in which these gains shaped human temperaments. A first effect, undoubtedly, was a considerable taming down of pugnacity.

Beyond doubt the first food growers were as ready battlers as their hunter forebears. But as interests shifted from hunting to cultivating, the fighting habit would receive less constant and urgent stimulation. Such folk would continue to fight savagely in defense, but their preference would be for dodging or lying low when enemies appeared. Also, bit by bit, they would lose the urge to roam. Others might enjoy the perils and thrills of the hunting or nomad life if they liked; these peasants would be content to remain tucked away in some snug valley close to their food supply.

Thus we notice the beginnings of the deliberate, tenacious temperament which marks peasants and farmers the world over. These beginnings were reinforced, moreover, by a factor in mentality which becomes increasingly important in human thinking from this time on. This factor is *force of habit* or, more accurately, *habit fixation*.

The phenomena of habit arise from the physical fact that the cortex or neopallium needs to be grooved somewhat, so to speak, *by use,* before its processes become effective. Human infants, colts, young birds and all young animals demonstrate this fact by their awkward, jerky and uncertain movements at the start of life. Their nervous channels are merely sketched in and not "grooved" as yet. But practice grooves the channels, and the youngsters gain smoothness of action—just as training gives deft, easy certainty to the movements of an athlete.

Thus efficiency is developed only in often-used and important actions; trivial or rare responses have no chance to become grooved in. All this is well enough, save for one pitfall. This is the fact that once a response is well grooved in *it is hard to change,* even if change would be highly advantageous; and the peril in this fact is intensified by the decrease in plasticity which comes with advancing age.

All brains are highly plastic at birth, and through childhood and youth learning and formation of new habits are easy. But the brain seems attuned to the proposition that a creature will have formed all the habits it needs by early maturity. Thereafter plasticity begins to diminish and habits become set.

As a consequence mature mammals can continue to learn and readjust their ways *only if their minds are kept stirred up by new experiences.* Among human beings an educated man, accustomed to using his reasoning powers, can absorb new ideas to the day of his death; but men who follow a plodding routine, such as farm labor or machine tending in mass production, may have their mental faculties set and rigid by the time they are thirty years old. Then nothing short of a smashup in their accustomed world can force fundamentally new ideas into their minds.

What little they learn is acquired early in life, and much of it is trash—folk tales, so-called explanations given them by ignorant adults, their own childish attempts to understand. By early maturity this mass of erroneous material has set into firm convictions, and thereafter they have enormous difficulty in wrenching apart familiar linkages of ideas in order to insert something new. Their feeling of difficulty is all but physical, akin to the wrenching effort required to master a correct swing in golf. In fact, the effort is so great that usually they refuse to go through with it. Rule-of-thumb tests and rubber-stamp conclusions are far more comfortable to use. They tend to reject any new idea or viewpoint as "outlandish" or "crazy," without really considering it. They will fight and die rather than change their minds about folkways and customs if among their fixed ideas is the notion that any way or custom has magic virtue or is otherwise "right."

Obviously the plodding routine of settled agricultural life would

fasten this cast of mind all but irrevocably upon the first peasants—
and thereby still another brake upon progress would be added to the
older one of tending to follow emotion rather than reason whenever
cherished beliefs are challenged. One combination of driving forces
has produced the beginnings of civilization; something similar will
be needed now to drive these beginnings above the habit-ridden
peasant level.

Happily for ease in tracing, we know today just where, when and
how these other forces came into play. The place is Mesopotamia,
and the story of what happened has been revealed by splendid work,
undertaken after the World War of 1914–18 ended backward Turkish
rule over the region and made intensive research possible.*

The new British and French authorities provided good working
conditions for archaeological parties, while the prosperity of the
1920s provided ample funds for research. Accordingly, a mass attack
upon prehistory in the region was made by opening up the huge
mounds—"tells," in the Arabic term—which contained the remains
of famous early cities such as Babylon, Nineveh, and Ur of the Chal-
dees, as well as sites which promised to reveal still older cultures.

Each site was laid open systematically, clear down to virgin earth
or rock. Thus all occupancy of the site by man back to the very first

*Only two challenges to this choice of locale exist. One is an inclination to favor
Egypt—but reasons for giving priority to Mesopotamia will appear in Chapter XIII.
The other challenge arises from a long-standing controversy about whether civilization
originated in Asia and spread to Europe (the Oriental hypothesis) or whether the
reverse was true (the Nordic hypothesis).

The Oriental hypothesis received its first thorough formulation, with careful weighing of all available evidence, from the Swedish scholar Montelius in 1899. The contrary
west-east view arose in Germany before the World War, as part of the doctrine that
the Nordic or so-called Aryan race invented all the good things in life. To account
for early progress in southwestern Asia, German scholars claimed that the necessary
inventions were made by Nordics who had migrated from the Baltic regions into these
lands long before the dawn of history. Today this doctrine is part of the official Nazi
creed.

Almost all scholars other than German condemn this doctrine as an outright flying
into the face of the evidence to gratify national pride. The German idea requires a vast
stretch of time, if only to allow for the necessary migrations of the Nordics from the
Baltic to southwestern Asia before 4000 or 5000 B.C. The German datings of finds
which revealed the beginnings of civilized life in Europe are correspondingly early—
even fantastically so, according to believers in the short chronology, such as V. Gordon
Childe.

These archaeologists believe that western Europe remained sunk in Mesolithic stagnation until substantially 3000 B.C. At this time, as Childe sets forth at length in his
Dawn of European Civilization (1925), the first peasants are supposed to have begun
their penetration of Europe with their neolithic arts; and this view is followed in the
accompanying text. A later and highly illuminating review of this question by Childe
may be found in Nature for September 24 and October 1, 1938.

was revealed, and all the painstaking precautions of modern archaeological technique were employed to gather all the light possible upon these early cultures.

At Erech, for example, German excavators uncovered three temples, each one built over the ruins of a predecessor. The topmost one contained so-called Jemdet Nasr culture from days before the Pyramids were built in Egypt. Beneath it was a Red Temple, so called from the color of the brick, and beneath the Red Temple was a Limestone Temple many centuries older. From beneath this temple the excavators sunk a shaft sixty feet deep to virgin earth and passed through no less than eighteen layers of prehistoric cultures. These finds are linked in turn with still older ones elsewhere, because the al'Ubaid culture at the bottom of the Erech shaft occurs at *upper* levels above still older relics in northerly sites such as Tell Halaf and Chagar Bazar.

An illuminating summary and appraisal of these findings was given by V. Gordon Childe in his presidential address on August 22, 1938, before the Anthropology Section of the British Association for the Advancement of Science. The address can be found in *Nature* of September 2 and October 1, 1938, and this address points out that the evidence gives a fair picture of the whole postglacial history of man in the region.

In point of dating Childe suggests that the al'Ubaid culture at the bottom of the Erech shaft was deposited probably not later than 4500 B.C. Dating the more northerly finds backward from this brings us in fair probability, Childe said, "well back into the sixth millenium B.C." Since the sixth millenium includes a commonly accepted date, 6700 B.C., for the end of the Ice Age, such a record certainly covers the time in which civilization grew out of hunting life. The story stands outlined, then, in time as well as in sequence of events; we *know* how civilization came to be.

Let us see, then, how this happened by making a short visit in imagination to the men of this time while they worked out this momentous advance!

CHAPTER XI

Sumerian Contributions to Civilization

IF THE FIRST FLOWERING of civilization occurred in Mesopotamia, as archaeologists now believe, so important an event deserves as accurate a setting as possible in both place and time; and archaeologists have worked out a fairly good setting in each respect by considering the geological history of the region during Pleistocene or Ice Age times.

The setting in place presents no problem. Geologists are sure that during the Ice Age all of Mesopotamia south of Hit was only in the making. The archaeological record shows how men moved into the newly made land from the first centers of neolithic culture in Asia Minor, Syria and Palestine, but it also shows that equally early beginnings were made farther south in a land known as Sumeria, and Sumer led in developing civilization.

The true story of civilization is to be found, then, when Sumer emerged from beneath the Persian Gulf. This emergence occurred because of two huge banks or bars of mud, sand and gravel which projected into the Persian Gulf from either shore in Ice Age times.

One bar had been built by an outwash of material from the Arabian plateau to the westward. The other had been built out from the eastern shore by the river Karun; and between them these banks or bars prevented the waves and tides of the Persian Gulf from disturbing the waters to the northward. Hence mud could settle out of the stagnant water on the north side of each bar, and this caused dry land to grow northward gradually from each bar.

The record suggests beyond much possibility of doubt that here on these growing bars is where full civilization was born. The next question is when this birth occurred.

A rough answer can be given by reckoning backward from a well-established fact of prehistory in Sumer.

The Sumerians believed that great floods occurred in the land after civilization had been well established, and they believed that the hero and god Gilgamesh rode out these floods in an ark. This tradition is supported to some extent by evidence of floods in some of the lower levels at Ur, at Erech and at other sites; hence civilization began *before* these floods. But floods could only have occurred if the rainfall was heavy, and the climate of Holocene or postglacial times offers only two probable times for heavy rainfall.

The times, in terms of European chronology, are known as the Bühl stadium and the Gschnitz advance; and the latter only is reckoned as occurring in Holocene time. Dates are uncertain, as explained in Appendix A, but the Gschnitz advance could have occurred after 4500 B.C., the date suggested by Childe for the first culture on this site. This would account for the Sumerian tradition of floods—and incidentally it gives us a rough dating for Noah and his ark, because Noah obviously is the Jewish equivalent of Gilgamesh.

Another necessary bit of setting for the origin of civilization here is the matter of the people involved.

The answer should rest upon positive evidence in the form of skeletal remains, and finds have been scanty indeed. But such finds as have been made suggest that the people belonged to the Mediterranean strain which descended with little change from the high-mentality stock of Mindel-Riss times; and they came in from the surrounding country, either east, west, north or all three, bringing with them neolithic arts. What happened next is reasonably well proved by the relics which Woolley found at al'Ubaid in 1922—and here is where we may let the story unfold before our eyes by imagining ourselves on the ground at the time.

For our observation point we choose a spot near the site of modern Basra, on the dry, solid edge of the Arabian plateau. Thanks to the postglacial change in climate, which has replaced the rain-bearing westerly winds of glacial times with parching hot winds, the entire plateau at our backs is rapidly becoming a hot desert. To the northeast, however, lies a broad marshy expanse that stretches as far as the eye can see. It seems to be all but steaming under the hot sun.

Its cover of reeds and rushes waves almost like a sea, thanks to an overhot breeze; laced through the green we see stretches of tawny, muddy water. Here and there a date palm relieves the flatness of the scene.

As we scan this sea of rippling green the region seems treacherous with its swampy dangers, yet tempting with its promises of food. The air is alive with thousands of game birds, and we imagine that the rich mud would yield fine crops if any patches of land are dry enough to be cultivated.

So, apparently, do the people of this day!

Here come four men now from the west. They are naked from the waist up, and they are sweating from the mere exertion of moving. For weapons they have slings and slingstones, bows and arrows, boomeranglike sticks, and maces—clublike affairs with heads of stone. The pear-shaped or *piriform* head of the mace is worth noting, because this shape seems to have been preferred throughout south-western Asia, whereas the Egyptians and many others preferred a disk shape.

As we join them they are manning a boat at the water's edge—a rude affair made by tying reeds into bundles with some sort of fibrous cord and then fashioning the bundles into an all but flat-bottomed boat. They have made it watertight by smearing it with bituminous pitch, and this bespeaks surprising enterprise for such seemingly rude folk. To get this substance someone must have visited the bitumen deposits many miles up the Euphrates near Hit!

Now off we go, pushing along with poles thrust against the mud bottom, through the reeds to get a bag of birds. The birds rise quacking, honking or cheeping on every hand; bows and arrows and throwing sticks soon bring down a good bag. But now comes a surprise. The men do not return to the high solid land to the west-ward, where presumably they live. Instead they push even deeper into the swamp. What can be drawing them, now that they have plenty of game for the day?

Soon we see their objective—a blisterlike bulge of reasonably solid land, several acres broad. It is thick with reeds, and a few scrubby date palms have taken root. The place seems to offer nothing save more game, but after we land we see what is attracting the party. There, a few feet before us, stand rude palm poles, set roughly upright a few feet apart and outlining four houses.

Are these men, then, building a camp of some sort? No; soon we gather from their gestures and speech that their ambitions run still higher. They are planning to live here and cultivate this patch of firm ground! Human culture is about to move in and take possession of this rich new marshland.

At present the men are adding some touches to the huts before returning home. Several poles are missing from the plan of the framework, but the men do not cut down the last good date palms on the islet for the needed poles. Instead they tie together bundles of extremely long rushes, set one end in the earth, then bend the free ends together and tie them. Thus the framework of a roof is achieved—the food trees are spared—and the whole task has taken only a few hours!

Back on the dry land to the west, where the tribe is still living, we could see the rest of the project if we liked. There we could note that these men are still unmarried; evidently they must provide homes before they can take brides. The intended brides are weaving rush mats, to be hung between the poles. Daubing the mats with clay and letting the sun bake the clay dry will provide four walls, quite all that is needed to make a home in this hot land of infrequent rains!

This little glimpse of entry upon the mud flat is purely imaginative as to incident—but the evidence uncovered by Woolley justifies every detail. Down at the bottom level of the excavation, on land which had barely emerged from the river in al'Ubaid times, Woolley uncovered the postholes for the huts, with relics of the mats.

To make a door these folk hung a panel to swing on an upright pole. The lower end of the pole was set in a scooped-out stone; there it would turn as though standing in a socket. Such stones can be found by the hundreds in these excavations. Finally, these first settlers were shrewd enough not to waste firm, tillable ground upon homes. They seem to have set the houses on marshy ground at the edge of the farm, and they tramped down bundles of rushes and clay (*terre pisée*) until they achieved a dry floor.

Such achievements were mere beginnings, however, compared to other developments which were forced by the special character of the land—and particularly by failure to provide certain essential materials.

First of all, the lack of wood and stone forced a rapid development of all clay-working or *ceramic* arts.

Relics from the primeval settlement of al'Ubaid near the site of ancient Ur prove that these people quickly became expert potters. They soon learned how to use the potter's oven, and beyond this they learned to use *slip*. That is, they made a pot of relatively coarse clay, then covered it with paste, or slip, of finely worked material. When fired the slip was watertight and usually showed a beautiful gloss. These people also painted on decorative designs which became an integral part of the pot when it was fired.

Extraordinary ingenuity went into making clay substitutes for implements that ordinarily are made of sharp stone or of metal. For a sickle they made a curved handle of wet clay and equipped it with teeth made of tiny sharp flakes of stone. When baked this implement cut grain well enough. They also made nails and pegs of baked clay. Such nails, of course, could not be hammered home. They could only be pressed or tacked lightly, but they served well enough for fastening up mats. These builders also developed, if indeed they did not invent, that most utilitarian building material, *brick*.

The value of brick for building, in a region devoid of both stone and wood, need scarcely be mentioned, save for one point. In this all-but-rainless land mere sun-dried bricks of adobe type were good enough for building. They lacked the waterproof consistency which can only be imparted by hot fire; hence they dissolved when exposed to storm or flood. But floods would ruin a community regardless of the brick used, so the lack of water-resisting power did not matter. The people could and did produce fired, waterproof brick whenever they wanted it for important structures such as temples.

Other developments were forced by lack of stone for tools and weapons.

To get good workable stone these people had to trade surplus foodstuffs for it with neighbors. Thus *trade, commerce,* came into being; and by trade we mean, not exchange of gewgaws and trinkets, but serious business, unremittingly pursued under the spur of necessity. And progress did not stop here, in this matter of overcoming lack of good stone! The lack also forced early use of *metal* and thus gave birth to the cultural stage commonly called *chalcolithic*—that is, combined use of copper and stone for tools. The word is from the Greek *chalcos* for copper or brass and *lithos* for stone.

During their life on higher lands these folk had become acquainted with surface deposits of copper ore, and in these deposits had occurred bits of metal sufficiently pure to be hammered into trinkets. Undoubtedly, just as did the American Indians around Lake Superior, these folk made such ornaments. Probably they discovered, too, that copper could be hammered to a sharp cutting edge and would hold this edge longer than would stone; but as long as stone was plentiful they probably did not bother to gather and work up scattered bits of the red metal.

Now, however, they could turn this discovery to good profit. Since they had to import stone they could just as well import the material that gave a better, stronger edge. Also their growing skill with pottery had taught them how to use hot fires and ovens, and somehow they learned that these same fires would *smelt* copper. Then they could smelt small pieces into a large lump and work up the lump into a knife, an ax or some other tool.

Not only did these people accomplish this; they displayed rare inventive genius by producing *socketed* axes, spearheads and chisels.

Previous to this time all blades and other cutting tools had been set into a notch or split in the handle. Such a mounting weakened the handle. Another defect which most peoples introduced into tools, once they learned to use copper, was fastening the tool to the handle with rivets. This was not sound design, because a smashing blow with an ax against a tree, for example, might well shear off rivets made of material as soft as copper. But now some brilliant thinker, fit to rank with any Edison or Marconi of our day, thought of providing a hole in the tool and setting the handle in the hole. Now the joint would hold until the handle itself broke.

This invention may seem simple to us, but the archaeological record proves that no other people thought of it for themselves. The socketed implement, therefore, is considered a veritable trade-mark of Mesopotamia. Archaeologists always look for the Mesopotamian contact, direct or transmitted, whenever socketed tools first appear anywhere in any culture in Europe or in Asia.

Next comes a development which seems to lie at the very heart of the Sumerian story—a development which has to do with human nature itself.

So far these peasants have been engaged with the foundations only of civilized living. They have adapted their older neolithic ways to their new surroundings and even made inventions to overcome lack of many raw materials; but all these advances are still on the low material level of winning the essentials of life. No discernable push toward higher achievements has appeared as yet.

Unquestionably, however, such a push did come, because here was one of the first places where men achieved highly civilized ways of living. Also a broad hint concerning the nature of the push has been turned up by Heinrich from deep excavations at Erech.

In the fifth and sixth layers above the first al'Ubaid relics a strikingly new type of pottery appeared, monochrome red or deep plum in color, together with other important cultural changes. These finds suggest strongly that some alien people moved in at this time and became dominant in Sumer.

Who were these people and where did they come from? Their own testimony can be taken from a résumé written out by one Berossus in the third century B.C. to preserve the ancient glories of this race.

According to Berossus a race of mermen, led by one Oannes, came out of the Persian Gulf with the arts of agriculture, metalworking and writing. "In a word," Berossus says, "all the things that make for the amelioration of life were bequeathed to men by Oannes, and since that time no further inventions have been made."

Less fanciful testimony appears in Holy Writ (Gen. 11, 2–4ff.):

And it came to pass, as they journeyed from the east, that they found a plain in the land of Shinar; and they dwelt there.

And they said one to another, Go to, let us make brick, and burn them thoroughly. And they had brick for stone, and slime had they for mortar.

And they said Go to, let us build us a city and a tower, whose top may reach unto heaven. . . .

Here do we not have an occupation of Sumer (Shinar in Hebrew) and brickmaking with thorough burning, because the work was to be important? And the Tower of Babel, here proposed—what was that but the familiar ziggurat or temple, in the form of stepped pyramid, which began appearing on the Sumerian plain after this new folk arrived?

Evidently, then, some fine day an expedition of strange people came rowing or sailing up the gulf, found the land good and took possession. Now, since the relics show that from this time on the culture in the land ran continuously into the historic Sumerian, archaeologists suspect that these invaders may have been the conquerors and organizers who energized the peasant life of the region and developed it into the high Sumerian civilization.

If so, and if they came by sea, these two facts give some valuable hints as to their temperamental fitness to achieve this advance.

Seafaring is a great selector of the hardheaded and practical in temperament—and of folk who have a good capacity for discipline and a knack for meeting emergencies with practical expedients. Others do not survive for long when they venture out upon open water, even if only for a coasting expedition. Hence on principle these newcomers should have been of a hardheaded doer or go-getter type—and just so they seem to have been.

Nowhere in their scheme of life as it unfolded later in Sumer did room exist for idle, vaporous speculation about the hereafter. They did what was necessary to keep the gods and the spirits in Nature in a favorable mood, and that was that for religion. In science and technology they applied some of the keenest intelligences known in the ancient world to anything which promised to be profitable; but thought for thought's sake seems to have had but little standing with them.

Most especially did the seafarer's hardheaded tendency to have everything shipshape and under firm control show up in the organization of community effort for life in Sumer, where everything depended upon irrigation of the land.

Irrigation from the river was, of course, the very basis of life in this rainless region. But irrigation canals required organized effort; and use of water had to be controlled, lest those nearer the source of supply take more than their share. This necessity for exact control, added to the necessity born of growing pressure from population upon the land, in turn enforced a well-defined system of land ownership. Thus, for the first time in our knowledge, arises a sharply defined idea of *property* and especially property in the land.

The original neolithic peasants had developed this idea in part. They wanted a property right in their dwellings, their tools and their stores of food, and they wanted it for limited periods in land as well. The idea that others could reap what they had sowed would have been intolerable. But there they stopped; they did not want perpetual ownership. This would have been senseless, because primitive agriculture quickly exhausted the soil, and every few years these early farmers abandoned their old farms and moved on to new land.

Here in Sumer, however, with a growing population and a strictly limited supply of good land, moving on was impossible. An owner had to work the same land all his life, and he passed on ownership to his son. Thus arose the idea of permanent property right in specific parcels of land; and since agriculture, food supply, lies at the root of all else in civilized living, this right became the most important of all. Not for nothing does our law consider ownership of land a man's *real* estate. The very word "real" in this connection is from the Latin *res,* the thing, the substance; and it comes ultimately from the primitive Indo-European root, the Sanskrit *ras* for wealth or property.

This idea would be sharpened in Sumer by the very fact that the Sumerians had won the land by conquest.

Conquerors always follow the principle that they have won all, own all and may dispose of everything as they see fit. Also they often give practical effect to this viewpoint by setting themselves up as *landlords,* or owners who stand above the actual possessors and workers of the soil. If they want a particular farm they may oust or slay the former owner, but more usually they apportion supreme ownership among themselves and let the former owners remain, as long as they pay *rent* in produce, services or, in later times, in cash to the landlord.

Many conquerors carry the landlord idea only far enough to set up members of their tribe as landowning nobles, but the Sumerians pushed the idea to the limit. They had come as a unified conquering army or navy; they saw that everyone was equally dependent upon efficient control of land and irrigation; and finally, among their mental patterns, was a strong religious faith, administered by intelligent priests. We know this to be so because their first great building in any important new city was not a palace, not a fort, but a ziggurat or temple. Intelligent priests may be assumed from the fact that the temples always were accurately oriented with the corners pointing south, west, north and east. A good understanding of astronomy was required for that.

Now all these mental elements combine to suggest a fine solution for the problem of control and organization to the Sumerians. They made *their god* the supreme landlord, with landowners of noble rank under him. They had a king, of course, who served as war chief and supreme authority; but all the evidence suggests that his most important function was that of high priest, because the temple was the true seat of government and irrigation control.

The Sumerian idea of rigid national discipline under religious authority also brought exactly the organizing strength needed for founding a political state.

At home the Sumerians needed only to maintain a sufficient number of their folk as a sort of standing army to fight off jealous neighbors and subdue domestic insurrection. Then they could wring enough from the abundant crops produced by the peasants to support the priesthood, the army and the potters, metalworkers and other artisans in their towns.

Abroad this army could keep trade routes open for getting the raw materials the Sumerians had to have and the luxuries they wanted. The army could also maintain strong trading posts at strategic points in foreign territory and escort trading caravans. All this was necessary in a day when almost any neighbor could be counted upon to seize what he wanted by sheer force if he could.

Thus the human story passes from beginnings into fruitions; the essential elements of civilization stood fairly born in Sumer. The outstanding element in it was the combination of limitations and opportunities presented by a mud flat—and if confirmation of this view be asked, it appears plainly enough from the fact that every other emergence of civilization directly out of barbarism *also occurred on a similar mud flat*. This was true in Egypt, as will appear later; it was true in China; and it was true of the other civilization, only discovered in comparatively recent years, which arose at this time. This addition to the roster of cultural beginnings is the *Indus civilization,* first described comprehensively in Sir John Marshall's *Mohenjodaro and the Indus Civilization* (1924).

Everything learned so far about it goes to show that it, too, was a river-flat culture, like those of Mesopotamia and Egypt.

It grew up in the Sind and Punjabi region, where the most important water supply is the runoff from the Himalayas through five rivers: the Indus, the Jhelum, the Chenab, the Degh or Rabi, and the Sutlej. Only two major sites are known—Mohenjodaro on the Indus and Harappa on the Rabi; but they are four hundred miles apart and hence speak unmistakably, as do outlying sites at Amri and Rupar, of a widespread culture. Moreover, the relics prove that this culture emerged in civilized living about when the Sumerian did, between the end of the Ice Age and 3000 B.C.

The towns were built of brick and ranked with those of Sumer, neither ahead nor behind, save that the brick was kiln dried and the towns do not seem to have been dominated by a temple, as the Sumerian towns were by ziggurats. Another point of cultural difference is lack of the stone door socket which Mesopotamia inherited from al'Ubaid days. But strong social control is manifest. Whenever either town was rebuilt after a flood a careful street plan was provided; individuals did not build where they liked. Sewage drains were installed, and the larger houses had both wells and baths.

Agriculture was by irrigation. The wheat was *Triticum compactum,* comparable to the *T. vulgare* we cultivate today; cotton took the place of Egyptian and Mesopotamian flax. Two-wheeled carts of a type which still can be seen in Sind were known, but metalworking was less advanced than it was in Sumer. These folk, for example, did not make socketed implements. The absence of abundant war implements bespeaks more peace than the Sumerians enjoyed.

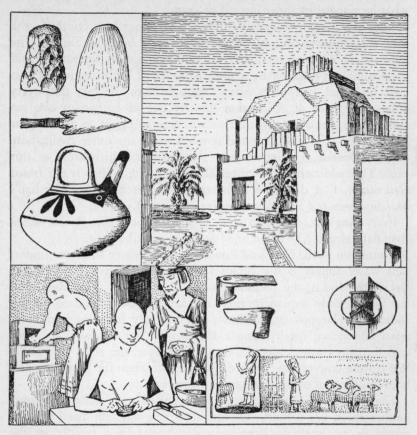

GLIMPSES OF LIFE IN BUSY SUMER

At the upper left are some of the fundamental implements needed for civilized city living, as they took form with the first inhabitants of the Sumerian mud flat. The panel shows a chipped stone hoe, a polished stone celt, a copper harpoon lashed to a stick and a pot with two distinctive features of the earliest style—a spout and painted decorations, fired on. At the upper right a ziggurat, or stepped pyramid, dominates the city of well-made brick houses and brick-paved streets equipped with drains and sewers. At the lower left a scribe writes a letter for a waiting trader by impressing wedge-shaped or cuneiform characters on a tablet of wet clay. An assistant prepares a little oven for baking the tablet when done. The highly distinctive products of Sumerian crafts at the lower right include two socketed battle-axes, a socketed double ax and a cylinder seal with its impression. Such seals were used to affix signatures in wet clay or hot wax throughout Sumerian and Babylonian times.

127

These people also wrote with a strange pictographic script, as yet utterly undeciphered. Their religion is evidenced by the existence of a three-faced prototype of the Hindu Siva, seated cross-legged in typical later Hindu fashion. The fantastic later Hindu gods therefore were not created by the Aryan invaders who created the Hindu civilization we know, in the second millenium before Christ. Apparently they combined their beliefs with a pantheon of gods which they found ready-made. The Hindu gods, then, like the carts of Sind, are "living fossils" which still testify today to the arts and beliefs of this ancient life at the dawn of historic times.

This culture would seem to clinch the proof, if clinching be needed, that our story of how civilization began is substantially correct. If the driving force was not just such an adaptation to the peculiar conditions found on river mud flats, the rise of the oldest civilizations in just such situations *and in no others* would be hard to understand. We seem justified then in believing that we know how and why men came to invent the arts, techniques and social arrangements that form the foundation of fully civilized living.

For an inquiry such as ours, however, this is a mere beginning. We still face the larger inquiry into *mental* aspects of this development. Material arts are not the whole of life. They are not even the larger part, once a culture rises above the level of attaining a bare living. Then more completely mental aspirations come into play. Men can think more of achieving happiness in this life above the level of brute existence. They devote more thought to the hereafter. The soul, the spirit, begins to expand in countless ways, and so the center of emphasis shifts from man's dealings with Nature to his dealings with himself and his fellows.

Now, with civilization fairly established, we stand at the place in the human story where this shift occurred. Incidentally we can also see ourselves fairly in the making, because ways of thinking which serve us for better or for worse started creeping into man's mental equipment at this time. And all these important developments can be attacked to best advantage by starting with the working basis of them —the formation and use of the ideas which man applies in shaping his mental life.

CHAPTER XII

The Controlling Force of Ideas

ACCORDING to the Oxford dictionary an idea may be defined as "a picture or notion of anything conceived by the mind"—and this test of recognition by the consciousness is enough to set ideas off from all other mental stuff such as emotional states and the raw data reported by sight, hearing and other senses. But ideas by no means count equally in building civilization. Mere recognitions of objects, of place and time relations and of simple cause-and-effect sequences have been standard mental stock from the beginning. The ideas which counted in building civilization were of the sort described in Chapter II as "reasoning in terms of abstract principle"—that is, reasoning which enables a musician to "hear" keys, rhythms and chords in a symphony or suggests a law of gravity at work behind the apparent motions of the sun, the moon and the planets across the sky.

For all practical purposes we can describe formation of such ideas in two steps. First the mind arrays the material of the problem in some logical arrangement—let us say a time sequence of events or appearances as they occur. Then, by drawing upon memory and constructive imagination, the mind tells itself, "If such and such a working force were behind all this, would it cause this sequence?" If the imagined pattern of causal force or working principle fits the data, the mind says, "Fine! This must *be* the cause or controlling principle!"

Here, then, we have the mental working method which, together with the manipulative abilities of the human hand, has produced all the practical differences between living like an ape and living as we do. But this working process, simple as it is in principle, becomes colored, warped and deflected in countless ways by emotional and other elements in human nature. Indeed, the human record has been

129

shaped more by these colorings and deflections than it has by intelligent thinking itself. Hence, now that highly intelligent thinking is coming to the front in man's story, it is high time to enlarge our earlier glimpses of these other elements into a definite working pattern for understanding human nature.

For the foundation of this pattern nothing could serve better than the psychological meaning of that time-honored term, "strength of character."

This term, like the terms mentioned in Chapter VIII for naming emotions, is no mere figure of speech. It expresses the important psychological truth that action turns upon the strength of intelligent character elements in our natures, as measured against the strength of urges from the brute side.

The man who is not accustomed to curbing his desires and whims yields to a comparatively mild emotional or animal impulse. So, likewise, does the brutish mind. It never has developed any worth-while, intelligent standards which could serve as curbs. In contrast, a man with highly developed reasoning power and a strong habit of self-discipline can control his emotional urges to almost any extent. Control can be exercised also by a strong emotional urge, such as religious asceticism, which dominates other urges.

Relative strength of the two natures is the key, therefore, to what man will think and do—and since brute nature is substantially the same in all normal individuals, the real key to thought and conduct is the quality and strength of the intellectual endowment.

A large part of this quality and strength consists in turn of the kind of tests which men use to test the truth or falsity and the value or uselessness of their ideas.

If thinkers always had been willing to accept as true only those principles which squared absolutely with all the known facts, all would have been well from the first. Progress would have marched with never a misstep or a setback. But mankind never has been willing to show such intellectual restraint. When a problem has defied search for the ultimate working principle thinkers have allowed fancy, untrammeled imagination, to fill the gap. They have invented fairy tales and accepted fanciful products of wishful thinking, such as faith in magic. Such explanations would have been fine if only they had been true. But they were not true. Many of them were violently wrong, and they led to perniciously wrong results, just as did faith in magic.

So also has man been incurably stubborn about clinging to the shoddy products of such shabby thinking, even after the validity of the ideas has been thoroughly and utterly demolished. James Harvey Robinson, in his magnificent study of human nature at work, *The Mind in the Making* (1921), attributes this stubbornness to sheer vanity. "We are incredibly heedless in the formation of our beliefs," he says, "but find ourselves filled with an illicit passion for them when anyone proposes to rob us of their companionship. It is obviously not the ideas themselves that are dear to us, but our self-esteem, which is threatened. We are by nature stubbornly pledged to defend our own from attack, whether it be our person, our family, our property or our opinion."

Still another aspect of tests for truth can be made plain by contrasting early ways of tackling problems with truly modern scientific thinking.

Thus far man has gathered new knowledge by the simple processes of observation and chance discovery of simple facts and principles. He noticed that clay became hard and waterproof when placed in hot fire; thus he achieved pottery. He noticed that between spring and spring twelve full moons came and went; this gave him his idea of the year. Beyond this his reasoning was naïve and childish.

The idea of impersonal natural forces was utterly beyond him. Everything had to be moved or caused by gods or spirits. They might be invisible, but they were visualized as having the forms of men, animals or of combinations of familiar objects like human-headed bulls or falcon-headed human bodies.

Truly scientific thinking also uses sheer observation and chance discovery, but its principal reliance is a technique as definite as the art of a builder while erecting a house. After getting an idea true science *tests* the idea by careful comparison of it with all known facts and even more by using it in *experiments*. If the idea works out exactly as expected, then and only then does it acquire standing as probably true; and then comes the acid test. This is the requirement that no exceptions or contradictions can be found.

Science does not permit a man to believe that a belief is true because he wants it to be true, or because someone tells him, "the gods have ordained it thus," or because he can point as astrologers do to numerous instances wherein a "principle" or a "control" *has* worked out. The test of validity is that the rule *always* holds good, with never a failure or exception. A rule is accepted as true only when nobody has been able to find an instance wherein it fails to work.

Many more aspects of these fundamentals will become apparent as the human story unfolds, but these observations will be enough at the start. With them we can organize our patterns of human nature by considering how mankind may be allocated roughly among "mental" types—or, to state the matter another way, how men may be distinguished by differences in *temperament*.

First, and overwhelmingly most numerous of all the types or temperaments, come the *habit ridden*—people who, like the first peasants considered in Chapter X, get set in their ideas, most of them wrong, as though their minds were so much concrete.

Such people may seem unimportant, because of their dullness, in a history of intelligence—but their overwhelming preponderance in any population makes them the most important type in all humanity. They do the hard, grubbing work of the world, and if they are kept contented they do it well. Neither is contentment difficult to provide in principle, because their wants are simple. A full belly, a reasonably comfortable shelter, a chance to gratify the animal instinct for rearing a family—historically this has meant the full circle of happiness for such individuals, with an occasional feast day or community celebration thrown in for spice. Given this much, they carry their share of the human load cheerfully enough. The Roman emperors learned the knack of getting such service from them long ago, with the formula *panem et circenses*, "bread and circuses"—and never were the emperors troubled with a popular uprising or a peasant's revolt.

Trouble has arisen constantly, however, with the habit ridden because most rulers have not been as intelligent as were the emperors of Rome. The more typical attitude has been one of greedy contempt, which saw this vast, dumb mass as a fine array of cattle, ready to be driven and exploited to the uttermost. From time to time the victims have either run out on the system, leaving it in collapse, or they have risen in revolt. Then the results were even worse, because habit-ridden folk lack the mental endowment needed to pursue their own interests to good advantage. Instead of following the dictates of reason they fall victims to the wiles of every demagogue and cultist who knows how to whip up emotions and prejudice.

The historic record will prove this time and again—in ancient Egypt, in even the Golden Age of Athens and throughout the history of Europe. But proof lies much nearer at hand in our own civilization. For an all-sufficient example of this weakness we need only consider the usual course of political campaigns, from national ones for the presidency to local ones for dogcatcher.

How many campaigns are fought out by sober discussion of the real issues? Not one in a hundred; practical politicians know that sober argument would break into spray like waves beating upon a rocky coast when it meets the stony immobility of habit-ridden minds. Instead the politicians seek to arouse the emotions of fear, hate, party loyalty and the like. They turn loose leather-lunged and brass-throated rabble rousers, for they know full well the ability of such solicitors to win elections in this supposedly intelligent democracy of ours.

Above this level come the folk endowed with mental flexibility and power enough to achieve changes in ideas and even at times to impress these changes upon their fellows.

Any accurate, detailed analysis would have to acknowledge that actually any two thinkers differ as sharply in mentality as they do in face and figure—but an understanding of the human record need not consider these individual differences. Mankind en masse can be understood well enough by grouping temperaments above the habit-ridden level into three classes —(1) the wishful, emotional or subjective personalities, (2) the so-called "pure thinkers" or intellectuals and (3) the restless, hard, *doer,* or driver type.

Each of these "temperaments" affords a beautiful demonstration of our principle that the quality of thought is profoundly affected by the balance between the intelligent and the brute, the relative strength of reason, emotion and impulse in shaping thought and conduct.

The *wishful* thinkers, the folk who "think with their hearts instead of their heads" or, more formally, the *subjective* thinkers, are an excellent illustration. They are marked most of all by a high intensity of "nervous charge" on the emotional side, a readiness of the emotions to flood up and swamp the less intense or less active powers of reason in their mental make-up.

For an explanation of how this type acquires its characteristics we need only note how it branches off from other types during childhood. The divergence occurs during a certain phase of development which all thinking parents recognize in, say, two-year-olds.

Most of us have noticed that children of this age show a sudden outburst of riotous fancy, with untrammeled flights of imagination— and many of us have been appalled as well by what seems a most barefaced willingness to lie!

Yet we should not be appalled. Little Johnny is not destined to be an incorrigible liar because when asked what he saw around the corner he replies, "O-o-h big fire—all the houses burned down, fire-mans come, people all roasted!" Mary is not willfully trying to deceive her mother when, upon being urged to eat her bread and milk, she says, "Won't! Nasty big spider in it!"

Such incidents simply mean that these children have come suddenly into possession of their powers of imagination but have not yet learned that imagination should be controlled by respect for fact. This lesson should be taught tactfully, carefully and firmly; but the only occasion for worry is when the *need* for this lesson does not arise. Such a failure suggests a lag in acquiring imaginative powers.

The more usual trouble is failure to bring this ebullience under control by reason and respect for cold fact. Some children, unfortunately, grow to adult stature with their emotions and imaginative faculties still undisciplined, still in nearly complete control of their lives and actions. They are the emotional, wishful thinkers.

This is not to say that such people cannot be effective or valuable. Quite the contrary; they often do splendidly for themselves and for mankind when they manage to find suitable stimuli and practical outlets for their emotional natures. Their troubles arise when they cannot find such stimuli and outlets or when they try to deal with life as they would like to have it, instead of as it is. The psychoanalyst tells us what happens then. Their emotional urges, faced with constant and bitter defeat, turn them in upon themselves; and all too often such people finish their days under the lash of torturing complexes and neuroses.

Next in our array comes those in whom reason reigns, without much drive from emotional force. Perhaps a better way to state their character would be to say that their interests and even their emotions are stirred powerfully by patterns of abstract understanding which leave most people cold. An outstanding example is Sir Isaac Newton, founder of modern physics and the man who worked out the law of gravity. To picture the driving force in such natures, a sufficient example is the difference in reactions to the night sky as felt by "the man in the street" and the astronomer.

To the layman the charm of astronomy lies in the brilliant array of stars twinkling jewel-like against the black velvet of the night sky, the soft silver moonlight and the mysterious and thrilling feeling of seeing to infinite distance throughout space. The professional astronomer is not insensible to all this; he merely adds another source of mental charm to these direct ones. Behind the direct appearances in the sky he sees in his mind's eye a mechanism of forces, planes, orbits and angles, which is all as real to him as though the heavenly bodies were actually wired together and being driven like a machine. The joy of the creator is his as he thinks of the mechanism—and rightly so, for this mechanism actually is the child of his own mind.

So it is with the biologist as he watches the play of principle which he has created to explain the myriad appearances and workings of life. The mathematician thrills to an equation which "works out" just as does a man who loves machinery to the purr of a sweetly running engine. Detection of abstract principle as the cause of events and appearances is a fundamental joy with people of this type, and it is well that this is so. If this type had not arisen mankind would still be living scarcely better than did neolithic peasants.

Lastly we come to the *doers,* furnishers of the great generals, the noted prime ministers of history and hardheaded men of affairs— merchants, manufacturers, mariners and explorers. The source of their inner driving power or urge to action has always been a mystery, and so it is today; but science probably is on the track of the secret now. The chances are that as we learn more about the workings of hormones such as adrenalin and acetylcholine we shall find that these folk are set on a psychological hair trigger which conditions them for action at the slightest challenge to their powers.

There, then, we have our types—and we must confess that they are highly artificial. No normal man has ever been entirely habit ridden or entirely habit free. Nobody has ever seen an entirely emotional thinker outside an asylum, and heaven forbid that we should ever be compelled to deal with a man who is purely a thinker! But even so, do not these types give order and system to our understanding of our fellow men? If we allow a proper amount of each "type" to any person we know, have we not gone far toward explaining his temperament?

It would seem so, provided we sharpen one concept as a sort of capstone to our analysis. We can still review with profit the array of driving forces behind all human activity, the steam, so to speak, which makes the engine go.

Some driving forces have been evident from the beginning—desires for food, shelter of a sort, a mate and the companionship and support of a group. To these was added need for clothing, as soon as man advanced enough from beginnings to move into regions which had inclement climate. Later on, with the advent of neolithic arts, came more sophisticated desires for security, leisure and freedom.

In all later times, however, and in all modern life, the most universal urge aside from these primitive ones seems to be the desire for *self-aggrandizement*. Throughout all ages we can see this urge at work with an infinite variety of detail, but also with an underlying sameness in psychic objective. We see the brutish, self-indulgent person seeking to emphasize his importance with rare and costly food, more dazzling beauty in his women and a resplendent, awe-inspiring home. The artist wants to surpass other artists, the philosopher to achieve fame for new understandings. The politically minded man wants higher office and more power, just as the man who takes money as a measure of worth wants an ever-larger fortune.

Beneath all these varieties of self-aggrandizement lies a still deeper one, at least with most people. Most people whose mental life rises above the concerns of the moment want a permanent place in the universal scheme, a place which will still be theirs when death closes their earthly career. To think that they have the divine gift of self-consciousness for a season and then must perish like a beast of the field seems unbearable. This gift must survive somehow and give continued existence beyond the grave. So thinking, they take courage to bear all ills, for better times will come.

From its very nature as the ultimate comfort and reward this religious hope has figured in all ages as the most potent driving force of all. It is highly fitting, then, that the oldest major example of ideas shaping destinies in all the human record should have this hope at its very heart. The example turns up in Egypt in a kind of religious and ethical thinking which set the Egyptians sharply apart from every other people we know in the early ancient world and gave Egyptian culture an enduring power unmatched, save only by Chinese culture, in all the purview of history.

CHAPTER XIII

History Begins in Egypt

THE PYRAMIDS OF EGYPT are a universally used symbol for deathless age—and yet they can be matched in one sense by the Egyptians themselves. Of all the peoples on the earth none came into civilized living earlier, and of all the peoples none save the Chinese have been as little changed by time. Today we can see Egyptians unchanged in physical type from those forebears in the very dawn of antiquity who erected the deathless Pyramids. The modern Egyptians live as their forebears did; and if the scene were freed of a few modern touches such as railroads and traces of Mohammedan influence such as mosques, any pharaoh would feel at home in the Egypt of today.

Now a handy explanation for this changelessness is the tag word "conservatism"—but the true reason lies deeper than any such tag. Other peoples have been conservative, but they have not endured. Change has been forced upon them, or they have even perished or been absorbed into other peoples.

Plainly, then, the Egyptians had something more than conservatism. They had something which *fitted them to endure,* and this something is not hard to name. Even a quick comparison of their ways and their historic record with the facts of human nature will show that they endured because even before the dawn of history they evolved a viewpoint, a religion and a philosophy which towered above the thinking of other peoples as one of their pyramids dominates the surrounding plain. Conquerors might come in, but when they did the superior Egyptian ways won them over; and so Egypt and the Egyptians lived on, immutable as their own Nile, through all history right down to our times. The record is one of the most impressive in all history of the sustaining value of a sound idea, suited to a situation and tenaciously held.

This idea, therefore, is the obvious key to an understanding of Egypt—and the nature of it fairly shouts at the visitor, from the Pyramids, the temples and the gods which raise their towering bulk above the Egyptian scene. To understand Egypt one need only understand *Egyptian religion,* together with its effect upon life and thought. This understanding, in turn, can be drawn readily enough from the primitive way of forming religious ideas.

In terms of thinking viewed as a process of forming patterns of understanding, primitive man got his religious ideas by shuffling familiar concepts into combinations that had awesome power. Adding the wings of an eagle to the body of a man gave that body power of far-reaching movement. Making the combination invisible added still more power. Winds could well be the breath of some gigantic creature—and so the process ran, until everything stood explained.

Inevitably such naïve thinking took coloring from its surroundings. Forest peoples placed gods in trees; dwellers on a barren, wind-swept coast placed their deities in the water and the air. So it was with the early Egyptians, and we need have no difficulty in identifying many a feature of Egyptian surroundings which exerted powerful influence upon Egyptian thought.

One such feature was perennially clear skies, with a blazing sun every day and glorious starlit nights. In all ages such skies have lifted men's thoughts heavenward. Practically every great religion originated in a comparatively rainless land, with perpetually clear skies that set off the glories of the sun, the moon and the stars.

Another distinctive feature of the Egyptian scene was its essential *kindliness.*

In most farming lands, the crop-giving spring rains usually come accompanied by high winds, thunder and lightning. In such lands men could imagine readily that the gods and spirits could be angry as well as helpful, and charms and sacrifices to propitiate them would be in order. But the Nile floods never showed such fits of temper. They simply rolled in every year with their rich gifts. Plainly, then, the gods or spirits who gave these floods were good, and this idea of goodness figured in Egyptian thought as far back as we know.

Still another kindly feature of Egypt was comparative freedom from hostile and predaceous neighbors. Beyond the Sinai Peninsula to the northeast Egypt was blocked off from Asia by forbidding desert. Desert lay to the westward as well. The Mediterranean barred invasion from the north as long as cultures were too primitive to undertake seafaring in force, and the headwaters of the Nile to the south lay at an immense distance from the first seats of Egyptian thinking along the middle and northern portions of the Nile. The Egyptian, therefore, escaped much of the pressure from neighbors which kept the Sumerians hardheaded, practical and militaristic in spite of equally clear skies and unfailing rivers. Along the Nile man had a chance to lift up his thoughts to the sky without interference from without and to elevate his concepts of life accordingly.

Thus a trend away from the savage and the fearful aspects of life got a good start in Egypt, and the trend was reinforced by another idea which pervaded all Egyptian thinking throughout historic times. This other idea was the hope for life after death—and this seems to have come, like the idea of good gods, from the play of special circumstance in Egypt upon primitive ideas about death.

According to modern understandings of the primitive mind, early folk did not visualize a complete divorce between body and soul as a result of death. The two were separated, yes; but the early thinkers believed that the soul returned to the body from time to time, re-animated it and used it to obtain food, drink and other satisfactions. Here was the reason for funeral gifts—and also for the common practice of tying the body securely, to keep the soul from using it to inflict harm upon living beings!

In most lands this danger was temporary because the body soon disintegrated. In Egypt, however, the narrow fertile valley of the Nile was bordered on either side by hot dry sands, and the Egyptians customarily buried their dead here rather than on the good farming land. But this hot dry sand *mummified* the bodies. Hence, to primitive ways of thinking, the soul could live indefinitely if only the relatives provided gifts of utensils and food with the burial and renewed them from time to time.

Thus a fundamental idea of immense importance in all later ages got its start in Egypt, and from that time on it set the Egyptians more or less apart from other peoples in early ancient times. This is worth noting well, because apart from this trend of religious thought the course of events here ran much as they did in Sumeria.

In Egypt the beginnings of civilized life arose much as they did in Mesopotamia, because of life upon a mud flat. Indeed, in the delta where the Nile was busily building land out into the Mediterranean conditions were almost the same as in Sumeria—scorching sun, steaming marshlands rich with game and, to each side, a solid mainland that was becoming desert. Hence the delta saw the same infiltration of folk and the same type of life—boats, reed huts and all. The folk brought in a version of the North African Capsian culture, with neolithic flints, bows and arrows and lively art.

Similar ways of living also prevailed in Middle and Upper, or southern, Egypt, where the Nile flows in a broad valley from ten to twenty miles across. This culture has been called *Tasian* since 1929, when Brunton and his associates published their discovery of it at Dier Tasa. With the Tasian may be grouped similar cultures found at Merimde in the delta and in the depression of the Fayum with its lake, the Birket-el-Qarun, west of Cairo.

Several features of the Tasian culture suggest that these people entered the Nile Valley before the Sahara was completly dried out. One feature was the decoration on their pottery. The patterns included crisscrossed lines, interlocked triangles, a herringbone effect and parallel lines running around the pot. Such patterns reflect the texture of basketry, and the Sahara could not have been completely dry as yet if basketry still remained alive enough to influence pottery style. Also the Nile Valley still seems to have had trees, because the Tasians are the one folk in Egyptian prehistory who made celts or stone axes suitable for cutting wood.

But if trees still existed in Egypt, the Tasian cultures can be dated at least roughly in terms of geologic time.

The last time trees could have lived in Egypt was during the Gschnitz advance of the glaciers, an event which some authorities date tentatively at about 4500 B.C. If the climate of Gschnitz time was not responsible, then these trees must be referred to the end of the Bühl—a time which is dated tentatively by many at 6700 B.C. Hence a large uncertainty exists, but at least we can say that the Tasian culture seems to have flourished sometime between 6700 and 4500 B.C.

The Tasian culture seems to have given way, when the trees disappeared from Egypt, to the *Badarian* way of life.

This culture has been known scarcely longer than the Tasian, since it was discovered in 1924 at El-Badari (*The Badarian Civilization,* Brunton and Caton Thompson, 1928, and later reports). It seems to have come in from the south, and it contributed nothing save in pottery. The Badarians made fine pieces with red bodies and black tops by firing the pot upside down, with its top masked from an abundance of air. They could use slip, and they produced a beautiful ripple finish, probably by stroking the wet clay with a blunt-toothed comb. The shapes had worked free from the basketry tradition and had become perfectly suited to the nature of the material itself.

The pace of progress quickened, however, when a new folk arrived and established the *Amratian* culture.

These newcomers seemed to have come in from the west. The racial type seems Getulian or Libyan and hence descended from the men of the Paleolithic Capsian. Rudeness is bespoken by a reversion to basketry ornamentation on pottery; crisscross lines filled with white were applied on a black background.

These people reacted, however, even more powerfully than the earlier ones to the spiritual suggestions from the surroundings— perhaps because the climatic change to dryness was completely established by this time. Amratian times brought extremely careful burial of the dead, with a complete array of gifts for life in the next world. The people dug wide graves, and in the space they built box-like tombs, with plenty of room alongside the body for the funeral gifts. Thus began the style of entombment which developed later into the *mastaba,* a two-part dwelling for the dead. In this structure an underground chamber held the mummified body, and a chapel on the ground level held gifts and charms.

Another development in spiritual ideas is suggested by the abundant images and representations of scorpions and crocodiles on amulets—animals for which the people certainly had no use in daily life. From this Egyptologists argue that the Amratians had clans or tribes, each one with an animal as its totem. Thus, many scholars believe, arose the later practice of endowing many Egyptian gods with animal heads. This was an echo of these clan totems.

A last item worth notice in Amratian life is the flintwork. Previous work, while good enough, had not developed much beyond the level attained by the first Cro-Magnons in Europe. The Amratians, however, produced pressure-flaked implements as fine as any such work ever done.

The distinctive spiritual life of Egypt had its start, therefore, in Amratian times, and the influences which made the full-fledged Egypt of antiquity came in with the next culture, the *Gerzean.*

This culture produced a quickening and an intensification of Egyptian development similar to that wrought by the intruding Sumerians in Mesopotamia—and for good reason. It came from southwestern Asia, with a wealth of new ideas and techniques from the fast-growing civilizations along the Tigris and the Euphrates as well as elements from Syria and Asia Minor.

Among the new techniques were pots decorated with painted

scenes of life along the Nile—an unmistakable evidence of contact with al'Ubaid painted ware, since this technique had been utterly unknown in Egypt down to this time. Another al'Ubaid feature was pots with spouts—a feature almost as distinctively Mesopotamian as a socketed ax. Such weapons did not appear, but the Gerzeans did bring the piriform, or pear-shaped, mace.

A vastly more important importation, however, was religious ideas from the Syrian cult of nature deities. First among these imported gods were Osiris and his son Horus. In Syrian belief both these gods had been slain in their first careers on earth; Osiris had been cut to bits by the fiendish Set. Both had been restored to life beyond the grave by magic, but the magic had to be renewed periodically, to renew this life. This is a religious parallel with the periodic death of vegetation at the onset of winter and its renewal in the spring; and this idea, with resulting fertility cults and fertility goddesses, flourished in Asia not only as early as scholars can trace but forward well into Greco-Roman times.

This idea obviously fitted in beautifully with Egyptian thinking—so much so that it became the predominant faith of Egypt in due time. But before this could happen—or for that matter, any other amalgamation of Gerzean with Egyptian—a long period of bitter struggle and shaking down was needed, to overcome the instinctive aversion felt by all primitive peoples for alien ideas.

This struggle was slow in developing, because at first the new-comers found congenial homes in the delta at the mouth of the Nile, and they did not disturb the Amratian settlements higher up the river. In time, however, the Gerzeans spread southward along the flood plain of the Middle Nile, until they encroached upon the Amratians. This meeting of Amratian and Gerzean filled the land and brought all Egyptians face to face with the fundamental problem of civilized living—the problem of devising social arrangements for enabling large numbers of people to live and work together in harmony.

Almost invariably such situations have been submitted to arbitrament by force of arms—and the rule held good now. A protracted struggle for supremacy occurred between the delta folk and those who lived farther south in the rocky gorge of the Nile.

The delta dwellers seem to have been the victors at first. They had the better culture, and their knowledge of copper working was backed up by acquaintance with the rich deposits in the Sinai Peninsula. They could march or, rather, row and sail along the Nile,

THE DAWN OF CIVILIZED LIVING 143

armed with devastatingly superior weapons. But also, as we might expect—human nature being what it is—a turn of fortune came after this victory. The northern clans undoubtedly settled down to enjoy the fruits of victory and became self-satisfied and soft. The southerners, after acquiring northern weapons and arts, reasserted themselves; and being the harder-bitten folk, thanks to adversity, they won in the end. Egyptian tradition names Menes, a chief of the Hathor or Cow clan, as the ultimate victor and honors him as the first pharoah and founder of the first dynasty. (Pharoah is the Hebrew name, made familiar to us through the Bible, for an Egyptian king.)

Modern scholars believe that Menes was a composite figure, built up by combining the achievements of several leaders; but the victory itself is clear. Every pharoah thereafter wore a double crown, signifying rule over both Upper, or southern, and Lower Egypt; and from then on the rule of the pharoahs ran almost unbroken for nearly 3000 years, down to the days of Alexander the Great. But this advent of the pharoahs was matched in importance by two other landmarks in the history of thought. One was the emergence of clean-cut religious beliefs among both the conquering Amratians from the south and the conquered Gerzeans of the north. The other was the beginning of written records, and with these the *dawn of history* in the technical sense of the word as a record of events preserved in writing. Let us consider them in this order!

The more important faith in these early days was, of course, the faith of the southern masters of united Egypt under Menes and later kings. This faith contained an array of old tribal totems erected into animal gods, but the core of it was worship of Re or Ra, the sun-god, the giver of the immortality which was striven for with mastaba tombs. This faith was remarkable for its clean-cut intellectual power and its daring concepts.

It sprang probably from the connection between the Nile floods and the northward movement of the sun in the early summer. Here was a fine suggestion for religious belief. The Nile was the fount of life in Egypt; the Nile's floods seemed brought by the sun; so the sun must be the supreme deity. Certainly it was worthy to be, what with its blazing glory and its scorching power!

But some similar trend of thought argued that if the sun was the king of all gods, so also should worship of the sun be reserved for kings. Peasants and commoners could content themselves with lesser gods; the privilege of soaring eagle-like to the heaven provided in the sky by Re was reserved for the king alone, or at best for the king and the greater nobles.

The faith was a proud one also, as befitted a ruling caste. While on earth the aristocratic worshipers of Re were children of the sun, his viceroys. They ruled with the same power and calm majesty that characterized the sun itself and in the spirit which the Egyptians called *maat,* a spirit of respect for right and justice; but they did this as an expression of their own godlike dignity and not because they had to win immortality as a reward for lives well lived. No question of *winning* immortality existed in this faith. With the proper charms and arrangements the princely worshipers commanded entry into the sun heaven as their *right*. Once there, they continued to rule just as they had on earth, as long as their mummified bodies were supplied with necessary sustenance on earth.

Meanwhile the conquered commoners were developing an equally satisfactory religion by combining the Egyptian idea of immortality with their Osiris faith. In this elaborated form the faith taught that the evil demon Set, after killing Osiris, had chopped him to bits and scattered the bits on the sea. The faithful sister-wife Isis of Osiris and his son Horus finally found the bits at Byblos—a significant location, since it was the historic point of contact by sea with Palestine and Syria—and by magic they restored Osiris to life. Horus vanquished Set, brought the whole quarrel to judgment before Thoth, god of justice, and Osiris was vindicated. Thereafter he ruled the kingdom of the dead, admitted those humans whom he thought worthy and granted resurrection to crops on earth every year.

Egypt, therefore, had a duality of faiths—but the outcome was a happy one. The rulers could enjoy their exclusive and supposedly superior faith; the commoners were happy with their beliefs. Thus Egypt enjoyed religious peace, an inspiring prospect of immortality for everyone and a benevolent attitude, without parallel in early antiquity, toward life and the rights of man.

The crowning achievement of this time, however, was the beginning, so important to all mankind, of *history,* in the technical sense of events recorded in writing.

This does not mean that men had not kept records before this time. It means rather that now the Egyptians began to keep records to *let posterity know what they did*. The motive behind this is obvious. A strong monarchy had arisen in Egypt, and strong monarchs like to pass on records of their deeds by placing recitals of their achievements on monuments, temples, palaces and their tombs. The Egyptian monarchs followed this impulse—and their records are the beginning of history, because these records, preserved in a dry climate, have lasted down to our day, whereas most other records of similar age have perished beyond redemption by us.

This impulse to preserve records also lent impetus, if impetus was needed, to develop writing into thoroughly usable form. The word "develop" is advisable here, because it would be a mistake to say that writing was *invented*. No such outright creation of the writing art ever occurred, unless we call paleolithic man's use of a picture to mean a reindeer an invention. It grew as language grew, in step with man's need for it; and the various steps can be traced easily down to this blooming of the writing art in First Dynasty times.

The next step above simple pictures was the one used on the Azilian painted pebbles. Pictures were reduced to symbols, and these symbols conveyed meanings. A symbol for a sun with three marks or dots could mean three days; a full moon, a crescent and another full moon could mean a month.

Such signs are called *ideograms,* and all peoples in all times who had reached even the beginnings of neolithic arts understood this method of writing. The American Indians knew it; Australian aborigines of today know it; and in ancient Egyptian times ideograms appear on the pots and in the tombs of Gerzean times.

From these simple beginnings ideographs were developed until they could express complex and abstract ideas by simply carrying forward the principle of symbolizing. The Chinese sign for "listen" was originally an ear between two doors, and either "happy" or "joy" was shown in Egyptian by a dancing man. Of course, as human thinking grew in complexity, thousands of ideograms would be needed for all the ideas if nothing was done to simplify the methods; but even before the First Dynasty came into power the Egyptians had overcome this difficulty. Instead of creating a separate sign for each new idea, they retained such old ones as were thoroughly useful —just as we use the sign $, even though we know how to write out "dollars"—and then they used *phonograms* or sound signs for other words.

These were simple in principle. Every idea the mind can conceive can be expressed in speech by uttering combinations of sound called syllables. In English we convey the idea "belief" by uttering two syllables, "bee" and "leaf." Now if we were in the Egyptian situation and did not care to invent an ideogram for this idea, we could convey the idea with a picture of a bee and another of a leaf—that is, with two phonograms. Similarly, by inventing signs for all the syllables in speech, we could write down any idea whatever. This is substantially the kind of writing the Egyptians had achieved by the time of the First Dynasty—a mixture of old ideographs which had proved worth keeping and an array of phonograms for the syllables of their speech.

All this occurred, archaeologists now believe, about 3000 B.C.—and Childe's *New Light on the Most Ancient East* (1934) accepts this date as correct with a margin of error amounting to not over two hundred years either way.* So close a result, reckoned backward over nearly five thousand years, must be accounted a triumph for modern historical research.

One more fact—or rather, one unsettled question—will round out the story of these Egyptian beginnings. The question is the highly intriguing one of how much Egypt may have learned from Sumer and how much Sumer may have learned in return, in these days when each center was creating civilization out of life on a mud flat.

The evidence is not clear, and scarcely any general agreement exists among scholars on the question. Some, such as Breasted, hold the simple view that the Egyptians produced their own culture, although they picked up useful Asiatic ideas which came through the delta. Others see a penetration of ideas, brought into the south by traders coming overland from the Red Sea through the Wadi Hammamat opposite modern Qûs, the ancient Coptos. Still others, such as Petrie and De Morgan, are inclined to see an actual invasion of Sumerians or Elamites by this route—an invasion which brought culture elements borrowed from Sumer, subdued and then strengthened the south and finally swept on to supreme power over all Egypt.

The one substantial bit of evidence that bears upon the problem is a noted ivory knife handle found at Gebel-el-Arak, south of Girgeh, in a predynastic deposit. The carving on it shows a victory won by the crew of one boat over another crew, and the victors are clearly Semitic or Sumerian. The leading conqueror is bearded and wears a cap and robe; he would make a fair Gilgamesh, a Sumerian hero who combined the deeds of Ulysses or Odysseus with the adventures

*The task of assigning dates to Egyptian prehistory turns upon a peculiar correlation of Egyptian time reckoning with ours and then applying the result to Egyptian records. An associated problem is that of dating all Greco-Roman records, as well as the earlier Egyptian, in terms of division between B.C. and A.D. The current solutions for these problems are explained in Appendix B.

of Noah. The carvings include a dog which is Mesopotamian in breed and not a typical Egyptian greyhound. The boat is high in prow and stern, a typical Sumerian craft.

Unquestionably, then, the south was in contact at this time either with Sumerians or with people who got the knife from the Sumerians, and the conclusion is supported by a strong infusion of Sumerian culture elements in the life of the First Dynasty. This occurred particularly in architecture. Pretentious building started in Egypt under the First Dynasty, and it started with Sumerian forms and techniques, columns and crossbeams, corbeled vaults, brickwork and the distinctive brick wall of flat panels set between buttresses.

All these features are seen to magnificent advantage in what is thought to be the elaborate mastaba or underground tomb of King Aha of the First Dynasty. It was discovered in 1937, and the discoverers, Walter B. Emery and Zaki Effendi Saad, thought that Aha might well have been the legendary Menes himself. The tomb was built in Sakkara, the cemetery of the capital city Memphis, which Menes was supposed to have founded; and it seems much more suitable in its imposing grandeur for a conqueror such as Menes than does the tomb at Abydos formerly ascribed to him.

A much less definite and far more puzzling hint of possible invasion is the only known instance of human sacrifice in Egypt. The same rite appeared in certain Sumerian royal tombs at Ur at this time, as will be noted later, and one possible interpretation of this evidence is that both Sumer and Egypt were conquered by people who practiced this rite. But if so, the savage practice was soon forgotten as the conquerors absorbed the spirit of Egyptian religion and Egyptian life moved forward to its first flowering, the state in which we find it at the dawn of history.

And now, with history fairly started in Egypt, what of the rest of the world at this significant date of 3000 B.C., some five thousand years ago?

CHAPTER XIV

3000 B.C.—A Milestone Date in Man's Career

THE START of written history in Egypt would be enough to make the date 3000 B.C. a milestone in the human record, even if nothing else happened. But other developments and changes were all but inevitable. Other lands could hardly fail to be affected by the flowering of civilized living along the Nile and in Mesopotamia. Thinking, too, would be influenced throughout all areas that were in touch with these cultures. The record hardly can be kept accurate and complete unless these far-flung repercussions are taken into account.

The first and simplest feature of the world situation to be considered seems to be the range of peoples and lands which would be affected by the rise of civilization in Egypt and Sumeria. This can be done readily, even though sketchily, by considering the farthest outposts known to us in which evidence of being influenced has been discovered.

Of these outposts the most remote one known to us, and also the key to the most far-reaching contacts, was lonely Anau, located on a somewhat sandy plain southeast of the Caspian Sea, in the present-day Russian Turkestan. If any Sumerian had been bold enough to journey here, he would have judged the place as lonely as we consider the most outlying Hudson Bay trading post in the Arctic.

Behind him lie the rugged mountains of Iran; before him lie sparse grass and sand, stretching like a limitless sea to the horizon. Here in the center of the lonely scene stands the village of Anau itself, on a slight mound. It is a miserable collection of small mud-brick huts; the natives are primitive longheads, akin to the type which eventually was pushed into Australia, the East Indies and poorer hill regions of India. They have learned how to grow wheat and barley, but they are only just acquiring domesticated breeds of oxen, pigs and sheep. They use microlithic stone tools; they spin thread crudely by using spindle whorls or little weights to stretch out a hank of fiber while it is being twisted into thread.*

Beyond Anau, in the grasslands to the north, live the nomads. There no civilized person would dare to go. He would not know how to win a living, and his chances of death at the hands of some of these fierce riders would be all too good. As a matter of fact, civilized people probably did not come this far. Trade goods seem to have passed from tribe to tribe, through descending levels of culture; Anau offers no evidence that the Sumerians ever appeared there.

Trade must have flowed, however, because the archaeological record shows a constant flow of metal weapons, trinkets and other "trade goods" akin to the gaudy trumpery which modern whites have sold for centuries to so-called savages. This trade gave the grassland nomads their knowledge of pottery, metal and, most particularly, their distinctive weapon, the *battle-ax*.

Axes designed for wood chopping and other peaceful work had always been thick and possessed a broad, sturdy blade. Battle-axes were longer, thinner and not heavy enough to tire the user or reduce speed of handling in battle. They were killing implements, pure and simple, and the badge of killers; and every migration of the grassland nomads was marked, as though by a trail of modern "Historical Site" monuments, by funeral offerings and other deposits of these weapons.

So also can ideas for pottery making and metalworking be traced from here clear into faraway China. In return for all these goods the nomads probably offered precious stones, picked up during their wanderings over Central Asia, and amber, obtained by trade with

---

*In all, three great periods of settlement can be detected. The oldest left a deposit of relics some forty-five feet deep, bespeaking an immensely long period of occupation. Raymond Pumpelly and Huntington, after a thorough study of this site, thought that the oldest settlement might date from 9000 B.C.; other estimates would indicate a beginning as far back as the time when the Cro-Magnons were entering Europe. Peake and Fleure, two good proponents of an antiquity more modest than Pumpelly assigned, date the first settlement at or after 4000 B.C. This would mean roughly a thousand years before the rise of the First Dynasty in Egypt and about the same length of time before authentic historic events can be identified in Sumeria.

An undated drought crippled this culture, but gradually a second culture filtered in, bringing new arts from the young civilization in Mesopotamia. Among its distinctive features were stone sockets for doorposts, red and gray pottery and copper daggers. Intense drought drove these people out. Peake and Fleure date this evacuating at about 2500 B.C., or a little more than two hundred years after the Egyptians had built the Pyramids and a strong kingdom had been organized in Mesopotamia by the Semite, Sargon of Akkadia. The third period had bronze and correlates with southern cultures which can be brought into historic time.

tribes living along the Baltic Sea in the vicinity of modern Prussia. Anau, therefore, was one of the most important contact points, despite its primitive culture, in all the world of 3000 B.C.

Another outpost in what must have seemed a fabled "Far West" to Sumerians was Troy, destined to be the scene, nearly two thousand years later, of the Homeric *Iliad*.

Here on a site slightly southeast of the Dardanelles another town of huts was growing up. Probably at the time it was not much ahead of Anau, but its destiny was to be far different. Even now, about 3000 B.C., this destiny was taking shape.

Already neolithic peasants from Asia Minor were filtering across the Dardanelles and the Bosporus, seeking new land in Europe. They were rude and uncouth as yet—more akin to Iroquois Indians than to the North American whites of colonial days—and at the time they did not provide much basis for trade. But they were opening up the new country, and in time they would obtain wares which the eastern civilizations wanted—especially Baltic amber and tin for bronze making from Bohemia. Then Troy, thanks to its superb position at one of the greatest crossroads in the world, would become one of the greatest trading cities of early antiquity.

Another crossroads like Troy, but far more important at the time, was the town Gebal ("mountain" in Semitic). Its better-known Greco-Roman name is Byblos, from which our word "Bible" comes. Here was a famous meeting place of Egyptian and Sumerian since earliest antiquity, because even before the dawn of history each of these great cultures traded with Gebal to get cedar from the Lebanon mountains behind the town.

The prehistoric inhabitants of the region were largely descendants of the original Mediterranean strain which had helped give birth to neolithic arts in this region. Shot through their record is evidence of using caves as sacred places, and a curious manner of sacrificing pigs over a perforated floor, which let blood drain down onto burials or sacred images in a lower chamber. Here, as Olmstead suggests in his *History of Palestine and Syria* (1931), may be the root of the aversion shown by later Semites, such as Arabs and Jews, for pigs and pork. These Semites took Palestine from the older inhabitants, and undoubtedly they would learn to abhor the animal used in these sacrifices.

By far the most important of these earlier outposts, however, was the island of Crete, the seat of the later Minoan seafaring culture which did more than any other to spread civilization throughout the western Mediterranean world of early antiquity.

Since 1900, when Arthur James Evans unearthed the evidence for this long-forgotten culture, knowledge of it has become reasonably clear; and discoveries in Egypt give a broad hint about the start of this first seafaring state.

Archaeologists have found that from the time when the First Dynasty was founded the emblem of the Fish Clan, formerly common in the delta, disappeared from Egypt. But this same emblem appeared at about this same time in the oldest pictures we have of boats on the Aegean Sea, and these pictures coincided in time with the beginnings of the Cretan, or Minoan, civilization. Can it be that this clan, disgruntled or perhaps driven out, settled in Crete and other near by islands and thus helped in founding the oldest maritime civilization on the Mediterranean?

Evans believes strongly in such an origin, and he has impressive parallels in pottery and other artifacts to back his belief. But a powerful case can also be made out for an Asiatic origin. The Cretan boats resembled the seaworthy Sumerian craft more than the Egyptian. Again, a prominent symbol in Minoan religion was the double ax, with two blades facing outward from a common shaft. This was ancient in Sumer when the Minoan state was founded, and it has been traced in deposits across Mesopotamia and North Syria to coastal locations from which it could easily have reached Crete. Other artifacts support this suggestion; and finally, the skeletal remains of the early population show both the longheaded Egyptian type and the rounder-headed Asiatic.

Such a mixture of type suggests strongly that Minoan civilization was a fusion of Egyptian and Asiatic cultures from the start. This would be natural enough in a seafaring state, and the later record of the Minoans showed ample ability to take and adapt whatever they liked from other civilizations. It shows too another common result of fusion, in comparative freedom from the incrusted, conservative formalisms of the parent cultures.

The Minoan religion seems to have been free from formalism and a crushing burden of ritual and priesthoods. Nowhere did the Minoans build huge temples or monumental statues of gods. They seem to have worshiped Nature gods headed by the fertility goddess or Earth Mother which Asia had worshiped since paleolithic times, and evidently they expected these gods to be content with ceremonies at simple shrines, tucked away in mountains, in woods and in the king's palace.

Minoan art also shows a clean-cut break with the formalism which ruled in Egypt and in Mesopotamia. In each of these regions subjects always were posed and treated according to rigid conventions; the only freedom allowed the craftsman was in details of finish and, to some extent, in his choice of detail to be included or eliminated. But the Minoans steered away from formalism; their instinct ran to a rather free and joyous naturalism. They tried to get swing and movement into their figures, and in their later art they decorated freely with plants and animals treated in a fresh, lively style that reflected a keen eye for natural beauty.

Throughout most of their history they relied upon their ships and their trade for security and wealth and attempted no grandiose conquests. During the middle period of their history they built fine palaces for their kings at Knossos (or Cnossus) and elsewhere, but these palaces were pleasure structures with spacious halls and corridors. They were not seats of warlike strength. The towns were compact and well built, but no Cretan community was fortified. The sea and stout fighting ships were Crete's all-sufficient protection.

This comparatively free and joyous viewpoint was to become, in due time, the foundation of classic Greek culture. But long before this happened the Minoans were to serve as advance agents of civilization throughout the western Mediterranean, perhaps even as far as Spain—and this service to mankind started almost immediately after the Minoan state was founded because of outstanding advantages, throughout the Aegean Sea to the northward, for maritime trade.

Probably nowhere in the world could a region be found which was better suited for providing a living to seafarers. The Aegean is literally studded with mountainous islands, the tops of a submerged mountain chain that runs from the Adriatic through Greece into Asia Minor; a mariner would be hard put to it to be completely beyond sight of at least a purplish peak on the horizon. The weather is usually inviting, the sea sparkling and relatively calm. Scattered among the islands and on the near-by coasts were copper on the island of Cyprus, for which the metal is named, marble, emery, obsidian, gold and other materials which the Mesopotamians and the Egyptians would take in trade for manufactured goods. The materials also provided a basis for local manufacturing.

The cultures which sprang up outside of Crete to use the advantages are usually called the *Cycladic cultures,* from the Cyclades Islands just east of Greece. These cultures stretched to the Troad, the domain of Troy, and they threw off influences which gave the Greek mainland its *Early Helladic* or pre-Greek cultures. Thus a generous heritage was provided for what later was to prove incomparably the highest flowering of artistic and intellectual impulses in history.

All these outposts together—Anau, Troy, Byblos and Crete, with the Indus Valley added to cover contacts to the eastward—give a reasonably good limit to the portions of the world which would be stirred by cultural influences from the new civilizations, not only in material arts, but in mental advances. Foremost among these mental advances was the beginning of a change from primitive, magic-ridden concepts of the universe to concepts which embodied the concept of *natural law,* the rule of unvarying principle rather than the whims of spirits and gods.

Fortunately we need not look far for the root of these beginnings. The record leaves no room for doubt that the concept of natural, invariable law arose first of all in connection with the heavens. The oldest of all sciences was *astronomy.*

Even in paleolithic times man undoubtedly had noticed a certain unfailing regularity in the heavens. But once man learned to notice this he would see also that the stars seemed to move as though they were fixed inside a huge hollow globe which rotated around the earth once a day. This globe also would have a slant, according to the observer's latitude, as shown on the following page.

Moreover, in this instance the gods or spirits of Nature never were capricious. However much they changed their minds about giving fair days or foul, good years or bad ones, they never changed their minds about having the stars rise in the east, follow a slanting course overhead and set in the west. The "law of motion" which governed the stars was invariable; it never changed.

The fact that men realized this by the time history dawned stands proved by a plain bit of evidence. At the time men oriented temples and other buildings accurately with the points of the compass, both in Mesopotamia and Egypt. They could not have done this unless they had identified the polestar, and this meant in turn that they understood the unvarying character of heavenly motions.

A second germ of scientific thinking, which stood born with the beginnings of astronomy at the dawn of history, was the rudiments

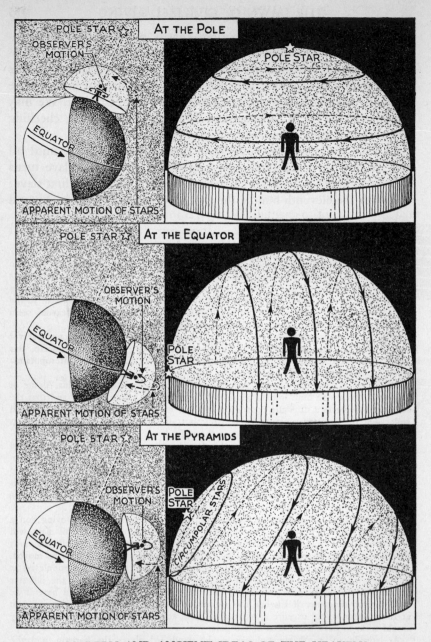

AT THE POLE

POLE STAR

OBSERVER'S MOTION

EQUATOR

APPARENT MOTION OF STARS

POLE STAR

POLE STAR AT THE EQUATOR

OBSERVER'S MOTION

EQUATOR

POLE STAR

APPARENT MOTION OF STARS

POLE STAR AT THE PYRAMIDS

OBSERVER'S MOTION

EQUATOR

POLE STAR

CIRCUMPOLAR STARS

APPARENT MOTION OF STARS

MODERN AND ANCIENT IDEAS OF THE HEAVENS

The accompanying diagrams illustrate one of man's loftiest feats of thinking—his idea of law and order in the heavens. The diagrams at the left show the modern version

Continued at bottom of the next page

of accurate counting and measuring—that is, *mathematics*. These beginnings ran almost alike in both Sumer and Egypt.

In each land, as commerce grew, a need arose for accurate counts of goods and obligations; and in each land counting seems to have arisen by making tallies or marks to record a finger count. We may summarize the result by imagining three slaves and a clerk checking in bundles of some commodity at a warehouse.

As each bundle passes, one slave turns down a finger, until all ten are down. As the tenth one goes down the second slave turns down one finger, to indicate the count of all fingers by the first slave; and with the eleventh bundle the first slave starts over again. Should

Continued from preceding page

of this concept, while those at the right show the ancient version. The relation between the two versions is shown in each pair of diagrams by the half dome which represents the observer's range of vision. Under the modern version the half dome and the observer move with the earth as it rotates upon its axis, and the stars remain fixed. In the ancient version the observer and the half dome remain fixed, while the heavens seem to move in a direction contrary to the real motion.

The actual and apparent motions can best be made plain by considering an observer stationed (1) at the North Pole; (2) on the equator; (3) at latitude 30° north, this being approximately the latitude in which the stargazers of Egypt and of Mesopotamia worked out their first ideas of astronomy.

At the North Pole the observer simply turns around once a day, and his "dome of visibility" turns with him. But his senses tell him that he is standing still and that the stars are moving in a direction contrary to his real motion. One star, directly overhead and called the polestar, seems to stand still; but all the others seem to move across the sky in horizontal circles, as shown at the right.

For an observer on the equator the field of vision sweeps around the night sky, and the zenith or overhead position moves with the field. Again this creates an illusion that the stars are moving. The stars will appear to rise in the east, climb straight up to the top of their courses and then go straight down until they set in the west. This is a striking contrast with the motion at the pole. It is vertical in place of being horizontal.

Obviously, then, an observer at latitude 30° north will see the stars moving "on a slant" somewhere between vertical and horizontal. To determine what this slant will be, consider what would happen if the observer on the equator in the middle diagrams moved toward the North Pole, taking his "dome of visibility" with him as he moved. While he was on the equator the polestar—that is, the one seemingly motionless star in the heavens—was on the northern horizon. As he moved northward the polestar would seem to climb up in the sky, toward the vertical position it would have if he should reach the pole. Meanwhile the seemingly vertical courses of the stars as seen at the equator would acquire a southward slant, toward the horizontal courses they would seem to have when seen at the pole.

At latitude 30° north the polestar would stand 30° above the horizon, and the courses of the stars near it (the so-called circumpolar stars) would be lifted above the horizon. They would never rise or set; they would simply fade from view whenever daylight blocked them out, and during the night they would wheel around the polestar. The other stars would follow the slanting courses shown.

the second slave use all his fingers, the third one would turn down one finger; and so the process would go until all the bundles were checked in. Suppose now that the count ended with this situation— shown from right to left, because that is the way we are accustomed to count:

THIRD SLAVE   SECOND SLAVE   FIRST SLAVE

This is our familiar number 111. The first hand at the right shows one bundle; the middle one shows ten ones, or ten; and the third or left one shows ten tens, or one hundred. The whole example is one of decimal notation, or counting by tens; and the choice of ten is considered by all scholars to be sufficient proof that finger counting lay at the root of all more sophisticated systems.

Of course so crude a method would not be used by any folk who were sophisticated enough to check goods into a warehouse. The clerk would simply keep tally marks on a sheet, probably in groups of five. For purposes of illustration we can translate the finger count given above into groups of tally marks. To show the progression from slave to slave we set down 111 marks in groups, but all the units which figured in the tens count, and all the tens which figured in a hundreds count are separated from the final count. The result follows:

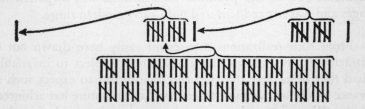

After this start the invention of digits, or separate signs to show each possible combination of fingers from one to nine, would complete the system; and the archaeological evidence shows that this stage was reached in Egypt by the First Dynasty and in Mesopotamia soon after al'Ubaid times. Mathematicians consider the decimal system of counting by tens lamentably defective and mourn the fact which gave rise to it—that is, that man has five fingers on each hand and based his finger counting upon groups of five. Six would have been far better. Then we would have "changed over" from units to the next higher count at twelve instead of ten.

This would have simplified decimal fractions enormously. At present we can write one half as .5, one quarter as .25 and so on with subdivision of halves; but we cannot write one third exactly or any of its subdivisions. Under a *duodecimal,* or "twelve" count, we could write one half as .6, one third as .4, one quarter as .3 and so on with subdivisions of halves and thirds.

The Sumerians realized this, and even before the dawn of history they adopted a compromise between the two systems. They counted decimally, or by tens, for small numbers; but instead of "changing over" from tens to the next higher unit at ten tens or one hundred, as we do, they changed at sixty. Sixty could be divided accurately into halves, thirds, fifths and subdivisions of these fractions. This handy "sixty" or sexagesimal count survives in our hours, minutes and seconds of the day and in the degrees, minutes and seconds used to measure angles and portions of the perimeter of a circle.

The beginning in counting naturally was accompanied by the beginnings of measuring—that is, of *geometry.*

Geometry was needed particularly in Egypt where the Nile floods obliterated many a landmark and boundary every year. Thereafter the fields needed resurveying, and the need for good methods naturally forced development of geometry. Engineering and construction also fostered this science. A surprising bit of knowledge, revealed in a recently discovered papyrus, was ability to calculate the cubic contents of a square pyramid. This formula was forgotten in later ages and was not rediscovered until early modern times.

From such realizations men could easily have drawn out or abstracted the realization that all Nature is subject to invariable law, had they been clear thinking and logical. But to expect such an advance would be to expect more than human nature has achieved even today. We still have far too much crystal gazing, tea-leaf reading and consulting of horoscopes to expect that the Egyptians and the Sumerians could have achieved a housecleaning of such mental rubbish because they had caught a few glimpses of natural law. The persistence of old superstitions stands proved by the naïve ideas entertained in Egypt and in Mesopotamia about how the earth was supported beneath the heavenly globe. The Egyptians imagined the earth as a flat disk that rested upon the backs of four elephants. The elephants stood on the back of a tortoise, and the tortoise swam in a sea; but ingenuity or patience gave out before the Egyptians provided a support for this sea. The Sumerians omitted the animals and simply imagined a flat earth swimming upon an unsupported sea.

Magic also figured in the subsequent development of astronomy.

The Egyptians seemed to have been contented with simple ideas which enabled them to tell directions from the stars and the sun and to keep track of the year. The Sumerians, however, got the idea that the stars, and particularly the planets, exercised direct control over the destinies of men. This constituted *astrology,* and the belief was typical of early nonscientific thinking that took ideas on hope or through faith, without demanding *test* or proof. The mistake was valuable, nevertheless, because it produced intensive, accurate study of the heavens and an astonishing development of sound knowledge mixed in with erroneous beliefs.

A similar mixture of sound and silly ideas was to be found in another science where clear thinking should have appeared as soon as anywhere. This science was the healing art, or *medicine.*

In medicine, if anywhere, we might expect men to think effectively, since health and even life itself always were at stake. But man did nothing of the sort. While we have no direct evidence to show where the medical art stood in attainment at the dawn of history, we can judge what it must have been in Egypt from its status there in later times, as revealed by the Edwin Smith papyrus.

This was a copy made in the seventeenth century B.C. of an older manuscript, and when fully published by Breasted in 1930 it revealed an astonishingly fine grasp of surgery. Procedures were practical within the limits of the day; and he was a good observer of important facts. He made the oldest mention we have of the brain, and he noticed that the brain controlled the movement of the legs. He knew that the heart drove something through the vessels which were connected to it.

If such a critical, observing spirit could have worked intensively, the steps from these observations to a rough understanding of the nervous and circulatory systems would not have taken long. A sound understanding of physiology could have been won at that early date. But just turning over the manuscript reveals why medicine did not make progress. The back offers charms, including one for giving an old man the youthfulness of twenty!

Babylonian medicine was in a worse state. The Egyptians at least could practice surgery; but a Babylonian who did so, or who tried out a new drug, did so at his peril. The punishment was dire if any treatment other than the orthodox magic was tried and failed to work a cure. Faith in magic, therefore, ruled man's thinking about medicine—and thereby progress automatically was paralyzed.

Examples could be multiplied, but to no good purpose. The record is plain enough that men had made a beginning, but a beginning only, toward sound, scientific ways of thinking. Much more pressure from circumstances and many more bitter experiences would be needed before this advance could make real gains against the dead-weight resistance of accustomed ideas.

From this it follows that the principal burden of any history of thought from this time on for many a long age will consist of the circumstances and experiences which work to break down these encrusted preconceptions, prejudices and mistaken attitudes. Happily, the very date 3000 B.C. is a milestone in this matter as well as in those which we have been considering. At this time the world saw the first stirrings of a dire but potent force which did more than any other single factor to drive men into better ways from this time on. We can well afford then to close our account of beginnings and usher in the new chapter of history, with consideration of this driving force. It may be identified with two words—"the nomads."

Almost all around the mud-flat homes of the first civilizations prowled these wandering herdsmen, ever ready to pounce in whenever stagnation and degeneration had weakened the fiber of a civilized folk and take over land, cities, people and all. Whenever this happened their fierce spirit and the smashing of old, comfortable ways with sword and fire gave a new impetus to thought and progress—and so these nomad invasions, despite their outward appearance as calamities, formed the real driving force behind progress. Some acquaintance with these nomads, therefore, is in order before they take up their historic roles; and those who deserve first introductory consideration are the immediate neighbors of the Sumerians, the Semitic folk of the Arabian Desert.

These Arabic nomads were Mediterraneans, and the various groups spoke a complex of Semitic languages; among the important tongues were Babylonian, Assyrian, Aramaic, Phoenician, Hebrew and Arabic. As the postglacial change of climate made Arabia a desert those who did not escape into surrounding lands were forced into nomadic life. To support their animals they used the thin blush of grass which appeared every spring between the central desert and the *Fertile Crescent* of better-watered land which looped around Arabia from Egypt through Palestine and Syria to Mesopotamia.

Since the desert land blended smoothly into this fertile crescent, without any natural barriers such as mountains to bar movement, the civilized peoples always had to be on guard against the Semites. A saving grace existed, however, in the fact that the Semitic population was small. Any civilized people could keep the raiders out as long as it retained its vigor and effective national organization of government and armed force. But equally, when a civilization became decadent the Semites were right at hand to take it over.

This fact will be dominant in Mesopotamian and Near Eastern history for more than a thousand years after 3000 B.C. But in addition to the ever-present Semite menace these lands lay under the threat of an immensely greater and darker storm cloud in the north. There was the land of the Indo-European nomads—folk who outnumbered the Semites ten to one and who had greater energy and drive, in keeping with the more invigorating climate in their latitudes. Even the Semites had to bow to these folk whenever the two met in determined clash, and so these northern nomads deserve the most extended introductory attention of all.

CHAPTER XV

The Nomad Energizers of Early Ancient Life

THANKS to one of Nature's coincidences, our present purpose of becoming acquainted with those whips of destiny, the nomadic white herdsmen of Asia, will take us once more to the very scene where man himself probably was born—the grasslands of Central or southwestern Asia. Half a million years, perhaps a million years or even more, have passed since that birth, but the scene itself remains unchanged. The same seas of grass stretch to the horizon; we notice the same streams bordered with occasional trees and feel the same sense of vast, empty loneliness. But now the human element is far different.

A million years or so ago Og and his fellows dodged about in constant fear for their lives while they picked up a miserable living from raw Nature. The present inhabitants are immensely better off. They have herds of cattle and of sheep—and horses too, which they ride like so many centaurs. Meat and milk, then, are assured, and hair, hides and wool for making clothes and shelter. They need only pick up flint and other materials needed for tools and weapons, to complete the essentials of a living. They have tents, and for fuel they can use dried animal droppings, eked out with wood now and then. The life is rude, dirty—for water is too precious to use for washing—and toilsome, but it is reasonably secure and immeasurably ahead of hunting life.

How these men achieved this mode of life can only be guessed at, in our present state of knowledge, but one portion of any guess can rest upon well-known fact. The nomadic life was possible on these Asiatic grasslands because here man found ancestors of both modern cattle and modern horses—reasonably docile species, each of them,

161

which did not object overmuch to an overlordship exercised by man. Soon men learned that such animals could be made to supply more than meat and hides. They would see calves and colts living on milk; and thanks to the comparative docility of cows and mares, men could manage to make themselves messmates of these youngsters. Thereby, all unwittingly, they would have decanted themselves upon their subsequent careers as nomads. Now milk, as well as meat, was a food; and to get milk they would have to care for their herds.

Many developments would flow naturally from this start—riding on horseback, matting wool into felt for garments and tents and developing harness for controlling the animals. Of greater interest now, however, are the twin questions of who those nomads were and what temperament and outlook they would bring to bear whenever they injected themselves into civilized affairs.

A thorough examination of racial origins would require dealing with the thorny problem of single or multiple origins of the human race, because some of these nomads were Caucasian or "white," while others were Mongoloid, as explained in Appendix A. Happily, however, this question was not important in the history of western civilization in 3000 B.C. The Mongoloids were off to the eastward, in contact with Chinese civilization; the nomadic neighbors of the western cultures were all white.

The whites were Mediterranean in physical type; they might well have descended from the primordial high-mental type of man in about this one locality. Also, even though they were split into many tribes, they were all but a unit in language. Each and every tribe of these white nomads spoke some variant of an Indo-European language, and this one fact gives a handy key to the tremendous later importance of these people.

Included in Indo-European is nearly every important language, aside from Semitic tongues, which is spoken by the white race today. In the Germanic or Teutonic division come German, Dutch, the Scandinavian tongues and English. The Romance group contains French, Spanish, Italian and Portuguese. Greek is included and also the Slavic language, including Russian. Most of the languages spoken by the peoples of India, together with Persian or Iranian, form still another branch. Even Gaelic and Welsh are included. Thus the sheer geographic extent of Indo-European languages indicates how, age after age, these nomads spread over Europe, into Iran and into India, subduing the earlier inhabitants and imposing Indo-European speech upon them.

And now for temperament, viewpoint and mental endowment!

Both the circumstances of nomad life and evidence from the later record prove that nomadic thinking diverged from the thinking done by earlier hunters and later peasants exactly where nomadic life diverged.

Hunters organized bands to capture a large animal or to fight off a common foe, but once the immediate object was attained, the organization fell apart until a new danger threatened or hunger prompted another hunt. Nomads could never let such disorganization occur.

They had to watch, night and day, to keep their animals together and to fight off wolves, hunters and perhaps herdsmen from other groups. The group had to move as a unit with its herds, in search of fresh pasture and more abundant water, whenever local resources had been exhausted; and always internal questions of rights and ownership needed settling. These necessities forced a feeling for *government,* or control of the individual by the judgment and the leaders of the group—and this government could not be the rigid, static control by tradition, custom and magic which ruled the minds of hunters. It had to be fresh minded and flexible enough to direct the power of the group wherever needed to meet emergencies.

This government also had to be democratic, under elected chiefs. No other kind could last; the fierce, proud spirit of the nomad never would tolerate rule by anyone who claimed authority by birth or wealth, or for any reason other than being the best man in the group for the job. Therefore each and every nomad, even if he was not a chief, had a voice and an interest in the government. He could vote for a new chief, and if an old one became unworthy, he could join in deposing or even killing such a leader.

This difference between nomads and hunters was matched by another between nomads and peasants in attitude toward other men and even entire peoples.

The peasant looked for his living to the soil and to the labor he gave to producing crops and domesticated animals. Fellow men—if raiders from other regions be excluded—were considered fellow toilers. If they let the peasant alone to pursue his plodding ways, he was willing enough to let them alone.

The nomad, in contrast, had exploitation grained into the very roots of his thinking by his practice of herding animals for a living, with aid from a skilled, courageous group of fellow nomads. Could the nomads help, then, substituting some group of strange men for animals in this pattern—and passing on from this to the idea that exploiting weaker men would yield an even better living than could be obtained from herding animals? The development is so natural, so obvious, as to be all but inevitable.

Of course this idea can hardly be counted as unique with nomads, although Menghin and others urge that the Sumerians and Egyptians did not begin to prey upon their neighbors until after they had received an infusion of nomad blood and ideas. But this question can be left until later; a point of more immediate importance about these nomads was their peculiar effectiveness in making their program good by skilled, organized fighting on horseback or in horse-drawn chariots. The *mounted warrior* marched with nomadism and democratic government throughout history. The Sumerians, the Egyptians and other Mediterranean folk knew nothing of such fighting until they learned it through bitter experience with invaders from the grasslands.

These aspects of temperament are enough to set the nomads apart from other types and to suggest their destined role in history. The next question about them is how and why they came to take up this role—and the answer grows, first of all, out of the geographic setting of their grassland domain.

Our previous examination of Eurasian climate after the Ice Age shows that it was dominated, in all latitudes north of India, Mesopotamia and the Mediterranean shores, by westerly winds laden with moisture from the Atlantic Ocean and the North and Baltic seas. As pointed out in Chapter IX, these winds covered western Europe with forest, thus choking progress in the region; and this forest extended eastward into Poland, northern Russia and to the Dnieper River in southwestern Russia, except for barer spots caused by rugged mountain, sand or loessal soil.

East of these limits the rain thinned out and could no longer support trees, with their heavy demands for moisture. It could, however, support grass. Hence vast seas of grassland rolled across Russia, into Central Asia and almost to China—and here the nomads had their domain. But these very circumstances, combined with mountain ranges, conspired to *keep the nomads confined* to this domain.

Herding of the nomad type is impracticable in forests, and because of this the nomads had little temptation, as long as these natural conditions endured, to cross the Dnieper and push westward into Europe. To the south the lofty snow-clad Himalayas and Pamirs were utterly impassable, and the high rocky plateau of Iran would not be inviting until after farmers had come into being and made it so. West of Iran came the tree-and-snow-covered ranges of the Caucasus and then the Black Sea. Passage around the east end of the sea was blocked by the rocky heights of Asia Minor and around the west end by forest.

This blocking in was fortunate for all concerned. The peasant folk to the southward were left undisturbed while they achieved the beginnings of civilization. The nomads profited by receiving products and ideas born from these beginnings and particularly from the ideas born in Sumer. From Sumer they learned use of metal, and this knowledge became the foundation of a distinct nomad culture which exploited rich deposits of copper in the headwaters of the Kuban River, in the Caucasus range east of the Black Sea. When the Sumerians invented wheels the nomads turned this invention to good account by using carts and wagons in their movements. For wheels they used disks cut from logs; and the wagons, probably supplemented with tents, served as homes.

Harmonious relations prevailed, then, between Indo-European nomads, the peasants of Asia Minor and the Danube, and the civilized folk in Mesopotamia at the dawn of history, about 3000 B.C. But after this time something happened to disrupt this harmony and start the nomads upon their disrupting, conquering and exploiting career over all Europe and southward even to Egypt in the end. What happened can be stated in two words—climate change—or even in one word, drought.

As explained in some detail in Appendix B, sometime after 3000 B.C. a world-wide change toward a drier climate set in. This change thinned out forests and dried up bogs in northwestern Europe, while it afflicted the grasslands with a dryness which amounted to devastating drought. Consequently the Indo-Europeans of the western grasslands and the Mongoloids toward the eastward began battering at the doors of their neighbors in search of escape, on all but a world-wide scale.

Chinese annals record the pressure from 2356 to 2208 B.C., if we may accept Chinese dating, and it fell much earlier with heavy force upon southeastern Asia. The historic consequences of this latter movement will appear throughout the later record of these lands, but soon after 3000 B.C. Europe began to feel the results. This European record, therefore, belongs in the world setting of conditions at and immediately after the dawn of history, and it may be sketched in appropriately at this point in the human story.

The main events are known well enough, because the movements of the nomads can be traced by characteristic funeral gifts left when they buried their dead, liberally painted with red ocher, beneath great mounds or tumuli. These mounds are called *kargans* in Russia; hence these invading nomads are commonly called the kargan or red ocher people, even though the Cro-Magnons and others also had used this pigment for burial as far back as paleolithic times. Another common term for them is the Corded people, from their later practice of ornamenting pottery with designs pressed into the wet clay with knotted cords. And always they left behind them a trail of battle-axes—made of metal as long as the nomads remained in touch with their source of supply, the basin of the Kuban River, and then of stone when metal became unobtainable.

In point of geographic location, the starting position for the invasion of Europe was the age-old line between forest and grassland, the Dnieper River.

Since the headwaters of this river in Poland received ample rain and snow from the west, its water supply was reliable; and even though its lower course debouched upon the grasslands, its valley was cut deep and wide into the adjoining flatlands by spring and autumn freshets, and the river water gave life to good grass even during the scorching Ukrainian summer. Hence the nomads could follow it with their animals to its headwaters in present-day Poland.

In the earlier days of good rain, forests made the land uninviting from here on. But now these forests thinned out, and the hard-pressed nomads could cross over the flat Polish watershed without much trouble to rivers which drained into the Baltic.

From there the sandy shores of the Baltic offered a fine corridor into Europe, and the relics tell us that many a migration of white nomads used this route. Many scholars believe that the original Nordics or Scandinavians came this way; so did many of the Celts and the later Nordics, called Teutons; and some groups even backtracked along this route in historic times. A wave of Celts did so and settled in Asia Minor in Greek times, and in early Christian times the Goths followed the Dnieper from their Baltic home to Crimean Russia. From thence they crossed the Danube and overthrew Rome.

Another route for invading Europe led across the passes of the Transylvanian Alps and the Carpathians, once increasing dryness had thinned the forests in these regions—and here, probably, is where the nomads first met the second racial and cultural element which went into founding the peoples of modern Europe.

As told in Childe's *Dawn of European Civilization* (1925), during all this time of nomad restlessness neolithic farmers were filtering through the Balkans and moving northward through the Hungarian plain and up the slopes of the Carpathians, leaving the peasant culture which archaeologists called *Danubian*. They could do this, although forests were choking culture farther west, because widespread deposits of loessal soil had been left by chill Ice Age blasts from the Carpathians and from the Alps. This soil is unfavorable for dense growth of trees, and so the farmers found open country.

This Danubian culture seems to have spread neolithic arts even as far as Denmark and France, ahead of the nomads. Hence the nomads always found a peasantry—thin and poor in spots, but nevertheless present—ready to hand for conquest and exploitation. Hence the cultural story of these times was much the same throughout Europe. First came the Danubian way of jogging along peacefully and establishing new farms and pit homes whenever the soil became exhausted in previously occupied areas. Then came the nomads and an end to this plodding, peaceful routine. With their arrival war and exploitation became an industry in Europe, just as these activities have remained a principal occupation there ever since. The nomads, organized by tribes in various regions, conquered the Danubians, warred with each other, and whenever they could they erupted into the more advanced peoples which bordered the Mediterranean.

But they were changed as well by this experience, for just as they altered life in Europe so did Europe compel them to alter their lives. This forcing was done largely by two factors—the forest, and the many mountain ranges and hills which cut the continent into small valleys and medium-sized basins.

With such physical conditions confronting them the nomads found their old, free roaming with herds impossible. They had to settle down and adopt the arts of the farmers. The little forest clearings and the thin scattering of peasants could not produce enough to let them live by exploiting the conquered folk. Thus Europe saw an enforced blending of agricultural and nomadic cultures and an amalgamation of the peoples, rather than a system of exploiters and exploited such as grew up in Sumeria when the Sumerians became masters of the al'Ubaid folk. The net contribution of the nomads to Europe, after all this had happened, was their fierce spirit and their gift for organizing governments of more or less democratic type.

This European record was, however, a mere backwash, a side show, compared to developments which were occurring back in the original homes of civilization!

There the larger trends of history already were taking shape in response to certain fundamentals of human nature which have proved almost all-powerful from then until now. First among these controlling forces was the basic urge, already noticed in Chapter XII, to achieve self-aggrandizement. Before the advent of fully civilized living, this urge had found little opportunity for gratification. Men were too busy on the whole, maintaining mere existence, or were too habit-ridden to think above the level of peasant mentality. Now, however, the highly developed cultures of Egypt and Mesopotamia had provided surpluses of food, labor and time which could be used for whatever seemed best. Hence the ambition to achieve enlargement of personality and power was unleashed, and it has remained so, driving individuals, communities and nations, the entire march of thought and history, in fact, ever since.

The open question at the time, of course, was what direction this urge would take. Another fundamental force in human nature provides the answer—an answer which later events verify to the hilt.

The record to date has shown mankind still almost completely habit-ridden and obsessed with faith in magic. This means in turn that individual aspirations will scarcely be astir as yet; men will think in terms of group interests and group magic and will seek their aggrandizement *through their groups,* rather than as free individuals. Hence history will be a story of group interests until something happens to break up this age-old way of thinking and release intelligence to do its work—and this "something" will have to be drastic indeed, to overcome the mental habits inherited from hundreds of thousands of years.

So says our viewpoint upon human nature, at least—and the test of whether we are right will be the record itself. Let us turn now to this record and see whether it bears us out!

PART IV

ANCIENT HISTORY—

The Warrior-Religious States

CHAPTER XVI

Slaves, Kings and Priests in Sumer

Most NATURAL DIVISIONS of history have a keynote, a dominating motive which can be stated in a happy turn or phrase—and this was done many years ago for the period which lasted some two thousand five hundred years after the dawn of history, by the American sociologist Franklin H. Giddings. He called this period the time of the "warrior and religious states," and he set forth his interpretation of the period in these terms:

So it came to pass that governments presently adopted certain policies that were characteristic of all early civilizations. The first step was an effort to bring under one central administration all adjoining regions which, together with the dominant city-state, formed a natural geographic unity. . . . Thus was created the national state. . . . Through this policy a strong military power was developed. Mere military government, however, was not enough. . . . Religion was still the dominant interest of the majority of men; and so religious unification also was attempted. . . . The medley of ancient faiths was blended in a national, organic religion, which was made to uphold the authority of the central power. . . . Such was the first stage of civilization.

No better clue could be asked to the entire spirit of the age, and beyond that, to the march of events for fully two thousand five hundred years!

At the basis of this spirit lay the age-old feeling, found in all primitive folk, of living not for and by themselves but as members of a group and by virtue of gifts won from the gods and the spirits of Nature by the group's magic. When the Sumerians, the Egyptians and others achieved the beginnings of civilized living they lost none of

171

this feeling. They carried it over into civilized ways of community life and they remained as convinced as ever that they prospered by the grace of the community's gods. Hence the heart and mainspring of every city and nation was the temple. The palace of the king or the governor and the countinghouses of the merchants might be important, but their owners had to propitiate the gods quite as much as did the meanest peasant or commoner. If ever anyone from the king down did anything which kindled the wrath of the gods, the consequences might be ruin for everybody.

So also did this domination of the group interest and the interest of the gods run through every private life. Details of clothing had social and magical significance; men dressed as the gods and the state prescribed, not as they saw fit. Individuals found their callings prescribed for them, without any chance to say aye or nay. A man born to the soil remained there all his life, except as he might be called to service as a soldier or as a laborer on a temple, a city wall, or a palace. Those who served in more intellectual callings had their work prescribed for them by the state religion and the inherited magic; never for a moment were they free to strike out on their own.

A particularly illuminating example of this attitude was the universal dependence for labor upon *slavery*.

Until recently the universality and persistence of this institution usually was explained as a product of necessity. Laborers could not be hired for money during early ancient times because money as we know it had not been invented and would not be for several thousand years. Only the sword, the whip and the spear remained, then, for bringing labor to the larger undertakings. Whatever labor force was needed was captured in wars or by slave raids upon primitive peoples. The ancients were supposed to have shut their minds to the brutality and inhumanity of the process because it was necessary and profitable.

Undoubtedly necessity and profit did suggest blindness to evils, just as they did in the American South before 1865; but today we can see clearly that the ancients also held slavery to be perfectly natural and proper.

In a day when every people considered that it lived by virtue of aids from its gods, issues of right and wrong as between different peoples were not matters for the peoples themselves to decide. Such issues were decided by the gods of the different peoples and by the same test which men commonly used, the test of superior strength. If the Egyptians fought with a Negro tribe in the Sudan, so did the

Egyptian gods fight with the Negro gods. When the Egyptians prevailed, as they usually did, this meant that their gods were the stronger. These gods, therefore, were plainly entitled to the services of the Negroes—and so the captured Negroes were enslaved.

The proof that this was indeed the logic of ancient times is the fact that it was accepted by the slaves quite as thoroughly as it was by the conquerors. They saw their condition as something which man had to accept just as he had to accept floods, droughts and other manifestations of divine wrath. They never even dreamed that a better social order might be possible.

In all these ways, then, Giddings' warrior-religious states took shape as veritable human anthills, with every ant taking up his appointed place. How well such states worked out would depend, of course, upon how serviceable the anthill philosophy proved to be in the long run; and it is high time now to see what the record shows. For our first example we need look no farther than that earliest of civilizations, the culture of the Sumerians.

This record tells us at once that throughout the formative period, when strength was needed to draw a strong civilized culture out of barbarism, the anthill philosophy on the whole worked well. Certainly it unleashed the technical talents of this people and gave the world many of man's most important inventions. One such invention already has appeared in socketed tools and weapons; among others now to come were probably the wheel, bronze working and large-scale architecture.

The story of the wheel is not known even in outline as yet, but first among the facts which point toward the Sumerians as inventors is their possession of two essentials for this feat—proved mechanical ingenuity, and a broad hint of the essential idea.

The Sumerians brought large quantities of timber for their buildings, and the buyers inevitably would see logs used as rollers in timber-cutting country. To mechanical geniuses like these folk the transformation of this hint into an actual wheel would be easy. Instead of using a whole log cut two cross sections, place an axle between and roll the load on the axle! Thus you get the desired result, yet your equipment is much lighter than an actual log.

Such an origin is highly probable, because the oldest vehicles we know have exactly this construction of wheels and axle joined rigidly and rolling together in their mountings beneath the vehicle. The wheels were either cut from logs or were made by nailing timber into a thick flat mass and cutting a disk from the mass. Either type of disk was equipped with a leather tire to help prevent splitting.

In their book *Peasants and Potters* Peake and Fleure suggest the possibility of another origin through the *potter's wheel*.

The potter's wheel is a device used to make pots truly round. The wheel is really a disk mounted on an upright axle and capable of spinning horizontally. To shape a pot the potter places his clay on the disk, sets the disk spinning with a foot drive such as we use on sewing machines and then draws his hand or a shaping tool upward against the spinning mass of clay. The upward motion shapes the clay from bottom to the top, and the spin carries the shape all around.

Now long before such wheels were known al'Ubaid potters had advanced from crude hand shaping to shaping on the *tournette* or "slow wheel," a pivoted plaque which the potter turned by hand as he shaped the clay. The resulting pot was nearly round, as seen from above, but not quite so; only a fast, powerful spin against a shaping tool could achieve true roundness. The idea of a fast wheel could grow naturally, however, from the tournette, and, once achieved, it could have been the germ idea for rolling motions in general.

Such ideas are mere speculation, obviously, but one fact about cart wheels and potter's wheels stands well removed from the charge of being merely speculative. The spread of these devices throughout the ancient world proved that they went hand in hand from wherever they had been invented. Since first the slow wheel or tournette, then the fast potter's wheel seemed to have been invented in Sumeria, a good probability exists that the cart wheel was invented there as well. This probability is strengthened, moreover, by the fact that oldest evidence we have of wheeled vehicles comes from this region, in finds of actual vehicles and, perhaps oldest of all, a rudely drawn chariot on a potsherd found at Tell Halaf.

Similarly the proved cleverness of Sumerians as metalworkers makes them logical candidates for the honor of inventing bronze. They had experience with the necessary materials—copper and tin—and they had the best incentive imaginable in a certain trouble they were bound to encounter in making socketed tools and weapons.

The easy way to make these tools was by casting them in a mold with a core of baked clay or other material to keep metal out of the socket space, but terrific heat—1981.4° F. or 1083 C.°—was needed to melt copper, the first metal used. Often the smiths did not get it liquid enough to fill the mold satisfactorily, and probably they made sockets by the laborious process of punching or drilling out the hole.

Some of these clever smiths, however, may well have noticed that some impure coppers melted at lower temperatures and gave better results in molding; and the evidence suggests strongly that at some-time during this prehistoric period they ran down the secret of this happy result. The impurity in the copper was tin. Therefore mix 10% of tin with 90% of copper, and you have *bronze,* an alloy that melts at a temperature 200°F. lower! By using this trick they could make the metal fluid enough to fill molds perfectly, and the alloy had another important advantage. Quenching it while still hot made the metal tough and malleable; then hammering it gave a cutting edge that held its sharpness far better than any copper.

It must be said here that archaeologists are not agreed about crediting this invention to Sumeria, but tracing back the routes followed by bronze working as the new art diffused throughout the ancient world points to Sumeria as a logical center. The argument from technical skill and need is reinforced by Sumerian leadership in a particularly fine type of work—the "lost wax" (*à cire perdue*) process of casting objects with fine surface decorations.*

In architecture and construction the Sumerians almost beyond question were the teachers of the early ancient world. The only possible rivals for this distinction were the Egyptians, and the evidence proves that they got their techniques from Sumeria. When they started large-scale building in First Dynasty times they used brick, not stone as they did later. They broke the façades of buildings into straight panels set between stout buttresses. The technique obviously gave strength, but the significant aspect to archaeologists was stylistic. The Sumerians are supposed to have developed it from the original al'Ubaid hut made of mats hung between poles, and some archaeologists claim that decorations on the walls of the early Egyptian buildings still echo these original mats! Not much question can exist, then, about who was pupil and who was teacher.

These achievements show beyond question that the anthill idea had value in many fields. But what now of weaknesses, of failure to support an enduring expansion of effort and progress?

The Sumerian record is just as clear on this question as it is about

*To start this ingenious process the worker prepares a core and covers it with wax; then he or an artist carves the decorations on the wax exactly as they are to appear in the finished metal. Next he applies a fine liquid paste of clay and plaster outside the wax, dries it and strengthens it into a mold. Finally he melts out the wax, runs in molten metal—and from the plaster of the mold the metal takes an exact reproduction of the carving on the wax.

strength. It shows beyond possibility of doubt that the anthill philosophy contained one weakness which led in the end to stagnation and collapse in every anthill state throughout history.

The trouble arose from shaping cultural programs not to serve man's needs but to win luck by pleasing the gods. Once a culture achieved a satisfactory level, men applied their further efforts not toward improving their own lot but toward winning more territory, building more and finer temples and otherwise serving this utterly mistaken aim in life. Sooner or later, of course, this formula failed to fit new conditions or even to remedy oppressive internal ills; and then, since nobody had any idea of meeting difficulties with common-sense solutions, the culture collapsed.

How true this was appears with grim clarity throughout the record of more than three thousand years, to and through the fall of the Roman Empire—and the Sumerian civilization offered no exception. Discoveries made since 1919 have shown plainly that once a satisfactory level of technology had been attained the creative urge declined; the craftsmen became more and more preoccupied with rehashing and overelaborating old techniques, and the various cities devoted their strength to quarrels with each other rather than to forging ahead.

The penalty of such decadence was inevitable, and with Semitic nomads right at hand it was not long in coming. After a debatable first conquest by white nomads about 3000 B.C.,* the Sumerians remained in command for a few centuries and then fell victim to another conquest—this time beyond question by Semitic nomads.

For several centuries after 3000 B.C. the Semites had been filtering into Akkad to the north of Sumeria and building up power as city

---

*This possibility is suggested by finding, just above the eighteenth level of relics at Erech, the one and only instance in the land of wholesale human sacrifice as a feature of royal burials. To provide a ghostly retinue of soldiers and servants in the hereafter, the king's servitors were led into the antechamber of the tomb and there they were slaughtered, together with draft animals for the chariots. When Woolley opened the tombs in 1928 there the skeletons were, scores of them, and all posted properly for serving the royal dead.

This rite contains an irresistible reminder of royal funerals among the Indo-European Scyths of south Russia as described by Herodotus some twenty-five hundred years later. These funerals were climaxed by impaling stuffed bodies of horses and of fifty Scythian youths on poles around the tomb. Hence we have no difficulty in following the argument of those who believe, with Menghin and others of the German school, that Sumeria was conquered by white nomads at this time; but the very plausibility of the idea lends weight to Childe's caution: "Such nomads have little of their own in the way of material culture that the archaeologist can hope to find, and always absorb the civilization of their victims. The foregoing suggestions are therefore scarcely hypotheses but are mere guesses incapable of either proof or refutation."

dwellers. Finally, about 2500 B.C., Sargon of Akkad conquered all Sumeria. He and his successors moved the seat of government to Akkad, and Sumerian leadership was gone forever. Even though the region had a few more flashes of glory, in the form of short-lived Chaldean empires, in the main civilization remained static until the days of the Greeks and the Romans.

Such an outcome shows plainly enough why every anthill state contained the germ of its own destruction; and Sumer was only the first of many states which proved this same truth, over and over again, on this same ground. When we of today ask lessons for ourselves from examination of man's early record we can find none more impressive than this dreary round of failures. Nothing will prove better how stubbornly mankind hugs erroneous ideas to the bitter end, right down to the time when everything based upon the idea lies in ruins and something new must be done because the old has vanished.

Just so did Americans cling to their crazy paper-profit boom prosperity of the 1920s until bankruptcies stalked the land. In just this way did fatuous democracies in the late 1930s cling to the faith that "nothing would happen" until the Nazi storm poured upon them; and in these mistakes these peoples did no more than copy an age-old error which they could have learned to understand well by simply mastering the lesson which was provided for them away back in the dawn of history.

The lesson becomes even more impressive when we turn to the one exception which proves how such stubborn error can be remedied by simply applying intelligent thought. This exception is given us by Egypt, the only one of these early ancient cultures which managed to endure with the same rock-ribbed indestructibility which marked the land's monumental pyramids.

As said before, the difference was due to an idea, an underlying philosophy of life which set Egypt off from other early ancient lands; and a happy explanation of the difference can be found in two inscriptions. The Egyptian one is the epitaph on the tomb of Amenemhet I, the pharaoh who established the Twelfth Dynasty about 2000 B.C.:

There was no citizen's daughter whom I misused, there was no widow whom I afflicted, there was no peasant whom I evicted, there was no herdsman whom I expelled . . . There was none wretched in my community, there was none hungry in my time. . . . I gave the widow as to her who had a husband, I did not exalt the great above the small in anything that I gave. Then came great Niles, rich in the arrears of the field.

The contrasting Assyrian inscription dates from more than a thousand years later, when ideas should have been correspondingly more advanced. But now consider these excerpts:

I am great and I am glorious, Assur-nasir-habal, King of Assyria;
In the beginning of my reign, in my first campaign my chariots and armies I collected; to the land of Narri I went:
Their spoil in abundance like the young of sheep I carried off; their corpses like rubbish on the mountains I heaped up; their cities I overthrew, I demolished, in fire I burned.
To a territory close by the town Khulun I passed; 260 of the warriors by the sword I smote down: Their heads cut off in heaps I arranged;
Bubu son of Bubua in the city of Arbela I flayed; his skin I stretched in contempt upon the wall. . . .
The rebellious nobles who had revolted against me and whose skins I had stripped off, I made into a trophy: some in the middle of the pile I left to rot: some on the top of the pile on stakes I impaled; of the officers of the rebels the limbs I cut off.
. . . to Kiuadu I drew near. I besieged and took the town; 3000 of their captives I consigned to the flames; their corpses into piles I built; their boys and maidens I dishonored; Hulai the governor of their city I flayed . . .

Thus the unbelievably ferocious record runs, over three columns of closely inscribed stone. Nowhere in it do we find a boast, after the Egyptian style, about beneficial public works, just rule or enrichment of life; blood, rapine, flayings and pillage fill it from end to end. And this monarch was no insane sadist; he was a typical Assyrian king.

And now—the reason for the temper of the Egyptian inscription, and the effects of this temper upon life in Egypt!

CHAPTER XVII

The Indestructible Culture of Egypt

Egypt's strength began with the founding of the First Dynasty about 3000 B.C.—but the full flowering and glory of Egyptian culture came about two centuries later, in the days of the Third Dynasty, under King Zoser and his brilliant minister Imhotep.

Imhotep, according to all accounts, must be counted among the all-time great of the human race. He was a physician—so much so as to be worshiped later as the god of medicine, as late as Greek times, under the name of Aesculapius. He changed the early Sumerian technique of building with brick into building with stone. Mathematics, astronomy and engineering, especially as applied to irrigation, flourished under his guidance; and this may well have been the time when the animal-drawn or *traction plow* was invented. Also, as explained in Appendix B, this reign may have seen establishment of the Egyptian calendar, the first nearly accurate one in all history.

But Imhotep must also be charged with releasing, all unknowingly, a germ of deadly disaster.

Because of universal devotion to winning immortality by providing security for the body, the crowning glory of each reign was the king's tomb; and Imhotep produced a masterpiece to insure immortality in the sun heaven of Re for Zoser.

Earlier kings had built brick underground tombs, now called *mastabas* after the Arabic. Such tombs had always been easy prey for grave robbers; but Imhotep thought he saw how to safeguard Zoser against any such mishap by taking a hint from the Sumerian ziggurat. He embedded Zoser's tomb in a stepped pyramid at Sakkara, near present-day Cairo. This huge mass, lying over the tomb proper, surely could keep robbers out; and he improved upon the ziggurat of brick

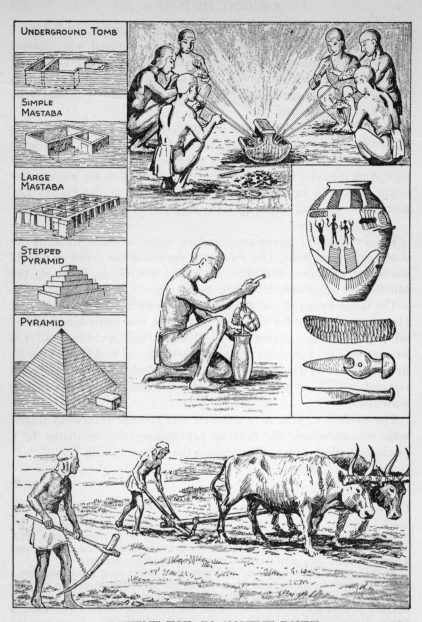

UNDERGROUND TOMB

SIMPLE MASTABA

LARGE MASTABA

STEPPED PYRAMID

PYRAMID

PATIENT TOIL IN ANCIENT EGYPT

Nothing bespeaks Egyptian willingness to toil more strikingly than does the care given to the dead. The sketches at the upper left of the opposite page show the evolution of tombs, as built by the powerful and the wealthy. The under-

Continued at bottom of the next page

and mud by making this monumental mass with stone. Probably he crowned it with a peak of polished granite, engraved with charms which would command the sun at its first peep over the horizon and ensure the king's life in heaven of the sun forever. This seems probable because later pyramids certainly were crowned with this type of tip and magic charm.

Thus the pyramid idea came to Egypt, and the Third, or Golden, Dynasty passed, with everything done that could well have been done under a warrior-religious rule to organize life to the best advantage. And then the vice of the Egyptian prescription for immortality began getting in its work, through the excesses of the Fourth Dynasty, otherwise called the Pyramid Age.

The Pyramids of Egypt are popularly taken to mean three of the scores that were built. The three still dominate the scene at Gizeh, southwest of Cairo, and they are called the Great Pyramid, the Middle and the Third, according to the size.

The Great Pyramid, and the oldest, was built by Cheops or Khufu. Herodotus gives us the Egyptian story that this stern king, during his fifty-year reign, closed all the temples and mobilized all the strength of Egypt in shifts of 100,000 workmen to build his pyramid. Each shift was on duty four months at a time, while the rest of Egypt sweated and all but starved in the effort to keep the huge working army fed.

The modern fashion is to consider this account somewhat tinged with sensationalism, but nothing can gainsay the testimony to a prodigious effort which still stands in the pyramid itself.

Continued from preceding page

ground chamber, with a separate room for gifts made by relatives after the burial, became the mastaba, an underground tomb with chapel above. This structure reached imposing size in the royal tombs of the First, Second and Third dynasties, then gave way to the pyramid, as told in the text.

At the upper right lung power and blowpipes, rather than a bellows, give a fire hot enough to smelt metal from ore. In the center the worker is twirling a drill, weighted with stones, to hollow out a stone vase. At the right center is a Gerzean painted pot with a boat. Below the pot are a Gerzean flint knife, a copper dagger with ivory handle riveted on and a chisel with a flange rounded to a handle. The bottom picture shows at the left a Third-Dynasty peasant looking up from his labors with the early type of Egyptian hoe, as that new invention, the plow, goes by. The plow was essentially nothing more than the hoe turned around and equipped with handles for the plowman. For many centuries the cattle were harnessed by simply tying the draft ropes around their horns.

There it is, 725 feet square at the base and 451 feet high; it was 482 feet high before it lost its tip. If it were hollow, the entire church of St Peter's at Rome could stand inside, on only about half the ground space. It contains some 3,057,000 cubic yards of stone, weighing perhaps 6,848,000 tons; and every last block of this unbelievable mass was quarried from the Mokattan and Tura hills east of the Nile, hauled across the river on barges, then dragged on sledges and perhaps rollers by sweating men, up an inclined causeway to the working level.

Amazing astronomical and surveying skill went into it as well. The four sides are faced within six inches of true to the north, east, south and west. This orientation insured that the sun charm at the top would face the deity squarely and command him every morning.

The builders also did well with the escape from the tomb to the circumpolar stars around the North Star or polestar.

The Egyptians called these stars the Eternal Ones and considered them to be the souls of departed kings. For his escape from the pyramid to this heavenly realm Khufu had a tunnel built to lead from near his actual tomb to an opening on the north face of the pyramid; and thanks to accurate alignment his soul, by continuing along the direction the tunnel set, would strike squarely in the center of this pharaonic paradise. Neither did Khufu's provision for his own eternal happiness cease here!

In addition to the towering pyramid itself he provided a magnificent array of temple grounds, farms, walls, and homes for priests, from the pyramid to an elaborate landing and water gate along the Nile. The priests and workers were to guard the tomb and furnish the king's body with everything it needed, forever.

Well, eventually Khufu died; we trust with serene confidence in his arrangements. After a short rule by one Dedefre, Khufu's brother Khafre or Chephren became king and built the Second Pyramid, slightly smaller than the great one. And then some sense of proportion or perhaps growing revolt in Egypt brought some sanity into these royal tomb-building efforts. Khafre's son Menkeure (Mycerines in Greek) contented himself with the much smaller Third Pyramid, and the orgy of misdirected effort came to an end. Scores of other pyramids were built, it is true, but they were on a reasonable scale.

The damage, however, had been all but done—not only through national exhaustion but through the aftereffects of the temple endowment which accompanied each pyramid, both the great ones of Gizeh and the modest ones which followed.

Egypt might have stood such an endowment for one king or two, or even a dozen. But now that the idea had taken hold such foundations were set aside for rulers during hundreds of years, and a host of less pretentious ones were set up every generation for nobles and high officials. Had this been allowed to continue indefinitely, all Egypt would have been parceled out and dedicated to the service of men long dead. To avoid this impossible outcome later kings began sanctioning redistribution of these endowments—cautiously at first but more boldly as the despoiled individuals were forgotten.

This remedy was far too feeble, however, and it came far too late to save Egypt from the consequences of this mistaken idea. During all the centuries of enslaving the country to the dead, royal authority had decayed and a feudal array of petty nobles had grown up. Quarrels between these nobles wracked the land, and finally the decay and breakdown in political life matched the breakdown in the endowments provided for the souls of the older rulers.

This decay stretched over several hundred years before its course was run, and if Egypt had been an ordinary warrior-religious state, the end of the course would have been complete ruin and conquest by some invader. But Egypt was not an ordinary state. By generating the hope for immortality and permitting two faiths, the solar and the Osirian, the Egyptians had provided scope for intelligent thought in a time of crisis, and now thought began coming to their rescue.

This thinking was inspired, according to Breasted,* by the very neglect and decay which had overtaken the early pyramids and all that went with them during the period of decline.

Long centuries ago, as Egyptians came to see the matter now, the entire nation had been enslaved to produce these assurances of immortality for the kings. Now here they stood, a melancholy array of deserted and crumbling ruins, all along the edge of the magic sunset home of the dead in the desert west of the Nile Valley; and from this eye-filling vantage point they delivered a cruel, mocking sneer at Egyptian hopes. If not even a king could save his soul after having poured the power of all Egypt into creating the necessary pyramid and temples, what hope could exist for lesser men?

For a time no encouraging answer seems to have taken shape, but fortunately the Egyptian temperament was tough enough not to be

---

*The latest work of this noted American Egyptologist, published after his death, is *The Conquest of Civilization* (1938). A more complete tracing of the religious evolution narrated here may be found in this author's *The Dawn of Conscience* (1933).

broken by despair. In papyrus manuscripts and various inscriptions left from the time, we can trace how thoughtful minds worked out a remedy for spiritual and political afflictions, through a revival of the respect for *maat,* the ancient spirit of right and justice, and a broadening and deepening of the Osiris faith, with its promise of immortality for everybody.

The share of *maat* in the problem becomes plain from its various meanings as Truth, Justice and Right. Often this mixture of meanings is cited as evidence of naïve inability to distinguish the concepts, but even if the Egyptians did mix them, were they naïve in doing so? Would not justice follow if truth were told—and if justice were done, would not right prevail and all be well? The Egyptians could hardly be called guilty of hazy thinking in that view!

Well, *maat* still remained the ideal of government, and all rulers paid lip service to it. But down to the days of despair the ideal had no teeth in it, as we say today of empty laws. It lacked a sanction, a penalty for violation. Under the old solar faith a king who possessed a proper tomb, the right services of food and other supplies and the proper magic charms, commanded entry into the kingdom of the sun-god Re regardless of what his rule had been. He paid no penalty for misconduct or misrule.

But that belief was dead now; it had been slain by those mocking, towering monuments of vast futility, the Pyramids. Kings, as well as others, had to turn elsewhere for their immortality; and where were they to turn? Why, to the alternative faith, the faith in Osiris which always had flourished in Egypt as the comfort of the commoners! Also, in this faith lay not only new hope for life after death but the very remedy needed for the ills of the time. The Osirian faith contained a sanction: it insisted that a man was judged in heaven upon his record in life.

How the kings and higher nobles came to join the humbler folk in this belief is not recorded; the only suggested reason is that no other hope remained, now that the internal confusion had cast down power and pride. Just so today do we see pride, once it has been utterly crushed, turning for comfort to ideals which it had scorned or put aside with amused contempt in its day of glory; and often pride is rewarded with new strength once it has undergone this chastening. Just this seemed to happen, at any rate, in Egypt through a period of a few hundred years in which the pendulum swung between gain and loss, then finally settled upon a rebirth of Egyptian strength.

The first resurgence of new hope came about 2000 B.C. when Amenemhet, whose epitaph we have noticed, came to power and founded the Twelfth Dynasty. The quality of his humanity, as expressed in his epitaph, is the more remarkable since he was subjected to embittering experiences throughout life. As a young man he had to battle his way through all the trials of civil strife to power over all Egypt, and in his old age he barely escaped a palace plot to assassinate him.

In spite of all this he held to his faith and left his successors a united, powerful realm. Semitic nomads who had seized parts of northern Egypt during the centuries of decay had all been expelled; the later kings kept them out with a line of fortifications across the Sinai Peninsula. The mines of Sinai were reopened, and something far more precious than copper or gems came from them, all unsuspected by anyone at the time. This new gain for mankind was *alphabetic writing.*

The value of this gain can scarcely be overemphasized. It substituted twenty or thirty signs for the hundreds or even thousands of signs which were needed for early writing. This in turn enabled anyone to learn how to write in short order instead of having to spend a lifetime in the work, as did the early scribes. Thus it became possible in principle for everyone to read and write, and from this came the possibility of universal education and an end to the dense ignorance, with all its habit-ridden and superstition-plagued prejudices, which always must rule an unlettered population. The story of this gain, therefore, is a fitting capstone for this period of regeneration in Egyptian religion and political power.

One of the most striking features of the story is the fact that the germ of alphabetic writing had existed in Egyptian writing almost from the beginning.

The Egyptians, like all other early peoples, used ideograms and phonograms. But they also had a simpler system for use in special cases. One such case would be a foreign name which could not be written in ordinary symbols. Another was the belief that certain names and words used in magic were too awesome or sacred to be set down in ordinary writing. We reflect this tendency when we say "The Awesome One" or "The Flaming One" instead of simply saying "God."

To deal with such situations the Egyptians employed the *acrophonic principle* of using the syllable signs to mean the first sound only of each syllable, in a style of writing called a *rebus*. Two such syllable signs or phonograms were the pictures of a bee and a leaf which could be used to set down the word "belief," as explained in Chapter XIII. Under the acrophonic principle the bee would be used to mean the "b" sound only (the sound which is vocalized in English as "buh"). The leaf would be used to mean "l" alone, and the two together, with a sign for "oo," could be used acrophonically to spell "blue" instead of conveying their usual meaning, "belief."

Now the Egyptians had an array of such signs, sufficient to write down all the words in their language. That is to say, they possessed alphabetic writing—and they could, if they wished, have dispensed with their whole cumbersome system for recording thought. Why, then, did they not do so? Well, why do we not write "through" as "threw"—or, even better, with a Greek theta (Θ) for "th" and perhaps with (Υ) for "oo" and get a three-letter word $\Theta R \Upsilon$? Habit holds us; and so it did the early writers. Also, beyond habit lay the exalted position of writing in early life. It was one of the mysteries, like magic. The scribes who practiced it had no more desire to simplify it than did a magician to explain his secrets to the mob.

But in Amenemhet's time, or soon after, an occasion arose for making just this simplification, in the turquoise mines of the Sinai Peninsula—and how we came to know this is one of the most unusual of the many recent triumphs in winning knowledge of these early times.

The story starts with mysterious inscriptions which were discovered around ancient turquoise mines in the Sinai Peninsula by Flinders Petrie in 1905. No Egyptologist could make anything of them until Allan H. Gardiner decided in 1916 that a certain sequence of signs meant Ba'laat (*balaat,* a goddess or "the lady lord"). Others quarreled with this and announced different views. Finally a Professor Martin Sprengling of the University of Chicago was asked to review a book which set forth Hubert Grimme's solution of the puzzle.

Sprengling, as he tells in the preface to his little book which made everything clear, was not an Egyptologist at all. He was a student of Arabic and of Islamic history; so to fortify himself for what he thought would be an ordinary scholarly book review he read up on the subject. Thereupon he saw the forest where the Egyptologists had only seen trees. The probable truth flashed into his mind, and he published his idea in what is scarcely more than a pamphlet, under

B A L T   B A L T   B L T

THE FIRST CLUE TO THE ORIGINAL ALPHABET

As the text explains, the alphabet probably was invented in the Serabit mines at Mount Sinai. Discovery of this fact began in 1916, when Allan Gardiner decided, from frequent use of the signs above, that they meant Balaat (goddess). Prof. Sprengling then used this and other hints to read the riddle, as explained below, for his reading of the inscription, "I am the miner Shamilat, foreman of mine shaft number four."

1   2   3   4   5   6
A   I   N   K   M   P   N
I   (AM) (THE)   BADGER (=MINER)

7   8   9   10   11   12   13   14
S(H)   H   M   AT   R   B   M   N
SHAMILAT(?)   FOREMAN

15 |||| 16   17   18
4   G   M   A OR SH
(No.) FOUR   MINE SHAFT

As an example of his work, signs 16, 17 and 18 at the end showed how he discovered the letter G. He knew M (18) from other readings, and sign 16 looked like a flower calyx. But in Semitic tongues both "gabi" and "Gib (h) ol" mean "flower," so the sign might mean G. Sign 18 was almost illegible but could be either a bull's head or a fish. He already knew that these signs meant (H) and S (H). But in Aramaic GMA meant mine shaft, and GMSH meant the same in Canaanite. Hence "mine shaft" seemed a safe reading, and, therefore, the flower almost certainly stood for G.

By similar study of many inscriptions Sprengling worked out all the signs which are shown in the second column at the right, following the Egyptian signs which might have been imitated in making them. The English names of the objects are below the signs. The right-hand column shows the Semitic writing and names for the characters which grew out of the rude Sinaitic script. The characters are those used on the Moabite Stone.

THE FIRST LETTERS

EGYPT	SINAI	LATER
BULL	BULL	ALEPH
YARD	HOUSE	BETH
FLOWER	FLOWER	GABI
DOOR	DOOR	DALETH
REJOICE	CRY OF JOY	HALLEL
CLUB	PEG	WAW
POOL	STICKS	ZAIN
FLAX	WRAPPING	JCHATL
HAND	HAND	YOD
WOOD	BRACE	KAFIS
TO BIND	LOOP	LOYAH
WATER	WATER	MAY
SNAKE	SNAKE	NAHASH
FISH	FISH	SAMEK
MOUTH	EYE	HAIN
CORNER	CORNER	PEHAH
LASSO	KNOT	QUAW
HEAD	HEAD	RESH
DESERT	TEETH	SHIN
CROSS	MARK	TAW

187

the title *The Alphabet; Its Rise and Development from the Sinai Inscriptions* (1931).

He did not go into the human "hows and whys" of what happened; he stopped with working out the means of the signs. But this suggests strongly enough what happened to bring the invention about.

For laborers Egyptians used natives called Seirites, and the course of events showed that the Seiritic foremen wanted to learn how to write. The Egyptian scribes were willing to oblige; but instead of trying to teach these unschooled desert men the full, elaborate Egyptian method, the scribes must have decided to short-cut the job by teaching only the alphabetic or single-sound letters.

Their teaching procedure can only be imagined, but the signs which came from it suggest how they must have gone about the task. Undoubtedly they made plain the idea of writing one sign for one sound and then writing as many signs as might be needed to indicate the pronunciation of a word. The only difficulty would be selecting the right signs for the sounds, because of differences in names between the two languages. For example, the Egyptian sign for the M sound was an owl, because the Egyptian word *mulak* for "owl" began with that sound; but the Seirites had an entirely different word for owl.

The scribes seem to have met this difficulty, however, very cleverly. Undoubtedly they simply showed an array of signs and let the Seirites pick signs for the sounds of Seiritic speech to suit themselves.

For example, the Egyptians used the diagram of a courtyard for their D sound. To the Seirites this sign suggested a house or *beth,* as they called a house; so this sign was taken as the symbol for B. Again, the Egyptians used a wavy line for N, because the sign meant a body of water, and their word for this began with the N sound. The Seirites recognized the sign, but their word for a body of water was *may*. The wavy line therefore became their M.

So the process went until the Seirites had worked out and learned an alphabet, the one commonly called by us the Sinaitic script; and eventually each people went home. The Egyptians probably thought they had done nothing beyond giving these folk a crude system, good enough for their simple needs but not at all elegant or refined. The Seirites undoubtedly were delighted and showed off their accomplishments to their neighbors. The neighbors picked it up, and the idea spread until it reached the city dwellers in north Palestine and Syria. These folk recognized the handiness of the method, polished it up, and so full-fledged alphabetic writing came into the world.*

Such an advance, added to the resurgence of Egyptian strength, might suggest that Egypt had achieved the beginnings of progressive thought. Unhappily, erroneous ideas did not surrender their power that easily! These Egyptian examples show how better ideas could and did arise out of anthill thinking, when pressure from circumstances forced them or some singularly happy situation arose, as happened at Sinai; but they show, too, that in these days such advances remained strictly limited. They went as far as necessary to deal with the difficulty in hand, and there they stopped. Before anything like a general freeing of thought could occur the entire mental structure based upon the anthill philosophy would have to crash. Then and then only would men be willing to adopt a fundamentally new approach to their problems.

The clean-cut proof of this, and a proof offered by the same land which produced the flashes of progress we have noticed, is an incident commonly called the *heresy of Ikhnaton.*

The author of this episode was a young Egyptian king who reigned from about 1380 B.C. to 1363. He came to the throne as Amenhotep IV (the name meant "Amon is satisfied," in honor of the most revered deity at the time), and he was one of those rare souls who saw straight through tradition to the essence of things and then tried to work out his straight thinking in actual life.

He saw that the essence of Egyptian religion was the hope for immortality and the judgment which the gods passed upon man's right to enjoy this boon; the rest, the bewildering array of animal gods and the meticulous and cumbersome ritual of the temples, was mumbo jumbo. Therefore he tried to set up a simple monotheistic faith, and for the god of this faith he chose what still was plainly the most important and all pervasive force in Egyptian life—the sun.

But his sun-god was not the old Re or Amon of the pyramid builders. He chose the sun disk, Aton, as his deity; and as part of his reform he took the name Ikhnaton ("profitable to Aton"). He also left the temple-smothered surroundings of Karnak and set up a new court with his pure sun worship at Amarna.

In all this he had done well. Beyond this, however, he showed all-too-common faults of the idealistic reformer.

*The further history of the alphabet, including the Phoenician share in spreading this writing over the western world, is discussed in Appendix C at the end of this volume.

For one fault, he neglected practical affairs. The vast collection of royal correspondence unearthed at Tell el-Amarna and published in 1915 is shot through with laments about the flouting and even the collapse of Egyptian power on important frontiers. Ikhnaton did not bestir himself, however, to stamp out these inroads.

For another fault, he failed to realize that his project would inevitably rouse up every priest in Egypt against him, as well as the natural allies of the priests, the nobles.

Reforms can prevail against such entrenched privilege only when the entire mass of the people is bent upon reform. In this instance, however, the people were *with* the priests and the old gods. The priests were their chief passports to salvation, and the people would not give up salvation without a fight! The moment they sensed what Ikhnaton was attempting, passion and prejudices flared up to swamp thought. His reform was doomed from that moment.

His power and prestige as king enabled him to ride out the storm personally while he lived, but the moment he died his temples and his sun-god were shattered, his hated name was erased wherever it had been set up in Egypt, and the country rolled back with a vast sigh of satisfaction into the old accustomed faith and ways. Not yet had the age dawned when any one man, even a pharaoh, could hope to change mental habit throughout an unschooled nation in one generation!

But if not even a king of Egypt had power enough to lead men into better thinking, what power could? Nothing, obviously, save the same kind of driving circumstance which had forced the birth of civilization!

Plainly, then, the full birth of reason will have to wait for a more or less complete breakdown of the anthill philosophy, a breakdown drastic enough to force men into thinking as individuals with clear-eyed intelligence instead of seeking solutions for their problems through magic and other operations of the group. No mere conquest of one state or people by another will serve. Such an event merely produces an exchange of masters; the pernicious philosophy rolls on unchanged. To produce a mental revolution the breakdown will have to occur for the masters as well as for the servitors, for the conquerors as well as for the conquered. Only when this happens will the pressure be sufficient to force a new mental approach to mankind's problems and open the way for a truly sound philosophy of society, one which places the individual ahead of the group and thereby enables men to seek a full measure of happiness by pursuing legitimate self-aggrandizement to the utmost.

This tells us in turn what to look for above all else in the historic record until it occurs. Out of all the welter of wars, conquests and collapses which will fill history from now on for more than a thousand years we should select those which work to produce the key to free thought, a breakdown of anthill living and thinking. It is time, then, that we turn to the world scene of 2000 B.C. and after to see whether any such breakdown is in the making. Since we know the state of affairs in Egypt at the time, let us turn for our first hint of breakdown to that other great center of early civilization, Mesopotamia.

CHAPTER XVIII

Preparations for a New Day in Thought

Fortunately for historic simplicity, the prospects for progress in Mesopotamia at and after 2000 B.C. can be set forth in terms of one state and indeed in terms of one man. The state was Babylonia, with its capital at Babylon, and the man was the great Babylonian ruler and lawgiver, Hammurabi.

Babylon got a start as a city in one of the periodic sweeps of neighbors over the land about 2050 B.C. Among those who seized a slice of the domain were the Semitic Amorites. They came into Akkad and established a modest capital at Babylon, near the ancient and still powerful city of Kish.

Soon thereafter Nature took a hand in shaping events by shifting the bed of the Euphrates away from Kish and past Babylon. This shift also drew the Euphrates to within a few miles of the Tigris, and there Babylon was, practically astride the two rivers over which all Mesopotamian travel and commerce flowed. The city waxed so powerful from this advantage that in 1918 B.C. its sixth king, Hammurabi, was able to make himself master of all the old realm and to bring the Babylonia of antiquity into existence.

Hammurabi's record and character have been well known since the nineteenth century from a wonderfully rich find of his correspondence, as set forth in L. W. King's *Letters and Inscriptions of Hammurabi* (1900) and later texts. This material proves that Hammurabi had every gift needed for rule, including the most important of all—an enormous capacity for handling administrative problems.

Hammurabi's letters prove that he kept an eagle eye upon everything, from government of a province to repairing gates and correcting injustices done to individuals. He waged war successfully; he acted as supreme judge and also as high priest; and he showed easily how these ancients kept their calendar in step with the seasons in spite of its inaccurate count of twelve moons to the year. One of the letters shows that the month Elul was enough out of step with the seasons to make a correction advisable, and Hammurabi managed this with the simple order: "Since the year hath a deficiency, let the month which is now beginning be registered as a second Elul." That is, since the months tended to get ahead of the seasons because the twelve-moon year was too short, the calendar was to be pulled back by having *two* Eluls that year.

Hammurabi's most memorable achievement, however, was his codification of all the old customary laws.

A copy of this code, carved on a stone shaft nearly eight feet high, was discovered at Susa in 1902. It gives us an amazingly illuminating insight into the life of the times. In it was the old *lex talionis,* or law of "an eye for an eye, a tooth for a tooth"; that is, any injury a man did was inflicted upon him exactly in kind. The code also distinguished carefully between classes. Killing a member of the ruling soldier class was punished by death; killing lesser members of society was punished by fines. But against these and other survivals of primitive law must be set many advanced provisions.

Women were protected in their property rights and given alimony if divorced. Scrupulous fulfillment of commercial contracts was required. If a slave married a free woman, the children were free. If a soldier was captured by an enemy and could not pay his ransom, the temple in his city was required to pay. Interest on borrowed money, modern businessmen might care to note, ran about thirty per cent a year; but the temples and large landowners made no charge, other than the annual rent, for advances of seed to their tenants.

Here, then, was early ancient rule at its best. But it showed characteristic early weaknesses as well. Hammurabi was wise, just and tremendously efficient, but he saw no farther than did any other early ancient. The warrior-religious or anthill idea of the state seemed quite all right to him; he saw no need for new invention or new philosophies. He gave the state order, system and administrative efficiency, and that was all. Progress received no impetus whatever.

Where then can we look for pressure of circumstances strong enough to force men into progress? One obvious possibility remains. Always around these centers of culture lurked those disturbing, disrupting folk, the nomads. Whenever civilization became too stagnant they could be expected to step in and create some kind of a stir, with perchance some impetus toward better ways.

So says our general understanding of history, at any rate—and the nomads will not disappoint expectation in this instance! Even before this time the Semitic nomads had visited the penalty of decadence upon Mesopotamia more than once. Babylonia itself was the product of such an inroad. Now, even in the days of Hammurabi's power, a formidable nation of Indo-Europeans, called the Hittites, was preparing to take up the same historic role.

The Hittite power got its start from an irruption of Indo-European nomads into Asia Minor at about 2000 B.C. or before. At this time this region had a distant reflection at best of Sumerian culture, and it was utterly devoid of military power. The Trojan or Troadic civilization in northwest Asia Minor looked to the sea rather than to this backland. Hence the nomads were opposed only by the easily conquered native Anatolians, and by perhaps 2000 B.C. the Indo-European peoples who became the Hittites or Hatti of antiquity were well established in the region.* The country was open, relatively dry and fine for horses; so the new state took shape as an aristocracy of mounted warriors, with the conquered Anatolians as subjects.

The first clear entry of the Hittites into civilized affairs came about 1758 B.C., when King Mursil or Murshilish marched southeast and captured Babylon.

Mursil himself soon withdrew, but other Indo-Europeans, the Kassites or Kasseans from Iran, kept possession of Babylon and became rulers of lower Mesopotamia. At about the same time other Indo-Europeans pushed into upper Mesopotamia, where the Euphrates debouches from the mountains onto the plain, and founded the Kingdom of Mitanni east of Carchemish. This intrusion displaced the Semitic Amorites or Amarru; and thereafter these displaced peoples, probably with Hittite and Mitannian adventurers as leaders, began carving out new kingdoms for themselves in Syria, in Palestine and eventually in Egypt.

Aside from the horrors of assault, plundering and burning during the initial conquest, the conquerors did not disturb the older in-

---

*This Indo-European origin was proved during the World War after much bewilderment over early finds of records in cuneiform script which nobody could read but which suggested a Semitic people. In 1906–07 and 1911–12, however, Hugo Winckler found tablets with Sumerian and Assyrian-Babylonian as well as Hittite. During the World War years Frederic Hrozný read these tablets and proved that Hittite was an Indo-European tongue. Thus he established the origin of these people. An excellent, popularly written account of the Hittite and Mitannian cultures can be found in Breasted, J. H.: *The Conquest of Civilization* (1938).

habitants overmuch. Once they subdued a region they built a square fortified camp, which often developed into a city, and to this camp they drew tribute from the near-by countryside and cities. Notable among these camp cities were the ones at Qatna, between Aleppo and Damascus, and at Kinza, later called Kidesh, "The Holy." This movement was completed when a band of these adventurers established great camps at Avoris, in the delta of the Nile, and at Tumilat, the "Land of Goshen" where the Jews dwelt during their sojourn in Egypt. From these camps the adventurers ruled Egypt. The Egyptians called them *Aek-khos,* "rulers of the barbarians"— and the later Greek version of this name, *Hyksos,* is also our name for these "shepherd kings" of Egypt.

So far the story seems no more than the old familiar one of nomads moving in and taking over decadent cultures. These Hittites, however, will prove different in two ways. First, unlike other nomads who made no cultural contributions of their own, the Hittites brought important advances in the material arts. Second, these contributions will help in due time and in a peculiarly backhanded way to break down anthill thinking and thereby force thought to become free.

The story of this twofold peculiar influence may well begin with the contribution made by the Hittites toward developing and spreading the use of iron.

Iron had been known before this but had not attracted much attention, for good reasons. Nearly pure metallic iron is not found in nature at the surface of the earth, as copper is; the only exposures are of ore, and Egypt and Mesopotamia did not offer even this much contact with the metal. Some Congo Negroes had ore and perhaps knew how to smelt it, but the Egyptians, Cretans and others who used iron at all tended to use the bits of the metal which could be found in some meteorites.* These they seem to have extracted and worked up into beads and ornaments.

In Asia Minor, however, good surface deposits of ore existed in the great bend of the Halys River. Sumerian trade contacts taught the Hittites the art of smelting, and before long they began to work up iron. Iron weapons gave them superiority in arms over any army they encountered. This superiority was enhanced by their success in combining the horse with the old Sumerian chariot in the formidable art of *chariot fighting*.

*Meteoric iron can be identified in relics by an admixture of nickel akin to the mixture which geologists believe exists in the central core of the earth.

Not so many years ago historians praised this achievement as amounting to an introduction of the horse to civilized lands, but a change to the statement as given seems necessary because of a discovery made by Langdon at Jemdet Nasr. In 1928 he reported use of an ideogram, "ass of the mountains," on a tablet found at that site; and this sign persisted with the unquestionable meaning of "horse" into the Babylonian cuneiform. The animal, therefore, seems to have been known even in prehistoric Jemdet Nasr days, and the Hittites cannot be credited with introducing knowledge of it. What they and other Indo-European invaders of Mesopotamia more probably did was to show how this fleet animal, when hitched to a chariot, gave devastating power on a battlefield—especially when the chariot was equipped with an iron scythe on each hub! The military value of iron and the horse naturally led to quick and widespread adoption of them, and this in turn led to peacetime uses of these new aids.

Now, having noted these additions to material culture, we may turn to the effect of them in hastening a breakdown of anthill thinking.

As our first observation we may note at once that nothing of the sort occurred among the Hittites themselves. It could not because of the policy they followed of fastening themselves upon existing cultures as masters and exploiters. This amounted only, as said before, to a change of masters; it did not in itself produce any breakdown. The Hittites did contribute, however, in a backhanded way, to making breakdown possible at a future date, by enabling the anthill philosophy to push on to its own destruction. This could happen now because of the increase in military efficiency which came from use of iron and the horse.

In the older days of foot soldiers conquest had been a relatively slow business, even when opposition was slight. Now mounted soldiers could move over the entire breadth of southwestern Asia in a single season, and the anthill idea of state aggrandizement was equipped to swoop where before it had been compelled to creep. The inevitable fruit of this would be a welter of wars, conquests and collapses through exhaustion and sufficient pressure here and there from collapse and despair to force men into freer ways of thinking.

All this is, of course, mere theory—but the record shows plainly enough how the Hittites themselves set this grim march going.

The march started, as has been said, with a conquest of Babylonia and a sweep across southwestern Asia and the Sinai Peninsula into Egypt. From then on the march toward exhaustion became a seesaw.

After each conquest the Hittites would hold their own for a time. Then, as soft living at the expense of their victim sapped their strength, the victim managed to throw them off.

The first recoil of this sort occurred soon after 1600 B.C., when Egypt gathered strength enough to oust the Hyksos shepherd kings. Thereupon the kings who accomplished this founded a magnificent court at Karnak, and as rulers of the Eighteenth Dynasty they made Egypt's power felt throughout the civilized world.

The founder of the Eighteenth Dynasty, Ahmose I, was an outstanding figure during his reign from 1580 to about 1557 B.C. After him came a succession of equally strong rulers: Amenhotep I, Thutmose I, Thutmose II, Queen Hatshepsut and Thutmose III (1483–51). This last monarch is often called the "Napoleon of Ancient Egypt." By his time the Hyksos rulers and their people had retired to Palestine; Thutmose sought them out and crushed them in their famed "last stand at Armageddon." The site now is called Megiddo, and the date of the battle has been fixed as May 14, 1483 (H. H. Nelson: *The Battle of Megiddo,* 1913). By this victory Thutmose made himself master of Palestine and Syria as well.

After Thutmose died, Egyptian power in Asia declined temporarily because the next ruler was Ikhnaton, the young king who devoted his reign to a futile attempt at religious reform; but recovery was almost immediate. The next ruler was Tutenkhamon, the "King Tut" who had the whole world talking in the 1920s about the splendors found in his tomb, and Tutenkhamon was followed, after a short reign, by the monarchs of the Nineteenth Dynasty—among them Ramses or Rameses I and II, the latter being identified by some commentators as the oppressor in the Biblical narrative of the Exodus. He reigned from 1292 to 1225 B.C., and he and his fellows of the dynasty confirmed Egypt in the old ways while re-establishing the Egyptian military power over the entire historic realm, with one exception. They could not regain power in Palestine and Syria.

During Ikhnaton's time the Hittites, under their able king, Suppilulyuma, had seized their chance to overrun Syria. Then they turned eastward and crushed Mitanni, thus producing the far-flung power which history calls the Second Hittite Empire. The Egyptian successors to Ikhnaton strove to recover Syria, and for many years these two leading powers in the world of that day waged war until mutual exhaustion compelled a peace, with a division of Syria, about 1270 B.C.

By this time the Hittites had all but fulfilled their historic destiny.

While they and the Egyptians had been locked in a devastating struggle other peoples had been gathering strength, and now an imposing array of new and ambitious tribes and nations began making bids for power. Assyrians, Medes, Persians and Greeks had their chance now to enter the world scene, and the Greeks delivered the *coup de grâce* to the Hittite power in 1190, by overrunning Asia Minor from the Aegean coast as far east as the river Halys.

This feat was overshadowed, however, at the time by the far more impressive rise of Assyria.

Throughout all earlier times Assyria has been a dependent province of whatever power ruled in Babylonia or Sumeria. By 1300 B.C., however, Kassite rule in Mesopotamia had become thoroughly decadent, and this gave the northern provincials an opportunity to bid for supreme power. The chance found them well prepared, both by discipline from natural surroundings and by national experience.

Their land was high and enjoyed cool nights as well as cool winters; vigor and ambition were not subjected to the steaming and the baking that sapped energy farther south. Their character was stiffened further by constant warfare with their neighbors—especially after the Hittites, the Mitanni and other Indo-European peoples came in. Thereafter they had been compelled to fight almost continuously to hold their own.

Under these circumstances they developed a strong military tradition, with their entire national life organized to support the army. This made them invaluable to Babylon, and Babylon made the mistake of relying upon them for defense. Thus no power existed to curb their king, Shalmaneser, when he decided in 1300 B.C. to throw off empty subservience to Babylon and seize the supreme power over Mesopotamia.

His chance was all the better at that time because Egypt and the Hittites were at the climax of their struggle in Syria. The Assyrians gladly let this process run its course while they built up their power at home and to the eastward. Thanks to this wise policy Assyria was in a splendid position to make a bid for world mastery when the Hittite Empire fell before invading Greeks in 1190.

The details of this struggle, the crushing power and ferocity of the Assyrian army and the far-flung successes won, need no attention in a history of thought.* A lesson may be drawn, however, from their

*One change contributed by Assyria—most people would not call it an advance—was an enormous increase in military efficiency. The Assyrian army was the first to be equipped throughout with iron weapons, and it was the first to make intensive use

example of a state so hated by all for its ferocious cruelty and its insatiable demands for tribute as to fall victim in the end to a general revolt by every nation in southwestern Asia. All the neighbors joined in a concerted drive to end this oppressive bloody rule once and for all, and Assyria was ripe to fall. She had converted her peasantry into soldiery and was living on tribute rather than her own produce. Once all tribute was cut off she was done, and the final debacle was as sudden as any such collapse in history.

In 616 B.C. Nabopolassar, subject king of Babylonia, revolted and kept the Assyrian army busy in the south. In 614 the Indo-European Medes marched down the Tigris from Iran and took the historic capital, Assur. Two years later the allies reduced the newer capital, Nineveh. Then in 609 they exterminated the last of the Assyrian army at Harran, in the mountains of Armenia; and the Assyrians themselves, in their dealings with many an unhappy city, had taught the allies what to do with Nineveh. They reduced this proud capital to a rubbish heap, and so it remained, a deserted mound, throughout all later times, until opened to the light again by the spades of modern archaeologists.

This collapse obviously left southwestern Asia wide open for new conquests, and they were not slow in coming. In fact, the lust for conquest moved on now to the logical climax of the anthill philosophy. Within less than a century all the Asiatic anthill states found themselves welded by force of arms into one super-anthill, one state spread by conquest over virtually the entire western civilized world by two related Indo-European peoples, the Medes and the Persians.

During the entire Assyrian period these Indo-Europeans had been filtering into the mountainous plateau which lay between the Asiatic

of siege machines. When the Assyrians attacked a city they customarily rolled besieging towers against the wall. Gangways from the tower gave their soldiers access to the top of the wall, and a direct assault could be delivered under cover of a cloud of arrows fired by concealed archers. If this failed, battering-rams in the base of the tower soon crumbled the sun-dried brick or poorly set stone in the walls, and through the breach the infantry poured to the final assault.

Another development of this time, important to scholars, was widespread use of *Aramaic* in trade and diplomacy, somewhat as Latin was the "universal language" in medieval Europe. The language was Semitic, and it got its spread because the speakers, a small tribe dispossessed of land by the Mitanni and the Hittites, took up the commercial role which the Jews pursued in later ages. In particular, they served as government clerks and agents for the Assyrian politicocommercial plunderbund. This gave their speech semiofficial standing, and from this time until the rise of Greek speech most writing was done in Aramaic. To a considerable extent native tongues like Hebrew became relegated to ceremonial and sacred use—so much so that many of our oldest versions of the Old Testament have Aramaic duplicates of the Hebrew.

grasslands and the northeastern border of Mesopotamia. They called themselves the *Arya* or *Airya,* and they gave the name Ariana to the high plateau which they occupied. Hence we get the modern name Iran for Persia. We might note also that these people constitute the only physical strain which can rightfully be called Aryan.

These folk had not moved as rapidly as had the Hittites in Asia Minor, because of the rougher country and a greater need for practicing farming themselves. History's first glimpse of them dates from about 1700 B.C., when some of them won mastery of the Punjab or Indus portion of India. After mastering the ancient civilization along the Indus they spread until they became the Hindu masters of the entire country.

At the same time a western wing was pushing into Iran, and some of the softer civilized nations of Mesopotamia began making the same mistake that Rome made nearly two thousand years later. They hired these fierce tribesmen as mercenaries, and the tribesmen acted as mercenaries so often do. They conquered a region for their employers, then took over mastery of it themselves—as loyal subjects of their employers, of course, but the employer dared not try to oust them! This course of events seems proved by the fact that Aryan names crop up constantly at this time as military commanders and local governors. The Egyptian correspondence found at Tell el-Amarna teems with such names, thus proving that Aryans had penetrated as far west as Syria and Palestine.

While the Assyrian power lasted it kept this infiltration from getting utterly out of hand, but in the Iranian highlands the Aryans were building up the tribes which were destined to overthrow all Semitic power in western Asia. Prominent in this group were the Persians or Parsa who settled near the Indian Ocean and held ancient Elam as their territory. The Medes lived in the northwest of Iran and the Parthians in the northeast. Beyond the Parthians to the north were the still other Aryan nomads who later were called *Daha* (enemies, robbers) by the more settled Aryans. The Babylonians called them Gimiri (Cimmerians), while to the Greeks they were Scyths or Scythians.

The fall of Assyria gave prominence to the Medes, both because of their share in the event and because as near neighbors they fell heir to much Assyrian territory. Sixty years later, however, the Persian king, Cyrus, revolted. A short fight gave him leadership of all the Iranians in 550 B.C.

Here was an event which gave all neighbors food for deep thought! The Medes had been dangerous enough before—and the Persians as well. Now their strength would be united under a ruler who plainly had the ambition to build himself up, and the probabilities were all against his being satisfied with having swallowed the Medes.

Babylonia, Egypt and Lydia, the Greek state which had succeeded the Hittite power, saw the menace instantly and planned to crush this upstart before he could weld his two nations into a firm empire. But diplomatic correspondence took time in those days; Croesus of Lydia wasted precious months consulting the oracle at Delphi; and while these states delayed Cyrus acted.

He turned on Lydia first and took both Croesus and his capital, Sardis, in 546. Then, leaving his General Harpagus to mop up, he rounded upon Babylon. This capital submitted in October 539. Cyrus then gave personal attention to eastern campaigns and was killed during one of them in 528. By the time this happened, however, the Persian Empire extended from the Black Sea to the Persian Gulf and the Red Sea, and from near India on the east to the borders of Egypt and the shores of the Aegean on the west. Three years later Cyrus' son, Cambyses, extended these boundaries even farther by conquering Egypt.

Now, with the anthill concept of government pushed to its climax of one world empire, what of human thought all this time?

A world empire might seem discouraging for progress, since it was the very opposite of the breakdown needed to free thought. But breakdowns and calamities aplenty had occurred during the long welter of struggle before the Persian triumph, and on principle, advances could have come out of this situation. Surely enough, an appraisal of the world scene shows several such gains. Let us see now what they were!

CHAPTER XIX

First Stirrings of New Viewpoints

Any search for mental gains which emerged from all the struggling in western Asia down to the days of the Persian Empire can utilize several simple guiding clues.

The larger, more powerful states were not likely spots for such achievements. When they were in a heyday of power they were well satisfied with everything as it was. When they were down they nevertheless had busy national lives and their dreams and plans for coming back again. Aside from Assyria none of them suffered the complete breakdown which was required to produce truly new ways of thinking—and Assyria was too utterly ruined to support anything at all save peasants living directly on the soil.

This leaves the smaller, humbler locations. By every test they were by far the most likely places to achieve mental advances. They had no visions of power, past or future; they lived by allying themselves with winners, seizing chances for profit when they could, and every now and then recovering from complete ruin of town and countryside. Such experiences would do most to shatter tradition.

Surely enough, it was just such smaller communities which produced the magnificent advances in thought which were made during this period of struggle. Our benefit of hindsight gives us the roster of them. Judea with its monotheistic religion, small communities of Medes and the Persians before their days of power, and, finally, certain new Greek cities which were taking shape around the Aegean, account for all advances in thought down to days of Persian world empire.

The necessary basis for tracing the rise of monotheistic faith among the Jews is a correlation of the Scriptural account with ancient history as worked out by the usual studies.

This correlation is extremely difficult, both because the early chapters of the Bible are all but completely blank as to date and geographic location and because identification of Hebrew names with those turned up in archaeological excavations presents many thorny problems. The first biblical figure who seems definitely datable in terms of secular history is Abram, later called Abraham, the father of the Jews—and the best link seems to be through Tidal, King of Goiim (Gen.: 13). If this monarch was Tidal the Hittite, Abram is placed in historic time between 1550 and 1450 B.C.—that is, in the same time which saw the Egyptian triumph at Megiddo in 1483.

This dating is a bit late, however, if another theory be accepted, that Abraham's grandson Joseph went down into Egypt in the days of the Hyksos and found a welcome from sympathetic fellow Asiatics. In such an event the Jews would already have been in Egypt during or before the days of Megiddo, and "the pharaoh who knew not Joseph" might have been an early ruler of the Eighteenth Dynasty. Such a ruler might well have been hostile to the Jews, along with all other Amu or Asiatics.

This is the more probable, since a little later the Tell el-Amarna correspondence of Ikhnaton's time shows the "Habiru" nibbling away at the Egyptian holding of Canaanite cities. The word was Babylonian for "stranger" or "outlander." This would match up splendidly with the idea of the Jews coming from the desert east and southeast of the Jordan, as the account in Exodus and later books has them doing—and the connection between "Habiru" and "Hebrew" is obvious. Excavations at Jericho show also just the destruction set forth in the Bible as occurring at this time.

From this time on, however, the march of events can be fitted into dated history without difficulty, and our record of human intelligence can turn to the growth of Jewish thought about God and man.

When the Jews came out of Egypt their understanding of God pictured a true tribal deity, a god who would fight for them against other peoples and gods as long as they obeyed his commands. He was equally ready to chastise transgressions of the law, and this remained the Jewish understanding of Yahveh during the conquest of Canaan and during their short career as a united nation under David and Solomon. Thereafter came a division, both in political life and in religion, and this division ran almost exactly with a significant physiographic division of Palestine.

The tribes of Judah and Benjamin lived on the high rocky backbone which separates the slope toward the Mediterranean on the west from the rift valley of the Jordan and the Arabian plateau to the eastward. The region was a commercial and cultural backwater, suitable at its best for sheep and horses; and the Judean shepherds could only watch while the other ten tribes, now called Israelites, waxed rich and reveled in the delights of sensuous Oriental faiths in the favored coastal lands.

But this contrast in opportunities for enjoyment proved to be the making of the hillsmen spiritually. The prophets led in this by preaching and thundering against the wickedness of the rich and their oppression of the poor, and they warned of dire punishment to come from deserting Yahveh in favor of Canaanite *baals* or gods. The hillsmen saw prophecy fulfilled when Samaria, the capital of Israel, fell to Sargon II of Assyria in 722 B.C. But the prophets warned that Judah had become tainted as well and would be chastised. Surely enough, Jerusalem fell to the Chaldean king, Nebuchadnezzar, in 586, and the Judeans were taken into the affliction of the Captivity by Nebuchadnezzar's act of transporting the population bodily to Babylonia.

To many Jews this transportation destroyed the power of their god Yahveh. In this they followed early ancient thought, which considered gods as tribal deities and their temples as the places where charms and sacrifices won their favor. With Yahveh's temple destroyed, and the Jews removed far from it, how could they obtain his help?

Their prophets had already pointed out the way.

During the last gloomy days of Jerusalem the prophet Jeremiah had been proclaiming that temples of stone and wood did not matter; Yahveh's true temple was in each man's heart. Now, in Babylon, some unknown prophet (whose teachings are embedded among those of Isaiah in the Bible) made this doctrine a message of hope not only for the Jews at that time but ultimately for all mankind.

He affirmed Jeremiah's doctrine that the consciences of men were the true temples of divinity, and he asserted that Yahveh was the Divine Father not only of the Jews but of all mankind. This was clean-cut monotheism and a clean break with all customary ancient ideas about gods; and the unknown prophet did not stop with this. He asserted what our own review of ancient history to date has proved abundantly—that men learn through adversity. Yahveh was purging his children, through bitter experience, of their follies; but the day would come when his chastened children would be fit to enter upon their good life and would do so.

Thus the Jews had a vision of a high spiritual destiny to sustain them throughout the Captivity, and the promise seemed to attain fulfillment when Cyrus the Persian took Babylon in 538 B.C. He permitted all Jews who so desired to return to Jerusalem and to take the sacred temple vessels which Nebuchadnezzar had brought to Babylon. Also he forbade his governors to interfere with the rebuilding of the temple. Thus it seemed to the Jews that the chance for a wholly new and hopefully bright life seemed open at last, with the necessary lessons learned, exactly as the prophet had foretold!

Unfortunately, realization of the prospect depended upon more than spiritual impulse. It depended upon compliance by human nature and compliance within the framework of ancient life, with its despotic subordination of the individual to the state, its dependence upon slavery and its reduction of most people to the completely habit-ridden level. The tiny Jewish nation, living by permission of the Persian power, could not rebuild life to match their ideal—and so, ere long, the ideal became formalized and lost its driving force. A new light had been lit and it still burned, but the task of spreading it throughout the world remained for stronger hands and more unflagging zeal.

Meanwhile a similar new spiritual light had been kindling among the Persians and allied Indo-European peoples. The faith took shape as *Zoroastrianism,* also mistakenly called *fire worship.*

The national or racial foundation for this faith was, as the last term suggests, a worship of fire and the sun. This was, of course, a primitive nature religion akin to the Egyptian cult of Re the sun-god, and it persisted among the Iranians until nearly the time of Cyrus. It was more than crude nature worship, however, because as far back as we can trace some ethical ideas seemed to have attached to it. Fire was not only a quickening and consuming force; as the Iranian acquaintance with more complex problems of conduct grew, fire also became something of a purifier. It burned away dross in human nature just as it consumed noxious substances in physical nature.

Now this was a fairly keen stroke of thinking for primitive minds to achieve, and it bloomed into a magnificent faith when Zoroaster or Zarathustra appeared at some uncertain date after 1000 B.C.

Zoroaster saw life and the world as a conflict between opponents, and his actors in this drama were Good and Evil, Ormuzd and Ahriman. Into this antithesis he took up the finer elements of fire worship.

Ormuzd was the flaming, brilliant principle of life and good. Ahriman was the devil of evil and destruction, and from the beginning of time he and Ormuzd had fought each other in all realms. In Nature Ormuzd fought to make the world beneficent and pleasing; Ahriman fought to tear it down with storms, plagues and natural destruction. Among men and nations Ormuzd battled to make them strong, wise and just; Ahriman, like Satan, toiled to ruin them with every wrong impulse and act.

The duty of man to himself, as well as to the gods, therefore was plain. If man wanted a good life, he should enlist under the banner of Ormuzd and lend his strength, by his own conduct as well as by his worship, to the cause of this good god. Thus men would hasten the day when Ormuzd would win the final victory and Ahriman and all his followers would be consumed in eternal flames. Thereafter life, both on earth and in the hereafter, would be happiness itself for Ormuzd and his people.

So lofty a faith hardly squares with later Greek accounts of the Persians as disgusting drunkards, loathsome sensualists and cruel beyond description in their statecraft. But such descriptions, it must be remembered, came out of the Greco-Persian Wars and undoubtedly contained a liberal dose of wartime propaganda. Evidence from the Persian side runs differently.

The inscriptions on the royal tomb of Cyrus and his successors reflect a high sense of a king's duty to his people. Inscriptions naturally put the best foot forward, but the point is, what the rulers consider to *be* the best foot. Again the Persian Empire survived long after Greek power and even Roman power had crumbled through internal decay. A nation of besotted, cruel and sensual monsters could hardly have achieved such lasting power. The high standing in India of the Parsees, the present-day followers of Ormuzd, testifies to the sustaining power of this faith. A final testimony to the power of Zoroastrianism was its standing in the days of the Roman Empire.

By the time of Augustus the Persian faith had given rise to a more pantheistic version called *Mithraism,* which was the favorite religion of the Roman army. Mithras was an earth-born god, a child of the highest and most mystic deities, who gave fertility and life after the manner of the Egyptian Osiris; and he was worshiped within the frame of the ethics and the larger philosophy of Zoroastrianism, with fire as his symbol.

And now we come to the most important single people in all the history of human thought—the ancient Greeks.

A splendid thumbnail appreciation of their place in the record of man's mental progress is the following from Harry Elmer Barnes's *Intellectual and Cultural History of Western Civilization* (1937):

The Greeks . . . did in some measure release men from the dead hand of tradition and the incubus of superstition. They introduced the scientific frame of mind and a thoroughly secular way of looking at life. The brilliance of Hellenic culture could not have been achieved unless it had reached what Professor Franklin H. Giddings called the "legal-liberal" state of civilization.

We have described the Oriental empires of Mesopotamia and Egypt as a military-religious civilization. . . . Centralization put an end to innumerable forms of local conflict and to untold and unnoticed wastes of energy, thereby liberating potent mental and physical forces for leisure-time activities. These activities produced literature, art and a rudimentary science, besides adorning and adding to the amenities of life. . . .

But the human intellect can make only limited progress under a military-religious regime, which is autocratic in essence and acts as a cultural steam roller, in forcing like-mindedness on the populations.

In the liberal-legal stage . . . the race learned to appreciate unlike-mindedness. It came to understand the value of doubt and skepticism, of individual and voluntary organization. It learned that *variation* and *criticism* constitute the lifeblood of man's progress. All this the Hellenes, and particularly the Athenians, realized.

So important a people obviously deserves careful introduction.

Indo-European nomads they were originally—tall, active blond folk, not at all the short swarthy Greek of today. The modern Greek is descended from the Mediterranean or Pelasgian stock which had held the land from paleolithic times, and still holds it, after the ancient or classic Greek had his day and disappeared. Perhaps the distinction can best be kept clear by calling the classic Greek what he called himself—a Hellene.

Their earliest history is still unknown, down to the time when a trickle of them appeared in Hellas, as later they called Greece. Since this new home had almost as much to do as the folk themselves with shaping the Hellenic temperament and career, it deserves careful scrutiny.

Hellas or Greece was a rugged mass of more or less parallel mountain ranges, hardly one hundred miles across, that projected three hundred miles into the Aegean and the Mediterranean from the southeastern corner of Europe. At the southeast end six ranges dipped beneath the sparkling blue sea to form capes, then the tops of submerged ranges formed two chains of islands that connected with Asia Minor.

Over this rugged, stony little land and the island-gemmed sea swept the winter rains and the bright, hot summer days of the Mediterranean climate. At times the little valleys that nestled between the rough gray ridges would be sparkling green with fresh grass, but more usually they showed the dusty gray green of a land that could do with considerably more water. On such a terrain agriculture was possible but not lush.

The cut-up nature of the land also insured small communities, one to a valley. Thus the Asiatic type of despotic military power, which drew soldiers and food from a broad open countryside, was impossible. Travel, communication and conquest were easiest when pursued by sea; hence the fresher, freer spirit of the typical maritime civilization was bound to enter into Greek culture from the start. Lastly, the climate, while hot, still was not debilitating.

Here, then, was a setting which offered a minimum of the natural influences that fostered despotisms in Egypt and Mesopotamia, and in it the Hellenes began to achieve a conquest, just as Teutonic invaders did some two thousand years later in the territories of Rome. Indeed, we even have two Romes in Mycenae and Tiryns, two mainland seats of Minoan power; and the story of old Asia cannot be joined to that of new Hellas more fruitfully than it can by using the story of these cities as the connecting link.

Since we have no Minoan records to help us we cannot say how these cities got their starts. They may have been simple trading posts which grew as Minoans were crowded off Crete, or a considerable population may have established strong cities after an earthquake wrecked Knossos at a time fixed by geologists as not long after 2000 B.C. Whatever happened, they were the leaders of the Minoan world by 1500 B.C., because Knossos, although rebuilt, never regained its primacy.

But this change unhappily carried an automatic penalty.

Had these people remained on Crete and other islands, they could ·have held off the nomad Hellenes indefinitely. But now the center of their power was on land, where the nomads could get at it, and all the evidence suggests that the culture was soft and decadent. The Mycenean art had exchanged the fresh creative spirit of the older Minoan for extravaganza and formalism in decoration. The cyclopean walls of the Mycenean strongholds also suggest softness. A vigorous land power takes the field and crushes the enemy; a power that shrinks to safety behind walls is half beaten before a blow is struck. Starvation, pestilence within the city and loss of raw materials from the surrounding countryside will do the job for the assailants, even though the walls themselves be invulnerable.

Of course for some centuries the walled strongholds could beat off the still thin population of Hellenes, but from the start the invaders began taking over weaker places. Probably, too, some states hired them as mercenaries against rivals, just as Rome imprudently taught the arts of war to Gothic and Teutonic barbarians. Certainly Knossos, the ancient Minoan capital, was captured, sacked and burned about 1400 B.C. by some combination of land and sea fighters.

If so, the blunder was fatal—particularly since the Hellenes were continually growing stronger through continual immigration from the north. About 1500 B.C. a fresh wave of immigrants called the Dorians came in behind the first and second ones, called the Acheans and the Ionians; and probably the new tribes pushed the older ones tight up against the Mycenean strongholds, just as later the Huns pushed the Goths across the Danube into the territories of Rome. This pressure gave the Hellenes determination enough to burst through all defenses, and about 1200 B.C. they managed to overthrow Minoan civilization.

Mycenae and Tiryns were stormed, and the Hellenes swept over the islands of the Aegean. Knossos had already been wrecked; now Rhodes and Cyprus fell. Still the tide rolled on. In 1190 B.C. the Hellenes crushed the Hittites and at about the same time they overwhelmed Troy. By 1000 B.C. they were masters of the west coast of Asia Minor. So complete was the ruin of Mycenean power the Hellenes even forgot these people, except for legends about the Cretan bull or Minotaur and the maze or labyrinth of King Minos.

By this victory the Hellenes laid the foundation of their later career. But this career took time in the shaping. More immediate effects were caused by the activities of the defeated and dispossessed peoples.

The great bulk of the population apparently suffered the fate of the conquered from time immemorial: they passed under the yoke of the new masters. This, however, was not as hard as it might seem. To the commoners yokes were nothing new. Minoan, Hittite or Hellenistic overlord—what mattered it which one ruled? The commoners plodded on in their habit-ridden ways, and in the fullness of time they would have their revenge. The dominant blond Hellene would pass or sink beneath the weight of a climate not suitable for him; the ancient stock would move quietly into his vacated place, and once more the age-old rule would be vindicated, the rule which says, "to men of the Mediterranean race, the Mediterranean shall belong." At least so Huntington says in his *Character of Races*—and nothing in the historic record says him nay.

The aristocrats, the wealthy and the energetic seem to have elected to flee. Probably they took with them a following of defeated Hellenic mercenaries and perhaps inhabitants of early Hellenic settlements which had been destroyed by the new invaders. This seems to many commentators a reasonable explanation for the mixed character of one horde which started coasting south along the seaboard of Syria into Egyptian territory. We know about them because Ramses III, lord of Egypt and Palestine at the time, left a record of how he dealt with them. About 1194, with campaigns by land and sea, he turned them back, as well as allied folk driven from Asia Minor; and the Egyptian account of this triumph closes with the despairing wail of the migrants, "Whither shall we go?"

One group did manage to remain in western Asia by seizing a home on the coast of Palestine. Philistines or "strangers" the backland Semites called these settlers, and we hear much of them through the Jews, who were mastering Palestine from the east at that time. Others turned west and seem to have become Etruscans of mainland Italy; still others may have planted civilization in Sardinia and Sicily, although scholars differ about this.

Thus the effects of the Hellenic invasion far outran the occupation of the new homeland. Like a huge wave which rolls hundreds of thousands of miles at sea after an earthquake or a volcanic explosion, the repercussions of the Mycenean disaster were felt throughout the Mediterranean world; and a last effect to be noted was the emergence of the Phoenicians as a world power.

Since the dawn of history these folk perforce had contented themselves with their Egyptian and inland trades; they could not challenge Minoan dominance in the Aegean and to the westward. During all this time they called their land Canaan and themselves Canaanites. Kinahhi and Kinahni are the terms used in the Tell el-Amarna letters. Other peoples often called them Sidonians, after their oldest important city Sidon, now Saida. The name Phoenician is Greek, from *phoenos* (blood red); it seems to have referred to sunburned complexion or perhaps to Phoenician "purple," the scarlet dye made from shellfish at Tyre.

Phoenicia's real chance came when the destruction of the Aegean sea powers threw the Mediterranean sea trade open for anybody who could capture it. The Phoenicians were shrewd enough to carry off the lion's share of the prize.

They wasted no strength in land warfare unless driven to it; they gladly acknowledged the overlordship of any glory-hungry king, Egyptian, Hittite or Assyrian, if the tribute he asked was not too high. In manufacturing they invented nothing, but they adopted every salable idea they could pick up from Egypt, Babylonia and Crete. Phoenician woolens and metalwork were prized everywhere. Sidon was famous for glassware, while Tyre gained immense wealth from Phoenician purple. Finally the Phoenicians rounded out their growth by establishing Carthage on the North African coast near Sicily. This colony in time outgrew the homeland in power; indeed, it held the distinction of being the last of all the Mediterranean powers which offered armed resistance to all-conquering Rome.

As navigators the Phoenicians were credited in their time with being the first to sail at night; they held their courses by sighting the polestar. No voyage was too long or too dangerous for them to undertake, provided it promised a profit. Herodotus tells that a Phoenician crew spent three years circumnavigating Africa, under a commission from Pharaoh Necho (Niku) in the seventh century B.C.

With their undoubted talents the Phoenicians could have made notable contributions to civilization, but unfortunately their motto was "nothing given save for a profit." They wrote nothing and told nothing which might enable other peoples to copy Phoenician methods. Their knowledge of geography they kept to themselves; and so, when Alexander the Great crushed their power by capturing Tyre in 333 B.C., they left no record other than in the accounts given by other peoples and in such relics as archaeologists can recover.

And now, with all these other peoples accounted for, what of the Hellenes themselves, the folk who had caused all this upset?

Nomads they still were in temperament—fierce, formidable and predaceous—but their scheme of life had been transformed by the necessities of their situation into the ways which the later Hellenes called the Heroic Age. In herding they had adopted the detailed care needed in rugged land, and they learned to practice agriculture.

To hold the new land each tribe usually fortified some hill near the center of its territory. Around this grew up such a village, town or city as the tribe might need, and here was the germ of the classic Hellenic state. The *polis* or city was the center; the *acropolis* or fortified hill (from *akros,* highest, and *polis*) was the stronghold.

Nomad government still persisted under an elected chief who led in war and in peace served as a *basileus,* a combined priest and king who conducted religious rites and presided over such government as existed. Usually this consisted of a council of elders or *boulē,* with an occasional assembly or *ecclesia* of all warriors to vote on important questions such as war.

Next came the nobles or *eupatrids.* These were the men who possessed or acquired wealth enough to maintain a chariot and horses and to buy armor from the more advanced lands. As time went on they became more important than the king. This was a natural consequence of settled life and the growth of governmental problems beyond any possibility of handling by one man. The council of elders became the legislative body. The king's military powers were transferred to an elected *polemarch* (pole-e-mark), while the growing civil business of the state was entrusted to an elected *archon* (ar'kon). The king himself was reduced to a mere high priest.

So life ran for several centuries, in the pattern already made familiar by the Hittites and other Indo-European invaders in Asia. Nothing in it suggested that the Hellenes were going to achieve any fundamental advances in culture or in thought. Indeed, once the shock of their initial conquests had died away the civilized world seems to have paid but little attention to them. We find no mention of their activities in the Bible and scarcely any in Egyptian or Mesopotamian records.

The important historic problem, therefore, is this: What happened to transform these half-peasant, half-nomad Hellenes into the most brilliant thinkers and artists in all history?

Nobody claims to know the answer in any detail, despite earnest study since the days of the Renaissance; but neither are we entirely in the dark. An outline, at least, of the answer can be given, beginning with the testimony of the Hellenes themselves.

PART V

ANCIENT HISTORY—

The Greco-Roman Climax

CHAPTER XX

The Dawn of Free Thought among the Greeks

WHEN WE OF TODAY ask from what source the ancient Greeks acquired their mental brilliance their literature gives us at least one broad hint of an answer. They hailed as pioneers in brilliant thought the Seven Wise Men.

These wise men were, by name, Thales of Miletus, Solon, Periander, Pittacus, Cleobulus, Bias and Chilon. Thales was a philosopher of scientific bent. The others were statesmen of a strange new quality. Most of them were poets or patrons of poets as well as statesmen, and all of them had splendid insight into the needs of the time.

Solon, for example, was an Athenian who humanized the laws of his city in 594 B.C. Bias was a legal counselor who flourished about 570 B.C. in Priene, in Ionia. When this city was faced with an overwhelming Persian invasion he advised the sane escape of a migration en masse and establishing a new and happy city in Sardinia. Pittacus was a hero of Mytilene in a war against Athens in 606. When his city offered him a reward he took only a small piece of land and devoted it to sacred uses. Later, when he was made despot or dictator for ten years, he established firm peace and wise laws and resigned quietly in 579, at the end of his term.

Chilon was an ephor or magistrate of Sparta in 560 or 556; he preached prudence and being ready for the future. "Know thyself" and "Nothing in excess" are some of his maxims. Cleobulus was a tyrant of Lindus in Rhodes. He was famous for maxims, poetry and riddles; we can date him from a letter written in 560 B.C.

Periander, who reigned as tyrant of Corinth from 625 to 585 B.C., was the one hard-boiled ruler in the lot, but he knew well how to make a state great and prosperous. He established colonies that protected and fed Corinthian commerce as far away as Macedonia. He strengthened the free citizenry by forbidding a large number of slaves under one owner. He fought overemphasis of city life by forbidding residence in the city to folk whose interest lay on the land.

Now a striking fact about this list is that, aside from Thales, each and every one of these sages achieved his fame by dealing wisely with the problem of how men could live together happily and profitably in political communities. This suggests in turn that something must have happened to set the Hellenes thinking about their ways of living as no people had ever done before, and the record reveals clearly enough what this "something" was. The Hellenes had brought about the complete breakdown of older ways which no other people had achieved.

The Hittites, the Medes and the Persians had fastened themselves upon existing cultures as masters and exploiters. Soon thereafter they were absorbed, just as the Chinese are said to absorb every conquering folk that enters the land. The Hellenes, however, had *smashed* the Mycenean culture, and so they were compelled to build from the ground up. They were inspired also to do so by their contacts with the rich cultures to the eastward and the south. Hence the array of circumstances needed to produce new thinking had come into being after many long ages, and the fruit of it was the birth of free thought among the Hellenes.

This process of new need prodding men into new ideas appeared first in the island and coastal states which undertook to develop maritime commerce after the Mycenean and Phoenician pattern, with piracy as a side line. Thinking was needed then, because the Hellenes were fitting the nomadic pattern of group co-operation, rather than the peasant principle of anthill organization, to life at sea. To work out this scheme they enlisted crews of men who also served as fighters, on shares in the profits—and this scheme of voluntary co-operation automatically stimulated thought, untrammeled by tradition since no tradition existed about such ventures.

Even more happily for mental stimulation, this necessity for thinking was bound to be permanent. Hellenic maritime effort could never grow into a tradition-bound activity dominated by an overwhelmingly strong ruling class, because the very nature of the cut-up Hellenic homeland prevented overaggrandizement of the rich and the powerful.

Entering also into commerce at this time was another profoundly important stimulant to thought—a new and growing use of money.

Money of a sort had been known, of course, since paleolithic times. Most people valued some few articles above all others and would accept them in trade when they did not care to exchange goods by direct barter. Gold and silver had been used for this purpose throughout historic times—and age-long experience with them had worked out a rough scale of values or *prices* in terms of silver and gold.

In early ancient times the metals actually were weighed out by the shekel or other unit of weight. Some coins had been made by the Assyrians by casting silver in a mold with a mark to show the weight, but nobody trusted them, because the mark was too poor to betray clipping or sweating with acid. But in the seventh or early sixth century B.C. the Hellenes of Lydia in Asia Minor learned how to mark pieces made of gold from deposits along the river Meander by stamping a clean-cut design on each piece with a die. The resulting sharp impression made cheating much more difficult, and this money could be accepted by talc, without the nuisance of weighing. The new coins were in widespread use by the reign of Croesus (560–46 B.C.) in Lydia and helped to create the aphorism "rich as Croesus!"

Trading benefited immediately through the improvement over clumsy barter. A more important effect, however, both to society and to thought itself, was the new possibility of subdividing both ownership and labor.

Up to this time a man of modest means had only two kinds of chance to be his own man. He could operate a family farm and barter his surplus output, above his own family's needs, for metal and other objects which he could not produce himself. He might also become an artificer or a craftsman, provided he did not need expensive raw materials. But in a day when free labor could not be hired for a money wage, because a convenient form of money did not exist, most production had to be carried on by large units worked by slaves.

The invention of money provided an alternative to slave labor, because with it workers could be hired for a money wage. Men did not swing over to this system immediately; of course slaveowners would continue to work their slaves. But free paid labor was possible now, whereas it had been impossible before—and here and there in certain cities and callings it did get a start. This automatically created necessity for thought, because arrangements had to be worked out for using this new device advantageously.

These new driving forces could not help bringing old social arrangements under question and particularly the concept which organized all life under control by the eupatrids or nobles. Here again the Hellenic situation was unusually favorable for thinking, because it upset the usual evolution of this class, even within itself.

In the older Mesopotamian and Egyptian cradles of culture the huge sweeps of fertile land had fostered a snowball type of evolution. The rich became ever richer at the expense of the poor; the stronger swallowed the weaker; and the natural end of the process was one ruler and one state dominating everything. In fact, even while the Hellenes were struggling with their problems their cousins the Persians had established exactly this type of superanthill over all southwestern Asia and Egypt as well.

Such an evolution was difficult, however, in the cut-up Hellenic homeland, and it was impossible as long as the Hellenic states were comparatively poor and consent of the citizenry was required for any large-scale effort. Under these circumstances the rich and the noble could only aggrandize themselves by working within the political framework of their city-states. Their road to power was winning office as archon or polemarch.

Older understandings of history selected this fact as important in stimulating thought, because it brought in democratic government. Newer views agree to the stimulating effect, but not through promoting democracy. Actually the results of democratic elections were not happy. Intelligent debate of proposals on their merits was impossible as long as the electorate was densely ignorant and prejudice ridden; the only effective appeal was appeal to passion. Hence the politically ambitious among the Hellenes turned more and more to raising mobs of excited commoners as their instrument of political aggrandizement. Many a measure was debated in council to the orchestration of a city filled with peasants and craftsmen shouting for the blood of an unpopular leader, judge or official.

Such turmoil, of course, could lead but to one end. The necessary outcome in any state is the strong man, the dictator, the man who can impose peace and order upon the factions by use of the iron hand. Within a century or so after 750 B.C. most cities had *tyrants* or dictators, and the so-called Age of Tyrants had begun.

The word "tyrant" has a horrendous sound in modern times, but at this time it simply meant "lord." Also, the tyrant was the real key which unlocked freedom of thought among the Hellenes. This was so because the tyrant owed his rise, as a rule, to support from the strongest mob, and always he had to keep a discerning finger on the public pulse. The same power which put him in could throw him out, if ever his policies and acts should unite the commoners and a sufficiently powerful faction of the nobles against him.

Tyrants, therefore, sought needed popularity by providing fine temples, joyous festivals and an enrichment of public life sufficient to produce general satisfaction. Outside the home state the tyrant strove to show power and achieve expansion, thus building up state pride. Fortunately for him and the world, this was easy to do by *colonizing* in new lands to the westward.

Colonization of new lands served as a superb safety valve for letting off discontent. If defeated factions were allowed to withdraw, they soon would be absorbed in building up their new homes; bitterness would die out, and soon only a tie of sentimental affection would remain between parent state and colonial child. Colonization thus became a strong instrument of state policy, and the fruit of it for civilization was a spreading of Hellenic influence far to the westward, even to Massilia, the forerunner of the modern Marseilles. This city was founded by Hellenes from Phocaea in Asia Minor about 600 B.C., just as Syracuse and Sicily had been founded by Corinthians in 734. Indeed, so dominant were the Hellenes in Sicily and southern Italy, the early Romans called the region *Magna Graeca* (Great Greece). At the same time, the Hellenes became eager maritime explorers throughout the Mediterranean and even along the Atlantic coast of Europe. In the fourth century B.C., Pytheas of Massilia is supposed to have voyaged as far as the Shetland Islands or perhaps even Iceland, later vaguely known to the Romans as *Ultima Thule*.

In this vast yet peaceful expansion many scholars see the final touch needed to free the mind of man in the trading and colonizing centers, Asia Minor and Sicily, with only one question unanswered. William Linn Westermann states this question as follows (page 10, Vol. I, *Encyclopedia of the Social Sciences,* 1930):

There is no possibility [he says] of answering the question whether the exploits of these unknown adventurers of the sea were an expression of an intellectual restlessness and curiosity already developed, or whether colonization is to be regarded as a factor in developing that exploring habit of mind which characterized Greek intellectual life for the succeeding four centuries.

No answer, however, is necessary, except as a nice refinement in analysis. The practical working fact was that the processes ran hand in hand, each feeding the other. Each one contributed also to the mental characteristic which constituted the very root of Greek mental brilliance. This characteristic can be named in a phrase as the *critical attitude*. An even simpler term is the one word *skepticism*.

Down to this time men had accepted beliefs without ever asking for proof. They would have expected lightning from heaven to smite them if they displayed such sacrilegious skepticism. Beyond this it never occurred to any two people to *compare their respective ideas,* in search of conflicts in theory. So set were all the peoples in their ways of thinking, they could face the most violent contradictions between cherished beliefs without ever suspecting that either belief might be wrong.

Until the Age of Tyrants and of colonization the Hellenes were as naïve as any Babylonian or Egyptian. But the economic and social ferments which had produced the Age of Tyrants had created a veritable habit of questioning all age-old and time-honored beliefs. That is, the Hellenes acquired the *critical attitude* which is the germ of the *scientific spirit*. And we know that the scientific spirit came alive at this time, because the record reveals a genuine "father of science" in the seventh and by far the most important of the Wise Men—Thales of Miletus.

Unfortunately, not a scrap of authentic detailed biography exists to throw light upon Thales; the nearest we can come to biographical detail are the statements that he lived from about 640 B.C. to perhaps 546 B.C. and he may have been a son of Phoenician parents from Tyre. We know, however, that his first achievements came in those ancient sciences, astronomy and mathematics, and they came also when these sciences were undergoing a burst of development in one of their two ancient homes—the short-lived Empire of Chaldea which arose upon the ruins of Assyrian power. Since this spurt of development may have contributed considerably to the achievements of Thales, it deserves attention prior to the sage himself.

Once the Assyrian despotism ended, Babylon enjoyed a short burst of glory under Nebuchadnezzar (604–561), the son of Nabopolazzar and the Hammurabi of his time. During his reign the city attained a magnificence which dazzled the ancient world. His new Temple of Marduk was a veritable brick mountain; his famous Hanging Gardens, a ziggurat with every terrace magnificently planted with flowers and trees, was another; and throughout the huge city craftsmen and merchants conducted one of the richest trades in all antiquity. His prowess in war was well remembered by the Jews, because it was he who conquered Jerusalem and carried its citizens into the Babylonian Captivity.

This was the time also when Babylonian or Chaldean astronomy achieved its greatest heights, with its ability to predict eclipses. Long study of the heavens and carefully kept records had taught the Chaldeans by now that eclipses came in a regular order of 29 lunar eclipses and 41 of the sun, 10 of these being total. This sequence was repeated every 18 years, 11 1/3 days, or one day less if five leap years occurred in the period. This was thinking of high quality, but it had one weakness which Thales was to correct.

Down to this time Chaldean and Egyptian stargazers had learned some facts about the motions of the heavenly bodies, but largely as a means to an end—either time telling, surveying or, most important of all, casting horoscopes. They did not care about scientific forces and laws, because they thought they knew well enough what these forces and laws were. Various gods and spirits were the moving forces behind the stars.

This explanation undoubtedly was given to Thales during the many years he was said to have spent traveling and studying Egyptian and Chaldean lore. But a full measure of growing Greek skepticism seems to have suggested a different answer to his mind at or about the time of his first recorded feat—predicting an eclipse of the sun in 585 B.C. and having the eclipse come off exactly as he said it would.

Thales' success with the eclipse must have given him a glimpse of law and order at work in Nature in this matter. He seems to have taken the hint and broadened it by asking himself the daring question, "If order rules here, why not throughout all Nature? Might there not be a beginning or arche, a source of power which creates all the appearance and phenomena that make up the universe?"

Neither did Thales stop with asking. He achieved an answer which he found satisfactory. How he got it we can only guess, because we know him only through scraps of mention by later philosophers; we have nothing written by him to guide us. Apparently, however, he was impressed by the Aegean itself—always restless and changing, yet ever the same—and also by the different states which water can assume, from solid ice to invisible dampness and cloudy steam. At any rate, he came out of his wondering with the answer that water was the arche, or source of all else in the world. Thereby he became the first man, as far as the records show, who worked out an explanation of the universe in terms of reasoned cause and effect rather than traditional folklore.

Beyond this Thales may well have added one final achievement—inspiring others to think and to delve for new understandings.

Whether he did so directly by urging or teaching we cannot say, but we do know that by the time he died, about 546 B.C., an entire group, later called the *Ionian* or *naturalistic* philosophers, was busily engaged, in the critical scientific spirit rather than with unquestioning acceptance of tradition, in studying the nature of the universe. The clear light of reason had been lit in the world after unnumbered ages of groping through the murky glow of tradition-ridden thinking and implicit faith in magic.

Today, accustomed as we are to scientific thought, such a feat may not seem so monumental. Its true importance will become apparent, however, the instant it is measured against the fundamentals of human nature and the general state of knowledge and thought among the Hellenes at the time.

Shallow expositions of Greek history, such as may be found in all too many a text, give a false impression that the new enlightenment led quickly to a golden age of progress. Actually this happened in only a few cities such as Athens, thanks to very special circumstances. Elsewhere, so sunk were most Hellenes in superstition-ridden mental stagnation that Harry Elmer Barnes could say with perfect justice in his *Intellectual History,* "the majority of the Greek city-states made no more contribution to the progress of civilization than did the Hottentots."

Another common misconception holds that the Hellenes were mental supermen, a race which was more intelligent than any people before or since their time. We have not a shred of evidence to prove that this was true, and plenty of evidence tends to prove this conception false.

At the time when Thales and his fellows started to use free, untrammeled intelligence only rich children received any education at all, and they did so from intelligent slaves or in private schools run by old poets or retired soldiers. Training was limited to reading, writing, the Homeric poems and simple arithmetic—necessarily, because as yet the store of common knowledge contained nothing more. Men who wanted to explore Chaldean and Egyptian wisdom had to visit these lands. To study the new philosophy a man had to visit a philosopher and live in or near his home.

Still another insight upon the general level of intelligence can be gained from that amazing Hellenic institution, the *oracle* of Apollo at Delphi.

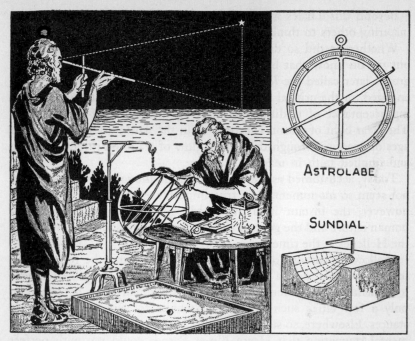

ASTROLABE

SUNDIAL

HOW GREEK ASTRONOMERS PROBED THE HEAVENS

The picture shows practically the entire equipment of a Greek "astronomical observatory"—crude angle-measuring instruments and an armillary sphere, on which the celestial equator, the ecliptic, and other astronomical reference planes were arranged correctly for the latitude of the observatory. Calculating was done by drawing on a bed of sand with a stick, or on a wax tablet; yet with such equipment the Greeks worked out the foundations of astronomy. The sundial shown is the hemispherical type which probably was invented by Chaldean astronomers in the seventh century B.C. It remained the standard type throughout antiquity; our type with a flat disc and slanting gnomen was a Middle-Age Moorish invention.

All Hellenes had unshakable faith in it. Nations sent embassies before making war or passing important laws; individuals presented pressing problems for answers. To the Hellene, asking Apollo at Delphi was as simple and natural as we think of the act of looking up a word in a dictionary, and he had the same unquestioning faith in the answer. Answers obtained by cities were treasured as precious state documents, sacred laws of the land, and a philosopher would be bold indeed if he dared reopen a question which had been settled conclusively in this fashion.

A final example of the prevailing superstition is the unverified but thoroughly probable story of an incident which arose from the same eclipse that gave Thales fame in 585 B.C.

At this time the westward movement of the Medes had brought them to the river Halys, which always had been accepted as the boundary between Greater Asia and Asia Minor. Thereupon the Hellenic Lydians to the west bestirred themselves against this menace. The Medes, never reluctant to fight, moved up an army; and in 585 the hostile forces confronted each other along the Halys. The rival leaders were about to give the word to engage, when lo! the gods began blackening the sun!

Now in Miletus at that very moment excited citizens were exclaiming about the man Thales, the man who had known enough to predict this event. But here on this dusty plain hundreds of miles away nobody had heard of Thales or his prediction. The plain portent of the eclipse was that the gods disapproved of this conflict, so the war ended then and there—a victory for superstition at the very time when reason was being vindicated in Miletus!

Superstition and ignorance, then, rather than brilliance and high mental power, provided the soil out of which Greek achievements were to grow—and this means that the story of intelligence has two sides from now on. Not only did it have to work its own way forward; it had to overcome the resistance which brute nature, tradition and habit-ridden minds always offer to guidance by clean-cut intelligence. What troubles arose out of this will be apparent enough as the record unfolds!

CHAPTER XXI

Beginnings of Philosophy and of Democracy

Lancelot hogben's book *Mathematics for the Million* (1937) gives a whimsical foretaste of what the Greek revolution was to mean in due time, with an episode in the life of Thales as a text. After Thales made a certain discovery, Hogben says, "he sacrificed an ox to the gods. It was a bad business for the ox. In the end, it was a bad business for the gods." Obviously this was so, because the Nature gods of the time, the ones who moved the stars and produced crops and weather, would have no functions left once scientific explanations for these phenomena were discovered.

Fortunately for thought, the philosophers kept pretty much to themselves, and the populace had no idea of the sacrilegious mischief which they were brewing. If even an inkling had leaked out, use of reason would have ended then and there. But philosophic reserve protected the philosophers while they pressed forward with Thales' problem of the *arche* or first cause. Their initial results were widely different and uniformly crude, but after some decades they came to favor the theory advanced by Anaximander (611?–547? B.C.).

Anaximander believed that the *arche* had to be something "unlimited"—what we might call a living force or a "soul of the universe." It used the tangible, visible substances of the universe just as a builder uses wood, stone and other materials. In Anaximander's universe a core of solid matter (earth) made the center of the world, and this core was surrounded by shells of water, air and fire, the last condensed in places as sun, moon and stars. The living *arche* presided over all this array and directed all changes which occurred in it.

This doctrine is worth noting well, because most later Greek thinking about the universe reflected it. So also did it show the later Greek tendency to work out a final, all-embracing answer before anyone could explain even minor details of the universe. These philosophers, we must remember, were still children in their use of reason—and like children, to whom the power of imagination comes at two years of age or so, they let their ideas run riot. Once any one of them got a theory, a pattern of understanding which seemed to fit the facts here and there, he pressed it to the limit and dealt with difficulties and contradictions just as children do, by overlooking or ignoring the harassing material.

Anaximander died when Cyrus the Great of Persia had possessed his empire for about thirteen years. Then this same Cyrus ushered in the next stage of Greek philosophy by his conquest of Lydia and the Greek cities along the coast of Asia Minor.

This Persian inroad crushed the first seat of Hellenic thinking and commercial development, and a host of brilliant men fled westward, to Greece in Europe and to the colonies in Magna Graeca—that is, Sicily and southern Italy. There Hogben's "bad business for the gods," the appeal to reason instead of myths and magic, went forward rapidly. Indeed, it even tended to *make a religion out of reason.*

The statement may sound fantastic, but even a momentary recollection of the mystic thrill to be had from contemplating the majestic wheeling of a star-studded night sky, or the play of tone in a masterly symphony, will make the idea sensible enough. To minds filled with Anaximander's doctrines might not such experiences seem like glimpses of the *arche* itself, the animating principle or "soul" which ran the universe? These thinkers were too naïve as yet to realize that such "principles" were abstractions which their own minds had created; they could fall easily enough into the idea of worshiping these principles as divine. At any rate, exactly this tendency appears in the doctrines of two southern-Italian philosophers, Pythagoras and Zenophanes.

Pythagoras (570?–500 B.C.) made principle or natural law the foundation of everything by holding that form or organization, rather than substance, was the basis of the universe. He was said to have been helped to his idea by noting the simple mathematical laws which connect the notes of music, and music, so far as he knew, was not "substance" at all. In pursuit of this principle he sought mystic relations between numbers and in geometric figures such as circles and triangles, and he established a brotherhood at Crotona to live according to his principles. This school is credited with several mathematical discoveries. Perhaps the best known is the Pythagorean theorem that in a right-angled triangle the square of the hypotenuse is equal to the sum of the squares of the other sides. Modern *numerology,* the so-called "science of numbers applied to names and fortunes," is a present-day reflection of Pythagorean doctrine.

Zenophanes of Elea (570?–480? B.C.) was noted principally for his denunciation of the accepted Hellenic gods with their human forms and attributes. "If oxen and lions had hands," he said, "they would make the pictures and images of their gods in their own likeness; horses would make horses, oxen like oxen. Ethiopians make their gods black and snub-nosed; Thracians give theirs blue eyes and red hair. . . . There is one god . . . like to mortals neither in form nor in mind."

This was bold thinking, indeed, in a day when denial of the gods was treason to the tribe and the state; but the religious aspect of Zenophanes' teachings was toned down by his follower Parmenides (540?–460? B.C.) into the *Eleatic doctrine* of an all-pervading and unknowable Reality, which never changes but only appears to do so before the fallible eyes and minds of men. This sounds horribly abstract, but the underlying thought in this Eleatic doctrine is simple enough. The Eleatics had caught a vague appreciation of the fact that behind all the changes and movements which made up the physical universe and the life of man stood an array of controlling natural laws which did *not* change. The real meaning of their high-flown language was that these laws formed the true Reality—that is, the true "essence of the universe."

Thus nearly a century of thinking gave philosophers the net result of establishing the principle that invariable law was the basis of the universe. But now inherent weaknesses in their methods began leading them not to new understandings but into unprofitable, sterile bickerings.

For one weakness, characteristic of amateur theorists in all ages, they did not appreciate the value of modesty and restraint in pushing an idea. The Eleatics in particular let their enthusiasm for unchanging Reality lead them into denying the existence of change and motion, and for this they were challenged fiercely by Heraclitus (540?–475? B.C.). He argued that the ultimate *arche* was fire and that the universe was an ever-changing flux, much as modern physics teaches that matter is electrical in nature and that the universe is really just a gigantic flux of energy. Seemingly fixed and stable objects actually had no more "real existence" than do waves on the surface of the sea. They come and in due time they are gone. The only reality is the restless, ever-changing flux which tosses up these appearances.

Now to modern ways of thinking no real conflict existed between the Eleatics and the fluxists. Each school was right in the positive portion of its doctrines. The universe is an ever-changing flux, but this flux utilizes unchanging substances and is controlled by unchanging laws.

This would have been plain enough to everybody had the clashing schools put their doctrines to the test of experiment. If they had worked out, say, the problem of why water boils, the Eleatics would have carried their point by proving the continued existence of water and of unchanging laws of boiling. The followers of Heraclitus would have had their flux in the change from liquid water to gaseous steam.

Unfortunately, the idea of appealing to test and experiment was utterly foreign to Hellenic philosophy—and for a most simple reason.

Such an appeal might have occurred to a practical man, one accustomed to working out his ideas with actual material. But these philosophers were gentlemen and rich men, every one of them—as a man had to be in those days, before he could indulge in the luxury of philosophizing—and they were under no compulsion, professional or economic, as a modern scientist is, to get answers. Moreover, the social prejudices of their times forbade putting their ideas to the test of experiment. This would have required manual labor on their part, and use of their hands to accomplish anything, even to prove a theory, was utterly beneath their dignity. Such work was for slaves; gentlemen worked with their minds.

Lack of practicality was to prove the death of Hellenic science in the end, as the later record will show. But this end was still far away, and our survey of Hellenic mental attainments at this time may turn with profit now to another immensely important development during this same time. This was the growth of *democratic government* in Athens.

Strikingly enough, one factor which seems to have contributed strongly to this development was the comparative poverty of the Attic homeland.

When the Hellenes first entered the Greek peninsula one of the few places which did not attract much attention was the peninsula of Attica. The rocky hillsides did not promise much for agriculture; the prizes to be won in the city and in shipping activities were not as rich as elsewhere. Gradually, however, this backwater peninsula drew human profit from its very poverty. The Greek historian Thucydides tells plainly how this happened:

Attica, of which the soil was poor and thin, enjoyed a long freedom from civil strife and therefore retained its original inhabitants. But Attica, through immigration, increased in population more than any other region. For the leading men of Hellas, when driven out of their own country by war or revolution, sought an asylum at Athens; and from the earliest times, being admitted to rights of citizenship, so greatly increased the number of inhabitants that Attica became incapable of containing them and was at last obliged to send out colonies to Ionia.

Thus the Attic population was leavened with some of the best and most progressive minds in Greece, for these would be the kind which tyrannical governments elsewhere would drive out, together with restless troublemakers. This was all-important, because it stored up intellectual power in the Attic temperament against the time, toward the end of the seventh century B.C., when Athens went through the common Hellenic experience of discontent, intrigue and tumult, leading to establishment of a dictatorial government under a tyrant.

The stored-up intellectuality was evidenced, even during this formative period, by two unusual attempts to make the older government work by reforming the laws. The first attempt, in 621 B.C., was an agreement by the dominant nobles to remedy the intolerable legal status of the commoners.

Up to this time all trials had been held before the Areopagus, an aristocratic council and court made up of nobles. Since no laws ever had been written out, the court could declare the law to be whatever it saw fit in any case. The fate of debt-ridden commoners haled before it by noble creditors can well be imagined. The great reform of 621 was to have the laws written out and made binding upon the court as well as all who appeared in trials.

A young official named Draco did the work, but the supposed reform inflamed the people more, rather than appeasing them. Slavery for debt and other overwhelming disadvantages for the poor were so drastic as to make the word "draconian" a synonym for harshness ever after. Clamor for reform mounted higher than ever and led to a second attempt—this time by a young man named Solon (638?–568? B.C.), the same who earned his status as one of Greece's Seven Wise Men out of this work.

The choice of Solon, rather than some older man, was the aftermath of as intriguing a feat as any to be found in history.

At the time, Athens had lost the island of Salamis, adjoining her harbor, to her westerly neighbor and rival, Megara—and also had bled herself white trying to regain it. To cut short further loss the Athenians had passed a law which forbade even mentioning Salamis under penalty of death. Solon, however, believed that the island must be regained or Athens would be strangled, and in 600 B.C. the Athenians were treated to a strange sight. A seeming madman appeared in the streets—a madman who dared urge another attempt upon Salamis! And so eloquent was he, so moving in his portrayal of all the island meant, that, law or no law, the Athenians resolved to try again!

The "madman," of course, was Solon; he took this means to remain alive while he preached his crusade. He was sound enough in his madness too. The Athenians retook Salamis, and Solon was the hero of the day. All Athens agreed, too, that he could reform the political situation if anybody could. He was commissioned to do so, and in 594 B.C. he proclaimed his new code and constitution.

Rarely did an oppressed people profit more from one stroke than did the commoners of Athens from Solon's code.

First of all he ordained debt relief. Those who had been enslaved or imprisoned for debt were released. These remedies were abolished for the future, and the interest rate on outstanding debts was reduced; the currency was debased. Solon also popularized the enforcement of laws by giving the election of judges to the *ecclesia* or general assembly; juries were appointed by lot from among all citizens.

These reforms occurred, it will be noticed, just nine years before the eclipse which gave Thales fame and stopped the war between the Lydians and the Medes. Hence popular government started out "neck and neck," so to speak, with philosophic thinking—but it proved much less successful.

The shrewder minded among the Athenians had bowed perforce to the storm in Solon's time, but later events showed that they had appraised democracy well and knew how to turn this new government to their advantage in the end. Let the rabble play with its new toy while the novelty lasted; then the smart fellows could set up glittering vote-catching programs and win all the power they wanted as a gift from the "sovereign people"!

Surely enough, within less than fifty years, just such maneuvering placed Athens under tyrannical rule by the political genius Pisistratus (605–527 B.C.).

Like Solon, Pisistratus got his start in the Salamis affair; he proved to be a popular military commander. He also had a magnetic personality, fine oratorical skill and a comfortable estate at Marathon. For party or following he chose the hillmen—not only because Marathon was in the heart of their country, but because they were the poorest and most discontented men in Attica and the best supporters for a revolution.

For years he built up his strength by shrewd service to his party and liberality to the poor, and the other parties wasted theirs, both in quarrels among their leaders and in permitting a cancerous growth of slavery at the expense of free labor. When discontent mounted again to explosive proportions by 560 B.C., Pisistratus judged that Athens was ripe for a dictator or tyrant. He seized the Acropolis. Leaders of the other parties fled, and from then on Pisistratus was boss or tyrant, save when he was driven out temporarily in 555 and again in 550.

To finance his policies he laid a flat tax of ten per cent upon income, and nobody could have spent the revenue more wisely. He relieved the men of his own party by wrenching them from their old error of trying to grow grain on their stony, hilly farms. He showed them that olives and grapes would be more profitable on such ground, and he lent them state funds to get the new crops going. To make up for the reduction in grain supply he established strong colonies along the Dardanelles and built up a trade of Athenian manufactures in return for grain produced in the Crimea. His foreign policy was the simple one of keeping peace with all neighbors and bending Athenian strength to building up Athenian prosperity.

Finally, he did not overlook those mainstays of popularity for a dictator or boss—eye-filling, pride-stimulating public works and abundant public entertainment. He fortified Athens and built a Parthenon or temple to the city's patron goddess Athena, the goddess of wisdom. He founded a public library and installed an improved water supply. Poets were encouraged; the annual Dionysiac festival was built up; also a great celebration, the Panathenaic festival, every four years; and Pisistratus is credited with sponsoring Thespis, an Icarian poet who founded drama.

The heart of the Thespian innovation was adding an answerer to the array of leader and chorus which had always chanted the songs and recitals in festivals. This gave a chance for *dialogue* and hence for drama. Thespis was also the first *showman* we know. To give his plays he took his props from town to town in a cart. In each town he recruited and trained a chorus, then gave a show with himself as the leading actor. Therein he proved far shrewder than most troupers. Popularity was assured in advance by having a large fraction of the townspeople in the show as chorus.

Thanks to these sound policies Athens was rich, cultured and powerful when Pisistratus died in 527 B.C.; on the surface the Athenian government had been a great success. Actually this success had been due to the genius of the tyrant, as troubled times soon proved. His sons Hippias and Hipparchus tried to carry on his rule, but in 514 Hipparchus was assassinated by Harmodious and Aristogeton, two youths who were always honored as national heroes thereafter. In 510 the Athenians drove Hippias from the city and called upon a popular citizen named Clisthenes for another dose of reform on the Solonic model. In 508–07 Clisthenes gave Athenian democracy a form which persisted to the end.

History must admit that Clisthenes had the right purpose in mind in what he did. He recognized that democracy could only be workable if political devices for whipping up mob passions were minimized, and one of the strongest of these devices was appealing to the clan spirit of the old blood tribes. The "tribal vote" could be turned out by clever politicians, just as modern politicians appeal to the Irish vote or the Italian vote in an American city.

Clisthenes therefore grouped the voters in ten new artificial tribes, each one named for a legendary hero. He changed the old *boulé* into a council of five hundred, each tribe selecting fifty members for one-year terms. Executive government was conducted by committees of ten, with one member from each tribe.

Clisthenes also introduced *ostracism* as a device for blocking would-be tyrants. He provided that any citizen who wanted anyone banished could write that person's name on an *ostraca,* or bit of broken pottery, this being the scrap paper of antiquity, and place the potsherd in an urn provided for the purpose. If enough votes accumulated, the person named was "ostracized" or "potsherded." That is, he was banished from Attica for ten years.

With this Clisthenian constitution adopted, Athens emerged for better or for worse upon its career as a full-fledged democracy, and this phase of development was completed almost immediately by a fiery trial which forged and tempered the state into a mighty nation. This trial was the *Persian Wars*.

During the preceding century, when the Persians under Cyrus

had overwhelmed the Ionian cities of Asia Minor, Pisistratus had contented himself with taking over Ionian trade rather than trying to fight the Persians. But soon after Clisthenes had reformed the Athenian constitution a great revolt against Persia broke out in all the Ionian cities, and this time the young democracy sent help to its fellow Hellenes. The revolt failed, and thereupon Darius I, called the Great, of Persia resolved to punish this upstart meddler from the west and launched the first Persian invasion of Greece.

This invasion was broken by the brilliant Hellenic victory at Marathon in 490 B.C. But everyone knew that the Persians would try again, and now occurred an illuminating instance of Athenian democracy at work. The hero of the incident was Themistocles (514–449 B.C.).

Themistocles argued that the victory at Marathon was a fluke; the small Hellenic armies could hardly expect to repeat the feat once the Persians came on with their entire strength. A navy, he said, was the thing. It could block Persian crossings of the Dardanelles, and if they did get across, it could harass or block their progress down the Greek coast. Also, a fine navy of two hundred triremes was easily possible for a state as wealthy as Athens. At the moment, the people were toying with the idea of voting themselves a bonus of one hundred drachmas apiece from the output of the silver mines at Laurium. For nearly a century these mines at Laurium, on the tip of the Attic peninsula, had been a powerful contributor to Athenian prosperity. They were exploited by slaves for the profit of the state, and the venture was successful enough to make Athenian silver money a favorite throughout the ancient world. Put that into a navy instead, said Themistocles, and the job would be done!

He carried his policy, and after the new Athenian navy had taken a leading part in crushing the second Persian invasion at Salamis in 480, Themistocles was the hero of the day. But now democracy was to have its odd way. Themistocles was a coarse, boastful fellow and perhaps not overscrupulous about bribetaking for official favors. At any rate, the Athenians seem to have found him insufferable after Salamis, and at some uncertain date after 476 they ostracized him. He sought the usual refuge of an unpopular Athenian—service with the Persian king—and he died in Magnesia in Asia Minor in 449, hated by the city which probably owed its very existence to him.

Meanwhile, however, this navy had done its part, not only at Salamis but thereafter, in giving Athens the leading position in the Hellenic world. Immediately after the Persians had been driven from the heart of Greece by the battle of Plataea in 479, Athens proposed a brilliant plan for ensuring safety thereafter to all the Hellenic states of the Aegean in the form of a permanent defensive league. The members were to pay regular dues into the treasury of Apollo on the island of Delos—hence the name Delian, of the league—and league affairs would be controlled by a sort of Senate composed of delegates from the member states. The league would unite all members in war, and in times of peace it would reimburse Athens for maintaining a navy on wartime footing.

Here was an advance in political institutions to rank with Athenian democracy itself, provided the league was administered wisely. The outstanding virtue of it was its constitutional provision for the *balance of powers* which has proved best in government throughout all later history. Individual cities could have tyrants or popular assemblies as they liked, but the league was to be ruled by responsible *representatives* of the member states. Such men might be expected to conduct the league's affairs wisely and thereby draw the petty city-states of the Hellenes into a strong nation—and also set an example of wise control by a selected assembly which could be incorporated to good profit in the government of every city-state.

It must be said, too, that the league got away to a flying start. For once the maritime cities and states were willing to lay aside their jealousies and allow one strong state to take the lead. In return Athens, for once, through her leading delegate Aristides, acted for the best interests of all. Aristides had the job of fixing the dues to be paid by all members, and so fair were his decisions that his scale of assessments stood up with scarcely a complaint or a question for nearly a century. Here, historians suspect, is where he got his cognomen "the Just."

All this gave Athens the rounding out of widespread power which she needed for a brilliant career, and the city lost no time in turning prospects into realities. The almost immediate aftermath of these arrangements was the "Golden Age of Athens."

CHAPTER XXII

Greek Thought Comes to Flower in Athens

THE GOLDEN AGE of Athens in the fifth century B.C. can be examined from many angles. The best approach, however, for a study of the mind at work seems to lie through the psychological texture and emotional color of Athenian life at the time. These elements in turn can be set forth readily by tracing the rise of Hellenic taste and skill in art out of older forms taken over from the original cradles of civilization.

In both Egypt and Mesopotamia a rigid, formal type of art spoke unmistakably of the anthill concept of life, a social philosophy which counted the individual as nothing and held gods, kings and the state to be everything. The homely doings of common people figure only in the retinues of the nobles and the kings. The one other subject which stirred the artist to creative effort was glorification of the gods by every device which the childish understandings of the age could suggest.

The supreme example of this psychology probably is the Assyrian winged bull. In it the flight of the eagle and the power of the bull were capped with the wisdom of man, embodied in a bearded human head—a sufficient testimony to naïveté in putting together attributes which would be impressive enough to constitute a god! The heavily formalized treatment of subjects, usually shown side on in statuesque pose, is equally eloquent of artists ridden by ritual and tradition. It tells us plainly that these artists would as soon have tried to picture a pyramid built upon its point as they would have tried to put anything of themselves or their feelings into their art.

This anthill viewpoint began melting away in Minoan and Mycenean art, as could be expected from the character of these cultures. In the maritime Minoan state the sailor citizen had to be more self-

235

reliant, more capable of thinking for himself, than did the human ant who lived in a ponderous, regimented state along the Nile, the Euphrates or the Tigris. The Minoan artist, therefore, could and did break away from complete obsession with gods, kings and the state. Throughout his art a wealth of flowers and similar decorations on pottery and metal objects bespeak his interest in the joys and doings of this earthly life.

But even with all this the Minoan at best was still an adolescent in art. He had a good eye for detail and a knack for expressing motion, but only rarely did he show any ability to achieve "sweep," "feeling" or "soul," as do those masterpieces which strike home a mood or message to the observer. Like the growing boy who loves tales of adventure and despises romance, tragedy and the clash of mind upon mind, the Minoan was factual, objective and "photographic" in his art. Nothing suggests any deep interest in the soul of man or in its struggles for satisfaction in this life and in the hereafter.

Now, however, the Hellenes were bringing into the world a viewpoint upon life which would place such interests at the very heart and center of artistic effort!

They were learning, through their philosophers, to want something better than the crude collection of capricious, clashing forces which made up the universe for their predecessors. They were striving for simple yet far-reaching laws which would endow all Nature with the same unified majestic symmetry that man sees in the nightly wheeling of the stars. Their position as citizens was teaching them that the individual does count in the social scheme; hence his interests, his joys and his sorrows deserve expression.

Hellenic art, therefore, mirrored all these trends in thought with ever-increasing power as growing wealth gave artists increasing support and as the artists learned how to work out their ideas in paint, in stone and in the wording of poems and dramas. Their feeling for the majestic symmetry found in natural law was expressed in the sublime lines and perfect proportions of Greek temples. In their statues they could express joy, despair, heroism or contemplation as well as standing, running or leaping. The noted *Discobolus* or discus thrower is not merely throwing a discus; he is striving with every fiber of his feeling and all his soul to make a *winning* throw. An aura of wisdom always sets off an Athena unmistakably from a voluptuous Aphrodite; nobody could mistake a statue of Hercules, charged as it would be with prodigious power, for the clean-limbed sun-god Apollo.

Such art proves beyond question that the Hellenes had all the mental capacity and emotional sensitivity needed to achieve a rounded, satisfactory life for all mankind. They had insight into human nature and the impulses which serve as mainsprings of human effort—an insight which seems almost uncanny when we read the dramas, the poems and the philosophic discussions of the age.

Between them the dramatists, the poets and the sophists had come by this time to understand man pretty much as modern psychology does. They saw him as a creature of brute impulses and animal passions, with intelligence presiding none too certainly over the lower nature. They recognized, too, that the fundamental driving force in man, once brute needs had been satisfied, was the urge toward *self-aggrandizement*—the craving to enlarge himself in the eyes of his fellows, to make himself more important.

All this might suggest that the situation was set for a rapid movement toward a truly satisfactory scheme of life for mankind. Unfortunately history gives a far different verdict. The facts of human nature likewise show readily why a happy outcome was impossible at this time.

When all is said and done the driving power in self-aggrandizement is the desire of the individual to aggrandize *himself*. Heretofore human effort had been cast in group actions, the kind of effort which we have called "anthill"; but in the ultimate analysis this was personal enough, even for the individual. He worked, thought and fought for his group, because to his way of thinking his fortune was wrapped up in the fortune of the group. Promoting the state and enlarging the power of the state's gods was the logical way to enlarge and enrich his own life.

Now, however, these Hellenes had seen themselves as *individuals*, the architects of their own fortunes. Therefore they acted exactly like a child with a new toy. They rode the new idea to death. In their enthusiasm for promoting individual interest they forgot that, after all, in civilized life a man can live *only within the framework provided by society*.

The fundamental needs of the situation therefore called upon these Hellenes to look to this framework, even before they thought of themselves. They had many an age-old evil to sweep away, certainly —slavery is one glaring example—before society could give them a really sound chance to aggrandize themselves. But they had caught a new idea, and like children they were off in hot pursuit of this glittering ideal of self-aggrandizement, without thinking out the full requirements of the problem.

The shining proof of this is the development which occurred in philosophy at this time—the rise of *sophistry*.

The Sophists—a term which meant "those who were wise"—were rebels against the old Ionian search for the *arche,* or secret of the universe. They ranged in temperament and ability from men of the loftiest ideals and highest integrity, such as Protagoras, Gorgias and Hippias, down to out-and-out tricksters and charlatans; but regardless of their characters they were in good general agreement about the proper use of philosophy. Let the putterers and the graybeards of the older schools spend their lives probing the universe if they liked; meanwhile, here on earth was man conducting his life, and the Sophist proposed to deal with man.

Now to explain or understand him—what profit lay in that? The Sophists proposed to persuade, move, sway and thereby control man. That is, they proposed to combine the functions of the teacher, the lawyer and the publicist. To do this required new arts—rhetoric, dialectic, oratory and the like; the Sophists addressed themselves to developing these arts. And all this wisdom they would teach to anyone who wished to acquire power over his fellow men, provided the pupil would pay a proper fee for the training.

The naturalistic philosophers had not been attracted to bustling commercial Athens with its fighting and its democratic brawls, but to the Sophists Athens looked like a veritable heaven. They swarmed in from everywhere, and in the days to come they became the fashion. Most rich families gave their sons a term of study with a Sophist to round out their education.

This development cannot be called other than good in principle. It focused man's attention upon the topic which should have engaged man's best thought since the start of the human career—that is to say, man himself, his nature and his needs. Most appropriately, too, this focusing occurred in the most suitable environment imaginable: the world's first democracy, where men were trying to conduct their affairs according to their own judgments and preferences instead of by prescription from magic and tradition.

As sophistry took shape, however, it had one disastrous weakness—a weakness which proved fatal for Athens in the end. Sophistry failed from first to last to see beyond its immediate objective. Never did it look beyond promotion of naked self-interest to the crying social needs of the time. This was to ruin Athens in the end, because society needed attention most of all.

At this time the Athenians were confronted, however well or poorly they realized it, with the fact that their first feat of freeing reason and democracy to do their work had brought a strange new control to bear upon the problem of whether a state or a culture could prosper or even survive.

Thus far through history, habit and emotional fixation through the national faith had been the cement of society. Men had been kept going regardless of dismal outlook, because they took it for granted that their lot was the will of the gods. It never occurred to them that they might strive for a better lot.

But now these Athenians had lit a new light with their doctrine that the individual citizen counted and was entitled to a voice in the conduct of the state. Once they did this, blind habit and faith imposed from above no longer would do. The scheme of society had to strike the *individual* as useful to him before he would be whole-heartedly loyal to it. He had to see where *he* was profiting in terms of the fundamental human quest for Leisure, Security and Freedom.

Superficially the Athenian state met this requirement superbly. After the Persian Wars every Athenian who qualified as a citizen was riding the crest of the golden wave, a wave rolled up by the fact that the Athenian navy had given Athens command of all Hellenic commerce, just as Athenian silver matched Persian gold as the favorite monies of the civilized world. But beneath this glittering surface the foundations of the state were far from sound.

Once the cement of blind faith and habit had been loosened and a state must depend for coherence upon satisfying its members, satisfaction must reach down to the very roots of society before the state can be called secure. But the Athenians proved utterly unable to see this. They were trying to make a democracy work upon an economic foundation of slavery, and if any truth ever has been proved in history, it is that this combination will not work.

The competition of slave labor drags down and utimately destroys free labor. When free labor dies the state loses its citizen defenders in time of war, and it has no middle class which is determined to make democracy work in time of peace. It has nothing but slaves and a slaveowning aristocracy, and such a combination can work only when held together by anthill discipline. It is hopeless as a social scheme for a democracy.

But no Sophist or other Athenian seemed to realize the menace in this unsound social scheme. The proof stands clear in the record—and fortunately for easy understanding the full story of what happened can be told in terms of one man, a man who ranks easily with Caesar and Napoleon in his influence upon history. His name was Pericles, and we can understand him best by commencing with his education and training for his life task.

He was born in a wealthy family in 490 B.C.—the year of the first Hellenic triumph over the Persians at Marathon—and he grew in the highly stimulating atmosphere of unfolding glory in Athenian art and literature. As a youth and a young man he heard the plays of Aeschylus (525–456 B.C.), first of the outstanding Greek dramatists. The next genius of tragedy, Sophocles (496–400 B.C.), came to manhood almost to a year with Pericles. Hence from boyhood on Pericles soaked up understanding of human nature from these masters, and his later career proved that he knew how to use this knowledge as a key to power with remarkable profit to himself.

For his formal education his parents generously gave him a term with each type of philosophy, the sophistic and the naturalistic, and from what we know of the latter we get a fine insight into the level of knowledge at the time. Our knowledge comes from our records of the views held by his teacher, Anaxagoras (500?–428? B.C.). Anaxagoras was a "reconciler," a man who strove to combine the Eleatic and the Heraclitean views into a sound scheme of knowledge.

Pericles was taught that everything was a combination of bits (*spermata,* or seeds). These bits are split, purified and recombined by the force of the original Mind or *nous,* the pure ruler of all life. The results of this action appear to the mind of man as motion—a view which has a strange prevision of modern doctrines held by the atom splitters and the Einsteins in modern physics! In astronomy Anaxagoras taught that the earth rotated and flung off stones; these stones, when heated, glowed and appeared to the eyes of man as stars. The sun was a mass of blazing metal as big as the Peloponnesus.

From these teachings we get a good measure of the state of knowledge at the time. Beyond this the relations between Pericles and Anaxagoras give us an accurate gauge upon the *status* of knowledge and education at this time.

Pericles retained Anaxagoras as a counselor all through life—and also had to defend him in the courts or by political pressure against many a charge of impiety and sacrilege. The doctrine about the sun was particularly objectionable, because to the populace the sun was the flaming chariot of Apollo. What would Apollo think if such insults were allowed to go unpunished, and would he continue his many benefits to man, such as the Delphic oracle and his beneficent habit of driving the sun daily across the sky to light and warm the earth? Such complaints showed that the way of the philosopher was not yet easy when he came close to state religion. The important fact, however, was that Pericles *could* defend his friend. A century or so earlier both men would have been executed out of hand.

In due time Pericles finished his education and entered public life, as superbly equipped for a statesman's career as ever any man has been throughout time. The Hellenes of his time described him as one of the handsomest of men and a magnificent orator. In his public appearances he was said to have radiated the dignity of a god.

His career as a young man may be covered by saying that he belonged to the "opposition party." His political creed was "Athens over all," whereas the dominant party held to the working combination of Athenian sea power and Spartan land power which had won the Persian Wars. In 461, however, the two powers fell into a bitter quarrel born out of highhanded actions by each one, and Athens launched the First Peloponnesian War (459–446 B.C.) to crush Sparta and make Athens the one dominant power over all the Hellenes.

The military events of the war were marked by Athenian maritime victory throughout; but on land, after brilliant opening successes, the tide ran strongly against Athens, and in the twelfth year of the war the Athenians had to cry quits. The discredited war party put forward its most popular member, young Pericles, as peacemaker, and in 445 B.C. he managed to get Athens out of the mess with a restoration of territories all around and a truce with Sparta which was to run for thirty years.

This diplomatic triumph made Pericles practically a political dictator in Athens, and he was in position at last to show how well or how poorly he understood the political and social needs of the state. It may be said at once that he missed his opportunity. Instead of taking the hard path marked out by Solon a century and a half earlier, the path which aimed at developing a sturdy citizenry, Pericles followed the lure of popularity through show and glory. He adopted the policy followed by Pisistratus—magnificent public works, gorgeous entertainment and a booming foreign trade.

The Pisistratean public buildings on the Acropolis had been reduced to a smoking rubbish heap by the Persians just before the Battle of Salamis, and restoration had been slow. Pericles dipped into the treasury of the Delian League and finished rebuilding everything on a breath-taking scale. Between 448 and 437 B.C. the architects Ictinus and Callicrates and the sculptor Phidias finished a new Parthenon. It was by far the most beautiful building achieved in all antiquity, if not indeed in all time. Pericles also provided long walls to connect Athens with her port, the Piraeus, five miles to the southwest; in the port were three magnificent harbors, one for commerce and two for the war galleys.

What amounted to a state theater was established by paying needy citizens the fee required for attending the national religious Dionysian festivals every year. Pericles also instituted pay for jury duty and other services to the state. This has often been criticized as amounting in effect to bribery of the electorate, but the press of government business and the relatively small number of citizens practically compelled it. Even the poor citizen had to serve almost continually in some capacity; he could not make ends meet without a few obols a day from the state. (An obol was 1/6 of a drachma; hence if the 4-drachma "owl" be considered analagous to the American dollar, an obol would be comparable to the American nickel. The bribe, if bribe it was, could hardly be called magnificent.)

For many years these policies seemed gloriously successful. The rich were getting richer, and even the poorest citizen was bedazzled by all the show. He was a member of the most powerful, glorious and brilliant state on earth—and what more could man ask than that?

Well, he could have asked for many things in the way of social reform to make the state secure, if only he could have foreseen the future! But he did not, and so Athens pursued her heady career of glory until destiny began presenting its bill for these mistakes.

During all this period the backland Hellenes, and particularly the Spartans, developed more and more hatred and jealousy of Athens. They feared the corrupting effect of Athenian luxury and sophistry upon their religion; they resented Athenian dominance of trade. At length a minor revolt in the Delian League, produced by some high-handed Athenian chicanery, drew in Sparta and caused all this rancor to boil over into the Second Peloponnesian War (431–421 B.C.).

Pericles, however, was not dismayed.

He could not hope for a victory in the field against the thirty thousand soldiers he knew the allies were planning to send against Athens in the spring of 431, but he saw no need of even trying to do so. Athens had long since outgrown dependence upon the country-side for food; the sea was her field, and she was drawing much of her grain from as far away as the Crimea. The countryside could be abandoned, then, to the attackers; Athens could stand behind her walls, with the open sea at her back and under her command. The well-known inability of the Spartans and other inland Hellenes to stay away very long from their home affairs would do the rest.

All this was sound strategy, but Pericles had overlooked the health problem of trying to withstand a siege in a city such as Athens.

All the architectural efforts of his time had been devoted to public buildings; the people still lived in miserable stone and plaster hovels, horribly crowded together. Sanitation was nonexistent; the open streets served as both sewers and garbage dumps as well as for travel. The Athenian addiction to open-air life and exercise had maintained a fair level of health even under these handicaps during normal times, but during a siege, with all Attica crowded in for refuge on top of the normal population, the menace to health was frightful.

As events fell out, it was precisely this menace which struck Athens down in the war. Plague broke out and ravaged the population until Athens could barely man all her walls. Then a second plague, a moral plague, boiled up. Pericles was brought face to face with the perils of leadership in a democracy such as Athens once calamity replaces prosperity. His inveterate enemies managed to play upon public resentment of the current tribulations and procured his con-viction and ousting from office on a charge of embezzling public funds.

The peanut politicians who had ousted him soon proved their in-ability to cope with the troubles of the time, and a repentant people recalled their great leader; but now he was broken and done. He is said to have survived one attack of the plague; but his two sons had died of it, and in the autumn of 429 either the plague, heartbreak, or both, carried him off with his lifework collapsing before his eyes. No Shakespearean or Greek tragedy ever offered a more perfect study in rise and fall than we have in this story of a brilliant but unsound Golden Age and its creator.

The rest of the Athenian career was a short, dreary epilogue of failure, and like the earlier chapters of the Athenian career the story had a brilliant leader as its center. Unfortunately, this leader was a persuasive but utterly unscrupulous young demagogue named Alcibiades.

The Athenians had patched up a not too onerous peace in 421 B.C., but Alcibiades preferred war as a setting for his undoubted military talents. He managed to achieve this end within eight years, and the resulting Third Peloponnesian War (413–403 B.C.) brought Athenian power to utter ruin.

During the war Alcibiades served as commander while affairs looked promising—and fled or even deserted to the Spartans when trouble loomed. One of his desertions left an incompetent in command of the attack upon Spartan's ally Syracuse, in Sicily, and in 413 B.C. the expedition was utterly destroyed. He was recalled for a time, but a slight defeat lost him his new ascendancy, and he retired to an estate on the Hellespont where he ended his days. Thereupon the mob completed its own ruin.

An unfortunate loss of life in the fleet due to storm brought a death sentence against the commanders. Thereupon men who were competent commanders fled to avoid so deadly a duty, and woeful incompetents sailed in 405 to give battle to the Peloponnesian fleet at the river Aegospotami, as the Athenians called the Dardanelles, in an effort to break open the blocked route to the Crimean grain supply. While waiting to force a battle the Athenians left their ships beached and unguarded every night, and at length the Spartans seized this easy chance, destroyed practically the entire fleet and had Athens at their mercy.

A short siege of Athens itself compelled surrender on terms which ruined the once-proud Queen of the Aegean. In 404 B.C. she gave up the remnants of her fleet, tore down her walls and accepted the dominance of Sparta by entering the Spartan League. The first large-scale experiment in democracy had had its century of glory, thanks to a few able men, and had sunk to ruin, thanks to its own weaknesses.

Such an event necessarily is an outstanding milestone in the human record—the more so, since the setback was not redeemed for more than two thousand years. A diluted form of democratic government was coming into the world stage at the time, it is true, in Rome; but it soon gave way to despotism. Popular government did not emerge again in strength until modern times in English-speaking lands.

Nevertheless, much that had been gained was not lost. The light of free intelligence had been lit in the world, and after Aegospotami it grew brighter, not dimmer. The chastened Athenians were willing now to study the nature and needs of human society, and so, after the Golden Age had collapsed in politics, they produced a Golden Age in philosophy. Art itself—sculpture, architecture, painting, drama, music —did not die.

From all this a keynote for the times to come can be struck without difficulty. The world of thought did not face any utter collapse, with a necessity for rebuilding from the ground up. Rather, it faced a necessity for reconstruction, of salvaging the good and correcting the evils which had generated the setback.

When we say this, however, we are speaking with aid from hindsight. We need not expect any such logical approach to the situation at this time. The Athenian philosophers, it is true, attempted to think the problem through, and with some success; but they were too deeply enmeshed in various evils of their day to discern many a needed change. Also, Athens was broken as a power; leadership in practical affairs had passed to stronger, ruder peoples. They could be expected to set the clock back with a heavy-handed return to "the good old ways," and mankind would have to fumble once more through many an error and heartbreak before it won back the lost ground and regained its chance to improve upon the Athenian experiment.

Just so did events fall out, commencing with a black reaction in government.

During the half century which followed the fall of Athens, Hellas was torn by Sparta's attempt to fasten her conservative stand-pat policies upon the Hellenic cities and the desperate resistance offered by these cities, under the leadership of Thebes, to this dominance. Epaminondas and the Thebans finally crushed Spartan power in the Battle of Leuctra in 371 B.C., but by then all the Hellenic states were exhausted and ripe for conquest by any sufficiently determined power. Such a power appeared in Macedonia, a half-barbarous land to the north of the Hellenic peninsula proper, and the conquest was completed in one generation by an outstanding leader, Philip of Macedon (383–336 B.C.).

Philip's son Alexander (356–323 B.C.) followed as king when only nineteen years old, not without suspicion of having a hand in the assassination of his father during a drunken court festival. His first act was to strike with all the power of Zeus himself hurling thunderbolts at the Greek cities which thought he would not be man enough to maintain his father's power; then within two years he took up his father's plan of breaking the Persian power by embarking, in the spring of 334 B.C., upon what turned out to be the conquest of the entire civilized world excepting India and China.

The details of his campaigns and battles, down to his death of fever in Babylon in 323 B.C. at the age of thirty-three, need not detain us; what counted most in the history of thought was his system of government.

Alexander knew men and history well enough to trust nothing save strong lieutenants and ample military force to hold his empire together. But he knew also how religion could help, especially in holding Asiatic peoples to an allegiance. Accordingly, as he penetrated deeper and deeper into Persian territory, he began insisting upon being honored as a god.

Until recent times this was considered simply the result of becoming intoxicated with success to the point of imagining himself a god, but many modern scholars see in this demand a clearheaded stroke of policy in thorough keeping with the thoughts of the times. Westermann expresses this view clearly in the *Encyclopedia of the Social Sciences:*

Alexander sent out from Susa a demand to the Greek city-states that each city place him among their city gods. The origin of this demand, to which the Greek cities agreed, is purely Greek. . . . It implies nothing as to any personal conviction on Alexander's part of his own divinity. The explanation is now generally accepted by historians that the measure was political. It relieved him of the embarrassment caused by the independence of the Greek city-states. . . . If recognized as a god in each of the city-states, he was thereby placed above the laws which its citizens might pass.

Neither would such a demand cause any wrench to Greek thought or religious convictions! As Westermann says, "the distance between gods and men had never been great in the anthropomorphic polytheism of the Greeks. To add one more god to the list of their divinities was not impossible or even difficult for them."

Beyond the benefits to be expected in Greece lay the immense value of being accepted as a god in Asia. There, where peoples considered the temples and the gods the mainspring of all life, a place in the Pantheon was worth as much as a strong garrison for maintaining the authority of a regime.

Thus in politics reaction was complete. The anthill concept of government had rolled back over the world. The only changes were

substitution of Macedonians for Persians and elevation of the conqueror himself to the status of a god. But this was the black side
of the situation. A bright side existed, too, in that with the Macedonians came Hellenic thought. Moreover, Alexander's very act of
deifying himself soon gave thought a freedom it never had enjoyed
down to this time.

Previously the only attacks upon the control of daily life and habits
by religion had been made by the philosophers. Considerable freedom of thought had been won in fact under Athenian democracy,
but it never had been conceded in principle. But now this authority
of religion was struck a deathblow in the minds of the new rulers,
the generals who divided Alexander's empire among themselves after
his death. They saw national and tribal deities for exactly what they
were in matters of politics—that is, as useful aids to authority. Hence
they enforced public respect for local deities and strove to elevate
themselves to that stature whenever possible, but they had no *moral*
zeal for such religion. A Ptolemy ruling Egypt might suppress a
defamer of Egyptian gods if the offender was haranguing crowds in
the streets, but if a philosopher did this among his fellow philosophers and his pupils of Greek race, why should a Greek ruler care?

The resulting slackness in enforcement of religious doctrine was of
incalculable benefit in freeing thought, and therein lay the setting
for the culmination of Greek science and philosophy. We are ready,
then, to see this culmination taking place.

CHAPTER XXIII

Athenian Philosophy and the Alexandrine Age

W‌E HAVE ACCOUNTED for the full blooming of Athenian philosophy *after* the end of Athenian political power as an instance of adversity proving better than prosperity as a teacher, and this can be justified by considering three men: Socrates, Plato and Aristotle.

They are ideal for the purpose, not only because they were by all counts the three giants of Greek thought but because they lived, roughly, a lifetime apart and among them covered the entire Golden Age of Athenian philosophy. Socrates lived in the dying days of Athenian political glory, and he suffered death in the end for alleged offenses against Athenian religion. Plato had a freer time between the fall of Athens and the rise of Macedonian power, and Aristotle was both the tutor of Alexander for twelve years after 347 B.C. and the beneficiary of his pupil's patronage throughout Alexander's life. Let us start our account, then, with Socrates (469–399 B.C.), who lived from the end of the Persian Wars until after the fall of Athens!

Socrates was a squat and ugly man, a veritable satyr among the handsome Hellenes of his day. Mentally he was a curious mixture of high moral viewpoint and serene, kindly temperament, with the qualities of a teasing, intellectual gadfly. His favorite method of philosophizing, later called the Socratic after him, was to let the other person talk, ask questions at appropriate points and gradually lead his opponent into contradictions which ruined his position.

In fundamental doctrine Socrates rounded out a trinity in which the naturalists and the Sophists formed the other two members. They had concerned themselves respectively with the nature of the universe and with swaying the minds of men; Socrates concerned himself with the *morals* of men and the *ethics* of society, all for the health of men's souls.

His prescription for preserving the health of the soul was the simple one of truth and justice—or, more sharply, the preachment that in knowledge lay the secret of both happiness and success. The man who knew the full consequences of his acts, first upon others and ultimately by recoil upon himself, would certainly do right, if only for his own ultimate good; and once all men had this guiding knowledge, all would be well with the world.

Therein Socrates placed his finger squarely upon what Athens needed above all else if the state was to endure. Knowledge—and particularly the knowledge that every act reacts sooner or later upon the actor for better or for worse—would have been the salvation of the state if only the Athenians had been willing to follow the light given them. So likewise did Socrates point out the road to new progress for philosophy, with his insistence upon use of the *hypothesis*—that is, setting up a theory and then testing it against facts to see whether it held water. Had the philosophers grasped the full meaning of his procedure, they would have been led into experimentation and so into a birth of modern science.

Socrates must be ranked, then, as one of the wisest of men throughout all time—but, as might be expected, he encountered the fate which all too often is the reward of being so far ahead of one's times.

During the "Terror" of 404, when the frightened Athenians drove competent men from Athens in droves before the final disaster of Aegospotami, Socrates was a member of the council, but he stoutly refused to make unjust arrests. Thereafter he was a biting critic of democratic follies, and finally, to drive him from Athens, a democratic leader named Anytus inspired charges against him of "corrupting the youth" and "neglect of the gods . . . and the practice of religious novelties." He confounded his enemies, however, by standing trial instead of fleeing. When a death verdict was rendered he accepted it, refused to accept a chance to escape and died, to complete the record of democratic folly as applied to him.

The second of the three philosophic giants, Plato (427–347 B.C.), had been a devoted young friend of Socrates in the latter's last years. He also taught Aristotle and thus served as a connecting link between these two. His life and his methods of teaching also linked the crude earlier Athenian education with the full flowering of schools during and after Alexander's day.

Socrates had taught, for example, by wandering about Athens talking to men and by discoursing in the homes of friends. Plato came from a rich family and could afford to devote his life to teaching philosophy. He did so in a regularly organized school which he founded—the famed Academy of Athens.

The academy was really a city pleasure grove, the *Accademia,* outside the city; Plato's school was named for it because the master taught his pupils by discoursing as they walked about in the grove. This academy soon gave rise to similar institutions during and after Alexander's time, and thus again Plato linked the old and the new. In the development of thought itself he occupies the same place—but not with equally happy results for mankind, if we may take the word of many a modern student of human affairs! A brief glimpse of his doctrine, as set forth in his dialogue *Timaeus,* will show why.

Socrates had taught that the real framework of the universe was Forms or Patterns of likeness and unlikeness, good and bad and the like; the universe men know through the senses is merely an "overlay" of appearances, organized on these Forms somewhat as individual beads are organized on threads to form a beaded pattern. Things and acts are good or bad, true or false, according to the "Form" on which they are strung. This doctrine sometimes is misrepresented because Socrates called a Form an *idea* or *eidos.* The word "idea" is often taken in the modern sense of meaning a *product of thought,* with the implication that all these aspects of reality are creatures of thought. Socrates meant nothing of the sort; hence the word Form is better than "idea" for a translation of his term.

In the *Timaeus* Plato carried this doctrine to heights that are all but unintelligible to anyone save a trained philosopher. A simplified version of the full doctrine can be offered, however, by starting with his teaching that in the beginning God made the soul of the universe out of three elements—Being, or sheer existence, Identity and Difference. These became the basis of all later Forms. Then God made the *body* of the universe out of earth, fire, air and water. Still later he made the subordinate gods and the reasoning part of man's soul. Thus the Universal Soul was the root of everything; but Plato did not exclude the senses from his scheme. They could detect imperfect aspects of reality from tangible objects and from physical motions and activities.

If this theory of the universe seems highly abstract and speculative, so much the better. It justifies the complaint of modern students that Plato represents the very height of the mistaken Hellenic tendency to spin ideas out of thought instead of building them up from proved facts. Anyone can see at once, for example, how Plato spun his "soul of the universe" out of his own thinking. The ingredients of this soul, Being, Identity and Difference, are simply labels for certain patterns of understanding which the mind uses in its thinking. Obviously, then, he erected his own working processes of intelligence into the foundation stones of the universe!

This was bad enough because it never could get anywhere; the next man could spin another doctrine, and each doctrine would be nothing more than mental cobwebs. But critics such as Hogben charge Plato with an even worse sin against valuable thinking, in his insistence upon "pure thought" instead of patient experimenting and testing as the source of knowledge.

Hogben complains bitterly in his *Mathematics for the Million* about Plato's attitude toward geometry. Plato taught that geometry was properly an exercise for the intellect, to be indulged in *for the exercise,* and he sneered at application of geometry to the affairs of men as a degrading business fit only for slaves. Thereby he set a fashion, according to Hogben, which has been the curse of mathematics from that day to ours. He changed it from a useful and therefore fascinating subject into a sterile and boring exercise in a vacuum. So likewise did he help to deflect Hellenic thought in many other fields from pursuit of the helpful and practical into useless and sterile "pure thinking"—and thereby, the critics charge, he contributed mightily to turning the brilliant Hellenic start in the use of reason into ultimate stagnation and failure.

Such criticisms seem more or less justified wherever Plato's influence can be traced in later thinking, and these evil tendencies were only partially corrected by the third and last of the first-rank Hellenic philosophers. This was Plato's star pupil Aristotle (384–322 B.C.).

Aristotle was as keen mentally as Plato, but some would say in our times he was "tougher minded," more "down to earth." At times he indulged in high-flown abstract speculations like Plato, but in the main he believed, as Socrates had, in building up knowledge by careful observation and careful reasoning about the facts observed. During his life he collected, sifted and presented practically all the knowledge that existed in his time, and even today his writings have what seems to us a seemingly modern flavor and viewpoint. No wonder that in densely ignorant medieval times, some fifteen hundred years later, Aristotle's texts seemed a veritable Bible of scientific knowledge!

Today we tend to follow the early modern scientists in their reaction against this attitude by dwelling almost entirely upon Aristotle's mistakes. These he made in plenty, but his errors were those which were common to his time, and dwelling upon them tends to obscure his important achievement of gathering together and organizing all this knowledge.

We tend also to overlook the service he rendered to mankind by instilling a measure of his own enthusiasm for knowledge in the young Alexander. Since Alexander in turn inspired his successors to carry on this devotion to knowledge in their respective domains, Aristotle undoubtedly launched a tremendous surge forward in human thinking. A final fact about his record is his establishment of a rival to Plato's academy in Athens after he had finished tutoring Alexander. His school was called the Lyceum from the *Lykeion* or Temple of Apollo, because he taught in the temple grounds.

After Aristotle formal philosophy advanced scarcely at all. He had built a well-rounded account of the universe and of man, one which was consistent within itself, provided certain errors were accepted as truth. To Hellenic philosophers, with their inveterate tendency to place intellectual consistency ahead of accurate, tested fact, this seemed to complete the task of philosophy. Why waste time trying to improve upon perfection?

This smug satisfaction was reinforced probably by a similar achievement in a parallel field. While the three philosophic giants had been rounding out—as they thought—man's understanding of himself and the universe, others had been drawing up the record of the past. Athens had given birth to *history*.

History in the form of fragmentary annals and records of events had existed almost since the dawn of historic days, but so far as we know, the first man who tried to draw a mass of existing material together into a connected narrative was Herodotus (484?–425? B.C.) of Halicarnassus, the so-called Father of History. His *History* appeared about when the first Peloponnesian War ended and Pericles was building the Parthenon, and the Athenians thought well enough of it to vote Herodotus a reward of ten talents, worth nearly twenty-five thousand dollars in American money.

Such enthusiasm is easily understood, because in this *History* Herodotus set forth the achievements of the Hellenes, and particularly the Athenians, in repelling the tremendous Persian invasions in the decade before he himself had been born. This in itself was not a novel idea, but his way of treating the theme was utterly novel.

Before starting the story of the actual invasions he had introduced each antagonist properly, and to do this with fitting richness of detail he had traveled over the entire civilized world for perhaps seventeen years, gathering his material. The result was a *History* that contained six books of "introduction" and only three that dealt with the main theme, but the six books were a fascinating mine of information about the peoples treated, their past, their customs and their beliefs. Even better, he was a master of vivid, clear and colorful writing, and the *History* read with all the charm of a novel.

He also had a keen respect for accuracy that showed throughout the work in his habit of earmarking statements as (1) something which he himself saw, (2) something told him by people he believed worthy of belief and (3) something told him which he put down for whatever it might be worth. Against this must be set the observation that he was not critical in the modern sense of trying to explain the whys and wherefores of the various customs and events he related. He simply told the facts without analyzing motives or evaluating outcomes.

But even while his *History* was taking Athens by storm this critical attitude was taking shape in the mind of "the father of *scientific* history," Thucydides.

Thucydides is a somewhat mysterious figure since we do not know when he was born or when he died. According to ancient accounts he was born about 471 B.C.; the internal evidence in his work suggests a later date, about 460. Internal evidence, chiefly failure to treat certain events, also suggests that he did not live beyond 399. But probable reasons for his scientific viewpoint are much clearer.

He came of a family which owned gold mines in Thrace and therefore was accustomed, as all people concerned with gold and money must be, to analyzing trends in public affairs. While he was still a young man the struggle between Athens and Sparta broke out, and he recognized immediately that this struggle would shake the world of the Hellenes. Thereupon he resolved, as he said in his *History of the Peloponnesian War,* to keep an accurate account of the struggle in order to help all those in later generations "who desire an accurate knowledge of the past as a key to the future, which in all probability will repeat or resemble the past."

Nobody has ever stated the true value of history more accurately and neatly, and his workmanship was a match for his loftiness of purpose. He took no one person's word, or even one side's word, for anything; all his material was sifted and checked by comparison of views from each side. In this he was helped mightily by a bitter experience of his own. In 424 he had been named a cogeneral in command of operations in Thrace, and the results had been disappointing. The Athenians thereupon banished him, and he spent years traveling and studying in the lands of the enemy countries.

As a result of all this Thucydides produced a work which is a model for all later historians in method, quality and purpose; it is one of the shining monuments to human thought at its best. Also, unfortunately, it was like the philosophy of Socrates in being far ahead of its time. Impartial judgment in partisan matters lay beyond the powers of ordinary human nature then, just as now. The Hellenes were as unable as most of us are to use "an accurate knowledge of the past as a key to the future" whenever this accurate knowledge crossed their partisan prejudices. Hence this monumental work had to drop into the hopper of material which could serve only as a leaven in superior minds here and there, while the main stream of thought rolled on in lower and less progressive levels.

In point of time this work ran with the later years of Socrates and the earlier ones of Plato—and so when Aristotle is added after Thucydides in the field of history, the record of Hellenic thought is brought down to the time when Alexander's successors began relaxing religious restrictions upon thought.

The age which resulted from this is commonly called the Hellenistic Age because of the world-wide spread of Hellenistic thought. It could as well be called the Alexandrine Age, both because Alexander provided the political foundation for it and because the center of progress was Alexandria, the new city which the Macedonian conqueror founded on the westernmost mouth of the Nile.

With his usual keenness for practical detail Alexander picked the site in 332 B.C.—a spot along the curving sweep of the African coast where the little island of Pharos provided shelter in its lee from the open water. The site also was some twelve miles west of the Canopic mouth of the Nile and therefore promised to be reasonably free from the silting which continually filled all harbors built on the mud-laden Nile itself. It was near enough, however, for easy communication with this river, either along the coast or through a canal, and it had an abundant supply of fresh water in Lake Mareotis, at its back.

Alexander did not live to see his city built, but his general Ptolemy, who took Egypt and Alexandria as his share of the empire after Alexander died, pushed the plan forward energetically. Indeed, the city all but pushed itself, because Alexander had ruined Tyre, the leading maritime city of the time. Abundant business, therefore, was waiting for the new port as soon as it was ready.

East of the port Ptolemy and his successors, also called Ptolemies, built a veritable fairyland of gardens and lagoons, dotted with palaces, and they added the crowning touch of an imposing Pharos or lighthouse at the east end of the island. It was said to stand four hundred feet high, or one third the height of the Empire State Building in New York City. The cost was reported as eight hundred talents or, on the basis of the Athenian talent, nearly two million dollars. And the Ptolemies were equally generous toward scholars and learning.

Even the first Ptolemy, who spent the latter half of his eighty-four years fighting off other Macedonian rulers who coveted Egypt, found time and money for establishing a library. His successor, Ptolemy Philadelphus (309–246 B.C.), maintained a court which for brilliance compared with the Versailles of Louis XIV, and he considered the library and the schools as among the chief glories of his reign. Under such auspices the Greek intellect came to full flower, with a level of attainments which was not surpassed other than in a few special fields until during the seventeenth century after Christ.

Perhaps the best instance of this came in astronomy.

Long before Alexandrine days the earlier astronomers had swept away the mumbo jumbo of the earth being supported by elephants, tortoises, the god Atlas or even a sea that floated in space. They realized that the earth itself might as well do the floating, and they gave it the logical form for the purpose, that of a sphere. We know when this idea took shape because Anaximander, a contemporary of the first philosopher Thales, taught that the earth was a cylinder; but soon after, Pythagoras of Samos taught that the earth was a sphere.

To explain the changing appearances of the heavens through the year Eudoxus of Cnidus (408–355 B.C.) had developed the geometric concepts of orbits and equatorial and ecliptic planes which astronomers still use, during just about the same years in which Plato was evolving his philosophy. By the beginning of Alexandrine days only two questions seemed to be left unsettled. One was the question whether the earth or the sun was at the center of the celestial globe. The other was the problem of explaining the motion of the five visible planets, or "wandering stars," which seemed to crawl about inside the celestial sphere like luminous flies.

The Alexandrians started their assault upon these problems in the most truly scientific spirit imaginable, with several decades of patient

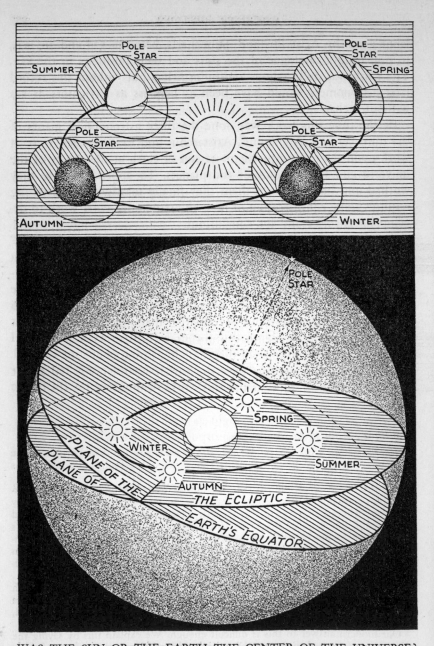

WAS THE SUN OR THE EARTH THE CENTER OF THE UNIVERSE?

The diagrams above show, at the top, the modern *heliocentric* theory that the sun is the center of the solar system. The lower diagram shows the ancient

Continued at bottom of the next page

labor given by Aristyllus and Timocharis, between 320 and 260 B.C., to preparing a catalogue of the stars and their positions in the sky. The work was dull, tedious and uninspiring, but without this record later astronomers would have been as helpless as navigators at sea without a chart.

By the time this work was done the three astronomical giants of the third century, Apollonius, Aristarchus and Eratosthenes, were at work upon the teasing problems of sun or earth at the center of the universe and the motions of the planets. To appreciate how they worked and how between them they finally managed to be wrong requires some consideration of how an astronomer *must* work to develop his theories and his conclusions.

Everyone can realize that an astronomer never can get "outside" his subject matter to view it in the round, in the way a biologist can examine a plant or an animal. That is, an astronomer cannot get outside the solar system; he is embedded in it and must do the best he can by looking out at whatever he sees. Having gathered in as much data as he can by observation, he must then set up a theory and test it by asking himself, "Does this theory explain every appearance I have found?" If it does the theory is true, so far as anyone can tell.

Now the accompanying diagrams show that under this test either the sun or the earth could be at the center of the universe (or of the

Continued from preceding page

geocentric view, which gave the earth this central position. Comparison of the diagrams will show why the ancients cannot be called foolish for taking this view.

For the first comparison a simple rotation of the earth upon its axis will explain day and night under either view. The ancients realized this, and many of them believed that the earth rotated. The seasons also can be explained equally well under either theory by taking into account the slant of the earth's axis relative to the plane of the *ecliptic*—that is, the plane fixed by the centers of the earth and the sun. Under either theory this slant places the Northern Hemisphere nearest the sun in June, farthest away in December, and at mid-distance in March and in September, thereby causing the seasons.

So far, then, the two theories are even. Now, however, comes the point which swung the ancients to the geocentric view. They knew that the North Pole points to the same star throughout the year—and how could this be, they asked, if the earth moved?

Our modern answer to this is difficult enough. We explain this by saying the stars are so far away that even the entire width of the earth's orbit makes no difference in the relative positions of the earth and the polestar. This concept is an extremely difficult one, and so we can hardly be surprised because the ancients preferred a view which served just as well, so far as they could tell, and did not require such a flight of fancy into all but infinite space.

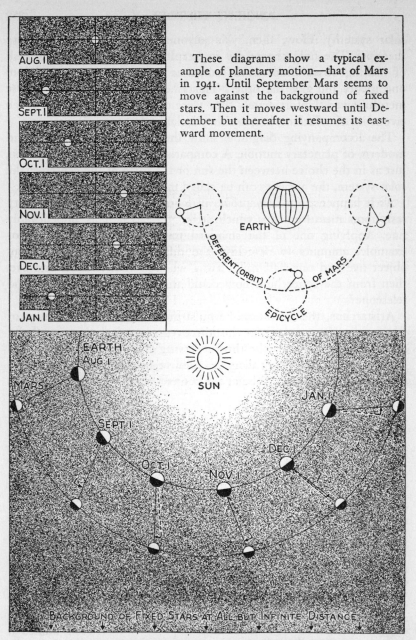

These diagrams show a typical example of planetary motion—that of Mars in 1941. Until September Mars seems to move against the background of fixed stars. Then it moves westward until December but thereafter it resumes its eastward movement.

AUG. 1
SEPT. 1
OCT. 1
NOV. 1
DEC. 1
JAN. 1

EARTH

DEFERENT (ORBIT)

EPICYCLE

OF MARS

EARTH
AUG 1

MARS

SUN

SEPT. 1

OCT. 1

NOV 1

DEC 1

JAN 1

BACKGROUND OF FIXED STARS AT ALL BUT INFINITE DISTANCE

THE PUZZLING MOTIONS OF THE PLANETS

Under the heliocentric view that the planets revolve around the sun this seemingly strange motion is explained by the respective positions of the planets

Continued at bottom of the next page

solar system). How, then, was anyone to choose between these theories? The only chance lay in keeping everlastingly at the task of making observations until sooner or later some fact fitted into one theory but not the other. This is exactly the procedure these men followed. Unfortunately they were doomed in advance to reach erroneous conclusions, because they lacked telescopes.

The accompanying diagrams show the two theories, ancient and modern, of planetary motion. A comparison will show that here, too, just as in the choice between the sun or the earth at the center of the solar system, the ancients can be called mistaken, but not stupid.

As it happens, our only proofs in favor of the heliocentric theory rest upon measurements which strike the layman as unbelievably fine. Applying one of the standard tests to the nearest star, for example, amounts to detecting the difference in direction of an object five and one half miles away when seen first from one eye, then from the other; and how could this be done without a good telescope?

Aristarchus, the astronomer who argued strenuously in favor of the correct theory that the earth moves around the sun, suffered particularly from this lack of fine observing equipment. As part of his attempt to build up his theory he tried to measure the distances to the sun and the moon. His methods were perfect in theory, but his

Continued from preceding page

in their orbits, as shown in the larger diagram below. The respective positions of the planets at the first of each month are shown joined by solid lines. The direction of the line for the *preceding* month is shown by a dotted line, and an arrow indicates the change during the month. These indications show why Mars appears to move eastward against the background of fixed stars, except when the two planets are moving practically parallel with each other. Then the earth's speed of 18 miles a second along its orbit enables it to pull ahead of Mars, which travels only 16 miles a second along a much larger orbit. Thus Mars seems to drop back or "move westward" during these months.

This theory, however, requires a background of stars at all but infinite distance, and the ancients were loath to accept this idea if any simpler one would explain this behavior of the planets. Apollonius worked out an explanation which did this, so far as anyone could see. He assumed an orbit for each planet, with the earth in the center of each orbit. But he did not have the planets move along these orbits. Instead what might be called a "center of motion" moved along the orbit, and the planet swung around it like a stone being whirled at the end of a string. While the planet was moving in the same direction as the center it would seem to move eastward against the background of the stars, but on the "back" part of each swing it would seem to move westward. In this scheme the orbit was called the deferent, and the circlings of the planet itself around its moving center were called epicycles.

crude instruments gave readings which made the distance to the sun figure out as only twenty times the distance to the moon, whereas it is actually 400 times as far away. Had he achieved a correct answer, he would have had a powerful argument in favor of the heliocentric theory, by showing that heavenly distances were enormous and suggesting why the polestar did not move. But his measurements suggested a relatively compact celestial mechanism, as called for by the rival theory.

Apollonius of Perga (about 265 B.C. to about 205 B.C.) championed the geocentric theory, and he needed no proofs at the time, because "common sense" seemed to be in his favor. He was confirmed, moreover, in it by using it—as he thought, successfully—to explain the motions of the planets.

The accompanying diagrams show the nature of this motion and explain it in terms of each theory, but they cannot show the final test of truth as between the two theories. This is the test of how well each theory works in actual calculation of planetary positions at any and all times, and here is where the geocentric theory won out with Apollonius. On this basis they could calculate positions which squared with everything he knew about planetary motions. He could not do so well with the heliocentric theory, and neither could anyone else; and so he would have been false to the spirit of science had he accepted the theory which we now know to be true.

Thus a fundamental error became embedded in astronomy—and not through stupidity, as we tend so smugly to believe, but because the techniques of the time were not sufficiently powerful to separate truth from error. What these ancients could do when problems lay within their powers is proved by Eratosthenes (276?–194? B.C.). He measured the size of the earth with amazing accuracy, and he did so with a method which was as ingenious as it was simple.

He learned that on the day of the summer solstice the sun shone straight down a well at Syene in south Egypt—that is, it was directly overhead. He therefore measured the shadow cast in a well at Alexandria on this same day and found that the sun stood 1/50 of a circle *south* of being overhead. This meant that Alexandria was 1/50 of the way north around the world from Syene. Since the north-south distance between the two places was five thousand stades, the circumference of the earth, therefore, was 50×5000, or 250,000 stades. If the stade (or stadium) be taken as 516.73 English feet, the circumference so obtained was 24,466⅓ statute miles. This is within 356⅙ miles of

the modern figure of 24,818½ miles for the circumpolar circumference
—an amazingly accurate result to get from shadows in two wells!

This record in ástronomy shows that the Alexandrine thinkers
could deal brilliantly with problems which lay within their powers.
But it shows, too, that they had reached the limit of these powers, as
long as they had no telescopes. Astronomy therefore fell into the same
state as philosophy. It became, as the ancients thought, a completed
and closed book. Systematizing replaced discovery, and of the sys-
tematizers, only two need mention: Hipparchus of Rhodes, who did
his important work between 146 and 126 b.c., and Claudius Ptolemaeus
or Ptolemy of Alexandria, who died about 161 a.d.

Hipparchus was the last of the creative astronomers. This was not
strange, since Hipparchus worked out about everything which could
be learned about astronomy without telescopes. He refined all previous star catalogues by years of patient observations, and he re-
measured all important astronomical constants, such as the inclination of the earth's axis to the plane of the ecliptic. He invented
trigonometry to help in his calculations, and he devised the system of
latitudes and longitudes which we still use on maps today. Also, as
was to be expected, he followed Apollonius rather than Aristarchus
in choosing the earth as the center of the universe.

Ptolemy was another Hipparchus, except that he lacked the spark
of creative genius. He gathered and compiled all previous work into a
tremendous study which now bears the name the Arabs gave it of
Almagest, "the Greatest." Unfortunately, in doing this he added nothing new of any value, and he did pick up many errors. Hence, when
astronomy "froze," so to speak, into a closed book, the Almagest, it
froze wrongly and progress was paralyzed until the crippling errors
were wrenched out in early modern times.

This record has been worth considering at length because it shows
beautifully what happened at this time, not only in astronomy but in
every field of thought. Astronomy had come to a dead end because
Hellenic thinking went only as far as observation, logic and argument
would take it; it never bothered to arm itself with powerful working
tools such as telescopes to help logic discover truth. So likewise did
the other sciences run into dead ends, for the same or similar reasons.
A splendid example is offered by medicine.

The Hellenes had made a good start toward really scientific medicine comparatively early in their career, thanks to the medical school
in the island of Cos and its most illustrious professor, Hippocrates.

This school had got its start roughly at about the time Thales of Miletus founded philosophy—that is, soon after 600 B.C.—and probably for the same reason. The Hellenes were putting together the medical lore obtained from the Egyptians and the Chaldeans and were applying the test of reason to the hodgepodge of practical observation, magic and outright covering up of ignorance with pompous mysticism. For doing this they were proceeding much as Thales had done. They tried to discover an *arche,* a beginning, a fundamental principle which would explain birth, growth and death and the difference between health and disease.

From out of our records of this effort looms dimly the figure of Hippocrates the man. According to Soranus he was born about 460 B.C., or just about the time Athens plunged into the First Peloponnesian War just before her Golden Age under Pericles, and he was said to have lived nearly a century. Beyond this we have almost no definite information; but the doctrines he laid down and their value to medicine are abundantly clear.

First and foremost he recognized, just as modern medicine does, that the key to success is making haste slowly. The human body is far too complex, and the penalties for mistakes are far too drastic, to permit roughshod application of theories conceived in advance. Study, observe, compare, test, preferably at the bedside, and be content to build your theories only when you can do so with proved facts; this is the proper spirit of medicine, and the Hippocratic school never wearied of preaching this doctrine. The Hippocratic literature consists largely of case results—symptoms, treatment and outcome—and the doctors were honest enough to record in most instances that the patient died!

The second fundamental tenet of Hippocratic medicine was another guiding star of modern medicine—reliance upon the healing powers of Nature. The physician served best when he helped Nature to help herself, and as part of the help these wise physicians insisted upon cleanliness, sanitation, temperance and general maintenance of health as the best insurance against disease.

As every modern medical man knows, such an attitude was the best possible intellectual foundation for rapid progress. But the slowness, patience and intellectual restraint which formed the core of the method were repugnant to the spirit of the days.

These Hellenes were like modern boys who acquire a new knife, gun or gadget of some sort. They had acquired a new mental tool, the power of reason, and they were bent upon obtaining quick answers with it. Even in medicine they insisted upon theorizing and generalizing before they knew enough about sickness to do so profitably, and they came out with just the erroneous and pernicious results that could be expected from such undue haste.

As a result the medical school which opened at Alexandria in 322 B.C. was saddled in advance with a "four humor" theory of disease, borrowed probably from the "four elements" of earth, air, fire and water, which the naïve physics of the day employed in its speculations. The "humors" were blood, black bile, yellow bile and phlegm (the modern mucus, and especially the mucus discharged by coughing). A proper combination of these humors meant health; an improper one brought disease or even death; and the function of medical treatment was to correct disorders in the functioning of the humors.

This was an improvement upon the Babylonian "possession by devils," as the cause of disease, in only one particular. It was not a sacred doctrine. It had been conceived by use of reason, and reason could correct the doctrine once the errors in it were recognized.

The Alexandrine school must be credited with starting to make such corrections even under its first professor, Herophilus (height of career about 300 B.C.). Herophilus believed in accurate data, and he believed in getting his data from the original source, the human body. He obtained bodies of criminals and dissected them before his pupils. He distinguished arteries and veins correctly. Unlike Aristotle, who had followed earlier doctrine in making the heart the seat of consciousness, Herophilus placed this function in the brain, and he understood that the nerves served for communications between the body and the brain.

Herophilus the anatomist was followed in the chair of medicine by a man with an equal flair for physiology, or *function,* as contrasted with anatomical *structure.* This man, Erasistratus, rejected the "four humor" theory in favor of *pneumatism,* a doctrine which often is falsely represented today as a belief that the arteries serve to carry air throughout the body.

This statement is correct as far as it goes, but to Erasistratus air was not "just air." It was the essence of life itself—an idea which the ancients obtained naturally enough from the fact that when a man stops breathing he stops living. Aside from this mistake Erasistratus did well. He distinguished sensory and motor nerves and guessed correctly that the convolutions of the brain served to add capacity.

He worked out the functions of the heart and made useful discoveries about bile, the spleen and the liver.

With such a start, and with benefit from continued experiment and observation, the Alexandrine school might well have worked itself free from preconceived theories and begun to grasp the real truth about the body. But unfortunately the very excellence of the start, with its bold innovations such as dissecting, was its undoing.

Of all scientists the physician is least free from control by popular prejudice and passion. He cannot work in scholastic seclusion as can the astronomer or the mathematician. His work lies among men—and, even harder, among men whose emotions and fears are aroused practically to the extent of swamping reason. They are aquiver with pain, ridden with fear of death for themselves or their loved ones and taut with anxiety concerning the fate the gods have in store for them. Hence any slightest action on the part of the physician which threatens to upset the luck of the tribe or the individual looses a flood of denunciation, passion or even mob violence. In Egypt dissection of dead bodies was particularly abhorrent because it prevented preparation of the body by mummification to serve as an earthly home for the departed soul.

The Alexandrine school therefore ran into trouble the moment it began promoting knowledge by dissection. While the Ptolemies were glad to encourage learning they did not care to let themselves in for civil disorder and they put the brakes on the medical school by forbidding dissection and other innovations which proved most offensive to local customs. Then and there the prospect for better medicine died. The later Alexandrine doctors were but little more than compilers and rehashers of old lore—and the one substantial achievement, if it could be called that, was the substitution of pneumatism for the older "four humor" theory of disease.

The record of progress stopping at dead ends can be capped off with two more examples of missed opportunity. The first is a footnote to the failures in astronomy and medicine, and it heightens tremendously the tragedy of the failure. Here these men were, keen thinkers who stood at dead ends for lack of the means needed to carry farther—and they had the key to entirely new realms of knowledge in their hands all the time, in their knowledge of the burning glass!

THE WONDER CITY OF THE HELLENISTIC WORLD

Created by order of Alexander the Great, the city of Alexandria was the wonder of its day for commerce and wealth, for freedom of thought and for the magnificence of its palaces, library and schools and temples. Dominating the sweep of splendid structures, stood the greatest wonder of all—the Pharos or lighthouse at the harbor entrance, a structure one third as high as the Empire State Building in New York City. Past it poured a steady outward stream of Egyptian wheat in sluggish round-bottomed cargo vessels, such as the one shown, to feed the teeming cities of the Mediterranean world; and in return came fine products from all this area, until the days when Roman power collapsed.

The burning glass was the same device we know—a lens which concentrates radiation from the sun sufficiently to set fire to paper and other easily ignited materials. Now anyone who looks through a burning glass can hardly fail to notice its magnifying power. Had the Alexandrians been experiment minded, any astronomer who noticed this power would have been struck by its value for sharpening his observations. The telescope would have followed easily, and thereby all technical difficulties would have been swept away. Progress could have marched with seven-league boots thereafter in astronomy. So also could they have given medicine that invaluable key to knowledge, the microscope. But they were not experiment minded. The burning glass remained a mere burning glass, and the opportunity was missed.

A last example, and perhaps the most suggestive of all, was failure to seize upon a wide-open opportunity to win the services of the steam engine.

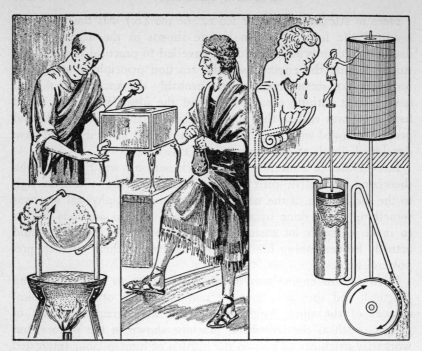

SLOT MACHINES AND STEAM ENGINES IN ALEXANDRIA

Three famous devices shown above illustrate the Alexandrian genius for gadgets. At the upper left one of the men is working a "coin-in-the-slot" machine in a temple entrance. When he drops the coin it will trip a lever, and a dash of holy water will fall into the devotee's waiting hand. At the lower left is Hero's toy steam engine. A shallow boiler delivered steam through two hollow uprights to a pivoted sphere and escaped from the sphere through two jets. Impact of the steam against the atmosphere caused corresponding recoil of the jets, and this sent the sphere spinning around on its pivots.

At the right is a "year-around" clock built by Ctesibius. A god's head on a temple wall wept tears which drained into a concealed container and gradually raised a float bearing a little manikin. As the manikin rose, it pointed to the hours of the day from bottom to top of a near-by cylinder. Once a day the container became full, and a siphon drew off the water. This let the float and the manikin fall into position for another rise next day.

The discharged water in its turn took care of a peculiar feature of Greek time telling. Instead of having twenty-four hours a day as we do and more or fewer hours of daylight according to season, the Greeks divided the daytime into twelve hours and made the hours longer or shorter according to season. These various lengths of hour were marked off on the cylindrical scale; and the water which came from the siphon once a day turned a paddle wheel. The wheel acted through gearing to turn the scale slightly and keep hours of the correct length for each day under the manikin's pointer.

Hero of Alexandria (about 100 B.C. or 100 A.D.) was the man who invented the form of steam engine shown in the accompanying diagram. This invention could not have led to practical devices as it stood, because the engine used the reaction principle employed in some modern steam turbines, and probably the ancients could not have built a turbine even if they had the idea. What they could have done was realize that steam could be made to do work, and people endowed with mechanical ingenuity such as theirs could have developed simple steam engines from this hint.

But the idea of a machine to do work not only was foreign to the theorizing speculative spirit of Hellenic science; it was utterly foreign to the *social* spirit of the times. Work of the hard physical sort was something to be done by slaves, and why should anybody bother to make a slave's lot easier? A philosopher or a scientist would actually be demeaning his abilities if he turned them to such preposterous tasks!

Hero's steam engine was doomed, therefore, to lead to nothing practical, and the same may be said of all the other mechanical devices of the time. The Alexandrians were great inventors of gadgets, such as the holy-water machine shown in the picture, but workaday machines to lighten the burden of human labor interested them not at all.

This indifference to practical concerns was of a piece with the final and probably most harmful defect of all in this brilliant civilization. The Alexandrians brought to disastrous completion the undermining of faith in the old gods which had started when Thales applied reason to the problem of the universe.

Inasmuch as the old gods were primitive nature deities, and no worth-while ethical code arose from worshiping them, this loss of faith was no evil in the realm of thought. But as noted already in Chapter XII, religious hope of some kind, true or false, is one of the most important mainsprings of human nature. As long as men feel they have an undying place in the universal scheme they have reason to go on with life and hold true to principle, however hard the road. Once this hope is impaired, the effects are disastrous throughout society.

The sensitive-minded feel a horror of extinction, akin to a child's fear of the night, and a bitter resentment at having been given conscious existence, only to lose it again. Others, who normally are held to their duties by religion, see little sense in doing their part toward the state or their fellow men if neither punishment nor reward can be expected in the end. The rich are content to get along as effort-lessly as possible; the poor plod on without the one consolation which had seemed to make life worth living. The hard-minded, rest-less "doers" remain active, but even they feel a touch of the general moral slackness. They concentrate upon their own self-interest of the moment, because the future holds nothing save extinction.

Now this destruction of the spiritual mainspring was going ahead rapidly in Alexandria. These Alexandrines were busy revamping life, thought and arts in the light of reason, but in exact proportion as they did this and sapped men's faith in the old gods so did they weaken the basis of spiritual life for most men. Probably they felt no lack themselves, because abstract truth itself can be emotionally satisfying to the truth-seeking type of mind; but such a substitution was impossible for uneducated peasants, habit-ridden craftsmen and heavily worked laborers and even for the soldier, the statesman and the man of affairs, the whole class of men who lacked the time and taste needed for philosophic speculation. When the gods became suspect in the minds of such men, the light of hope went out.

Thereby the gain from the Alexandrian freeing of reason to do its work was almost exactly balanced by the loss of spiritual power and energy; the one cut away the other. And this fact just about closes the account for the Greek contributions to human progress.

The Hellenes must be honored always as the people who burst the shackles of magic-ridden conservatism and thereby freed reason to do its work. Beyond this they created glorious art, the foundations of education and respect for rights of the individual. As final credits to their account stand the first large-scale experiment in history with democratic government and the creation of a rounded even though imperfect science in Athens and finally in Alexandria.

All these must be counted, however, as mere beginnings, if we measure their effort against the fundamental test of success—provision of maximum opportunity for individuals to enlarge and enrich their stature in life. The Athenians had come to understand this domi-nating need of human nature, but they did nothing effective to bring society into line with it, even by their experiment with democracy. Industrial and farm slaves ground away their lives as hopelessly as ever. The chance to develop the whole modern time-and-labor sav-ing technology of using machinery in place of men was missed. Science ran from a brilliant start to a dead end. In the domain of the spirit the old faith was dying, but neither the Athenians nor the Alexandrians provided any substitute.

Plainly, then, even though the light of reason had been lit in the minds of men, the task of following it to better ways still remained to be worked out. The age-old story of circumstances driving men into progress would have to be repeated, and before this could happen the new circumstances would have to arise. Meanwhile nothing could be expected save a general plodding along in the old anthill conception of life, embellished somewhat with Greek arts and Greek thought.

So, at least, says our concept of human nature—and just so did events fall out. History is plain enough about this and utterly simple as well. The only change from the situation after Alexander's day was substitution of one supreme power for another, when Rome replaced the Macedonian power as ruler of the western world. To Rome, then, we must turn for the next chapter in the human story, the final plodding along in ancient anthill ways until new forces began to shape a new way of life.

CHAPTER XXIV

Rome Rises to World Mastery

Throughout modern times historians have perplexed themselves mightily over the rise and fall of Rome, but today a clearer knowledge of what actually happened and a vastly improved knowledge of human nature combine to offer a comparatively simple explanation. A distinguished student of human mentality through the ages, Lynn Thorndike, gives this explanation splendidly in his *Medieval Europe* (1920). He states that probably the fundamental reason for the fall of Rome was that the Roman Empire was founded on the ruins of states and civilizations that had already declined. The empire was a patchwork of cultures which had nothing to give to sustain the whole; it possessed little new life of its own; it was the last stage in the ancient history of the Mediterranean basin.

This amounts to saying that Rome was a receiver in bankruptcy for ancient civilization, and this view just about eliminates all mystery concerning the rise and fall of Rome. In the realm of political power Rome was able to duplicate around the Mediterranean the earlier rise of Assyria in southwestern Asia, because of weakness in the rival states; but Rome had no more power to endure than did Assyria or any other ancient anthill state. In economics and material culture Rome pushed a life based upon slavery to the broadest and richest level ever attained; but, as always, the cancer of slavery and other anthill weaknesses ruined this attainment in the end.

Meanwhile and all unwittingly, Rome performed the truly useful functions of a good receiver.

By conquering all rivals Rome washed up many an old evil and imposed a universal brotherhood upon mankind in Europe, with a clean sweep and a chance to start anew. At the same time she organized and preserved most of the best elements in ancient cultures for use in new patterns. She provided a matrix in which the Christian faith could and did bring its woefully needed corrective for the most fundamental evil in ancient life by bringing in the idea that the individual, rather than the group or the state, was the supreme concern of human society, thereby giving men an incentive for striving throughout life. Finally, by virtue of her very collapse, Rome gave men in Europe a clean sweep and a chance to start anew—with the best of the ancient cultures plus the Christian faith as a heritage.

In this light, then, we may review the Roman story, beginning with the origins of the people themselves.

They practiced a culture called Villanovan, from a little village in Bologna where the type remains of the culture were uncovered in 1853–55. This culture contained a fusion of Alpine agricultural elements with Indo-European nomad practices. The practice of cremating the dead was Alpine, as were the methods of building homes and towns. Apart from use of dry land instead of lakes, Villanovan construction methods were foursquare with those used in the pile-dwelling or terremare settlements built by Alpines in the valley of the Po in 2000 B.C.

The speech, however, was Indo-European, bespeaking a descent from grassland nomads. The Villanovans also used the horse, and their tribal organization embodied the normal principles of strong group organization under elected chiefs. Important matters were decided by an assembly of all citizens, and for convenience the citizens usually were divided into ten groups, each one called a *curia*. The fact that Rome had thirty curiae, as far back as we can trace, is taken to mean that the Roman community had been created by amalgamating three previously existing groups.

Such a fusion of nomad and peasant is just what had been occurring throughout Europe after 2500 B.C., as set forth in Chapter XV, and this dilution of nomad spirit with plodding peasant temperament helps explain why the Villanovans lacked the mental alertness of their Indo-European cousins the Hellenes. Another reason was the lack of stimulating contact with highly developed civilizations; the Italy of those early days saw no more of culture than do the natives of west Africa in our time. Neither was this defect remedied when these backland Villanovans received a strong infusion of culture at the time the Hellenes smashed the Mycenean culture about 1200 B.C.

In recent years these cultured immigrants have been identified definitely as the people the early Romans called Etruscans. The tracing turns, first of all, upon the very Latin name Etruscan for these people. If this name is boiled down by omitting vowels, as the Semites and Egyptians did, and leaving off the endings, it becomes T-R-S. This is the exact name the Egyptians gave to one of the groups of "sea wanderers" which Rameses III kept out of his dominions. The next mention of the people is in Herodotus. He tells how a people in Lydia was afflicted by drought and decided that every other person, as chosen by lot, would have to find a home in a new land. The exiles found their way to north-central Italy and became the people the Hellenes called the Tyrsenians. This name again yields T-R-S—T(y)RS(enians). (A later change, common in Greek, of "rs" to "rr" gives the present name Tyrrhenian to the sea between Italy and Sicily, Sardinia and Corsica.) This account does not reflect a driving out by the Hellenes, but Herodotus did not even know his own people's share in this history. Naturally he would not know how the Etruscans were driven forth by the Hellenes. The Latin name Etruscan completes the chain of evidence from etymology.

The archaeological record leaves no doubt about the identification or the connection of these people with the Mycenean disaster. Etruscan art, building methods and technology are all unquestionably Asia Minor in type, with a strong Hittite flavor and many reflections of ancient Mesopotamian culture. The evidence was made conclusive in 1926 by discovery of a cemetery with unmistakably early Etruscan culture, in the island of Lemnos near the Dardanelles.

These wanderers were firmly established in the center of Italy and northward by the eighth century b.c., with exactly the culture to be expected. It was a hardheaded and practical combination of work, hard-driven trade and, as the cornerstone of its power, the maintenance of dominating naval power in the Tyrrhenian or Tuscan Sea. The intrusion of such a culture is the last factor needed to explain why the Romans never acquired the mental brilliance of the Hellenes. Had the original Villanovans been compelled to work out a culture for themselves, they might have profited mentally. But they acquired their culture ready-made from the Etruscans, and with it they acquired their hardheaded, heavy-handed temperaments.

One circumstance did operate, however, to lift them up from the level of peasant peoples and start them forward toward their historic destiny. This was the geographic nature of their homeland.

There was a little plain called Latium, traversed by the river Tiber.

Here some Villanovans established a village on a hill later called the Palatine, near an island that offered an easy crossing of the Tiber. The village was a convenient point for trading with both Etruscan merchants who came overland from the north and with Etruscan and Greek sea traders who came up the Tiber to the head of navigation at the island. Also it offered a rallying point for the farmers of the neighborhood whenever other Latin peoples, notably the Sabines, or the Etruscans came on raids into the Latin plain.

This last fact goes far to explain the later sturdiness and genius of the Romans for solving problems practically. These villagers were underdogs in a most exposed position. If they were to hold their own, they had to keep the entire tribe organized as an army, with every able-bodied citizen ready at a moment's notice to leave his plow or his tools and take up his appointed place in the military machine. From this sprung the Roman martial spirit and the stern discipline and military ideals of the early Romans.

The second result from being underdog was learning a lesson which escaped the too easily successful Hellenes. Never for a moment could the early Romans indulge in the supreme self-confidence of the typical Hellenic state. In their dealings with their neighbors the Romans fought and won when they could. But if a neighbor was too powerful to be beaten, the Romans were willing to conciliate and compromise if possible. This shows strongly later on, when their favorite stratagem if they could not *beat* a neighboring Latin tribe was to propose a *union* of the tribes.

Their hard-bitten early career also had taught them somehow to adopt a singularly fortunate political expedient, one that did much in the next few centuries to shape the Roman career. This expedient was the unusual degree of power given to the Senate, or Council of Old Men.

A council of elders that acted more continuously than did the general assembly of all warriors was common in Indo-European government. It gave rise to the Hellenic *boulē* and the Anglo-Saxon *witan* or *witanagemot*. The Roman situation among powerful foes seems, however, to have fostered an unusually high development of this institution. Undoubtedly consultation was needed constantly about questions of trade and relations with neighbors; yet the farmers could not afford to be leaving their fields at all times for this purpose. Hence undoubtedly they looked more than did most rudely civilized people to their elders to handle such matters, and so the Senate became more than usually important in their lives.

Thus the Romans insured themselves continuous guidance by the most skilled and seasoned members of their community, and Roman policy had a steadfastness and unswerving determination to achieve goals which were rare among ancient peoples. Still later, when the Roman people achieved a share in the government, the Senate provided what the Athenians had so sadly lacked—a seasoned, conservative counterbalance to the easily swayed passions of the mob.

The story of Rome's rise to world power from these beginnings is too well known to need rehearsing here. We need only place it in world time by saying that it began about 500 b.c. at just about the time Clisthenes gave final form to Athenian democracy, with the expulsion of the Etruscan kings who had fastened themselves upon the young nation. It was completed in 168 b.c., when the Ptolemies escaped dethronement by acknowledging themselves vassals of Rome. From 149 to 146 b.c. Rome turned westward again, to obliterate Carthage and run plows over the city site; and in that same year rebellious Corinth was burned. Thereby the political liquidation of older cultures was complete. The future was in the hands of Rome alone, and from now on the Roman story becomes important to the student of human nature.

The earlier rise had offered nothing particularly distinctive; scarcely anything other than geography set it apart from early predatory adventures such as the rise of Assyria. But from now on we have our first good insight, thanks to records far superior to those left from earlier cultures, of how such a state handled its problems—and, most instructive of all, how and why it was doomed to fail in the end because of unavoidable and fatal weaknesses in its predatory anthill concept of how a state should be organized.

First among these weaknesses was the grim fact that the very completeness of Rome's success had already destroyed the strongest forces which hold a predatory anthill state together.

The very essence of the anthill idea is that in proportion as the state succeeds it will transfer the burden of daily toil from the backs of the conquerors to the conquered populations and to slaves, and thereby it robs itself of a loyal citizenry of free toilers. By 146 b.c. this destruction was all but complete, not only in the original Roman territory but throughout Italy.

Even if nothing else had happened, the conquest of veritable empires of land and establishment of slave industry upon them insured that a humble citizen farmer had scarcely a chance of earning a living from his farm. The large estates, worked by hordes of slaves captured in the wars, produced and sold grain at prices which could not possibly yield the independent operator a living. He might struggle along for a few years, borrowing all the while—then his farm would be sold or taken over to satisfy his debt, and one more recruit was added to the mob which lived on private or public charity in the cities and, most of all, in Rome. This economic pressure was abetted by vicious administration of the Roman system of land ownership, by which the rich and influential men who ran the state could dispossess the peasantry, and thanks to both forces Rome deliberately destroyed the landholding tie which bound her humble citizenry to the state.

A predatory state still has cementing forces, however, as long as it has military problems. The army, the navy, or both, can replace peacetime toil and land ownership as an occupation for the citizens. But now Rome had no more military problems other than those of policing her conquests and holding her frontiers against barbarians, and these tasks could be performed by a relatively small professional army. Therefore even these ties were lost in the Roman state.

Meanwhile the aristocratic and trading classes were degenerating rapidly in moral fiber through addiction to brutal "get-rich-quick" exploitation of the Roman conquests.

Some aristocrats piled up wealth as plantation owners, shipowners and traders, but the favorite prescription for getting rich quickly was outright plunder of a captured province. The Roman tax system was beautifully designed for this. The republic asked a certain tribute from a province. How the governor raised it was his business, as was also the matter of *how much more* he managed to obtain.

This business of getting rich quick at provincial expense was refined and broadened at this point by another device. Governors could try their own hands at milking a province if they wished, but more usually they employed professional extortioners called tax farmers or *publicans*. A newly appointed governor received bids from unemployed publicans for the privilege of raising his required tribute and his personal cut on top of that. The successful bidder raised both sums without bother to the governor, other than requesting occasional torturings, executions and village burnings to speed up collections; and how much was raised *above* the required sums was the publican's business.

With such a system in force an ambitious Roman could well afford to spend the equivalent of half a million dollars in bribing the unemployed mob with games and food to elect him to any office which led by custom to a provincial governorship. Julius Caesar and many others are said to have spent most all of their personal fortunes on this step in their careers, but they could afford to because they regained the fortune and a much larger one on top of it once they got their clutches on a rich province.

Common fairness requires explanation that none of this was provided for *positively* by the law. The Senate's legal record was perfectly clear. The statute books showed a beautiful array of laws, all set up to insure just treatment for the provinces. What the Senate conveniently forgot to do was to *enforce* these laws.

A perfect example of the Roman system was Crassus, "the richest Roman of them all," in the early days of Julius Caesar.

As a young man Marcus Licinius Crassus managed to survive being on the wrong side politically in a time when losing an election all too often meant losing one's lands and one's life as well, by proscription. Later, when his side came up, he bought in the estates of the proscribed losers at bargain prices. During this time he did well also with his personally owned fire department and salvage corps, the only one in Rome. When a house took fire Crassus turned out his firemen and offered the owner and his neighbors fire-sale prices for the properties. If the owners sold—and usually they did—the men went to work. Often they were successful enough to salvage a fine deal for Crassus.

Finally this splendid model of a successful Roman businessman became consul, together with Pompey, and set off for the east to work whatever human gold mines he could find. The unsubdued and as yet unmilked Parthians, as the heirs of the Persians now were called, looked like good prospects; so he started a war against them. But for once retribution overtook the Roman formula for getting rich quick. The Parthians captured Crassus, and according to the traditional story handed down by the Romans themselves the Parthians told Crassus that for once he was going to get all the gold he could possibly stomach. Then they made good the promise by melting the gold and pouring it down his throat.

As a final commentary upon conditions of the time we have the fate of the few men who attempted to stem the march of the vicious and corroding forces in Roman life. Sufficient justice is done the record by considering only three men—the popular leaders and would-be reformers, Tiberius and Gaius Gracchus, and the orator, statesman and philosopher, Marcus Tullius Cicero.

Tiberius Gracchus (163–133 B.C.) was elected tribune, or representative of the people for 133 B.C., and immediately attempted to reform the administration of the land laws in the interest of independent farmer citizens. He lasted out his first term but was assassinated by outraged "conservatives" when he stood for re-election. Twelve years later his younger brother Gaius (153–121 B.C.) became tribune and pushed the same reforms but met the same fate. This was the last sincere attempt made in republican Rome to curb or correct the ruin of the old-time farmer.

Cicero (106–43 B.C.) also died a victim of the times but had a much happier time before his end. His public career as a lawyer and holder of offices up to his consulship in 63 B.C. has been called that of a trimmer, a man who tried to run with the hares of reform while hunting with the hounds of plunder; but the fate of the Gracchi had proved that an officeholder could hardly do anything else if he cared to live long enough to accomplish any good. Cicero apparently hoped to do a bit of good here and another bit there, as opportunity afforded, with the idea of reforming the state from within.

If mental endowment had been enough for this task, Cicero certainly was the man who could have succeeded.

He was the greatest orator Rome ever produced; most scholars agree that his only peer in all history was the Athenian Demosthenes. Throughout his life he did much to foster love of Greek literature and art, and even though he was no more able than any other Roman to add anything to Greek philosophy, he did manage to blend Greek ideas with the practical needs of the Roman situation into a polished, resigned attitude toward life. Even today we can find no better formula than Cicero gives us for living and dying like a gentleman— provided we have the wherewithal for gentility to start with. (Cicero was as helpless as all other Romans to explain how wealth could be acquired unless a man was born rich or got a chance to steal wealth from a conquered people.)

In politics the climax of his career was his consulship, and the high light of his consulship was his struggle with Catiline, a dissolute young noble who had staked his fortune upon winning the consulship in the election which went to Cicero. Rather than accept ruin as the fruit of defeat, Catiline planned to seize power by armed rebellion. Cicero forestalled and defeated this with several masterful orations which stirred the rich conservatives into driving Catiline from Rome. This was the last time, however, when the republican ideal showed even a spark of vitality. Almost immediately after Cicero's consulship stronger, more ruthless men began following Catiline's plan, and this soon brought the end for the polished, gentlemanly orator.

The first of the would-be dictators, Julius Caesar, spared him; but in 43 B.C. the partisans of Caesar's nephew Octavian decided that the danger of oratorical blasts against them and their schemes required proscription of Cicero. Accordingly he was murdered, and his head and his hands were nailed to the orator's rostrum in the Forum—a sardonic end for the greatest orator and philosopher Rome ever produced!

But more than a man died with Cicero. He is the last man on the record who showed any devotion to the earlier ideals of Roman government, and his fate can be taken as a token and symbol that republican Rome was dead save for the final deathblow. It had been slain by failure to comply with one fundamental requirement which human nature imposes upon all governments, the requirement that the state should appeal to the minds of its members as being worth preserving.

Now not even the aristocratic plunderers felt any devotion to Rome; the plunderbund had failed, even for them. The provinces had been bled white, and the more greedy of the plunderers, lacking other victims, had turned to plundering their fellow Romans. The system was simple enough—win an election from the mob or, failing that, lead in an army and then proscribe, murder and plunder all opponents. This plan drenched Rome with blood under Marius and again when Sulla tossed out the Marian party. By that time wealth was more of a danger than a source of satisfaction.

When conditions reached such a pass only one remedy remained— the dictator; and this need ushered in the era of the Caesars and the beginning of the empire.

The story of how Julius Caesar (102–44 B.C.) built a reputation as the conqueror of Gaul and then crossed the Rubicon to make himself master of Rome is familiar to everyone. So too is the story of how self-styled patriots assassinated him in 44 B.C. and how his would-be successors, Antony and Octavian, fought to win mastery of Rome. Octavian, as we know, won by defeating the fleets of Antony and Cleopatra in the Battle of Actium in 31 B.C., and it is not hard to understand the joy which arose over the news that the Roman world now had a prospect of peace and order under one master.

A joyful Senate named Octavian commander of the army and governor of such provinces as he wanted to control personally and voted him the titles of *Princeps* (first citizen), *Augustus* (the august) and *Imperator* (commander in chief). Thereupon Octavian justified every hope by plunging wholeheartedly into a program of reform.

In place of plunder-greedy governors and publicans he set up a paid administration of government tax officials and administrators. Men he named as governors were to *govern,* not to plunder. And to fill the cup of joy to overflowing in the provinces, a substantial portion of the tribute now was remitted in the form of roads, aqueducts, temples and other needed public works.

To these reforms Octavian—or Augustus, to give him the name which history employs—added specific emotional stimulants for Roman morale.

One stimulant was the time-honored dictator's device, eye-filling public works; before his death Augustus was able to boast that he found Rome a city of brick and left it a city of marble. Another stimulant was a revival of Alexander's program of treating the ruler as a god. In following this idea Augustus was more modest than Alexander—or perhaps more sensitive to possible public insight into the stratagem—in that he did not openly seek deification of himself. He rather asked the Senate to deify his predecessor with the imperial idea, his uncle Julius Caesar. This the Senate did, and Julius Caesar served as the emperor god while Augustus lived. The Senate also deified Augustus immediately after he died. Soon thereafter the Senate began making emperors gods even while they lived, and a citizen attested his loyalty not by saluting the flag but by offering a sacrifice to the emperor.

This stratagem is much misunderstood in our time because our judgments are based upon the Christian objection to this rite, but judgments can be kept straight by remembering that the emperors cared little about beliefs and convictions. The worshipers could make the sacrifice which constituted worship with tongue in cheek if they liked, provided they were discreet about their mental reservation. The point was that they must *make* the sacrifice and thus help along the real objective of giving the ignorant mass of the population a moral and emotional tie to the Roman state. Refusal to do this was not so much actual blasphemy against a god as it was a species of rebellion against the state.

In yet another feature of empire organization Augustus followed precedent, this time from both Persia and the Roman Republic.

Cyrus, Darius and all other competent Persian monarchs had

recognized that the nerves of their empire were *roads,* both for the movement of troops and, even more important, of news and orders. In their day of armies that relied on the nomad type of mounted warrior a good road *surface* was not important; the great need was for bridges over all unfordable rivers, and wells or other sources of water supply not more than a day's march apart. In addition, royal messengers needed relays of fresh horses—or, even better, relays of both horse and rider, which could pass a message along at top speed day and night. This was the system of *posts,* from which we get our term "post rider," "post haste" and "post office."

The Roman Republic needed and developed this system, but it needed good road surfaces as well, to speed the march of its infantry legions and their supply trains. As far back as 312 B.C., in the days of the consul Appius Claudius, a first-class road, the Appian Way, had been started south from Rome toward the region where the Samnite Wars were raging. By the time of Augustus Italy was crisscrossed with fine roads of the straightaway "over hill and over dale" Roman model, and he and later emperors pushed development of the system until it reached the farthest frontiers of the empire.

Thus far Augustus was on solid ground and using time-tried devices for strengthening a regime. They proved effective as well. Augustus and the empire were rewarded with a burst of new confidence, new industry and a flowering of Roman thought, such as it was, in the Golden or Augustan Age of Latin literature.

This "Age" had begun even before the time of the first emperor, with Cicero and with Julius Caesar's model of straightforward writing, *The Gallic Wars.* Other ornaments of this time had been the historian Sallust (86–34 B.C.), who wrote of Catiline's conspiracy, Lucretius (96?–55 B.C.), author of a philosophic poem *De rerum natura* (The Nature of Things), and Catullus (84–54 B.C.), famed for his love poems. Now these pioneers in the literary use of Latin were followed by the best-known Latin writers of all, men who were deliberately encouraged by Augustus and his home minister, Maecenas, as ornaments of the Augustan reign.

Among the poets critics are at odds in choosing between Vergil (Publius Vergilius Maro, 70–19 B.C.) and Horace as the King of Latin verse. Vergil's best-known work was his *Aeneid.* The hero Aeneas was presented as a wandering hero, like Ulysses in Homer's *Odyssey,* but his adventures really celebrated the achievements of Augustus. Next in fame probably come Vergil's *Georgics,* poems

"THE NERVES OF ROME"—FAST TRAVEL ON SUPERB ROADS

Invincible legions may have conquered the world for Rome, but the Roman roads held the conquest together. They were superbly built of stone slab, with rubble shoulders and deep ditches for drainage. Foot travelers, including troops, used the shoulders, with the officers walking on the high curb. The pavement was used by wagons, chariots and couriers of the imperial messenger service. All who traveled on official business could obtain fresh horses every few miles at posting stations, and so they could move at a gallop all day and for as many days as needed. In the background is a frontier garrison post and wall with blockhouses. The *limes* which guarded the German frontier and the walls which held off the Picts and Scots in northern Britain were of this type.

which celebrated the beauties and joys of country life. Horace (Quintus Horatius Flaccus, 68–8 B.C.) wrote *Odes, Satires* and *Epistles* which give a penetrating and fascinating picture of life in the Augustan Age.

Next to these two leaders in critical esteem come Sextus Propertius (50?–15 B.C.), a poet of love, Tibullus (54?–19 B.C.) and Ovid (43 B.C.–18 A.D.). Ovid's *Metamorphoses* wove ancient mythology and other material into a fascinating poem as long as Homer's *Odyssey*. The remaining giant of the period was the historian Livy (59 B.C.–17 A.D.). He was a fascinating storyteller and our chief source for information about the earliest days of Rome, but unfortunately he cannot be trusted without corroboration. Like all these Augustan writers he felt the eye of Augustus upon him, and he took good care to provide the pride-stimulating, morale-rousing material which the emperor demanded. Consequently he buried the hard, none-too-pleasing truth all but completely beneath his romantic tales which Macauley's *Lays* have passed on to us.

This propagandizing defect is well worth noting. It ran through the work of all these men and is a sufficient badge of what this Golden Age really was—a period of sophisticated, polished thought produced practically to order, just as were the architectural glories of Rome, and utterly lacking in the spontaneity, the devotion to truth and the beauty of simplicity which marked the best Greek writing. Thus the standard psychological test for any age, its literature, gave ample proof that Augustus had not created a new age or opened a new era; he had simply cleaned up the old culture and given it a new lease upon life.

Neither could any emperor have done more, Roman civilization being what it was.

Not much could be done about the peasant farmer except by attacking slavery and the capitalists who worked huge plantations with slaves. Augustus could hardly attempt that—especially when he would have to begin with himself, as the biggest plantation owner of all! The Senate had provided for supporting his imperial establishment by allotting all Egypt, the "Granary of the Empire," together with several other provinces, as the emperor's personal domain; and he was expected to support his imperial power and grandeur out of the tax revenues and the personal returns from this domain. The arrangement was a perfect example of Roman genius for exploitation, and it also had the effect of chaining Augustus and all his successors to the exploitive system.

The situation was even worse concerning the *spiritual* sources of hope, the wellsprings which draw spirit and courage from the very foundations of man's emotional nature.

Here, thanks to Hellenic destruction of faith in the old gods, the educated classes everywhere were undergoing the soul-searing experience of fearing that man could expect no end other than the grave.

Once such a fear sets in, one of the two reactions is inevitable. The harder minded manage to "forget it"—but usually at cost of becoming utterly worldly minded and materialistic. The more sensitive, imaginative and emotional minds feel again a child's fear of the night, intensified now with adult powers of imagination and accompanied by soul-sickness and a fierce resentment against the colossal injustice of such a fate.

Both of these reactions had become strong in the Alexandrian culture of Ptolemaic days, and now in the days of Augustus they were permeating the intelligent stratum of the entire Roman world. True, Hellenistic philosophers had tried to fill the gap, but the very quality of their substitutes proves how futile philosophy is as a substitute for a warm, firm faith in a just hereafter.

A soul-sick Roman could take up the somewhat heroic attitude of the Stoic, who held that man was caught in a trap and could save nothing but self-respect. To do this he must renounce all affections and all yearnings which led to attaching emotional value to anything in life. Then, come what may, he could at least keep his chin up and not be reduced to a weeping or a cringing caricature of a man.

So stern a doctrine could serve those who were strong minded enough and proud enough to place self-respect above all other values in life, but these very requirements show why Stoicism could never satisfy the great mass of softer-minded, more emotional members of the population. A much more popular doctrine was Epicureanism. "Eat, drink and be merry, for tomorrow we die," is the familiar paraphase of it; and while this is somewhat unjust to Epicurus in its baldness, it is the substance of the meaning the Romans got from his doctrine. The doctrines of the Cynics amounted in substance to revenging one's self upon Fate by sneering at everything.

The visible evidence of the yawning gap in the Roman spiritual scheme was the widespread popularity of mystic faiths, faiths which offered something more appealing than the crude folklore deities of the official pantheon. The goddess Isis of Egypt enjoyed enormous popularity, especially when Asiatic fertility-cult ceremonies were grafted onto the faith. This was only natural, for to the Romans, even as for us, Egypt wore an aura of unbelievable antiquity and wisdom in matters of magic and mystic faith.

Another popular deity was Serapis of Alexandria. This god had been all but deliberately put together by the Alexandrian thinkers to meet the need for a deity, out of elements taken from Egyptian, Greek and Asiatic faiths. The synthesis was in part honest, a belief by these thinkers that they were discovering the true essence of God that lay at the heart of all the jangling faiths, but our knowledge of psychology tells us that Serapis consisted mostly of wishful thinking. A god must be had—and so he might as well have the attributes which men in various lands had found most attractive.

The soldiers, oddly enough, showed widespread preference for the Persian faith of Mithras, a faith which is misrepresented today as fire worship. One reason undoubtedly was that by now the army had drawn a hodgepodge of faiths into its ranks. Sheer comparison of beliefs had revealed the emptiness of them to the soldiers, and the disillusionment was helped along by the military duty of knocking over barbarian gods, as well as bashing in barbarian heads, whenever the barbarians seemed to need such treatment. We can well understand why soldiers would turn to the faith which was mystical and beyond damage by sword, spear or siege engine in its central image of god.

These changes of the Augustan Age closed all but the last chapter of the Roman record and of ancient life as well. Everything possible had been done to clean up ancient life, but the cleanup was not enough. Certain evils still had to run their course and bring the old to an end before the new could appear. How they did so will close the story of ancient times.

CHAPTER XXV

The Collapse of Rome and of Ancient Life

WHEN AUGUSTUS DIED in A.D. 14 he had ruled as Princeps, or First Citizen, for forty-one years. During that span of time Rome had enjoyed peace and good government for the first time in more than a century, and the emperors who followed him managed to conceal the inherent weaknesses of the state for two centuries more. The only obvious weakness was the problem of obtaining a new princeps or emperor when the reigning one died.

Augustus never had dared to settle this with a definite provision by law, because in theory he had been elected by the Senate, and the Senate would name his successor. To settle the matter practically he had adopted Tiberius, a child of his wife by her first husband, as his son and had given Tiberius the duties of a sort of junior emperor. The Senate made Tiberius emperor when Augustus died, and this expedient of mingled adoption by the emperor and election by the Senate remained the legal method of choosing an emperor almost to the end of the empire.

The associated problem of what to do about intolerable emperors was met by the age-old expedient of assassination. This accounted for the three evil emperors, Caligula, Nero and Domitian, who were mingled with thirteen good ones down to the death of Marcus Aurelius in A.D. 180; and so on the surface the empire seemed invulnerable and destined to last forever. Nevertheless, several significant symptoms revealed that decline was proceeding inexorably.

Perhaps the most obvious symptom was a steady depreciation of the currency, achieved by alloying the silver coins with lead.

This began as early as the reign of Nero (A.D. 54–68), and traditionally the debasement has been put down as just another item in the long list of Nero's evil deeds. Modern historians know better. Nero had no choice in the matter. The known silver mines were all

285

but exhausted, and the existing supply was rapidly being locked up in luxury articles or shipped to the Far East in payment for luxury articles. The only way Nero could stretch the remaining supply far enough to provide the coins needed for daily business throughout the empire was by diluting the silver with lead.

This trouble grew worse, not better, after Nero's reign. From museum collections of Roman coins we know how steadily the evil progressed. The coins of Augustus' time were pure, but even after nearly two centuries of good government the coins issued by Marcus Aurelius contained twenty-five per cent alloy. Two generations later the content of precious metal was *only five per cent*.

The result of this deterioration was a twofold whipsawing of prices, with accompanying demoralization of industry, finance and government. Each debasement caused a rapid rise in prices, with strain upon imperial finance and private industry. Between such crises prices drifted steadily lower as precious metal continued to vanish from circulation, and the amount contained in each coin became worth more. But as prices fell so did the yield from taxes, returns from investments and enterprises, everything; and the ever-growing scarcity of coin compelled taxgatherers to take tribute more and more in kind, principally in foodstuffs.

Another sign of the times was the failure of attempts to revive a free citizenry during and after the reign of Nerva (A.D. 96–98). In an attempt to re-establish a sturdy, free peasantry Nerva bought large tracts of land and parceled the land out in small farms to settlers. Part of the money came from the imperial treasury; the rest he provided from his own fortune. He also set up a fund for making loans to farmers, probably at about five per cent, and he planned to spend this interest, as it was paid, upon the support and education of poor children. This was to be done in part through state schools and partly by paying poor parents who either gave birth to children or adopted orphans. Nerva also established a rising scale of pay to officials in government service, according to the number of children they had.

Nerva's successors continued these policies but without accomplishing any improvement whatever. They could loan money, or even give money, to small farmers all they liked; but they could not give the small farmer ability *to earn a living* as long as he faced competition from huge slave-worked estates. These estates were the real cancer that needed cutting out—but they could not be cut out, because they were the very body of the empire. The empire had to stand or fall with them.

Still another insidious evil was "race suicide"—the unwillingness or inability of the upper classes to reproduce their numbers. Part of the reason, undoubtedly, was the enervating, debilitating effect of luxury and all too often vicious luxury; but part also was sheer soul-sickness, a reaction to the unanswered question: "What is the use?" "Eat, drink and be merry, for tomorrow we die" remained the only answer to life that the Roman could see, and the more intelligent and sensitive the person was, the less reason he or she could see for projecting children into this empty round.

The plain proof that the evil was widespread was the constant injection of provincials into high office as the Roman stock continued to fail and a constant extension of citizenship to provincials, in order to maintain the fiction that the Roman government and army were made up of citizens and to broaden the base of taxable persons. Finally one of Rome's worst emperors, Caracalla, made everyone in the empire a citizen in 212. In theory this gave legal effect to the proposition that all men are brothers, but the ironical, practical reason for the change was far different. Caracalla made it solely to increase the number of taxpayers.

Until very recent years history tended to minimize the extent of these evils during the second-century time of good emperors. The assumption was that conditions could not have been as bad as the evidence suggests, because life seemed to run smoothly. But once human nature is taken properly into account, the reconcilement between bad underlying conditions and smoothness of everyday life presents no puzzle whatever.

Americans had a good demonstration of how human nature reacts to coinage change in 1934, when President Roosevelt cut the theoretical gold content of the dollar from about 1/20 of a troy ounce to 1/35 of an ounce. His opposition complained bitterly about "59-cent dollars," but the man in the street continued to accept a paper dollar as *worth* a dollar. That was force of habit at work, and just so did habit hold everyday life reasonably steady, in spite of pressure from growing evils, in the Roman Empire of the second century.

Meanwhile two forces, one destructive and the other constructive, were taking shape for their roles in the final collapse. They were respectively the increasing menace of German barbarians and the rise of a new hope for man from the teachings given by a humble carpenter of Nazareth during the reign of Tiberius.*

*Some of the perplexities involved in assigning this dating, as well as the history of our division of historic time into "B.C." and "A.D.," will be found in Appendix B.

The first real trouble with the Germans came from an emigration of the Nordic Goths from their home on the Baltic shores, back along the historic migration route of the Dnieper, toward the Black Sea.

What started this movement is not entirely clear, although many scholars ascribe it to an unfavorable change of climate. The effects, however, are perfectly clear. As the Gothic migration flowed along, men, women and children all moving in search of new homes, it thrust the local tribes aside quite as a ship throws off waves to either side—and the displaced tribes were flung against the breakwaters of the Roman frontier.

The first serious shock of this sort came in the second half of the second century after Christ, when the Marcomanni and the Quadi were pushed against the Danubian frontier. By dint of eleven years of warfare (166–78) Marcus Aurelius was able to hold these tribes off, and in the reign of Caracalla (211–17) the pressure shifted to the east, where the Goths now were assailing the trans-Danubian province of Dacia. For fifty years sporadic warfare occurred, with occasional forays of the Goths into Dacia and even across the Danube, as well as incessant piratical attacks upon sea-borne commerce. The peak of these attacks was the capture and sacking of Thessalonica (the modern Saloniki) in 269. Finally, in 275, the emperor Aurelian bought peace by ceding Dacia to the Goths.

During these troubles the western Germans made frequent forays across the Rhine. In 270 they even crossed the Alps and raided Italy, and in 273 the Franks swept across most of Gaul on a tremendous raid. Then the peace with the Goths stabilized the eastern frontiers and gave the emperors a freer hand to deal with the barbarians in the west.

This "dealing," however, could not follow the stern old "blood-and-iron" practice of republican Rome, for the good and sufficient reason that Roman soldiers of the old stamp no longer existed. Ever since the days of Augustus the legions had been filled with Bithynians, Egyptians, Spaniards, Britons, anybody who was willing to accept the emperor's pay—and worst of all, the best soldiers were Teutonic barbarians, kinfolk of the very people who now must be kept out! Here was a dilemma indeed, more especially since the ever worse finances of the empire could not match in pay what the barbarians could seize in plunder!

Faced with such a problem, the emperors took refuge in the age-old policy which the first Romans had followed when conquest proved impossible. They compromised with German tribes which could be repelled, by giving them lands and accepting them as *foederati,* or allies settled within the empire. This policy was at best a transparent attempt to put a good face upon a hopeless situation, but as long as the emperors had to pit Germans against Germans to hold the frontiers, they probably were wise in giving the defenders a stake in the empire by establishing them in Roman territory.

This meant, of course, that the Germans actually were masters of the situation. Once they realized this, they had only to put forth their hand and the empire was theirs. No greater tribute to the power of habit can be found in all history than is afforded by the German failure to realize their power. None of them assailed the empire seriously until after the middle of the fourth century after Christ.

And now for the positive force, the new hope offered by Christianity!

The rise of the Christian faith during the same time is a universally known story, save perhaps for one feature, the true nature of the constant friction between the Christians and the Roman state. The trouble did not arise from any Roman or imperial antipathy to Christianity as a faith. The root of it was the Roman demand for emperor worship as a mark of loyalty to the state.

To the Christian this was an abhorrent rite, a denial of God. The Roman, however, could see no sense whatever in this attitude. He knew that he was free to worship Serapis, Jupiter, Isis, Mithras or any other god as he liked, once he had done his duty as a Roman by offering a sacrifice to the emperor. What ailed these stubborn Christians, to bring about their stiff-necked attitude? Their talk of denying God seemed absurd, because no god was denied; the claim must be a cloak for something else, and that something, probably, was treason.

So argued the Roman, and once he got this idea he was quite willing to accept embroideries upon it, such as tales that "the flesh and blood of Christ," which formed the substance of the central Christian rite, really was obtained by slaughtering children. Such cannibalism went well with treason, and many an intelligent Roman was immensely puzzled when he found such charges had no foundation whatever in fact. What could the Christians be concealing if they were neither cannibals nor traitors?

This puzzlement—and also the nonferocious, nonbigoted spirit of the imperial government toward Christianity—stands forth clearly in a noted exchange of letters between Pliny the Younger (A.D. 61?–113?), while he was governor of Bithynia in Asia Minor, and the emperor Trajan. Pliny wrote:

It is a rule, sir, which I inviolably observe, to refer myself to you in all my doubts; for who is more capable of guiding my uncertainty or informing my ignorance? Having never been present at any trials of the Christians, I am unacquainted with the method and limits to be observed either in examining or punishing them. Whether any difference is to be made on account of age, or no distinction allowed between the youngest and the adult; whether repentance admits to a pardon, or if a man had been once a Christian it avails him nothing to recant; whether the mere profession of Christianity, albeit without crimes, or only the crimes associated therewith are punishable, in all these points I am greatly doubtful.

In the meanwhile, the method I have observed toward those who have been denounced to me as Christians is this: I interrogated them whether they were Christians; if they confessed it I repeated the question twice again, adding the threat of capital punishment; if they still persevered I ordered them to be executed.

These accusations spread (as is usually the case) from the mere fact of the matter being investigated; and several forms of the mischief came to life. A placard was put up, without any signature, accusing a large number of persons by name. Those who denied they were, or had ever been, Christians, who repeated after me an invocation to the gods, and offered adoration, with wine and frankincense to your image, which I had ordered to be brought for the purpose, together with those of the gods, and who finally cursed Christ—none of which acts, it is said, those who are really Christians can be forced into performing—these I thought it proper to discharge. Others who were named by that informer at first confessed themselves Christians, and then denied it; true, they had been of that persuasion but they had quitted it. . . . They all worshiped your statue and the images of the gods, and cursed Christ.

They affirmed, however, the whole of their guilt, or their error, was that they were in the habit of meeting on a certain fixed day before it was light, when they sang in alternate verses a hymn to Christ, as to a god, and bound themselves by a solemn oath, not to any wicked deeds, but never to commit any fraud, theft or adultery, never to falsify their word, nor deny a trust when they should be called upon to deliver it up; after which it was their custom to separate, and then reassemble to partake of food—but food of an ordinary and innocent kind. . . . I judged it so much the more necessary to extract the real truth, with the assistance of torture, from two female slaves, who were styled deaconesses; but I could discover nothing more than depraved and excessive superstition. . . .

Trajan's reply was a fine revelation of the usual imperial spirit, especially in prohibiting active search for Christians or use of anonymous information against them:

The method you have pursued, my dear Pliny, in sifting the cases of those denounced to you as Christians is extremely proper. It is not possible to lay down any general rule which can be applied as the fixed standard in all cases of this nature. No search should be made for these people; when they are denounced and found guilty they must be punished; with the restriction, however, that when the party denies himself to be a Christian, and shall give proof that he is not (that is, by adoring our gods), he shall be pardoned on the ground of repentance, even though he may have formerly incurred suspicion. Information without the accuser's name subscribed must not be admitted in evidence against anyone, as it is introducing a very dangerous precedent, and by no means agreeable to the spirit of the age.

In this exchange the perfect showing is made of the hardheaded, world-wise Roman who cared nothing for any religion he knew and could not understand anyone dying for a god. Equally obvious too, from the failure to mention spiritual values, was the Roman inability to understand that a new light had been lit in the world—a light which would have given the empire exactly the vitality it needed if only the emperors had managed to realize this. But they would not, or could not, grasp this fact—and their charge, the empire, continued to fail while the new faith gained ground steadily, because it gave men exactly the message the whole world wanted.

The Roman failure to appraise all these forces correctly becomes slightly more understandable, when we recollect that throughout the third century the state was driven to utter distraction by a parade of internal troubles. Not only had the economic and social fabric degenerated steadily; anthill history had repeated itself with an outbreak of ruthless rule by naked force. Throughout the third century a parade of military adventurers, the so-called "barracks emperors," had marched their legions from the frontier upon Rome and reigned as emperor until deposed and slain by the next adventurer. During the seventy-three years between the death of Severus and the accession of Diocletian in 284, no less than twenty-three men held the imperial power. Eight of them had ruled jointly, two and two; but even with each of these reigns counted as one, the average tenure was less than four years.

Diocletian was the ruler who ended this intolerable state of affairs by instituting what plainly was a "last gasp" expedient. He swept away the last pretense of the old constitution and substituted a naked tyranny of the age-old Oriental type.

In the field of economics he reverted to a rigidity which could not have been surpassed even in the Egyptian days when Khufu was enslaving the nation for the erection of his pyramid. Diocletian met—or tried to meet—the dwindling away of farmers and even of skilled craftsmen in the cities by decreeing that sons must follow the occupations of their fathers. The son of a fisherman must be a fisherman; sons born to carpenters had to be carpenters.

In the field of government he wisely recognized that the Roman problem was too big for any one man to handle personally. The task had to be divided, and in the division Diocletian brushed aside sentiment about Rome in favor of accepting the hard fact that Rome never had been the true center of imperial power, other than by its possession of the military force required to rule the world.

From the very start the principal supplies of both food and manufactured goods had come from the East and from Africa. Gaul, Britain and Spain were important, but not nearly as much so as Egypt, Syria and Asia Minor. The emperor who wanted to keep a watchful eye upon his sources of strength would be well advised to set up his court somewhere in this area.

Military policy also suggested leaving Rome. The city no longer was a strategic center. The military problem lay along the Rhine and the Danube now, and the proper place for a ruler was somewhere just south of the Alps. There he would be buttressed by these mountains against sudden frontal attack but would be close enough to act promptly when trouble developed on either frontier.

Diocletian gave effect to these considerations by dividing the empire into an eastern and a western portion. He took the richer eastern portion for himself and fixed his seat of government at Nicomedia on the eastern shore of the Bosporus, where the all-important land connection between Europe and Asia crossed the water route between the Danube and the Nile. In 286 he named Maximianus to rule the Western Empire, and he faced Rome with the brutal fact that her day was done by fixing the seat of this empire in northern Italy, at Milan.

His last provision for government recognized that naked self-interest of strong leaders would name the emperors from now on. His plan provided that each emperor, the eastern and the western, was to be an *Augustus* or, in the Greek term, a *Basileus*. Each Augustus also was to name a junior, to be called a *Caesar;* and the hope was that whenever either Augustus died his Caesar would step instantly into his place, with strength enough at his command to beat off any attempt by the surviving Augustus to seize the realm.

With all these matters arranged Diocletian tackled the most grievous problem of all, reanimating the morale of both the army and the civil population.

As a military man Diocletian knew that once an army began seeking its own self-interest a death knell had sounded for the state and even for civilization itself. The most fundamental duty of a soldier— getting killed, if need be, while protecting the state—was a complete denial of self-interest; but how were soldiers to be brought back to this duty now that self-interest, naked and undisguised, had become the ruling principle of every Roman?

Diocletian was judge enough of human nature to know that no "appeal to reason" would do. How could it, when reason said plainly that a man who sacrificed himself for a state such as the empire had become was a fool? The only workable alternative was the age-old expedient of reason-swamping *emotional* appeals, devices and policies which would whip up the spirit of hurrah and bring men back to their old-time blind loyalty to the gods and the king. Accordingly Diocletian tried to bolster up the emotional appeal of the state by giving dazzling magnificence to his role as god emperor.

Part of this policy was an application of terror to the Christians and all who might be tempted to adopt the new faith, through a savage persecution. As a positive build-up he carried the pomp and trappings of an Oriental monarch, previously adopted in part by a predecessor, Aurelian, to stupendous heights.

By dressing in purple robes, a blaze of jewels, and strewing gold dust on his hair, he sought to be the visible image of a god. Eight lackeys carried his train when he entered his throne room, preceded by fanbearers and servitors spreading perfume. Everyone in the room remained sunk to the floor until the Awful Presence was seated, and so likewise was the Presence made felt throughout every detail of court life. Everyone lived under the shadow of a god.

Such a mountebank performance could only be called preposterous and insane did we not have the far grimmer explanation that it was the only expedient left, as long as Rome remained an anthill state. It could even be called a stroke of genius if only Diocletian had shown genius by recognizing the one source of moral strength the empire had left within its borders—the Christian faith.

By this time Christianity had won the adherence of a large majority of the downtrodden—that is to say, the rank and file of the population. More importantly, it had won most of those who had conscience, sensitivity and social sense enough to give loyalty to something outside their own selfish interest. Christians, then, could bring the dying empire the loyalty it needed, and Diocletian established his own measure as a statesman when he persecuted the faith instead of enlisting it in the cause.

This blindness was only partially redeemed by the recognition which came, finally, a few years after Diocletian resigned office in 305 to end his days with a little peace and quiet.

The immediate result was a dogfight for the divided empire, a dogfight which resulted finally in victory for a claimant from Britain and Gaul—Constantine, later called Constantine the Great. He it was who wedded the two forces of the empire and Christianity, and Christian records ascribe this change to a vision he beheld the night before he was going to give battle at the Milvian Bridge near Rome to his western rival, Maxentius. The vision showed him a cross blazoned in the heavens and the admonition *"In hoc signo vinces* (In this sign shalt thou conquer)". Next day, October 28, 312, he routed the rival army and became undisputed master of the Western Empire; and next year (313) he issued the Edict of Milan, which granted freedom of worship to Christians.

Historians have argued endlessly over the genuineness of this conversion. Doubters urge that Constantine did not accept baptism until many years later and that throughout his later reign he acted like a politician seeking advantage from Christian strength rather than behaving like a genuine convert. They urge also that Diocletian's successor in the east, Galerius, had given Christian freedom of worship, with resulting benefit to himself, well before either the battle at the Milvian Bridge or the Edict of Milan. Constantine, they say, was only profiting from this example.

Such arguments, however, do not affect the historic evaluation of Constantine. Whatever his personal beliefs may have been, *in hoc signo vinces* was a hard political fact. The cross was the only salvation in sight for the tottering empire, and Constantine had been wise enough to accept this fact.

Had he been willing—or even able—to carry this acceptance through into a program of new economic and social practices, he might even have regenerated the empire, just as Egypt had been rejuvenated about 2000 B.C. But Constantine made no such attempt.

After making his concession to the new order, for the rest of his policy he clung to the old idea by following Diocletian's policy of absolutist government, a dazzling court and a capital on the Bosporus. For this capital he preferred the Greek city of Byzantium on the west shore to Diocletian's choice of Nicomedia on the east shore, and Byzantium, renamed Constantinople for him and rebuilt to rival Rome itself in grandeur, remained the capital of the Eastern Empire to the end.

This amounted to renouncing the last hope for the empire, because the only chance lay in substituting the *spirit,* not the form, of Christianity for anthill concepts. This Constantine failed utterly to do—and, even worse, he reversed this desirable policy by trying to formalize and regiment the new faith. Far from adopting the wise course of letting the new faith do its work as a regenerating spiritual force, he tried to bring it, like everything else in the empire, within his control and then enforce it as the official religion for all.

This Romanizing, legalizing tendency had all but immediate results for the worse within the faith itself, especially in the church's dealings with problems of orthodoxy and heresy.

From the days of the Apostles on, the church fathers had been faced with grave challenges here, as various peoples had been won to the faith and had sought to graft their viewpoints and temperaments upon it. During the first century after Christ many of the Jewish converts saw in Christ their promised Messiah, and they tried to keep the faith a nationalistic property of the Jews. Condemnation of this on the ground that the faith was open to all men led to various heretical sects that insisted upon the Jewish viewpoint.

The great problems of the second century arose from attempts made by various mystic faiths, collectively called Gnosticism, to combine Christianity with their doctrines. In order to keep the Christian faith clearly separated from these combination doctrines the church fathers had laid down a Rule of Faith a man had to believe if he was to be considered a Christian.

During the third century the faith was troubled by a strong tendency to apply the rationalizing speculative spirit of Greek philosophy to Christian beliefs. The principal source of argument was *trinitarianism,* or the belief that the Father, the Son and the Holy Ghost were three in one. This contained a mystery, a concept which could not be rationalized, because to the Greek mind three could not be three and yet one. Three parts could form one larger unit, as do the leaflets of a shamrock leaf; but either they had to remain separate as parts, and so were not entirely one, or they had to fuse into one, and so the three parts would be lost.

So, at least, the philosophically minded Christians argued, while the orthodox insisted that the Trinity did exist and was *both* one and three. Now nobody need take a position on the doctrinal point involved in order to see that the orthodox party held the *psychologically* sound position. They were insisting upon a mystery, an article of faith which lay beyond justification by reason, and as a pure matter of psychology this was eminently sound. A religion without a mystery is not much of a religion. It does not give man the thrill of feeling that he is in touch with a larger Reality which transcends human reason and therefore has power which mankind lacks to help and to save. The rationalizing tendency, if carried through, might have left Christianity with but little more emotional power than had been possessed by Greek philosophy.

If left to itself, Christianity would have settled this difficulty with no more bitterness than had resulted from the Gnostic and earlier controversies. But now Constantine thrust himself into the situation with his legalizing program, by taking official action concerning the Trinitarian controversy immediately after he conquered the eastern empire and won mastery of the entire Roman world in 323.

At the time, the church in Alexandria had been torn for several years by arguments between the orthodox bishop, Alexander, and the presbyter Arius over the question of the Trinity. Arius held that God was one and eternal and had created Christ as his son before the beginning of the world. This satisfied the Greek passion for unity since it postulated one God and one only, but it brought the orthodox party up in arms because it reduced Christ to the status of a created demigod.

The quarrel attracted attention throughout the Roman world, and Constantine felt impelled to take a hand lest this new ally of his, the church, be riven. He was not yet baptized himself, much less entitled to speak as a clergyman, so he decided to call a general council of bishops and to give official sanction to whatever view the council adopted. The orthodox view prevailed and was formulated as the Nicene Creed—largely in terms of an older creed from Caesarea which stated the accepted doctrine—while Arianism was condemned as heretical.

If nothing more had been done, Arianism might well have died out as a minor heresy. But this time Constantine placed the official power of the empire behind the orthodox position by banishing Arius and all bishops who did not accept the decision of the council. This stern action, added to previous edicts against older heresies, announced to the world that all must believe as the emperor said, under penalty of punishment by imperial laws; and this remained the policy of every emperor after Constantine.

This was bad enough in itself, but it was not the limit of the mischief. Once the emperors took this position they automatically created a weapon which could be turned against them. Any leader or community which was against the emperor but did not care to base opposition upon political grounds could stir up a *doctrinal* quarrel. Thus theological questions often became rallying points, like a flag, for nationalistic sentiments and for the schemes of political intriguers; to doctrinal enthusiasm or even fanaticism was added political passion. Religious controversy from then on all too often seemed a product of hell rather than an attempt to promote devotion to a Heavenly Father and a loving Saviour. As only one sorry example, this same Arian heresy kept the Christian world torn into factions during all the soul-trying centuries of the final Roman collapse—with what loss of healing power and chance to inject Christian spirit into the new states which followed Rome, nobody can guess.

Thus Constantine missed the last fair chance the empire had to save itself, and nothing remains but to close the record with the story of the final ruin, at the hands of Teutonic barbarians. All in all, their so-called "invasions" were more of a taking over, a picking up of control as control fell from paralyzed Roman hands, than a conquest; and the complete illustration of this is the story of the people who delivered the actual deathblow in the west.

These people were the Goths, the folk who had established themselves in southwestern Russia and in Dacia under the peace made with Aurelian in 275. The driving force which set them in motion was the impact of a terrible new invasion from the Asiatic grasslands.

The invaders were Mongoloid Huns, driven perhaps by drought and attracted undoubtedly by hopes for plunder. After ravaging the lands of the Ostrogoths or Eastern Goths they fell upon the western group, the Visigoths of Dacia. These people fled southward across the Danube and begged to be accepted as settlers within the empire. The eastern emperor Valens agreed, and had he been able to restrain the rapacity of his officials, he might have acquired a valuable buffer against further inroads from the north. But his officials cheated and squeezed the new settlers until in 378 they revolted.

Valens moved against them, but in a terrible battle at Adrianople on August 9, 378, his army was routed and he himself was slain.

His successor Theodosius first defeated the Goths, then wisely persuaded them to resume their position as *foederati* along the lower Danube. He kept his promises to them, and they in turn helped him suppress a usurper in the Western Empire. In 395, however, he died— one year after the young Alaric had become king of the Goths—and the new eastern emperor Arcadius was foolish enough not to flatter Alaric with high office in the empire. Alaric promptly vented his disappointment by leading his people on a terrific raid.

Thanks to natural strength and stupendous walls Constantinople itself held out, and at length Arcadius placated Alaric by offering the Goths the province of Illyricum (roughly the eastern coast of the Adriatic) as a home. This drew the Western Empire into the crisis because this land belonged to the west; Arcadius had craftily given away what was not his to give. This threw the burden of keeping the Goths satisfied or subdued, as might be necessary, upon the western emperor Honorius, and of all men imaginable he was the least fitted to bear so heavy a responsibility.

He was honest enough at heart, perhaps; Honorius tried in his edicts to lighten burdens and hold the empire loyal. But he was a weakling and a coward, with the added failing, common to such men, of preferring crafty flatterers to strong men as advisers and lieutenants. Finally, his court exemplified the utter decadence of the Roman stock in that his one strong general, Stilicho, was not a Roman but a Vandal. In the inevitable struggle with the Goths Honorius would have to pit German against German, Stilicho against Alaric, and Stilicho would have to fight with Latin intriguers busily poisoning the emperor's mind behind his back.

Stilicho beat back several forays across the frontiers, but with ever greater difficulty because of poor quality in the army and lack of imperial support. But instead of being grateful Honorius listened to intriguing insinuations that Stilicho was to blame. Accordingly he had Stilicho assassinated (August 23, 408) while the populace butchered the unsuspecting soldiers of the army.

Alaric answered this insanity by marching straight upon Rome. Outside the city he was received by a deputation which both offered him bribes and reminded him of the enormous population opposed to him. To this he made his famous reply, "The thicker the hay, the easier it is mowed." Nevertheless, so great was the awe which Rome still inspired in all minds, he hesitated about attacking and finally consented to accept a huge ransom, a home for his people and Stilicho's position as commander of the Western Empire's armies.

Now Honorius redoubled his idiocies. Once Alaric retired, the emperor let his flatterers persuade him that the Goth was afraid, and he refused to honor the ransom bargain. Alaric advanced again, and Honorius promised to pay; Alaric retired, and again the emperor repudiated the bargain. This was more than enough for the Goth. He marched upon Rome; disgruntled slaves within the city opened the Salarian gate, and on August 24, 410, Alaric led in his Goths to take their fill of plunder.

A few historians take this event as marking the end of the Western Empire. Actually it was only one episode in the dismal record of dissolution, but it was a landmark, nevertheless, for the shock it gave to the entire civilized world. From Britain to Egypt, and from Gibraltar to farthest Mesopotamia, men could not have been more astounded had the moon tumbled from the heavens. The general reaction was that nothing less than a direct act of God could explain such a catastrophe. The only questions were what god had acted and why.

The still numerous pagans asserted that the long-suffering gods of Rome had taken their revenge at last. For the orthodox Christians, St Augustine spoke up with his famous work *The City of God*. In this book he set forth the view that similar disasters had occurred before but God would continue to care for his children. Orosius wrote *Seven Books of History against the Pagans* to prove that the error lay in allowing pestiferous pagan beliefs to persist. To accomplish this he piled up as partisan and prejudiced an array of evidence as can be found in all literature; but later ages swallowed it, and so arose the view that pagan imperial Rome had been without a parallel for monstrous vice, depravity and iniquities beyond power of description.

Thoughtful, balanced Romans shuddered but thought that the storm would blow over, and Honorius produced yet another twist in his eel-like policy. He raised not a finger when the Goths withdrew to southern Italy with their plunder. There Alaric died, probably of fever, and his followers buried him in the bed of a little river, the Busento; and now, after all the damage had been done, the emperor devised a colossal face-saving expedient. He offered Alaric's successor Athaulf (or Adolph) what he should have given Alaric—command of the Western Empire's forces.

What these forces were, nobody knew; the Goths themselves were all-powerful at the moment. The real point to the offer was the "commission" to expel the Vandals from Gaul and Spain. This the Goths proceeded to do, exactly as Honorius had hoped they would. By 418 they had conquered southwestern Gaul from the Loire to the Pyrenees, and by 429 they had driven the Vandals completely out of Spain into Africa.

Honorius died in 419, probably thinking that he had solved the problem of the Goths satisfactorily and perhaps never realizing that he had all but completed the ruin of the Western Empire. Southwestern Gaul was gone, and after 429 the Vandals seized and despoiled Africa with a savagery which has made "vandalism" a byword ever since. The harassed provincials of southeast Gaul actually invited the Burgundians to move in and establish themselves, hoping thereby to obtain a government strong enough to end the anarchy and brigandage which had resulted from collapse of the imperial power. The Franks spread westward from the middle and northern course of the Rhine, while the rude Angles, Saxons and Jutes began taking over England after the last imperial forces were withdrawn in 442.

In the Italian peninsula the imperial court tried to maintain authority with a mercenary army of Germans, but the army, naturally, was master of the court and made and unmade emperors at will. One last flash of spirit was shown when Attila led the Huns on a devastating raid as far west as central France. The imperial general Aëtius marshaled a force of provincials and Germans and inflicted a crushing defeat upon the Huns in 451 near Troyes. This was the engagement which is called mistakenly the Battle of Châlons.

But this general, "the last Roman of them all," earned Stilicho's reward for his achievements. The emperor Valentinian III listened to jealous intriguers and had Aëtius assassinated in 453. Two years later the Vandals sacked Rome, and in 476 the commander of the mercenary imperial army, Odoacer, ended the whole dismal farce. He swept the emperor of the moment, Romulus Augustus, out of office and took over the rule himself. To give himself legal status he arranged with the eastern emperor to act as a nominal vassal of the court at Constantinople, but apart from this shadowy allegiance even the fiction of imperial power was at an end in the west. All Europe faced whatever the future might have in store under its new masters, the various German nations. The book was closed on antiquity; the dawn of the Middle Ages had come.

PART VI

MEDIEVAL HISTORY—

The Forerunner of Modern Life

CHAPTER XXVI

The Dawn of the Middle Ages

THE TURN OF HISTORY from antiquity into the Middle Ages is time honored but also tricky—so much so as to prompt not a few modern historians to condemn the entire concept of a "Middle Age" as a false intrusion between ancient and modern times.

In *The Middle Ages* James Westfall Thompson says, "Antiquity ended with the Roman Empire. The modern period began with it. The Roman Empire was the link between ancient and modern European politics, institutions and culture." As to the term "Middle Age" itself, which was first used as far as we know in 1469, Thompson ascribes it to a belief among scholars of that day that the whole interval between ancient times and their own was an interlude of darkness, a "middle age." This, Thompson claims, was utterly untrue.

Nearly every art and technique of today has its roots in Greek and Roman culture. Modern arts and sciences, modern laws and the very essence of modern thinking and philosophy stem directly from Greek use of reason and from the Christian faith which grew up under the Roman Empire. The idea of a "Middle Age" can only be justified as a period of transition which did not begin at any definite date such as A.D. 476 and which certainly is by no means ended yet.

A somewhat sharper definition can be given, however, to the term "Dark Ages," for the opening centuries of this period.

If the Middle Ages was a period of working over the old material into a new mold, the first phase necessarily was a complete melting down of the old. The mere stagnation and breakdown under the empire had not been enough. The old culture had to pass through a crucible fiery enough to separate the sound metal from the dross and leave mankind in a position to rebuild with sound metal alone.

Such a trial meant continued decline, violence and misery, until the liquidation of the old was complete—and the centuries required for this liquidation form the Dark Ages.

This melting down started, however, almost without perceptible change or shock.

Perhaps the most rapid and striking *apparent* change was an all but complete disappearance of city life, except in Italy. Still, this decline looks greater than it was. The decay was already well along toward completion before ever the barbarians dealt the empire its deathblow. Many a city was all but deserted and even had farms appearing inside the city walls when the barbarians took over; they merely hastened the end.

In Italy, where the sea provided contact with the surviving Eastern Empire, some cities managed to keep going, albeit as shrunken shadows of their former selves. In Spain, Gaul and Britain, however, city life and commerce based upon money virtually disappeared. To survive, men drew together into the old primitive economy of self-contained local units—peasants growing food, craftsmen producing needed goods, and all doing so under the eye of a lord who regulated all the affairs of the little local anthill. The western world reverted practically to the economic life of First Dynasty days in Egypt; yet the Romans did not mind, because even this crude economy was preferable to the evils of the empire, especially the exhausting, merciless squeeze of imperial taxes. Salvian of Marseilles reflected this feeling in his book *The Governance of God,* with the statement, "So far are the barbarian Goths from tolerating such evil taxation that not even the Romans who lived under Gothic rule are compelled to endure it, and hence the one wish of all the Romans in those parts is that it may never be necessary for them to pass under Roman rule again."

The redistribution of land to provide the barbarians with homes and farms also proceeded with a minimum of shock. This was possible because the newcomers could obtain all the land they wanted without dispossessing any private owner. All they had to do was occupy the enormous tracts formerly held directly by the imperial government and commonly called the *fisc*. The Romans also had developed a system of landholding which suited barbarian ideas perfectly.

In legal theory the Romans owned land as people do today. The land belonged to the owner, and he could do as he liked with it as long as he paid his taxes and obeyed the law. Actually this free ownership had been disappearing steadily, owing to humble Romans seeking protection from the rich and the powerful through the process of *commendation*.

Under this process a poor man *commended* himself as a client to a rich *patron* by agreeing to perform services in return for protection and aid. The agreement did not transfer ownership of land in the eyes of the law, but actually it had much the same effect. The client was seeking protection for his property as well as himself from his patron, and he could not disregard the patron's wishes about his land. Usually he acquired the status of a *colonus,* a man granted a living upon the land of the state or of a rich proprietor. These *coloni* had been the empire's "colonists" on the frontiers, and by the easy device of forcing them to remain on the land they had been given they became the prototype of the medieval serf.

Commendation fitted beautifully into the barbarian ideas of life and government. In their wilder days the Teutonic barbarians had an institution called *comitatus* by the Romans, which was a warlike equivalent of the peaceful patron-client relation. The members were sworn followers of a chief in war. They fought and died together in support of their chief, and he in return shared the fruits of victory with his band.

Commendation therefore was a ready-made device for giving effect to the bond of the comitatus in taking over control of a region. First of all, the tribe or group possessed itself of the imperial fisc and the lands of those Romans who had been foolish enough to resist. The king and perhaps a few chiefs became the supreme holders and patrons for the others—or, in the later terminology, lieges or liege lords. The followers became clients (later called vassals), and the land held subject to this bond was called a fief (or, in the later English terminology, a "fee"). Roman holders fitted themselves into this arrangement by commending themselves to the liege of their district.

This arrangement obviously was the foundation of the later *feudal* holding—and it differed from Roman commendation only in the chief's right, held over from barbarian days, to call his vassals into his service in time of war. One other feature of the system is also worth noting carefully, because it was the source of much trouble later on. This was the provision for supporting the king himself and his retinue of persons who did not receive holdings of their own.

To accomplish this the king simply retained a generous slice of the fisc as *crown land* and lived upon the proceeds from it just as Augustus and his successors had lived upon the revenues from Egypt and other imperial holdings. This worked well enough as long as the fisc remained by far the largest holding in the kingdom; then the king would remain the most powerful war lord, as he should always be. But when fiscs shrank, as inevitably they did through divisions between sons, gifts to the church and to powerful lords in return for extra services, the king became no better than his chief tenants in power. Much of the confusion and near anarchy which marked the later phases of the Dark Ages arose directly from this lack of power in the central government.

And now for the positive forces which were at work, urging men toward a new society while the old was sinking into oblivion!

One obvious force was the renewal of group enthusiasms and loyalties, carried over from old tribal spirit. This renewal was by no means happy in all its results, since a favorite outlet for such enthusiasm was war—but still, almost any fount of group loyalty was better than the contemptuous and even bitter indifference with which Romans had come to view the state. Another potent force for good was the loss of profit in that age-old social cancer, slavery.

The intelligent slave and the highly accomplished house slave, both of which were to be found in swarms in ancient Greece and Rome, never had figured as profit earners. They cost as much as members of the family to maintain. Often they were treated as members and in time were given their freedom. The only profit makers were the agricultural and industrial slaves who were worked in gangs on highly productive soil or in heavy industrial tasks which did not call for much skill or initiative.

Such opportunities for using slaves had declined sharply in the later days of the empire, and they became virtually nonexistent in the barbarian kingdoms. Industry was dead except for household and manorial production, and the center of agriculture had shifted from the hot, fertile lands bordering the Mediterranean to northwestern Europe, with its sharply seasonal climate. The brute power of slave gangs was not efficient in meeting the demands imposed by such climate upon agriculture, and no city markets existed for mass production of foodstuffs if they had been grown.

Slavery gave way, therefore, to medieval serfdom, with serfs bound to the soil like a Roman *colonus* but still having a stake, such as it was, in their own future. Their lot was dull, miserable and deadening to mental development; but even so, it was not so much worse in this respect than was the lot of the master. He had a certain rude luxury, the excitements of war and the thrill of feeling important; but his sources of mental stimulation were no better than those of the serf, and the serf shared with him in the hope of eternal salvation held forth by the Christian faith.

This last fact introduces by far the most potent force of all for creation of a new order—Christianity, and the spokesman for the faith, the Church!

During all the troubled times of Roman decay and collapse the Church had gained immensely in prestige and power, since it had been not only the one remaining source of comfort but also the only strong institution of any sort in the land. When prefects and governors became powerless to enforce law and justice men appealed to the priests and the bishops; and these authorities had a sanction or penalty more potent even than prison for enforcing their decisions. They could excommunicate offenders and thereby condemn them to hell. Therefore, when the Western Empire collapsed entirely the Church stood forth as the only effective civil power as well as the spiritual mentor of the Roman world.

Fortunately, a considerable measure of this authority could be exercised over the barbarians as well, in restraint of their most savage impulses to ravage and plunder, because most of the Germanic tribes had been converted by this time. *Unfortunately,* this situation was poisoned by the persistence of the Arian heresy.

Most of the missionaries to the Germanic tribes had been adherents of the Arian party, and the barbarians therefore were Arians. This automatically set up a wide spiritual gulf between them and the western Romans, because Rome had held solidly to Trinitarianism throughout the controversy; and this cleavage poisoned what otherwise would have been a happy situation of barbarian and Roman being drawn together toward the ideal of a universal brotherhood fostered by a universal church. Actually they were held apart as Arians and Catholics, as Trinitarians now were being called, in addition to their separation as barbarians and Romans. Thereby regional and folk antipathy, rather than brotherhood, were bred into the thinking of the new states in their most impressionable formative days—with most unhappy results for Europe right into our own times.

Another unhappy circumstance was the necessary involvement of the Church in feudal landholding and thereby in the political schemes and quarrels of kings and chiefs as well.

From the very start of organized churches under a hierarchy, the organization had been supported by gifts and tithes from the faithful. These practices still remained in force, but now, in times when many a bishop bore the burden of maintaining law and order in addition to his spiritual functions, this support was not enough. The bishoprics needed lands of their own, not only to support the clergy but to support armed retainers in the only way possible at the time—giving a man land in return for his agreement to render military service whenever necessary.

This necessity in turn raised a host of plaguing problems concerning the relations of the Church to the kingdoms.

Each king insisted, naturally, that a bishop who held land should bear his share of the kingdom's military burden as did every other lord. The bishops insisted that their position was special, and the result was unending argument, punctuated by cancellations of land grants and immediate regrants as the balance of power between the kings and the clergy swayed with the political situation and the state of opinion within each kingdom.

This problem was complicated further by the rise of the bishop of Rome to leadership within the western orthodox or Catholic church.

Almost from the start these bishops enjoyed special prestige within the Church, partly because of Rome's importance and partly because of the connection between the apostle Peter and the Roman Church. The western orthodox church held the conviction that Peter had been selected by Christ as head of the church on earth and had established the Roman Church. The bishop of Rome was the obvious heir to Peter's authority, according to this view, and therefore was the rightful primate, or first bishop, in all Christendom. He was also coming to be known as the Pope, from the Latin *pappa* for father.

Other bishops resisted this claim, particularly the bishops of Constantinople. They held that the primacy had been established in Rome because Rome was the capital of the world at the time but that it followed the transfer of supreme imperial authority to Constantinople under Constantine. The situation was complicated further by the fact that the actual rulers in the west now were Arians, and the Arian clergy refused to accord any dignity at all to the Catholic bishop of Rome.

The inevitable result of all this was certain secular policies which marked the papacy throughout early medieval times. The first was a persistent attempt to enlarge the direct holdings of land as a source of much-needed economic and military strength. The popes came gradually to insist also that they held this so-called "patrimony of Peter" not from any earthly sovereign but from God. Thus they claimed temporal sovereignty as well as spiritual authority over the papal lands.

Another cardinal feature of papal policy was winning the barbarians from Arianism to the orthodox faith. Until this was done the pope's spiritual authority would scarcely extend out of Rome, and his hold upon the patrimony would be utterly insecure. But such a conversion by missionary methods seemed hopeless. The only hope seemed to lie in the rise of Catholic princes and kingdoms capable of displacing the Arian power, and the popes were committed in advance to playing politics with such Catholic princes and kingdoms in order to achieve their larger aim of a united Christendom.

Still another highly important development in the Church at this time was *monasticism*.

This institution began, so far as the records show, with the hermits of the third century after Christ. These were men whose souls rose in rebellion against the rottenness of life and consciousness of personal sin to an extent which prompted flight from all mankind into desert wastes. There they lived practically like beasts, subjecting their bodies to every hardship and even to torture, in a wild desire to achieve purity of soul. The earliest ones known to us were St Anthony (251–456?) and St Paul of Thebes (251–356?).

In these days when the Roman world was being torn by the struggles of the barracks emperors and life seemed a hollow mockery to all too many intelligent people, this example attracted hordes of imitators, both male and female, until the desert was all but alive with them. St Pachomius, an ex-soldier (292?–346?), was the first man, so far as the records show, who recognized the many evil effects of mass hysteria, personal degradation and loss of Christian effort which flowed from the practice. His remedy was organization into groups with a program of work and a community of life which sustained sanity. About 340 he gathered many hermits into a co-operative community on the island of Tabenna in the Nile and so established the first Christian monastery.

St Basil (329–79) established similar institutions in Asia, under a *Basilean rule* or discipline which still is fundamental in monasteries of the Greek Orthodox Church. The Western Empire received an impulse toward monastic life through St Cassian (about 360–435) and St Martin of Tours (about 316–97). In the decades immediately after the rise of Frankish power under Clovis, St Caesar of Arles (died 542) established many monasteries, and St Benedict (about 480–543) gave western monasticism its fundamental rule with his discipline for the establishment which he formed at Monte Cassino, halfway between Rome and Naples.

The Benedictine Rule was a superb combination of requirements for health of mind and body with celibacy and the idea of spiritual perfection. The diet was plain but ample; conversation and even manifestations of happiness were permitted. The prescription for keeping physical nature subdued was ample work.

The development of monasteries proved invaluable during the trying times of the Dark Ages through providing a rallying point for the spiritually minded, but it had the unfortunate corollary of drawing such people out of everyday life and weakening spirituality throughout the general population by that withdrawal.

Behind all these institutional developments within the Church, stood a corresponding mixed development of helpful and hurtful ideas and viewpoints.

On the constructive side stood the overwhelming fact that in principle the Christian faith contained everything needed to effect the change from ancient ways to modern within a few generations.

First and foremost, Christianity offered a complete remedy for the soul-sickness which had poisoned enthusiasm and initiative in the more sensitive and intelligent members of society. Moreover, the insistence of the faith upon the importance and dignity of the individual offered a potent solvent for such evils as slavery and inhuman regimentation under imperial law. These evils were utterly incompatible with the spirit of Christianity; as this spirit grew the evils had to dissolve and disappear, if through no other action than the workings of conscience in Christian individuals.

Unfortunately, the spirit of Christianity was not free to work its saving transformations either with the barbarians or the Christian Romans.

In the fields of morals and social conduct Christianity is a discipline of the spirit that brings brute nature into behaving in conformity with the Golden Rule, "Do unto others as you would be done by." Such an abstraction was utterly beyond the grasp of barbarian thinking. The new Teutonic masters of Europe were little better than children mentally. They were ignorant, credulous and more interested in wonders and miracles than they were in exact knowledge, and they had a savage's or child's preference for a personalized, concrete interpretation of the universe rather than the Greek's instinct for abstract principles.

Roman or Catholic Christianity could only accept this spirit with the hope of melting it in good time, and meantime wisdom seemed to call for giving the barbarian mind a personalization of evil with which it could fight. Satan, patterned almost exactly after the evil Ahriman of Zoroastrianism, became a real force in religious life. An impressive armamentarium of spells and charms grew up for dealing with him, and the business of foiling the devil became a major interest in later medieval life. The finer task of dealing with the evils in man's own soul was slower by centuries in winning its place in the everyday Christian life of the barbarian peoples.

Meantime Christianity was hampered in its dealings with the more intelligent and sensitive-minded Romans by an unfortunate aversion to knowledge and even to use of intelligence for advancing knowledge. This tendency was the inevitable consequence of the fact that the faith had come at a time when defeat and despair were overtaking mankind's efforts to live in the light of Roman government and Greek philosophy. The church fathers quite naturally had urged men to turn from vain Greek thinking to Christ as the one solid value in all the world, and this viewpoint held over into the days when men had smashed the old evils and had a chance to begin building anew in the light of the Christian dispensation.

Many handicaps existed then, as Europe faced its new future, and during several centuries these handicaps were to seem more important than the slow working of constructive forces. This weary period of seeming stagnation therefore is the next phase in the reconstructing of civilization. To complete our setting for it we owe a glance to the rest of the world scene at this time. We need only consider two features—the surviving fragment of Roman imperial power, the Eastern Empire, and the rise of Islam, the states and peoples together which followed the teachings of Mohammed.

The position of the Eastern Empire—or the Byzantine Empire, as the Latins were coming to call this state, from the ancient Greek name Byzantium—was extremely simple.

The natural strength born of superb strategic situation, which had enabled Arcadius and Constantinople to hold out when Honorius and Rome were overwhelmed in the west, still held good. The empire fortified its position further by taking over the age-old source of strength in the Mediterranean, sea-borne trade. This was enough, if necessary, to maintain a strong power even though its holdings might be reduced to the one focal point, Constantinople. Neither did the people themselves see the empire as a holdover remnant of ancient days! They called themselves Romans and dreamed of the days when they would re-establish the world-wide power of Constantine.

Actually, of course, this was only a dream, in more ways than one. Not only did their empire lack the military and social power to establish so vast a fabric; by now they themselves were Romans only in name. The move to Constantinople had placed them back in the Greek sphere, and Greek culture, always fascinating to the Roman mind, had overwhelmed them. They spoke Greek even though the law courts insisted upon Latin for a time, and they exchanged the Roman sense of natural discipline and instinct for practical group action for old-time Hellenic factionalism. They held together for a thousand years only because of their superb geographic position and the powerful momentum still left in their inherited culture.

Islam, in contrast, was a far more dynamic force in world affairs.

The origin of this faith with Mohammed, and the impetus for the conquests which resulted from it, are simple enough in outline.

Mohammed was born about A.D. 571 in Mecca, and he was named Abul-Kassim. His historic name Mohammed is a title which means "praiseworthy." His character can only be deduced from his career and his writings, but it seems to have been distinctly neurotic. He was a dreamer and a mystic, a sensualist and a fighter by turns; his ideas were a syncretism of material from other faiths. Neither did the ideas set his neighbors afire! In 613, when he was forty years old or more, his only converts were members of his family, one cousin and one friend.

How, then, did he manage to win the entire world of Arabs to his faith during the nineteen years of life which remained to him?

This happened because of a stupid action taken by the Meccans and Mohammed's shrewd response.

Mecca was living at the time on pilgrims to its various idolatrous shrines and by trade. Neither of these activities were being hurt by Mohammed's preaching, but about 616 some rich Meccans were foolish enough to think that he should be suppressed. They threatened to boycott his clan unless it ousted Mohammed, and although his clan stood by him, he elected to make his famed *hegira* or flight to the near-by city of Medina. He left on September 22, 622.

In Medina Mohammed found a people heavily sprinkled with Jews, who had no love for Mecca. He gained followers rapidly and soon felt strong enough to proclaim a *jihad* or holy war against Meccan caravans. The Meccans resisted but were finally beaten, and in 630 Mohammed was able to enter his old home as a conqueror.

From now on the new faith spread like wildfire, and for good reason. It coupled a delightful paradise after death with a program of plundering unbelievers during life on earth—a combination which was bound to attract an enthusiastic following from among the nomad Arabs once the followers of the prophet had proved their power by taking Mecca. Against this following stood only a thoroughly decadent Persian state in the northeast and elsewhere the Christian Eastern Empire; and the empire was in no shape to hold its outlying possessions.

The emperors had harried Palestine, Syria and Egypt because of various heresies and had imposed a crushing tax load as well as the Roman system of economic exploitation by the rich. These lands therefore were glad enough to see the empire and all its works thrown out, and they offered feeble resistance or none to the Mohammedan advance. Difficulties over religion were avoided by letting a conquered people retain any faith it liked on payment of a surtax.

The empire managed to stay the advance only at the mountain border between Syria and Asia Minor, while the first solid resistance in the west was offered by the Visigoths in Spain. But they had been torn by bitter strife between the Arian clergy and the king ever since King Reccared had embraced the Catholic faith in 586. They had harried the Jews mercilessly, and all western Africa was filled with exiles who welcomed an opportunity to help overthrow the Visigothic government. The Mohammedans, therefore, had every advantage from the time they entered Spain in 710 until they were thrown back out of France by Charles Martel and the Franks in 732.

Now let us see how this external setting, combined with the forces within Europe itself, began the slow and painful process of erecting a new order upon the ruins of the old ways!

CHAPTER XXVII

The First Shaping of Medieval Life

FORTUNATELY for historic simplicity, the first phase of transition from Roman to medieval can be traced largely in terms of one twin development. This was the rise of the Frankish power, and with it the Papacy, to the seeming dawn of a much-desired new order, when Charlemagne and Pope Leo III between them launched the Holy Roman Empire on Christmas Day, A.D. 800.

These events began with the appearance of a much-needed Catholic barbarian king, instead of an Arian, in Clovis, king of the Franks. He was converted in 496, or exactly twenty years after the extinction of the empire in the west. Thus the rise of the Franks ran almost exactly with the entire span of early post-empire history.

The events themselves need little attention down to 800 A.D. The half-tacit, half-acknowledged alliance of the Franks and the Papacy supported each other's interest against Mohammedan Moors from Spain, a last Teutonic irruption into Italy by the Lombards and intrigues by the Eastern Empire against the Papacy. The Moors were turned back by the Frankish king's chief officer, the mayor of the palace, Charles Martel, at Tours on an undated Saturday in October 732. Later Pope Zacharias helped cure a growing weakness of the Franks by endorsing the ouster of the original but degenerate Merovingian line in favor of Charles's son, Pepin the Short, as king. This first Carolingian king (so called from Charles Martel) broke the Lombard power and gave Romagna and the Campagna to the Papacy as Peter's patrimony. The Papal-Frankish march to power came to a peak under Pepin's son, Charles the Great, or Charlemagne (742–814; acceded 768).

Here was one of the strongest characters in all history—an in-

314

vincible warrior, a superb statesman and a fine friend of learning. By dint of thirty years of war he forced Christianity upon the heathen Saxons in north Germany and spread the Frankish empire from the Pyrenees to the Elbe and the Middle Danube and down the north half of Italy. In this last accession he included a protectorate sovereignty over the papal lands. Throughout this vast realm he maintained firm authority, in spite of wretched roads and turbulent local lords, by hawklike pounces upon his major enemies and a remarkable organization of trustworthy lieutenants. He attached the English monk Alcuin (735–804), one of the few learned men of the time, to his court and supported Alcuin's far-reaching program for educating the clergy and fostering learning. Charles himself set an example by learning to read and write Latin and Greek in his middle age.

The climax came when Charles was attending mass in St Peter's in Rome on Christmas Day 800. Pope Leo III unexpectly interrupted the service to place the famed Iron Crown of Lombardy upon Charles's head and to hail him in terms which the crowd in St Peter's Square took up—"Carolus Augustus, crowned by God, mighty and pacific emperor!" The terms "Augustus" and "emperor" showed clearly enough what was in everyone's mind. After centuries of turmoil and misery the *pax romana* of the old empire was to be restored, while the words "crowned by God" promised a new imperial spirit imbued with the spirit of Christianity.

This coronation is counted as the birth of the Holy Roman Empire, although the term "Holy" was not created until the coronation of the emperor Otto in 962—and the hope of such a temporal overlordship, to match the spiritual leadership of the Pope, remained alive in Europe for many years. But the brightness of the hope was matched only by the impossibility of fulfillment.

These men had caught a vision without realizing what would be needed to convert the vision into a reality.

For one need, no empire could be held together long without rapid communication and transportation over good roads by land and reliable shipping by sea. The Romans had possessed both, but in Frankish days the Roman roads were considered mere sources of building stones, and the Franks had no ability at all as seafarers. Another and even greater need was a population which had some comprehension, from mighty lords down to humblest workers, of national unity and discipline. Not even a superman could hold an empire together overlong unless he had some co-operation from his people. Charlemagne's empire, however, was a congerie of jangling tribes, in which the highest general sense of social organization was a sort of dumb loyalty to the local lord, the parish priest and perchance the bishop of the district.

An even more pressing need for an empire was revenue—and preferably revenue in money, since this was the only resource flexible enough to give freedom of action throughout a realm. But commerce and the use of money were all but dead in the Europe of Charles's day. The only resource of any consequence was land, and the feudal system of land ownership did not envisage taxation in money. A landowner's obligation to his overlord or lords was paid in military service, and a king such as Charlemagne was supposed to support himself, his retinue and any enterprises such as schools from the revenues he obtained from his *fisc,* or crown land.

This system offered a king little chance to finance improvements, and it became worse generation after generation if successive kings had to divide the royal holdings to provide for sons. Charlemagne owed much of his strength to the death of his only brother, four years after their father Pepin had died, and the resulting inheritance of an undivided fisc. But his situation was exceptional. The normal expectation was continual division of the fisc—and so, unless the crown lands could be enlarged every generation by conquest, forfeitures and other acquisitions, the necessary financial foundation for an empire was lacking.

The whole idea of a revived Roman empire, therefore, was an empty dream—and the proof of this appeared strongly enough through Charlemagne's grandsons.

Charlemagne's heir, Louis the Pious (778–840), had been his only surviving son when the great emperor died in 814, and thereby Louis had acquired an unimpaired fisc; but he was not man enough to curb quarrels among his sons over their prospects even while he lived. After he died in 840 the Frankish empire became a cockpit of civil war until the trouble was settled by the famous Treaty and partition of Verdun in 843.

This treaty attempted to preserve the idea of the empire by allotting the title of emperor to the eldest son Lothair. Lothair also took what seemed the most strategically located portion of the fisc—the central strip along the Rhine, the western Alpine region and northern Italy. If this portion had been stronger than all the others put together, the empire might have been saved; but unfortunately for this hope, Lothair's brothers had won practically equal shares. Louis or

Ludwig of Bavaria won everything east of Lothair's share—a domain which stretched practically to the Poland and Jugoslavia of our day. Charles, called the Bald, won a share roughly equivalent to modern Belgium and France.

Now the imperial power was worth only what Lothair could make it worth against these rivals, and this amounted to nothing at all. Neither did the trouble stop here. This division had to be followed by others in later generations, and by the time the ninth century had run, the disintegration of central authority was virtually complete.

Heirs of Charlemagne's blood still lived and claimed kingly authority in each of the three realms, but their fiscal holdings were overshadowed by those of many a duke, count and lesser lord. The only authority that counted really was the strength of each lord's castle, the valor, fidelity and strength of his retainers and his own skill as a fighter, intriguer and administrator. The situation was one of practical anarchy, as may be judged from Taine's classic description in his *L'Ancien Régime* (Durand translation, The Ancient Regime):

In this epic of perpetual warfare only one regimen is suitable, that of a body of men confronting the enemy, and such is the feudal system; we can judge by this trait alone of the perils which it wards off and of the service which it enjoins. "In those days," says the Spanish general chronicle, "kings, counts, nobles and knights, in order to be ready at all hours, kept their horses in the rooms in which they slept with their wives. The viscount in his tower defending the entrance to a valley or the passage of a ford, the count of the border, thrown as a forlorn hope on the burning frontier, sleeps with his hand on his weapon. . . . His dwelling is simply a camp and a refuge; straw and heaps of leaves overspread the floor of the great hall; here he rests with his armed horsemen, taking off a spur if he has a chance to sleep.

Thanks to these braves, the peasant . . . enjoys protection. He is no longer to be slaughtered, no longer to be led captive with his family, in herds, with his neck in a pitchfork. He ventures to plow and to sow, and to rely upon his crops; in case of danger he knows that he can find an asylum for himself, and for his grain and cattle, in the circle of palisades at the base of the fortress. By degrees necessity establishes a tacit contract between the military chieftain of the donjon and the early settlers of the open country, and this becomes a recognized custom. They work for him, cultivate his ground, do his carting, pay him quittances, so much for house, so much per head for cattle, so much to inherit or to sell; he is compelled to support his troop.

People accordingly lived, or rather began to live, under the rude, iron-gloved hand which used them roughly but which afforded them protection. The seignior, sovereign and proprietor maintains for himself, under this double title, the moors, the river, the forest, all the game; it is no great evil, since the country is nearly a desert, and he devotes his leisure to exterminating large wild beasts. He alone, possessing the resources, is the only one that is able to construct the mill, the oven and the wine press; to establish the ferry . . . or purchase a bull; and to indemnify himself he taxes for these or forces their use. If he is intelligent and a good manager of men, if he seeks to derive the greatest profit from his ground, he gradually relaxes, or allows to become relaxed, the meshes of the net in which his villeins and serfs work unprofitably because they are too tightly drawn. Habit, necessity, a voluntary or forced conformity, have their effect; seigniors, villeins, serfs . . . in the end adapted to their condition, bound together by a common interest, form together a society, a veritable corporation. The seigniory, the county, the duchy becomes a patrimony which is loved through a blind instinct, and to which all are devoted. It is confounded with the seignior and his family; in this relation people are proud of him; they narrate his feats of arms; they cheer him as his cavalcade passes along the road; they rejoice in his magnificence through sympathy. If he becomes a widower and has no children, they send deputations to him, to entreat him to remarry in order that at his death the country may not fall into a war of succession or be given up to the encroachments of neighbors.

The same disheartening sinking from poor to worse also was overtaking the one other strong element in society, the Church, during this dreary time. Thanks to the entanglement of the Church with the feudal system as the only available source of land and defensive strength, the hierarchy became all but completely secularized save for the ordination of its members as clergymen. Bishops often rode out with their troops and fought as stoutly as any feudal lord; more than one pope died leading an assault or in a defense which failed to hold out a foe from the Vatican, St Peter's and the stronghold of San Angelo.

Indeed, in the ninth century the Papacy became a football of Roman municipal politics, with rival factions throwing each other out and their popes with them. Perhaps bottom was touched with the grisly incident which followed the death of Pope Formosus in 896. His successor, Stephen VI, had the body disinterred, clad in full pontificals and tried before a packed court for uncanonical practices. After condemnation the fingers which had conferred the blessing were cut off and the body was thrown into the Tiber. A few months later John IX became pope, had the body fished out and gave it decent reinterment.

Even the monasteries suffered from the general decay, with sad loss of morals and involvement in world affairs. Some of them had *lay abbots*—noblemen who led the daily life and the fighting without becoming priests, just as many a bishopric had a lay bishop who held the episcopal fiefs for the same purpose.

Meanwhile, as civil society decayed, what civilization remained suffered from the age-old trouble which always came in such times— barbarian inroads over all the open frontiers.

In the east the Germans had long been troubled by the Slavs, an old amalgamation of Indo-Europeans and Alpines which had held the northern slopes of the Carpathians and now was spreading in all directions. This troublesome spread was intensified by continual pressure upon the Slavs from Turkish and Hunnish folk in Central Asia. Several centuries earlier Justinian had employed one of these tribes, the Avars, to fight another, the Bulgars; and when he dismissed them they seized Hungary and gave no end of trouble until Charlemagne and his son Pepin crushed them in 791–96. Then late in the ninth century another of these tribes, the Magyars, pushed through the Slavs and seized the Hungarian plain, where their Hunnish relatives had settled several centuries before under Attila. From this center they delivered harassing raids into Germany, Italy and even Burgundy, until the Germans crushed them in the Battle of the Lechfeld, August 10, 955.

This trouble was as nothing, however, compared to the continual hell which beat upon the northern and western coasts from out of the mysterious Northland! On almost any summer day some doomed community would descry gaily striped sails on the horizon—then beneath the sails would appear the dreaded Norse dragon boats, finer and faster than any previous watercraft known and filled with pagan blond warriors, the fiercest fighters by far in all Europe. Into some convenient river these Norsemen would come and beach their boats. Then would follow a visitation of sword, fire and pillage that left the countryside a stripped, smoking ruin. No power in Europe seemed able to stop these Norsemen, Northmen or Vikings ("Creekmen") as they called themselves.

During the first half of the ninth century the Norsemen confined their raids to the summer months and wintered at home. Then Harold Fairhair became active and gave the raids an entirely new character, especially after he defeated his rival chiefs in a sea fight at Hafrsfiord in 872 and became master of the entire Norse coast. Defeated chiefs had their choice of accepting his yoke or finding

AT SEA WITH "THE TERRORS OF THE NORTH"

Here a crew of Vikings, far out at sea, are "shooting the sun" at noon in
their crude way. The helmsman holds the sun straight abeam, and one rower
holds a bowl of water on the thwart. When the water stands evenly in the bowl
the boat is level, and the commander then marks the length of shadow cast by
the gunwale on the thwart. The longer the shadow, the farther north the boat
is—with due allowance, of course, for the season of the year. Such a determination of latitude may seem unbelievably crude to us, but the Vikings made it serve
for voyages as long as to Iceland and to Greenland.

homes elsewhere, and the second choice was the popular one. Instead
of merely raiding English and Frankish lands the Norse began
settling down in regions that suited them and raiding the country
round about. Truly the end of everything seemed at hand now that
these pirates were taking over the land!

Superficially the situation seemed like another impending fall of
Rome or conquest of Mesopotamia. Beneath the surface, however,
existed strong forces akin to those which pulled Egypt out of trouble
time and again. The Europeans of those days, for all the rudeness
of their culture, had plenty they were willing to defend with their
lives if necessary. They had their stakes in the land. They had their
Christian hope for salvation, and they still had plenty of the old
barbarian fighting spirit.

All these powers began rising now and offering resistance according to an ancient plan, the Caesar type of strong man. Petty dictators took charge here and there and began building up the power which was needed to restore peace and order.

One of these strong men—and at the same time one of history's finest monarchs—was Alfred the Great of England (848–99).

Alfred faced hostile settlements of Danes toward the northeast from the moment he became king of Wessex (West Saxon Land) in 871. For several years he maintained a heartbreaking war against them, until he managed to coop them up in a fortified camp at Chippenham, near the present Bristol. Thereupon he showed his genius by offering a compromise.

He proposed that the region north of the Thames and east of the old Roman road (now called Watling Street) should belong to the Danish king Guthrum and his people. Guthrum was to accept Christianity and acknowledge Alfred as his overlord. Guthrum agreed, and this peace, called the Treaty of Wedmore, turned the Danes from harriers of the land into defenders while exposing them to the Christian solvent for their fierce temperaments. Also it freed Alfred to rebuild life in his kingdom.

The foundation of the new order was a government which derived power not from the capricious loyalty of feudal vassals but from an organization of *shires* or administrative districts. The administrative head of each shire was a shire-reeve, later called a *sheriff*. He presided over the shire court, collected the fines and dues for the king and administered the crown lands within his jurisdiction.

This reform was possible because the exhausting Danish wars had all but wiped out the local lords; the survivors were happy to accept any arrangement which promised peace and order. But the real virtue of the plan was the strength it gave the central government. This government now enjoyed revenues *as a government,* and these revenues passed intact from king to king with the succession. They were no longer personal to the king, as the Frankish fisc had been, and subject to constant weakening by subdivision among the king's sons. Thus out of the fires of bitter adversity the English drew a lesson which no Teutonic people had ever learned before, and from this time on England began to display strength not only as a kingdom but in developing a distinctive and virile English culture.

Alfred himself laid the foundations of this culture, just as he had founded efficient government.

As a young man he had been stirred by the songs of the gleemen in his father's hall, and he was determined that his people should continue to have the patriotic stimulus of this racial heritage. For this purpose he compiled a record of Anglo-Saxon achievements which continued for three centuries as the Anglo-Saxon Chronicle. He also compiled the epic poems of his race. One of these, *Beowulf,* has survived and gives us our oldest picture of Anglo-Saxon temperament and speech. He had Anglo-Saxon translations made of such standard reference works as Bede's *Ecclesiastical History,* the *Seven Books against the Pagans* by Orosius, the *Consolations of Philosophy* by Boethius, and *Pastoral Care* by Pope Gregory I. By doing this he made the first break with use of Latin for all writing and helped bring about early use of English as a literary language.

Meanwhile the same lesson concerning government was being learned across the English Channel under Count Odo of Paris.

Odo inherited two elements of strength when he became ruler of Anjou and Blois in 886. One was the fine record of his father Robert the Strong, a lay abbot of St Martin's of Tours, who had been made Count of Anjou and Blois and defender of the region between the Seine and the Loire by Charles the Bald in 860. Robert had been killed fighting the Norsemen in 886, and Hugh the Welf, another abbot, had held the post until his death; but the memory of Robert lived to give Odo prestige when he succeeded Hugh.

The second element of strength was a remarkably simple but effective expedient which Charles the Bald adopted in 862 for checking the Norsemen. As seamen they had pushed their raids inland by sailing up the rivers. To stop this Charles simply built fortified bridges across the rivers. Thereafter the Norse ability to raid swiftly and depart was replaced by the necessity of first besieging and carrying these protecting bridges. An energetic defense at such a rallying point automatically protected all the country upstream from the bridge.

One of these bridges in Odo's charge was at Paris, and there Odo proved himself a worthy son of Robert by holding the bridge and Paris through a memorable ten months' siege laid by the Norsemen in 885–86. He also unwittingly put himself in line to be king of the western third of the empire through the contrast he afforded with the miserable successor to Charles the Bald, Charles the Fat. This blubbery weakling came, supposedly, to the rescue in September 886—and he relieved Paris by the disgraceful expedient of buying off the Norsemen. He had grace enough to give Odo the titles Count of

Paris and Duke of the Franks before he returned to his German lands, but his day was done. Not much more than a year later the disgusted western Franks and the Germans together declared Charles deposed, and Odo was crowned king of the western Franks on February 29, 888.

Odo then wore out his strength until he died on New Year's Day 898, defending his title against Charles's legitimate successor, Charles the Simple; but he learned his lesson. Just before dying he advised his brother and heir Robert to let the bauble of kingship go to Charles. From that wise policy came the kingdom of France, with Odo's house of Capet furnishing the kings directly or through branches as long as France retained kings.

Robert and his canny descendants, Hugh the Great (reign 922–56) and Hugh Capet, built up their power while the Carolingians faded until Lothaire, the last of the line, died in 986. Thereupon the Frankish nobles elected Hugh Capet king. He founded what later became the strongest and most absolute monarchy in western Europe.

Thus two strong monarchies arose out of the ruin created by the Norsemen. Others were created by the invaders themselves, beginning in the years when Odo's brother Robert was contenting himself with building the power of his house.

During this time the Norsemen were actual masters of the Channel coast between Flanders and Brittany, and in 912 Charles the Simple bought peace as Alfred had done. By the Treaty of Saint-Clair-sur-Epte he granted this region as a fief of France, while the Norse leader Hrolf or Rolf agreed to become a Christian and a vassal of the French king, with the title Duke of Normandy. Thereafter, as often happens when marauders acquire a stake in the land, these Norsemen—or Normans, as they now came to be called—became a tower of strength in northern Europe.

In political administration they exhibited the highest sense of discipline and unity Europe had known since the days of early Rome. Perhaps they remembered the discipline of the sea, or perhaps centuries of incessant war had insured that practically any Norse leader would be of first-rank caliber. But whatever the reason, Norman dukes and lords were conspicuously successful in maintaining and enlarging their domains.

Not only did they make Normandy the leading power in France; within a century and a half all England was Norman as well. In the Mediterranean a group of forty Norman knights on a pilgrimage were invited into a local quarrel in southern Italy in 1016. Before long the forty, with some recruits from home, seized the heel and the toe of Italy, ousted the Mohammedan Saracens from Sicily and made the region into Norman principalities. In all these expansions they spread a rule of iron, but also they gave the arts of peace a chance to develop behind a screen of Norman lances, swords and shields.

Neither were they backward as leaders in this development! Wherever they went they showed striking ability to absorb local culture and energize it. After less than a century in France the Norse were intensely French in spirit but more active than ever the Franks had been. They developed such North French industries as weaving to humming activity, and they converted old Roman architecture into their own Norman style of building. The Danish Norse in England became equally English within this same century, and within a century after the conquest of England the English Normans had become Englishmen as well and were lending their peculiar energies to building a strong and distinctive English culture. The Norman dukes in Sicily usually were strong patrons of the Arab learning they found there, and under their rule Europe gained what probably was its first university, at Salerno.

In addition to these local contributions the Norsemen gave all Europe a new zest for exploring and a new idea of seafaring.

When everything is considered the Norse must be counted the greatest seafarers of all times. Instead of building clumsy arks or floating castles, as all previous seafarers had done, they built graceful, light craft, exquisitely molded for speed and ability to ride out storms. Whereas other peoples dreaded the open sea, the Norse loved it. As navigators they were without equal at that time. They did not mind crossing the North Atlantic to Iceland and Greenland, steering by the stars at night, and by day judging latitude from the length of shadow cast on a thwart when the sun was at its highest. To make landfalls in thick weather, they released ravens and followed the bird's flight to land. From them came the seafaring ability of the later English, the Breton French and the Dutch mariners, while even the Italians and the Portuguese of the south owed much to them. The southerners first became competent to sail the Atlantic when they adopted Norse ideas in their shipbuilding and caught some measure of Norse daring at sea.

Because of all these contributions some modern historians consider the Norsemen the most important single force among all the

THE TOPMOST EXPERIMENT IN DARK AGE EDUCATION

Here the greatest teacher of the early Middle Ages—Gerbert (950–1003) of Aurillac, afterward Pope Sylvester II—is concluding the education of a class in the cathedral school at Reims by showing how musical tones are created. He is showing that the pitch of a tone depends upon the length of the wire or other vibrating medium which gives off the tone. Longer lengths give lower tones; shorter lengths give higher tones. This simple demonstration, which today would be given in a high-school introductory course in physics, was the crowning bit of knowledge imparted in the tenth century and rightly so. Nothing more could be taught, because nothing more was known.

factors which turned the tide in Europe from degeneration toward renewed progress in the tenth and eleventh centuries. But history cannot disregard the regenerative force exercised by the Church once partial restoration of civil order gave it a chance to work.

Perhaps the most striking instance of churchly influence at work was the *Cluniac reform,* so called because the driving force behind it was the preachers trained and sent forth from a monastery established in 910 at Cluny, near the Jura Alps. These preachers carried a message which fitted the times as a key fits a lock.

Most of the evils had come about because no strong authority, national or imperial, had existed to maintain peace and order. Now, however, Europe could envisage a remedy which earlier ages had lacked. Even though earthly authority had failed men still could expect God and His Son to establish just rule on earth. So far this had not been done; but the Cluniacs had a convincing explanation for this, one drawn from the Hebrew prophets. Mankind had displeased God by allowing worldly life and even the lives of God's particular servants, the clergy, to become corrupt and evil. Let mankind prove to God that it repented its sins by cleaning up these evils, and God would see to it that his just rule became effective!

Such an appeal can never stir an entire population as long as the powerful leaders are satisfied with conditions and the majority of the people still have hope. But now despair had swamped hope throughout Europe and laid men wide open to any emotional appeal which offered a remedy for intolerable conditions. Here was just such an appeal—and it swept the continent, not only with a new spiritual urge within individuals but with the even more formidable conviction that rulers and clergymen who displeased God were responsible in a large degree for the miseries of mankind!

This new conviction lit a fire which no sensible ruler cared to defy. A tough-minded feudal lord might decide that he could push the consciences of his subjects to revolt and still keep his authority with military power, but he took care, unless he was a complete fool, not to outrage the general conscience to a point which would bring denunciation from the Church and Church-inspired action by neighboring lords and his sovereign to end his wrongdoing by force.

This awakening of general conscience was matched, slowly but still surely, by a more formal growth of ethical ideas in the form of *medieval law*.

In general, medieval law was a blend of Roman and barbarian ideas reworked in the spirit of Christian doctrine.

Roman law had rested, as did all else in the state, upon the theory that the will of the sovereign was supreme. Whatever the emperor commanded was the law. But this view that "law is the expressed will of the sovereign" was tempered by two other principles.

From their early days the Romans had inherited a body of principles, the *jus gentium* or "law of the peoples," which they considered valid for non-Romans and in civil controversies between Romans and non-Romans. This *jus gentium* therefore constituted a sort of "right" which all men enjoyed by sheer virtue of *being* men, and the emperors usually respected this charter of elementary human rights.

The second principle was that of *equity*.

The Romans recognized that any body of formal law, however carefully drawn, would produce occasional injustices. When this happened the sovereign or his representatives should intervene and set aside the formal law in favor of doing justice. This intervention was the process of "giving equity."

All these principles, and all the vast mass of edicts and decisions that dealt with the intricacies of Roman life, had been reduced to fair order by jurists such as Papinian (died 212); and the results were set forth in the *Theodosian Code* of Emperor Theodosius II in 438, only twenty-eight years before the extinction of the Western Empire. Thereafter the codification of the law was completed in the Eastern Empire under Justinian, in the magnificent *Corpus Juris Civilis* or "Body of the Civil Law." The Corpus consisted of a Code (529, in twelve books), which contained all edicts and similar formal pronouncements; the Institutes (533), a brief statement of controlling principles; the Digest or Pandects (about 433), which analyzed decisions or precedents; and the Novels (565), which set forth Justinian's own laws.

Meanwhile the Teutons had been following the universal primitive view that law expressed established custom. Even in the comparatively sophisticated times of Anglo-Norman law in the eleventh and twelfth centuries, a common test of validity for a law or right was that "the memory of man runneth not to the contrary." Kings and other magistrates could explain and interpret while applying such customary law, but they were supposed to leave it unchanged except with the consent of the elders, the full assembly of warriors or, in later days, some respected body of important men.

As the barbarian folk became more sophisticated and began acquiring acquaintance with Roman thought they caught the Roman idea of law as an expression of sovereign will. But they were still too fiercely free in spirit to grant any such sweeping power to an earthly sovereign. Also, the priests who explained the idea of sovereignty took good care to give another twist to the principle. They set up God as the sovereign who gave commands; his will, as expressed in the Bible and through the Church, was the supreme law. From this the priests drew the further conclusion that the customary rights enjoyed by men under barbarian law and the *jus gentium* of Roman law actually were two different forms of God's charter of rights for man, and no king or lesser man could transgress whichever one applied without risking the wrath of God.

As for the power of equity, kings should continue to exercise this under guidance from God, and to insure this guidance the medieval lawyers devised a most ingenious expedient. The "keeper of the king's conscience"—that is, the priest who heard his confessions— usually was known as the *chancellor,* and who could guide the king better in doing equity than this same priest who knew the innermost secrets of his soul? The chancellor therefore became the chief adviser in such matters, and when the king no longer could keep up with the press of such business he usually delegated his powers of equity to his chancellor. This practice is reflected even today in the common name "chancery" for a court that exercises the power of equity.

Of course in the rude days of early feudalism the hardhanded lords did not trouble their minds much over such finespun theory. The actual working law often was what the Germans called *Faustrecht* ("fist right," or in more idiomatic English, "the law of the strong right arm"). But even in these rude days most of the lords felt fear enough of this abstract law to seek some gloss of legal justification for their actions. And this rude respect for right was only a dim foreshadowing of the power the concept developed as the turbulence of raw feudalism gave way to more settled institutions.

In these later days the very heart of governmental and social philosophies was this doctrine that man had certain rights conferred by God —rights which no sovereign could set aside or transgress—and this idea became an even stronger rallying cry against tyranny and oppression of every kind. Thus in principle one of the most important of all the needed changes from ancient to modern was taking shape even in this supposedly "Dark Age." These rude European thinkers were overthrowing the anthill principle that man exists for the group. Now the individual was winning recognition as the fundamental unit of society, with certain inalienable rights granted by God which no king or group could transgress. By working from this foundation, a foundation which the Greeks had missed despite their mental brilliance, mankind could build a truly satisfactory social framework for giving scope to the urge for self-aggrandizement. Within such a framework individuals would work and contribute as they never would do in an anthill society, because now they could feel that some individual reward was guaranteed to them.

When we say this we are, of course, anticipating events by many centuries. Recognition of the individual was taking shape in principle at this time, but in principle only. In practice the recognition still was of the rudest quality, and it was overlaid by many a mistaken concept. The distrust of knowledge and of life which had arisen from the spiritual emptiness and despair of Rome's dying days was still almost all-powerful; the leaders of thought still insisted that the only worth-while objective in life was winning salvation in Heaven. The social framework which would give scope to individual search for self-aggrandizement still remained to be built, almost from the ground up.

Nevertheless, the new light had dawned, and the burden of history from now on will be the story of how men learned through many a bitter trial to follow it more and more. Moreover, history has an outstanding marker in events and in time for this change.

How long these rude beginnings would have taken to bear fruit if left to themselves, nobody can say now, because at this time the world setting of Greek, Latin and Islamic rivalries boiled up into a series of continent-wide convulsions. The convulsions were the Crusades, and out of them came a fusing of ideas and a stirring of new impulses which transformed Europe within a few centuries and set in train the regenerating force of new respect for the individual as the unit of society.

CHAPTER XXVIII

The Crusades Transform Europe

THE ORIGIN OF THE CRUSADES is simple enough and an outstanding example, as well, of how the emotional forces in human nature can work to make history. The entire movement was a logical capstone to the Cluniac reform, a flowering of the new enthusiasm for Christian ideals; and this flowering took the form of military expeditions to the Near East, partly because of the martial spirit of the age and partly because a rallying cry lay available for use in the status of pilgrims to Jerusalem.

Under the Arab Mohammedans this status had been agreeable. Far from being intolerant, the Arab caliphs welcomed visitors, especially those having cash; and in 807 the two greatest representatives of the rival faiths, Harun-al-Rashid and Charlemagne, had achieved a splendid working arrangement. The Moslem caliph gave Charlemagne the right to protect the Church of the Holy Sepulcher and pilgrims traveling to it. Charlemagne agreed not to interfere with pilgrimages made by Mohammedans to their holy places in Jerusalem. Thereafter, aside from a short burst of trouble in 1010 with the mad Caliph Hakim, pilgrims enjoyed peace until the Seljuk Turks took Jerusalem in 1071.

The Seljuks were not fanatic but they were rough, and they had inflicted a crushing defeat on the Eastern Empire at Manzikert that same year. Thereafter the empire kept up a continuous outcry against them, with the idea of enlisting help from the Latin west for its endangered territory in Asia Minor.

This clamor found sympathetic ears among laity and clergy alike in western Europe. Both nobles and commoners within the laity were feeling the urge to "do something for God," in keeping with Cluniac preaching, without being quite able to reach the heights of regenerating their moral natures. Service to God within the familiar frame of a military adventure had potent appeal. Behind this stood the more hardheaded appeal of the Norman success in winning a kingdom in Sicily and southern Italy. A formidable force of Norman and French younger sons, and even lords who saw no prospects for improving their holdings at home, saw a bedazzling chance to repeat the Sicilian success in the rich Near East.

The clergy found special attractiveness in the adventure, not only through gaining Jerusalem but as part of the Church program for Europe.

As part of the Cluniac movement for regeneration of social and spiritual life the Church wanted to suppress the torment of constant feudal fighting. But the reformers knew the laity well enough not to preach against fighting itself. Instead they pressed a flank attack throughout the eleventh century by insisting throughout France, where the Cluniac influence was strongest, upon the so-called Truce of God. This "truce" was launched at the Synod of Elne (1027) in southwestern France, with prohibitions of private warfare from noon Saturday to sunrise (prime) on Monday, under penalty of excommunication. Later the closed season for fighting took in various holy days and seasons such as Lent, and it lasted from Wednesday evening until Monday morning. By the twelfth century scarcely a quarter of the year remained available for private wars.

This program was still largely in the making, however, in these days, and a crusade to Asia looked like a beautiful expedient for drawing off fighting from Europe. Warriors could well afford to observe the Truce of God at home as long as they could get all the fighting (and plunder) they wanted by warring upon the infidel enemies of Christ.

An equally strong commercial motive existed in various Italian trading cities but especially in Venice and Genoa.

These cities had grown gradually out of the wreckage of the Western Empire and competed with Constantinople in carrying Oriental goods to supply such western markets as existed. In this trade they suffered a heavy disadvantage since they had to obtain much of their wares from their senior competitor, and the obvious remedy was to establish trading centers of their own in western Asia, where they could contact producers and caravans from the Far East directly. A successful crusade almost certainly would yield them such establishments.

The underlying situation, therefore, was highly favorable for military effort, and all these factors were brought to a head when Pope Urban II, on November 26, 1095, issued a fiery call for a crusade at the Council of Clermont in France.

His call to war was a masterly appeal to all the existing impulses, especially when he added remission of sins for all who took the Cross. The upshot was an all but explosive response, once Europe had digested the terms of the call.

To the lay mind Urban had offered a complete and glorious solution for every doubt and trouble, both worldly and spiritual. Rich lands to be seized and held—in God's name; plunder and women to be had for the taking—as part of God's work. Sins, crimes and debts at home would be escaped, for to the crusader all would be forgiven.

At the very thought of all this, emotion came welling up until in susceptible minds caution, prudence and reason were swamped and the individual found himself swept almost as in a dream to take the Cross. Everywhere in Europe the reaction was the same—dazzled bewilderment at first, then a growling murmur that rose to a shout as the vision took hold. *"Deus vult!* (God wills it!)"—the cry would ring out, and from that instant on men were ablaze with crusading fervor.

The actual course of the crusade, from 1096 to 1099, is a splendid demonstration of such an emotional explosion at work.

Urban had set midsummer of 1096 for assembly of the forces, but when Peter the Hermit and others set the populace afire with their preaching the serfs, peasants, criminals and petty figures generally could not wait. As soon as spring came and made traveling possible they dropped tools, took the roads to the Danube and started backtracking along the prehistoric route which the first neolithic peasants had followed from Asia Minor into Europe three or four thousand years earlier. Gradually the migrants coalesced into five enormous mobs which moved as so many hordes of locusts, devouring everything they encountered as they pressed forward to God's work.

The first two mobs, led by Peter the Hermit and Walter the Penniless, passed through Hungary in May and reached the assembly point, Constantinople, in July. But these two were all that the Magyars of Hungary could stand. When the third and fourth mobs poured in during June the Magyars slaughtered them. The fifth delayed its fate by tarrying long enough in the Rhineland to massacre ten thousand Jews, then met its Hungarian death in August. Meanwhile the eastern emperor, Alexius Comnenus I, freed his capital of the human plague by shipping the mobs across the Bosporus, into the teeth of the Seljuk Turks. By October nothing but heaps of bleaching bones scattered through western Asia Minor told of this first wave. Peter the Hermit escaped because he remained in the eastern capital.

The armed and disciplined forces of the major leaders moved in better order, according to schedule, during 1096 and were assembled in Constantinople by May 1097. The chronicler Fulcher estimated the strength at 600,000; Urban set it at 300,000; modern scholars such as Ernest Barker prefer a more modest figure of 150,000. But even so, these burly, armored braves, clanking about Constantinople with their heavy Frankish longswords, were frightening enough—and Alexius was glad to see them off in May and June, after wringing a reluctant oath from the leaders to recognize him as suzerain of all lands they conquered.

Thereafter the record outdoes romance for hardship, adventure and *outré* turns of fortune. For seven months the crusaders besieged Antioch, on the north Syrian coast, and suffered almost as much as the besieged from lack of food, weather, hardship and disease. Then they took the city, and almost immediately a Seljukian army penned them in to stand a siege in their turn. They were reduced to eating rats and melting away from disease, when the priest Peter Barthélemy announced that he had found the spear which had pierced Christ on the cross—a spear which reputedly had been hidden under the altar of a church in Antioch.

Enthusiasm born of this find enabled the wracked, emaciated force to throw off the siege and open the road to Jerusalem. The walls of the Holy City rose before them in July, and on the fifteenth they took their goal by storm and celebrated the victory with an appalling massacre of inhabitants. Horses splashed in blood to their knees, according to a chronicler. During all the slaughter the crusaders took care to chalk their names or signs on the doors of the houses that pleased them—a summary but effective way to acquire property. *"Deus vult!"*—it was all God's work, and a perfect demonstration of what can happen when the brute in man is unchained in a spiritual cause.

After the conquest many of the crusaders left for home, and those who remained set up a government under Godfrey de Bouillon (1060–1100) as Defender of the Faith. So also were crusading orders formed—the Knights Templars and the Knights of St John or Hospitalers—and the conquerors settled down to impose the iron hand of western feudalism and fanaticism upon Palestine.

They did not succeed in the end because they gave more strength to fighting among themselves than they did to holding Palestine. In less than two centuries, despite support from six more crusades, the Moslems threw all Christian power out of Palestine, and the crusading effort, in point of military and political objectives, ended in failure. All these later crusades are more important, however, to the historic record than they are to the history of thought. The effect of crusading upon European thought and life was touched off effectively by the First Crusade. The later efforts need not be considered.

In direct effect upon thinking and life the most important immediate result was the contact with the rich old Roman imperial culture, as seen both in the Eastern Empire and under Mohammedan rule in Syria and Palestine. The crusaders of higher rank, accustomed to life in drafty, cheerless castles with rush-strewn floors and the general barrenness of a modern lumber camp, saw elegant palaces with tinkling fountains, luxurious furniture, luscious gardens and silk-clad women and slaves—altogether something comparable to paradise being enjoyed right here on earth. The lower ranks saw imposing cities, churches ablaze with gold and jewels, public gardens, shops filled with rich merchandise, amazing bridges, aqueducts—again a vision of paradise to humble men such as they.

Once seen, such sights never could be forgotten. Neither could the urge to strive for such delights back home be downed. Certainly men who could overawe the empire and conquer the infidels could live as well as these weaker men—and this, by hook or crook, they proposed to do. This desire not only brought commerce alive in western Europe; it completed the new day for the commercial activities of the Italian cities. Out of the First Crusade Venice and Genoa had won direct trading centers of their own in eastern cities and were in strong position to acquire and transport wares for the western market, without yielding any of the profit to the empire. Western Europe behind them had become a clamorous market—and best of all, the traders found a fine way to pay for the imports. The East was glad to exchange its wares for the fine woolen cloth which northwestern Europe could produce.

Neither did these cities monopolize the benefit. After they had transported eastern goods and placed them on the main roads in Europe, opportunities existed for other traders to handle the goods in retail lots. The return demand for wool also gave manufacturing a start in the woolgrowing centers. Together these new chances for profitable activity stimulated the rise of cities and towns. The Rhine, long a "bishop's way," began to become a "merchant's way," with towns becoming rich all along its course; towns grew up in Flanders to spin and weave wool in payment for Oriental goods. Northern Italy developed inland Lombard cities—Milan, Pavia, Mantua and others—which were able within a century to stand up for their rights as well as could Venice or Genoa against any overlord.

Meanwhile the more thoughtful among the crusaders were equally impressed by the manifest richness and supposed depth of imperial or Byzantine and Moslem knowledge. Instead of the meager array of parchment rolls which passed for a goodly collection in a European monastery, they saw huge libraries and thronged schools. They had been making guesses on a childish level at the riddles of the universe; now they met astronomers, mathematicians, doctors and other scholars who could assure them with a superior smile that all such questions had been answered long ago. The inevitable result was a burning desire to plumb this knowledge and a persistent effort, once they returned home and were at peace, to do so from the Saracen scholars still left in Sicily and the Moorish centers of learning, such as Cordova, in Spain.

To do this required not only to have dealings with the hated Moslem infidel but translation of texts from Arabic into Latin. This "long way around" seems absurd, because the original writing had been in Latin and Greek, tongues which should have been familiar to western Europe; but recovery from the Arabic was necessary because of the vast difference between Christian and Mohammedan rulers in their attitude toward learning.

Since the fall of the Western Empire Rome had been indifferent or even hostile to any learning other than theology. In the sixth century Justinian had dealt learning in the Eastern Empire a deadly blow by closing the schools in Athens and virtually driving all scholars other than lawyers and theologians into exile in Persia. In each center this reactionary policy grew naturally from thinking that man should concentrate upon winning eternal life in Heaven without much thought for life on earth, but learning suffered grievously.

In contrast, the Arabs were not only tolerant to all thought which accepted political domination by the Mohammedans but they displayed an Alexandrian or Ptolemaic attitude toward learning. In place of austere Christian disdain for knowledge of the earth they considered learning an enrichment of their culture, and the caliphs of Baghdad, in particular, welcomed scholars of all creeds and races to their capital. Persians bringing Byzantine learning, Jews with hidden tomes of ancient Greek lore, Hindus with their independent knowledge—all were welcomed and set to fusing their knowledge in the common pot of Arabic lore.

The contrast, both in attitude and results, between Christian and Moslem had shown forth strikingly a full three hundred years before the First Crusade, in the difference between the limited success achieved by Charlemagne with his Christian schools and the brilliant flowering of knowledge under his Moslem contemporary in Baghdad, Harun-al-Rashid. Even by Harun's time most of the important Greek works had been translated into Arabic, and Jewish, Persian and Arab scholars were developing their own versions of the thought. At the same time knowledge utterly beyond the ken of the ancient Greeks was coming in from India and even distant China.

One such gain was the germ of the magnetic compass. The history of this device is obscure, but the Chinese seem to have used a lodestone as an interesting toy. They used it on land instead of at sea, and the Arabs seemingly did not value the device any more highly. This cannot be counted as stupidity, since all seafaring was done by coasting with steady monsoon winds, and no real need existed for a compass. The real contribution was having the idea at hand where western seafarers could pick it up when they began to need such guidance.

Another immeasurably important addition to western knowledge was Hindu mathematics. Indeed, no serious guilt of overstatement could be attached to the claim that without this contribution modern science and machine-age industry could hardly have been attained. Both science and industry rest today upon accurate, efficient mathematical calculations of dimensions and quantities, and we can make them only because the Hindus and the Arabs broke away from the idea which had all but paralyzed progress in mathematics since Alexandrine days.

The trouble here had been the Hellenic objection to using zero as a number. How, the Hellenes had asked, could a sign for *nothing* be used as a sign for *something*? It could not, in one sense; but the Hellenes overlooked one highly important use. Zero could be used in a number system to mean "nothing here," as we do when we write 4, 40, 400, 4000, 40,000. Here we have used only one digit, 4; but it has five different meanings, thanks to the zeros. This number writing is easy, no matter how large the number, whereas the Greek system and the Roman one after it produced such horrors as CDXVIII, meaning 418. The sheer labor of writing numbers in Greek fashion choked mathematical progress until the Hindus devised the use of zero.

How the Hindus attained this happy system is not known, but Hogben offers a plausible explanation in *Mathematics for the Million*. He says that Hindu mathematics was developed by practical-minded men who wanted efficiency and simplicity in mathematics and did not let logical niceties stand in their way, after the fashion set by the Greek philosophers. The Arabs were of like mind, and so between them the two peoples brushed aside one of the greatest handicaps which mistaken thinking ever had imposed upon itself.

This new and practical kind of arithmetic and algebra was set forth even in Harun's time by Mohammed ibn Musa al-Khowarizmi, and his text gave the west both the science and the name of algebra, from the Arabic *al-jebr*, meaning to bind together. During this same reign Geber or Jabir (Abu Musa Jabir ibn-Hayyan, 721?–813?) produced some hundred works on chemical manipulations. These books inspired Europe with the idea of alchemy, a parent of modern chemistry.

By the time of the First Crusade this growth of knowledge had come to a glorious culmination.

During the century between Harun and the First Crusade Avicenna (Abu Ali ab-ibn-Sina, 979–1037), a physician and philosopher in Persia, produced his *Book of Recovery*, setting forth in Arabic his version of Aristotle. His *Canon of Medicine*, in five volumes, embodies Aristotle's version of Hippocratic medicine, later Alexandrian work and the Roman knowledge of Galen. So well did Europe think of it that the universities of Louvain and Montpellier used it as late as 1650. At the time of the First Crusade Omar Khayyám, "the Tentmaker," was bringing Al Khowarizmi's algebra to a new high level of efficiency, revising astronomical tables, devising an improved calendar and meanwhile writing his charming *Rubáiyát* in praise of joyful living. His birth date is not known, but he died in 1123.

Thus a rich harvest of learning awaited European exploration— and a trickle of scholars, which soon enlarged to a flood, swallowed religious prejudices long enough to study in Moslem universities, particularly in Spain. Thanks to them, Latin translations of Arabic works began pouring into Europe.

A start on this work had already been made by a curious character, Constantine the African (1020?–1087), just before the First Crusade. He turned up in the court of Roger Guiscard of Sicily as Roger's secretary about 1071, and he followed Roger to the health resort at Salerno. Then he became a monk at Monte Cassino, where he died, and during these years he translated many Arabic works by African writers. He compiled a treatise on Aristotelian physics, another on philosophic definitions and several medical books from Isaac Isreali (855–955, called in Europe "Isaac the Jew"). He also extracted a tome on medicine from the works of Ali ibn-al-Abbas (called Holy Abbas in Europe; died 994).

These translations spread like wildfire, and soon they were followed by a flood. A magnificent source was Toledo in Spain, which had fallen to the Christians in 1085, just before Constantine the African died. Archbishop Raymond maintained a splendid corps of translators to work into Latin the riches of the Moslem universities from 1125 to 1151. From their labors Europe acquired Arabic versions of the most important Roman and Greek works. The leader of these workers was Gerard of Cremona (1114?–1187); others were Adelard of Bath, Robert of Chester, Herman of Germany, John of Spain and, lastly, Alfred the Englishman (about 1225).

Another quick result from this stimulus was enlargement of various old cathedral and monastery schools into the beginnings of universities and, somewhat later, the foundation of new institutions.

The University of Paris, including the Sorbonne, and Oxford and Cambridge universities in England were typical products of this movement, while the University of Bologna was the first one in Europe to receive a charter as a self-governing institution of learning (1158). Most of these schools, being church institutions, still restricted their curriculum to the medieval *trivium* of grammar, rhetoric and logic, followed by the *quadrivium* of arithmetic, geometry, music and astronomy, and theology as a culminating study; but medicine and the liberal arts began to creep in. This tendency was especially marked under Norman rule in Sicily and southern Italy.

Roger II of Sicily (reigned 1101–54) made a notably liberal gesture by inviting the young Moorish geographer Idrisi (1099–1154) to his court in or about 1125. Idrisi brought with him all the geographic knowledge which had been gathered since the day of Ptolemy, and he and Roger made a strenuous effort to enlarge this knowledge during the following twenty-five years. They supplemented Idrisi's personal knowledge, gathered by traveling from Portugal as far east as Asia Minor, by sending observers into more distant lands to study and report. By January 1154 the results had been compiled into an imposing treatise with a large world map and seventy-seven smaller ones. Idrisi called it *El Rojari* after his patron, but the scope of it is revealed better by the full title, *The Going out of a Curious Man to Explore the Regions of the Globe, its Provinces, Cities, and their Dimensions and Situation*. The work was crude and more descriptive than scientific; geographic locations were fixed more by travel time than by astronomical observations of latitude and longitude. Nevertheless, it was a beginning for scientific geography in Europe.

A significant footnote to this geographic effort is the oldest known mention of the magnetic compass in Europe. An English monk and teacher, Alexander Neckam, spoke of it twice about 1180 in two of his encyclopedic treatments of the new knowledge. The quotation from his book *The Uses of Things* runs as follows:

When they cannot see the sun clearly in cloudy weather or at night, and cannot tell which way their prow is tending, they put a needle above a Magnet which revolves till its point looks North and then stops.

Plainly, then, the sailors as well as the geographers were on the track of new ways—another fruit of Arab contacts!

Meanwhile this enrichment of knowledge was being paralleled by a corresponding relaxation of austerity and enlargement of gaiety in the lives of the noble and the rich. Oriental silks and muslins added gaiety to attire; spices, sugar, watermelons, apricots, lemons and other fruits enriched the diet. Traveling singers, called *trouvères* in Provence and *troubadours* in the north, wandered over France, singing romantic songs and being treated as favored guests in the castles they visited. Poetry became rich with color and romantic interest. The idea of chivalry—valor in war, tenderness for women and knightly honor at all times—came into bloom.

Even the serfs and the commoners shared to some extent in these benefits. Their meager joys were enlarged by traveling jugglers and the growth of *miracle plays*—Bible stories and tales of the saints, staged on festival days for the moral uplift of the population. They also derived profit from quickened economic life. A succession of lucky harvests, coupled with freedom from baronial wars, might yield the serf enough to purchase his freedom. Many a rural commoner established himself in a happier lot by escaping to a growing town and finding a place there.

Finally, behind all these obvious gains, occurred a steady growth of the legal and governmental ideas which lay at the heart of medieval law. Especially was this true in England. Indeed, England led the world at the time in this field by finding practical expedients for reviving *democratic government,* without the weaknesses which had ruined the Athenian experiment some fifteen hundred years earlier.

The immediate foundation of this movement was the practice begun by William the Conqueror, after his seizure of the throne in 1066, of issuing charters granting certain rights to citizens and also to cities and towns. Henry I and Henry II continued this practice and also organized the administration of justice by establishing royal courts and sending *king's justices* on regular tours or *circuits* to supervise local courts. In 1215 a momentous advance in principle was added when the outraged barons, clergy and other powers of the realm confronted the infamous King John with his choice between giving a written guarantee to respect lawful rights or facing war to the death. With all England against him John could only give the guarantee, and on June 15, at the little Runnymede Brook near Oxford, he signed the Great Charter, or *Magna Charta,* which bound English royalty to respect English rights.

The Great Charter contained nothing beyond the rights granted in its predecessors save for sharp definitions intended to block John's well-known shiftiness, but by its very nature it constituted an immense advance in principle. Previous charters had been royal *grants,* freely given and presumably alterable or revokable at royal pleasure. This charter was a contract with every powerful person in the kingdom, and in legal theory no king had power to change it unless the contracting powers of the kingdom gave their consent.

During this same time England was developing efficient methods for financing the government with taxes in place of the unworkable feudal scheme of crown land and feudal military service.

General taxation as a substitute for feudal dues had started obscurely in the ninth and tenth centuries in the form of the *Danegeld* —a general levy upon wealth to raise the enormous bribes with which the rulers of harried lands hoped to buy off the Viking raiders. English kings had used the device *and* the name to raise revenues in emergencies long after the Norse raids had ceased, whenever they thought that a feeling of emergency would produce willingness to pay; but in time the device became unworkable, and kings were without an excuse for levying general taxes until the keen legal mind of Henry II supplied two new expedients during the latter half of the eleventh century.

In 1159, when Henry contemplated fighting to obtain the feudal rights of his wife Eleanor of Aquitaine in southern France, his chancellor Thomas à Becket had suggested that many knights and higher lords might like to pay a *scutage* or "shield fee" (from the Latin *scutum* for shield) instead of performing actual service. The revenue from this could be used to hire fighters. Henry accepted the idea, and it proved enormously popular; so Henry and his successors drifted into the habit of levying scutages instead of calling for feudal service, unless the emergency was grave enough to demand the full fighting strength of England.

Henry's second form of tax was the *Saladin tithe*—a levy of one tenth of all personal property in England, which the Great Council authorized in 1187 to finance the Third Crusade. This was the old Danegeld type of levy, but it bore a new and popular name and hence gave such levies a new lease on life. With these grants added to the increasing use of scutage the outlines of general taxes plainly were growing out of feudal government.

These taxes differed, however, in two tremendously important respects from the autocratic taxes levied in Roman times. For one difference, all of them were outside the feudal contract and hence not legal, *unless consent was given* by the vassals to the extra imposition. The second difference was the desirability of having them paid in *money,* and this would be utterly impossible except as newly revived commerce stimulated use of money and provided the wherewithal for payment. Kings therefore had a direct financial interest, aside from their revenues from charters and monopolies, for fostering commerce and the seats of commerce, the chartered towns.

Accompanying these developments as an enforcing agent came the rise of the British *Parliament.* (The term "Parlementum" from the French *parler,* to speak, seems to have been used by Matthew of Paris in 1246 for a meeting of the French Great Council.)

The British type of parliament began to grow out of the King's Great Council of dignitaries, when it was summoned in 1265 to pass upon a demand from the extravagant Henry III for a huge grant of money. The powerful Simon de Montfort, leader of the dissatisfied peerage, forced inclusion of representatives from the towns. This was the first recognition of the nonnoble commoners in the national deliberations of England. This gain was confirmed, and this initial evolution of English government was completed, in the reign of Henry's son and successor, Edward I, sometimes called "the Justinian of England."

Edward, like his Byzantine prototype, was hard, grasping and imperious; but he had the knack of his better forebears for thinking in terms of practical law. He also knew well how to read the signs of the times, from the moment he acceded in 1292. England was determined to have her charter; the barons were determined to have their say about the conduct of affairs and the granting of levies upon the kingdom. The only problem was to work these demands together into a practical scheme of government with, of course, as much royal power as possible, and by the end of his reign in 1307 this had been accomplished.

The form of English government was set by the Model Parliament of 1295. This parliament included not only the great bishops and lords but two proctors from the lower clergy of each diocese, two knights from each shire and two citizens from each city or borough. This parliament accepted the doctrine that once these representatives had voted a grant the levy was binding upon the entire kingdom; no one could plead feudal right or lack of personal consent against it.

Next year the church properties were brought within the plan by a characteristic bit of Edward's strategy. The clergy stood upon a papal bull of 1296, which forbade payment of taxes by churchmen to any civil authority. Edward did not inveigh against the action. He said in effect, "So be it. But those who withdraw from duty to the kingdom withdraw from its protection." This amounted to outlawry—and Edward, the clergy well knew, was strong enough to make the policy stick. They observed the letter of the bull by paying their share of the levy as gifts, but they paid and continued so to do thereafter.

So likewise does much of our civil law, especially laws concerning real estate and property held in trust, date back to statutes of Edward's reign. He also gave English courts their historic organization into four divisions—a Court of Exchequer to deal with questions of revenue, a Court of King's Bench for criminal cases, a Court of Common Pleas for civil cases, and a Court of Equity for exercising the king's prerogative of relieving injustices or lack of justice under the common law.

Taken together, this development of Parliament and English law is one of history's finest examples of how successful new institutions, new patterns of human organization and understanding, are worked out. England had accepted the fundamental principle of democracy—consent of the governed to the measures of the government—but the result was as different in character and strength as could be imagined from the Athenian experiment of the fifth century B.C.

In that distant time Clisthenes had injected untried theory in his constitution of 508-07 B.C., and every departure he made from the sound reforms of Solon had worked badly. He had introduced ostracism to get rid of would-be tyrants; the citizens had used it to silence critics whose criticisms should have been heeded and to banish leaders who insisted upon unpopular but necessary measures. He had placed all power in the hands of the citizenry, unschooled as it was, and thereby he had made demagogues the actual rulers of Athens.

In contrast, the English experiment had been hammered out step by step, often by dint of frightful conflict, and every item in it had been tested by ripe experience before it went in. The government had a powerful source of responsibility, in the kings and the great lords, in place of an irresponsible, chaotic mob in supreme authority; it admitted less skilled and seasoned elements, such as town governments, only as they forced admission by proving their power and their value to the state. Yet at the same time the way was open for such admissions whenever they should be justified, and this conservative but reasonably steady enlargement of the democratic principle has remained the keynote of English constitutional development from Edward's day to ours. One of the undying glories of the English people always will be this achievement. Athens may have invented the principle of democracy, but England discovered how to make the principle workable.

And now, against these gains made during the crusading period, stands the other side, the darker side of the story!

Naturally these gains were not achieved without cost in struggle against bitter opposition and cost in suffering as well. Europe had her forces of ingrained conservatism, blind prejudice and fierce bigotry as did Athens, Egypt and all other lands wherein the powers of reason had tried to assert themselves during earlier times. The shining example of what these powers could do is the record of western Europe's greatest scholar at the time when the Crusades commenced in 1095—Peter Abélard, hero of the dramatic and piteous love affair with Héloïse.

Born at Pallet near Nantes in 1079 of a noble family, Abélard proved flamingly brilliant as a student in various cathedral schools. While studying in Paris under William of Champeaux he beat the master in debate and was expelled in punishment. The same triumph crowned his studies under the noted Anselm at Laon, and students flocked to him in preference to all other masters. By 1115 student clamor practically forced his appointment as canon and master of the cathedral school of Notre Dame in Paris.

Then he and Héloïse, niece of the canon Fulbert, fell in love, had a child and were secretly married. The enraged Fulbert invaded Abélard's room at night and inflicted brutal mutilation upon him. Abélard hired bravos to retaliate but sought refuge for himself by becoming a monk in St Denis, while Héloïse became a nun. Thereafter love could only express itself in letters.

But the students would not let Abélard alone. He tried to be a hermit; they followed him, and a school grew up at his hermitage. Neither could the jealous and fearful ecclesiastics let him alone. The fierce "fundamentalist" and preacher of the Second Crusade, Bernard of Clairvaux (1090–1153), had Abélard's views condemned as heresy at Sens in 1141, and the badgered scholar died April 21, 1142, while on a journey to Rome to plead his cause. Héloïse lived until 1164, and the two still lie in the famous tomb in Père la Chaise cemetery in Paris, a perfect monument to brilliance and love struggling against medieval asceticism and bigotry and a monument as well to the eagerness of students to learn, even in that dark time.

Abélard founded no doctrine and left no "school"; his best-known work, *Sic et Non* (Yes and No), was simply a compilation without comment of opposite positions taken by the church fathers on theological questions. But the very compilation was a challenge to thought. For this reason Abélard is sometimes called "the father of Aristotelianism" in Europe.

This can fairly be said even though a portion of Aristotle had been used consistently in western schools as a textbook for dialectic, the "art of reasoning correctly." This fragment, the first part of the *Organon,* had been translated into Latin, with commentaries, by "the last Roman scholar," Boethius, just before the fall of the Western Empire. What Abélard did was show what power could be gained in argument and analysis by using the logical principles laid down by Aristotle. Thereby he not only set students ablaze with enthusiasm for mastering Aristotle; he made them thirst for more knowledge of all these amazingly keen old Greeks, pagans though they were.

By this same token, however, Greek learning inevitably would become the first battleground behind conservatism and progress, between the Dark Age concept of a society organized entirely to win salvation and one organized to give scope to individual lives. Reaction could look with a somewhat kindly eye upon change in worldly life; this would not deflect *thought*. But when men began to change the objectives of thought itself, this surely was nothing less than the devil at work, slipping in his soul-destroying poison! Such contamination would have to be fought to the death.

So indeed the issue took shape. Not rapidly at first, because the scholarly seekers after new light did not realize themselves what they were doing! Only as they went on would some older ideas become suspect—and then and then only would trouble come. Let us see now how this worked out!

CHAPTER XXIX

Beginning of the Struggle for Free Thought

How and why twelfth-century enthusiasm for Aristotle can be called the parent of modern thinking appears clearly enough from the nature of the problem the medieval thinkers raised for themselves when they sought to work the teachings of the ancient Greek master into their own patterns of thinking. They fancied that their task amounted to reconciling the teachings of their new enlightener, the pagan Aristotle, with the tenets of the orthodox faith. Actually they were questioning the very foundations of all faith, all knowledge and all understanding.

This was inevitable, because the essence of Aristotle was reliance upon reason while the essence of Christian orthodoxy was acceptance and belief upon faith. Now reconcilement of reason with faith is the most fundamental problem any man can set for himself. To deal with it requires, first of all, a comprehensive theory of human nature, one which explains what man's mind is and how it works. Next this theory must be brought into satisfactory relation with God, for the essence of the problem is to explain how the mind can "run free" when it is applying reason and yet be bound to and controlled by God when God's grace and will are at work. This in turn raises the questions of what God's nature might be and how this nature is related to both the physical universe and the mind of man.

The philosophy which came from applying Aristotelian logic to such questions is known as "Scholasticism." We call the thinkers Scholastics—and in our day the fashion is to sneer at Scholasticism as a sterile business of debating how many angels could dance on a needle's point. Truly enough, it was abstract, philosophical and subject to the ironclad requirement that all arguments *had to end in triumph for orthodox Christian doctrine.* But even so, men also must learn to walk before they can run, and the Scholastics, little as they realized the fact, were giving rise to modern thinking.

One of their first steps in this direction was learning the difference between two fundamental ways of gaining knowledge. One way was by the *inductive* or *synthetic* method of collecting, testing and sieving out facts, then building the facts into large understandings. The other was the *deductive* or *analytic* method of reasoning down from an assumed general principle to detailed explanations of facts; and the two approaches were thrust upon these medieval thinkers in unmistakable clarity by the characteristic mental bents of their new Greek mentors, Aristotle and Plato.

Aristotle was practical, Socratic and inductive or synthetic in his handling of problems, especially in his encyclopedic treatment of biology, astronomy and other sciences. Hence he is often called "the materialistic philosopher."

Plato created a speculative dreamworld in which mind alone counted—nay, in which mind *was* the real world, the only True Reality. God was the Supreme Mind and gave everything, even sticks and stones, whatever true reality they had. The *seeming* reality which men see and feel was only a set of appearances which the senses of man caught as a sort of reflection from the inner essence. Aristotle held a similar view of God as the supreme driving force of the universe, including man, but he gave separate existence to free will. He might be said in modern terms to have considered God as the steam in the steam engine, whereas Plato said there was no real engine. What we call an engine was simply the form our senses give to the reflections we catch of the steam at work.

At the same time the Scholastics had a knotty problem upon which to try out these approaches in the question of *free will*—that is, whether man has some power within him which can do as it sees fit, or whether the decisions which seem like products of free will actually just register orders from God, much as a marionette obeys pulls on hidden strings.

Until now Christian thinking had seemed comfortably set on this problem by the decision reached after a famous fifth-century controversy between Augustine of Hippo and Pelagius over the Pelagian heresy. This heresy arose when an earnest monk named Pelagius came to Rome from Scotland and was shocked, when he cried out against the licentiousness of Roman life, to receive the excuse, "The flesh is weak." He replied roundly, "You can be good Christians if you will"—and for his later amplification of his position he was challenged by Augustine.

Augustine's contention was that human will is powerless to achieve the Christian life and salvation unless imbued with God's grace, first by baptism and periodically thereafter by other sacraments. Pelagius replied, "Why then need a Christian bother, under this view, about good works or good living? If he has grace, he has it—if not, his case is hopeless; and effort would not count in either situation. You must grant man free will, or he has no logical reason for striving to win salvation." Augustine replied that the situation was twofold. God, through his grace, gave men the chance to be saved, and so grace was indispensable. Thereafter man had to justify the gift of grace in his conduct. This was the view which the Church pronounced orthodox.

Now, however, Aristotle gave this view a rude shock. By admitting even a slight bit of free will, he seemed to be a Pelagian. Even worse, when the Scholastics applied Aristotelian logic to Augustine's views they found that the bishop of Hippo had left many a loose thread in his argument. Hence they were more perplexed than ever—nor did they find light when they sought help from infidel sources. The Moslem divines were equally baffled by this problem of free will. The best the Christian scholars could find was two brilliant minds at work upon this problem in the half century after the death of Abélard in 1142. One was a Spanish Moor whom they called Averroes; the other was the rabbi in Cairo who was called Maimonides by the Christians.

Averroes (properly Abul Walid Mohammed ibn-Ahmed ibn-Mohammed ibn-Rushd, 1126–98) developed his thought by translating Aristotle with comments of his own, and these comments were strongly Platonic in flavor. He believed in an all-pervading God-mind which gave off an emanation into the universe. Men were intelligent because of this emanation, and they enjoyed immortality through the return of their shares of emanation to God when they died. This emanation therefore corresponded closely to Augustine's views about God's grace, but this view left no room for individual free will or even for wholly individual immortality, since each man's portion of "emanation" returned to God at death.

Maimonides (Rabbi Moses ben-Maimon, 1135–1204) set forth his views in a massive three-volume work, *The Guide for the Perplexed*. In this work he achieved a reasonable reconciliation between Aristotle and the Jewish Bible by assuming a limited and separate amount of free will in each man. This sufficed for many choices and decisions, but for complete life and for the existence of the universe God's will also was necessary. This Divine Will supported the universe and kept the various celestial spheres of Aristotle's cosmology turning in their appointed courses; so also did it support the lives of individual souls. Thereby Maimonides provided a reasonably good basis for explaining the mixture of free will and dependence upon God which the Augustinian doctrine required.

Thus, thanks to a Moor and a Jew, the Christians had suggestive treatments of their problem—and a long and difficult story may be telescoped, in its purely intellectual phases as a problem in thought, by considering the answer achieved by the brilliant Thomas Aquinas (1225-74), creator of so-called Thomism. We call him "Thomas" here while referring to him as a living man, although the proper name in general is *Saint* Thomas because of canonization in 1323.

Thomas was born of a well-to-do family at Aquino near Naples, and he was educated in the historic Benedictine monastery at Monte Cassino; but in 1244 he forsook the Benedictines by becoming a Dominican friar. Thereafter his official life was spent in the schools of Naples, Paris, Cologne and Rome, but his lifelong personal purpose was solving the scholastic problem of reconciling Aristotle and the Bible—or, more broadly, of proving a consistency between the existence of human reason with its supposedly "free will" and the existence and providence of God. This he accomplished in two monumental works—*Summa contra Gentiles* (The Summation against Pagans, 1259–64) and the *Summa Theologica* (written after 1265 and unfinished at his death; Reginald of Piperno wrote the end).

In the work against pagans—really against pagan or Greek reliance upon reason—Thomas proved the reconcilability of reason with faith in God. He held that both existed somewhat like two sides of a shield or a coin and each must be exercised to fulfill the complete destiny of man. Man tries, and should try, to do what he can with his power of reason by applying it to the data furnished by his senses and by using his ability to select, arrange and modify. But when he has done all he can he reaches a vast array of problems which baffle reason, and for his adjustment to the universe and his destiny in this field of thought he must rely upon beliefs accepted on faith. These beliefs, Thomas said, have been given man by God through revelations.

Now this may be called dry medieval scholasticism, but apart from particularized theological doctrines about God and revelation this is precisely the view which is held by most advanced scientists of today. Science has come closest, perhaps, to grappling with its ultimate problems in the field of physics (including astrophysics), and all leading physicists today recognize that knowledge can go only so far before it comes to problems which defeat human understanding.

We talk glibly enough, for example, about "infinity" and "eternity." We even use these concepts mathematically; but who can really *understand* them or grasp their essential nature? We may extend space and time as far as we like in imagination, but after we have done our best to make such an extension all we can say about the real nature of either infinity or eternity is, "It lies beyond that uttermost extension which we have just imagined." In our grapplings with these ultimates we can only stand upon some explanations which we take on faith, just as we must in our dealings with the origin of man's self-consciousness. This is precisely the conclusion which Thomas reached in the *Summa contra Gentiles*.

In the *Summa Theologica* Thomas gave an amazingly keen foreshadowing of our new understandings about the nature of man.

Thomas said that in essential nature man is a wellspring of urges and desires, which is precisely the understanding being reached today by modern psychologists. As long as the urges and desires which are not destructive are gratified man prospers in body, mind and soul, but when these gratifications are blocked or denied man withers and dies—a proposition which is the soundest of modern psychology, particularly in psychoanalytic and psychiatric views of mental trouble.

Man's social problem of dealing man to man therefore becomes one of arranging for uttermost gratification to each man, subject only to the limitation that no man should gratify his own urges at the expense of his fellows. The man-and-God problem arises, for man's share in it, because among man's deepest desires is a yearning for eternal life. But when man attempts to find his way to this end he is in the realm of thought that lies beyond the grasp of reason. He must rely upon faith in the providence of God. Concerning free will, Thomas said that it existed and could *turn* man toward salvation or damnation but it could not *achieve* salvation by its own power. For this God's grace, or gift of power to live in God's way, had to be added to man's free will—an addition which God made for all who sincerely wished it. Then the will, as modified by grace, could achieve a Christian life on earth and salvation in heaven.

This example of scholastic doctrine gives a fair idea of how these medieval thinkers came closer than many a modern psychologist, writer, and preacher of uplift to setting forth the true nature of man. Thomas also ranged into explanations of government and science which were extremely penetrating and acute, considering the limitations of knowledge in his day and the necessity of squaring every statement with orthodox dogma. Meanwhile, however, more voluminous work in these fields was done by encyclopedists such as Albertus Magnus, Vincent of Beauvais and Bartholomew de Glanvil (called Bartholomew the Englishman).

Albert (1206–80) was a busy Dominican friar and master of schools in Paris and in Cologne, yet during his well-occupied life he found time to compile all the knowledge of his day—Aristotelian, Christian, Moslem, Jewish, everything he could find. He is accused today of childish credulity, and certainly his work bristles with phoenixes, unicorns and other fabulous outrages upon sober fact. Had he applied his own (and Aristotle's) dictum of relying upon direct observation of Nature, he would have avoided a host of elementary errors.

Still, a busy churchman such as Albert could hardly have roamed the world and tested everything for himself. He could only work with material which others had gathered, and certainly he performed a valuable service by organizing all the existing knowledge and pseudo knowledge of this day for use by other scholars. Taylor says in *The Medieval Mind* that his writings represent, perhaps more fully than those of any other man, all the knowledge and intellectual interest of western Europe in the thirteenth century.

Vincent of Beauvais (1190–1264) was keener than Albert as a systematizer but much less voluminous. Bartholomew the Englishman wrote in an engaging style which made him the leading exponent in his day of "popular" or "Sunday supplement" science.

These men complete the list of deductive or analytic Scholastics who reasoned from an accepted Christian starting point to detailed explanations, save only for Duns Scotus (1270–1308), the man who stood midway between these deductive thinkers and those of inductive or synthetic bent who all unknowingly were giving birth to modern science.

Duns Scotus was a Franciscan friar from Oxford who devoted himself wholeheartedly to testing out everything for himself, so far as he could, before accepting it as true. One of his feats was spending a bleak winter in Paris working out astronomical calculations on the wall of his friar's cell for lack of better working facilities. His more intellectual contribution was his insistence that the deductive method could get nowhere in the end because it could only come back, after all the argument, to the starting point, its original premise. The only way to gain increased knowledge was to gain new facts.

This typically modern viewpoint found expression also in two other medieval pioneers of scientific thought—Roger Grosseteste (1175–1253), bishop of Lincoln, and the noted Franciscan monk, Roger Bacon (1214–94).

Grosseteste was altogether phenomenal for his time. As a bishop he had plenty of administrative duties to fill his days, yet he gave considerable care to development of learning from the Arabic. Also he realized that use of Arabic tests was a second-best approach to knowledge. Since Greeks had been the founders of Arabic knowledge, translations should be from the original Greek in his opinion, and he gave effect to his belief by translating a considerable portion of Aristotle. He attempted mathematical treatment of all physical and astronomical phenomena and revived use of the lens for studying light. He was also the teacher and inspirer of Roger Bacon.

Bacon has been regarded as the first and only true scientific mind of his age—probably because of a forecast in one of his letters:

Ships will go without rowers and with only a single man to guide them. Carriages without horses will travel with incredible speed. Machines for flying can be made in which a man sits, and skillfully devised wings strike the air in the manner of a bird. Machines will raise infinitely great weights, and ingenious bridges will span rivers without support.

A legendary aura of brave struggling alone in an ignorant and persecuting world also has attached to Bacon. More penetrating and accurate appraisal such as may be found in George Sarton's *Introduction to the History of Science* (1927) paints a different picture. Bacon was assailed by the fundamentalists of his day—as scientists still are—but he was not persecuted for his science as such. He was involved in questions of discipline and policy which had the Franciscans in a turmoil, and his studies were made a convenient handle for getting at him on the charge of unworthy intellectual pride.

He made some discoveries, but nothing like the monumental ones sometimes credited to him. His supposed rediscovery of gunpowder, for example, was actually a testing out of current information about this substance. His really important merit was his clear understanding that the true road to scientific knowledge lay through testing and experiment—an understanding which he voiced eloquently enough:

There are four stumbling blocks . . . which hinder well nigh every scholar: the example of frail and unworthy authority, long-established custom, the sense of the ignorant crowd . . . and the hiding of one's own ignorance under the pretense of wisdom. In these, every man is involved and every state beset. For in every act of life, or business, or study, these three worst arguments are used for the same conclusion: This was the way of our ancestors, this is the custom, this is the common view: therefore it shall be held. . . . If these three are sometimes refuted by the glorious power of reason, the fourth is already ready, as a gloss for foolishness; so that, though a man know nothing of any value, he will impudently magnify [his scanty knowledge], and thus, soothing his wretched folly, defeat truth.

Bacon is important finally as a splendid example of why these medieval scholars succeeded in achieving the true scientific viewpoint after the most brilliant of Greek philosophers had failed to do so. The secret of medieval success may be stated in one simple phrase— willingness *to work with one's own hands* in search of truth. Men like Bacon were friars or monks and trained to consider personal labor dignified, not slavish. The tendency to "try things out," to build brick by brick whether mentally or physically, came as naturally to them once they caught an idea as did Plato's tendency to employ lordly thought without work to a Greek philosopher.

By its very nature such thinking was destined to become the central battleground between the older viewpoint and the new. Deductive Scholastics could enjoy a relatively free hand, even on quite daring flights of inquiry, because they were considered safe. As Duns Scotus pointed out, they were chained to their starting point and had to come back to good orthodox views in the end.

Inductive thinking, however, contained spiritual and social dynamite, because nobody could say where it might lead or what consequences might come from beginnings such as those made by Grosseteste and Roger Bacon. Hence, as the new viewpoint gained momentum and attracted more followers, it was bound to bring every shocked conservative in Europe up in arms.

Since this battle will be the very crux of the change from ancient to modern, an accurate appraisal of these conservative forces is in order before the actual struggle is taken up.

Included among them were most of the rich and the successful, the established men who instinctively resented anything new lest it disturb the order which they had found completely satisfactory. We of today need not be smug about the existence of such reactionaries in medieval times. We have all too many of them in our own midst, ever ready to apply the damning labels "red," "anarchistic" or "government handouts" to any proposal whatever for grappling with crying evils of the day before they give even five seconds of time to informing themselves about either the problem or the proposal. Medieval Europe also possessed many an emotional thinker of the William Jennings Bryan type—men who had arranged concepts which pleased them into a delightful pattern and who were willing to persecute anyone who disturbed their self-arranged universes. To all these age-old enemies of thought must be added an emotional tension or strain which was peculiar to the Middle Ages and which kept passions and fear perilously near to swamping reason at all times. The pattern of heaven and hell, God and devil, which the Church held forth kept most men in a constantly keyed emotional state that ranged from ecstasy to terror as the extremes of this pattern were contemplated.

The ecstatic, pleasurable state bore glorious fruit in Gothic cathedrals, medieval literature and art, religious charities and a flood tide of childlike faith in constant miraculous intervention by God in even the most trivial affairs of men. At the other extreme stood the gloomy, terrifying pictures of the devil, with his constant machinations, and the torments of hell. Men fed their minds on such portrayals as the following, of what occurred to the damned in the flame-shot darkness of the pit:

. . . in that same black darkness they see black things as devils, that even maul them and afflict and harass them with all kinds of tortures; and tailed drakes, horrible as devils, that devour them whole and spew them out afterward before and behind. At other times they rend them in pieces and chew each gobbet of them, and they afterwards become whole again, such as they previously were, to undergo again such bale without recovery, and full well they see themselves very horrible and dreadful; and to increase their pains the loathsome hell-worms, toads, and frogs that eat out their eyes and nostrils, and adders and water-frogs, not like those here, but a hundred times more horrible, sneak in and out of the mouth, ears, eyes, navel and at the hollow of the breast, as maggots in putrid flesh, ever yet thickest. There is shrieking in the flame and chattering of teeth in the snowy waters. Suddenly they flit upon the heat into the cold, nor ever do they know of these two which is worst for them, for each is intolerable. . . . And this same wan hope is their greatest torment, that none have any hope of recovery, but are sure of every ill, to continue in woe, world without end, even in eternity. Each chokes the other, and each is another's torment, and each hateth another and himself as the black devil; and even as they loved them the more in this world, so the more shall they hate them there. And each curseth another, and gnaws off the other's arms, ears and nose also. I have begun to tell of things that I am not able to bring to any end, though I had a thousand tongues of steel, and told until they were all worn out. (Cited from a medieval theologian by S. M. Brown in *Medieval Europe*, 1932).

This constant emotional strain was characteristic enough to lead Henry Osborn Taylor into making it the very basis of the medieval psychological state. Certainly it set the emotional color of the age, and it added a very special peril to free thinking with its concept of the devil lurking everywhere, seeking to entrap men with every insidious device possible. Who could tell, then, when one of these free thinkers spoke up with some seemingly mild thought, whether he might not actually be one of Satan's snares for the unwary?

And now comes one highly important reservation which must be made during this roll call of opponents to free thinking. Among these opponents we cannot count the Church as a whole.

It is quite true that tremendous opposition came from many churchmen—priests and abbots here, bishops there and popes at the top. But so also did the Church furnish practically every man who stood *for* free thought. From the start of the development of free thinking almost to its culmination it occurred within the Church.

Another common error which must be cleared away, if the Middle Ages are to be understood aright, is the idea that the Church over-awed the minds of men and froze the impulse toward thought. If ever such an overawing occurred, it was only in the despairing times when the Western Empire was sinking to its end and during the Dark Ages which followed. Certainly from the beginning of the Crusades on, plenty of men could be found who were willing to speak out stoutly enough for their ideas of right and truth.

The dour Bernard of Clairvaux, the same man who preached the Second Crusade and hounded Peter Abélard to his end, was just as formidable when speaking to his superiors. He even dared address a Pope in these stern words:

I do not find that St Peter ever appeared in public loaded with gold and jewels, clad in silk, mounted on a white mule, surrounded by soldiers and followed by a brilliant retinue. In the glitter that environs thee, rather wouldst thou be taken for the successor of Constantine than for the successor of Peter.

Bishop Grosseteste was equally outspoken for the right. One of his last acts was to return a quaint but resolute protest to a demand from Innocent IV in 1253 that one of Innocent's nephews be given a living in Grosseteste's see of Lincoln. "I decline to obey," the up-standing English prelate replied. "Filially and obediently, I oppose; I rebel."

The Church cannot, then, be counted as a unit on any side. In this matter it was truly a "Catholic" or "universal" institution; it mirrored all thoughts and all trends. Official actions depended there-fore upon the men in power at the time and must be weighed in the light of this fact, just as must the acts of cities and nations. Only if this is remembered carefully can the record of the next few cen-turies be read aright.

With this said we have the lines drawn for the battle to come, the battle which carried human thinking from the ancient pattern through the medieval transition to modern types of thinking. For general understanding the record will be sufficiently complete if the story of the struggle opens with the status of thought and life in the thirteenth century.

CHAPTER XXX

The Medieval Climax

THE THIRTEENTH CENTURY is often pronounced the summit of the medieval achievement, and the state of the times in Europe justifies the opinion. In Paris, for example, the bishop and his devout burghers were finishing their monument to God, the Cathedral of Notre Dame, as the century opened. The schools were drawing students from far and wide; and during the century those three giants of scholastic thought, Thomas Aquinas, Albertus Magnus and Duns Scotus, were to complete important parts of their lifework here.

So likewise, in the neighboring cathedral cities, other Gothic "poems in stone" were thrusting their walls and spires heavenward, and into every carving and every soaring vault and rib went an ingredient never before used on such a scale by mankind. These cathedrals were no monuments to despotic power, heaped up by slave labor. They were erected by free men toiling for the glory of God and their city; each one felt that he was putting in something of himself to stand for all time with every stroke he added to the gorgeous structure.

Another addition to the spiritual setting was the formation of *mendicant orders* of *begging friars.*

The first of these orders was the *Franciscan,* a fruit of the Christ-like ministry of St Francis of Assisi (1182–1226). A son of a rich merchant family, he had taken holy orders in his early twenties—but not to live as a protected priest or monk. Rather, clad in cast-off garments and living entirely on charity, he spent his life ministering to the poor in city slums. Others of like mind were attracted to him, and in 1209 Pope Innocent III sanctioned his plan for organizing these followers into an order of *Franciscans,* commonly called Gray Friars from the color of their habits.

357

These clerics were not to be sheltered monks, hidden away from the world in search of their own salvation. They were to be "begging brothers" or friars, living on a portion of the alms given them and dispensing the rest to aid and comfort the poor and the distressed. The order took on like wildfire, and all through the early thirteenth century these Gray Friars or Franciscans came thrusting into the worst cesspools of misery in Europe, bringing their message of spiritual comfort and such help as they could marshal from the devout.

In northern France and Flanders looms were busy working up English wool into the Flemish cloth which the Orient took in exchange for spices, silks and other luxuries. Glassworking was growing too—as it was in German centers, together with the distinctive German art of metalworking. Everywhere the growing cities were winning charters from their rulers, charters which granted trading and manufacturing rights. Merchants were forming trade guilds to conduct the industries and commerce of their cities, while other guilds or fraternities were forming as mutual aid societies to help members in distress, provide masses for deceased members and perform civic services such as providing needed bridges and roads. Throughout Europe the roads and trails were filled with pilgrims and students, confident that any abbey or great house where they stopped for the night would give them food and lodging, in Christian deference to their errands.

This generally fair scene wore the superficial aspect of a culmination, a bringing to fruition of a proper plan for the life of mankind. Beneath the surface, however, it was no culmination. Rather it was a matrix, superficially rounded out but actually containing ferments which were working steadily toward new ways. These ferments existed in practically every phase of life—economic, political, scientific and spiritual—and nobody can say which phase was most important. Any review of them should begin, however, with the economic forces, because they provided the basis for everything else.

The medieval scheme of economic life had rested always upon service in the station and the calling to which God had appointed every man, and this service was to be free from taint of self-aggrandizement and profit seeking.

The Church had permitted monasteries and church treasuries to make small loans, on interest, to distressed individuals and to accept deposits, repayable on demand or over a term of years, as a sort of an annuity; but commercial profit was frowned upon and usury was forbidden. Lay governments, except those of Lombardy and Cahors, had made banking and loans impossible in the early Middle Ages, and the laws generally forbade engrossing (monopolizing) and forestalling, or buying commodities on their way to market to shorten supplies and raise the price. No such thing as free trading was thinkable. Kings granted charters to towns to trade, manufacture and hold fairs, but no one other than feudal lords could presume to engage in such activities without a charter. Usually a chartered town formed a merchant guild to which a restricted number of citizens was admitted, and no one else could enjoy the benefits of the charter, except as servants or employees of guild members.

This iron scheme of economic organization had begun perforce to soften when the new commerce with the Orient grew up in the twelfth century. The Italian trading cities naturally led in this since they derived the first profit and therefore most strength from handling Oriental goods. Genoa had founded the bank of San Giorgio (St George) in 1108 to receive deposits and transfer funds, and in 1157 Venice had opened a "chamber of loans," through which citizens could invest in the enterprises of the Venetian state. During the twelfth century the crusading order of Knights Templars also developed an extensive banking business throughout Europe. Crippling restrictions upon charging interest for commercial loans were simply forgotten in these enterprises, and so the beginnings of capitalistic banking and financing were laid down as well as the beginnings of capitalistic commerce.

These developments received a tremendous impetus when the Venetians unscrupulously diverted the Fourth Crusade of 1202–04 against their chief trade rival, the Eastern Empire, and substituted the Normans of Sicily and southern Italy for the Greek emperors. The chance for this shrewd maneuver arose out of Venice's role as transporter of men and supplies for the Crusades.

For the Fourth Crusade Venice was asked her price for transporting 9000 knights, 4500 horses and 20,000 foot soldiers, with provisions for a year. The price was 85,000 silver marks of Cologne, or 53,266 troy pounds of silver (worth at 1938–39 bullion prices about 275,000 dollars), and one half of all conquests. The crusaders could not pay, and finally the doge Dandolo offered to wait for the silver if the crusaders would subdue various troublesome pirates along the Adriatic coast. The crusaders did so, and once involved in the region they swept on to the capture of Constantinople in 1204.

This gave the Latin peoples command of the empire's resources and trade, with a tremendous boom for Venetian, Genoan and other Italian commerce. It also opened many secrets of Byzantine arts and manufactures for western imitation. The Venetians became the leading glassmakers of Europe, while silk growing and working spread throughout northern Italy, strengthening the cities of Lombardy and Tuscan cities such as Florence and Pisa.

Meantime a similar if less rich development of city commercial effort was occurring in the north, with a march of events which led to formation of the noted Hanseatic League. This organization included German trading cities around the Baltic, others headed by Cologne on the old trade route along the Rhine, and German traders scattered from London to Novgorod in Russia.

The first-known associated action of these cities occurred in 1229 when thirty of them, headed by Cologne, made a treaty with a Russian prince concerning their trade to Novgorod. Cologne was the leading city in trade at the time, having won a charter to trade in London as early as 1157; but for convenience the allied cities named Wisby, on a little island off Sweden, as their headquarters. The headquarters were shifted to Lübeck in 1293, when the league had developed a policy of sharing advantages in foreign ports. By this time the league also had built up a naval force to suppress pirates and enforce respect for league rights everywhere. During the latter part of the sixteenth century this league became the greatest maritime and commercial power in the north, just as Venice was in the south, and it held this position until well after the discovery of America.

During this same period changes in commerce were being matched by growing curiosity about the sources of Oriental wealth and a marked tendency to make distant journeys for exploration.

The outstanding feat of this sort was performed by the Polos of Venice—Maffeo, Nicolo and Nicolo's son Marco (1254?–1324). The two elder Polos were traders from the Venetian quarter in Constantinople to points of contact with Far Eastern caravans, and in 1260 they joined the return journey of a party of envoys to the Pope from Kublai Khan (1216–94), to visit the great Mongol's new conquest, China. The Khan was delighted with them, especially since they promised to help along his plan for unifying China by substituting Christianity for the many conflicting local faiths. They came home with the Khan's greetings to western rulers and a letter asking the Pope for missionaries and for instructors in western arts.

Unfortunately, all Europe was in a turmoil when the Polos reached home in 1269, and not until 1279 were they able to leave again, taking young Marco and two missionary priests. The priests soon quailed from the awesome journey ahead and turned back—with what consequences to world history through failing to Christianize China at this time, nobody can say—but the Polos pressed on and reached the court of the great Khan after three and a half years of travel.

Kublai was disappointed by the lack of Christian instructors but turned to Buddhism for China's new official faith, and he pressed all the Polos into his service as imperial envoys. They spent many years in this service and did not return home until 1295.

We know nothing of them thereafter until September 7, 1298, when the Genoese captured Marco in a naval battle with the Venetians. While held prisoner he passed the time dictating his adventures and memories of China, and so the world received *The Book of Sir Marco Polo*—a tale of unbelievably rich lands which set the imagination of Europe afire.

Coupled with this urge to explore by land was an array of bolder ventures at sea, particularly into waters which we are told all too often the mariners were afraid to explore—that is, the mysterious waters of the Atlantic beyond the Straits of Gibraltar.

Actually the Arabs had preserved accounts of ancient voyages around Africa; and even in the twelfth century, after the First Crusade, Roger of Sicily's geographer Idrisi had fortified this material with an account of the "Lisbon wanderers"—eight relatives who were blown to sea and, after touching on several islands, reached the coast of Africa. In 1270 Lancelot Malocello had reached the Canaries, and in 1291 a strong expedition led by the Vivaldis of Genoa had passed beyond these islands. So did a Catalan expedition from Majorca in 1346, and the end of the fourteenth century produced the romantic tale of the Englishman, Machin. He was said to have eloped with one Anne d'Arfet from Bristol about 1370 and been storm-blown onto islands far off Gibraltar and Africa. Accounts thereafter are conflicting, but some of the crew and perhaps Machin reached Africa and were enslaved by the Moors. An account of their adventure reached Europe through a ransomed fellow slave in 1416.

The navigators of the fourteenth and fifteenth centuries therefore knew at least the first stage in what "lay out beyond," but the fate of the Vivaldi and Catalan expeditions gave grim warning that deadly perils of some sort lay beyond. Word came back of each one sailing

In the figure (labels as shown): 60°W, 45°W, 30°W, 15°W, 0°, 15°E, 30°E, 45°E

Newfoundland
PREVAILING WESTERLIES
45°N

Azores Is.
Madeira Is.

30°N
23½°N
T. of CANCER
Canary Is.
C. Bojador
N.E. TRADES
15°N
C. Verde Is.

EQUATORIAL DOLDRUMS
EQUATOR
C. Palmas
PORTUGUESE EXPLORATION
0°

S.E. TRADES

15°S
23½°S
T. of CAPRICORN

30°S
C. of Good Hope
C. Agulhas

BEST SAILING ROUTE AROUND AFRICA
PREVAILING WESTERLIES
45°S

AFRICA
ON THE
WORLD MAP WITH THE
MEDICEAN (LAURENTIAN)
PORTOLANI (1351)

THE PROBLEM OF CIRCUMNAVIGATING AFRICA

In the upper right-hand corner of this diagram is the presumptive foundation of late Middle Age attempts to circumnavigate Africa—the surprisingly good knowledge of the continent's shape which stands revealed in the atlas commonly called the Laurentian or Medicean portolani of about 1351. The larger diagram shows why this circumnavigation was hampered, not by ignorance or cowardice, but by natural conditions which made this voyage one of the most hazardous of any in the history of seafaring.

As the diagram shows, the northeast trade winds blew a ship along bravely enough to the Canary Islands; the job was to beat back again, gaining perhaps only one mile in eight or ten of zigzagging back and forth across the wind. Beyond Cape Bojador lay the equatorial doldrums, a belt of steaming hot thundershowers, with only vagrant breezes in which a ship might lie for weeks without making progress. The navigators who ultimately pushed south to the Cape of Good Hope encountered even worse troubles south of the equator. Once the men battled through the doldrums they had to beat their way for perhaps 2500 miles (as far as from New York overland to San Francisco) against the southeast trades; and once beyond the equator, they had to do this off a coast which offered scarcely a drop of water or a morsel of food all the way. The wonder

Continued at bottom of the next page

south from the Canaries, and that was the last the world ever heard from either expedition.

But this fate did not stir up ideas that these parties had "sailed over the edge of a flat world" or had been boiled to death in the equatorial sea or met some similar weird fate. Common sailors may have entertained such notions, but trained navigators knew better. They realized that they were tackling what modern seamen pronounce one of the toughest sailing assignments in all the world. The accompanying map sets forth the nature of the difficulty and makes plain why Cape Bojador came to be considered a natural "farthest south" for safe navigation.

Such activities were bound to produce momentous consequences in time. How they did can best be appreciated, however, by providing as a background the story of darker forces at work in this same thirteenth century—forces which did as much by oppression and obstruction as did the positive urges toward better ways to make the final transition from medieval to modern all but explosive in force. The center of the trouble was the constant quarreling between popes and Holy Roman emperors for supreme power in the Church and in Europe.

For many centuries Central Europe and Italy had been torn by wars between popes and Holy Roman emperors, over which one had the last word in feudal control of the lands within bishoprics and the patrimony of Peter and also in the naming of new popes. The bitter Investiture Conflict (1075–1122), over whether the emperor or the pope had the right to name bishops, drenched Europe with blood for two generations before the Concordat of Worms reached the sensible compromise that the emperor was to invest bishops with their temporal feudal powers while the pope gave the ring and crozier which conferred spiritual power.

The method of naming new popes likewise underwent evolution,

Continued from preceding page

was, not that they were slow in getting around Africa, but that they ever did so; and the crowning proof that this was an astounding feat is the fact that even the fine clipper ships of the nineteenth century never attempted this voyage. Instead they coasted along South America, as shown, until they caught the prevailing westerlies of the southern hemisphere. This maneuver undoubtedly would have occurred to the Portuguese once they reached the Cape of Good Hope in 1487; and it would have led to the discovery of America, if Columbus had not forestalled them.

rather than being established and accepted, until late in the Middle Ages. In the early days the nobles and, to some extent, the clergy of Rome named the popes; the College of Cardinals was not created and given the power of election until 1059. For several centuries thereafter it was an open question whether this college, general church councils or the pope had final authority over the Church.

At the turn into the thirteenth century the Papacy had been gaining almost steadily in this struggle for nearly a century, and in the early 1200s the papal throne was occupied by one of history's strongest popes, Innocent III (reign 1194–1216).

Innocent probably had more temporal power than any pope before his time or after. Not only did he have the emperor-to-be, Frederick, as his ward; the Eastern Empire, with its Greek faith, had been brought to heel by the Latin conquest of Constantinople, and nearly every king in Europe had been brought to acknowledge Innocent as feudal overlord. The list included the rulers of Sicily and Naples, Sardinia, the Christian Syrian states, Servia, Bosnia, the Scandinavian states, Castile, Leon, Navarre, Portugal and (in 1213) John of England. Only Philip Augustus of France held out, but he usually could be enlisted, if advantage showed, in papal political projects.

In contrast with all this power stood the seemingly feeble position of the boy Frederick.

Frederick had been only three when his father, the Hohenstaufen emperor Henry VI, died in 1197. The boy was also king of Norman Italy and Sicily, Henry having conquered this realm in 1190; and so, by virtue of an old agreement with these Normans, Pope Innocent III assumed guardianship in 1198. The Germans, not caring for a child emperor, elected Philip of Swabia and then Otto as emperor, and Innocent crowned Otto in 1209.

The two fell out immediately, however, over Otto's adamantine determination to seize the boy Frederick's domain, and all Europe became engulfed in war. On Frederick's side were the Pope, the Hohenstaufen or Ghibelline party of Germany and Philip Augustus of France. Otto's Guelph party had as allies Flanders and John of England. But the Guelph cause was crushed by Philip's victory in the Battle of Bouvines (1214), and now Innocent and his youthful emperor seemed to have everything their way. Frederick next year took the crusader's cross, although naturally without moving at the time, and he settled an old vexing question by confirming the papal claim to the lands left by Mathilda of Tuscany nearly a century before.

But Innocent was utterly mistaken in this boy. Frederick was only biding his time. He remained docile until Innocent died in 1216 and through the mild reign of Honorius III (1216–27). Gregory IV (1227–41) was sterner, however, and threatened to excommunicate him unless he made his long-deferred crusade. Frederick therefore conducted the sixth of these now outworn enterprises (1228–29), but he did so largely by making treaties favorable for Christians with the Saracens. Then on his return he showed his hand by crushing the revolt which Gregory had been trying to stir up against him in the Tuscan and Lombard cities.

This quarrel ended in a truce which lasted until 1235, and Frederick used the time to strengthen his position. He realized that as between Germany and Italy he might better hold the latter, so he left Germany drift and concentrated upon Italy. His measures were truly remarkable for the time.

First, for a legal basis, he pushed the revival of Roman law which had been started by his grandfather, Frederick Barbarossa. Both Fredericks valued this law for its exaltation of imperial authority— a doctrine which later gave rise to the pernicious "divine right of kings" to do as they pleased because God had made them kings. But the change brought immense improvement in procedure. The Roman type of trial by evidence before judges was substituted for the medieval trial by battle or ordeal; the Roman law of property and contract gained ground.

Frederick also promoted agriculture, introducing Saracen plants such as dates, cotton and sugar, and established thoroughly modern but just taxation, payable in money rather than feudal dues and services. He abolished serfdom, chartered universities, and by authorizing dissection of an executed criminal once every five years, he revived study of anatomy at the point where the Alexandrian anatomists had been stopped by the Ptolemies some fourteen hundred years before. In his court Saracen and Jewish scholars were as welcome as Christians, and from his court Leonard of Pisa made Europe acquainted with the convenient Hindu-Arabic arithmetic.

The end of his reign was, however, as medieval and gloomy as this interlude had been bright and modern. The touch-off to the trouble was the one blind spot in his modern outlook. He could not stomach the idea of free cities managing their own affairs. This threw the Lombard and Tuscan cities into the camp of the Papacy, and the Papacy, always anxious to improve its temporal position in Italy at the expense of an emperor, egged on the cities. The situation boiled over on March 20, 1239, when Gregory IX excommunicated Frederick; and from then until Frederick died in 1250 Italy was tortured as few lands ever have been by devastating war.

During all this troubled time the mounting passions and the papal sense of need for stern dealings with all opponents were producing an ever harder attitude toward dissent and heresy. The change was accelerated also by a development which struck the popes as particularly menacing—the rise of heresy among the *laity*.

Throughout all these centuries when heretics had been clerics for the most part, the Church had been content to condemn their doctrines and excommunicate the culprits if they continued to preach heresy. The old pagan faiths had survived in backward districts, with "Black Masses" and pagan festivals or "Black Sabbaths" led by priests dressed as goats and supposedly able to work magic; but the Church had done little about this beyond pronouncing such gods manifestations of the devil and calling the whole business witchcraft. During the twelfth century the empire had taken to burning heretics, but even this must be put down largely to a blind, ferocious dread felt by rulers of independent thinking among their subjects.

At the beginning of the thirteenth century, however, the all-powerful Innocent III felt strong enough to commence cleansing the lay population of heresy, beginning with the most obnoxious and widespread one—the Albigensian or Catharist heresy of southern France.

These heretics were spiritual heirs of the second-century mystic Manicheans of western Asia crossed with the ascetism of third-century hermits. They believed in solving the problem of evil by as complete an approach to race suicide as possible and rejected the sacramental system of the Church in favor of mystical spiritualism. For decades the Church had sent missions among them, but when Innocent found them still obdurate he decided to turn the familiar device of a crusade against them and summoned their liege lord Philip Augustus to the work.

To Philip and his land-hungry nobles the call was a godsend. An army led by Simon de Montfort, grandfather of England's famous Simon, fell upon the heretics like so many wolves. What Innocent intended as an Albigensian crusade became an appalling massacre, and when the crusade proper (1209–19) was over the war went on as a business of conquering feudal fiefs. The result was all but complete extirpation of Provençal or southern French culture and of the *langue d'oc* (the language in which the word for "yes" was *oc* instead of the northern Frenchman's *œil,* parent of the modern *oui*). Only the name of the speech survived in the provincial name Languedoc.

Still, Innocent's object was accomplished, and now he turned to permanent measures for surpassing heresy to replace the scattered and often lukewarm activities of the bishops. The Lateran Council of 1215 required an agreement to exterminate heretics in the corona-tion oath of every king and tightened control of the laity by making confession compulsory. He died next year, and his successor, Hon-orius III, was less energetic; but Gregory IX (1227–41) pushed the organization of antiheretical campaigning to completion by develop-ing the Inquisition.

The Inquisition acted both through commissions sent into sus-pected districts and Holy Offices established in important centers. At the outset of each campaign a period of grace was allowed in which heretics could make their peace with the Church, and then active extirpation commenced. The procedure was secret, drastic and without appeal. Accusation was taken as all but sufficient proof of guilt; torture, an age-old feature of Roman law, came into use. Once a heretic was convicted the inquisitors pronounced an anathema upon him, confiscated his lands and turned him over, with a recom-mendation of mercy, to the civil authorities. The Church counte-nanced no shedding of blood, so the proceedings were closed by burning the heretic or heretics to death on a Sunday, usually before a cathedral, as part of a public "act of faith" (*auto de fe* in the familiar Spanish term).

Thus ferocity came into the discipline of the Church, a sorry match for the bloody political troubles in Italy. It must not be supposed, however, that the progressive spirits of the age accepted this change with lamblike meekness! Dissidence grew stronger, not weaker, under pressure from iron repression. This was inevitable, the times being what they were. A light had been lit which was too strong for any power to quench, and the existence of reaction simply meant that this light had to shine in many a fierce battle and over many a scene of anguish instead of being able to lead men peacefully and steadily to better lives. Moreover, the battle lines had already been drawn, however dimly, in this same thirteenth century. The story of the next two centuries, the fourteenth and fifteenth, will be the shap-ing of this battle and the crash of medievalism.

CHAPTER XXXI

The Medieval Dissolves into the Modern

ONE SIMPLE CONSIDERATION will give the actual tangle of events which ushered in modern ways complete consistency with the principles of human nature. Gains will come rapidly in fields of thought and effort where changes are easy, but the pace will be slower wherever the change can come only after acquiring new techniques for investigation, or the perception of even elementary truth will be difficult or the resistance offered by conservatives is bitter.

Because of this the first and most rapid swing to modern standards occurred in literature and art—in general, the amenities and aesthetic enrichments of life. Commerce, industrial arts and their handmaidens, navigation and geographic discovery, came along at the next most rapid pace. Science, with its need for new techniques and fundamental concepts as a prerequisite for advances in definite knowledge, advanced only slowly; while political and religious institutions, being the most heavily saddled of all with the dead weight of ignorant mob prejudices and the passions and vested interests of leaders, were slowest of all to advance. This suggests that the story of change be followed in this order—commencing with the intellectual, literary and artistic advance which is commonly called the *Renaissance* or "rebirth."

Before we allow ourselves to use this term, however, we should note that modern scholarship pronounces the notion of a literal "rebirth" completely untenable, at least if the rebirth is considered as occurring in the fourteenth, fifteenth and early sixteenth centuries. This view was the child of the utterly exploded notion that the Middle Ages contained nothing but dreary ignorance, darkness and stagnation. Lynn Thorndike, author of *Science and Thought in the*

368

Fifteenth Century (1929), expresses particular scorn for this view. H. O. Taylor, author of *The Medieval Mind,* is tempted to wish that the term could be abolished as misleading and historically false. Preserved Smith's *Age of the Reformation* (1920) presents the more conservative view that the Renaissance is a useful term for the culmination of preceding advances, partial in the fourteenth century and coming to full bloom in the fifteenth and early sixteenth centuries. He adds that a definite change, amounting to an awakening in some ways, did occur in the fifteenth century—and this may be seen in literature by comparing Dante, "the dawn light," and "the two morning stars," Petrarch and Boccaccio.

Dante Alighieri (1265–1321), son of a moderately well-to-do burgher family of Florence, was modern in that he wrote in Tuscan Italian and practically created the art of writing poetry in that tongue. But his monumental allegory of Hell, Purgatory and Heaven, *The Divine Comedy,* was thoroughly medieval in theme. The modern features in it are the zest and feeling in the text and the respect shown for the great minds of antiquity by placing them in the highest and least tormenting parts of Hell.

Francesco Petrarch and Boccaccio broke with all this by treating themes of interest to earthly life. Petrarch (1304–74), a modestly circumstanced priest and canon lawyer until middle life, wrote on a wide variety of subjects from classical to current politics, both in Latin and exquisite Italian verse; when he became a diplomat for despots of Milan he was the most famous poet living in Italy. Giovanni Boccaccio (1313–75), a natural son of a Florentine banker, spent his early life pretending to dabble in business but writing both prose and poetry to please a lost love whom he celebrated as Fiammeta, just as Petrarch addressed Laura; then the frightful havoc wrought by the Black Death steadied him into his prose masterpiece, the *Decameron.*

In this collection of tales told by aristocratic refugees from the plague who had gathered in a country palace he gathered together tenderness, coarse ribaldry, adventure, cruelty, every facet of current thought, into a marvelous mirror of the times; and not only that, he inspired a host of writers to do likewise. Geoffrey Chaucer (1340?–1400), "the father of English poetry" who wrote soon after Boccaccio died, helped himself liberally to the Italian's material, sometimes by merely translating it; and the influence of the *Decameron* can be traced through a long line of later first-rank writers.

Neither did these two "morning stars" content themselves with setting writers afire with enthusiasm for fresh, lively treatment of current themes. They busied themselves throughout their lives in another enthusiasm which caught on like a craze in their time—unearthing manuscripts by ancient authors who could gratify this new zest for treatment of "here and now" life. Monasteries all over Europe were combed by a swarm of literary detectives, and news that an important manuscript had been discovered ran through the literary world as much as would word today that a copy, say, of a third-century New Testament had been turned up.

The lifetimes of Petrarch and Boccaccio, therefore, may fairly be set down as seeing the full blossoming of that literary Renaissance which has been called falsely the Revival of Learning. Now too began the later habit of considering Latin and Greek the backbone of a gentleman's education. This was true in those days, when the only authors who reflected polish and elegance in living were the ancients who had written in those tongues.

As a last fruit from the seed came the attitude toward life which was called Humanism. This was a mode and manner of living which today we would call "cultured." It included an understanding taste for art, ability to converse with intelligence and sophistication, and the notion that fierce scrambling and brawling were undignified. From this movement came the convention that a gentleman should be able to write a sonnet to his lady as well as wield an effective lance and sword in war. Courtliness of manner was added to ruthlessness in advancing the interest of one's estate; lace and velvet were added to masculine attire as well as feminine.

It should be said also that a much darker stream came into life with Italian Humanism. These scholarly gentlemen were rapidly learning scorn for the old ascetic Christian morality, but they were not acquiring new moral controls. A gentleman did not indulge in street brawls or country wars. He hired an assassin to do his dirty work, while open quarrels between gentlemen became formalized in time into the duel. Within a century after Petrarch's death Niccolo Machiavelli (1469–1527) was expressing such views in his book *The Prince*. Here was set forth the doctrine that the only morality which bound a ruler was the success of his state; broken words, monumental injustices and cruelties and assassinations were all proper if they made the state strong.

This change in literature proceeded without serious opposition because Middle Age opinion was not touchy when sacred matters were not involved. Also, the very conservatives who would fight progress in other fields were natural patrons of the arts.

For the same reasons no definite opposition arose when this same humanizing tendency spread into painting, sculpture and architecture. The pace here was slower, however, because of the greater expenses involved and greater technical difficulties. Indeed, aside from Giotto (1276–1337?), a contemporary of Dante, first-rank new work in these fields began appearing only at the *end* of the fourteenth century, or about when the pioneers of the literary Renaissance had died. The fourteenth century saw only the *birth* of Donatello, Brunelleschi, Ghiberti, Fra Angelico, Della Robbia and Van Eyck.

Toward the end of the fourteenth century, however, the Italian trading cities were wealthy enough to unleash these more costly arts—most of all in Florence.

Here the heart of the new artistic impulse was enriching the city with beautiful structures. The Florentines built a charming Baptistry in the thirteenth century and started a new *Duomo* or cathedral in 1298 (without completing it until 1878!). These buildings were true civic enterprises, both in financing and because design and construction were decided by holding a competition for the design of a mural, a pair of doors or whatever feature was needed at the moment and awarding the job to the creator of the winning design. These competitions seem to have brought the Renaissance into lusty life in architecture and art in the early fifteenth century.

Lorenzo Ghiberti (1378–1455) accomplished this in bronze casting with two sets of bronze doors for the Baptistry. On the first set he worked more than twenty years; then from 1425 to 1452 he created the second set, which Michelangelo said a century later were fit to be the gates of paradise.

Renaissance architecture got its start from a loser in the competition for the first pair of doors, Filippo Brunelleschi (1379–1446). After the award to Ghiberti in 1403 Brunelleschi, then about twenty-six, tramped off to Rome to study the ancient ruins. With him went young Donatello, later the "father of Florentine Renaissance sculpture," and when the two came back Brunelleschi won a commission to place a dome on the Duomo. The dome was a Roman or classic architectural device, but Brunelleschi gave it a treatment which created the Renaissance in architecture.

Roman domes had always rested solidly upon the supporting walls and did not "soar" when seen from the outside. Brunelleschi interposed a circular drum between the walls and the dome and thus "got his dome up" into the clear, where it could appear to soar. He also added to the appearance of soaring or reaching heavenward by drawing the top up to a point and crowning it with a cupola. The most familiar American example of this style is the dome of the national Capitol at Washington. A comparison with the low dome of, say, the Pantheon in Rome will show the change in feeling which Brunelleschi achieved.

From this dome Brunelleschi went on to further developments in his use of Roman forms, columns, arches and the like in a new spirit of buoyant joyousness. He shaped his rooms, halls and windows to make for rich living here and now, with ample wall space for decoration. The Roman forms which had been pre-eminently suitable for temples and fortresses now found perfect expression in the palace. Rulers and rich men such as the Medici saw this instantly, and building in "the new antique manner" spread rapidly all over Italy.

Meanwhile the sculptor Donato Donatello (1386–1466) was shaking free from medieval stiffness and formalism in pose and figure into use of truly natural figures which nevertheless conveyed overpowering expression of ideas. His equestrian statue of the mercenary general Gattamelata is a true man seated naturally upon a true-to-life horse, yet as one contemplates it both man and horse blend into an impression of *military prowess,* of generalship.

In this same period that strange boy genius of painting, Tommaso Guidi (1402–29), commonly called Masaccio, was studying how to get the feeling of sweep and movement into his canvases and also how to create the illusion of space and depth with *aerial* perspective— that is, altering shades and hues according to whether an object shown was near or far. His masterpiece, the fresco Tribute Money in the Brancacci Chapel, was used for a century as an object lesson in how to achieve such effects. Leonardo da Vinci, Raphael and Michelangelo were among the many masters who learned valuable lessons from it. Masaccio also was a devoted student of surface anatomy and introduced the nude into Renaissance art.

Paolo Uccello (1397–1457) devoted his life to achieving *linear* perspective with foreshortening and drawing the composition of the picture to a point on the horizon. Domenico Veneziano (1400–61) is noted for bringing to Italy the monumental advance achieved by the pioneer Flemish artist Hubert Van Eyck (1366?–1426)—mixing pigments with oil instead of water. Luca della Robbia (1400?–82), in addition to being a great sculptor, worked out statuary and tile ornaments in glazed terra cotta, thus making possible rich ornamentation in a medium much less costly than marble or bronze.

These achievements account for the transition to modern concern with man and promotion of human happiness as the major concern of art and architecture. It had come as said in Italy because there is where economic change had been going forward rapidly and producing wealth enough to support the new art and humanism. These changes can be surveyed sufficiently in terms of three cities—Venice, Genoa and Florence. Venice comes first, because it showed least change from the medieval policy of repression and rigid control.

The Venetians, realizing that firm organization was the secret of success, had placed their entire trading, shipping and manufacturing and political life within a framework of control as rigid as an Oriental despotism. At the basis of it was the Great Council (*Maggior Consiglio*) which named all officials; only those who were in the council in 1296 or whose ancestors had been members since 1172 were eligible to be members. Above this was a Senate of prominent citizens, which acted as a legislative body, and a terrible Committee of Ten. This committee had extraordinary powers to suppress conspiracy and breaches of morals; it acted in secret without consulting anybody, and often its victim was dead before any of his friends realized that he had been arrested. At the top of the structure was the *doge* or duke, named for life by the Council.

Manufacturing secrets were guarded as jealously as state secrets, especially in Venice's great glass industry. In 1291 the industry had been moved en bloc to the island of Murano, because of danger to the city from the intensely hot fires used, and there the glassworkers were all but enslaved. Death was the penalty for taking a secret of glassmaking abroad—a penalty enforced with an assassin's stiletto, wherever the culprit might seek refuge, if no other means proved possible.

So likewise did Venice insist upon monopolizing the most profitable trade routes, with the most powerful fleet in the Mediterranean backing up the insistence. Smashing such repression was almost a first prerequisite for modern life, and this milestone was not passed effectively until England crushed Spain's attempt to maintain a Venetian type of trade control by defeating the Spanish Armada in 1588.

The only formidable opposition to this monopoly came from Genoa. But this opposition was not so important in developing thought as was the fact that ultimately it failed. The failure occurred because Genoa did not organize her effort with the ruthless efficiency shown by Venice and also because she permitted pernicious rivalry by feudal families within the state. These families, notably the Dorias and the Spinolas, often wasted as much strength fighting each other as they devoted to struggling with Venice.

This gave Venice the victory in the end, but also it worked in a backhanded fashion to lend a new impetus to progress. It gave the defeated factions a powerful incentive to explore in search of new trade routes and opportunities. Successful discovery not only would escape pressure from Venetians; it would gain the jump on the "ins" at home in exploiting new markets. No mystery exists, then, in the fact that the earliest of the great maritime explorations were led by Genoese mariners, Columbus and John Cabot among them.

Long before these voyages, however, growing interest in bold seafaring brought a notable aid to navigation in new portolani or sailing charts in place of the older peripli or "sea-route maps."

The *periplus,* inherited from the coasting voyages of ancient times, was a simple list of sailing directions, such as "row two days, then cut across open water to mountain peak on the south horizon." But not long after the compass came into use during the first century of crusading, the Italian mariners began developing the *portolano,* a real sailing chart. This showed coast lines as a modern chart does, and it bore a pattern of crisscrossed lines to help in laying compass courses.

The oldest known portolano is the Carte Pisane (about 1300, from Pisa); it shows evidence of having been drawn from peripli. The oldest dated example we have is the Carte Vesconti of 1311—a well-drawn and surprisingly accurate chart of the Mediterranean. Later ones gave information outside Gibraltar, and the Laurentian *portolano* of 1351 shows a surprisingly good shape for all of Africa. Where the makers got the information is utterly unknown, but there it stands, and it could hardly have been a blind guess. Either the makers contacted some survivor of the lost Vivaldi or Catalan expeditions, or they learned about the east coast from Arabs who were known to have coasted as far as Madagascar and who may have rounded the southern tip.

We come now to the third city, Florence, which contributed notably to economic development at the time. Excellent symbols of the Florentine contribution were the first two great Medici, Giovanni and Cosimo. Giovanni de' Medici (1360–1429) got his start by acting as the "man behind the scenes" in a revolt of the powerful wool carders' guild against the oppressive policies of the aristocratic government in power at the moment. He was *gonfalonier* of justice at this time, but he and his descendants must have studied the success of Pisistratus in Athens to good profit, because beginning with Giovanni, the Medici preferred to be the bosses behind puppet officials. Giovanni did this and left immense actual power as well as an ample banking fortune. After he died in 1429 his son Cosimo (1389–1464) made the Medicean house one of the great powers in Europe.

Cosimo, later called the Elder, was uncanny in his ability to finance winners in political quarrels all over Europe and to collect when victory was achieved. At home he kept the turbulent Florentines in what was amazingly good order for them by intriguing them with popular civic projects and no doubt by commissioning a quiet assassination when this seemed the best way to dispose of a troublemaker. He was exiled once but was soon recalled, and throughout his career he was a generous patron to the Florentine geniuses of Renaissance art. His grandson Lorenzo (1449–92) carried this tradition to heights that earned him the soubriquet Lorenzo the Magnificent.

This sketch of the early Medicean grandees, down to the time when Columbus discovered America, introduces the familiar modern figure, the individual financier and capitalist.

Florence was a natural site for the appearance of the individual capitalist, because the city dealt in small, costly wares, and the field for individual effort and reward was large. Such opportunities still were exceptional, however. Florence had set a pattern, but medieval repressions had to be smashed throughout Europe, not merely in one city, before individual capitalism could become widespread.

This raises the question of what forces were at work to produce this smashing, and so we come logically to changes in the most difficult fields of all—politics, government and spiritual affairs.

One supposed milestone in this field was the fall of Constantinople to the Turks on May 29, 1453. This event often is selected as a marker for the division between the Middle Ages and modern times because nineteenth-century and earlier views of the Renaissance as a genuine rebirth ascribed outstanding importance to it. Fleeing Greek scholars were supposed to have taken precious manuscripts with them, revealed these documents to a barely awakened Europe and thereby helped mightily to kindle the blaze of enthusiasm for classic art, knowledge and ways of living.

Actually Constantinople had been combed for everything which it could offer ever since the Fourth Crusade culminated in the Latin or Norman Conquest in 1204. When the city fell this time in 1453 Europe was interested and somewhat shocked, but when several popes urged a crusade the appeal fell upon deaf ears. Venice preferred scooping in Byzantine trade to restoring a competitor to power; other European powers were too busy with their own concerns to go trooping off on a holy war against the Turks.

Indeed, in northwestern Europe kings were dealing with two new instrumentalities of warfare which between them would destroy feudalism entirely by the sixteenth century, through ending the value of the armored, mounted knight. These new instrumentalities were the longbow and gunpowder.

The longbow, almost as high as a man and wielded by putting the entire weight of the body into drawing a yard-long arrow to its head before letting fly, had come into military use substantially under Edward I—and it was a match for the Roman short sword in effectiveness. A longbowman could discharge several arrows while a crossbowman was winding up his weapon to let fly one bolt; range and accuracy were superior, and power was sufficient, in the bowman's phrase, "to try out the joints in a knight's armor." The knights of France were utterly baffled by this new menace when they first met it at Crécy (1346), and they found it worse when they reached the absurd conclusion that fighting on foot had something to do with English power. This led them, both at Poitiers (1356) and again at Agincourt (1415), to make the insane mistake of dismounting and clanking ahead on foot, weighed with all their metal, into the deadly hail of gray-goose-feather cloth-yard shafts.

The net result was to make the common soldier practically the fighting equal of the mounted knights. Hence English kings had less incentive to maintain an expensive, turbulent nobility and more reason for strengthening the life of the yeomanry, the class of sturdy, non-noble but free farmers who could wield the longbow.

Gunpowder, too, came into use—some accounts say at Crécy—in crude cannon. But in the state of the art at the time, this new force was all but as dangerous to its users as to the foe, when applied in weapons. The first really effective use was in blowing down gates and demolishing walls and thus reducing the military value of feudal castles; the Spanish matchlocks of the early sixteenth century were the first reasonably effective firearms for hand use.

Meanwhile spiritual affairs had been going through grievously trying times ever since the death of Frederick II in 1250.

The Papacy had sought support from the French after that time, and the upshot, after many years of tangled politics and fighting, was withdrawal of the papal court from Rome to the shelter of French power at Avignon for nearly three fourths of a century, beginning in 1305. This action, called by non-French Christians "the Babylonian captivity" or "the Exile," was followed after Pope Gregory XI (1370–78) returned to Rome September 27, 1370, by the Great Schism (1378–1417). French, German and Roman factions set up rival popes, and Christianity entered the fifteenth century with the intolerable situation of having *three* claimants for the supreme spiritual authority. This situation was liquidated by Sigismund of Hungary, king of Germany and the Romans but not yet crowned emperor, through the Council of Constance (1414–18). The council elected Cardinal Otto Colonna as Martin V and thereby healed the Great Schism of the West in a formal sense. It failed utterly, however, to heal the rancors and clamors for change which had sprung up throughout Europe.

The most prominent outcry had been raised by the Minorite or Spiritual party of the Franciscans, with their demand for *evangelical poverty*—that is, abandonment of riches, glitter and show and return to the apostolic simplicity of the fathers. The first outcry had been suppressed by the Inquisition, but during the days of the Great Schism it was fanned into a blaze again, notably by the English Franciscan John Wycliffe (1320?–84), or Wyclif of Oxford and vicar of Lutterworth.

He began by simple inveighing against worldliness, excessive tribute to support clerical luxury and lack of spiritual force in the Church. He attached the people of London to him with his eloquent preaching, and when he was put on trial before the Bishop of London the public created an uproar that stopped the proceedings. Wycliffe then sent out "hedge priests" to preach without churches, and when charges were laid against him for this he began asserting that salvation could come to men directly from God, without need for priestly intervention. To help people find salvation he and two associates translated the Bible into English. Together with Chaucer's contemporary poetry this translation did much to fix the form of the English language.

Wycliffe died of apoplexy before any action was taken against him, but his doctrines were taken up and preached in less extreme form by John Huss (1369–1415) of Bohemia. The Council of Constance called him to account for his views, under a safeguard from Sigismund. When he appeared Sigismund was away, working on the resignation of the three popes; and the council, after pronouncing Huss a heretic, declared that safeguards to heretics were invalid, and Huss was burned to death. When Sigismund returned he had to swallow the breach of his safeguard or see the council break up without results.

As to Wycliffe, the council had to content itself with ordering his body dug up and burned, and with this the issue of evangelical poverty was thought settled once and for all. It did not appear as a major heresy for a century. But the reactionaries in the Church deluded themselves when they thought such an issue, once alive in the minds of men, could be suppressed by sword, prison or stake.

The delusion became even more reprehensible within half a century, when the most powerful stimulant to thought since the birth of skeptical reasoning among the Greeks came into the world with the invention of *printing*.

The origin of this art, which burst forth in Mainz, Germany, in 1456–57, is obscure. Printing from blocks was known to the Chinese in the ninth century; a book found in Kansu in 1900 shows a date translatable as May 11, 868. Pi Sheng used movable type in 1041–49, and the Japanese had printed pictures from blocks since at least A.D. 770. No connection has been shown between this Oriental art and European printing, but block printing was used in an English print dated 1423.

To achieve the full printing art from this, three steps were required —use of paper, already provided by development of linen paper in the fourteenth century; a suitable ink, which came about by adopting the Van Eyck oil pigments of the early fifteenth century; and cutting the blocks into single letters for convenience in setting or, better yet, casting the types in metal. Tradition credits Johann Gutenberg (1398?–1468) of Mainz in Germany with accomplishing this synthesis of arts, but the record is obscure because the early printers worked in secret and imitated manuscript as best they could, to avoid probable suppression by the powerful guilds of manuscript workers.

No uncertainty exists, however, about the explosive spread of printing once "the secret of Mainz" leaked out. A printing establishment was set up at Subiaco near Rome in 1464; Venice received the art in 1469 and Paris in 1470, while William Caxton set up the first English press in Westminster in 1476. By 1490 Venice alone had a hundred printers, and by the end of the century perhaps nine million copies of books had been printed, so eager was Europe to obtain the product of this marvelously inexpensive new process for spreading the written word.

With printing doing its work in such fashion, reactionary medieval-ism stood doomed. It could not stand overlong, now that intelligent men everywhere had easy, relatively inexpensive access to the accumu-lated thinking of the ages, capped by current demand for reform and change. How long the overthrow might have taken had nothing more happened nobody can say. As events fell out, we need not even bother to guess. Within half a century after the invention of printing the change to new, free thought was precipitated with all but ex-plosive violence by the discovery of America.

Since this event is one of the most important milestones in all his-tory, it deserves tracing in all detail from the onset of the forces which led to it. Those who have weighed the matter most carefully tend to start the story on June 21, 1380, the fateful day when Venice captured the entire Genoese fleet at Chioggia. Thereafter Venice was undisputed Queen of the Mediterranean, and the Genoese had to find new trade routes around Africa if they were to escape Venetian domination.

Since Genoa now lacked strength to do this for herself various Genoese mariners sought patrons elsewhere, and early in the fifteenth century they found one after their hearts' desire in Prince Henry of Portugal (1394-1460).

Henry had won fame serving with his father and brothers against the Moors, down to their crowning feat of capturing Ceuta, across the strait from Gibraltar, in 1415. He also took holy orders and com-manded the Order of Christ, with which Portugal had replaced the disbanded Knights Templar. In 1419 he was made governor of the Algarve (southwest Portugal), and he settled down at Sagres near Cape Saint Vincent for what proved to be his lifework of laying a firm foundation for modern navigation and maritime exploration.

The records offer no reason to suppose that Henry cared about finding a sea route to India; the Genoese who flocked into his service would be the only ones who had that interest. Henry seems to have been intrigued by the fabled kingdom of Prester John, a land of Christians far to the south of the Moors. The real basis for this belief may have been the Coptic Christians of Ethiopia, and Henry, know-ing nothing of Africa beyond the Sahara, could well believe that he could contact this realm by sailing beyond Cape Bojador. But whatever his motives, he showed first-rank genius in his attack upon the problem.

He realized, for example, that such exploration would require vessels that could sail much closer into the wind than could the craft of the day, so he pushed development of the *caravel,* a knife-prowed craft with lateen sails which did well in such sailing. He wanted the best charts and navigating methods he could get—so, Christian leader as he was, he used Arabs and Jews if they could lend real knowledge. Beyond this he wanted stouthearted captains, men who would balk at nothing in searching out the secrets of the African coast.

His first two expeditions stuck, however, at Cape Bojador. After the second failure Henry, according to the chronicler Azurara, was told by the commander, young Gil Eannes, that several mariners had pronounced the cape impassable. Thereupon Henry treated Gil to some plain talk:

The Infant [Portuguese for prince], calling Gil apart, charged him earnestly to . . . pass that Cape . . . even if he could do nothing else. . . . "You cannot find," said the Infant, "a peril so great that the hope of reward will not be greater, and in truth I wonder much at the notion you have all taken on so uncertain a matter—for . . . you tell me only the opinion of four mariners, who came but from the Flanders trade . . . and know nothing of needle [compass] or sailing chart. Go forth, then, and heed none of their words, but make your voyage straightaway."

Gil Eannes lived up to this ringing charge by rounding the dreaded cape in 1434. Then, with the spell of Bojador broken, discovery pushed on until Diniz Diaz rounded Cape Verde in 1445. Now, unhappily, the Portuguese found that Negro slaves were highly profitable, and Henry's high purpose was lost in prosecution of this brutal business. What he thought of it is not known, but the thought of the time suggests two possible reconciliations. Undoubtedly his revenues had been depleted by his costly expeditions, so that profit from any source was welcome—and beyond this the Negroes, however hard their lot otherwise, were being given the boon of Christian salvation. The sad part for Henry was that the full fruit of his effort, the circumnavigation of Africa, was not achieved until twenty-seven years after his death in 1460.

Renewed interest in a sea route pushed this feat through, however, in 1487. In that year Bartholomew Diaz conquered the terrific pull south from the equator, and when he stuck fast in head winds and storms at the present Cape of Good Hope he adopted a daring expedient. He sailed far out to the southwest, on a gamble, caught a gale from the west, and when he saw land again the coast line trended northeast! He had rounded the tip of Africa, and from Arab accounts he knew that beyond this lay an open route to India!

He turned back at Algoa Bay and set every church bell in Lisbon clanging when he sailed up the Tagus in December 1488 with his news. The baffling cape which he had named *Cabo Tormentoso* (the Cape of Torments) was renamed *Cabo de Boa Esperanza* (Cape of Good Hope), and all Portugal looked forward to becoming the equal of Venice in the rich Oriental trade.

And now for the climax, to be provided by Columbus! We may take up his story when the bells were ringing in Lisbon for Diaz's success in rounding the Cape of Good Hope.

Columbus was present, and to him these joyful bells were ringing out the ruin of hope. They meant that Portugal would devote herself to this new route and would give no further ear to a project he had been trying to promote—the project of reaching Japan or India by sailing due west.

This project could not be called a new idea, since Eratosthenes of Alexandria had envisaged it and had estimated the distance almost exactly. This we know from his regretful remark: "If it were not that the vast extent of the Atlantic renders it impossible, one might even sail from the coast of Spain to that of India along the same parallel." Columbus had drawn his idea, however, from Ptolemy, and Ptolemy had made the earth much smaller than had Eratosthenes. He also overestimated the size of Asia, and the combined effect of these two errors was to place Japan about where Mexico actually is. Sailing across the northeast trades over the intervening distance promised to be as easy as the going around Africa had proved tough.

This, however, was something he could not persuade any ruler to believe. In this the rulers were not blind or foolish, as we are given to think with our benefit of hindsight. After all, Columbus' idea depended upon Ptolemy being right, and actually both Ptolemy and Columbus were very wrong. Columbus would not have had a chance in the world to succeed had not the Americas been in his way and saved the day. Moreover, the rulers had good reason for doubting Ptolemy, since the astronomers had been finding this authority more and more unsatisfactory about the planets for at least two centuries.

Even worse, Columbus had been making his own way hard by the high terms he demanded. Columbus wanted to be made an admiral for the voyage, to have one tenth of all precious metals secured and to be viceroy of all lands discovered—an office which would have made him as powerful as any king if the voyage turned out well. All in all, then, it was sheer good fortune for Columbus, to say nothing of the world, when Isabella of Spain turned softhearted in 1492 and let him have his chance.

He sailed from Palos on Friday, August 3, 1492, and what happened then until the landing on October 12 is well known to every school child. He had discovered a "New World" in the geographic sense, and by the shock to thought the world over he had also opened a new world to the mind of man. Now even the dullest dolt in Christendom could not help realizing that old ideas, already under heavy suspicion, would need drastic overhauling to fit them in with this amazing new discovery—and once that realization began fermenting in the thought of Europe, medieval thinking was dead. The curtain had risen upon modern times.

MIND THROUGH THE AGES

PART VII

MODERN HISTORY

The Rule of Reason

CHAPTER XXXII

First Fruits of the Modern Period

INEVITABLY the shock which Columbus gave the world with his monumental discovery would touch off many of the powder mines which had already been set in European thinking, but as said in the preceding chapter, the order of explosion would depend upon the difficulty of achieving change. The first and simplest effect would be a simple spirit of high adventure, of hope for finding new fortunes just over the horizon. The decades to come were to be primarily the "Period of Great Voyages," the "Age of Maritime Discovery."

Happily enough for simplicity in tracing, the period has excellent historic unity in that most of the developments center about Spain or at least involve Spanish power as a controlling element, and the period comes to a reasonably logical close when Spanish power was crippled by the defeat of the great Armada in 1588. The march of thought for this period may well begin, then, with Spanish reaction when Columbus returned with his great news.

Spain's first hope was to get rich quick after the thoroughly medieval pattern set by Venice of a rigid trade monopoly. Coupled with this were vague ideas of settlement in what at the moment were supposed to be backward portions of Asia; but no Spaniard had any idea of winning wealth through toil. These lands were heathen and, as such, fair game for Spanish arms. The Spaniards proposed to carry the boon of Christianity to them on the point of a sword and to enrich themselves with plunder while doing so.

Immediate and emphatic opposition came, however, from Portugal, with a thoroughly medieval argument but one which Spain could not ignore. Portugal claimed prior right to all overseas discoveries, by whomever made, by virtue of an existing agreement with all the princes. How this agreement was reached and what came of it was told quaintly by one Robert Thorne, "A merchant of London who dwelt long in the city of Sivil (Seville)," when England's ambassador to Spain asked for light upon the transaction in 1527. Pertinent extracts from the Hakluyt Society's reprint of Thorne's letter follow:

. . . In the year 1484 the king of Portingal minded to arm certain Carvels to discover this Spicerie [i.e., India]. Then forasmuch as he feared that being discovered, every other prince would sende and trade thither, so that the cost and peril of discovering should be his, and the profit common; wherefore first hee gave knowledge of this his minde to all princes Christened, saying that he would seeke amongst the infidels newe possessions of regions, and therefore would make a certain armie; and that if any of them would help in the cost of the sayd armie, he should enjoy his part of the profite or honor that might come of it.

Nowe they say, that all the Princes of Christendome answered, that they would be no part of such an armie nor yet of the profit that might come of it. After which he [the king of Portugal] gave knowledge to the Pope of his purpose, and the answere of the Princes, desiring him [i.e., the Pope] that seeing that none would helpe in the costes, that he would judge all that should bee found and discovered to be of his [the king of Portugal's] jurisdiction. . . . The Pope not only granted that all should be discovered from Orient to Occident, should be the Kings of Portingal, but also, that upon great censures no other Prince should discover but he. And if they did, all to bee the kings of Portingal.

. . . In the year 1492 the king of Spaine . . . armed certain Carvels . . . and then discovered . . . La Dominica, and . . . Cuba . . . When the king of Portingal had knowledge, he sent to the King of Spaine, requiring him to give him the sayd Islands. . . . At the same time it seemeth that out of Castil into Portingal had gone for fear of burning . . . infinite number of Jewes . . . and carried with them infinite number of golde and silver. So the king of Spaine . . . answered . . . that to be obedient to which the Pope had decreed, he would give him [the king of Portugal] the sayd Islands of the Indies. [But] forasmuch as it was decreed betwixt the sayde kings, that none should receive the others subjects fugitives, nor their goods, therefore the king of Portingal should pay and returne to the king of Spaine a million of golde or more, that the Jewes had carried out of Spaine to Portingal & that in so doing he would give these Islands, and desist from any more discovering. And not fulfilling this, he would not onely not give these Islands but procure to discover more where him thought best.

It seemeth that the king of Portingal would not, or could not with his ease pay this money. And so not paying . . . he . . . consented to the king of Spaine, that touching this discovery they should divide the world between them two.

The fruit of this diplomatic claim and counterclaim was the Treaty of Tordesillas (June 7, 1494). This agreement, confirmed and later amended by various papal bulls, resulted in Pope Julian II's noted *line of demarcation* of January 24, 1506. This line girdled the earth through both poles and a point 370 leagues west of the Cape Verde Islands, cutting the earth into hemispheres. All discoveries in the same hemisphere with Europe were to be Portugal's; Spain had right of discovery and exploitation in the other hemisphere. In terms of land areas Portugal's half included the eastern part of Brazil as far west as Rio de Janeiro and the mouth of the Amazon, all of Asia, the East Indies, except the eastern tip of New Guinea, and Australia, except the east coast. Spain had the Americas, except Portuguese Brazil, and the Pacific Ocean almost as far west as Japan.

Such a division, with the accompanying idea that it was enforcible against both the natives and European nations, was about as medieval as anything that could be imagined. So also was the formation of Spain's historic colonial policy.

For a decade the colonial administration was left largely to Columbus, with well-known and unfortunate results. He was driven by the lust of his royal backers for gold, silver, jewels and spices, and he wore his life out seeking them, never realizing to the day he died (May 20, 1506) that he was dealing with a new continent and not with outlying portions of the Far East. Such colonies as he planted spent their time in seeking gold and maltreating the Indians and succeeded only in being an expense to the Spanish crown.

At length in 1503 the disgusted Ferdinand established a House of Trade (*Casa de Contratación*) in Seville, with a complete monopoly, after the Venetian pattern, over all colonial trade.

To this Ferdinand's successor, the Hapsburg Charles I, added a Royal and Supreme Council of Indies in 1517, to exercise legislative and judical authority over the colonies. Under this council all trade came to be conveyed by two fleets a year, one plying to and from Porto Bello on the Isthmus of Panama and the other serving Vera Cruz in Mexico.

When the Philippines were added to Spain's possessions after 1521, they were served by the grueling annual voyage of the Manila galleon across the Pacific to a connection at Panama. From one third to one half of the crew surrendered their lives to scurvy on each voyage, and year after year, at Manila galleon time, Panama prepared hospital beds for the survivors as well as pack mules to carry the royal tribute to Porto Bello. Annual treasure fleets, plying between Panama and Peru, completed the nautical machinery for colonial exploitation.

This policy was rounded out within the Americas by half a century of exploration and conquest. Amerigo Vespucci (1451–1512) was the first to add his name to the roster of Spanish discoverers, although no man was less entitled to such a distinction. He was an agent of the Medicis, in charge of the financial backing that gave Columbus his second voyage, and naturally he kept his principals well informed concerning discoveries. He claimed to have gone on voyages, and perhaps he did; but if so, he was an astonishingly poor geographer, because he contradicted himself from letter to letter. But some of his material came to the notice of the learned professor of geography, Martin Waldseemüller (1470?–1521), then working in St Dié on a new geography and map of the world. Waldseemüller took Vespucci's claim to have discovered the continent of America at face value, and in describing the parts of the world (1507) he said:

. . . Another fourth part has been discovered by Americus Vespucius [Vespucci's name Latinized] . . . Wherefore I do not see what is rightly to hinder us from calling it Amerige or America, after its discoverer, Americus.

The name took on, and so geography took unto itself representations which were tantamount to frauds. More genuine work was done by Vasco Núñez de Balboa (1475–1517), who crossed the Isthmus of Panama and sighted the Pacific on September 25, 1513. From the east-west lie of the Isthmus he called this ocean the "South Sea," and the Spaniards used this term even as late as the Treaty of 1819 which settled boundaries with the United States. On land the Spanish empire was rounded out by the astonishing conquests made by Hernando Cortez (1485–1547) in Mexico, between 1519 and 1521, and by Francisco Pizarro (1471?–1541) in Peru from 1524 until he was assassinated by an associate in 1541.

North America was given some attention by Juan Ponce de León (1460?–1520), Francisco Vásquez de Coronado (about 1500–54) and Hernando De Soto (1496?–1542). But Ponce de León, after combing Florida for the Fountain of Youth, fell mortally wounded in an engagement with the natives in 1521. Coronado combed the southwest of the United States from 1540 to 1542 for the fabled golden Seven Cities of Cibola and was degraded and disgraced after he failed to find them. De Soto fought his way from Florida to Missouri and Arkansas from 1539 to 1542, in search of gold, but at length died of his hardships and—no doubt—unwillingness to face his backers with news of failure. Thereafter this seemingly goldless land of North America drew no attention from Spaniards north of Mexico, until Franciscan and Jesuit missionaries began penetrating California, Arizona and Texas in the seventeenth and eighteenth centuries.

This record of reactionary policy and blind greed for gold is relieved, however, by the high spirit and daring of the navigators who completed a first blocking in of man's knowledge of the world. Of all the men who battled storms and scurvy at sea, natives while abroad and greedy backers at home, two must suffice here for samples— Vasco da Gama (1460?–1524) and Fernão de Magalhães (1480?–1521), or Magellan, to give him the better-known Spanish form of his name.

Vasco da Gama was a Portuguese veteran of many wars and not a navigator, but he had the iron will needed to drive an expedition along the tremendous pull around Africa, to contact with India, in 1497–98. The climax to his feat came when the expedition, riddled with scurvy and heartsick over grueling hardships, encountered a terrific storm off the east coast of Africa. Da Gama met clamors that he turn back by seizing and throwing overboard all maps and navigation instruments other than his own. Then he announced, "See here, men, that you have neither master nor pilot. . . . Henceforward let no one speak to me of putting back, for know from me of a certainty, that if I do not find information which I have come to seek . . . to Portugal I do not return."

His was a specimen of the iron wills that drove men through to a knowledge of the world. Magellan was a man of the same stamp but having a vastly different motive. He also was a Portuguese veteran who had been maimed while fighting and who was cashiered for trading with the Moors when he recovered. He knew Portuguese navigating secrets, and to seek revenge, as well as a livelihood, riches and glory, he offered Charles of Spain a most cunning proposition.

The basis of the proposition was well stated by Robert Thorne in his letter about Spanish and Portuguese maritime policy. The point lay in deliberate falsification of charts, to bring desirable lands on each nation's own side of the line of demarcation:

For these coasts and situations of the Islands, everyone one of the Cosmographers and pilots of Portingal & Spayne do set after their purpose. The Spaniards toward the Orient because they [the islands] should appear to appertain to the Emperour; & the Portingals more toward the Occident for that they should fal within their jurisdiction. So that the pilots and navigants thither, which in such cases should declare the truth, by their industrie do set them falsely everyone to favor his prince.

Magellan's proposition was that many of the Spice Islands or Moluccas lay east of the line in the Pacific and hence in Spanish territory. He knew, he said, for he had been in those waters—as he had, in a location which we reckon as longitude 130° east. Spain was forbidden, of course, to use the Portuguese route around Africa; but Magellan proposed to reach and claim these islands by sailing west across the Spanish zone—that is, across the Pacific.

Charles liked the idea, and on August 10, 1519, Magellan set out from Seville in his flagship the Trinidad and four others. He spent more than a year probing the Argentinian coast, especially the Rio de la Plata, and waiting for the southern summer—and then spent thirty-eight days after October 21, 1520, beating through the straits which bear his name, to a glimpse of the open ocean beyond. "Thank God our Lord," he exclaimed at sight of Balboa's South Sea. "It is true, señores, that we have lost two vessels, that our provisions are wasted . . . but even if we are reduced to eating the leather on our ships yards, we will go on!"

He was right about the leather, and he could have mentioned sawdust and rats, because both were added to the menu before the scurvy-rotted, decimated crews sighted Guam on March 6, 1521. With health restored by fresh food the expedition pushed on until the great commander was killed in a native squabble on April 27. But he had circumnavigated the world personally at the time, for he was killed on Mactan in longitude 124° east—nearer Europe than his previous "farthest east"—and his lieutenant, Juan Sebastian del Cano, finished the epic journey with one vessel, the Vittoria, and thirty-eight men by dropping anchor in Seville September 9, 1522.

The voyage did not win the Moluccas for Spain, but it did win the Philippines. Now Spain's maritime record was complete. She settled down to her medieval policy of rigid monopoly and ruthless exploitation, particularly of the gold and silver which even then was making her incomparably the richest and most powerful nation in Europe, and for half a century this power awed all other nations into accepting the situation. New developments in commerce, trade and settlement had to wait until this power was broken.

Spain had no chance, however, to enjoy her riches in peace, because even while Magellan was making his epochal voyage another of the European powder mines had exploded, with world-shaking effect.

into the beginnings of the movement called by Catholics the Protestant Revolt and by Protestants the Reformation.

The powder for this explosion was the old Franciscan issue of evangelical poverty, and even while Spain was winning the Americas a new fuse was being laid to the powder by two great Humanists— the German, Johann Reuchlin (1455–1522), and the Netherlander, Desiderius Erasmus (1466?–1536).

Reuchlin came into the situation innocently enough, through his defense of Hebrew as a fit subject for study against violent attacks made by a converted Jew, one Johann Pfefferkorn, upon such studies. Reuchlin's defense of Hebrew was pronounced heretical, and a copy was officially burned in public. Two German Humanists, Crotus Rubianus and Ulrich von Hutten, thereupon produced a collection of ostensible letters from priests and others praising this action, and in these Letters of Obscure Men (1515) they packed all the ignorance, prejudice, worldiness and bigotry that could be found among Reuchlin's opponents. The satire was as one sided as the attitude it portrayed and terribly coarse in its humor, but it produced an enormous effect throughout Germany upon the less intelligent classes.

Meanwhile quieter but equally potent fanning of discontent had been coming from Erasmus.

Erasmus had spent an intensely unhappy childhood in an orphanage, having been the natural son of a priest. He was ordained as a priest but worked as an editor for the first printing firm in Switzerland. While he never openly assailed the church, his urbane, polished personal writings set up telling contrasts between the spirituality religion should have and the existing decadence and materialism. Among the more intelligent his works wore away respect for authority as dripping water gnaws at a stone.

Thanks to all this, Germany was in an explosive state of mind when the spark was applied by Martin Luther's objection to indulgences.

In principle the indulgence merely remitted temporal punishments —penances and public rebukes imposed by the Church upon sinners who had purged themselves spiritually by sincere repentance. They had been given for some centuries as rewards for crusaders and as features of Church jubilees, but as papal policy became more and more materialistic in the late fifteenth century the new printing press was used to print copies of indulgences offered on flimsy pretexts, and the papers were hawked throughout Europe. Many of the hawkers were not over careful about emphasizing the need for *sincere* repentance to make the indulgence effective, and in the popular mind these printed slips came to be a sort of bargain-counter trafficking with God. One simply paid the price and did as one liked, subject only to finding a complaisant priest to hear one's confession.

For some years the young Augustinian friar Martin Luther (1483–1546) had been getting worked up more and more over this popular reaction as he heard it in the confessional, and in 1517, when a Dominican friar, John Tetzel, was selling indulgences in the neighborhood, Luther exploded. He prepared ninety-five theses or propositions arraigning the entire practice together with other abuses of spiritual authority, and on October 31 he nailed a copy of the theses to the church door in Wittenberg. Another copy went with a strongly worded letter to the archbishop.

Luther expected a fiery debate, and he got it. But neither he nor the pope of the day, Leo X (1513–21), thought they were going to explode a mine beneath the Church with their controversy over this comparatively trifling issue. Leo dealt patiently and thoughtfully with the problem, but his handling of it was perverted by intermediate zealots, while Luther's attitude was conditioned throughout by the tension and strain of his own maladjusted personality. He was a man of violent emotions and strong physical passions who was continually wracked by inner conflict between a strongly sexed nature and his vows. His only relief had been through fierce devotion to duty—and now, with all Germany crackling with excitement over the argument, he plunged ahead like a locomotive out of control, until he allowed himself to advance his famous doctrine that man's faith in God was enough to win God's grace and no priestly intermediation or sacrament was needed. When the pope condemned this doctrine Luther, on December 10, 1520, publicly burned the bull of condemnation.

This was rank heresy, rebellion and an assault upon the very foundations of the Church. It was not dealt with immediately and drastically, because all Europe was absorbed at the moment in the election of a successor to the emperor Maximilian I—an election which Charles I of Spain secured by outbribing every rival for the honor. But once the Spanish king became Charles V of the empire he called a diet to meet at Worms to deal with the matter and also to consider a similar revolt which Ulrich Zwingli had been stirring up in Switzerland since 1518. The diet heard Luther, allowed him to go under his safe conduct and then authorized the emperor to issue the Edict of Worms (May 25, 1521) which condemned Luther to a heretic's death.

But sympathizers with Luther and a strong group of malcontents among the German nobility now were willing to fight over the issue, as Germany had fought the Papacy through many an earlier century. The elector Frederick of Saxony sheltered Luther in his castle, and Luther spent his time writing hymns, arranging a modified church doctrine and service and translating the Bible into German. The German populace at large, outside Charles's Hapsburg domains, was with Luther; and Charles forced the issue to a "rule or ruin" outcome by declaring war.

The result was nearly a generation of intermittent fighting, until finally Charles realized in 1555 that the Lutherans were still strong enough to hold out indefinitely. He gave up then and signed the Peace of Augsburg, which allowed each German state to have whichever faith it preferred, Lutheran or Roman Catholic.

With that act the ideal of a Universal Church, which had persisted since the Resurrection, stood shattered; Christians now were to have a voice in the selection of their faith. This does not mean that any such thing as *religious freedom* had come into the world. States were to have a choice, but once the rulers and other powers in each state made their choice everyone in the state had to conform.

Neither had any spirit of tolerance arisen. If the Protestant states did not go to the length of establishing a medieval inquisition, this was due, more than to anything else, to the fact that the Inquisition was an institution of the old church. Trials for heresy continued, and dissidents and Roman Catholics suffered for their faith in Protestant countries just as heretics had under the Universal Church. John Calvin (1509–64), the leader of the revolt in Switzerland, was as savage as the notorious inquisitor Torquemada (1420–98) of Spain; at least two centuries more had to pass before the idea that an *individual* could choose his church would become general.

Nevertheless, a strong start in this direction had been made, and another momentous advance toward free thought and action was brewing through growth in English naval strength. Indeed, this was the development which did most after the Peace of Augsburg to usher in modern times through destruction of monopoly of the New World.

The fathers of this strength were the two Henrys, the Seventh and the Eighth, and the basis of it was shrewd development of English naval ships and tactics.

The Henrys, in common with all navigators, had seen that on the

Atlantic oars had no place; ships had to rely upon sails alone and have rounded, high shapes that could not accommodate rowers but could ride out storms. Beyond this they saw, more clearly than did any Spanish or Mediterranean nation, that the secret of offensive power lay in *cannon*. The southern nations used cannon, true, but only for preliminary attack; their main reliance was in coming alongside, boarding and finishing the fight hand to hand. The Henrys built and armed their ships and trained their crews to keep out of boarding distance by skillful sailing and to win the fight with fire power alone. Boarding could follow if desirable, when the foe was crushed and in no spirit or condition to resist.

The two Henrys had not tried out their idea in actual warfare; they preferred, as long as no one challenged them, to build up and conserve their strength. They had indulged cautiously in exploration from the year 1497, when the city of Bristol had sent out the Genoese-born and naturalized Venetian, Giovanni Caboto (John Cabot, 1450–98), who discovered Newfoundland and Cape Breton Island; but they had kept out of Portuguese and Spanish territory.

The English dreamed rather of finding a route to the East through the Arctic Seas north of Norway and Russia (the Northeast Passage), through or past North America (the Northwest Passage) or both; and when Elizabeth acceded, the search to the northeast was being pushed actively by the Muscovy Company, an organization chartered in 1555 with a monopoly of any trade it might develop.

Elizabeth continued this policy officially. Unofficially she cut into Spanish profits by letting slip her "sea dogs of Devon," a breed of mariners from southwest England who were little better than pirates but who also were skilled seamen and redoubtable fighters. The most famous and successful of them was Francis Drake (1540?–96). Drake crowned his exploits by plundering ships and raiding towns along the entire coast of South America, from Cape Horn to Panama. Then with Spanish power well roused behind him he thought the fittest course home would be Magellan's track around the world, and so he was the first Englishman to circumnavigate the globe. He reached England in November 1780, having spent three years on his memorable voyage.

The Spaniards naturally were furious over such exploits, but for many years they let Elizabeth put them off with shifty promises to "do something" about these pirates. The principal reason for this complaisance, probably, was a supposedly cunning policy which obsessed Philip II, the thoroughly stupid son of Charles, who came

to the Spanish throne when Charles abdicated after the Peace of
Augsburg to end his days with a little rest and quiet.

Philip's dream was to bring England back to the Catholic faith,
after Henry VIII had broken away in 1534 because the Pope refused
to grant him a divorce from his first wife, Catherine of Aragon. This
dream had got a good start in 1554 through Philip's marriage to
Henry's daughter Mary, who had remained a Catholic, and when
Mary became queen in 1553 the desired return seemed assured.
Mary's untimely death in 1558 had been a check, but Philip fondly
thought he could redeem this by winning Mary's Protestant sister
Elizabeth.

Philip had sounder reasons also for avoiding war with England
through many years, because he was having trouble not only with the
French but with a plaguing hornets' nest in one of his own domains,
the Netherlands.

The trouble had started when the northern provinces, commonly
called Holland, had developed a strong swing to Lutheranism under
Charles V. Philip, being stupid enough to think he could succeed in
stamping this out after his much more capable father had failed,
loosed the ferocious Duke of Alva upon the province as governor.
Alva burned, massacred and imprisoned, but instead of submission
he achieved a flaming revolt in 1567.

The heroisms of this revolt, with cutting of dikes, Dutch ships sailing over flooded fields to the rescue of cities and Dutch burghers
skating over frozen canals to the fight, are well known. But for many
years the fight was a bloody draw. The Dutch could not shake off
Philip; he could not subdue them. But in 1580 he strengthened himself by seizing Portugal, and his prospects improved further in 1584
when the Dutch leader, William of Orange, was assassinated. France
also was plainly headed for civil war over the prospect of having a
Protestant, Henry of Navarre, for king.

Elizabeth knew well that once Philip had profited from these turns
he would take revenge for all his wrongs. She acted first, therefore,
by making an alliance with the Dutch in 1585. She also permitted the
execution of Mary, Queen of Scots, on February 8, 1587, to rob
Catholic intrigue of its rallying point.

This wrong roused Philip to instant action, more especially since
Mary had named Philip's daughter as her heir. He started accordingly
to prepare an Invincible Armada, which with its own force and with
troops from the Netherlands would dispose of England once and
for all.

England trembled, but nobody flinched—least of all, the seamen who would have to bear the brunt of the defense. Not only did they have high confidence in their ships and tactics; they had tested out the fighting abilities of the "Dons" on blue water and felt able to thrash any number of them. Drake more than justified this confidence when he was sent out early in 1587 with twenty-four ships to reconnoiter the Spanish activities. He ravaged the West Indies in the spring, then sailed boldly into Cádiz and "singed the Spanish king's beard" by burning the entire fleet and all the stores which Philip had been gathering there.

This delayed Philip a year, but in the summer of 1588 the Armada finally sailed—132 warships, 40 transports, 7400 sailors and 19,000 soldiers, the mightiest force of its kind ever assembled. Pitted against it were 197 light English ships, but they were fast, nimble sailers and they bore more cannon than did the Spanish craft. Above all, they carried *seamen,* not soldiers, and they were officered under Drake as vice-admiral, by such veterans of the Northwest Passage as Frobisher and Davis and others equally redoubtable. The fight was to be between a true navy and a floating army; and it turned out just as this difference suggested it would.

Upon reaching the English Channel the Duke of Medina-Sidonia deployed his vessels in a magnificent half-moon, seven miles across from tip to tip; then he started east to pick up troops from the Netherlands, with a wind from the west at his back. In this insanely weak formation he sailed past Plymouth, where Drake and many others of the English were lurking, on July 20; and the moment he passed, the English swarmed out to reap the fruits of this folly. Having the weather gauge, they could bear down within cannon range, deliver shattering broadsides and then hold up, leaving the Spaniards utterly unable to beat back into the wind and board. They could concentrate strength as they liked against any ship in the long thin Spanish line, and so they managed to "pluck the feathers" of the Armada one by one.

After the harassed and baffled Spaniards reached the seeming shelter of Calais on July 22, the English on the twenty-ninth sent fire ships on a northeast wind into the clumsy fleet. When the wind changed, and the Spaniards sought relief by sailing into the North Sea, the English delivered another "feather-plucking" attack as long as their ammunition held out. By now the Spaniards thought only of flight around the north end of Scotland and home, but now the elements took a hand. Savage gales piled up many of the vessels on the

Scottish and Irish coasts; two thousand bodies were washed up on the beach at Sligo Bay alone. In the end only fifty-three shattered, useless vessels ever reached a Spanish port.

So died the myth of Spanish might on the water and the attempt by Spain to perpetuate medieval monopoly over the sea. From now on the oceans of the world were to be free, and the day of modern free maritime commerce had dawned. The English could and did explore and trade as they liked, subject only to control of ports by hostile powers. The Dutch, virtually free though not acknowledged so as yet, worked their way into the nominally Spanish trade of Portugal and so acquired the original Portuguese possessions in South Africa and the East Indies. The French began bestirring themselves at sea, and in all the welter the medieval maritime powers—Venice, Genoa, and the Hanseatic League—simply disappeared.

With this change the ebullient, high-spirited, emotional era of golden expectations may be said to have ended. Plenty of adventure and upset were still to occur, but now the emphasis had shifted. The world had broken through the iron medieval mold of monopoly at sea, and the problem now was to make the most of the opportunity. Politically, the dominating motive was a scramble for colonies. Commercially, the keynote was development of settlement and trade. Technologically, the dead hand of self-satisfied monopoly had been removed, and victory in the race now would go to the swift—that is, to the best equipped. Mercantile and even national power now enlisted in the drive to achieve progress; commerce and science began to strike their stride; and what came of this new drive is the central story of at least the next century.

ASTRONOMERS AND THE LONGITUDE PROBLEM

The upper picture shows how medieval and early modern astronomers achieved a fair degree of accuracy in measuring the positions and movements of heavenly bodies with large observing instruments. The one in the foreground is an *azimuth quadrant* of the type used by John Hevel or Hevelius of Danzig (died 1687). It could be set to any vertical angle and horizontal bearing.

The lower diagram shows the ancients determined longitude by the local time at which eclipses were seen. The moon is just entering the earth's shadow, and every observer will see this event at the same instant. But the *local time* will be different, according to the observer's east-west location on the earth. Observers at A and C will know from this difference in local time that they are halfway around the earth from each other. The observer at B will know that he is halfway between A and C. Passage of the moon across fixed stars could also be used. The weakness of the method was inability to tell precise local time.

CHAPTER XXXIII

Freedom of Thought Hits Its Stride

DURING THE CENTURY which saw Spain's losing struggle to maintain the universality of the Catholic Church and her own commercial monopoly of the newly discovered lands, science had been pressing forward as best it could, but the pace had been slow because scientists had not yet acquired efficient working methods, or even efficient mental attitudes toward their problems. They were still steeped in Greek and medieval lore—and while they were coming rapidly to realize that much of this knowledge was faulty, they had not fully appreciated the need for an entirely new approach by experimentation with adequate instrumental equipment, along the lines suggested by inductive thinkers such as Duns Scotus and Roger Bacon.

An excellent first example of this situation is the record of early modern struggles with two related problems in astronomy.

The first problem was the demand from navigators for good determinations of *longitude,* or east-west locations around the earth, just as latitude or north-south locations had been determined since early Egyptian times by observing the height of the polestar or the sun above the horizon.

Longitude could not be determined by any such direct method because, unhappily, the east-west location of an observer on the earth created no difference in the appearance of the heavenly bodies. The very wheeling of the heavens (really the rotation of the earth) presented the same configuration of stars at some time of night all around the earth, and how were men to tell locations east or west from an array of heavenly bodies which looked the same everywhere?

One method, known since ancient times, was observing heavenly events such as eclipses and noting the difference in time of night or day at which these events were seen from widely separated parts of the earth, as explained by the accompanying diagram. Greek knowledge of this method is proved by Ptolemy's lament that it had not been used freely:

Hipparchus . . . in the case of a few cities . . . has transmitted to us the elevations of the north pole. [By this Ptolemy meant the elevation of the polestar above the horizon.] Distances . . . have for the most part been reckoned only in a rough and ready general way, especially those from east to west; not so much from carelessness . . . as from the small number of simultaneous observations of lunar eclipses at different places that have been duly recorded; like that which was seen at Arbela at the 5th hour and at Carthage at the 2nd.

Navigators, however, wanted some method which they could use every day rather than once or twice a year at best. The heavens offered them events which could be used as well as eclipses in occultations, or passages of the moon and the planets across stars, and in the changing positions of the planets relative to the moon and the stars. To use these methods, however, two conditions had to be met—first among them, observation far finer than the unaided human eye could achieve. On the equator an error of one degree of angle in making a measurement meant an error of about 66⅔ miles in east-west location, while an error of one minute in fixing local time meant an error of more than sixteen miles in location. Such errors might well mean the difference between making a landfall or missing it, with a possibility of being wrecked on a coast in a storm or missing a tiny island where desperately needed food and water could be found.

To achieve more accurate observations astronomers used large observing instruments, such as shown in the accompanying picture. This helped greatly in working on land. Such instruments could not be used, however, at sea—and this difficulty had the astronomers stumped. The remedy lay, of course, in using the magnifying power of lenses and thus getting fine observations with small, handy observing instruments. But training in optics did not form a prescribed part of an astronomer's education at the time, and as matters fell out, the needed invention of the telescope was not made by an astronomer at all. It came from a spectacle maker more than a century after Columbus had made his memorable voyage.

The other condition was exact knowledge of when these events would take place, calculated well in advance and furnished to navigators in *almanacs*. This task, however, had baffled astronomers for several centuries, because they based their calculations upon the Greek theory of planets moving in epicycles, and this theory had broken down continually ever since the days of Ptolemy.

In an effort to make this theory work the Arabs had added more epicycles and motions to the Ptolemaic scheme, until they were using some sixty motions, and the computation of planetary positions became a mathematical nightmare. This was evidenced by a striking remark made by Alphonso X the Wise (reign 1254–84), of Castile, while he watched his Arab astronomers preparing the first European almanac, the *Alphonsine Tables,* in 1252. Fifty of them toiled for a year over the computations, and Alphonso was moved to remark that "had he been present at the Creation, he could have given the Almighty some advice." Plainly he appreciated the need for a simpler theory of the solar system.

But even the prodigious toil required was not the worst feature of the theory. After all the labor which had been put in on the Alphonsine Tables they soon began getting out of step with the actual positions of the planets! Johann Müller (1435–76), or Regiomontanus, went through the whole weary business again and in 1474 produced the tables which Columbus used, but within a few decades *his* calculations were no good.

By the sixteenth century every astronomer in Europe realized that something was sadly and fundamentally wrong with the Ptolemaic theory, but what to do about it? A Polish physician and cathedral canon, Nicolaus Koppernigk (Copernicus, 1473–1543), decided to tackle the problem according to the theory advanced by Aristarchus that the sun rather than the earth was the center of the solar system, and as he died he released to the world his book *On the Revolution of the Heavenly Bodies* which set forth this view.

This book is commonly hailed as giving birth to modern astronomy. Actually it did no more than revive the old Greek controversy on the subject. Copernicus did not advance one jot beyond Aristarchus, except for giving the world abundant proof that Apollonius and Ptolemy had gone wrong. His orbits were circles; he retained the enclosing globe of fixed stars, and he estimated the distance to it from the earth at only a million miles. Tables based on these assumptions could not have stood up better than did earlier efforts. Lastly, he did not explain why the polestar did not seem to change position, as it should have if the earth actually moved in an orbit.

This objection led the greatest astronomer of the next half century, Tycho Brahe (1546–1601) of Denmark, to reject the Copernicus theory. Instead he adopted the old Egyptian compromise that all the planets except the earth revolved around the sun and this solar system encircled the earth. This was valueless, but the rich collection of splendid observations he made were not. His devoted pupil, Johann Kepler (1571–1630), spent years calculating possible solar systems that would fit Brahe's data; then in 1609 in his *Astronomia Nova* he presented the world with the essential parts of a satisfactory solution. He used the Copernican theory but changed the orbits from circles to ellipses, with the sun at one focus, and he proved that calculations made according to this theory explained every planetary motion known.

Kepler therefore was the real father of modern astronomy, and the slowness of the advance was caused, we can see now, by two handicaps. For one, while these men knew that accurate observation was the key to their problem none of them made a flank attack by developing use of the lens to improve accuracy. Had they done so, they might well have discovered certain small movements of the stars which would have settled Tycho Brahe's objection to the Copernican theory. Again, Kepler's calculations were extremely laborious because his mathematical techniques were limited. Had he possessed knowledge of logarithms—a mathematical aid which was invented, ironically enough, by the Scottish mathematician, John Napier (1550–1617), just as Kepler was finishing his work—he might have saved half a lifetime in reaching his conclusions.

The same kind of halting, hampered advance was evident in the field of medicine and surgery.

These subjects had been in a strait jacket for lack of sound fundamental information from the days when the Ptolemies had clamped down on dissection of human bodies, about 300 B.C., until this restriction began to be relaxed by Frederick II and later rulers. By the time Columbus discovered America a modest amount of dissection was permitted in Italy, and in 1543, the same year that saw publication of the Copernican theory, a milestone in the development of medicine was passed. Andreas Vesalius (1514–64) of the University of Padua published *The Structure of the Human Body*.

With this one text Vesalius put anatomy on a modern footing. By treating only what he had seen and proved he swept all the Greco-Roman guesswork into the rubbish heap. His superb illustrations—prepared, it is said, with help from Titian—drove home the new knowledge to those who could not study in the dissecting theaters of Italy.

From that day on the appeal on any question about human anatomy was to the human body—not to what Galen said or Hippocrates said or to the word of any other guesser who had been dead a thousand years and more. Ambroise Paré (1517–90) achieved a like substitution of sanity for superstition in surgery. Of all his achievements the most significant probably arose from running out of supplies for dressing wounds after a battle. He used water and clean bandages, only to have the wounds heal better than those which had been treated with hot oil. From this he recognized that cleanliness, not heat and oil, was the secret of healthful healing. So also did he devise many ingenious operations, to be performed in a trice, as operations had to be performed in those days before anesthetics were known. Surgery still was a crude and barbarous art when Paré died, but at least it was on the road to better ways.

These advances, however, came noticeably in the field of bodily *structure,* which the eye could see just as an astronomer could see a star. *Function,* the physiology of living processes which could not be seen, still remained largely a mystery and a field for guesswork—the more so since, as we know, the road to understanding function lay through chemistry and microscopy. Physiology could not march ahead, abreast of anatomy and practical surgery, until these sister sciences had gained some degree of working power.

This dependence upon other sciences is made even clearer by the one advance achieved in physiology during this epoch of early progress—William Harvey's feat of discovering the circulation of the blood. Harvey (1578–1657) studied under Jerome Fabricius (1537–1619), the founder of embryology, during the time of Queen Elizabeth; then, while serving as physician to James I of England, he unraveled this great mystery. He proved that arteries, instead of carrying air or "vital spirit," carried blood from the heart to the tissues; the veins carried it back. Then the blood passed from the venous side of the heart to the arterial side, not through pores or a septum, as was thought at the time, but through the lungs.

This discovery laid the foundations of modern physiology, because until the circulation of the blood is understood no physiological process can be explained aright. But Harvey could make it, in spite of backward chemistry and nonexistent microscopy, because this circulation can be established by appeal to structural features of the body and mechanical principles. Harvey proved it by comparing the cubic capacity of the heart with that of all the blood vessels, then measuring the output and intake of blood at each stroke of the heart in animals and showing that the blood *had* to circulate in order to account for the phenomena he had observed. He missed the important link of connection between arteries and veins through the capillaries; many years passed before Marcello Malpighi (1628–94) added this item of knowledge by observing blood cells passing through capillaries on the surface of a frog's lung with a microscope. Harvey did not explain the nature of blood purification with oxygen in the lungs. This *could* not be done until the French chemist Antoine Lavoisier (1743–94) established the nature of oxidation between 1777 and 1785, almost exactly the period of the American Revolution.

These examples are enough to show what was needed most before science could begin making rapid progress. One need was for advance on all fronts, in order that each science might draw upon the others for help. New equipment and powerful working techniques were needed in order to see what lay beyond discernment by the naked eye and to test and analyze phenomena which could not be traced out by simple observation and manipulation. Behind all these needs stood a psychological one, a need for adjusting *thought itself* to the entirely new kind of problems which confronted scientific minds. Since this need underlay all others it deserves consideration first.

Even a casual survey will prove that ancient and medieval thought had been concerned largely with descriptive studies of things as they were, of a static world and a scheme of life which did not change. Now thinkers were confronted with a dynamic world and with changes and the forces which produced change, and they needed a new approach to engineering, mechanics and physics.

The difference is symbolized neatly by the ancient ability to fix latitude from the unchanging polestar and the modern art of using clocks and time to fix longitude. Again, the ancients understood the principles of *statics* which controlled the design of a temple or a bridge; they were childishly wrong in their ideas about falling bodies or the forces which made a pump work. Even worse, their mathematical methods were utterly unable to cope with the problems of movement and change.

A thought-provoking suggestion about how the early modern scientists gained the needed change in viewpoint is offered by Lancelot Hogben in his book *Science for the Citizen*.

He points out that during all the sixteenth century soldiers and, above soldiers, their rulers, had been confronted with a difficult puzzle in learning to use that new device, the cannon. They had no trouble with point-blank fire over short ranges; the difficulty came in laying for bombardment over longer ranges, in such fashion as to bring the shots accurately upon the target.

This was a problem in the mechanics of falling bodies, since shots were fired on an angle upward and then curved down in the latter part of their flight until they fell upon the target. The Greeks had laid down some rules for such motion, but experience proved that the Greeks had only guessed at the rules and had guessed wrongly to boot. What, then, were the correct rules that would enable an artilleryman to lay his cannon properly?

Certainly the element of timing is correct in this suggestion, for cannon were just becoming powerful enough to raise this problem with insistent force when the dynamic viewpoint first appeared clearly in the lifework of the Italian genius, Galileo Galilei (1564–1642).

This son of a brilliant but needy Florentine noble made his first important discovery in 1581 while studying medicine in the University of Pisa. He timed the swings of a swaying lamp hung in the cathedral, by counting his pulse, and found that the time remained the same no matter how wide or narrow the swing. He experimented with the phenomenon and found that neither the material in the pendulum nor the width of the swing made any difference; the time of swing depended only upon the *length* of the swinging arm.

Thus Galileo discovered the first reliable timekeeper—the *pendulum*—and it *was* reliable, because by cutting the arm at the proper length the pendulum could be made to swing once in any fraction of a day the experimenter might desire. Galileo was a medical student at the time and not interested in astronomy, geography or navigation. Hence he did not apply his pendulum to give workers in these fields an improved clock either then or in 1589, when the attention won by his invention of a hydrostatic balance led him to accept a post as lecturer on mathematics in Pisa and to devote his life to mechanics instead of medicine.

Galileo addressed himself to the problem of falling bodies the moment he became a lecturer at Pisa in 1589. This was when he was supposed to have disposed of Aristotle's rule that heavier bodies dropped faster, by dropping balls of different weights from the leaning tower of Pisa; but modern authorities such as Lane Cooper and Wohlwill pronounce this episode an exaggeration and also an injustice to Aristotle. (A compact review of this question can be found in Professor E. N. de C. Andrade's lecture to the Royal Institution, as printed in *Nature* of July 2, 1938.) What Galileo certainly did to solve the problem was to deduce the laws of falling bodies by timing heavy balls as they rolled down an inclined plane.

From these experiments he learned that the rate of fall grew faster, or was accelerated, second by second, and he measured the rate of acceleration. He learned also that the "up-and-down" path of a projectile was not along a circle or an ellipse but along another type of curve, a parabola. Thus he discovered the essential facts needed to work out the law of gravitation. He missed discovering this law himself, but his findings formed an important part of the material which Newton used nearly a century later in discovering gravitation.

Galileo's studies of this sort, in mechanics, are counted by most competent historians of science as his most important contribution to knowledge. This runs counter to the shallower and more popular view that Galileo's best work was done as an astronomer and even as the inventor of the telescope. Actually the telescope was the child of the older technique of accidental discovery and not the fruit of a newer genius such as Galileo's. It came, not out of astronomy's needs, but from those homely devices, spectacles.

The advent of printed books after 1455 had brought about widespread demand for spectacles as a reading aid for the elderly. Spectacles were lenses, and to combine lenses into a telescope requires only that one lens (the objective) be used to gather in and condense light from the object seen, while another (the eyepiece) is placed at a proper distance from the first to transmit the condensed image to the eye in such a way as to enlarge it. The traditional story has it that this combination of lenses was hit upon accidentally by Hans Lippershey, a spectacle maker of Middleburg in the Netherlands, in 1608.

He was examining two lenses, one in each hand, and happened to bring both of them in line with his eyes *and* with a distant church steeple. To his astonishment the steeple "leaped at him" as though it stood immensely nearer. He tried again, then fixed the lenses to a frame instead of holding them, and he had the first telescope. On October 2, 1608, the States General or legislative assembly of Holland considered his application for a patent, then, after a test on October 4, granted a patent and nine hundred florins on October 6. So runs the story, although it must be said that two other makers of spectacles, Zacharias Jansen and James Metius, had petitioned this same meeting of the assembly for the same patent.

Galileo heard of the new device in June 1609. He made one, and in 1610 he discovered the craters of the moon, the phases of Venus and, most disturbing of all to traditionalists, spots on the sun. This was a deathblow to the doctrine that the sun was the image of perfection, but a verdict of heresy and error was hard to bring in when anyone could see the spots for himself by simply looking through a smoked glass and a telescope.

To round out Galileo's record of monumental achievements mention should be made of still another discovery which arose because of difficulties experienced in pumping out mines.

At that time pumps were of the vacuum type. Each upstroke of the plunger created a vacuum, and the water rose in this vacant space. Physicists explained this by Aristotle's dictum that "Nature abhors a vacuum." Once an "emptiness" was created Nature rushed anything available into the space, and since the construction of the pump limited the available material to water, up the water came.

The trouble with this view was that the action could not be made to raise water higher than between thirty-two and thirty-three feet. This led Galileo to remark in his usual sarcastic fashion that evidently Nature did not abhor a vacuum over any greater distance. Then, as was also usual with him, he set about supplying a better answer.

His idea was that pumps worked because of atmospheric pressure. The winds offered proof enough that such pressure could be exerted, and Galileo thought that the air pressed upon the water around the pump. When a vacuum was created the air pressed water up into the vacant space, and the action ceased when the weight of the raised water balanced the pressure. To prove this he thought of using another liquid, mercury, which was thirteen times as heavy as water. If mercury could be pushed up only one thirteenth as high as water by pump action, his theory would stand proved.

Galileo was near the end of his days when he thought of this, but his pupil Evangelista Torricelli (1608–47) finished the experiment in 1643 and thereby invented the barometer. This invention led almost immediately to a host of discoveries. By having a relative take a barometer up the Puy de Dôme in central France in 1648, Blaise Pascal proved that atmospheric pressure decreases with height above sea level. Otto von Guericke (1602–86) invented the air pump about 1654 and proved with his famous Magdeburg hemispheres that teams of horses could not pull apart these large metal cups once the air had been pumped out from inside them.

While he was mayor of Magdeburg he also astounded the good citizens of Magdeburg by installing a water barometer to project above the roof of his house. The device was arranged so that high atmospheric pressure, which accompanies bright days, would push the top of the water above the roof and buoy up a little wooden manikin into view from the street. When stormy weather (and low pressure) approached the manikin dropped out of sight, and so the good burghers of Magdeburg wondered whether their mayor was in league with the devil. Actually Von Guericke was laying the foundations of meteorology or weather science, and the Grand Duke Ferdinand of Tuscany pushed this development by equipping monasteries throughout his domain with barometers and requiring the monks to keep records of weather and barometric pressures.

In many ways, then, Galileo is a true milestone of thought, marking with his own achievements and through his inspiring effect upon others the change from the static to the dynamic, and from the observational to the experimental, in scientific procedure.

His lifetime serves as a marker, too, for dating another much-needed advance—development of mathematical procedures which had power enough to cope with problems in dynamics.

The accompanying illustration shows the idea of *conic sections* which Apollonius of Perga developed in ancient times to describe certain common curves and curved figures. These served finely as long as such matters were merely intellectual curiosities, but applying them in astronomy and physics placed an enormous burden of work upon men such as Kepler and Galileo when they used these curves to explain the motions of planets and falling bodies. The diagrams also show the next development with which René Descartes (1596–1650) eased the burden, with his *analytic geometry*.

He "married algebra to geometry," as has been said, by "telescoping the conic sections of Apollonius into an algebraic equation." With this new method a simple algebraic calculation replaced all the drawing, measuring and "cut and try" procedures which had been necessary in such problems.

A similar change came into arithmetic, with vast benefit to businessmen as well as scientists, out of a battle royal between *abacists* and *algorists*. The abacists were the conservatives, the men who clung to the clumsy Greek and Roman arithmetic. The difficulties of an astronomer may be imagined when he had to multiply by *duplations* or doublings—that is, doubling again and again until he reached the desired multiplication. To multiply by 15, for example, he doubled three times (thus multiplying by eight), then added all his results, plus the original figure—and all in clumsy Roman (or similar) nota-

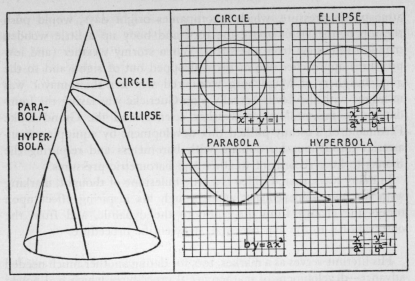

CIRCLE ELLIPSE

$x^2 + y^2 = 1$

$\dfrac{x^2}{a^2} + \dfrac{y^2}{b^2} = 1$

PARABOLA HYPERBOLA

$by = ax^2$

$\dfrac{x^2}{a^2} - \dfrac{y^2}{b^2} = 1$

CIRCLE

PARA-
BOLA ELLIPSE

HYPER-
BOLA

A MATHEMATICAL KEY TO MODERN SCIENCE

These diagrams show how Descartes substituted algebra for geometry, as explained in the text, and thereby reduced many a calculation which had taken weeks or even months to a matter of a few hours. Such ability to save time helped modern science to march with giant strides.

tion. The computation follows for 107 × 15—with the neat modern method for comparison:

(First duplation, 107×2)	CVII×II=CCXIIII	
(Second duplation, 214×2)	CCXIIII×II=CCCCXXVIII	
	=CDXXVIII	
(Third duplation, 428×2)	CDXXVIII×II=DCCCXXXXVI	
	=DCCCLVI	

Adding,		MODERN
	CVII	107
	CCXIIII	15
	CDXXVIII	535
	DCCCLVI	107
	DDCCCCCCLXXXVVVIIIIIIIII	
Simplifying,	MDCVI (=1605)	1605

Division was done by the reverse process of halving. To avoid these tedious processes men usually used a calculating frame or abacus, such as may be seen in some Chinese laundries—hence the name abacists for the conservatives. The opponents were named for algorism, the Arabic term for the new reckoning.

Today arithmetic, including long division and decimals, is taught to youngsters in the primary grades. In the fifteenth and early sixteenth centuries arithmetic was a college subject. Students could learn the new arithmetic with Arabic numerals, up to long division, from German experts called *Rechenmeister* (masters of reckoning); but one father, on asking whether this training would be sufficient for his son, was advised that the boy could learn long division best if he attended an Italian university. Educational facilities were a little better in the days of the early Stuarts of England, James I and Charles I. The noted shipbuilder Phineas Pett, who kept a diary until 1638, tells how he decided that the new reckoning would help him in his work. But he did not have to visit Italy to learn. By his time long division with Arabic numerals was being taught in Cambridge University.

These pioneer changes during Galileo's lifetime may be assigned for the most part to the first half of the seventeenth century. They may be said to have reached a first culmination in the latter half, in the work of four supreme geniuses: Huygens, Leibnitz and England's scientific ornaments, Robert Hooke, the supreme tinkerer, and Sir Isaac Newton, the supreme thinker. Christian Huygens and Gottfried Leibnitz of Holland and Germany might also be called fathers of the first modern synthesis of science, because they drew together the work of Kepler, Galileo and many others into modern physics.

Physicists and mathematicians will always claim Huygens and Leibnitz as geniuses in their fields, but the less erudite can always honor Huygens (1629–95) for giving astronomy, navigation and kindred arts far-reaching improvements in telescopes and clocks. In 1655 Huygens, with his brother's help, made the first large-sized astronomical telescope; and two years later he made the first good pendulum clock, thereby achieving an improvement which the genius of Galileo had passed by.

With these gains in equipment, added to Kepler's clearing up of astronomical theory, the way was open for settling the geography of the earth. Observers made rapid progress in working out longitudes; the continents which had looked like amorphous lumps on sixteenth-century charts began taking crisp and much more accurate form. This work was helped along now, also, by new and powerful government support and new organized effort by scientists. So striking was this development, the latter part of the seventeenth century could well be called "the age of observatories and learned societies."

All the most important maritime nations acquired observatories, either national or in connection with universities, to prepare good almanacs and other aids to navigation and geographic studies. Leyden University was first (1632); Copenhagen came next (1637–57); then Paris (1667–71) and Greenwich, near London (1675).

Learned societies for arts and literature had sprung up like mushrooms in Italy during the Renaissance, and the Academy of Natural Secrets appeared in Naples in 1560. It was suppressed, but the Accademia de Lincei, founded in 1603, still survives in Rome. Galileo was an honored member. Leipzig gained a similar strong institution in 1651, and the Royal Society of England was organized formally in 1660 and granted a royal charter on July 15, 1662. The French Academy of Sciences followed in 1666. These societies not only speeded interchange of ideas, discoveries and criticisms among members and correspondents; they began carrying the burden of publishing scientific papers and supporting research.

Gottfried Leibnitz (1648–1716) can best be appreciated by those who lack training in higher mathematics as a continental counterpart of Newton, and this observation brings us to the two English giants of the period, Hooke the tinkerer and Newton the thinker.

The title of "tinkerer" given to Hooke (1635–1703) is no reflection upon his abilities as a thinker. Had he not been overshadowed by Newton, he would be considered as one of mankind's first-rank thinkers. As matters fell out, he is remembered rather for his superb mechanical genius. A waspish, jealous little man he was, tortured by neuralgia and gallstones during his later years; but he had Galileo's knack for getting an idea, then scoring a bull's-eye with an experiment, a device or a machine which would give effect to the inspiration.

In timekeeping he completed Huygen's idea of using a coiled spring for driving power by using a fine, coiled *hairspring,* in place of a pendulum, to provide correct intervals of time. This made possible modern watches and later led to the spring-driven chronometer which could stand tossing on shipboard. He also invented a device for cutting the teeth of gear wheels and escapements accurately. From Galileo's time on, scientists had used lenses to observe tiny objects; Hooke combined all this earlier work into an efficient compound microscope. The complete record of his achievements reads almost like a catalogue of scientific apparatus; invaluable heritages from Hooke are to be seen in every modern laboratory.

Hooke was an equally keen thinker in larger matters of principle, but here he was blanketed by the broader, keener genius of Newton (1642–1727), the man who was born, as though destined to carry on the torch of science from Galileo, in the same year which saw the death of the Italian master.

Isaac Newton was the son of a gentleman farmer and never throughout his life did he have to worry about his livelihood. His early brilliance won him a Cambridge professorship in mathematics in 1669, and the government, alive to the value of scientific genius for once, gave him an easy well-paid post as director of the mint from 1699 until he died. Psychologically he is extremely interesting to psychoanalysts. He never felt even the slightest interest in women; all the forces of the usual sexual impulses seem to have been sublimated, in the psychoanalytic term, into passion for science. He was an even-tempered, concentrated, living thinking machine—and he proved his worth the year he was graduated from Cambridge (1665) by producing "the greatest engine of all for physical research," differential and integral calculus.

This powerful mathematical method does for motion and change what geometry does for studies in space and arithmetic and algebra do for calculating with numbers. In this achievement he stood on the work of others, and Leibnitz made the same epochal achievement independently; but Newton gave it to England, in his lifetime the most progressive country of all in science.

At about the same time he used his new calculating methods to see whether Galileo's laws of falling bodies would explain the orbital motions of the moon. They came within sixteen per cent of doing so, but to Newton this was no better than "completely wrong." He laid his calculations away for nearly twenty years; then a new (and more nearly correct) distance between the moon and the earth was published, and Newton recalculated the problem. It worked out exactly; he had discovered the law of gravitation. He said nothing about it until the astronomer Halley asked his opinion about some views Hooke was airing at the time on this problem. Newton quietly set forth the truth of the matter, and when the astonished Halley asked how he knew, Newton replied he had calculated it. Halley pressed him to publish his calculations, so Newton did, together with all the rest of his monumental work, in his epochal book *Philosophiae Naturalis Principia Mathematica* (Mathematical Principles of Natural Philosophy, 1687). This book, commonly called *The Principia,* probably is the greatest single contribution ever made to science.

It set forth the application of Newton's mathematical methods to mechanical problems and thus set physics upon an unshakable foundation for later research. It performed a like service for astronomy, with his mathematical methods and his law of gravitation. His researches on the nature of colored light are classical.

In general he was the first scientist who refused, almost without exception, to make any guesses. When he ran out of facts which he could prove he stopped his development of a subject. Notably he refused to guess about the nature of gravitational force. Kepler had guessed that the planets were held in their orbits by magnetism, and he was wrong, because the laws of magnetic action across space are not the same as those of gravitation. Newton's wisdom is proved by the fact that even today nobody has any idea about the cause of gravitation, unless we say that Einstein's speculations about warped space amount to a cause. But Einstein himself says, as Newton did, that his theories simply describe how gravitation *works*.

In the few instances when Newton allowed himself to guess he guessed wrong or partly wrong. He made a guarded suggestion that matter might be made up of atoms like "hard, round, massy particles," much too small to be seen in a microscope. This idea stood up for two centuries, but these "hard particles" have given way now to the electrical theory of matter.

He guessed that light might consist of tiny corpuscles shot out from hot bodies. Huygens challenged this with the claim that light was waves in a weightless, invisible "luminiferous ether." Newton's theory held the field until several nineteenth-century discoveries, notably radio, seemed to give it a deathblow. In the early twentieth century the wave theory was shaken by discoveries concerning X rays, and today scientists are trying to combine the two theories into one, with a highly mathematical treatment of light as sort of tiny energy bundles, called *photons,* borne through space in waves.

After Newton modern science can be called fairly born, with a beginning at least of equipment in telescopes and clocks, a mathematical technique powerful enough to handle necessary computations and a discipline which relies upon vigorous, experimental proof and eschews guessing. It also had theories and trends which guided most of its progress for two centuries, because not until the 1890s and our own times did fundamentally new ideas appear. Only a few items need be added to complete an elementary sketch of modern beginnings in the physical and natural sciences.

One important item is the reason for the lag in development of chemistry and the biological sciences behind the pace set in astronomy and physics. The reason can be named simply enough as *difficulty of observation and study*.

Galileo, Newton and their kind were dealing with movements of heavenly objects, falling bodies, air pressure—phenomena which they could at least control experimentally. Now the chemist who was interested in combustion could "see wood burn," but he could not see the causative process at work—the molecules of oxygen combining with those of carbon and hydrogen in the wood to produce the burning. The physiologist could detect the difference between the dark venous blood that entered the lungs and the bright arterial blood which emerged. He knew also that the lungs took in and expelled air. What he could not see was the essential processes—removal of carbon dioxide and replenishment of oxygen in the hemoglobin of the blood.

Since chemists and biologists stood baffled in this fashion at the time, they could only fall back upon explanations inherited from older days. Primitive peoples had met such problems by explaining every mysterious happening as the work of a "spirit." The ancient Greeks had trimmed down the supernatural element by calling these mysterious working somethings "essences" or "ethers"—and nothing better had been developed even by the eighteenth century.

Burning, for example, was accomplished by a "spirit of fire" or *phlogiston,* which flowed in and out of combustible substances. A body was hot or cold according to the amount of "heat spirit" or *caloric* which it possessed. The difference between life and death turned upon whether a body did or did not possess "vital spirit."

Today we are taught to wonder that men could be so naïve, childish and blind to the truth, especially when the triumphs of Galileo, Kepler and Newton were a living demonstration of how science should be advanced. Actually the chemists and biologists achieved creditable progress, considering the inherent difficulties in their problems. They kept working to improve their knowledge of the supposed essences and spirits by studying what seemed to be the most logical place to find them, the invisible air; and even before Newton was fairly started on his lifework Robert Boyle (1627–91) of Oxford and his assistants, Robert Hooke and John Mayow, had made some valuable discoveries.

These men placed burning objects and living animals in confined spaces and found that the fire went out or the animal died when about one fifth of the air was consumed. From this they concluded rightly that air is a mixture of gases and only one of the gases supports fire and breathing. But they did not prove their theory by isolating this gas—an oversight which was natural enough, since nobody at the time knew how to go about such a task.

For more than a century "pneumatic chemists," as such experimenters were called, continued to pick up isolated bits of knowledge, which proved immensely useful later; their tragedy, as we can see now, was that they failed to hit upon some key phenomenon, some bit of knowledge which could *not* be explained under any older theory but which did point the way to the truth, and these chemists did not succeed in making their difficult experiments yield such discoveries until about the time of the American Revolution.

Since biology and physiology above the level of descriptive natural history consist quite largely of chemistry applied to life processes, the block in chemistry obviously held back these other sciences. Biologists and physiologists were handicapped also by technical difficulties in developing their needed opposite to the telescope, the *microscope*.

It is true that they had the germ of the needed instrument, because lenses had been used for observing minute objects since early times. The British Museum has one found in Nineveh and used before Greek times. Galileo used simple microscopes, and the first compound one, with a combination of lenses, seems to have been made in 1590 by Zacharias Jansen, one of Lippershey's rivals with the telescope. The whole fascinating subject of microscopic life was opened up by the first outstanding microscopist, Anthony Leeuwenhoek (1632–1723), during Newton's lifetime.

The microscope suffered, however, from the technical difficulty of *chromatic aberration*—which means that the simple lenses used refracted and focused the various colors of light differently. An attempt to achieve high magnifying power could do so with light of *one* color, but other colors did not come to focus at the same point, and they blurred the image. This trouble could be dodged, fortunately, in telescopes by using mirrors in place of lenses, but microscopes had to have lenses, so that light could be shone through both the object being observed and the optical system. The remedy for chromatic aberration was not found until an English optician and optometrist, John Dollond (1706–61), found that if crown and flint glass are combined properly in a lens one kind canceled out the chromatic aberration from the other. Thereafter high magnifying power was possible.

A final important aspect of thought at this time is man's ideas about *himself* as a thinking creature during this whirl of inquiry into nature and the physical nature of mankind. A one-word name for such ideas is *psychology,* and what happened in this field of thought is an illuminating example of how at any given time mankind tends to apply a dominant trend from a leading field of thought to all subjects under investigation. This was particularly true of psychology in these seventeenth-century days.

Progress had been made in precisely those subjects which were mechanical and structural, while discovery fumbled and lagged in dealing with questions of invisible function. The idea of structures and mechanisms, therefore, was dominant in seventeenth-century thinking. "Find the mechanism and explain it," was the battle cry of science, and men now tried to do this even for human intelligence and emotions.

For their point of attack they selected the brain, correctly enough, as the seat of thought—and then in the brain they tried to find the "mechanism" which produced thought and that something which they called "the soul." René Descartes, the father of analytic geometry, said that the pineal gland was the physical mechanism of the soul. Newton's one peer as a mathematician, Leibnitz, came out with his idea of *monads*. In his doctrine, roughly stated, each atom of matter had its own share, as Plato would have said, of the universal "world soul"; and when the atoms of the body were put together these fragments of soul co-operated and produced the soul of man. The brilliant philosopher Baruch Spinoza (1632–77) advocated a similar but more keenly reasoned reflection of Platonism.

A more solid line of thought was developed by the Englishmen Thomas Hobbes and John Locke. Hobbes (1588–1679) was interested more in society that he was in single persons; his noted book *Leviathan* was a picture of government as a vast, interacting mechanism, with human beings as the cogs. Still, it reduced human nature and human thinking to a mechanistic process, and Locke (1632–1704), the contemporary in psychology of Newton in physics, developed a sound basis for this view with his *tabula rasa* or "blank state" theory of the untrained brain and mind.

Locke's idea, as set forth in his *Essay Concerning the Human Understanding* (1690), was that the brain at birth had no "mental tendencies" whatever. It was rather like a smooth, sloping sheet of clay in a field, before the clay has been exposed to washing from rainfall. But just as rain grooves the field with little scorings that develop finally into deep, mature gullies, so, Locke said, does experience groove the tissues of the brain. Then thought follows these grooves, just as rain follows the gullies it has carved in the clay.

Now this process corresponds exactly in its workings to the modern doctrine of *conditioning* and *habit formation*. Locke was right, then, in this much of his speculating. Where he went wrong was, first, in overlooking the inborn organization of the mind, the sketched-in "grooves" and organization of brain and mind which are inherited. Second, he tried to make this mechanical process and others derived from it cover nearly every aspect of human thought. Later psychologists took after him, and for two centuries since Locke's time they have followed this will-o'-the-wisp, with the result of seeing system after system come to shipwreck on the rock of self-consciousness, the phenomenon which stubbornly refuses to be reduced to the workings of a mechanism. Only in our time, thanks to the pioneer work of Freud, are psychologists working back to man's inner nature as a creature of urges and desires, but thinly controlled by intelligence, as the basis of psychological theory.

All in all, then, the record was a mixed one. Freedom of thought had hit its stride effectively in astronomy, in mathematics and in physics during the sixteenth and the seventeenth centuries. It lagged badly in chemistry and in biological subjects. In psychology it was partly right and partly wrong.

In this state let us leave scientific thought for a time and trace another important development in this period. While the early modern scientists were learning how to make intelligence really effective in coping with scientific problems, society also was enlarging the medieval recognition of the individual as the fundamental concern of society. The Middle Ages, however, had gone only far enough to assure the individual his chance for salvation; otherwise most men formed a dumb, ill-privileged mass like so many cattle at the base of the social structure. But throughout early modern times economic and social forces have been moving to bring new freedom and new opportunities for self-aggrandizement to that meek and humble figure, "the common man," the sweater and toiler who carried the burdens of life and got next to nothing in return.

This of course meant progress in the greatest social need of all— spreading the benefits of thinking throughout the race instead of reserving the lion's share for a privileged few. Let us see now how this momentous development took shape!

CHAPTER XXXIV

Commerce and the Common Man

UNTIL NOW not much has been said about the dumb, sweating army of men who carried most of the load throughout every age—and for a sufficient reason. From the earliest days the very nature of the human brain insured that habit would clamp down upon intelligence and freeze the ability to get new ideas or learn new ways, unless a man had both time and energy to spare for thinking and some driving need for doing so. But these were precisely the requirements which most men could not meet.

In the business of the food hunt society had advanced far above the hunting and primitive food gathering of prehistoric days; the land could support a vastly increased population. But unfortunately for mankind population had increased about as rapidly as did techniques of food production and manufacture of other necessities. Hence the race as a whole still was pressed to utmost exertion if it was to get along. From dawn to sunset was the rule—and had to be the rule—for working on the farms. The same rule held in city shops, in the monasteries and wherever the work of the world was done. Hence the workers had neither time nor energy left for education, thought or anything outside their toilsome daily grind.

Moreover, no improvement could be expected until three social advances had been worked out successfully.

The first and most fundamental need was for increased *productive capacity,* for advances in method which would enable the common man to do his share of the world's work in less time and so win leisure enough to permit self-improvement. That is to say, having made one such advance in prehistoric times by inventing agriculture and thereby creating ancient civilization, mankind now needed to pull productive capacity ahead of natural increase in population.

Once this need was met the second need would arise, as the so-called *problem of distribution*. Before the common man could benefit from increased productive capacity he would have to get his share of the enlarged production, and he would have to wring this share from his betters, since they would naturally look upon the gain as belonging entirely to them. The idea of sharing it would seem as strange as would the notion of sharing with the cattle in the fields.

Third and most difficult of all, the common man would have to learn how to use his opportunity aright. This can fairly be called the most difficult part of the problem, because up to this time the record of failure had been complete on every occasion when the commonalty won a voice in the conduct of affairs. The Athenians had let demagogues and the fallacious lure of avoiding work through using slaves lead them to their ruin. The plebeians of Rome had let the Senate lead them to world conquest and the ruin of the peasant class through the fruits of conquest. The chance opened by the First Crusade had been muffled horribly.

Now, however, after all the ages of repression, economic and social conditions began to develop these needed changes in favor of the common man. Moreover, the trends which produced these gains are not hard to identify. They are called in history the Commercial Revolution and the Industrial Revolution, and to them should be added a political counterpart, the English, French and American revolutions. These events, added to developments in science, were enough to set a pattern which still controls our twentieth-century life.

The Commercial Revolution consists broadly of the transformation from feudal and community effort to individual effort as the mainspring of production, and reliance upon money profit and money wages as the main driving force. These transformations began, as the record has shown, with the Crusades, and they achieved their early modern form by early Renaissance times in Italy. Thereafter only two events need be considered until the defeat of the Spanish Armada in 1588 opened opportunities for all nations and launched the full rush of change. The first of these events was the scourge of plague, the Black Death, which swept in devastating waves over Europe during the fourteenth century.

The full extent of this horror can scarcely be imagined now. Many villages and even some cities were all but depopulated. People often fell as though struck with an ax when the fever came. Out of a total

European population estimated at about one hundred million, Hecker estimates plague deaths at twenty-five million or more. The city of Florence, with what then was an enormous population of one hundred thousand, probably lost that many through the century. But this horror had its constructive side as well, grim though the process was. It cut through accustomed feudal ties by slaying commoner, lord or both, and it compelled recruitment of labor by offering at least the beginning of a money wage.

The second transforming force in this period of the Commercial Revolution was the flood of gold and silver which the Spaniards wrung from the helpless natives of Mexico and Peru. The Spaniards used much of the metal to finance their military and other activities throughout Europe; the release of gold and silver in abundance cheapened these metals, relative to other commodities and to services, and the result was a drastic inflation of prices which worked incalculable good throughout European commerce and industry.

The word "inflation" has an ugly sound in the twentieth century because the effects usually are disastrous, but in the sixteenth century it ended a disease which had been hampering Europe at least since the reign of Nero (A.D. 54–68). Commerce and industry can only be widespread and healthy when money is the medium of exchange, and money required gold and silver as a base. But Europe had been all but starved for gold and silver ever since Nero had debased the Roman currency in order to get cash enough for daily business.

This condition had kept prices and wages distressingly low and also restricted freedom of purchase. A man who earned only a few pennies a day could not buy much even though prices were correspondingly low. He lacked the actual coins needed to make a variety of purchases. But now abundant gold and silver inflated this shriveled, restricted economy, and both manufacturing and commerce boomed throughout Europe.

Opening of opportunity in America after 1588 naturally lent tremendous impetus to this growth. One immense gain was new foods, notably the white potato. Although this plant came from tropic latitudes, its home was the bleak, chill Bolivian plateau, more than two miles above sea level. Hence it was well adapted to northern latitudes in Europe, and it yielded much more food from an acre of land than could any grain or any meat animal. Such an addition was invaluable. The Spanish Americas also furnished sugar and molasses, and when the north Europeans became active in the seventeenth century they enlarged and cheapened the supply of timber, salt, fish and furs by imports from the west.

Best of all from the social point of view, the Americans offered an escape from the pressure of population upon these gains. Heretofore any benefits for the common man from increased productivity had been largely canceled by increased population. But once the restrictive Spanish monopoly was broken the peoples of northwestern Europe found relief from this drag, for the first time in their history, through emigration to North America. Some went voluntarily to seek new opportunity or escape persecution; undesirables were deported as bound servants; and all these processes together began relieving population pressure upon the food supply and the gains from increased productivity.

From this same colonizing effort came other gains for the common man, gains which were forced by unescapable necessity. This happened even though overseas trade and colonizing efforts still were ridden by the medieval idea of monopolies granted to strong individuals and to large stock companies. This was neither stupid nor reactionary. It was the only possible way, conditions being what they were.

No shipping "lines" existed as yet to handle small shipments; anyone who wanted to trade overseas had to use his own ships or chartered ones and had to have business enough to warrant shipload cargoes. Marine insurance was only getting a start in the Netherlands, so the shipper had to be rich enough to stand heavy losses. Pirates flourished, and no government as yet made any great effort outside of European waters to suppress them. Monarchs and other influential persons tended rather to wink at such depredations in return for a share in the profits. Indeed, one of Elizabeth's earliest problems in shifty diplomacy came when Lady Killigrew, the mother of Elizabeth's vice-admiral for Cornwall, and a band of retainers plundered a Hanseatic League ship off the Cornish coast. Elizabeth hanged the retainers but shuffled the proceedings about the mother until the league lost interest in the case.

Strong resources were required, then, for overseas ventures, and the same was true for colonizing efforts. Governments still left this work to private companies. Monopolies, therefore, were inevitable. Without them the prospects for profit would hardly overmatch the expenses and the risks.

The strengths and weaknesses of this system showed up strongly in the first colonizing ventures in North America. Sir Humphrey

Gilbert and Sir Walter Raleigh made the first of these and with equally disastrous results.

Gilbert (1539?–83) had the sound idea of planting a colony to exploit the cod fishery on the Grand Banks, and on August 5, 1583, he started the first English colony in North America at St John's, Newfoundland. But on his way home he was lost in a storm at sea, and his colonists saw no reason for staying in bleak Newfoundland when they could just as well sail out from England to catch cod, so they gave up in disgust. Raleigh, a half brother of Gilbert, had been interested in this venture, and a year after Gilbert's death he sent an expedition to explore the more genial coast of the present-day Carolinas.

The report was highly favorable, and Raleigh sent out colonists to Roanoke Island in 1585 and again in 1587 under John White as governor. White's granddaughter, Virginia Dare, was the first English child born in North America (August 18, 1587), but when White returned to the colony after a three-year absence in England to procure supplies, he found only the word CROATAN carved on a tree and not another sign of people or colony. Neither has anything more been learned to this very day.

During the succeeding reign of James I strong trading companies of London, Plymouth and Bristol tried their hand. In 1607 the Plymouth Company sent George Popham and one hundred and twenty men to repeat Gilbert's venture with a colony at the mouth of the Kennebec River in Maine, but after Popham returned to England the colonists got to thinking of the hard winter ahead and what they would get out of the venture even if the company did get rich. As a result of this thinking they "built a faire pinnace of thirty tons," the Virginia, and sailed away to England.

In this same year the London Company planted a nondescript mixture of gentlemen fortune seekers and jailbirds, one hundred and four in all, in Virginia, and so started Jamestown. But the gentlemen spent their time hunting gold; the jailbirds gave more attention to fighting and clamoring for food from the company supplies than they did to working; and the colony would have starved had it not been for doughty Captain John Smith (1580–1631). This soldier of fortune had been sent as one of the councilors, and when his superiors proved unable to control the situation he took charge and brought some order out of chaos with his famous dictum, "He who will not work shall not eat."

His outspoken criticisms of the management brought dismissal in

1609, and the colony languished until the iron-willed Sir Thomas Dale arrived as governor in 1616 and tobacco was found to be an easy road to wealth. Meanwhile Smith hired out to the Bristol Company for adventures north of Virginia. But bad weather and pirates foiled three ventures, so when he offered his services as pilot to the dissenters who sailed in the Mayflower in 1620 they considered him a hoodoo and would have none of him.

As events turned out, this was terribly bad judgment on their part, because Smith almost certainly would have steered them away from their worst errors. They had a grant of land in New Jersey from the London Company and an advance of seven thousand pounds, repayable in seven years. Had they reached their land, their first winter would have been easier than it was; and almost certainly they would have reached this land had Smith been in charge. He would hardly have let the captain of the Mayflower hang off the elbow of Cape Cod for weeks, trying to beat into head winds, until he had to land his passengers in Cape Cod Bay to get them ashore before winter.

Even if Smith had not been able to prevent this error, once there he would have put them on New England's best road to wealth— fishing. He always had said "the main staple from hence to be extracted . . . is fish," and he knew exactly how to work the trade. A cargo of high-flavored salt cod would bring ten shillings the quintal in Spain, yielding a handsome profit on the season's expense. Then the vessel itself could be sold in England, and the proceeds would buy all needed supplies for next year and leave a profit besides. But the pilgrims were landsmen, not seamen, and they struggled for years with farming and fur trading until the Massachusetts Colony, which settled around Boston in 1630, started this sure-fire triangular trade and achieved prosperity with the "sacred cod" and New England-built ships as the backbone of the effort.

Thus a half century and more of failure was required to prove the folly of the naïve idea that men would work like so many serfs in a wilderness to produce wealth for a distant company. Serfs had worked in this fashion at home under the watchful eye and iron hand of a tough-willed feudal lord and a Church which made obedience the serf's passport to heaven. The same idea could be made to work in tropical lands, with Negro slaves doing the actual toil, but it simply would not do with free men in North America.

They had to be given a stake of their own in the land before they would put in the necessary effort and devotion, and the real strength of the English colonial effort was the unwitting wisdom of the Stuart rulers in peopling these colonies with dissenters and misfits. The Pilgrims and the Massachusetts Puritans made a go of their ventures; so did Lord Baltimore's Catholics in Maryland after 1632. William Penn built the most successful colony of all with Quakers, beginning in 1681 in Pennsylvania; Oglethorpe succeeded in Georgia even with such poor material as jailed debtors and bankrupts in and after 1732. These colonists succeeded because they had to. England was closed to them, and the colony was their only chance.

Still, hard as their lot was, these people had found opportunity open to them; a new chance for the common man had arisen in the world. What now of effects upon those left at home, both the lowly and those in high places?

The lowly profited to some extent through diet enriched with New World foods and through a general quickening and broadening of productive and commercial life. The benefit was limited, however, because the merchants and the grandees ran true to form, the form usually displayed when prospects arise for achieving wealth without too much effort. These leaders thought as better-placed men always had since the very dawn of civilized living. They were the "betters," the "upper classes," and as such they were entitled to the cream of social effort. The commoners had to have enough to get along, just as cattle had to be fed, and in the colonies this allowance had to be generous. But the leaders had no intention of letting this process get out of hand. Once the colonies proved able to stand on their own feet, that would be enough; thereafter England could start skimming the cream off the colonial effort.

The skimming process, called the mercantilist system, was easy enough to set up—on paper. England simply provided by law where and in what articles the colonists might trade. Many articles which England wanted and could not produce herself, or which she could resell profitably in Europe, were "enumerated"; this meant that a colonial ship could not land or sell them anywhere but in England. Among them were tobacco, furs, rice, indigo and naval stores (resin and turpentine). The English manufacturers were protected by forbidding the manufacture of most articles in the colonies. The colonies were allowed enough foreign trade to get the money they needed for their purchases of English manufactures, but the authorities kept a jealous watch to see that the colonies did not earn too much.

This process was to bring the punishment of the American Revolution in due time, but a more immediate evil result was the corroding effect upon the beneficiaries themselves of too easy wealth, too easily won.

Since trading privileges and monopolies were the order of the day, English court life became an incessant scramble to acquire these passports to wealth through favoritism or bribery, either with cash or a share in the profits. Under the Stuart kings down to 1688 corruption spread like a plague through all officialdom, and England even countenanced piracy as long as English ships were not victimized. Pirates such as the notorious Henry Morgan were given shelter in Jamaica and North Carolina as long as they brought in plenty of booty from their harryings of Spanish towns; Morgan was even knighted, ostensibly for "war services," in 1674. Altogether, the situation was all but foursquare with the rottenness of republican Rome after the civilized world had been conquered and the Roman plunderbund set to work exploiting its conquests.

For a brief period an Augustus of a sort appeared in William, the king who, with his wife Mary, replaced James II in 1688. William gave English commercial and political life a dose of Dutch honesty. He redeemed the old clipped and depreciated English money in honest coin and founded the Bank of England (July 27, 1694). Marine insurance got a good start among brokers who gathered in Lloyd's coffeehouse during his reign, and William took a flint-hard stand against further dealings with pirates. He allowed a period of grace until 1700 in which English pirates could forsake their ways; after that they were to be hanged out of hand. New York's Captain Kidd was a victim of this policy.

In May 1699 he had sailed in the galley Adventure, a ship financed by Lord Bellemont, governor of the middle colonies, the Lord Chancellor of England, the First Lord of the Admiralty, two secretaries of state and Robert Livingston of New York. His instructions were to attack pirates and the French; actually he attacked East Indian ships, knowing, as he thought, how to read between the lines of his instructions. He probably was the most astonished man in Christendom after his return when Lord Bellemont shipped him to England as a pirate, and he continued to protest to the day he was hanged (May 23, 1701). At that, the principal count against him was not piracy but murder, through striking a seaman with a bucket—an act which would not have been noticed for a moment in any other shipmaster. Quite probably his noble backers were glad to have this charge pressed rather than piracy, because a thorough airing of Kidd's backing might have drawn William's dour eye in their direction.

Reform was checked, however, after William died in 1702. Four dull and stupid monarchs, Queen Anne and the first three Georges, let the system run on without a check. England grew richer and more corrupt, and society acquired the same glittering, heartless artificiality which always has marked periods of high decadence.

Honest work and honest service became "stupid" and "unfashionable." The mark of a gentleman was his ability to waste, squander and then recoup his fortune through securing some extortionate monopoly or profitable privilege. The merchants and merchant companies were more hardheaded, but they were being beaten wherever they met free competition from hard-driving Yankee ships, and crews that worked on shares, out of New England. The restrictive laws were their only salvation and they knew it, so they pressed constantly for more restrictions.

Had the methods of production remained the same, this degeneration could only run on, as it always had, into revolution or destruction; and it did run into the revolt of the American colonies. But throughout the eighteenth century a revolution of another sort had been brewing quietly in England—a technical revolution, as profound as the creation of ancient civilization or the foundation of newly invented agriculture or the rise of modern commerce, science and political states out of feudalism after the Crusades. Here in England economic forces were slowly but surely pressing men out of age-old methods for doing the world's work with animal, wind and human power into the use of mechanical power and the methods of the Machine Age. The course of the Commercial Revolution was crossed and transformed by the power of the Industrial Revolution.

The textile industry is often cited as leading in this so-called Industrial Revolution. Certainly this industry was the first one to make extensive use of power-driven machinery, but the heart of the innovation, the steam engine, was the child of coal mining.

Coal had been used in Britain since Roman times—as coal ashes in Roman ruins prove—and a monastery grant of land in 852 provided for rent to be paid partly in coal. But intensive use of this resource did not begin until the expansion of commerce, shipping, population and, above all, ironworking during the time of Elizabeth began to exhaust England's forests and force use of coal.

The constantly rising demand for coal forced ever deeper mining, and the deeper the shafts went the more difficult was the job of keeping them pumped out. A handsome profit awaited anyone who invented a better pump, and in 1698 Thomas Savery invented a crude steam pump. Newcomen's engine of 1705 was an improvement upon Savery's crude device, and it proved good enough to win wide use, both for pumping out English coal mines and to force the blast in iron-smelting furnaces. James Watt's invention of 1763 was a logical culmination to these earlier inventions, because it came about, as Watt himself said, as an improvement upon the Newcomen engine.

Meanwhile the textile industry was undergoing an expansion and an evolution which made the steam engine a highly welcome aid in this field as well as in coal mines.

The expansion had come through constantly rising demand for more cloth and cheaper cloth, both at home and in colonial trade. The first result from this demand was the "putting-out" or cottage system of production. Under this system men who had the necessary capital and outlets for goods had thread spun upon contract, then furnished the thread to weavers who worked in their own homes in small towns throughout the weaving districts. This avoided restrictions imposed by the old guilds and the government in the larger cities. At the same time the cottage weavers could live for much less than did city workers, and the cost of the cloth was correspondingly low.

The pressure for more output and lower cost brought a slow but steady accumulation of mechanical improvements—Kay's flying shuttle in 1733, imperfect roller spinning of cotton in 1741 and Hargreave's spinning jenny in 1770. The jenny worked eight spindles at once, and Richard Arkwright soon added rollers and water power. In 1779 Samuel Crompton combined all these devices into the spinning mule. In 1785 Edmund Cartwright produced a power-driven loom, while Thomas Bell invented cylinder printing of calico.

Once such quantity producers were available, use of the steam engine to drive them was inevitable, and the chain of events which created the Machine Age was complete. A striking feature about this highly important step in the Industrial Revolution was that it came just when the political revolution in the American colonies was drawing to a close; and both revolutions, the political and the industrial, were accompanied by a *mental* revolution against the whole structure of monopoly, privilege and mercantilism. This revolution was given voice by Adam Smith (1723–90) in his epochal book, *The Wealth of Nations*. It was published in 1776, the same year which saw the American Declaration of Independence.

The keynote of this time, therefore, was plainly one of revolution. The commoners were determined to win their share in the good things of life, by violence if necessary. Also for the first time in history they were in a position to make such a fight with some prospect for success. The pattern of economic life was built now of free labor, paid a money wage, in all activities that counted most. Also this labor had to be reasonably intelligent and co-operative. Should anyone doubt this, let him try to imagine successful operation of a machine-equipped factory with a gang of slaves driven by the whip, or even a force of oxlike medieval serfs! Slavery and serfdom were all but complete anachronisms now. They survived only where civilization was still medieval, as in Russia, or where semi-tropical climate could make utterly unintelligent gang labor profitable, as in raising the American cotton crop.

But if a co-operative attitude was needed in all ranks of labor this automatically gave labor its chance to demand a price for its co-operation. Moreover, labor had a mental pattern now, a precedent to guide its thinking along these lines. The lower ranks of society could envisage doing in the political and economic realms what their forefathers had done in the religious revolutions of the sixteenth century.

CHAPTER XXXV

Mental and Political Revolutions in the Eighteenth Century

THE IDEA of connecting the religious revolution in the sixteenth century with the political revolutions during the eighteenth century as links in one continuous chain may seem at first glance an over-simplification of history. From the standpoint of tracing human nature at work, however, the connection is clear enough. It emerges unmistakably once a common misconception about the religious revolution is cleared away.

The effect of the religious revolts is often misunderstood as a freeing of individual thought and initiative in the Protestant countries. It had no such effect, because neither thought, initiative nor religious preferences were freed. What the revolts *did* accomplish for the common man, in Protestant and Catholic countries alike, was to *create the mental pattern* of criticizing and judging the policies of the ruling classes.

A population which gave blind obedience to the word of authority as being tantamount to the word of God was poor material for resistance to unjust political and social policies. Under such a mental regime the downtrodden peasant or the abused sailor would think of resisting an earthquake or a stroke of lightning about as quickly as he would think of rebelling against his lot. But once such a population had been through the experience of having religious faith questioned and perhaps rearranged by its betters, it could and did pass easily to wondering whether other institutions might not stand in need of change. It was ripe mentally to demand relief and, if prodded sufficiently, to support revolts.

In this way the populations of Europe received invaluable mental conditioning, to use the psychological phrase, from the religious question. Whether anything would come of this would depend, of

429

course, upon many other circumstances—how hard or easy life was on the whole, whether the commoners led completely habit-ridden lives or followed more stimulating occupations such as seafaring. How such differences worked out can be shown beautifully by comparing the course of events in France and in Great Britain.

The simpler of the two examples is the French, because of clean-cut adherence in France to the principle that the strong and the competent rule the weak and incompetent.

Always the race has had stronger men and weaker, wise men and fools, saints and knaves; and always its social institutions have shaken down into a framework wherein the strong ruled the weak. The only question in any age has been what constituted strength—brute physical power, prowess in war, superior craft and cunning and, latest of all, the power of wealth at work in commerce.

In France the circumstances of successful agriculture and need for strong armies to hold land frontiers had preserved the feudal array of strength from king through noble and knight to peasant and serf with but little intrusion by the powers of wealth and commerce. This conservatism was reinforced as well by the tradition, held over from Roman and barbarian days, of the distinction between the conquerors and the conquered, the rulers and the ruled. The only changes were in name.

The Frankish or Burgundian warrior, together with the Roman knight who managed to hold his own, had become the French noble. The conquered Gallo-Roman population had become commoners, and pride of caste still ran deep as between the two classes. France had her *bourgeoisie,* or townsmen engaged in commerce and hand manufactures, but since the genius of France had run to agriculture and war the bourgeoisie had nothing like the power it held in the intensely commercial Italian cities and now in the new commercial powers, the independent Netherlands and England.

Thus a strong, entrenched ruling class, steeped in medieval conservatism and pride, made prospects rather dark for the common man. He was hampered also in pushing his cause by the very conservatism which goes with agriculture. Through all the religious troubles of the fifteenth and sixteenth centuries the French peasant had clung to the ministrations, saints, shrines and miracles of the mother church. Protestantism had gained a following among the bourgeoisie of the towns, but a particular twist of French history under Henry IV had all but isolated this infection.

Henry of Navarre (1553–1610) this prince had been when the death of Henry III in 1589, without a Valois heir, made him the rightful king of France. But Henry of Navarre was a Protestant, and Catholic France would not have him until he made his historic change of faith in 1593. *"Paris bien vaut une messe* [Paris is well worth a mass]," he said, when convinced that the resistance in the capital would collapse if he became converted; and so it did when he became a Catholic. He was crowned February 27, 1594, and thus he founded the Bourbon branch of the Capetian line; the Pope absolved him September 14, 1595, for past errors, and then he set about rebuilding his faction-torn kingdom.

Henry was shrewd enough to see that full freedom of worship for his former coreligionists would be highly irritating to his predominantly Catholic kingdom. He therefore issued an Edict of Nantes (April 13, 1598), which granted full freedom of conscience and complete civil rights to Protestants but restricted Protestant public worship to designated towns where it had been established and to the castles of Protestant nobles. Some two hundred towns were named "places of safety" for Protestants, and they were given authority enough in these towns to make the safeguard effective.

This arrangement reduced friction between the Catholics and the Huguenots—as the French Protestants were called, after the Calvinist leader Hugues of Geneva—but it also drew many of the smart skilled craftsmen out of contact with the French Catholics and reduced stimulus to thought by that much. The separation also reduced the continual contacts which might have broken down prejudice. Each party, therefore, remained highly suspicious of the other. Such a thing as an alliance of Huguenot townsmen and Catholic peasants to promote their interests against the nobles was utterly impossible.

The common man, therefore, lacked strength to fight his own cause; his chance lay rather in the gradual decay of energy, initiative and intelligent understanding of government among the nobles. This decay set in because the growth of royal power steadily deprived the nobles of genuine functions in French life.

The feudal knight who fought to protect his estate, or for his suzerain when he wanted to or had to, had given way to the professional common soldier, paid by the king from royal revenues. Nobles served, of course, as officers in this army, but not by virtue of their rank; professional skill came first. The king's judges and officers were taking over administration of justice and collection of taxes, and the nobles more and more were becoming mere parasites upon their lands and idle butterflies sunning themselves in the light of royal smiles at court.

They also completed the vicious effects of this trend by developing class arrogance and an absurdly artificial array of distinctions to replace their lost genuine attributes of rank. Their forebears, who had proved their right to distinction with their spears, swords and good right arms every year of their lives, had been content to let the king's valet warm the king's shirt at the fire before the king put it on of a cold morning; in the foppish court of the seventeenth century the right to perform this service was quarreled over and jealously regulated. Toward the end of the eighteenth century a state of distemper in the king's mistress's poodle was much more important than widespread starvation among the peasantry.

Once the nobility reached this state it was a hollow shell, ready to collapse at the first hard push—and the push was brewing beneath all the superficial brilliance of French court life. France's political and economic position was steadily becoming weaker relative to Britain's, through failure to press vigorously the new wealth producers, colonization and overseas trade. Discontent was growing, and loyalty was vanishing rapidly. Meanwhile the intellectual and ideological groundwork for revolution was being plowed by a group of scientists and social doctrinaires known collectively as the Encyclopedists, because many of them contributed to the French encyclopedia edited by Denis Diderot (1713–84).

Pre-eminent in this group was the brilliant, witty, acid François Marie Arouet, known to literature by his pen name Voltaire (1694–1778). With one pointed phrase Voltaire could and did expose many a folly and injustice of the times in such fashion as to burn the thought unforgettably into the minds of men. If ever anyone could slay with the pen Voltaire was the man. When his long life ended all France except the court itself held the regime in contempt and was ready to see it overthrown.

Meanwhile pressure of circumstances was setting up an instructive contrast to the French trend in both England and the Netherlands. Of the two the Netherlands were on the whole more progressive.

Not only had the Dutch gone through the mental shake-ups of the Protestant revolt and their struggle to win independence from Spain; they came out of these trials with a fortunately large Catholic minority in their population. This blocked any high degree of Protestant intolerance. Neither did the Dutch muzzle their press, as did every other nation, in the interests of a dominant party and religion. Rather, the Netherlands became a haven of refuge for dissidents from everywhere and Europe's center for printing all new and advanced ideas. For more than a century these advantages enabled the Dutch to exercise an influence far out of proportion to their size as a nation.

England stood midway between this advanced position and the conservative attitude of France. English royalty was jealous of its authority as head of the Anglican church. Dissenters had nothing like the Huguenot rights under the Edict of Nantes, and the narrow-minded, shifty and mean James Stuart, who succeeded Elizabeth in 1603, believed thoroughly in the divine right of kings. He improved upon French policy only by letting dissenters set up colonies in America.

Against conservatism was arrayed the lawless tradition of the Elizabethan sea dogs and a merchant class which far surpassed the French bourgeoisie both in activity and determination to go its own way. Behind both of these indefinite forces stood the English Parliament, with a spirit far different from that of the French town councils, called parlements, or even the French Estates General. The English Parliament could look back upon many a tussle with kings, beginning in the days of the infamous John, and it was quite willing to tussle again whenever any king tried to push it too far.

James avoided this mistake, but his son Charles (1600–49) lacked his father's caution and soon embroiled himself hopelessly with his Parliament. This event is often represented as a rising of the English spirit of freedom. It was anything but this. The real driving power behind the parliamentary cause was a blend of hardheaded business and stern theology which is commonly called Puritanism. Another name for it is the philosophy of *sanctified work*.

The typical Puritan was exactly what his name indicated—a man who believed in "purifying." He wanted to purify his own life by stripping from it all vanities, all weaknesses of the flesh and all silly gauds and luxuries. He wanted to purify religion as well, by a similar stripping out of pomp, ceremony and the sensuous appeals of music, rich vestments and the play of light through mellow stained glass. Hence he was not a dissident, as the independents were; he stayed within the Anglican church but clamored for "purification" of it.

Psychoanalysts explain this as a sort of sublimation. The Puritan almost invariably came from non-noble, nongraceful walks of life in which these amenities were hopelessly lacking. The Puritan con-

vinced himself that this lack was a virtue, and then, like most sublimated personalities, he erected his reconciliation to his lot into a
supreme passion.

He was doomed to a life of work—so work became the passport
to heaven. Man was not placed upon earth to live an enjoyable life
or a kindly life. He was to live a *productive* life, productive in material goods and tangible gain, and the measure of his gain was to be
found not in the richer lives and minds but in the cold figures provided by *double-entry bookkeeping*.

This form of business control was developed by Luca Pacioli (1440?–
1515?), and it had a most peculiar effect upon the philosophy of
human productivity. Without it the guildsman or the lord of the
manor could and did think of productive activity in terms of materials to be brought from far places, output of goods for use, human
beings toiling and needing food and care in order that they might
toil effectively. For these vivid, dynamic elements double-entry bookkeeping substituted lifeless rows of figures in a ledger. Living, toiling
men were replaced by "wage cost" in business thinking. The glow
of satisfaction which a medieval craftsman got from a well-made
piece of cloth or from the play of light through a new variety of
glass was represented now by "material cost."

Double-entry bookkeeping is perfect for showing rise and fall of
money values in the productive process, but it does so by shutting
out the epic *human* values. It has no technique for showing men
braving heat and fever to get oil out of a Venezuelan jungle, the high
enthusiasm that drove a Union Pacific railroad across prairie, mountain and desert to marry the Atlantic and Pacific coasts of the United
States or the bleak, sunless toil, overhung with the constant threat
of being entombed alive, which produces the world's coal. As Harry
Elmer Barnes says in his *Intellectual and Cultural History of the
Western World,* the ledger probably did more than anything else to
give a special slant and stereotype to business morality.

But the very lack of human warmth was what commended such
a philosophy to the Puritan. Work well done was man's passport
to heaven, and the double-entry ledger cast up this account perfectly.
It also ignored, as the Puritan thought it should ignore, the silly
weaknesses of the flesh and the lust for soft comforts and sensuous
blandishments which deflected men from their true mission in life.
With the ledger's findings as his guide the Puritan master could drive
his men as mercilessly as he drove himself.

All this may sound like an arraignment of Puritanism for hypocrisy. It is not; the Puritan was as sincere as any monk or hermit. He drove himself as hard as he did anyone else. Furthermore, the Puritan had a driving power which neither intellect alone nor emotion alone could match, because he had managed to fuse both with his sublimation of pleasure into work in his philosophy.

Charles therefore was bucking against one of the most potent spiritual forces men ever created when he challenged Puritanism in its stronghold, the Parliament, with his claim that he could tax Puritan commercial effort at his pleasure. Worldly men of the Italian humanist type might have shrugged and paid as the easiest way out. French thinking, reminiscent of the Roman, might have accepted the exaction as the will of God; but the Puritan rose up in flaming wrath.

Neither was the wrath a mere selfish guarding of possessions, as has often been charged. It ran far deeper. Charles was challenging the very roots of the Puritan's spiritual convictions when he sought to trim off the fruits of sanctified work. He was cutting not so much at the Puritan's pocketbook as at the Puritan passport to heaven. So he brought upon himself the blazing power of this curious blend of spiritual fervor with hardheaded, driving commercial instinct, and he paid for his mistake with his head.

Now we may well ask wherein the common man gained anything from this, and history's answer is that he gained nothing at all at the moment. Rather he lost, if enjoyment of life counted for anything. Once Charles's head fell beneath the ax on January 30, 1649, Puritanism could and did give full rein to the attitude which, as a wag put the matter, "objected to bearbaiting not for the pain to the bear but for the pleasure it gave the spectators." The iron Puritan clamped down upon every joy and pleasure in England, and eleven years later Charles II had only to walk into the kingdom to be received with the joy that sight of a rescuing ship creates in men shipwrecked on a desert isle.

Nevertheless, both profit and power came in the end and abundantly. Some of it showed up throughout Charles II's reign. He was a Stuart and as inclined to be as pre-emptory as any of his forebears, but "he had no desire," as he said, "to resume his travels" in exile. Hence he took good care not to rouse the sleeping lion. His brother James II, who succeeded him, had not been as well seasoned by "travels"—and so, after a brief reign from 1685 to 1688, James got out of the kingdom just one jump ahead of English wrath. Thereafter no

English king dared defy English convictions concerning political rights.

This respect for political rights enabled the English to replace revolution with evolution from then on in their government, and William, who followed James as king, remedied many old abuses as part of his program for conciliating all-powerful interests in England.

His record for cleansing and promoting commerce has already been reviewed. To heal factional religious discontent he persuaded Parliament to pass a Toleration Act (1689). This act allowed all dissenters except Catholics and Unitarians to hold services, once they took the oaths of allegiance and supremacy which acknowledged William as lawful king. The two faiths mentioned were excepted because Catholics formed the party of the ousted Stuarts; Unitarians were considered next to atheists and hence men whose oaths would be of no value. Printing was thrown open to all by allowing the old Licensing Act to lapse on May 7, 1695.

This particular liberty came in good time to aid expression of all the thinking which had accompanied these developments, about the principles which should control men's activities and lives. Most of this thinking, as it happened, turned around the idea of a *social contract.*

The essence of this view, the idea that men agreed together upon their forms of government and the governing practices and customs of life, reflected the actual truth that the *consent* of mankind was necessary for the success of any social institution. The more precise idea of a *contract,* a formal agreement, obviously overshot the mark. In actual truth, men lived and worked together because they *found* themselves together. Consent to existing institutions was expressed by failure to resent or resist; dissent took the form of revolt. Only occasionally did men establish outright contractual relations through charters and written constitutions.

Nevertheless, this fictitious "social contract" was highly useful for organizing thought about social relations, and the important attitudes taken could be, and were, expressed in terms of it. These attitudes can be grouped with sufficient accuracy as (1) conservative, (2) progressive and democratic and (3) sentimental and romantic.

The conservative thinkers took one of two views. The ultraconservatives who thought at all about such matters, and the well-placed leaders who never thought about anything other than ways and means for preserving their positions, stood flatly on the medieval viewpoint that they held their powers by divine right. God had made one man a king and another man a peasant. Any question of either status was blasphemous and wicked; men should accept God's appointments without debate or demur.

The less hidebound conservatives admitted the existence of a social contract, but after considering the ignorance and obvious incapacity of the common man as he then was, this group could not envisage granting him any voice in enforcement of the contract. Hobbes set forth this view in his *Leviathan* at the time when Charles I and Parliament were squaring off for their life-and-death struggle. Hobbes said that men had made a social contract when they set up kings, but once they did so they had surrendered their natural rights into the king's keeping and should abide by his decisions.

Progressive and democratic theorists granted the existing incapacity of the common man but insisted that this defect could and should be remedied by pursuing two interrelated broad policies. The common man should be given an enlarged share of the wealth and so be given the power needed for self-improvement, and his abilities should be improved by education. Locke, coming a generation after Hobbes, voiced this view, particularly as to education—and in general, education was the principal reliance of this group. It came ahead of democratic government, because the vote was a dangerous weapon in the hands of ignorant men, while intelligent ones could advance their interests even without the right to vote.

The radical romanticists and sentimentalists, men who thought with their emotions far more than they did with their powers of reason, were sure that "natural man" was "a noble animal." He had been warped by cruel and unjust treatment; reverse this policy, and man's innate nobility would appear in his actions and his life. Jean Jacques Rousseau (1712–78) gave the world a supreme example of such thinking in the eighteenth century under the catchwords, "Liberty, Equality, Fraternity," which became the motto of the French Revolution and later of the French Republic.

Thinking about economics and workaday affairs remained mercantilist—that is, in favor of state control—as long as industry worked by hand and manufacturing output remained limited. But in England this theory had a silent foe in the Puritan viewpoint, and overthrow of it came when the Industrial Revolution took shape.

The intellectual essence of this revolution was *invention of machines,* and inventors would not consent to see state licensing and monopolies granted to court favorites skim the cream from their efforts. The economic essence of the revolution was *capitalism*— provision of money in large amounts for the new machines and factories. The men who furnished this money, either as individual owners or as subscribers to stock, had no patience with the idea of business being milked for the profit of the state.

All these ideas found expression in Adam Smith's *Wealth of Nations* (1776).

In this book Smith voiced the bitter but unescapable truth that self-interest or, more bluntly, selfishness, was the true mainspring of human activity. From this he argued that the best way to achieve efficiency in every productivity lay in unchaining this force and allowing every man to do his utmost to promote his own interest. Under such a system of free competition the best men and the best ideas would inevitably win, while prices would be brought down to the lowest level which would provide remuneration for everybody concerned.

Smith's view has been known since his day as the doctrine of *laissez faire* or "let alone," and it was not mere coincidence that such a view should be voiced concerning economics in the very year that saw the Americans demanding to be let alone politically. Neither demand could have been made with compelling force much earlier than this; the colonies were not strong enough, nor was industry, until this time. But now each of these parties *was* strong enough to insist upon having its way—and so it did, in these years of the 1770s. The mercantilist system simply dissolved in England, and the colonists won their way, through the American Revolution.

The American Revolution did not explode until after the French had been driven from Canada in 1763. Until then the colonists needed the protection of the British Navy, and they knew it; so for a century and a half they suffered economically under the grievous restrictions of the mercantilist system. During this time, however, their opportunity was being prepared by French indifference to colonial strength and the ever-growing disparity between French and British naval strength. By 1754, when the French and Indian War broke out, the British colonies had about one and a half million people and Canada scarcely more than one hundred thousand Frenchmen—odds of fourteen to one. The result was inevitable.

Thus the French can be said to have bowed themselves out of America with their own errors. A final instructive contrast between

French and British ways can be drawn from the difference in outcome between the American and the French revolutions.

As is well known, the American Revolution followed all but automatically—once the French menace was removed—and it was plagued with a generous load of impractical and selfish demagoguery, woodenheaded stupidity and rank incompetence in high places. But its leaders—Washington, John Adams, Thomas Jefferson, Benjamin Franklin, Gouverneur Morris and men of their stamp—were seasoned in the British sense for the practical in politics, and they were steeped as well in philosophic studies of past successes and failures in government. Therefore they managed not only to pull the revolution itself through to success, but afterward they established a government which, by the test of results to date, must be called one of the most successful in all history.

The French Revolution, like the American, was an overhauling by violence of the outworn political structure, but the violence was an aftermath. Every essential change came about through sheer collapse of the old regime. It had run its stupid course of wasting national strength upon grandiose, imperialistic efforts to dominate Europe, upon a profligate court and a parasitic nobility, without achieving colonies and foreign trade enough to support the folly. In 1789 the royal treasury was virtually empty, even after every possible source of revenue had been milked to the limit. Louis XVI had only one recourse left. He had to call a meeting of the long-neglected Estates General and invite it to devise a program for carrying on.

The commoners—that is, the only real producers which France had—demanded release from intolerable feudal restrictions and oppressions as the price of continued effort. The nobility did not resist; it had no good reason for doing so, since the game was played out. A new order was set up, and all might have been well had Louis been able to accept the new order wholeheartedly and then name strong men to administer the government fearlessly and fairly, with every effort bent upon building up the peasantry, the craftsmen and the merchants while keeping a firm hand upon the demagogues.

But Louis could not, or at least did not, find the right kind of men among the decadent nobility, and the popular side was equally lacking in seasoned competent administrators. The popular leaders were either flaming demagogues or impractical doctrinaires, men who parroted the sayings of Voltaire and Rousseau and failed to realize that demagoguery is the most pernicious of poisons in a new democracy. Louis also let his silly queen, Marie Antoinette, and equally silly noblemen persuade him that help from Austria would strengthen his position, and that piece of folly touched off the Reign of Terror. Thereafter events ran their well-known course from bad to worse, until the nation was only too glad to let Napoleon take charge as First Consul in 1799, then as emperor in 1804.

From Napoleon France obtained both a generation of bloody wars that gained her nothing in the end, and a combination of governmental and economic policies which has seemed to suit the national genius from that day to this.

This outcome in France completes the record of revolutionary change during the late eighteenth century, and from then on for nearly a century economic development was marked by ever-growing use of machinery and *laissez-faire* economics, while world politics was dominated by British sea power.

The British Navy compelled Napoleon to forego any idea of matching Britain's world-wide trade in manufactured goods and confined France to the area which her armies could control. After the fateful Battle of Waterloo in 1815 France accepted this situation, and from then on she concentrated upon building up an orderly, satisfying life within her own borders, with security valued more than riches and fineness placed ahead of abundance. Machinery was used, but not as in the United States and Britain, to an extent which all but stifles fine handwork. In government France treasured the watchwords of the revolution—Liberty, Equality, Fraternity—in theory, but in practice the French turn in time of trouble to the single strong man.

Meanwhile Britain, the United States and toward the end of the century the newly created German Empire under Bismarck and the Hohenzollerns led the pace in developing the Machine Age.

In detail this story is the familiar one of railroads, steamships and all the other inventions which have produced the mechanical marvels of modern life. It is a story, too, of immense expansion in wealth and population and of tremendous gains for everyone, shot through with many evils and many failures to use the new forces for the best interests of mankind. The changes in technological aspects of life in this one century probably amounted to as much as all previous changes put together, since the very dawn of civilized life.

But the detailed story of these changes, magnificent and far reaching as they were, scarcely belong in a study of human intelligence. What counts here is trends and enlargements in viewpoints, understandings and ways of thinking. These deserve study with double care because of the well-known difficulty experienced by every generation in seeing itself against the entire pattern of human development. The people of any time tend to see their own ways as the only ones, their own ideas of the moment as eternal principles. Only by the most thoughtful care and comparison with history and the fundamentals of human nature can the really permanent elements in thought and life be sorted out from the transitory and the true status of the times be appraised.

This is just as true in our times as any other. We do have, however, one good clue which enables us to characterize our thinking in all the features which set it off from the thinking done in previous ages. Our social and economic philosophy has taken its dominant theme from the same influence which has come to dominate workaday life. The machine has come to be the pattern for thinking, just as it came to be the favorite device for working. Throughout the nineteenth century and well down into our times men have tended to explain everything in terms of mechanisms.

We are justified, then, in calling this stretch of time the period of the mechanistic spirit. Also, since this spirit has set the tone for our twentieth-century life, we should trace its rise in detail throughout the nineteenth century, in order to provide background for appraising our own times and a starting point for attempting to catch a glimpse of what the future may hold in store.

CHAPTER XXXVI

The Mechanistic Spirit of the Nineteenth Century

CHARACTERIZATION of the nineteenth century as predominantly "mechanistic" in spirit might be logical enough, even without considering anything beyond use of the machine; but an intellectual counterpart for this use tinged all scientific and philosophic thought as well. This counterpart began, as noted in Chapter XXXIII, in devotion to structure in studies during the sixteenth and seventeenth centuries. It came into bloom at the turn from the eighteenth into the nineteenth century, with success in achieving firm foundations for chemistry and biological subjects and with new vistas opening in physics because of enlarged knowledge of electricity.

One beginning of success in chemistry was achieved by the Swedish apothecary, Karl Wilhelm Scheele (1742–86). He isolated a gas (now called oxygen) which supported fire and breathing. A dilatory publisher held up his book *Air and Fire,* which described his discovery, until 1777; and meanwhile the same discovery was announced by Joesph Priestley (1733–1804), an English clergyman who devoted his spare time to chemistry.

On August 1, 1774, Priestley obtained a gas, which he thought to be the long-sought phlogiston, from an experiment which had been under the noses of everyone all this time. Medieval alchemists had known that red oxide or precipitate of mercury would give off gas when sunlight was concentrated upon it with a burning glass. Priestley did this, collected the gas in his newly invented pneumatic trough and proved by tests that it was the "vital air" or "dephlogisticated air" which supported fire and breathing.

Before this the eccentric English nobleman, Henry Cavendish (1731–1810), had applied sparks from the newly developed electric machine to water and collected two gases. One he did not identify. The other he called "fire air" (we say hydrogen), which burned with great heat in ordinary air and left a dew in a collecting vessel. This was extraordinary, since water (dew) had always been considered a primal element since the days of Thales, and this upset provided the clue to the badly needed pattern of understanding which made sense out of all these mysteries.

If water was not an element but a compound of "fire gas" with something, all other "elements," "essences" and "spirits" were automatically brought under suspicion. The suspicion was deepened when the "other gas" in water was found to be Priestley's and Scheele's new gas. Water could be torn apart into these two gases; put these two gases together properly, and they produced water. This supposedly primal element, one of the supposed foundation stones of the universe, was just a simple chemical compound of hydrogen and oxygen—H_2O, as we say today.

Here was a challenge to all chemists, a challenge as electric as the spark which had torn water apart, to overhaul all of their fundamental ideas—and from 1777 to 1783 the genius of Antoine Laurent Lavoisier (1743–94) worked out the chemical process involved in burning or combustion, in breathing, in smelting metals and in the production and destruction of water. All these processes turned upon combinations of oxygen with other substances, principally carbon, hydrogen and the metals.

Whenever the combination occurred heat was produced. This was true in the flames of a furnace and equally so in the body of a living animal. It was true, but over a long period of time, when oxygen combined with a metal to produce a rust or an ore. The process could be reversed by applying heat, as in smelting ore down to a pure metal, or by applying an electric spark, as in the destruction of water. Oxygen and oxidation explained all these processes; the "essence of fire," or phlogiston, was a figment of the imagination.

Soon after Lavoisier's day the American-born Count Rumford (Benjamin Thompson, 1753–1814) disposed of the similar "spirit" or "essence" of heat, the so-called *caloric* of earlier physics.

While supervising the boring of brass cannon in Munich he insulated the metal carefully, to prevent inflow or outflow of "caloric." But the metal still gained heat in exact proportion to the speed of the boring. Count Rumford, therefore, told the Royal Society in

1798 that in his opinion there was no such substance as caloric. Heat was simply motion, the vibration of molecules in the heated substance.

This hint was developed quickly into the modern explanation of heat as the product of vibration in the molecules of a substance. The faster they were made to vibrate by chemical or mechanical means, the hotter the substance got. When they communicated this vibration by contact or otherwise to other substances they lost some of it and became cooler, while the other substance gained vibration and "became hotter." The supposed "calorific essence" was simply a transfer of vibration from the molecules of one substance to those of another substance.

With "caloric" challenged in this fashion, just as "phlogiston" had been discredited by Lavoisier, the time-honored pattern of understanding which employed "essences" and "spirits" was all but destroyed in chemistry. Between 1803 and 1808 the English schoolmaster and chemist, John Dalton (1766–1844), ended the old ideas completely with his *atomic theory*.

The idea that matter was made up of tiny atoms had been a part of chemical thinking since the days of the Ionian philosophers, but until now nobody had clinched the idea with striking *proof*. Lavoisier had gone far toward doing so when he weighed all the materials, including gases, which he put into an experiment and found that he had the same weight of materials in the end. But even so the materials did not have to be made up of atoms, to satisfy this test. Now Dalton proved that no other structure of matter would meet the test of comparison with known *facts* by pointing out an essential difference between *mixtures* and chemical *compounds*.

Powdered sulphur and iron filings can be mixed in any proportion desired, but the product remains a mixture. The iron can be teased out with a magnet, and both the iron and the sulphur are found unchanged. But if the two be fused by heat into a chemical compound, the proportions no longer were haphazard. They always were simple ratios between the amounts of the substances, as tested by weight.

This could only happen, Dalton argued, if matter was made up of atoms and these atoms carried their respective weights with them into chemical compounds.

Dalton pushed this idea over the whole range of known compounds, and always it held true. He had to multiply his weights for sulphur and iron by eight, making them 32 and 56, to allow for compounds involving lighter elements (oxygen, atomic weight 16, and hydrogen with a weight of only 1), but once this array was complete the conclusion was unescapable. Matter had to consist of atoms that had definite comparative weights and combined in simple, definite proportions.

In such fashion the old patterns of understandings were pushed aside in favor of the newer *mechanistic* pattern, which interpreted the characteristics and behavior of matter as an affair of definite atoms responding to definite physicochemical laws. Fire, breathing and all these other mysterious phenomena had been fitted into the framework which Kepler, Galileo, Newton and Huygens had created for the planets, for falling bodies and for some aspects of light; and men now had good reason to believe that this framework of physicochemical law would serve to explain all Nature and the entire physical universe, from the humblest microscopic plant or animal to the hottest sun or the most distant star in the universe.

This idea was reinforced at the time by brilliant successes in harnessing the mysterious force, electricity, and in unraveling the relations between electricity and magnetism.

Luigi Galvani (1737–98) got the idea of "galvanic electricity" in 1790 from touching the muscles of a dead frog with copper and iron. Alessandro Volta (1745–1827) proved that the frog was not essential by placing these metals in acids or salts and producing "voltaic" or "current" electricity from the first "electric battery." From this beginning Hans Christian Oersted (1777–1851), Michael Faraday (1791–1867), Joseph Henry (1799–1878) and many others developed our modern mastery of electricity, with all its wonders of electric power, electric lighting, the telephone, the X ray and the radio.

In the latter half of the century faith in the universality of the mechanistic concept was fed by two superb feats of scientific thinking—the magnificent telescoping of light, magnetism and electricity into one phenomenon by the genius of Clerk-Maxwell, with radio as one fruit of the achievement, and the discovery of the electronic nature of matter, first detected by radioactivity.

Clerk-Maxwell (1831–79) achieved his triumph by brilliant use of mathematics, and it cannot be explained in nonmathematical terms, but some hint of its greatness can be set forth.

The idea held that all these phenomena consisted of stresses and strains in an invisible, weightless medium, the *luminiferous ether,* which pervaded the universe. These effects tended to radiate outward from their sources, somewhat as "waves" travel along a shaken rope, and always at the same speed—186,000 miles a second. One variety of strain could either radiate across space as electrostatic charge or follow wires as electric current; another type caused the phenomena of magnetism. One special class of extremely rapid, short vibrations caused light.

Clerk-Maxwell used this last idea as the basis of some predictions, and these predictions bore fruit soon after his death. He said that if light consisted of short waves, longer waves capable of causing electromagnetic effects should exist. In 1887 Heinrich Hertz (1857–94) found these waves; a few years later Guglielmo Marconi (1874–1937) developed use of them into *wireless telegraphy,* parent of modern radio.

Also, waves shorter than those of light should exist. In 1895 Wilhelm Roentgen (1845–1923) found some of them; today we call them, as Roentgen did, X rays. Still others constitute *ultraviolet radiation,* an invisible part of sunlight which causes marked effects, such as tanning and burning of the skin and conversion of certain fatty substances into vitamin D.

But if electrical disturbances accounted for so much, might not matter itself be electrical in nature? The answer "Yes" began appearing in 1898, when Madame Curie and her husband announced discovery of *radium.* This substance seemed to be continually exploding, giving off energy that caused definite electrical, chemical and physiological effects; yet it did not seem to lose weight or undergo change of any sort. This behavior seemed to defy all previous understandings of matter, but in the early 1900s J. J. Thomson (born 1856), William Rutherford (1871–1937), Niels Bohr (born 1885) and others produced a solution, as they thought, of the riddle.

The emanation of energy consisted of electrified particles, much smaller than any atom, and atoms themselves were made up of these particles arranged like suns and planets in solar systems. The different properties shown by the different chemical elements were due to different numbers and arrangements of the electrified particles within the atoms; when some of the particles escaped from substances such as radium they caused the effects called radioactivity. The original idea that radium did not lose weight proved false. Weight was lost, but so slowly that the loss had not been detected at first.

Here, then, seemed to be a prospect of complete fulfillment for science's age-old dream since Thales started scientific thinking back in the sixth century B.C.—the dream of one theory, one primal substance which by its workings would explain everything in the universe!

Science seemed to have this substance now, in electricity. Particles or atoms of positive and negative electricity (protons and electrons) explained matter and its behavior. The behavior of matter thereafter stood explained by physics and chemistry, and physics and chemistry in time could be expected to explain life and even thought. Could any prospect be fairer or rest more solidly upon tested knowledge?

Biology had been slow about joining this march at the start of the century, owing to special technical difficulties; but after a quarter of the century had passed success began crowning efforts to explain life from the mechanistic viewpoint.

In 1828 Friedrich Wöhler (1800–82) ended all doubts about whether laboratory methods could duplicate the intricate substances elaborated by living plants and animals. He synthesized the nitrogenous waste product, urea, and knowledge of this compound proved the key to understanding a host of others. In 1838 M. Schleiden (1804–81) drew together all previous evidence, added some of his own and convinced botanists that the ultimate unit of plant life was the cell. Next year his friend Theodor Schwann (1810–82) proved the same theory for animal life and thus gave biology sound working units comparable to Dalton's atoms in chemistry.

In 1859 Charles Darwin (1809–82) gave biology the far-reaching doctrine of evolution with his monumental study, *The Origin of Species*. Next year Louis Pasteur (1822–95) disposed of all lingering vestiges of belief in spontaneous generation—that is, the idea that worms, germs and other lowly creatures sprang from mud, "primordial slime" or any source whatever other than previously existing life. Pasteur also opened the way for modern surgery and control of infectious disease with his "germ theory"—that is, the discovery that infections came from the presence and transmission of microscopic one-celled plants (bacteria) and animals (protozoa).

Of course many phenomena remained stubbornly unexplainable on any mechanistic hypothesis. Darwin was balked by some problems, as explained in Chapter III, and always biologists were reminded of a subtle but unmistakable difference between "living" and "nonliving" substances and processes. Even the lowliest of plants and animals seemed to have urges and drives which were utterly lacking in all lifeless organisms and processes; every living thing plainly had something which all nonliving things did not. Still biologists did not despair. They had come far with mechanistic doctrines in a comparatively short time, and they believed that, given time, they would enjoy equal success with these remaining problems.

Thus the mechanistic concept proved as fruitful for biology and medicine as it had for astronomy, physics and chemistry, and during the nineteenth century it came to dominate men's ideas about economics, human society and human thought as well.

Especially was this true in the field of economics. As thinkers viewed the hurly-burly and the scramble to get ahead and win fortunes with the aid of the new machines, they became more and more convinced that Adam Smith had been right with his doctrine that men were essentially automatons driven by self-interest in all their economic activities. His "laws of selfishness" seemed to explain the current scene without a hitch or a flaw, and economists of the so-called Manchester school developed his theories until economics came to be called "the dismal science."

One such "dismal doctrine" was offered by Thomas Robert Malthus (1766–1834). He pointed out that man, like every other living thing, tended to reproduce his kind and increase his numbers faster than he could improve his supply of food. The natural checks upon this process were disease and starvation of the weakest, and the race would always have a marginal population which was just barely escaping death by starvation, unless something was done about it. He proposed to attack the situation at the source with birth control, and of course was howled down as a monster of immorality. Babies came from God, and man should not interfere. But once this correction had been made, in the name of morality, the Malthusian doctrine became highly popular in certain circles. Since misery, low wages and semistarvation were biologically inevitable, nothing need be done about them.

Of similar import was "the iron law of wages," propounded by the English financier and economist, David Ricardo (1772–1823). He held that people would not pay much more than production costs for goods, and this small excess constituted a fixed fund from which owners had to draw their profits and laborers their wages. Hence whatever one party gained the other must lose, and since owners had both the power to take the lion's share and could recruit workers who would accept a starvation wage from Malthus' "marginal population," the prospects for labor inevitably were gloomy.

Darwin's "survival of the fittest" was a doctrine of biology, but it fitted admirably into this scheme of economic thought. How could anyone complain about the rich getting richer and the poor getting poorer, when this was the fundamental law of Nature? Let the struggle go on, then, with the best men winning and the rest finding their proper level, down to those who lived on the brink of starvation! It was all as inevitable and as irremediable as the belching coal smoke which stained every manufacturing community and the drab hovels in which the "marginal" workers lived.

From such views of economics and the similar doctrines in biology nineteenth-century thinkers passed easily to a completely mechanistic concept of human society, the view that social relations are machine-like reactions of living automatons to circumstance.

Biology contributed a neat hierarchy based upon the cell. Cells were organized into tissues, tissues into organs and organs into "organisms," or complete living individuals. Sheer momentum of thinking along this line suggested that individuals were bound likewise into communities and communities into societies. The science of economics suggested that biological laws such as survival of the fittest held over as well, and so a mechanist concept of society was all but complete. Add a few special "laws" to reflect and emphasize the social point of view, and the result would be a full-fledged *sociology* or science of society!

The great English systematizer and encyclopedic writer, Herbert Spencer (1820–1903), can fairly be called the high priest of this view. Certainly no man labored harder to interpret society as an out-and-out mechanism obeying invariable law, and his influence upon nineteenth-century thought was enormous. Neither did Spencer shrink from pushing the mechanistic concept to its ultimate limit of application. He did his best to interpret the mind and thinking of man mechanistically, and from him as much as from anyone the infant science of psychology took its dominating viewpoint.

Here, however, the mechanistic concept met its first check. Workers such as Wilhelm Wundt (1832–1920) spent their lives trying to reduce thought to an array of physicochemical responses of nerve and brain to external and internal stimuli, but as explained in Chapter IV, all such attempts came to shipwreck on the problem of self-awareness. Try as they would, psychologists could not fit this phenomenon into the mechanistic framework, and as long as they could not accomplish this their science stood without a foundation. Wundt's brilliant American pupil, William James (1842–1910), tried to remedy the defect by making self-consciousness his central fact and telling how it worked, but in 1891 he stated his opinion of the results and of psychology as a science, as quoted in Chapter I.

This check was warning enough that in psychology, at least, the mechanistic concept would not do; something lay here which could not be explained in terms of a machine. Now it happens that this first thin wedge of a nonmechanistic viewpoint has been driven deeply enough since James's time to demolish any prospect of reaching ultimate truth through such thinking. Therefore we of the mid-twentieth century face a need for rearranging our fundamental concepts from the ground up. But this has not happened because of any setback or check in a science as young and untrusted as psychology. The need for change has arisen out of setbacks which began developing at this time in those supposedly most solid and trustworthy of all sciences, astronomy, mathematics and physics.

One setback was lack of progress toward explaining the law of gravity; the one gain made was realization that this force was *not* magnetic or electrical in nature. For another check the planet Mercury persistently refused to complete its movements around the sun in precisely the time called for by astronomical theory; it was always late. In still another field geologists insisted that the earth was hundreds of millions of years old; but the physicist, Lord Kelvin (William Thomson, 1824–1907), insisted as stoutly that even if the earth started as a white-hot gas, it would cool to the deadness of the moon in a score or two million years. Geology simply could not have more time.

These checks seemed trifling, however, measured against science's many successes; Kelvin, toward the end of his life, called them "tiny clouds" on a fair horizon. Indeed, the discovery of radioactivity cleared away all difficulty for the geologists. This process alone seemed able to provide all the heat needed to maintain life on the earth for billions of years. But alas for self-satisfaction, the other clouds *grew* instead of vanishing, until they threatened the concept which formed the very foundation of the mechanistic philosophy.

This concept, as we have seen, was that of a universe built out of electrified particles organized as atoms and responding to, or forming part of, a universal flux of energy. But twentieth-century work with this idea—work which is known dimly to the general public under the catch title, "the Einstein theory"—has led to a most surprising result. As physicists plunged deeper and deeper into the subject, with their atom smashing and their artificially induced radioactivity, they found that they could not make any sharply defined mechanical concept fit the proved facts.

Under Newtonian and nineteenth-century views (now called "classical," so rapidly has progress marched in this field) any phenomenon could be described accurately in terms of three "dimensions" in space and a fourth measure—often called a "dimension"—time. Einstein made the first breach in this view when he pointed out that space cannot be considered as an all-pervading, fixed and static something. It is subject to warps and perhaps to fluxes or flows. Therefore what seems to us to be motion of an object in response to some force, such as the force of gravity, may really be an object standing motionless in space while space is being subjected to a warp or a flow and carrying the object with it.

If this idea seems "contrary to plain sense," that is splendid; such an impression shows how science is being compelled to realize that "plain sense" cannot explain the universe. This realization has been sharpened in dealing with the atom, by need for accepting the principle of *indeterminacy*. This principle is "pure mathematics" in its very nature, but a slight nonmathematical hint of its import is this: if we want to fix an atom or a particle accurately in time at "now" or at any definite instant, past, present or future, we cannot say accurately where it *was* or *will be* in space at the selected instant. If we want to pin it down in space, we cannot say whether it "is there now," "was there some time back" or "will be there at some future time." Thus the atom cannot be pinned down accurately. Nature in its very heart, the atom, is "unpinnable," indeterminate, unknowable in all details by the mind of man.

Such an outcome opens up entirely new vistas for thought, with its warning that we must learn to think in terms of "indefinites" and "indeterminates" in place of supposed "certainties" about the universe. But before we can consider this prospect with profit we should bring experiences with the mechanistic concept in other fields of thought down to date, and particularly thought about economic and social affairs.

In these fields, high optimism reigned throughout the nineteenth century, despite many a "tiny cloud" on the horizon.

One of these "clouds" was a seeming inability to press forward evenly to ever greater productivity and profit. Instead business seemed to be cursed by *cycles*—alternations of boom times with collapse and depression. Several of these "cycles" ran their course in the nineteenth century, and economists were puzzled mightily even to *explain* them, to say nothing of suggesting how to *eliminate* them.

Variations in world supply of gold and the tendency of costs, inventories and capital investment to outrun wages were favorite explanations. Nobody advanced seriously the *human* explanation that the boom was a species of self-intoxication, a feeding of hope for yet more profit upon profits as they came in, until, like the drunkard, business had to face a "morning after." Unchained, intoxicated selfishness as the driving power behind the business cycle was far too "thin-spun" for a mental discipline which thought in terms of account books, stock inventories, balance sheets and cost records—that is, in terms of money rather than men.

Business was plagued also, as was politics, by constant social unrest. The trouble here with the smug application of mechanistic views to human beings and human society was that men, after all, are not mere economic and social automatons. The rich and powerful employer of labor might tell himself (and society) all he liked that his workers were "hands," "items of labor cost" and subject to "the iron law of wages." The workers declined to accept this view. They insisted, in the quite outworn medieval fashion, that they were *men* and, as such, they had some inalienable rights. Also, being men, however stupid, and not sheep, they did what they could to obtain these rights. Strikes and riots were frequent in the miserable crowded centers of industry, and while these could be repressed with cooperation from the civil and military authorities, nobody cared or dared to carry repression too far. Great Britain remembered the fruits of too blind stubbornness in the American Revolution; the entire world remembered what happened to the old regime during the French Revolution.

Then, too, employers were human and not mere "driving economic forces." Most of them preferred contented workmen to maddened, starving wage slaves, and when business enterprises gathered resources enough, wage increases, shorter hours and better working conditions were passed on to the "hands." During the end of the century most of the trouble which occurred was caused not by the older type of personal employer but by the impersonal corporation run by someone who saw only an accountant's report or the size of the dividend checks and sent out peremptory demands from London or New York for lower cost and more profit, with never a thought of human values.

A much more powerful relieving force, however, throughout the century was the constant opportunity for *expansion*—expansion into new lands and expansion into new enterprises which seemed to increase sales, work, profits and wages in all but snowball fashion.

Great Britain had enormous outlets upon new land in Australia, Canada and elsewhere and in pushing British manufactures and investments throughout the world. The United States had the vast domain of the West to fill up and a rich export trade to Europe. France, after the Napoleonic Wars, had a stable population which could meet its needs with French resources and felt only effervescent discontent over political irritations. Short, comparatively bloodless revolutions settled these matters.

Germany became a major power when the empire was formed with but limited land and resources. Trouble was avoided, however, for nearly half a century, thanks largely to the shrewdness of the "blood and iron" chancellor, Prince Otto von Bismarck. Bismarck saw that Germany's chance lay in developing manufactures for export and in doing so "the German way"—finding out what people wanted and selling it to them at low prices, rather than imitating the more lordly ways of Britain of pushing good quality at good prices. Low prices abroad required low wages at home, but Bismarck, hard though he was, saw the right answer for this. Instead of suppressing discontent with clubs, bayonets and bullets, he soothed the workers with social legislation—state medical care, old-age insurance and housing.

Japan was only starting her marvelous rush from complete feudalism to full-blown modernity in the latter half of the nineteenth century. The remaining powers were living largely in the older ways and felt but little pressure as yet from the new economy. The political situation seemed reasonably stable, then, the world over, with British naval power controlling the seas of the world and other nations finding reasonably satisfactory places in world economy.

Behind all this, and most soothing of all, was the phenomenal and seemingly unstoppable rise in the general level of living. Machinery more than vindicated itself here, by freeing man from scarcities imposed by physical Nature and opening the way to progress as far as men had intelligence enough to go.

Without machinery, men on the Atlantic coast of North America would have been compelled until the end of time to spend months sailing around Cape Horn to reach the Pacific coast of the continent or to spend an equal time trekking overland. With machinery, men could and did cut a canal through the Isthmus of Panama to shorten the sea voyage, and steamships lent more speed. For land travel men flung railroads across the continent, and today airplanes swoop from coast to coast in less time than was needed a century ago for a trip from New York to Philadelphia.

Before the advent of machinery periods of scarcity amounting even to famine were inevitable whenever crops failed. Hand labor with animal power never could pile up a sufficient surplus to carry a population comfortably over a bad year. Neither could supplies be moved from one part of the world to another in quantity enough and with speed enough to relieve major shortages, with horse-drawn wagons and wind-driven ships. Today American flour relieves famines in China; in normal times Argentine beef and Australian mutton feed Europe; Brazil supplies coffee for the world. The American farmer's problem is to find markets for his produce rather than to produce enough for bare minimum needs.

Until the nineteenth century almost all men toiled from sunrise to sunset, as did most women and all too many children, and even then mankind achieved at best a thin margin above minimum needs. Today a forty-eight-hour working week is the maximum needed in any decently organized land. Most occupations in the United States can meet every demand with a forty-four-hour week, and every student of such matters agrees that less than forty hours would be enough, if only truly efficient economic and social organization could be achieved. Yet this short week produces enough to meet all daily needs and a surplus sufficient to support universal education, a rich program of scientific and artistic work and an amazingly far-flung program of government activity—including the seemingly unavoidable outlay for military armament and the grueling burdens of war.

Men felt, therefore, that they could afford to overlook evil in the faith that before too long remedies would be found, and so life turned from the nineteenth into the twentieth century with as serene prospects as ever the race enjoyed. The halcyon times continued, too, for more than a decade; and so, in the cultural and intellectual sense, the real transition to newer times came not with the arbitrary calendar change from the 1800s to the 1900s but with the fateful years of 1914–18.

We of today need not be told what a Pandora's box of trouble the World War of those years unloosed upon mankind.

Not only did the destruction of life and wealth place a heavy drag upon progress in Europe and kindle rancors which boiled over again in 1939; the war brought to ominous thunderheads all the "tiny clouds" in economic and social affairs which had seemed so trifling before 1914. Boom and depression on a world-wide scale; unemployment and social unrest; depreciation and downright collapse of currencies; these tested the nineteenth-century pattern of industry and commerce until some observers wondered whether it would stand the strain. And then, as a capstone of trouble, came the most dangerous flare-up in modern times of the outworn ambition to confine mankind once more within the paralyzing pattern of the anthill state.

In these trials, and in what is being done about them, lies the true historic burden of the twentieth century, for to us has fallen the task of dealing with these troubles. To us, too, has fallen the task of readjusting our thinking to such strange patterns as relativity and indeterminacy in science, the unexplainable self-awareness of man, and the possibility of replacing scarcity with abundance in economic life, once we learn to use our technological powers aright. What we do and fail to do in dealing with these problems will determine not only our immediate future, but the rating which future generations will give us in history.

Let us try now to see how we measure up against this challenge!

CHAPTER XXXVII

The Twentieth Century and Its Outlook

To appraise our times as future generations will weigh them for their contributions to progress we need only one simple test, one measure of value. We need only ask what mankind has always wanted and how close we come toward satisfying these wants.

To organize this test we may set down as proved by our long review of the past that all human striving can be classified in terms of three objectives. One has been meeting primary requirements for life, such as food, shelter and clothing. The second, lying in the social realm, has been winning some degree of security, leisure and freedom for carrying on with the third and most deep-lying objective. This is the urge for self-aggrandizement, the insatiable desire in every normal individual to enlarge his life and his importance in every way possible. Taken together, these three objectives provide a yardstick for measuring the attainments of any people or period.

Now how do we measure up against this yardstick?

We may say at once that the first objective of meeting primary requirements has been all but attained.

In technology, the ways of getting the world's work done, we have won substantial victory in the fight man started untold ages ago, when he first sought to improve his lot by chipping a rude tool out of a stone. Our technology is sufficiently powerful to meet all the primary needs of the race without compelling man to devote all, or even half, of his waking hours to the task. Improvements will come, doubtless, and they will transform technology in all its details, but they cannot improve *in principle* upon this fundamental achievement. Man's large problems in the future will lie in dealing with himself, not with physical Nature.

456

This means that our times face their test in their dealings with the second and the third larger objectives of the race. The problem of the day is learning how to overcome these dragging forces in human mentality which keep us from entering upon enjoyment of the new richness made possible by technological advance. We must find really effective ways for overcoming the poisoning of intelligent thought by emotion, passion and prejudice. We must learn remedies for vanity of opinion and stubborn, blind selfishness of purpose. Above all we must rid ourselves of inherited viewpoints, shibboleths and rule-of-thumb tests and learn how to see our problems truly in the light of our new knowledge about human nature.

For an example of needed mental reconstruction we might as well take the foundation of our current thinking about economic life— Adam Smith's *laissez-faire* view of man as a sort of living automaton, driven by the *profit motive*.

Let us start by agreeing at once that our times should not and *could* not seek to do away with the profit motive. Our civilization is geared firmly to it; any failure of the motive to function would entail untold confusion, suffering and setback during several generations of readjustment. What we should do is learn to see the system in its true light, as a driving force which the race has elected to use, just as it uses steam and electricity, and not as a god which rules every aspect of our lives and must not be questioned or challenged in any way.

Our first step in learning to see aright is ridding ourselves of the notion that the profit motive is either fundamental or indispensable.

We hear much today of threatened government bankruptcies here and there about the earth, the collapse of business under tax loads and the end of the profit system. Such events would be close to utter catastrophe for many an individual, certainly; the person who has lost all takes small comfort from the fact that society carries on. But from the social point of view, the standpoint of the race rather than of individuals, predictions of disaster from such calamities overlook historic precedent.

Suppose the profit system should collapse—what then? For many of us this would mean ruin, certainly, but would it mean ruin for the race and the end of civilization? History says otherwise; it denies that hope for profit is anything like the all-important and indispensable driving force which we of today consider it to be.

The most enduring civilization on record, that of Egypt, was carried on by religion and custom, not by hope of profit. The brilliance of Ionian and Athenian achievement sprang from intellectual and emotional interests, not money ones; commercialism, the lure of profit, proved a wrecking force, not a constructive one, in the end for Athens. Europe achieved the medieval reconstruction down to the time of the Crusades with profit frowned upon as an evil, not honored as a leading objective in life.

Coming down to recent times, as all of us know Germany went through a complete collapse of money values between 1918 and 1923, yet German economy emerged and showed ample strength within a few years. Then, starting in 1938 and 1939, Germany shook the world with its ambition for dominance, and the strength for this was not born of hope for personal profit at all. Competent neutral observers of the German military effort were struck most of all by the all but fanatic zeal of the young Nazi soldiery for furthering the ideal of *weltmacht,* of *Deutschland über alles.* In addition to reviving the political and economic institutions of the ancient anthill state Hitler plainly had succeeded in bringing back the psychological motivation of these times. In the ideology of the Nazi rank and file we have a living example of the group thinking, the enhancement of self through enhancing the realm and its gods, which drove life on in ancient Sumeria, Egypt, Babylonia, Assyria and all the other anthill states clear through the Roman Empire.

From all this we can see plainly the nature of the mistake Adam Smith made when he considered profit a fundamental motive. He mistook a variant, a twist taken in his time by the true driving force, for the force itself. The true force is the urge for self-aggrandizement. Money profit happens to be the means brought in by the commercial and industrial revolutions to achieve this end; but even so, it is only a means to an end. What men really want remains unaltered. They still strive, just as they have striven in all past ages, to win richer lives, positions of power and the esteem of their fellows. We happen to measure these efforts today by figures in an account book and on dividend and pay checks, but this is far from indispensable. Mankind has used other measures in the past and, if need be, can devise other measures in the future.

Once we realize this we can really begin to use the profit motive intelligently just as the engineer uses the driving forces of steam and electricity. Most of the workaday tasks of the race—producing and moving the world's goods and measuring the worth of routine personal service—can be measured and driven forward by means of money. But we have gone beyond this to trusting the profit motive in activities where it is a menace, not an incentive.

We corrupt true human values when we measure a lawyer's worth by the size of his fortune, not by his contributions to law and justice. We poison life for the majority of young people when we let them gain the notion that the supreme aim in life is to get rich. Human endowments being what they are, not one in a thousand of our young people can attain this ambition, and they only doom themselves to disappointment when they dedicate their lives to trying.

Above all, we postpone the day of abundant living when we leave provision of the primary necessities to an economic system which is designed to produce profit at every step, instead of being dedicated to producing maximum quantity at least cost. Our economic thinking cannot be called sound until we learn, for example, to reward the farmer in proportion as he produces food *cheaply,* instead of compelling him to get along only in proportion as he can force prices *up.* The statement may sound paradoxical, but Henry Ford is an outstanding example of how the seemingly paradoxical is the true road to better living. His career shows how to use the profit motive intelligently, instead of letting it misuse and defeat human need.

Another example of crying need for mental reconstruction exists in our whole scheme of regulating life, as we find the scheme drawn up in civil and criminal law.

Civil law, with its hairsplitting technicalities, its interminable procedures and its frequently empty results of judgments that yield nothing, has advanced far too little from the condition pictured in Charles Dickens' *Jarndyce vs. Jarndyce.* That biting satire was the common-sense answer to Blackstone's smug praise of the law as "a perfect engine" for achieving justice. Perfect it may have been, if justice consisted only of weighing abstractions in a vacuum, rather than adjusting rights and conflicts between living human beings who had a way of dying while the law unraveled its tortuous procedures. Dickens' tale of a case that dragged on until scarcely a shred of the rights at stake was left for the grandchildren of the litigants showed how "perfect" Blackstone's justice was in actual practice, and our civil law still has all too much of this taint today.

To this the lawyer's stock reply is, "What would you do about it?" The problem admittedly is difficult, because civil rights and duties are enormously complex, and adjudication of them is correspondingly intricate—but what of that? Inventors and engineers conquered com-

plex problems when they gave us the radio and the airplane. Navigators, manufacturers, merchants, physicians and architects have
brought difficult problems into line with the needs and the tempo
of the age. Why should the lawyer be exempt from expectation that
he do likewise?

Criminal law is in a far worse state; it still is but little better than
medieval, or even ancient Roman, in its spirit and procedures and in
the philosophy which expects to curb crime with fear of punishment,
"making examples" and "making the punishment fit the crime."

These ideas square well enough with medieval scholastic ideas of
personal moral responsibility or with ancient Roman or early modern
notions of man as an essentially intelligent creature. They are given
the lie, however, first of all by the utter failure, through all ages, of
fear as an effective deterrent. Pickpockets plying their trade in the
shadow of the gallows on Tyburn Hill is one well-remembered
example; well-educated, well-to-do young "thrill criminals," those
who steal and even murder "for the excitement," are another.

A still more fundamental error is the psychological one of "making
the punishment fit the crime." This envisages the criminal as an
intelligent person who weighs possible profits against possible penalties, and the theory is he can be deterred from light crimes by
light penalties, while heavier penalties are needed to prevent the most
serious crimes. Occasionally a criminal fits this pattern, but not often.
Most of them yield to urges which spring from warped, defective
personalities or from faulty social conditioning, without weighing
consequences at all.

This one psychological fact is enough to show that the law should
make the punishment fit the *criminal* and not the crime. This does
not mean dealing mawkishly with criminals, excusing them because
they "never had a chance" or "are good to their mothers." It means
assessing the criminal accurately as to future potentialities for good
and evil and dealing with him accordingly. It means, too, dealing
heavily rather than lightly with many a light crime. This should be
done to cure the lamentable weakness in our present law of being
utterly unable to *forestall* crimes by those of known and ineradicable
bent.

Of course what *should* be done and what *can* be done are vastly
different matters. We might well shudder at the mere thought of
giving our present-day police, courts and juries the right to lock up
anybody as a *potential* criminal, but this objection only shows what

society should do if we are to rid ourselves of ineffective medieval criminal law. It should bend every effort to acquiring police and courts which *can* be trusted to fit treatments to criminals instead of crimes and thereby come within sight of providing really adequate protection against crime.

A similar need for drastic overhauling to bring institutions into conformity with human nature exists in the field of *education*. Here in this activity of giving the young a better approach to life than their parents enjoyed lies the true hope of the race; but education itself needs considerable overhauling before it can serve this purpose with true effectiveness.

One crying need is for better education of the educators.

We take it for granted that our teachers know *what* to teach—that they have a correct understanding of the facts they impart to the young. We have a handy method, too, for testing the correctness of this assumption. Most states and cities provide curricula for their schools, laying down what shall be taught and how. But these curricula offer many a shock and surprise. Not so long ago one Texas city, noted among educators for progressivism, prescribed in its curriculum that children be taught how the Phoenicians *invented* the alphabet. Not only had the authors of this curriculum failed to hear of Sprengling's work; they apparently had heard nothing of knowledge gained about the history of the alphabet at any time after Herodotus gave this mistaken credit to the Phoenicians in his *History* twenty-four centuries ago.

Today we are concerned with soil conservation. Modern science has most illuminating knowledge of how soil takes on characteristics from climate—knowledge which would suggest to anyone the folly of trying to misuse soil and climate together, as Americans did when they created a "dust bowl" in the Southwest. Such knowledge would provide an invaluable foundation for training in conservation; it is well suited to the understandings of young children; but scarcely a curriculum in the country prescribes this knowledge. The young still are taught the old sterile notion that soil is a mere storage bin with characteristics fixed by whatever was left in the locality during past ages.

Such failures to keep up with advancing knowledge are trifles, however, compared to the need for revamping education until it becomes really effective in *shaping human character aright*.

Education should continue to impart knowledge—the more the better, provided the knowledge is *correct*—but its larger task is to give real understanding of human nature and psychological conditioning which is based upon this understanding rather than upon outworn and mistaken notions of man as a creature ruled by intelligence. Education should sweep out this mistaken notion and teach children instead to understand that their primary difficulty will lie not with use of intelligence but with control of the inherited brute in their natures. Also, since self-interest is the accepted mainspring of our society today, children should be "conditioned," in the psychological term, to pursue self-interest intelligently.

The word "conditioning" is used instead of "training" because training implies an appeal to intelligence, an effort to *convince* children that the man who pursues his own interest "regardless" brings calamity to himself and society in the end. This is the method we have used for hundreds of years, and failure with it is bespoken all too eloquently in every community every day. Society's safeguard should reach deeper by far, and it lies ready to use whenever we care to use it. It is *social conditioning,* ingraining of desirable attitudes into the so-called "instincts," training of the sort which keeps even the hardest and most unscrupulous of men from appearing in public without his trousers.

The distinction between this and training is subtle but real enough. In practice it turns largely upon *timing,* the period in life when the training is imparted. Training is timed for ages when use of intelligence has been established; conditioning is most successful in the plastic period of young childhood, when the child's most fundamental patterns of understanding are taking shape. This is when the child is stamped with either anthill subservience, the Hellene's vivacious skepticism, the medieval respect for God and fear of the devil—or the modern idea that money is the lifeblood of commerce and gaining wealth in money is man's chief purpose in life.

Here undoubtedly is where we touch upon the most fundamental of all changes needed if we are to profit from our new knowledge. Rearrangements of laws, economic institutions, education and all the specific aspects of human effort can do their part; but a program for achieving really intelligent living can only succeed fully if it has at its very foundation a wise conditioning of the race with so-called "social instincts" and norms of conduct which really fit the true facts of human nature.

So also do we see here the full reason why such a program cannot be worked out overnight, by one or two political administrations, or even by one generation.

This necessity for early shaping shows well enough why the schools alone never can achieve successful social conditioning, try as they will. A sound program of conditioning must start before school years, in the nursery, and this means that parents must either be conditioned or at least brought to realize the need for conditioning their children aright. The difficulty of doing this, throughout a population which still is thoroughly conditioned in nineteenth-century thinking, is obvious and a sufficient example of why social change lags far behind manifest need for readjustment.

Nevertheless, the race has been reconditioned in the past, and it can and will be in the future. The only question is whether it will wait, as it always has, until driven by the whip of calamity or whether men will seize their twentieth-century opportunity to use our new and clear understandings of human nature for adjusting society accurately to man's characteristics and needs.

But not even a soundly adjusted society will be enough if man is to enter upon the full heritage which is rightfully his by virtue of his endowment of intelligence. Society is only a means to an end and not an end in itself. It exists to serve *man the individual,* and the measure of its service is full when it has given every individual a full chance to achieve the utmost his capabilities permit. But when all this has been done one adjustment—or readjustment, if we prefer—will remain to be accomplished. This is the adjustment of the individual to society and, even more, to himself, to the limitations imposed upon him by the social framework and to his ultimate destiny as a creature born to live a term in the worldly scheme and then depart therefrom forever.

Happily we have all the endowment needed, in both knowledge and command of Nature, to commence finding a real and satisfying solution for this problem after long ages of fumbling with it in the light of mistaken theories and principles.

For one happy prospect we are in a position to see clearly now that much of the thwarting of legitimate individual self-aggrandizement has been caused by unreasoning, unnecessary, and even destructive application of standards which arose out of folklore, outmoded viewpoints and mistaken theories, rather than from clear-eyed understanding of human nature and its needs. We have mentioned one such maladjustment in our training of the young in the idea that they aggrandize themselves only in proportion as they get rich. Riches may have been the one passport to self-aggrandizement in the heyday of nineteenth-century *laissez-faire* economy; but at best this passport could be obtained and used only by an exceptional few. We can arrange matters better now. Once we employ our technological powers to bring about an economy of abundance, human beings can live comfortably as to all primary necessities without being rich. Then they can and should be conditioned from the cradle onward to seek satisfaction in terms of *accomplishment,* of discharging their responsibilities well, whatever their lot in life. This will place self-aggrandizement upon terms which every man can meet, whether he serves as scientist, merchant or ditchdigger.

Another bright prospect is offered for individual happiness by the sheer adequacy of our techniques as opposed to the constant thwarting suffered by the best minds in past ages. A sufficient example of this evil is that tragic figure of a man thinking far ahead of his times, Leonardo da Vinci (1452–1519).

Here was the true mastermind of the Renaissance—a painter equal to the best in all time, a first-rank engineer and possessor of a scientific flair as fine as the genius of a Galileo or a Newton. But most of his most cherished dreams were stifled at birth by the inadequate techniques of the times. He foresaw the airplane and tried to build flying machines, but he could accomplish nothing because the times could not provide him with a suitable engine. He sensed the truths which lie at the basis of modern geology, but not even in ten lifetimes could he have gathered the evidence needed to prove his ideas correct, and nobody else had gathered it. And always over him hung the shadow of the Inquisition, ready to thwart and punish any undue boldness in making reason rather than tradition the test of truth.

Today men of Leonardo's stamp enjoy far different prospects. They have at their disposal all the rich resources of modern scientific knowledge. They live in an age which values and encourages advances rather than seeking to stifle them. Society also can provide the means. Let a man need an eighty-ton electromagnet and a flood of electric power to advance knowledge by smashing atoms—both the magnet and the power are provided. Will a two-hundred-inch telescope solve problems which a one-hundred-inch instrument cannot unravel? One of the Foundations for advancing knowledge provides the money and says also that when astronomers have done their best with this telescope, funds for an even more powerful one will be available.

But entirely apart from such large satisfactions, the simple process of conditioning with so-called "social instincts" attuned to real human nature will open an entirely new era of opportunity to seek happiness. After all, most of the misery in the world is caused by maladjustment, not by adverse circumstance—or so it is today, at least, when modern technology has the ability to banish physical want for the race. In the past the race has tortured itself with its seeking after false gods—blind glorification of the nation and its idols spread with fire and sword, the self-stultification of search for God through asceticism, the pursuit of wealth for wealth's sake. Once we learn to seek happiness where it is free for all, in self-aggrandizement through *accomplishment* according to the abilities given us, the miseries and pulling at cross purposes which still torture the race will seem a nightmare as far removed from daily experience as do the privations of the cave man.

And now we come to the most important prospect of all—man's reconcilement with his ultimate destiny, his seeming place in the eternal scheme!

In the past this reconcilement has been achieved through religious hope for life eternal. In recent centuries the growth of science has seemed, to unthinking minds, to challenge the validity of this reconcilement; but now in our time we are coming to see more clearly than did either the intellectually proud, mechanistic-minded scientist of the past century or his prejudiced, unwilling-to-think opponent from the fundamentalist wing of religion, how slight a challenge really exists. Science rather provides as valid a basis for religious hope as could be asked.

Today we see clearly that a mystery lies at the very heart of man's nature—a mystery which nobody can explain. But if something unexplainable exists there, we are placed fairly upon our warning that we do not know all. The limits to which we can see are *not* the limits which, in the realm of First Causes, actually circumscribe man. Something lies beyond the farthest range of our limited vision, and upon the clear existence of this something religion can base its teachings and its hopes, without possibility of challenge from science.

This realization is fortified by the very position in which science finds itself, in its knowledge that when it comes down to the very foundation of all its concepts, its views of the atom and of energy, it must accept relativity and indeterminacy as set forth in the preceding chapter.

But if science must accept indeterminacy at its very heart, how can scientific knowledge be used, with any logical justification, to establish *determinate* or "completely known" conclusions about anything? It can only take us "as far as its powers go," and it knows now that its stopping place is far from being "the end of the line" for Reality, the full nature of the Infinite and the Eternal. Man is part of an ineffable something which transcends understanding; he would be both foolish and arrogant if he attempted to push his limited understandings to a claim that he knows the full measure of his destiny.

Even today we voice one fragment of this truth when we say that biological evolution is not complete. This statement can be taken narrowly to mean such trifles as reduction of wisdom teeth, or even failure to develop them, in keeping with reduction of the jaw, as intelligence increases; but can we not imagine that mental evolution can occur as well and give the stock new powers and new vistas of understanding in times to come?

Indeed, we have glimpses of such powers appearing, just as they have appeared in past times, in so-called *prodigies* and the rare thinkers properly called *geniuses*.

The most familiar type of prodigy perhaps is the mathematical one. He can glance at a pageful of figures and give the answer instantly. He can remember and add all the numbers on a hundred-car freight train as it speeds by. Another feat is being shown fifty or a hundred numbers and stating the cube root of the entire sum as soon as the last number has been given. Now the significant feature of this ability is the answer given when someone asks how he "works out" these problems. He usually replies in effect, "I don't know. The answer just comes to me."

Here, then, we have the existence of a mental power, ability or intuition which clearly stands outside the scope of ordinary thought. This same type of superior thinking seems to make geniuses such as Shakespeare, Bach, Beethoven, Michelangelo and others of their kind. We might imagine them producing one masterpiece, two, or even half a dozen, by the laborious "cut-and-try" methods used by lesser minds. But they could not have achieved the sheer volume of output which stands to their credit with step-by-step creation. They must have been helped along by having the right idea, the happy turn "come to them" as it comes to the mathematical prodigy. They must have had something which we can call an *intuitive* approach rather than the approach of "think it through."

But if such qualities can appear even occasionally in such rare minds this is proof enough that our ordinary thinking is not the limit which can be attained by human minds. The course of evolution might well make this type of intuitive thinking, rare as it is today, the commonplace of tomorrow and broaden it until all men can apply it over all their living. A strange world would result—a world in which everyone was a Beethoven in music, a Shakespeare in drama and a prodigy in mathematics—but it is not at all inconceivable. Indeed, as rigidly scientific a thinker as Alexis Carrel set forth precisely this prospect in his *Man the Unknown*. But if and when this comes to pass, we may well hope that as a part of the new endowment man will see a satisfying place for himself in the universal scheme of things, a place as far beyond our ken as would have been the airplane or the radio in the Pliocene days of man's beginnings.

Altogether, then, man has ample material out of which he can draw reconciliation to his destiny. Once he does this he will have power enough to press forward indefinitely to heights which we cannot even imagine today, and this seems as sound a note as any with which to end our survey of "Mind through the Ages."

Appendix A

Current Theories Concerning Modern Human Races

In the days before the mechanisms of biological inheritance were understood students had to guess at racial relations as best they could. Most systems were based upon easily seen characteristics such as skin color, shape of head and type of hair. Today we know that such characteristics run only partially with inheritance, and they are subject to change according to climate, diet and other cultural circumstances. The true characteristics of race are those transmitted by the genes, and older tests of race must be re-examined to determine which of them meet this requirement.

The test by skin color is, of course, the familiar division into white, yellow, black, red and brown. This test was devised by Johann Friedrich Blumenbach (1752–1840), the founder of anthropology, and it is completely unscientific because skin color can change with difference in climate even in one individual's lifetime. The white man who "burns black as coal" in the tropics is one example; a better one is the dark color which the Hindu blood cousins of the fairest whites have acquired in a few thousand years. Color is reliable only in combination with more permanent characteristics such as the straight hair and the slanting eyes of the Mongolian or the woolly hair and the broad nose of the Negro. A few of Blumenbach's combinations of this sort are, however, still considered valid.

A fair general agreement exists that races such as the Australian aborigines and the Bushmen and Hottentots of South Africa are genuine racial types and stand close to the assumed "original type" of hominid or "thinking man." This type is woolly haired and is equivalent roughly to the term Negrito—a term which does *not* mean Negro.

468

The Negro is recognized as a genuine racial type, well advanced above the primitive level but otherwise extremely puzzling. His black color is a recent adaptation to tropical heat, because it only develops strongly *after* birth. His flaring nostrils also seem a recent change, to permit adequate intake of oxygen from the hot, moist air of his equatorial home. Other skeletal features, such as jutting jaws and the peculiar Negro shinbone, seem more fundamental; but nobody has offered a satisfying reason why the Negro should have these features while other races do not.

The white and Mongoloid types are considered well advanced. They also present, together with the Negro, the question of single or multiple origin—that is, whether only one ancestral type of *Homo sapiens,* or modern man, arose from earlier hominid stock or whether whites, Mongoloids and Negroids arose separately.

The tendency is to leave this question open, pending additional evidence, and be content with a theory of *polycentric development* that is, the view that whether or not whites, Mongoloids and Negroids had separate ancestors, these races worked out their early *careers* in different centers. A typical view of this sort, which takes in the important finds of Peking man at Choukoutien, the Mount Carmel skeletons and the finds of very ancient modern types in England, is offered by Franz Weidenreich. He suggests that the modern races seem to have been found earliest in four centers of development— the most primitive type, such as Australian Bushmen, in southeast Asia; the Mongoloids in east Asia, perhaps with an inheritance from the Sinanthropoid-Neanderthaloid stock; the whites in southwest Asia and the Negroes in Africa [*Biomorphosis* (1938) p. 1].

The feature which is most generally used for tracing racial affinity is *skull shape,* long, round or medium (or *dolichocephalic, brachycephalic* and *mesocephalic,* from *kephale,* head, and *dolicho,* long, *brachy,* short, and *meso,* in the middle). These prevailing shapes are indicated by *cephalic indices,* or ratios of breadth to length. The higher the ratio the more nearly round is the head; an index of 100 would mean a completely round head. An index down to 83.1 remains roundheaded; from there to 75, medium-headed; all indices below 75 mark longheadedness.

This craniometric test still enjoys good standing when applied correctly, but many questions about its fundamental certainty as a test of race have been raised by recent studies such as those made by T. Wingate Todd and associated workers.

Todd's group has found that the skull does not grow at an invariably uniform rate all around—that is, as a balloon swells when inflated. Instead it has three separate directions of growth—from front to back, from side to side and upward—and growth may proceed at the same rate or at *different* rates in each of these directions. In well-fed healthy children the rates of growth in these dimensions remain neatly teamed, and the head will be more or less round in adult life, subject somewhat to racial inheritance. But poor food, bad health and heredity, or all three, may break up the teaming. Upward growth may be retarded in keeping with slackened body growth. Sidewise growth may be slowed down. But front-to-back growth persists; apparently, ample size fore and aft is most important in a pinch.

The result of such warped growth may be a longheaded adult, even though the child comes of a roundheaded race. Conversely, longheaded peoples can acquire more rounded heads, as Franz Boas once announced was happening among American-born children of longheaded Jewish immigrants, whom he tested in New York City. The most modern findings suggest, however, that Nature tends to attain middle ground when diet and health are good in childhood. That is, so-called racial tendencies toward extreme longheadedness or roundheadedness seem to trend toward the medium shape.

An ingenious theory of races and racial distribution, based upon the relation between food and head shape, is W. Griffith Taylor's view that extreme longheadedness was and is a mark of extremely primitive culture, whereas people of more advanced culture tend to be more roundheaded.

The most primitive types of man, according to Taylor, are marked by dolichocephaly. That is, they have a head breadth less than three fourths of the length (cephalic index of less than 75). This type is found today in a *shatterbelt* of isolated patches far from the center of origin. Examples are the aborigines of Australia, certain peoples in south India, the Bushmen and Hottentots of South Africa and the Greenland Eskimos. In undesirable corners of the earth, where they were driven by later, more roundheaded folk, they are living testimonials to the "original man."

From these extremes the peoples, toward an assumed Eurasian center of origin for the races, show rounder and rounder heads and also more and more advanced cultures, until the central zone contains the almost roundheaded Alpine type of man.

This relation between culture and head shape fits many of the facts but not all. One difficulty is the fact that the ancient Egyptians, who were fully as advanced as Mesopotamian Asiatics, remained persistently longer headed. So also did one of the most dominant white types, the Nordic, even when set down as conquerors among rounder headed folk.

More reliance may be placed upon A. C. Haddon's classification by hair into (1) the woolly type (*Ulotrichous*), (2) the wavy or frizzy type (*Cymotrichous*) and (3) the straight-haired type (*Leiotrichous*). Hair character is fixed by the cross section, being straight when the cross section is round and more and more curly as the hair becomes flatter, and it seems to run with race. But in order to obtain a classification broad enough to cover seemingly known races, Haddon had to use head shape in addition to hair type; so his test is far from sufficient in itself.

Another attack upon the problem was offered by R. B. Dixon of Harvard in 1923, in his *Racial History of Man*. Dixon's theory was that no one feature was sufficient to identify a race. But he thought also that if any particular *combination* of head measurements was persistent this combination might be a reliable test of race.

For his combinations he used three measurements— head *shape*, or ratio of breadth to length, with three classifications: long, medium and round; head *height,* classified as high, medium and low; and shape of the nose, whether narrow and sharp, medium or broad and flat. Now the three classes of each feature can yield $3 \times 3 \times 3$ or twenty-seven combinations in all, but Dixon proposed to consider all "medium" types as blends and used only the eight combinations of the extreme types. To these combinations he gave names, and these names correspond fairly well to recognized races. His racial types may be tabulated as follows, using the letter symbols shown:

Cranial Index—L, long, B, broad; Head Height— H, high, Lo, low; Nose—N, narrow, W, wide.

Proto-Australoid	L, Lo, W	Mongoloid	B, Lo, W
Proto-Negroid	L, H, W	Palae-Alpine	B, H, W
Mediterranean	L, Lo, N	Ural	B, Lo, W
Caspian	L, H, N	Alpine	B, H, N

Dixon recognized, however, that these types did not match up well enough with seemingly well-established racial strains to be considered fully satisfactory. His Caspian type, for example, corresponds to the tall blond Nordic of other schemes, but the existing Nordic stock also contains strains which fit better into the proto-Negroid group. This might be all right in point of color, since a few thousand years in the North probably would bleach out the skin, but why does this stock not show a trace of the much more persistent woolly hair of the Negroid?

Still another test which now intrigues science greatly is *blood type*.

A fine short explanation of this test is a translation, in *Antiquity* of December 1935, of an article by J. Millot of the Sorbonne in Paris, and we can do nothing better than follow this, with excerpts of the high points.

Millot explains first that blood consists of corpuscles, red and white, which float in the serum, or liquid part of the blood. Normally the red corpuscles remain free from each other, but if the blood from an animal be injected, the corpuscles come together, or agglutinate. This may happen also when blood from two humans chosen at random is mixed; this result is called isoagglutination. This phenomenon Millot explains as follows:

The simplest explanation, and the one most usually given at the present moment, is that isoagglutination results from the reciprocal action of two kinds of substances whose chemical nature, however, remains completely unknown; the one called agglutinogen is contained in the red corpuscles, the other, or agglutinin, is in the serum. Analysis has shown that there are at least two different agglutinogens, conventionally called *A* and *B* and capable of being present in the red corpuscles either singly (*A* or *B*) or together (*AB*), or not at all (*O*); certain individuals therefore have only *A*, and others have *B*, and others both agglutinogens; while yet others are totally devoid of either. It is this which is described somewhat inaccurately (but which has found its way into scientific parlance) as the existence in the human species of four blood groups—group *A*, group *B*, group *AB* and group *O*, this last containing neither *A* nor *B*.

To the agglutinogens of the corpuscles correspond agglutinins in the serum which are distinguished by the Greek letters α (or anti-*A*) and β (or anti-*B*). The same blood never possesses agglutinins active in the presence of their opposites; or in other words, the serum of a given individual never agglutinates its own corpuscles. . . . Accordingly the serum of bloods belonging to group *A* contains, not agglutinin α which agglutinates *A*, but agglutinin β; and it is the serum of group *B* which contains agglutinin α. The group *AB*, possessor of two agglutinogens, can never have agglutinins, whilst group *O* possesses at the same time both α and β. From this it follows that the complete formulas of the blood groups are *A*β, *B*α, *ABO*, *O*αβ. . . .

If one brings together the blood of two people belonging to the same group there is no result—the blood mixes normally. If on the other hand one brings together blood samples from group *A* and *B*, α will react with *A*, β with *B*, and agglutination will ensue.

This phenomenon is used to control blood transfusions by testing donors for type before giving their blood to patients. But this fact is also a valuable test of race, because blood type is inherited. As Millot says, "If the father and mother belong to group *A*, all the children may belong to group *A;* if they belong to group *O*, all the children will belong to group *O;* if the parents do not belong to the same group—if, for example, one is *A* and the other *B*—the children will differ and be *A, B, AB* or *O*." Recognition of these facts has resulted in curious applications of them. It has made it possible, for instance, to restore to their respective mothers newly born infants who had been mixed up immediately after birth. Above all it has been used in medicolegal practice to investigate paternity.

Now during the World War the biologists L. and H. Hirzfeld, while in army medical service in the Far East, noticed that the percentage of each blood type found in a population could be used as a test of race. From this, according to Millot again:

They established three categories: One marked by a high percentage of subjects of group *A* and a low percentage of *B* and including the majority of European races (European type); a second showing on the contrary a high percentage of *B* and a low one of *A*, comprising Mongoloids and Ethiopians (Asio-African type); and a last category containing approximately equal quantities of *A* and *B*, comprising Russians, Turks, Arabs and Jews (intermediate type). This discovery, published in 1919 . . . emphasized the great ethnological interest of blood groups.

This, in bald outline, is the principle of the blood test, and anthropologists are trying out the idea the world over. But the work is new as yet, and no definite theories of race have emerged from it.

All these considerations are taken into account, together with much original material, in the theories advanced in Carleton Stevens Coon's *The Races of Europe* (1939), principally concerning the strains or races of white men.

Coon follows the view that skeletal features, such as head shape and stature, tend to pass by inheritance but change in response to favorable and unfavorable environment. Stature, for example, increases with favorable environment and health conditions. This is proved strikingly by records kept at Harvard for several generations, with an abundance of families recorded for three or more generations. Grandsons almost invariably are taller than their grandfathers. Stunting from unfavorable conditions is seen characteristically in all Arctic regions and most strikingly in Iceland and Greenland, where conditions were good during the Middle Age settlement by Vikings, then bad, then good again. The skeletons from the bad period show stunting, but recovery was prompt when times became better.

Another such plastic response is a tendency toward roundhead-edness with good times. This occurred in the original longheaded Cro-Magnon stock of Europe when the Ice Age ended, with the result of producing the roundheaded strain which Ripley called Alpine (Chapter IX). It can also be traced during historic periods of good times in Europe during the Middle Ages.

A third important plastic effect comes from *crossing* different strains. If other conditions are favorable, a cross or hybridization results in exaggerated male characteristics. This is shown in skeletons by rugged eyebrows, massive jaws and long limb bones—exactly the features which marked the Cro-Magnon—and this fact leads to Coon's view that these people descended from the Mount Carmel cross between high mental and Neanderthaloid types, which produced Skhul man.

With these tendencies as a basis, Coon offers a theory of races which he warns is highly tentative but which seems to explain many otherwise highly puzzling facts.

Coon's basic strains of the hominid stock are two. One is the high mental type (called Mediterranean by Coon) which we know existed in Mindel-Riss times, as explained in Chapter V. At the same time the earth had seemingly less-changed descendants of the prehominid or early hominid types such as *Pithecanthropus* and *Sinanthropus*. Neanderthal man was a highly specialized descendant from this type, with brutalized features which equipped him to withstand glacial cold. He died as a pure type, or was killed off, at the end of the Ice Age.

The pure high mental or Mediterranean strain survives today in two main branches, each with three subdivisions. One is the *modern* Mediterranean, at home around the shores of this sea and typified by Arabs and discernible strains in Latins, Greeks and others. (This is the one strain called Mediterranean in Ripley's classification of whites.) One branch, the Danubian, carried neolithic arts into Europe, in Coon's opinion, and this branch formed crosses with the earlier Alpine population. Another, the Cappadocian, provided the original peasant population of Asia Minor.

The second main branch of Mediterraneans provided (roughly) the white, Indo-European-speaking nomad population of the Central Asiatic grasslands. One branch, the Irano-Afghan, occupied Iran and India with the Aryan culture. Another, the Corded Folk mentioned in Chapter XV, provided the original waves of nomads into Europe, and a third, the Atlanto-Mediterranean, turned back into the domain of the first great branch and probably corresponded roughly to the megalithic folk described in Appendix D.

Meanwhile the more rugged and perhaps more ancient strain of hominids had provided a strain which crossed with the high mental type at Mount Carmel (and perhaps elsewhere in the Far East) to produce Skhul man. From this one (or two) cross came two principal strains. One divided further into Mongoloid (including American Indian) and a complex of Lappish and Ladogan arctic folk, at home now in the northernmost part of Europe and Siberia. The other was the strain called Cro-Magnon in Chapter IX.

This strain was dominant in Europe during the Ice Age, although Mediterraneans, typified by the Combe-Capelle skeleton, were there also—and toward the end at least of the Ice Age a strain descended almost without change from Skhul man. The Predmost skull, which typifies this strain, is almost at one with the Skhul cranium.

With better times at the end of the Ice Age, these strains became roundheaded and persisted, both as the pure Borreby, Tronder and Alpine types of mesolithic times and through crosses with both neolithic peasants and with nomads, into modern times. The most important of these crosses, between nomad Corded Folk and Danubian peasants, produced the tall blond Nordic of north Germany and Scandinavia.

Another highly important cross between Alpines, Cappadocians and Irano-Afghans resulted in a peculiar emphasis of features called *Dinaricization*. This is an extremely round skull shape as seen from above. As seen from the side the skull is flat in back and rises almost to a peak instead of a dome at the top, while the nose is strongly arched or hooked. These Dinaricized folk now spread from the Dinaric Alps along the Mediterranean into Syria and into Asia Minor as far as Armenia. They form the *Armenoid* type, which many older schemes considered the most recent and physically most advanced type not only of the Alpines but of all modern man.

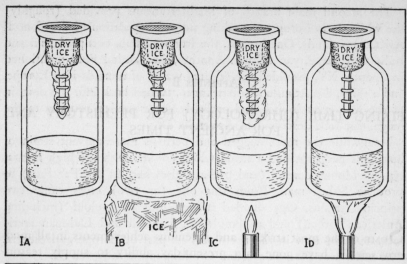

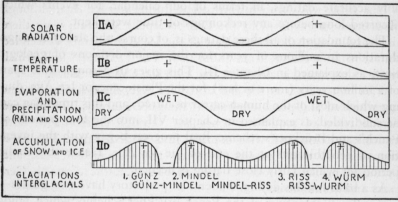

SIMPSON'S FOUR BOTTLES FOR EXPLAINING THE ICE AGE

Sir George Simpson explains the Pleistocene Ice Age by saying that ice and snow accumulate when weather is *somewhat* cold but *not* cold enough to check evaporation of water from the oceans. To demonstrate this theory during a lecture before the Royal Institution on December 10, 1937, he used four bottles, with a bit of dry ice in each cork to chill an ice gatherer below. The control bottle (IA) at room temperature formed some ice. Chilling the next bottle (IB) checked evaporation from the water in the bottom, and *less* ice formed. Warming the third bottle (IC) increased evaporation, and *more* ice formed. Strong heating of the fourth bottle (ID) cleared away all ice.

To apply the theory demonstrated with the bottles to explaining the four glaciations of the Pleistocene Ice Age Simpson assumed a twofold pulsation in the amount of heat given by the sun (IIA). At four critical times (IIB and IIc), while the temperature was high enough to cause good evaporation but low enough to form abundant ice and snow, periods of glaciation would occur.

Continued at bottom of the next page

FIXING TIME (CHRONOLOGY) FOR PREHISTORY AND FOR ANCIENT TIMES

SOME of the most striking and ingenious achievements in all modern science have gone into present-day ability to supply reasonably accurate datings, in terms of our calendar, for events which occurred long before any reckonings of time were kept.

The foundation of all these datings is, of course, the ability to assign durations in millions of years for the major divisions of geologic time, as explained in Chapter III. This gives us a rough time span of a million years (more or less) for the Pleistocene, or Ice Age, during which most of the human career occurred; and this time span can be subdivided, as explained in Chapter VII, into the four periods of Penck's and Brückner's scheme. Real progress began with the invention of neolithic arts at the end of the Ice Age. Hence this is the period for which fairly close dating is needed.

As a basis for this dating, students of prehistory have two guides— a postglacial extension of the Penck-Brückner scheme, which holds fairly well over all of Eurasia and Africa, and an extremely accurate dating worked out for these events as they occurred in Scandinavia.

Penck's scheme describes the breakup of the Ice Age as an oscillation between reintensifications of the cold (with *advance*s or *stadia* of the glaciers), periods of increasing warmth (*retreats* of the glaciers) and periods of stable climate (*pauses* in the glacial retreat).

Continued from preceding page
Between these four periods would occur interglacial times. The first and the third would be *warm* and dry, because they were due to high temperature; but the third would be *cool* and dry, because it was caused by deficient evaporation, not by heat (IID).

No advance, however, regained all the ground lost in the preceding retreat. The events follow (beginning with the earliest):

Achen Retreat or Oscillation—a period of alternating advances and retreats, but on the whole a retreat; some northward shift of the prevailing trade and westerly winds, with dryness in southerly regions.

Bühl Advance—increased cold in glaciated regions, southward shift of winds, increased rain in southwest Asia and Africa. This stage consisted of a threefold oscillation called Bühl I, II and III. Thereafter came an unnamed retreat.

Gschnitz Advance—similar to the Bühl, but less intense and soon followed by a retreat.

Duan Advance—the last advance. Today we live in the post-Duan retreat.

Glacial advances and retreats in just about this sequence occurred in Scandinavia and have been dated with all but uncanny accuracy by Baron de Geer of Sweden and his associates and pupils by means of *varve-dating* or *geochronological dating,* a technique applied to the laminated or banded deposits left in the lakes formed by water from glaciers.

Throughout the warmer months the outflow of muddy water from a glacier into a river or lake deposited sediment—mixed sand, dirt and clay—on the bottom of the watercourse. Then winter froze the surface water; the stream flow was not active, and no coarse, heavy sediments were carried. During this quiet period the fine silt which never settled out of the water in the warmer months dropped to the bottom and formed a layer of pure clay over the coarser deposit. Thus a double layer of coarse and fine material was formed each year.

The double layer is a varve, and the key to correlating varves in different deposits was the fact that some summer layers were thick while others were thin. The thick layers obviously were laid down in wet years, when sediment was abundant; thin ones marked dry years. De Geer discovered, moreover, that wet years and dry years *never came in exactly the same order* over any considerable number of years. Therefore, if the same sequence of thick and thin varves occurred in two different deposits, the respective portions of the two deposits must have been laid down in exactly the same years. This permitted linking different deposits together in time and so constructing a calendar of postglacial time.

The result of these studies was the discovery that the icecap underwent four periods of shrinking but held stationary during three inter-

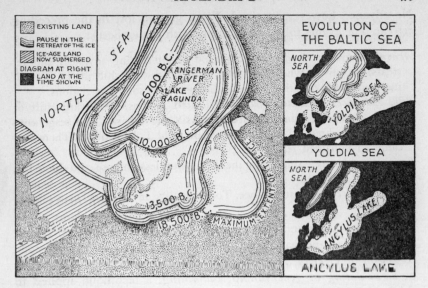

THE END OF THE ICE AGE IN SCANDINAVIA

The left-hand picture shows the step-by-step retreat of the last or Würmian icecap from Scandinavia, as traced by De Geer with his varve dating. The dated lines mark halts or pauses in the retreat, when moraines were formed. The moraines and retreats are named as follows: 18,500 B.C.—Brandenburg Moraine, followed by the Daniglacial Retreat; 13,500 B.C.—Pomeranian or Mecklenburgian Moraine, followed by the Gotiglacial Retreat; 10,000 B.C.— Fennoscandian Moraine, followed by the Finiglacial Retreat and the Ragunda Pause; 6740 B.C.—End of the Ice Age at Lake Ragunda, as explained in the text. The lower diagrams show accompanying changes in land and sea over the site of the present Baltic Sea. The retreat uncovered land which had been depressed by the weight of the ice; salt water flowed in and created the Yoldia Sea. Then the crust of the earth recoiled from the depression and temporarily elevated the land. This cut off the sea and formed the fresh-water Lake Ancylus. The excess elevation soon subsided, and salt water re-entered, forming the Littorina Sea. Modern changes thereafter changed this body of water into the present Baltic Sea.

mediary pauses. Finally the icecap shrank back into two mountain valleys above Lake Ragunda in northern Sweden and quickly disappeared. The splitting of the cap seemed to De Geer to be a satisfactory event to take as the end of the Ice Age.

The remaining problem was to tie in this event satisfactorily with some known historic date. For many years this baffled De Geer, although he believed that his uncertainties amounted to less than a thousand years. But in 1933 his daughter, Countess Ebba de Geer, announced successful solution of the problem, thanks to dating of postglacial river deposits in Sweden and some help from Huntington's studies of the giant Sequoia tree rings in California. She gave the date of the Ragunda split as 6740 B.C. From here the reckoning goes back to 10,000 B.C. for the Finiglacial pause, 13,500 B.C. for the Gotiglacial and 18,500 B.C. for the beginning of the retreat from the Danish moraine.

Many scholars quarrel with details of the work, and for the present, at least, round-number dates are safer than De Geer's exact ones. Large uncertainties also exist concerning correlation of phases in this retreat with the findings of Penck and Brückner concerning the retreat of the Würmian glaciation to the present limits in the Alps. But the accepted facts are complete enough to provide at least a provisional dating of post-Würmian time and modern man's early career in Europe. The following scheme of events and dates, taken from Peake and Fleure's *Hunters and Artists* (Corridors of Time), is a fair sample of modern thought upon the subject.

Modern man's entry into Europe is proved by relics to have fallen within the latter part of the Würmian glaciation, and the spread of the Early or Lower Aurignacian culture over Europe is assigned to the time called the Achen oscillation in the Alps and the Daniglacial retreat in De Geer's scheme. This stretch of time lasted, in round dates, from 18,000 B.C. to 13,500 B.C.

This oscillation was followed by three halts in the retreat of the ice (Penck's Bühl I, II and III). Peake and Fleure make these stages agree with the Scanian, Finnish and Ragunda pauses in De Geer's chronology. This would date the Bühl as lasting from 13,000 B.C. to 6700 B.C. During this time European man practiced a sequence of cultures which culminated, in classic French terminology, in the Magdalenian. Thereafter postglacial or modern conditions superseded the Ice Age climate and men in Europe fell into the stagnant epipaleolithic or mesolithic culture (Chapter IX).

This ends the direct use of De Geer's scheme. Thereafter the record used consists of climate changes which resulted from removal of glacial influence, and the generally accepted scheme of changes for northwest Europe is that of a Norwegian, Axel Blytt.

Blytt based his scheme upon the reappearance of trees—first the cold-climate aspen and fir, then beech and oak as the climate improved. This evidence led him to set up four great climatic periods, called Boreal, Atlantic, Sub-Boreal and Sub-Atlantic. The following description of them follows Blytt, but the dating remains that of Peake and Fleure.

The *Boreal* period lasted until the Ragunda split about 6700 B.C. It was still subglacial in character, with dry, warm summers and cold winters. The characteristic vegetation was aspen and fir.

The *Atlantic* period brought a full, genial release from glaciation. Mild winters and warm summers were accompanied by moisture enough to create peat bogs over much of Europe. On bog-free land the characteristic trees were hazel, beech and, in the warmest regions, oak. This period lasted until after 5000 B.C., and even east of the Dnieper River in Russia, where today moisture thins out, the rainfall seems to have produced rich grasslands.

The *Sub-Boreal* period was marked by persistent reduction of moisture about 4500 B.C., due to a slight increase in glaciation; Penck and Brückner call this increase the Gschnitz advance. In western Europe this dried out most of the bogs and enabled oak forests to make a complete conquest of the region. In Asia the dryness amounted to an all but devastating and permanent drought after perhaps 2700 B.C. or 2600 B.C., with tremendous consequences in driving nomads out from Central Asia.

The *Sub-Atlantic* period set in about 850 B.C., with an increase of moisture but not of heat. This change choked the Alpine passes, which previously had been open, with snow and ice; hence it is often correlated with the Duan advance of the Alpine glaciers which closes the Penck-Brückner chronology. It produced corresponding changes in cultures which are well within the view of history.

J. G. D. Clark, in *The Neolithic Settlements of Northern Europe* (1936), gives a substantially similar dating as follows: *Pre-Boreal,* and the Yoldia Sea, until about 7500 B.C.; *Boreal,* and the Ancylus Lake, to 5000 B.C.; *Atlantic Period,* and the Littorina Sea, to 2500 B.C.; *Sub-Boreal Period,* and the Baltic Sea, to 800 B.C.; *Sub-Atlantic Period* thereafter.

Probably the first stirrings toward neolithic arts occurred in Mesopotamia and Egypt during the Boreal period of Blytt (Ragunda pause of De Geer, Bühl III of Penck and Brückner). But the same change which brought the genial Atlantic period to northwest Europe undoubtedly brought devastating drought to these southern cradles of civilization, and then came the developments described in Chapters X, XI and XIII.

During these times men also began to keep records by years, but unfortunately these records cannot be translated directly into terms of our calendar of years because of the crude reckoning used for the year in these times. All the earliest civilized peoples reckoned years by moon counts, twelve moons to the year. This method was obvious and natural, but it was also highly inaccurate.

Twelve *synodic* moons—that is, moons counted against the sun, which means against the year—last only 354 days, 8 hours, 48 minutes and 33½ seconds. This is about eleven days short of a full year. Hence each such year starts eleven days sooner than it should, and in three "twelve-moon" years the calendar gets a full month ahead of the season. It says February, for example, when the season is still January, and this continues for about thirty-three years, until the calendar comes right with the seasons again.

This did not bother early peoples. They started a new count or inserted an extra month in the year whenever the calendar got badly out of step. We have an instance of this being done in Hammurabi's time (Chapter XVI); it was a regular practice with the early Greeks and Romans. The real trouble is ours, in trying to reckon in our count from such years.

The scribes did not preserve a record of when corrections were made or by how much. Even worse, they kept no running count of years from any starting year; such a running count was not kept until the ancient Greeks began keeping a record of Olympiads, or four-year periods between the Olympic festivals. Instead early ancient records were kept "in years of the king." A typical dating of this sort is "the seventh year of King Alulim."

Perhaps a hundred years later another King Alulim might come to the throne, and the scribes of his time might or might not mention that this Alulim was the great-grandson of the first one. Thousands of years later we find the records of the two Alulims. Are they one and the same man? If not, how far apart were their reigns? If a statement in moon years is given, what does it mean in actual years, when the count might have been changed several times during the interval?

Such a muddle seems hopeless, and so it would be, save for one fortunate circumstance. The ancient Egyptians were forced to reckon time in *solar* years rather than moon years, and hence they kept a count which can be tied in with ours.

The circumstance which forced the Egyptians into this practice, so fortunate for us, was simple. They depended for crops not upon seasonal temperatures and rainfall but upon the annual flooding of the Nile, and this came at about the same time every year—earlier if the flood was good and later if it was poor. Hence to be ready, and also to judge their prospects, they had to keep accurate track of the year. The old moon count would not do, but how were they to achieve a better count?

Necessity sharpens men's wits, and once this need for better timing arose, some genius noted the needed timekeeper in the sky. He saw that year after year, just when the Nile flood started, the Dog Star or Sirius was rising just at dawn in the east. Moreover, on the average, the very day the flood reached Memphis, near the present-day Cairo, Sirius came to its *heliacal* rising—that is, it rose with the sun. (The term "heliacal" is from the Greek *helios* for sun.)

Next this genius counted days between heliacal risings and found that they numbered 365. There, then, was the measure of time between "Niles," as the Egyptians called the annual floods; so the Egyptians devised a calendar of 365 days to the year and placed their New Year's Day upon the first day in the month of Thoth, on this magic day of the heliacal rising. Thus they achieved a good reckoning for the year—the first in all human history!

Unfortunately for us, the Egyptians kept their records by reigns instead of dating from a fixed year, and so for us the records are a jumble; but fortunately a slight error in their calendar gives us a basis for straightening out the jumble. This error consisted of using exactly 365 days for the year.

We know today that the earth's journey around the sun, and also the sequence of the seasons, is complete in 365 days, 5 hours, 48 minutes and 46.08 seconds. This length of time is called a *tropical* year, because it is the time taken by the sun to return to a tropic at solstice or to the equator at equinox. Now this is more than 365 days, and every four years the excess amounts to almost a day. Therefore we insert a leap day into the year to keep the calendar from getting ahead of the seasons, just as Julius Caesar did when he established the Julian calendar in 46 B.C.

The excess, however, is not *quite* a full day. Hence we must omit leap years occasionally, under the plan promulgated by Pope Gregory VIII in 1582, to prevent overshooting the mark and falling *behind* a day every 128 years.

The Egyptians made no such corrections, and so their calendar moved one day ahead every four years. In 120 years New Year's Day was a full month ahead of the heliacal rising, and so it moved, right around through the seasons, for four times 365 years, or 1460 years. Then, on the 1461st year, everything came out right again, with Sirius, sun, earth and New Year's Day all in proper relation to each other. All this was known, of course, to the later Egyptians, and when the ancient Greeks learned about this situation they called the 1460-year interval a *Sothic cycle,* from their name Sothis for the Dog Star.

The error caused no inconvenience, since each generation would use this calendar as it then stood. The important feature about the cycle is that the Egyptians themselves mentioned three occasions in terms of the Sothic cycle. The record of Manetho mentions that a new Sothic cycle started in a year which we can identify as either 139 A.D. or 143 A.D. in our reckoning. We also have a statement that Rameses I of the Eighteenth Dynasty started his reign at the beginning of a Sothic cycle. For a third tie-in we have a statement in a papyrus found at Kahun in 1899 that Sirius rose heliacally on the first day of the eighth month Pharmouthi, in the second year of Senusert or Senwosri of the Twelfth Dynasty.

These statements give us three clues for arranging Egyptian records according to our dates. By reckoning backward from 143 A.D., the preferred choice between the two later Sothic dates, astronomers compute that earlier Sothic cycles began in 1316 B.C., 2776 B.C. and 4236 B.C. Most Egyptologists assign Rameses I to the cycle which began in the thirteenth century B.C. and place Senusert one third of the way back in the next cycle.

The remaining problem is how much time to allow for the reigns before Senusert. The only good way to answer is to decide when the Sothic-cycle calendar began and then fit the reigns into this span of time.

From the very nature of the calendar it must have been established at a time when the new year came with the heliacal rising of Sirius—that is, about 2776 B.C. or 4236 B.C. Since the calendar was in use by 2776 B.C., the simplest assumption is that it was started on the previous date, 4236 B.C. But in 1927 Scharff pointed out a formidable objection to this view.

The records do not reveal reigns enough before Senusert to permit dating the First Dynasty much earlier than 3000 B.C. But First Dynasty culture was primitive in many ways. Writing was just taking shape, and the Egyptians were just learning the principles of large-scale architecture. Yet the assumption that the calendar started in 4236 B.C. asks us to believe that *more than a thousand years before the First Dynasty* the Egyptians were sophisticated enough to have figured out the length of the solar year! This, said Scharff, is unbelievable.

To this objection believers in the early date retorted that the calendar was in use before 2776 B.C. When *could* it have been invented, if not in 4236 B.C.? Scharff answered with an argument based upon the assumption that the date 2776 B.C. in all probability falls into the time of the Third Dynasty.

This dynasty included Pharoah Zoser, who ruled just before the Great Pyramids were built, and Zoser's chief minister, Imhotep. Imhotep, from all accounts, was one of the greatest of men in all antiquity, and he produced a veritable Golden Age of achievement in Egypt. This reign, therefore, is the one which on principle should have seen invention of the calendar, and the seeming earlier use could have been a simple correction of old records to fit the new dates. We do that today when we say that George Washington was born on February 22, 1732, although the calendar in use when he was born made the date February 11, 1731. Archaeologists are inclining more and more to believe that Scharff found the right answer to the problem.

Egyptian prehistory often is dated according to a scheme devised by Flinders Petrie late in the nineteenth century. The scheme uses sequence dates, often written S.D.; the final version of it is given in Petrie's *Prehistoric Egypt* (Corpus of Pottery, 1920).

Petrie based his scheme upon a progressive degeneration in the handles of the sides of certain pots. The handle shrank to an ornament and then to a mere meaningless wriggle. Petrie worked out the evolution of other cultural features which marched with this change and found that the record covered the entire period from the earliest times he knew down to early historic days. He therefore planned a scale of one hundred "sequence dates" or divisions to cover these developments. He placed the earliest culture at Sequence Date or S.D. 30, leaving thirty dates open for earlier cultures whenever they might be discovered, and he placed the Third Dynasty, the oldest one he could fit definitely into history, at S.D. 80. This left twenty dates open for carrying on the scheme into later times.

Obviously this scheme gave no clue to actual dates; it merely arranged the cultures in proper order. But today S.D. 80 has been brought into our chronology in terms of years as equivalent to the Sothic date 2776 B.C. At the earlier end Petrie assigned S.D. 20 to the Tasian culture, and this may correspond to the last occurrence of moist climate over Egypt during the Gschnitz advance of the glaciers. Peake and Fleure assign a tentative dating of 4500 B.C. to this event, but as yet the Gschnitz cannot be considered dated with any degree of certainty.

The remaining problem in chronology is tying in the Egyptian record—as worked out into spans of years—and Greek and Roman chronology into our reckoning with its division, at the birth of Christ, into B.C. and A.D.

This division was proposed by Dionysius Exiguus, a learned Roman abbot, in 633 A.D. He considered that this year was the same as the 754th year since the founding of Rome. But two uncertainties are involved, the first being the difficulty of dating the life of Christ in the scheme of Roman years.

The Nativity can be placed roughly in the reign of Augustus and the Crucifixion in the reign of Tiberius, but the only accurate reference to time in Scripture is the fact of the Crucifixion on Friday, the fourteenth day of the Jewish month Nisan. This month was started on the day when the equinoctial new moon was seen, and astronomers can reckon back for thousands of years and tell which years would bring the fourteenth of Nisan on a Friday. Unhappily, the Jews did not *reckon* the month from a calendar. They started it when the priests actually *saw* the new moon, and cloudiness may have caused a day's error.

Weighing all the evidence, the choice seems to lie between A.D. 29 and A.D. 30 for the Crucifixion, provided one remaining problem is settled. This is correlating Manetho's date for a new Sothic cycle (which we can reckon backward from our times) with the count of Roman years used by Dionysius Exiguus in selecting his year A.D. 1. This is difficult, because several counts of Roman years exist. Dionysius used the count given by Varro, which would place the Nativity in the 753rd year of Rome. Other (and seemingly better) counts give the 750th year, subject to the uncertainty above as between A.D. 29 and A.D. 30.

The latter uncertainty can be dealt with by choosing either date as a matter of historical judgment, and the count of years reckoned as A.D. is clear. The four-year uncertainty as between 753 and 750 in the Roman count runs backward, however, through all the years B.C. Modern preference leans slightly toward saying that Dionysius was wrong, that Christ was born in 8 or 7 B.C., and correlating Sothic reckoning accordingly. A minor trouble is that Dionysius started his A.D. 1 on Annunciation Day (March 25) *before* the Nativity, whereas the later *vulgar* Christian reckoning which we use started this year on January 1 *after* the Nativity.

DEVELOPMENT AND SPREAD OF THE ALPHABET

THE EARLY SEMITIC refinements upon the crude Sinai script fell into two families, the northern and the southern. The northern, composed of Aramaic, Phoenician, early Hebrew and Moabite, was the important one for the western world. The early character of it is known from an inscription on the tomb of Ahiram of Gebal or Byblos, the Moabite stone and a Phoenician inscription of Abi'baal.

The Ahiram inscription was found in 1922 by Montet and is often dated as of the thirteenth century B.C. This is disputed, but the articles found in the tomb forbid a dating later than 1000 B.C. The script is almost identical with that of the Moabite stone, a ninth-century monument to the exploits of King Mesha. The Abi'baal script also is ninth century, and its angular character and the slant of the letters in all these specimens show a clear adaptation of the Sinaitic characters to carving on stone from right to left.

Probably the most intriguing question that still remains open about this early history of the alphabet is raised by a discovery made in 1929 at Ras-Shamra, the site of the important early seaport Ugarit and of the modern Latakia. The find was a clay tablet, apparently written in an alphabetic cuneiform. Professors Bauer and Dhorme worked out the reading of the tablet and found a Semitic alphabet of thirty characters; the signs had been adapted from Akkadian cuneiform. From names mentioned in the tablet the date of it seems to be about 1500 B.C. This comes sometime after the date of the Sinai inscriptions, and so priority could hardly be claimed for it. Zellig S. Harris, in his review of the question in the 1937 *Report of the Smithsonian Institution,* inclines to the belief that the Ugarites got the *idea* of the alphabet from Phoenician users who were developing the

Sinai script, but he proposes that the Ugarites preferred to adapt cuneiform signs which they knew to the new way of writing.

The principal changes after this Semitic early history were the use of unneeded Semitic consonant sounds for all-important Greek vowels and a wholesale turning around of the right-to-left letters to fit better into Greek writing from left to right. These changes are shown in the accompanying diagram and explained by the text following.

1. *Canaanite-Phoenician or North Semitic.*—This script is shown on the opposite page at the right of the Sinaitic characters. The letters have the highly developed ninth-century forms found on the Moabite stone, although the Greeks probably received a less-developed script. This earlier script, however, is only partially known from material found at Byblos in 1930 and after.

The names given for the letters are from the Jewish. This is legitimate, because the Jews used this script until after they acquired their present letters during the Babylonian captivity. The Canaanite script appears, for example, on the Siloam tunnel inscription from King Hezekiah's reign (522?–586 B.C.) and in the letters found at Lachish (published in 1935 and later) which date from before 588, when this town was besieged by Nebuchadnezzar of Babylon.

This developed Semitic script of twenty-two letters contains two variations of the *t* sound—Thav and Tsadi, *th* and *ts*—which are not identified in the original Sinaitic script. The letters show the effect of writing from right to left by having most of the dominating upright strokes at the right of the sign. Smaller strokes were then made toward the left. Simple reversal of this process changes many a seemingly strange Semitic character into a familiar one. Examples are E, F and K.

2. *Transition to Greek.*—According to Greek legend the Phoenician letters were brought to Greece by the hero Cadmus of Tyre. Twentieth-century discoveries have increased the probability that the legend, minus certain heroic and supernatural embellishments, is substantially true. The Cadmus legend has the hero land first on the island of Thera, and this island has yielded some of the oldest Greek inscriptions known. Cadmus then was supposed to have founded Thebes in Boetia and established the first Greek script.

In support of this legend we know that various changes from the Phoenician, too numerous to be shown in the table, resulted first in a *western* (Boetian or Cadmian) script. Agreement of this crude Greek script with the Semitic writing found at Byblos suggests the

CANAANITE-PHOENICIAN			GREEK			LATIN		
(Aleph)	⌿	ALEPH	⋏	A	a	ALPHA	A	AH	A
(Beth)	⟨	BETH	⟨	B	β	BETA	B	BAY	B
(Gabi)	⌐	GIMEL	⌐	Γ	γ	GAMMA	C	KAY	C
(Daleth)	◁	DALETH	◭	Δ	δ	DELTA	D	DAY	D
(Hallel)	⟩	HAY	⟩	E	ε	EPSILON	E	EH	E
(Waw)	YY	VAU	⊣	...	..	(DIGAMMA)	F	EF	F
...	...	....	...	...	...	....	G	(Old C)	G
(Zain)	⚌	ZAYIN	I	Z	ζ	ZETA	...	(Used Last)	...
(Jchattl)	⯐	CHETH	⊟	H	η	ETA	H	HAH	H
?	⊞	THAV	...	θ	θ	THETA	...	....	...
(Yod)	⌐	YOD	Z	I	ι	IOTA	I	EE	I
...	...	...	...	...	..	....	...	....	J
(Kafis)	⋏	KAPH	⋋	K	κ	KAPPA	K	KAH	K
(Loyah)	⌐⌐	LAMED	⋀	Λ	λ	LAMBDA	L	EL	L
(Mem)	⋎	MEM	⋔	M	μ	MU	M	EM	M
(Nahash)	⋎	NUN	⋎	V	ν	NU	N	EN	N
(Samek)	⧧	SAMEKH	...	Ξ	ξ	XI	...	(Used Later)	...
(Hain)	O	AYIN	⊙	O	ο	OMICRON	O	OH	O
(Pehah)	⌐	PE	...	Π	π	PI	P	PAY	P
?	⫟	TSADI	...	...	...	....	...	....	...
(Quaw)	φ	KOPH	φ	...	..	....	Q	KOO	Q
(Resh)	⌐	RESH	⌐	P	ρ	RHO	R	AIR	R
(Shin, Sin)	W	SHIN	⧣	Σ	σ,s	SIGMA	S	ESS	S
(Taw)	×+	TAHV	⊥	T	τ	TAU	T	TAY	T
			∪	Υ	υ	UPSILON	V	OOEH	U
			...	...	..	....	...	....	V
			...	Φ	φ	PHI	...	....	W
			...	X	χ	CHI	X	EEX	X
			...	Ψ	ψ	PSI	...	....	...
			V	...	..	....	Y	EUEE(Ü)	Y
			....	Ω	ω	OMEGA	...	....	...
			...	...	...	....	Z	ZAYTA	Z

DEVELOPMENT OF THE ALPHABET

thirteenth century B.C. as a date. This script was the parent of both the Ionic script shown in the table and of Etruscan and Latin.

The first change was a transitional one of writing the lines in alternate directions, with each new line begun below the end of the preceding one. The Greeks called this style *boustrophédon* or "ox-turning," from the resemblance to the back-and-forth movement of an ox and plow in making furrows across a field. During this state letters such as E were made *with* the direction of the line, as either

Ǝ or E. The exclusive left-to-right style was not established until the fifth century B.C.

The remaining changes took account of the fact that Greek speech differed from Semitic in its greater emphasis upon vowel sounds—that is, variants of the sounds we indicate in English by *a, e, i, o* and *u*. The Canaanites had not developed signs for these sounds because Semitic speech is keyed to its consonants, but the Greeks could remedy this lack because the Phoenician script contained several consonant signs which were not needed in Greek.

3a. *Greek: vowels.*—The Greek signs for vowels were taken from Semitic signs for the weak consonants "(*h*) ah," "(*h*) ay" or "(*h*) eh," "(*ch*) eth," "(*h*) ayin," and from "(*y*) od."

In Semitic the indicated *h* sounds ranged from a weak breathing, like that of the *h* in "honor," to a deep growling or guttural, as in "hrrumph!" and "dj-h′ ug!" Omitting these *h* sounds, as a Cockney does with "(h)aitches" in English, exposed the following vowel sounds. Thus two *a*'s were obtained, from aleph and ayin; the Greeks used the first for *a* (alpha), and the second for *o* (omicron). The sound *heh* gave *e* (epsilon). The sound *i* was already contained in *y*, as shown by the detailed pronunciation of *y* as "oo-eye."

The sound *cheth,* with a peculiar growled *h,* evolved differently in western and classic Greek. The westerners combed out the explosive "breathing" which became our *h;* the Ionians selected the component which become long *e* or *eta* (ayta) in their alphabet.

The final vowel sign for *u* was obtained from the Semitic vau when "phi," the Greek *f,* was developed as a variant of "pi." This left the vau sign for (hard) *f* unused, and omission of *f* from "fau" (or "few") left "eu" or *u* (upsilon). The name "digamma" for this sound is misleading. It was a late term and was derived not from the *sound* of the character but from its *appearance* as a "double gamma" —that is, a gamma with an extra stroke.

The sign omega (Ω) for very long *o* (as in obey) was invented by the eastern Greeks by cutting off the bottom of omicron (the *o* as in open) to obtain a parallel to the difference between eta and epsilon. The Greeks added the new sign after all the others—hence the saying "from alpha to omega," meaning "from beginning to end."

3b. *Greek: sibilants.*—The Greeks managed to muddle these handsomely before they settled upon characters of their own.

Sibilant *s* sounds were contained in the Canaanite samekh and shin, with the variant "sin." (Hebrew shows the last two as ש *shin* and ש *sin.*)

The Greeks used the sign and place of shin for their plain *s* but used the name sigma from samekh. From the end sound of samekh both the eastern (classic) and the western Greeks obtained the sound *k-si*. The easterners retained the samekh sign for this sound, modified into Ξ ; the westerners used X.

3c. *Greek: phi, chi, psi.*—The sign phi (Φ) obtained its name from pi (Π) through a simple change in sound; the character was adopted from the Phoenician *koph,* which was not needed in Greek. The Greek name phi for *f* is preserved in English in such words as Phoenician and philosophy.

The sound *chi* was a variant of the end sound in the Phoenician *samekh.* For a sign the western Greeks used an archaic kaph (Ψ), later refined into Ψ. The easterners used X. English spelling preserves this relation between the *sign* and the *sound* chi in words such as "cholera."

The sign and sound *psi* were coined in eastern Greek to use the western Ψ for chi to advantage. This sign is remembered in English in such spellings as "psalter."

4. *Transition to Latin.*—Discoveries in recent years have established that the Latin alphabet came from *western* Greek through the Etruscan, probably during the seventh century B.C. This origin accounts for Latin use of the sign X for chi and survival of koppa as Q. The Semitic vau still persisted in western Greek and appeared in Latin as F, while yod was preserved as *y.* The Romans took only the early signs for vowels. Thus eta and omega found no place in the Latin alphabet. The most complex changes during the transition from Greek to Latin concerned the *k* sound.

The early Greek practice, which the Etruscans passed on to the Romans, had been to represent the *k* sound by kappa before *a* and by koppa (later abandoned) before *u.* We still follow this rule with *q* (our form of koppa), by always writing *u* after it. For *k* sounds not followed by *eu* the Romans used gamma (Γ, pronounced as *k* but written in a rounded form as *c*).

Thus the Romans had three letters for one sound and none for hard *g,* as in get. They corrected this absurdity in part by keeping *c* for a *k* sound but adding a tail to it for the harder sound. Thus they created *g.* They gave this letter the place of *z,* which they did not use at first, in the alphabet. Later, when they took to using many Greek words and needed a *z,* they tacked it on to the end of the alphabet, where it still stands. The Romans spelled out phi, chi and psi with combinations of letters, as we do, and they simplified the Greek Υ into V.

5. *Transition to English.*—The mature Latin alphabet was taken over into English without change except for *u, v* and *j*.

The Romans had used the *v* sign for both the *u* and the *v* sounds; in English we use a rounded sign, like the early Greek upsilon, to distinguish *u*. The letter *j* appeared in the ninth century after Christ as a distinguishing form for the second *i* in *ii* (*ij*); when printing was invented it came into some use as a capital I. "Julius" for the Latin "Iulius" is one example.

The letter was not completely accepted, however, until the seventeenth century, when the *dj* pronunciation grew up. No *j*'s are to be found, for example, in the earliest King James Bibles.

The Anglo-Saxons added *w* for their sound "wen." The name "double *u*" reflects how the sign was made by linking two *u*'s, made in the Latin form as *v*'s.

THE PREHISTORIC SETTLEMENT OF EUROPE
IN NEOLITHIC TIMES

THE DOMINANT NOTE in neolithic Europe during the establishment of the present peoples was struck by wave after wave of nomads pouring over the earlier neolithic population and fusing with it to form the peoples who filled the stage at the dawn of European history.

The physical races are indicated in Appendix A and in the main text. There remains, however, to be noted here several waves of cultural influence which were important in prehistory. First among them was the *megalithic* (great stone) *culture* which worked up along the Atlantic coast and along the northern coast as far as Scandinavia and northern Germany.

Wherever they went these people built tremendous stone dolmens and later passage or "trench" graves of stone. Such structures were built in Palestine before the Semitic Canaanites and Phoenicians took over the land. They can also be found around the Black Sea and as far east as India, and wherever they are found they challenge interest because of the very immensity of the effort these people put into the tombs they built for their dead and for the fact that these tombs served *all* the people. They did not spring from the vainglory and power of a chief or king, like the pyramids in Egypt. They were community tombs which accommodated all the dead of a group. Hence the entire community must have been driven by a deep faith in their efficacy.

When we view the relics of such efforts, as we see them at Stonehenge in England and Carnac in Brittany, we are awed by the evident amount of work given to the structures. With aid from copper chisels, at best, these folk quarried out huge slabs of stone, often larger than a man, then moved them on rollers or sledges to the chosen site for the tomb. There they set up the slabs to form sides, and they capped the structure with huge stone or stones, large enough to provide even modern masons and modern machinery with no mean feat of handling.

At first these graves took the form of a *dolmen*, or simple chamber of square or rounded shape. Usually this chamber was covered with earth to form a mound, at least up to the capstone; an entrance was left at one side and blocked with a stone. Later these folk built tombs with a long passage for access. In time this became a passage with alcoves, and finally the tomb was reduced to a *cist grave*, or long trench dug in the ground and lined and roofed with stone. This series, worked out by Montelius of Sweden, is our key for detecting successive phases of the megalithic culture.

Who were these people who gave so much patient toil to their provision for the dead? The early dolmens remind scholars of the tombs which gave rise to the mastaba tombs of Egypt; hence many archaeologists argue that these people were protodynastic Egyptians combing the seacoast for gold. Montelius took this view of them; so have Obermaier, Perry and others. Peake favors a Sumerian origin, not only because of seafaring but because in later structures these builders used corbeled vaulting. He thinks that they combed the coast for deposits of metal and calls them the *Prospectatores*.

V. Gordon Childe, in his *Dawn of European Civilization*, opposes all these theories with the simple view that this whole culture developed in Spain and Portugal. These people could have obtained the original idea of winning life after death with tomb burial from Egypt through North Africa. Thereafter, in Childe's view, they simply spread gradually along the coasts as the desire for new homes drew them to new lands. Myres also took this view in the *Cambridge Ancient History*.

These megalithic folk made no cultural contributions, however, of any particular value; apparently the cult of the dead absorbed most of their thoughts and energy. The student of human nature sees in them a superb example of how obsession with magical ideas can sterilize creative effort, and the remaining point of interest is modern attempts to date these folk.

Many archaeologists think that the circles of huge stones which still stand at Carnac and Stonehenge were calendar-keeping structures. They were arranged, according to this theory, to show the sun at its "farthest north" on the day of the summer solstice on a line between two sets of stones and to detect other days similarly. But the procession of the equinoxes, caused by the circling of the earth's axis once every 25,000 years around a north-polar point in the sky, causes a change in the direction of such lines of sight from century to century. Computing the difference between the line today and the line shown by the stones should tell, therefore, when the stones were set up. Sir Norman Lockyer dates Stonehenge and similar monuments at about 1500 B.C. by this method.

The remaining influences which bore upon Europe during this time were trade contacts and movements.

One of the most striking movements was that of the bell-beaker folk of Spain. They learned to make a peculiar bell-mouthed type of pottery ornamented with a fine herringbone pattern, and they left a trail of this pottery all along the trade routes they followed from Spain to the Baltic coast, apparently to obtain amber. Bronze working came up the old Danubian route from Troy, drawn particularly by deposits of tin in Bohemia. The local folk learned the art and established a famous bronze-working center at Aunjetitz. This center developed, according to Childe, between 2200 and 1650 B.C.

Later ironworking became prominent at Halstatt and achieved a distinctive product—a short two-edged sword which could be used either for cutting or for stabbing. This weapon proved much more deadly than the long, thrusting rapier used in the eastern Mediterranean. It may well have been the parent of the short sword with which Roman legionaries later conquered the entire civilized world west of Iran.

Another highly important aspect of European prehistory is the establishment of Indo-European speech over the entire continent. The actual spread has been accounted for in the main text (Chapter XV), but modern views about the nature of the language itself seem worth a bit of notice here.

Most modern philologists are convinced that Indo-European speech arose on the Asiatic grasslands from blending two older tongues. One was Uralic, the speech of the original postglacial inhabitants of the region. This speech was akin to the parents of modern Finnish, Magyar, Turkish and kindred tongues of the Ural-Altaic family; it also contributed an intensive use of vowels and root words expressing the most fundamental concepts such as family relations. The second element consisted of importations from Mediterranean and Mesopotamian regions, with names for many plants and animals and features of agriculture and metalworking.

This blended speech diverged early, as the nomads spread in various directions, into eastern and western divisions. This division is marked by the change in certain guttural sounds—in the East (Sanskrit, Hindustani, Iranian, etc.) into sibilant sounds and in the West into k sounds. This is the so-called Satem-Centum (pronounced Kentum) division, from the Zend and the Latin respectively for "one hundred." An example is various words for "dog"—*Kyon* in Greek and *canis* in Latin, for the Centum division, and *çao(n)* in Sanskrit and *zuon* in Lithuanian, for Satem speech. The western division was shaped further, some scholars think, on and near the plains of Hungary, as nomads amalgamated with Danubian Mediterraneans; and from there it spread Celtic, Latin and Teutonic tongues over Europe.

INDEX

Where folios in an item are not in sequence, the most important references are given first.

Abacists, 408
Abbas, Holy, 338
Abélard, Peter, 343–4
Aberration, in lenses, 415
Abi'baal script, 487
Abnormal mentality, brain waves, 39
Abram or Abraham of the Jews, 203
Abstract principle, in thought, 15, 73, 129
Academy, French, of Science, 411
Academy of Plato, 250
Acadian-Caledonian revolution, in geology, 27
Acceleration, in physics, 406
Accomplishment, as social motive, 464
Acetylcholine, 85
Acheans, 209
Achen oscillation or retreat, 478, 480
Acheulean culture, hand ax, *picture*, 78
Acquired characteristics, 25
Acrophonic principle in writing, 185
Acropolis, 212; Athenian, 242
Actium, battle, 278
A.D., in dates, 486
Adams, John, 439
Adelard of Bath, 338
Adobe brick, 121
Adrenalin, 85
Adrianople, battle, 298
Aegean Sea, 151–2, 209
Aegospotami, battle, 244
Aerial perspective, 372
Aeschylus, 240
Aesculapius, 179
Aetius, 300
Afghanistan, bread wheat, 110
Africa, as home of early man, 49, 56, 76; circumnavigation, 211, 363, 380; *map*, 362

"Age of Tyrants," 218
Agincourt, battle, 376
Agriculture: beginnings, 108–10, 124, 126; Danubian, 167; Roman, 274–5, 282, 286; medieval, 306
Agulhas, Cape, *map*, 362
Aha, King of Egypt, 147
Ahiram inscription, 487
Ahmose I, of Egypt, 197
Ahriman, 206, 311
Air, as "vital essence," 263; modern study, 414–15
Airya, 200
Akkad, 176–7, *map*, 106
Alaric, 298–9
Albertus Magnus, 351
Albigensian heresy and Crusade, 366–7
Alchemy, 337
Alcibiades, 244
Alcuin, 315
Alexander the Great, 245–6, 252, 211
Alexandria, Egypt, 254, *picture*, 265
Alexandrine Age, 254–69
Alexius Comnenus I, 333
Alfred the Englishman (translator), 338
Alfred the Great, 321–2
Algae, 22, 27
Algebra, 337, 408
Algorists, 408
Almagest of Ptolemy, 261
Almanacs, 401
"Alpha to Omega," 490
Alphabet, 185–9, 487–92
Alphonsine tables, 401
Alpine race, 89, 470, 471, 474, 475
Alps, 27
al'Ubaid culture, 116, 117–22, 142, *map*, 106

Alva, Duke of, 395
Amarna, Egypt, 189
Amarru, 194
Amber trade, 149, 150, 495
Amenemhet I, 185, 186, 177
Amenhotep, 197
America: discovery, 379, 381–2; exploration, 386, 388–90, 394; name, 388
American Indians, 475
American Revolution, 438–9; accompanying developments, 415, 419, 427
Amorites, 192, 194
Amphibians, 27, 32
Amratian culture, 141
Amri, 126
Analysis, as approach to knowledge, 347
Analytic geometry, 408
Anatolian race, 89
Anatomy, 263, 372, 402–3
Anau, Turkestan, 148–50
Anaxagoras, 240
Anaximander, 225, 255
Ancestor worship, 82
Ancient Period and History, 171–300. See also particular topics such as Assyrians, Astronomy, by name.
Ancylus Lake, 481, map, 479
Anemone, nervous system, 29
Anesthesia, mental effect, 10–11
Angerman River, map, 479
Anglo-Saxon Chronicle, 322
Anglo-Saxons, 299, 300
Animal co-operation, 71
Animism, 80, 81
Anne, Queen of England, 426
"Anthill" principle of social organization, 173, 235, 246–7, 274; Nazi Germany, 455, 458
Anthony, Saint, 309
Anthropoidea, 35, 41
Anthropology, 468
Antioch, 333
Antony, 278
Anytus, 249
Ape, 14, 41, 56, 64, diagram, 34
Ape man, 46
Apollonius of Perga, 257, 260, 408
Appalachian Revolution, 27, 32
Appearance and reality, 221–2, 225–6, 250, 296, 347, 465–6; infant's perception, picture, 13
Arabia, 49, 56, 76, 108; Semites, 159–60
Arabic culture, 159–60, 313, 335–6, 361, 474
Arabic numerals, 336–7, 365, 410

Aral Sea, 67, 68
Aramaic, 199, 487
Ararat, Mount, map, 106
Arcadius, 298
Arche, in Greek philosophy, 221
Archeozoic era, 27
Architecture, 147, 175, 236, 242, 243, 371–2
Archon, 212
Area needed by primitive family, 66
Areopagus, 229
Ariana, 200
Arian heresy, 296, 307
Aristarchus, 257, 259–60, 401
Aristides, 234
Aristogeton, 232
Aristotle, 248, 249, 251–2, 344, 346, 407
Aristyllus, 257
Arithmetic, 155–7, 336, 408
Arkwright, Richard, 427
Armageddon, 197
Armenian (Armenoid) race, 89, 475
Armillary sphere, picture, 223
Army. See in index Warfare
Arouet, François Marie, 432
Arrow straighteners, 96
Art: beginnings, 94, 95–8, 99; early ancient, 151–2, 208, 235–6, 235–7; Renaissance, 368, 372
Artifacts, 49, 76
Aryans, 115, 200, 475
Asia: as cradle of mankind, 45–6, 48–9, 51, 55–6, 59; climate, 67, 73, 481; cultural contributions, 111, 113, 125, 141, 171, 186–9, 195, 329–35, 359, 419; peoples, 88–9, 105, 159, 161, 469, 471, 475. See also Arabic culture
Asia Minor, 108, 113, 194–5, 198
Association areas, 37, 42, 44, diagram, 34
Assur-nasir-habal, 178
Assyria, 198–9, 178, 217
Astrolabe, diagram, 223
Astrology, 158
Astronomy: beginnings, 125, 153–5, 158, 191, 402; Greek, 221, 223, 240, 255–61; modern beginnings, 399–402, 406–7; present problems, 450–51
Aswan, map, 106
Athens, 228–30, 232, 238, 248–52, 335
Atlantic climate, 480, 481
Atlanto-Mediterranean race, 475
Atom, in science, 240, 444, 451
Aton, sun-disk god, 189
Attica, 228
Attila, 300, 319

Augsburg, Peace of, 393
Augustan Age of Latin literature, 280–82
Augustine, Saint, 299, 347
Augustus, 279–85, 299, 486
Aunjetitz, 495
Aurelian, 288
Aurignacian culture, 92, 480, *map,* 93
Australian aborigines, 468, 470
Australopithecus, picture, 45
Auto de fe, 367
Avars, 319
Avebury, Baron, 111
Averroes, 348
Avicenna, 337
Avignon, 377
Avoris, Egypt, 195
Axon, nerve, 31
Azilian culture, 98
Azimuth quadrant, *picture,* 398
Azores, *map,* 362

Babel, tower, 123
Babylon and Babylonia, 192, 194, 198, 199, 200–01, *map,* 106, Chaldean empire, 220–21; science, 159, 221. *See also* Sumerian culture and people
"Babylonian Captivity," of Jews, 204–5; of Papacy, 377
Bach, 466
Bacon, Roger, 352–3
Bacteria, 22, 27
Badarian culture, 140
Baghdad, 336
Ba'laat, 186, 187
Balboa, Vasco, 388
Baly, E. C., 19, 22
Baltic, 481, *map,* 479; migrations, 166; race, 89
Banking, 359
Bank of England, 425
Barbarians, Germanic, 287, 297–300
Barometer, 407
"Barracks emperors," 289
Barrell, J., 18
Barter, 94, 217
Barthélemy, Peter, 333
Bartholomew de Glanvil (the Englishman), 351
Basil, Saint, 309
Basileus, 212, 292
Basketry, 112
Batons de commandement, 95
Battering-ram, 199
Battle-ax, 149, 166
B.C., in dates, 486

Beethoven, 466
Begging friars, 357
Behaviorism, 37
Bell, Thomas, 427
Bell-beaker culture, 495
Benedict, Saint, 310
Benedictine Order and Rule, 310
Benjamin, tribe, 204
Beowulf, 322
Berger rhythms, 38–9
Bernard of Clairvaux, 344, 355–6
Berossus, 123
Bias, 215
Bible, 203, 377, 393, 492
Bile, in Greek medicine, 263
Binocular vision, 35
Biology, as a science, 413–14, 447; beginnings of life, 18–19, 21–4; cells, 447; chemistry of life, 19, 447; heredity, 5, 19–21; life eras, 26–8; mutations, variations, and species, 24–5; reproduction, 21; specialization, 41; vitalism, 24
Birds, 27, 32–3, *diagram,* 31
Birket-el-Qarun, 140, *map,* 106
Bismarck, Otto von, 453
Bitumen, 119
Black, Davidson, 47
Black Death, 419
"Black Mass" and "Black Sabbath," 366
Black race, 88, 468
Black Sea, 67
Blood, 158, 264, 304, 472–3
Blumenbach, J., 468
Blytt, A., 480
Boas, F., 470
Boats. *See in index* Ships
Boccaccio, 369
Boethius, 344
Bohemia, 10, 495
Bohlin, B., 47
Bohr, N., 446
Bojador, Cape, 363, 379–80, *map,* 362
Bologna, University of, 338
Bone industry, 77, 93
Boreal climate, 480, 481
Borreby race, 475
Boston, 423
Bouillon, Godfrey de, 333
Boulē, 212, 232, 273
Boule, Marcellin, 95
Bourbon kings, 430
Bourgeoisie, 430
Boustrophedon writing, 489
Bouvines, battle, 364
Bow and arrow, 98

Boyle, Robert, 414
Brachycephalic head, 469
Brahe, Tycho, 401–2
Brain, 29–40, 44; evolution, 43–5, 52; knowledge of, 158, 263; "storm," 39; waves, electric, 38–9
Brandenburg moraine, *map,* 479
Brazil, 387
"Bread and circuses," 132
Bread wheat, 110
Breasted, J. H., 146, 183
Breathing, 263, 443
Breuil, Abbé, 95
Brick, 126, 147, 179
Bristol Company, 423
Britain. *See* England and Britain
British Isles, in Ice Age, *map,* 93
Bronze, 174, 150, 495
Brooding reflex, 33
Brooks, C. E. P., 74
Brown race, 468
Brückner, E., 73, 477
Brunelleschi, 371
Brunton, G., 140
"Brute nature" of man, 7, 16, 130
Bühl advance or stadium, 478, 118, 140, 480
Building construction, 75
Bulb of percussion, 78
Bulgars, 319
Burning, 443
Burning glass, 264–5
Bushmen, 468, 470
Byblos, 144, 150, 487, 488, *map,* 106
Byzantine Empire. *See* Eastern Empire, Roman
Byzantium, 295. *See also* Constantinople

Cabot, John, 374, 394
Cadmus, 488
Caesar, 278, 292
Caesar, Julius, 276, 278, 483
Caesar, Saint, 310
Cahors, 359
Cairo, 179, 181
Calculus, 412
Caledonian revolution, in geology, 27
Calendar: early ancient, 131, 481–2, 193; Egyptian, 482–3; Julian, 483; modern (Gregorian), 483
Callicrates, 242
Caloric, 414, 443–4
Calvin, John, 393
Cambridge University, 338, 410, 412
Cambyses, 201

Canaan and Canaanites, 210, 203, 489
Canary Islands, 361, 363, *map,* 362
Cannon, 376, 394, 405
Cannon, W. B., 84
Cano, Juan, 390
Capetian kings, 323, 430
Capillary circulation of blood, 404
Capital and Capitalism, 172, 217, 282, 375, 437–8, 440, 448–9
Cappadocian race, 474, 475
Capsian culture, 98, 140, 141, *picture,* 96
Captivity, Jewish, 204, 488; of Papacy, 377
Caracalla, 287, 288
Caravel, 380
Carbohydrates, 19
Carbon, 19
Carboniferous Age, 27
Carchemish, 194
Cardinals, College of, 364
Carmel, Mt., *map,* 106; early man, 6, 90, 474, 475
Carnac, 493, 494
Carolina, 422
Carolingian kings, 314
Carpathian Mts., 167, 480
Carrel, Alexis, 466
Carte Pisane, 374
Carte Vesconti, 374
Carthage, 211, 274
Cartwright, E., 427
Caspian race, 471
Caspian Sea, 67, 148
Cassian, Saint, 309
Cassino, Monte, 310, 338, 349
Catalan Expedition, 374
Catfish mentality, 30, 83
Catharist heresy and crusade, 366
Catholics, Roman, 307, 308. *See also* Christianity
Catiline, 277
Caton-Thompson, G., 140
Catullus, 280
Caucasian race, 6, 88, 162
Causality, 14, 15, 64, 129
Cave men of Europe, 91, 94–8, *picture,* 99
Cavendish, Henry, 442
Caxton, William, 378
Cedars of Lebanon, 150
Celestial globe, 153
Cell, in biology, 447, 22–3; nerve, 29, *diagram,* 31; reproductive, 24–5, *diagram,* 20
Celtic, horse, 97; language, 496; race, 166
Cenozoic era, 27, 28
Central nervous system, 30

Centum speech, 496
Cephalic indices, 469
Ceramic arts, 120
Chagar Bazar, 116
Chain reflexes, 32, 33
Chalcolithic culture, 121
Chaldean Empire, 220–21
Châlons, battle, 300
Chancelade race, 92
Chancellor and chancery, 327, 328
Change, in philosophy, 227, 412
Character: "strength of," 130; training, 461
Characteristics, acquired and inherited, 25
Chariot fighting, 195
Charlemagne, 314, 319, 330, 336
Charles V, emperor and king of Spain, 387, 390, 392
Charles, of England: I, 433, 435; II, 435
Charles Martel, 314
Charters, English, 340, 341, 342, 359
Chaucer, Geoffrey, 369, 377
Chefren, 182
Chemistry, 413–4, 442, 446
Cheops, 181
Child mentality, 11–15, 39, 63, 80, 94, 133, picture, 13
Childe, V. Gordon, 115, 146, 167, 494, 495
Chilon of Sparta, 215
Chimpanzee, 14, 24, 64, diagram, 50
Chin, in man, 44
China, 105, 126, 165, 149, 360–61, 378
Chioggia, battle, 379
Chippenham, siege, 321
Chivalry, 339
Choukoutein cave fossils, 47
Christ, birth, 486
Christianity: beginnings, 287, 289–91, 293; Constantine recognizes, 294–6; medieval, 307–11, 325–8, 349–50; monks and hermits, 309–10; orthodoxy and heresy, 295–7, 366–7; Papacy, 308–9, 363–4, 377–8, 392–3; Protestantism, 391–3; social and philosophic aspects, 294, 295, 310, 326–8, 349–50
Chromatic aberration, 415
Chromosomes, 19, 21
Chronology: geologic and prehistoric, 26–8, 73, 146, 477–82; historic, 482–6
Chronometer, 411
Churingas, 100
Cicero, 276–8
Cimmerians, 200
Circle, diagram, 409

Circuits, in administration of justice, 340
Circumpolar stars, 182, diagram, 154
Cire-perdue casting, 175
Cist graves, 494
City of God, The, 299
City-state, 171, 212
Civilization: beginnings, 105–16, 481–2, map, 106; fundamental needs, 108, 168, 190–91; historic highlights, early, 117–28, 137–53, 148, 159, 171–3, 185, 195, 196–8, 215–6. See also Decadence and regeneration; Economic organization; Political organization; Progress; Social organization; and various historic cultures by name
Civil law, 342, 459–60
Clark, J. G. D., 481
Class distinctions, 426, 430, 432
"Classical" mechanics and physics, 451
Clay-working, 120–21
Cleobulus, 215
Clerk-Maxwell, James, 445
Clermont, Council, 332
Client, in Roman landowning, 305
Climate: preglacial and glacial, 55, 67–8, 74, diagrams, 75; Mediterranean type, 107; modern, 101, 105–8, 164, 165, 480–1
Clisthenes, 232, 343
Clocks, 405, 410; water, picture, 266
Clothing, 69, 93, 112, 135, 370
Clovis, 314
Cluniac reform, 325, 330
Cnossus, 152. See also Knossos.
Coal, 426
Cod fishery, 422, 423
Code of Justinian, 327
Coelenterates, 27
Colonization, 219, 385, 387, 397, 421, 424
Colonus, Roman, 305
Color, as race test, 468, 472
Columbus, 374, 381–2, 387, 401
Combe-Capelle man, 92, 475
Combining weights, in chemistry, 444
Combustion, 414, 443
Comitatus, 305
Commendation, in land ownership, 305
Commerce: beginnings, 94–5, 121, 125, 146, 148–56, 495; ancient, 150, 152, 165, 193, 210–11, Greek and Roman, 216–7, 231, 239, 254–5, 272, 275, 286; medieval, beginnings, 304, 316; Byzantine empire, 312, 359–60, 375–6; Crusades stimulate, 331, 334; Italian cities, 331, 334, 359–60, 373, 379; modern,

Commerce—*Cont'd*
beginnings, 368, 375, 379–82, 385, 387, 390, 397; evolution, 418–28, 434–5, 437–8, 440, 448–9, 451–4; *principles,* money, use of, 172, 217, 420; monopoly and free trade, 358, 373, 385, 387, 390, 394, 397, 419, 421, 424–8, 437–8; profit motive, 358, 434–5, 448–9, 451–2, 457–9
Commercial Revolution, 419, 458
"Common man, the," 132, 417–19, 435, 439, 452
Common Pleas, Court of, 342
Compass, magnetic, 336, 339
Concordat of Worms, 363
Conditioning, in psychology, 33, 416, 462
Confession, Church, 367
Congo, 195
Conic sections, 408
Conquest, impulse from nomads, 167
Conscience and right, 183, 204–5, 248–9, 325–6
Consciousness, or self-awareness, 11, 12, 24, 36, 37–8; emotional coloring, 84–6, 129–30, 133–5; mechanistic interpretation, 6, 24, 37–8, 416–7, 449–50, 466
Conspicuous waste, as mark of social distinction, 426
Constance, Council of (1414–18), 377–8
Constantine, 294, 296, 297
Constantine the African, 338
Constantinople, 295, 312, 375–6
Constructive imagination, 14, 64, 68, 129
Contract, social, 436–7
Coon, C. S., 473
Co-operation: animal, 71; social, 70–72
Copernicus, 40
Copper, 121–2, 142, 152
Coptos, 146
Corals, 27
Corded Folk, 166, 475
Cordova, 335
Corinth, 215–16, 219, 274
Coronado, 388
Corpus juris civilis, 327
Cortex, of brain, 35
Cortez, Hernando, 388
Cosmic rays, 25
Cosmos, early ancient ideas, 157–8. *See also* Universe
Cottage industry, 427
Cotton, 126
Council of elders, 212, 273
Counting, 155–8
Coup de poing, 77

Courts of Justice, 229, 328, 365; English, 321, 340, 342
Craniometric test of race, 469
Cranium, evolution, 51
Crassus, 276
Crécy, battle, 376
Cretan bull, 209
Crete, 150–52, 208–9, *map,* 106
Crime, remedies for, 7, 460
Crimea, Greek grain trade, 231
Criminal law, 459, 460–1
Critical attitude, 207, 220
Croesus, 201, 217
Cro-Magnons, 90, 92, 100, 166, 474, 475, *pictures,* 96
Crompton, Samuel, 427
Crossopterygians, 32
Crotona, 226
Crown land, 305, 321
Crusades, 329–35, 359, 419
Crustacea, 27
Ctesibius, 266
Cultivation (agric.), 109, 110
Cuneiform writing, 487, *picture* of method, 127
Curia, Roman, 271
Curie, Marie and Pierre, 446
Curiosity, 63
Customary law, 327
Cycladic cultures, 153
Cycles, in business, 452
Cylinder seal, *picture,* 127
Cymotrichous race, 471
Cynics, 283
Cynodonty, *diagram,* 50
Cyprus, 152, 209
Cyrus I, 200–1, 205, 206, 226

Dacia, 288
Daha, 200
Dale, Sir H., 84
Dale, Sir Thomas, 422–3
Dalton, John, 444
Dandolo, 359
Danegeld, 340
Daniglacial retreat, of fourth glaciation, 480, *map,* 479
Dante Alighieri, 369
Danubian culture, 167, 474, 475
Dardanelles, 150, 231
Dare, Virginia, 422
Darius I, 233
Dark Ages, 304–29, 343–5
Dart, Raymond, 45
Darwin, Charles, 447

Darwinian theory, 25
"Dawn Light" of the Renaissance, 369
Dawson, Charles, 53
Decadence and Regeneration: early ancient, 176-7, 182-6, 193-4, 209; Greek, 267-9; Roman, 270, 275-8, 282-4, 286-9, 291-2, 297-300; medieval (Dark Ages), 318-25, 328; modern, 424-6, 431-2, 439
Decameron, 369
Decimal notation, 156
Dedefre, 182
Deductive approach to knowledge, 347, 353
Defender of the Faith, 333
Deferent, 259, diagram, 258
Degrees of circle, 157
Delian League, 234, 242
Della Robbia, 371
Delta, in Egypt, 139, 142
Demagogues, 132, 230, 343, 439
Demarcation, line of, 387, 389
Democracy: beginnings, 163, 218; Greek and Roman, 228-30, 232-5, 241-4, 268, 271, 274, 277; modern, 340, 341-3, 436-7, 462; perils of demagoguery, 132, 218, 230, 243-4, 439-40
De Morgan, J. J. M., 146
Descartes, René, 408, 416
Desert horse, 97
De Soto, Hernando, 388
Destiny of man, 466
"Deus vult," 332
Devil, 311, 345, 354
Dialectic, 238
Diaz, Bartholomew, 380; Diniz, 380
Diderot, Denis, 432
Diet, head shape affected, 470, 471, 474
Digest, of Justinian, 327
Dimensions, in physics, 451
Dinaricization, 475
Dinosaurs, 27
Diocletian, 291-4
Dionysiac festival, 231
Dionysius Exiguus, 486
Dipsomaniac, 32
Disharmonic head, 91
"Dismal Science, the," 448
Dispositions (primitive thought), 82
Dissection, 264, 263, 365, 402
Distribution, as social problem, 419
Divine Comedy, 369
"Divine right of kings," 365, 433, 437
Division of the Roman Empire, 292
Dixon, R. B., 471

Dnieper River, 164, 166, 288, 481
Doge, of Venice, 373
Dogs, domestication, 99
Dolichocephalic, 469, 470
Dollond, John, 415
Dolmens, 494
Dome, in architecture, 371
Domesticated animals, 99, 110
Dominance in heredity, 21
Donatello, 371, 372
Dorian Greeks, 209
Dorias, of Genoa, 374
Double ax, 151, picture, 127
Double-entry bookkeeping, 434
Draco's laws, 229
Drake, Francis, 394, 396
Drama, 231-2, 339
Drill, Egyptian, picture, 180
"Drinks like a fish," 32
"Driver type" of mentality, 133, 134
Drosophila melanogaster, 19
Drought, 105, 107, 149, 165, 481
Drunkenness, confirmed, 32
Duan advance, 478, 481
Dubois, E., 46
Duel, 370
Duns Scotus, 351-2
Duodecimal arithmetic, 157
Duplations, 408, 409
Dutch language, 162
Dutch War of Independence, 395
Dynamics, 404, 412

Eannes, Gil, 380
Ear, diagram, 45
Earth: age and history, 17, 25-8, 450; ancient views, 157-8, 221-2, 225, 255, 257, 260-1; medieval views, 363, 381; size, 260-1
Eastern Empire, Roman, 292, 311, 330-34, 359-60, 375-6
"Eat, drink, and be merry," 283
Ecclesia, 212, 230
Eclipses, 221, 224, 398, 399
Ecliptic, 255, 257, diagrams, 256, 261
Economic Organization: beginnings, 54, 92, 94, 121, 125, 172-3; Greek and Roman, 277, 279, 282, 292; Industrial Revolution, 426-7; principles, group control, 172-3, labor's interest, 217, 239, 418-19, 454, laissez-faire (mechanistic interpretation), 438, 448-9, 541-4; money and profit motive, 358, 434-5, 448-9, 451-2, 457-9; scarcity and abundance, 454, 456, 459; sound

Economic Organization—*Cont'd*
　adaptation to human nature, 458–9,
　463–4. *See also* Commerce
"Economy of abundance," 454–5, 456, 464
Edict of Milan, 294
Education: Greek, 222, 249–50, 252;
　medieval, 315, 338, 344, 365; *picture,*
　325; modern, 410, 437, 461–2
Edward I, England, 342, 376
Edwin Smith papyrus, 158
Effective level of nervous tension, 35
Egg cell, 21
Ego. *See* Consciousness
Egyptian culture and people, *map,* 106;
　beginnings, 92, 107–10, 126, 137–47,
　Mediterranean racial stock, 89, 470–71,
　473, megalithic, Minoan offshoots, 494,
　151, Syrian contact, 144, 150; *de-*
　velopments, agriculture, 109–10, 138,
　179, *picture,* 180, architecture, 175, 179,
　astronomy, 153, *diagram,* 154, 157–8,
　402, calendar and chronology, 179,
　482–5, commerce and trade, 141, 146,
　150, 152, 210, 254–5, *picture,* 265,
　government, 142–3, 183–5, industrials,
　140–41, *pictures,* 180, mathematics,
　155–7, medicine 158, 262, 263–4,
　slavery, 172–3, writing, 144–6, 185–8;
　history, chronology, 140, 482–5, dynastic
　(pharaohs), 143, 179–83, 185, 176–7,
　195, 197, 201, 203, 210, Ptolemaic and
　Roman, 254–5, 274, 282; *mental forces,*
　conservative ("group") thinking, 137,
　168, 171–2, 189–90, 235, ethics, 137–9,
　144, 183–4, 189–90, science, 153–8,
　220–21, religion, 138, 141, 142, 143–4,
　147, 183–4, 189–90
Eighteenth Dynasty, 197, 203, dating, 484
Einstein theory, 413, 450
Elam, 200, *map,* 106
Elders, council of, 212
Eleatic doctrine, 227
Electric brain waves, 38–9
Electricity, 445, 446–7
Electrocoagulation of brain, 39
Electronic theory of matter, 446, 447
Elizabeth, of England, 394, 395, 403,
　421, 426
Elliot-Smith. *See* Smith, Grafton Elliot
Ellipse, *diagram,* 409
Elne, Synod, 331
Embryology, 403, *diagram,* 34
Emery, 152
Emery, W. B., 147
Emmer, 110

Emotion: cause, physical, 84–6; control,
　130; emotional personality, 133–4; in-
　telligence affected, 81, 130, 132–4, 239;
　medieval importance, 332, 354–5; mod-
　ern view, 416–7, 457
Emperor worship, 279, 289, 293
Encyclopedists, medieval, 351; French,
　432
England and Britain: beginnings, 51, 52,
　53, 55, 56, 77, *map,* 93; *developments,*
　commerce and trade, 292, 358, 394,
　397, 421–25, 427, 433–6, 440, 448–9,
　453, democracy, 340–3, 436–7, gov-
　ernment, 321, 340–3, 433, 435–6, In-
　dustrial Revolution (Machine Age),
　426–7, 437–8, 440, 448–9, 451–4, law,
　327, 340, 342, literary beginnings, 322,
　369, 377, navy, 393, 396–7, 440, North
　American colonies, 421–4, 433, 438–9,
　printing, 378, 436, science, 351, 402–3,
　410, 411–17, 442–8, taxation, 322, 340–
　41, 342; *history,* Anglo-Saxons, 300,
　Danes (Norse), 320, 324, Alfred the
　Great, 321–2, Normans, 323, 324,
　Anglo-Norman kings, 340–43, 364,
　long bow and gunpowder (Crécy) 376,
　Tudors, 393–7, Stuarts, 433, 435, Wil-
　liam and Mary, 435, American Revolu-
　tion, 438–9, nineteenth-century growth,
　440
English language, 162, 322, 369, 377, 492
English Revolutions, 419, 435–6
Engrossing, 359
Entelechy, 24
Eoanthropus dawsoni, 53
Eocene, 28, 36
Eoliths, 77
Epaminondas, 245
Epicureanism, 283
Epicycle, in astronomy, 259, 401, *dia-*
　gram, 258
Epilepsy, 39
Epinephrin, 85
Epipaleolithic culture, 101, 480
Equity, 326, 327, 342
Erasistratus, 263
Erasmus, Desiderius, 391
Eratosthenes, 257, 260, 381
Erech, 116, 118, 122–3, 176
Erect posture, 42, 52
Eskimos, 77, 96, 470
"Essences," in science, 414, 444
Eternity, 350, 466
Ether, in physics, 413, 414, 445

Ethical thinking: early 138–9, 172–3, 183–5, 189–90, 203–7; Greek and Roman, 216, 238–9, 248–9, 267–9, 282–4, 287; medieval (Christian), 307, 310–11, 325–8, 349–50; modern, 370, 429–30, 433–5, 436–7, 457, 461–4

Ethiopia, 107, 110

Etruscans, 210, 272, 489

Eudoxus of Cnidus, 255

Eupatrids, 212

Euphrates, R., 108, 192, *map,* 106

Europe: as early home of man, 47, 49–54; climate evolution, 55, 73–6, 101–2, 480–81; Ice-Age life, 92–102, 480, *map,* 93; neolithic life, 150, 167, 493–6; nomad intrusions, 166–8; races, 89–92, 473–5, 493–6. *See also* cultural aspects, nations, and peoples by name

Evangelical poverty, 377, 391

Evans, Sir, A. J., 151

Evil, in religious thought, 144, 184, 206, 311, 354–5

Evolution, biology, 25, 447. *See also* Man; Mentality

Exchequer, Court of, 342

Exodus, 197

Experience, learning from, 33–4

Experiment, in science. *See* Science

Exploitation, economic: early 163–4, 167, 275–6, 282, medieval, early modern, 373–4, 385–90, 424–5; nineteenth century (laissez faire and profit motive), 427–9, 433–5, 448–9, 451–2, 454–5, 457–9

Exploration: ancient, 149, 211, 219; medieval, 324, 360–63, 374, 379–82; modern (from discovery of America), 381–2, 389–90, 394

Eyck, Van, 371

Eye, 29

"Eye for an eye," 193

Fabricius, J., 403

Faith and reason, 35–8, 225–7, 346–50, 449–50, 465–7

Falling bodies, 405, 406, 412

Fall of Rome, 299, 300

Family, origin, 71

Faraday, Michael, 445

"Father of English Poetry," 369

"Father of History," 252

"Father of Scientific History," 253

Faustrecht, 328

Fayum, in Egypt, 140

Fear, 84, 85, 86

Fee, in land, 305

Felt, 162

Fennoscandian moraine, *map,* 479

Ferdinand, King of Spain, 387

Ferdinand of Tuscany, 408

Fère-en-Tardenois culture, 98

Ferns, 27

"Fertile crescent" in S.W. Asia, 160

Fertility goddesses, 97, 142, 151

Fertilization, 21

Feudalism, 305, 308, 317, 328, 376, 420

Fief, 305

Finger counting, 155, 156

Finiglacial retreat, 480, *map,* 479

Finnish, language, 495

Fire: earliest uses, 47, 65, 68, 72; "fire air," 443; true nature, 205–6; worship of, 205–6

Firearms, 376

First Causes, 465

First Dynasty (Egypt), 143, 145, 147, 175, 484

Fisc, of land, 304, 305

Fischer, E., 19

Fishes, 27, 30, 32, 33, 35, 83; brain, *diagrams,* 31, 35

Flake tools, 77, 78

Flanders, 335, 358

Flanged tools, *picture,* 180

Flax, 112

Fleure, H. J., 101, 149, 174, 480, 485

Flintworking, 64, 78, 93, 141

Floods, Mesopotamian, 118

Florence, 360, 371, 374, 375, 420

Flowering plants, 27

Flux (philosophy), 227

Foederati, 289

Food gatherers and producers, 92

Food supply, 59–60, 66, 108–10, 124–5, 420, 454

Force of habit, 113–4

Ford, Henry, 459

Forehead, 43

Forestalling, 359

Formosus, Pope, 318

Forms, Socratic, 250

Fourth dimension, 451

Fourth Dynasty (Egypt), 181

Fra Angelico, 371

France: *beginnings,* 74, 77, 78, 89, 480, Cro-Magnons, 91–101, neolithic, 167, 493–4; *developments,* arts and amenities, 324, 339, 378, commerce and trade, 324, 358, 359, 453, government, 322–3, 344, 430–32, 439–40, 453,

France—*Cont'd*
    language, 162, 367, schools and universities, *picture,* 325, 337, 338, 343–4, 357, science, 325, 403, 407, 408, 411, 432, 443, 446, 447; *history* (incl. Gaul), ancient, 219, 288, 300, medieval, 313–5, 317, 320, 322–3, 331, 364, 366–7, 376, 377, modern, 395, 430–32, 438–40, 453
Francis, Saint, of Assisi, 357
Franciscans, 357–8, 377, 391
Franklin, Benjamin, 439
Franks, 288, 300, 313, 323
Frazer, Sir G. J., 80
Frederick of Saxony, 393
Frederick II, Holy Roman emperor, 364–6
Freedom of press, 433, 436
Freedom of thought: beginnings, 63–4, 68–73, 81; early ancient gains, 130–31, 172, 176, 190, 196, 201, 202; Greek gains, 207, 216–22, 236–7, 239, 241; medieval struggle for, 311, 335, 343–5, 346–56, 379; modern, 392, 398–417, 429
Free-field decoration of pottery, 113
Free trade: medieval restrictions, 358–9, 373–4, 375; modern evolution, 385, 387, 390, 397, 421, 424, 427–8, 438
Free will, 346, 347, 349, 350
"Freezing" (fear), 84
French and Indian War, 438
French language, 162
French Revolution, 419, 439–40
Freud, Sigmund, 417
Friars, orders of, 357–8
Frizzy-haired race, 471
Frogs, 27
Frontal lobe of brain, 43
Frontal region of brain, *diagram,* 34
Fruit fly, 19
Fulcher, on Crusades, 333
Funeral gifts, 96, 139

Gaelic, language, 162
Galerius, 294
Galileo, 405, 406, 407, 408, 415
Galley Hill man, 52, 78, 88, 92
Galvani, 445
Gama, Vasco da, 389
Games and play, 63
Garden culture, 111
Gardiner, A. H., 186–7
Garrod, D., 90
Gases, modern studies, 415
Gattamelata, statue, 372
Gebal, 487, 150

Gebel-el-Arak knife, 146
Geber, 337
Geddes, P., 24
Geer, Baron de, 478–9, 480
Geocentric theory of solar system, 257, 260
Geochronological dating, 478–80
Geography and exploration: medieval, 338–9, 360–63, 374, 379–82; modern, 381–2, 388, 389–90, 410–11
Geologic eras and time, 25, 27, 450, 477. *See also* Earth
Geometry, 157, 251, 408
Genes, 21, 25, *diagram,* 20
Genius, 466
Genoa, 359, 331, 373, 379, 397
George, Kings of England, 426
Georgia, 424
Gerard of Cremona, 338
Gerbert, *picture,* 325
Germ cells, 19, 21, 23, 24–5
Germ theory of disease, 447
German barbarians in Roman times, 288–9, 297–300, 314
Germany and Germanic lands: *beginnings,* 51, 74–6, 89, Cro-Magnons, 92–8, 100, neolithic, 115, 150, 166, 167, 495; *developments,* arts and crafts, 358, 440, commerce and trade, 150, 335, 360, 453, 495, feudalism, 304–6, 307, language, 162, 377, law, 327, printing, 378–9, science, *picture,* 398, 402, 407–8, 410, 443, 446, 447, 449; *history,* early, 166, 288–9, 297–300, medieval, 304–6, 316–17, 319, 332, 363–5, 377, modern, 391–3, 453, 458
Gerzean culture, 141–3, 145, *picture,* 180
Ghiberti, 371
Gibbon (ape), 41
Giddings, F. H., 171
Gilbert, Sir Humphrey, 421–2
Gilds (Guilds), 358, 427
Gilgamesh, 118
Gimiri, 200
Giotto, 371
Gizeh, 181, 182, *map,* 106
Glaciation, 73–6, 93, 476–80
Glassworking, 358, 360, 373
Gnosticism, 295
"God of medicine," 179
Gold, monetary use, 217, 420
Golden Age of Athens, 234–45
Golden Age of Latin literature, 280–82
Goldenweiser, A. A., 81

Good and evil in religion, 138, 144, 183–4, 204–6. *See also* Christianity
Good Hope, Cape of, 380, *map,* 362
Gorgias, sophist, 238
Goshen, Land of, 195
Gothic cathedrals, 354, 357
Gotiglacial retreat, 479
Goths, 166, 288, 297, 300
Gourd type of pottery, 113
Government. *See* Political organization
Grace, in theology, 347, 350
Gracchi, of Rome, 276–7
Grapes, Greek cultivation, 231
Grasslands, 42, 49, 55, 107, 161, 164
Gravitation, 406, 412, 413, 450, 451
Gray Friars, 357–8
Great Britain. *See* England and Britain
Great Pyramid, 181
Great Schism, 377
"Great Voyages, Period of," 385
Greek culture and people: *beginnings,* 152–3, 198, 201, 207–9, 211–12; *developments,* art, 152, 231, 236–7, calendar, 482, 486, democracy, 218, 228–34, free thought, 207, 216, 218, 220–22, 225–6, 247, history created, 252–4, language and writing, 162, 370, 488–91, philosophy and science, 221–2, 225–8, 238–9, 240, 245, 248–52, 255–68, religion, 222–3, 225, 240–41, 246–7, 267–8; *history,* 207–9, 218–9, 228–34, 240–45, 254–5, 274; *mental forces,* 152–3, 215–6, 237–40, 247, 267–8
Greenland, 470, 474
Greenwich observatory, 411
"Gregarious instinct," 71
Gregory VIII, Pope, 483
Gregory IX, Pope, 366, 367
Gregory XI, Pope, 377
Gregory, W. K., 44
Grimaldi race, 92
Group feeling, 71, 168
Grosseteste, Roger, 352, 353, 356
Gschnitz advance, 118, 140, 478, 481, 485
Guam, island, 390
Guericke, Otto von, 407
Guidi, Tommaso, 372
Guilds, 358, 427
Gunpowder, 376
Günz glaciation, 73
Günz-Mindel interglacial, 73
Gutenberg, Johann, 378
Gyri, of brain, 35

Habiru, 203

Habit, 113–14, 132, 239, 287, 289, 417
Haddon, A. C., 471
Hadendoa, 109
Hafrsfiord, battle, 319
Hair, as racial test, 89, 471
Hairspring, 411
Halstatt, 495
Halys R., 195, 224, *map,* 106
Hammurabi, 192–3, 482
Hand ax, 77, *picture,* 78
Hand, effect upon mentality, 36, 42
Hand mutilation (magic), 95
Hanging Gardens of Babylon, 220
Hanseatic League, 360, 397
Harappa, 126
Hargreaves, J., 427
Harmodious, 232
Harold Fairhair, 319
Harran, battle, 199
Harris, Z. S., 487
Harun-al-Rashid, 330, 336
Harvard graduates, growth studies, 473
Harvey, William, 403
Hatshepsut, Queen, 197
Hatti, or Hittites, 194–8
Head shape, as race test, 469, 471, 475
Hearing, 44, *diagram,* 34
Heart, 85, 158, 263
Heat, 443
Heavens, apparent motion, 153
Hebrew, 199, 203, 487
Hedge priests, 377
Hegira, 312
Heidelberg man, 51, 88
Heinrich, 122
Heliacal rising of Sirius, 483, 484
Heliocentric theory of the solar system, 256–7, 258
Hell, medieval concept, 354
Helladic cultures, 153
Hellas and Hellenes, 207, 209
Hellenistic Age, 254–69
Henry, of England: I, 340, II, 340, 341, VII, 393–4, VIII, 393–4, 395
Henry, of Navarre (IVth of France), 395, 430
Henry, Joseph, 445
Henry the Navigator, of Portugal, 379–80
Heraclitus, 227
Hercynian revolution, 27, 32
"Herd instinct," 71
Herding and herdsmen, 161–2, 163–4
Heredity, 5, 19
Heresy, 295, 366
Herman of Germany, 338

Hermits, 309
Hero of Alexandria, 267
Herodotus, 252, 176, 181, 272, 461
Heroic Age, in Greece, 212
Herophilus, 263
Herrick, C. J., 38
Hertz, H., 446
Hevelius, *picture*, 398
Hezekiah, 488
Himalaya Mts., 27
Hindu arithmetic, 336, 365
Hindus, 128, 200
Hindustani, 162, 496
Hipparchus, astronomer, 261, 400
Hipparchus, Athenian tyrant, 232
Hippias, Athenian tyrant, 232
Hippias, sophist, 238
Hippocrates, 261–2
Hirzfeld, L. and H., 473
Hisan, month, 486
History, written, 141, 144, 252–4
Hit (Mesopotamia), 108, 117, 119
Hittites, 194–8, 209, 216, 272
Hobbes, T., 416, 437
Hoe and hoe culture, 111, *pictures*, 127, 180
Holocene, 74
Holy Abbas, 338
Holy office (Inquisition), 367
Holy Roman Empire, 314, 315, 363
Hominidae, 35, 41, 42, 43, 49
Homo neanderthalensis, 52
Homo sapiens, 9
Honorius, 298–300
Hooke, Robert, 410, 411, 414
Horace, 280
Horse, 97, 161, 164, 196, 271
Horus, 142, 144
Hospitalers, 334
Hottentots, 468, 470
Housing. *See* Shelter
Hrozny, Frederic, 194
Hugh Capet, 323
Hugh the Welf, 322
Huguenots, 430
Humanism, 370, 391
Human nature: *basis, physical*, 7, 16, 81, 84–6, 130, 132–4, 239; *characteristics and needs*, 108, 128, 135–6, free will, 346, 347–50, individual aggrandizement, 168, 190–91, 328, 393, 417, 463–7; religious hope, 136, 183–5, 267–8, 282–4, 307–10, 465–6, social conditioning, 462–3; *understanding of*, Greek, 236,

237, 238, 239, medieval, 350, modern, 4–9, 416–17, 449–50, 457–67
Human sacrifice, 147, 176
"Humors" in Greek medicine, 263
Hunger, 83
Hungary, 319, 496
Huns, 297, 300, 319
Hunting life, 92
Huntington, Ellsworth, 101, 149, 210, 479
Huss, John, 377
Hutten, Ulrich von, 391
Huygens, C., 410, 413
Hybridization, in man, 91, 474
Hydrogen, 443
Hyksos, 195, 197
Hyperbola, *diagram*, 409
Hypothesis, 249

Ice Age (Pleistocene): cause, Simpson's theory, *diagram*, 476; climate effects, 73–4, *diagram*, 75; dating, periods, and end, 28, 73, 105, 477–80; man during, 49, 91–101, 475
Iceland, 219, 474
Ictinus, 242
Ideas, 129–31, 250
Ideograms, 145
Idrisi, 338, 361
Ikhnaton, 197, 189, 203
Imagination, 15, 43, 64, 133
Imhotep, 179, 485
Immortality, hope for, 136, 144, 183, 267–8, 282, 310
Imperator, 279
Indeterminacy, 451
India, 77, 105, 162, 200, 336, 379, 381
Indians, American, 475
Individual interest. *See* Human nature
Indo-European languages, 162–3, 495–6
Inductive approach to knowledge, 347, 353
Indulgences, 391, 392
Indus civilization, 126
Infant psychology, 11–15
Industrial Revolution, 419, 458
Infinity, 350, 466
Inflation and debasement, monetary, 230, 285–6, 420, 458
Inheritance, in biology, 21, 22, 25
In hoc signo vinces, 294
Ink, printing, 378
Innocent, Popes: III, 357, 364–5, 366; IV, 356
Inquisition, 367
Insanity, brain waves, 39

Insects, 27
Instincts, 32
Institutes, of Justinian, 327
Insurance, marine, 421, 425
Intelligence, 3, 4, 6, 10–16; development, 43, 56, 61–4, 66, 68–72, 78; emotion colors, 81, 130, 132–4, 239; Greek, 222; mechanistic explanation, 416–17, 449–50. *See also* Consciousness; Human nature
Interest on money, 193, 358
Interglacial periods, 73
Intuitive knowledge, 466
Invention, 15, 68, 69, 78, 173
Investiture conflict, 363
Ionian philosophers, 222
Ionians, 209
Iran, 68, 105, 110, 200, *map,* 106. *See also* Persia and Persians
Iranian language, 162, 496
Irano-Afghan race, 448
Iris, of eye, 29
Iron, 195, 495
"Iron law of wages," 448
Irrigation, 124, 126, 179
Isaac the Jew, 338
Isaiah, in Bible, 204
Isis, 283
Islam, 312–13
Israelites, 204
Italian language origin, 162
Italy: *beginnings,* 76, 89, 92, 98, 107, 152; *developments,* commercial city-states, 331, 334, 359–60, 373–6, 379, explorers, 360–63, 379, Renaissance, 369–73, schools and learning, 338, 349, 378, science, 365, 402, 405–7, 410, 411, 445, 446; *history,* 308–9, 314, 315, 316, 318, 319, 324, 364–5, 379

James, of England: I, 403, 422, 435; II, 435
James, William, 4–5, 449, 450
Jamestown, Virginia, 422
Jansen, Z., 406, 415
Japan, 378, 453
Jastrow, J., 81
Java ape man, 46, *diagram,* 50
Javelin throwers, 96
Jaw, 43, 47, 51, 52, *diagrams,* 50
Jefferson, Thomas, 439
Jellyfish, 27, 30
Jemdet Nasr, 116, 196, *map,* 106
Jeremiah, in Bible, 204
Jericho, 203

Jerusalem, 205, 204, 333
Jews, 195, 203–5, 488
Jihad, 313
John of England, 340, 364
John of Spain (translator), 338
Joly, J., 26
Jordan, river and valley, 204
Joseph, in Bible, 203
Judah, tribe, 204
Judgment after death, 184
Julian II, Pope, 387
Julian calendar, 483
Jury, Athenian, 230, 242
Jus gentium, 326
Justinian, 319, 327, 335, 342
Jutes, 300

Kahun papyrus, 484
Kargans, 166
Karnak, 197, *map,* 106
Karun R., 117, *map,* 106
Kassites (Kasseans), 194
Kay, John, 427
"Keeper of the king's conscience," 327
Keith, Sir A., 5–6, 43, 90
Kelvin, Lord, 450
Kennebec River settlement, 422
Kepler, J., 402, 408
Keying, mental, 83
Khafre, 182
Khowarizmi, al, 337
Khufu, 181, 182
Kidd, Capt. William, 425
Kidesh, 195
Killigrew, Lady, Cornish pirate, 421
Kinahhi and Kinahni, 210
King's Bench, Court of, 342
King's justices, 340
Kinza, 195
Kish, 192, *map,* 106
Knights of St John, 334
Knights Templars, 334
Knossos, 152, 208, 209
"Know thyself," 215
Köhler, W., 14
Kropotkin, Peter, 71
Kuban river culture, 165, 166
Kublai Khan, 360

Labor: ancient, 109, 172, 217, 239, 267, 274–5, 292; medieval, 306–7, 339–40, 359, 365, 376; modern rise, 418–20, 427–8, 448–9, 452, 454, 456–7, 464
Labor-saving tools, 111
Lachish, 488

Ladogan race, 475
"Laissez faire," 438, 440, 457
Lamp, in Ice Age, 98
Land, ownership, 124, 275, 277, 286, 304, 305, 342
Landlord, origin, 125
Land plants, 27
Langdon, S., 196
Language, 60, 72, 162
Langue d'oc and langue d'œil, 367
Lappish race, 475
"Last Roman of them all," 300
Laterau Council (1215), 367
Latin, 162, 496, 370; alphabet and writing, 491-2, diagram, 489; literature, 280-82
Latin conquest of Constantinople, 359-60
Latin plain, 272-3
Latitude and longitude, 261, 399, 410, picture, 320
Latium, 272
Laurentian portolani, diagram, 362, 374
Laurium, 233
Lavoisier, A., 404, 443
Law: early ancient, 192, Greek and Roman, 229, 230, 326, 365; medieval (incl. English), 326-8, 340-43; modern, 7, 459-61
Lay abbots and bishops, 319
Leaning tower of Pisa: Galileo's experiment, 405
Leap year, 483
Learned societies, 410-11
Learning from experience, 33
Lebanon mountains, cedars, 150
Lechfeld, battle, 319
Leeuwenhoek, A., 415
Left-to-right writing, 490
Leibnitz, G., 410, 411, 412, 416
Leiotrichous race, 471
Leisure, 108
Lemnos, Etruscan settlement, 272
Lemur, 41
Lens, 264-5, 352, 406, 415
Leo X, Pope, 392
Leonard of Pisa, 365
Letters of Obscure Men, 391
Leuctra, battle, 245
Levalloisean knife, 78-9, picture, 78
Leviathan (Hobbes) 416, 437
Lévy-Bruhl, L., 81
Lex talionis, 193
"Liberty, Equality, Fraternity," 437
Libraries, 231, 255
Licensing Act (press), 436
Liege lords, 305

Life, 18-24, 26-8, 444. See also Biology
Life after death, hope for, 136, 144, 183, 267-8, 282, 310
Light, in science, 413, 445
Limes, Roman, picture, 281
Linear perspective, 372
Line of demarcation, 387
Linnaeus, 9
Lippershey, Hans, 406
"Lisbon wanderers," 381
Littorina sea, 481, map, 479
Locke, John, 416, 437
Lockyer, Sir Norman, 495
Loess, 76, 167
Loewi, O., 84
Log houses, 111
Logarithms, 402
Logic, of Aristotle, 344
Lombardy, 359, 360
London Company, 422, 423
London skull, 53
Longbow, 376
Longheaded man, 469, 470, 474
Longitude, 261, 399, 404, 410, diagram, 398
Lorenzo the Magnificent, 375
Lothair, Holy Roman Emperor, 316
Louis XVI, of France, 439
Louis the Pious, 316
Lubbock, Sir John, 111
Lucretius, 280
Luther, Martin, 391, 392, 393
Lutherans, 393, 395
Luxor, map, 106
Lyceum, in Athens, 252
Lydia, 201, 217, 224
Lyell, C., 28

Maat, 144, 184
MacAlister, R. A. S., 96
Macauley's Lays, 281
Macedonia, 245. See also Alexander the Great
Maces, 119
Machiavelli, N., 370
Machin, Henry, 361
Machine Age, 426, 437-8, 440
Madeira, map, 362
Maecenas, 280
Magdalenian culture, 97, 480, picture, 96
Magdeburg hemispheres, 407
Magellan, 389
Magic, 80-83, 85-6, 130; progress retarded by, 80, 100-02, 159, 222-3; typical practices, 48, 95, 171, 222-3, 366, 493-5

Magna Charta, 340
Magna Graeca, 219, 226
Magnetic compass, 336, 339
Magnetism, 445
Magyars, 319, 495
Maimonides, 348
"Mainz, Secret of," 378
"Making the punishment fit the crime," 460
Malocello, Lancelot, 361
Malpighi, M., 404
Malthus, T. R., 448
Mammals: Age of, 27; brain and nervous structure, 33, 35, diagram, 31; curiosity and play, 63.
Man: ancestry and development, 41–54, 28; brain development, 29–40; early career, 59–70; races of, 51–2, 88 92, 468 75. See also Human nature
Manchester School, in economics, 448
Mandible, 43, diagram, 50
Manetho, 484
Mantua, 335
Manufactures. See Commerce and Trade; Industrial Revolution; Machine Age
Manzikert, battle, 330
Maps, 374, 410, diagram, 462
Marathon, 231, 233
Marble, 152
Marcomanni, 288
Marconi, G., 446
Marco Polo, 360–61
Marcus Aurelius, 288, 6, 286
"Marginal population," in economics, 448
Marie Antoinette, 439
Marine insurance, 425
"Maritime Discovery, Age of," 385
Marseilles, 219
Marshall, Sir John, 126
Marston, Alvan T., 53
Martel, Charles, 314
Martin, Saint, of Tours, 309
Mary, Queen of Scots, 395
Maryland, 424
Masaccio, 372
Mas d'Azil, 98, painted pebbles, picture, 96
Massachusetts colony, 423
Massilia, 219
Mastaba, 141, 179, 494, diagrams, 180
"Mastery over Nature," 64
"Materialistic philosopher, the," 347
Mathematics: ancient, 155–8, 251; medieval and modern, 336, 365, 402, 404, 408–9, 412

Matthew of Paris, 341
Mathildan lands, 364
Matmaking, 112
Matter (substance), in philosophy and science, 221, 226–8, 250, 413, 446–7, 451
Matthew, W. D., 49
Mauer jaw, 51, picture, 50
Mayflower, 423
Mayow, John, 414
Mecca, 312
Mechanical power, 426
Mechanics, in science, 404–6, 412
Mechanistic theory: applied to man, 16, 19, 23–4, 416–17, 449–50, 465–7; economic and social, 441, 448–9, 451–2; scientific, 416, 442–8, 450–51
Mecklenburgian moraine, map, 479
Medes, 198–201, 216, 224
Medicean portolani, diagram, 362
Medici, de', 374–5
Medicine and surgery, 158–9, 179, 261–4, 337, 338, 365, 402 4, 447
Medicine men, 81
Medieval Period and History, 301–82. See also topics such as Crusades, Law, by name
Medina, 312
Mediterranean, as cultural region, 76, 105
Mediterranean climate, 107
Mediterranean race, 89, 92, 471, 474–5; Pelasgian of Greece, 207, 210; Indo-European nomads, 162; Semites, 159–60
Megalithic culture, 475, 493
Megiddo, 197
Memory, 14, 33, 43, 129
Memphis (Egypt), 147, map, 106
Mendel, G., 20; laws, 19, diagram, 20
Mendicant orders, 357
Menes, 143, 147
Menghin, Oswald, 77, 164, 176
Men Keure, 182
Mentality: basis in brain, 30, 32–3, 37; development, 42, 44, 61–6; ideas (rational thought), 129–31; "types," civilized, 109, early ancient, 172, 184–5, Greek, 207, 215–16, 220, 222, modern, 428, 429, 435, 438–40, 457–67, possible future, 466. See also Consciousness; Intelligence; Temperament
Mercantilist system, 438, 424
Merchant guilds, 359
Merimde, Egypt, 140
Merovingian Kings, 314
Mesocephalic head, 469

Mesolithic culture, 101, 480
Mesopotamia, 108, 109, 117, 157, 235
Mesozoic era, 27, 28, 32–3
Metal, early use, 121
Meteoric iron, 195
Meteorology, 408
Metius, John, 406
Michelangelo, 466
Microliths, 98
Microscope, 404, 411, 415, 265
Migrations, 165–8, 210–11, 288, 297–8, 300
Milan, 292, 294, 335
Millot, J., 472
Milvian Bridge, battle, 294
Mind. See Mentality
Mind in the Making, 131
Mindel glaciation, 73
Mindel-Riss interglacial, 73–4, 78
Mining, technology stimulated by, 407, 426
Minoan culture, 150–52, 208–9, 235–6
Minorite controversy, 377
Minos, labyrinth, 209
Minotaur, 209
Minutes of circle and of time, 157
Miocene, 28
Miracle plays, 339
"Missing Link," 46
Mitanni, 194, 197
Mithraism, 206–7, 283–4
Moabite stone and script, 487, 488
Model Parliament, 342
Modern Period and History, 385–467. See also topics such as England, Exploration, by name
Mohammed, 312
Mohenjodaro civilization, 126
Molar teeth, 51
Mollusks, 27
Moluccas, 390
Monasticism, 309
Money, 172, 217, 286, 304, 420, 452
Mongoloid race, 88, 162, 469, 471, 475
Monism, in physical theory, 446–7
Monkey, 37, 41, diagram, 34
Monogenetic theory of human races, 88
Monopoly, 358, 373, 385, 387, 390, 394, 397, 421, 424–7, 438
Monotheistic religion, 189, 204
Montelius, G. O. A., 115, 494
Moon months, 193, 482
Moon, origin, 17
Moraines, 74
Morals, Socratic teaching, 248

Morgan, Henry, 425
Morgan, T. H., 19
"Morning Stars" of the Renaissance, 369
Morris, Gouverneur, 439
Mosaic disease virus, 22
Mosses, 27
Motion and change, 227–8, 404, 412
Mountains, origin of, 26
Mount Carmel. See in index Carmel, Mount
Mounted warriors, 164
Movement, brain center, diagram, 34
Mud flats, as cradles of civilization, 117, 119, 126, 128, 139
Mugharet-es-Skhul (cave), 90
Müller, H. J., 24
Multiple origin of mankind, 469
Multiple proportions, in chemistry, 444–5
Multiplication, in arithmetic, 408, 409
Mummification, 139, 141
Murano, isle of, 373
Mursil (Murshilish), 194
Muscovy Company, 394
Mutations, 24–5
Mycenae, 208, 209, map, 106
Mycerines, 182
Myelin sheath, diagram, 31
Myres, 494

Nabopolassar, 199
Nantes, Edict of, 430
Napoleon, 440
"Napoleon of Ancient Egypt," 197
Nativity, 486
Natural law, 153, 221, 226
"Natural man a noble animal," 437
Natural selection, 25
Naturalistic philosophers, 222
Navigation. See Seafaring
Navy. See in index Warfare
Nazi ideology, 458
Neanderthal man, diagram, 50, 52, 54, 92–3, 474
Nebuchadnezzar, 204, 220
Necho, pharaoh, 211
Neckam, A., 339
Negrito, 468
Negro and Negroid: 88, 468; iron used in Congo, 195; slavery, 380, 423
Neogenesis, laws of, 11
Neolithic Age and culture, 111, 115, 150, 474, 475, 481, 494
Neopallium, 33, diagrams, 31, 34
Nero, 285
Nerva, 286

Nerves and nervous systems, 29–33, *diagram*, 31, 158, 263
Nesting reflex, 33
Netherlands, 395, 397, 421, 432–3
Neurilemma, *diagram*, 31
New Stone Age, 111
Newcomer, 427
Newfoundland, 422
Newton, Isaac, 410, 411–13
Newts, 27
Nicene Creed, 296
Nicomedia, 292
Nile, 107, 138, 482
Nineteenth Dynasty, of Egypt, 197
Nineveh, 199, *map*, 106
Nitrogen, 19
Noah's ark, 118
Nobility, decadence, French, 430
Nomads, 105, 109; Indo-European, 160, 161–8, 475, 481; Mongoloid, 165; Semitic, 159–60, 194
Nordic race, 89, 115, 166, 471, 475
Normans and Normandy, 323–4; Norman conquest of Constantinople, 359–60
Norsemen, 319–24
Northeast and Northwest Passages, 394
"Nothing in excess," 215
Notre Dame de Paris, 357
Nous, in Greek philosophy, 240
Novels, of Justinian, 327
Nude, in Renaissance art, 372
Numbers, 226, 336–7
Numerology, 227

Oannes, 123
Obermaier, 100, 494, *picture*, 96
Observatories, 410–11, early, *pictures*, 223, 398
Obsidian, 152
Occipital region, *diagram*, 34
Ocher, red, 165
Octavian, 278–9
Odo, Count, of Paris, 322
Odoacer, 300
Oersted, H., 445
"Og, the first man," 60
Oglethorpe, 424
Oil painting, 372
Old Testament, Aramaic versions, 199
Oldest rock, 18
Olfactory bulb, *diagram*, 34
Oligocene, 28
Olives, Greek cultivation, 231
Olympiads, 482
Omar Khayyám, 337

Oöcyte, 21
Oracle of Delphi, 222
Oratory, 238
Oriental hypothesis of civilization, 115
Origin of man, 48
Origin of species, 25
Origin of Species (Charles Darwin), 447
Ormuzd, 206
Orosius, 299
Orthodoxy, 295
Osborn, H. F., 18–19
Osiris, 142, 144, 184
Ostracism, 232, 343
Ostrogoths, 297
Overpopulation, as biological and mental stimulus, 65–6
Ovid, 281
Oxford University, 338
Oxidation, 404, 414, 443
Oxygen, 19, 442

Pachomius, Saint, 309
Pacific Ocean, early voyages, 387, 390
Pacioli, Luca, 434
Padua, university, 402
Pain, 33
Painted pebbles, 99–100, 145, *picture*, 96
Painted pottery, 142
Painting: cave man, 97; Renaissance, 371, 372
Palace, Renaissance, 372
Palae-Alpine race, 471
Palate of mouth, 44
Paleozoic era, 18, 27, 28, 32
Palestine: *beginnings*, 6, 90, 108, 110, 150; *history*, 194–5, 197, 200, Jews, 203–5, Philistines and Phoenicians (Canaanites), 210–11
Panama, 388
Pandects, of Justinian, 327
"*Panem et circenses*," 132
Papacy, 308, 318, 363–6, 377
Paper, 378
Papinian, 327
Parabola, 406, *diagram*, 409
Paranthropus, diagram, 45
Paré, Ambroise, 403
Parietal region, 44, *diagram*, 34
Paris, 321, 338, 378
Parliament, 341–2
Parmenides, 227
Parsees (Parsa), 200
Parthenon, 231, 242
Parthians, 200, 276
Pascal, Blaise, 407

Passage graves, 493
Passion, emotional nature, 86
Pasteur, Louis, 447
Patrimony of Peter, 309, 314, 363
Patron, in Roman landowning, 305
Paul, Saint, of Thebes, 309
Pavia, 335
Pavlov, Ivan, 33
Peake, H. J. E., 101, 110, 149, 174, 480, 485, 494
Peasant temperament, 113-4, 163
Peking man, 46, 47, *diagram*, 50
Pelagian heresy, 347
Pelagian race, 207
Peloponnesian Wars: First, 241, Second, 242-4, Third, 244
Penck, A., 73, 477, 480, 481
Pendulum, 405, 410
Penn, William, 424
Pennsylvania, 424
Pepin the Short, 314
Percussion, bulb, 78
Percussion flaking, 93
Periander of Corinth, 215-6
Pericles, 240-43
Peripli, 374
Perry, W. J., 109, 494
Persia and Persians, 68, 162, 198-201, 205-6, 216, 335
Personality. *See* Mentality; Temperament
Perspective, 372
Peter's patrimony, 309, 314, 363
Peter the Hermit, 332
Petrarch, 369
Petrie, Flinders, 146, 186, 485
Pett, Phineas, 410
Pfefferkorn, J., 391
Pharaoh, 143
Pharmouthi, Egyptian month, 484
Pharos, of Alexandria, 255, *picture*, 265
Phidias, 242
Philip Augustus, 364, 366
Philip of Macedon, 245
Philip II of Spain, 394, 395, 396
Philippines, 387
Philistines, 210
Phillips, J., 28
Philosophy, 221-2, 238, 240, 248-52, 346-51
Phlegm, in Greek medicine, 263
Phlogiston, 414, 442, 443
Phoenicians, 210-11; alphabet, 487, 488, *diagram*, 489
Phonograms, 145, 186

Photons, 413
Photosynthesis, 19
Physics: Greek speculation, 221-2, 225-8, 264-5; medieval, *picture*, 325, 352; modern, 404-8, 410, 411-13, 442, 443-7, 450-51
Physiology, 158, 263, 403, 414
Pictographs, Indus culture, 128
Pile dwellings, Po valley, 271
Pilgrims, medieval, 330, 358
Piltdown man 51, 52, 78, 88, *diagram*, 50
Piracy, 216, 421, 425
Piraeus, 242
Piriform mace, 119, 142
Pisa, 360, 405
Pisistratus, 231
Pithecanthropus erectus, 45, 46, 47, 88, 474, *diagram*, 50
Pit houses, 112, 167
Pittacus, 215
Pizarro, Francisco, 388
Plague, 243, 419
Planetary motion, 255-60, 401, 402
Plasticity, nervous and mental, 33, 114
Plataea, battle, 234
Plato, 248, 249-51, 347, 416
Play, 15, 63
Pleasure and pain, 33
Pleistocene, 28, 73. *See also* Ice Age
Pliny the Younger, quoted on Christians, 290
Pliocene, 28, 49, 55, 67
Plow, 111, 179, *picture*, 180
Plymouth Company, 422
Pneumatics, physics and chemistry, 415
Pneumatism, medicine, 403, 263
Poetry, medieval, 339
Points d'Aurignac, 93
Poitiers, battle, 376
Poland, 166
Polarized-membrane theory of nervous action, *diagram*, 31
Polemarch, 212
Polestar: astronomical theory, 153, *diagram*, 154, 182, 257, *diagram*, 206, 401; in navigation, 211, 400
Polished stone, 111
Political Organization: "anthill" (warrior-religious or group), 171-3, 125, 192-3, 195-6, 198, 458; city-states, 171, 212, 215-16; democracy, 163, 218, 228-30, 232-5, 271, 273-4, 341-3; despotism (Persia, Alexander, Rome), 198, 245-7, 278-80, 282, 285, 288-9, 291-4; medieval, 304-6, 315-18, 321-3, 326-8, 340-

43, 365, modern, 368, 429-36; representative government, 234
Polycentric development of mankind, 469
Polychrome art, 97
Polygenetic theory of human races, 88
Pomeranian moraine, *map*, 479
Ponce de Léon, Juan, 388
Pope. *See in index* Papacy; also individual popes by name
Popham, George, 422
Population, 65-6, 417, 421
Porto Bello, 388
Portolani, 374
Portugal, 385, 386, 387, 395, *map*, 362
Posts and posting service, 280, *picture*, 281
Post-Würmian time, 74, 480
Potato, 420
Potsherds, 113
Potter's wheel, 174
Pottery, 112-13, 120, 140, 166, *pictures*, 127, 180
Power, mechanical, as economic and social force, 426
Pre-Boreal climate, 481
Precession of equinoxes, Stonehenge dating, 495
Predmost man, 475
Prejudice, emotional stimulant, 86
Press, freedom of, 433, 436
Pressure flaking, 93, 141
Prester, John, 379
Prevailing westerlies, *diagrams*, 75
Prices, 217, 286, 420
Priestley, Joseph, 442
Primary Era (geol.), 28
Primates, 36, 41, 42, *diagram*, 34
Primitive thought, 80-83, 86, 138, 139
Princeps, 279
Prince, The (Machiavelli), 370
Principia (Newton), 412-13
Printing, 378-9, 406, 433, 436
Prodigies, 466
Productive capacity, as key to progress, 418
Profit motive, 358, 457-9, 464
Prognathism, 43
Progress, 64-6, 67-73, 79; backwardness from faith in magic, 54-5, 80-83, 86-7, 100-2; civilized living with agriculture, tools, 105-9, 110-11; community life, (city, state), 124-6, 148, 171-3, 207; *fundamental needs*, food surplus, shelter, clothing, 97, 108-9, 418-19, leisure, security, freedom, 108-9, 135-6, mental,

spiritual, aspirations, 96-7, 135-6, 239, 267-9, release from custom-ridden thought, 157-9, 168, 176. *See also* Freedom of thought; Human nature; Political organization; Scientific thought; Social organization; and specific advances and events such as Alphabet, Crusades, Democracy, by name
Propertius, 281
Property rights, 124
Prophets, Jewish, 205
Prospectatores, 494
Protagoras, 238
Proteius, 19, 23
Proterozoic era, 27, 29
Protestantism, 391-3, 430
Proto-Australoid race, 471
Proto-Negroid race, 471
Protons, 447
Protozoans, 22
Provençal culture, extinction, 366-7
Psychology, 4, 6, 7, 38-9, 416-17, 449-50. *See also* such topics as Child mentality, Intelligence, by name
Ptolemies, Egyptian rulers, 255, 274
Ptolemy, astronomer, 261, 381, 401
Publicans, 275
Pumpelly, R., 149
Pumps, 407, 427
Punishment, in criminal law, 460-61
Punjabi, 126
Puritans, English, 433
Putting-out system, 427
Pyramids, 181, 183; stepped, 123, *picture*, 127
Pythagoras of Crotona, philosopher, 226
Pythagoras of Samos, astronomer, 255
Pythagorean theorem, 227
Pytheas of Massilia, 219

Qatna, 195
Quadi, 288
Quadririum, 338
Quaternary Era (geol.), 28
Qûs in Egypt, 146

Ra, sun-god, 143
"Race suicide," 287, 366
Races of mankind, 51-2, 88-92, 468-75
Radio, 445
Radioactivity, 451, 18, 26, 450
Radium, 446
Rage, 84
Ragunda Lake and Pause, 479-81
Raleigh, Sir Walter, 422

Rameses or Ramses, pharaohs, 197, 210, 484
Range needed by primitive family, 66
Rapier, prehistoric, 495
Ras-Shamra script, 487
Raymond, Archbishop of Toledo, 338
Re, sun-god, 143
Real estate, 124, 342
Reality, 221–2, 225–6, 296, 347, 465–6
Reason, 250, 347–50. See also Intelligence
Reccared, 313
Receptor-effector nervous system, 29
Recessive characteristics in heredity, 21
Rechenmeister, 410
Red ocher, funeral use, 166
Red race, 468
Reed boats, 119
Reflex, 30, 33, 83
Reflex arcs, 30, diagram, 31
Reformation, Protestant, 391–3
Regeneration, cultural. See Decadence and regeneration
Reginald of Piperno, 349
Regiomontanus, 401
Relativity, 465
Religion: beginnings among primitives, 80–82, 131, 138–9; early ancient, 171–2, 151, 235; emperor worship, 246, 279, 289, 293; need for, 136, 267–8, 282–3; present and future status, 465–7, 38; specific faiths, Egyptian, 138–9, 144, 183–4, 189–90, fire worship, 205, Greek, 225, 226–8, 246, 267–8, Hindu, 128, Jewish, 203–5, Minoan, 151–2, Mithraism, 206, 283–4, Roman, 279, 282–4, Sumerian, 125, Syrian, 142, Zoroastrianism, 205–6. See also Christianity
Religious freedom, 246–7, 289, 393, 431, 436
Renaissance, 368–73, 375–6, 419
Rent, 125, 193
Representative government, 234, 341, 342
Reproduction, in biology, 22, 27
Reptiles, 27, 32–3, diagram, 31
Republic. See Democracy
Reuchlin, Johann, 391
Revival of Learning, 370
Revolt, Protestant, 391–3
Revolution, geologic, 26
Revolution, political. See by name, as American R.
Rhetoric, 238
Rhine R., 288, 335
Rhodes, 209
Ricardo, David, 448

"Richest Roman of them all," 276
Riddle, Oscar, 23
Ripley, W. Z., 89
Riss glaciation, 73
Riss-Würm interglacial, 74
Riveted tools, 122, picture, 180
Roads, Roman, 280, picture, 281
Roanoke Island, 422
Robbia, della, 371, 372
Robert of Chester, 338
Robert the Strong (France), 322
Robinson, J. H., 131
Rock, oldest, 18
Roentgen, W., 446
Rogari, El, 339
Roger Guiscard, 338
Roger II of Sicily, 338
Rolf, Duke of Normandy, 323
Roman culture and people, 270–300; appraisal of contributions, 270–71, 303; calendar and chronology, 482; economic organization, 274–6, 279, 285–6, 292; Latin language and literature, 280–81, 496, 491–2, 370; law, 304, 326–7, 365, 367, 460; roads, 280, picture, 281; social organization, 270–1, 272, 274–5, 278, 279–84, 286–7, 292, 304–5; sword, 495; temperament, 272, 273. See also Eastern Empire, Roman
Roman Catholicism, 307, 308
Romance languages, 162
Rome, city of, 272–3, 279, 281, 292, 299, 300, 378, 486. See also Roman
Romulus Augustus, 300
Roundheaded man, 469, 470, 474
Rousseau, Jean Jacques, 437
Royal Society, 411
Royal tombs, Erech, 176
Rubianus, Crotus, 391
Rumford, Count, 443–4
Rupar, 126
Rutherford, W., 446

Saad, Zaki Effendi, 147
Sabre-toothed tiger, 56
Sacks of Rome, 299, 300
Sacraments, 347
Sahara, 49, 76, 107
Saint. See by name
Saint Clair-sur-Epte, Treaty, 323
Sakkara, 147, 179, map, 106
Saladin tithe, 341
Salamis, 230, 233
Salerno, 324, 338
Sallust, 280

Saloniki, 288
Salvian of Marseilles, 304
Samaria, fall, 204
"Sanctified work," 433
San Giorgio, bank, 359
Sanitation, early, 126, 127, 243
Sanskrit, 496
Sargon of Akkad, 177
Sargon II, of Assyria, 204
Saros, 221
Satan, 206, 311, 355
Satem speech, 496
Savery, T., 427
Saxons, 300
Scandinavia, 162, 166, 477–9
Scanian pause, of Ice Age, 480
"Scarcity, economy of," 453
Scharff, 484, 485
Scheele, K. W., 442
Schleiden, M., 447
Scholasticism, 346–50, 353
Schools and Universities, 250, 252, 324, 338, 365, 411
Schwann, Theodor, 447
Science: beginnings, 124, 153–5; Greek, 220–2, 228, 249, 261–4, 268; medieval, picture, 325, 335–9, 347, 351–3, 365; modern, 368, 399–417, 442–8, 450–51, 464; principles, experimental method, 228, 249, 265, 351–3, hypotheses, 249, intellectual rigor, 131, 225–8, 263, 413; mathematical aids, 404–5, 408–10, 412–13; ultimate limitations, 350, 449–51, 465–6
Sculpture, 94, 371, 372
Scutage, 341
Scyths, 176, 200
Seafaring: ancient, 123, 150–52, 210, 216, 219; charts and maps, 374, 410; compass, 336, 339; Italian, 360–63, 374, 379; latitude and longitude, 399–404, 410; Norse (Viking) 324, picture, 320; Portuguese (incl. Henry the Navigator), 379–81, map, 362, 389; Spanish, 381–2, 385–8, 389–90
Seasons, 259
Secondary Era (geol.), 28
Seconds of arc and of time, 157
Security, 108, 109
"Seeing red" (rage), 84
Seirites, 188
Seleucia, 221
Self-aggrandizement. See Human nature
Self-awareness, self-consciousness. See Consciousness

Self-esteem, 131
Seljuk Turks, 330
Semantic center in brain, 44, diagram, 34
Semites, 159–60, 176–7; alphabet, 186–9, 487–91, tables, 187, 489; Amorites (Amurru), 194; Assyrians, 198–9; Babylonians, 192–3; Aramaic, 199; Islamic Arabs, 312; Jews, 150, 203–5; Palestinian predecessors, 150; Phoenicians, 150, 203
Senate, Roman, 273
Sense centers of brain, diagram, 34
Sense impressions, 11, 12
Senusert (Senwosri), 484
Sequence dates, 485
Serabit mines, 187
Serapis, 283
Serfdom, 305, 306, 340, 365, 428
Sergi, G., 89
Set, god, 142
Seven Books of History against the Pagans, 299
Seven Wise Men, 215–16, 229–30
Sexagesimal arithmetic, 157
Shakespeare, 466
Shalmaneser, 198
Shamans, 81
Shatterbelt of primitive races, 470
Shelter, 92, 93–4, 111–12; caves in Europe, farming promotes, 109; first houses, 111; mud-flat (reed and rush) homes, 119–20, 140; nomad, 161, 165
"Shepherd Kings" of Egypt, 195
Sheriff, first, 321
Shinar, land of, 123
Shinn, Millicent, 12
Ships and boats, 119, 147, 324, 380, 393–4, pictures, 265, 320
Shire, origin, 321
Shrew, brain, 35
Sibilants, letters for, 490
Sic et non, 344
Sicily, 219, 226, 324, 338, 364
Sidon and Sidonians, 211
Siegecraft, Assyrian, 199
Sight, 36, brain center, diagram, 34
Sigismund of Hungary, 377–8
Silk growing, 360
Siloam tunnel script, 488
Silver, monetary use, 217, 420
Simiidae, 35, 41
Simon de Montfort, 341, 366
Simple reflexes, 32, 33
Simpson's Ice Age theory, diagrams, 476
Sinai, Mount, map, 106

Sinai Peninsula, 93, 110, 142, 185, 186–8
Sinaitic script, 188, 487
Sinanthropus Pekinensis, 46, 47, 88, 474
Sind, 126
"Singeing the Spanish King's beard," 396
Single origin of mankind, 469
Sirius, 483, 484
Siva, origin, 128
Skeletal tests of race, 89
Skeleton, 27
Skepticism, 220
Skhul race of men, 90, 475
Skin color, as race test, 88, 468, 472
Skull, 43, 48
Slavery: ancient, 172–3, 217, 239, 267, 274, 306; Negro, 380, 423
Slavic languages, 162
Slavs, 319
Slip, on pottery, 120
Slow wheel, in pottery, 174
Smell, 36, *diagram,* 34
Smelting, Egyptian picture, 180
Smith, Adam, 438, 448, 458, 427
Smith, G. Elliot, 36, 42
Smith, Capt. John, 422
Smith, Preserved, 369
Social conditioning, 462
"Social contract," 436–7
"Social instinct," 71
Social organization, 69–73; basic needs, 108, 128; group control ("anthill"), 171–3, 125, 189–90, 192–3, 239, 291–4; individual interest recognized, 217–18, 239, 310, 328, 417–19, 428; mental and spiritual controls, 239, 248–9, 267–8; present-day gains and needs, 454–67; *viewpoints and theories,* medieval, 304–6, 307–8, 328, 358–9, modern economic, 428, 429, 434, modern mechanistic, 449, 452, 454, sound adaptation to human nature, 8, 239, 462–3. *See also* Decadence and regeneration; Human nature; Labor; Political organization; Progress
Sociology, 449
Socketed tools, 174, 122, *picture,* 127
Socrates, 248–9
Solar system, 17, 255–60, 401–2
Solar year, 482, 484
Solo River, hominids, 46
Solon, 229–30
Sophistry, 238, 240
Sophocles, 240
Sorbonne, 338
Sothicycle, 484, 485, 486

Soul, 4, 61, 81, 128, 267, 283; Christian views, 291, 310, 325–6, 346–51; mechanistic explanations, 416–17, 449–50, 37–8
South Africa, as cradle of man, 42–3, 44, 48, *picture,* 45
South Sea, 388
"Sovereign will," in law, 327
Space, 14, 451
Spain, 98, 300, 313, 338, 385–9, 390, 392–7
Spanish Armada, 395–7, 419
Spanish language, 162
Sparta, 241, 242
Spartan League, 244
Spearman, C., 10, 11, 12
Specialization, in biology, 41
Species, origin of, 24–5
Spectacles, 406
Spectral tarsier, brain, 35, *diagram,* 34
Speech, 44, 47, brain center, *diagram,* 34
Spencer, Herbert, 449
Spermatozoa, 21
Spice Islands, 390
Spindle whorls, 149
Spinning, 112
Spinolas, of Genoa, 374
Spinoza, B., 416
Spiritual aspirations, 69, 81, 128, 267–8
Sponges, 27
Spontaneous generation, 447
Spores, 22
Spouts on pots, 142
Sprengling, M., 186–8
Stade (stadium), 260
Staffs of office (magic), 95
Stagner, Ross, 6
Stanley, W. G., 21, 23
Star catalogues, 257, 261
Stars, 153, *diagram,* 154, 259–60, 401–2
"Starvation wage," in economic theory, 448
State. *See* Political organization
Steam engine, 265–7, 426
Stepped pyramid, 123, *pictures,* 127, 179
Steppe horse, 97
Stereoscopic vision, 35
Stilicho, 298
Stoicism, 283
Stonehenge, 493, 494
Stone tools, 93
Straight-haired race, 471
Strength of character, 130
Stuart kings, of England, 423–5, 433–5
Sub-Atlantic climate, 480, 481

Sub-Boreal climate, 480, 481
Subjective personalities, 133-4
Sublimation, Puritan, 433
Suess, Eduard, 26
Sumerian culture and people, 117-26, 173-77, *map*, 106, *pictures*, 127; *beginnings*, 117-23, 115-16, 481; *developments*, agriculture, 124, architecture, 175, 147, arithmetic, 155-6, astronomy, 125, 153, 157-8, brick, 121, commerce, 121, 125-6, 147, 148-9, 150, 151, 165, 494, claywork (ceramics), 120-21, metalworking and tools, 121-2, 165, 151, political and social organization, 125, 173, 176-7, pottery 120-21, 174, religion, 125, 139, wheel, 173-4, 165
Summa contra Gentiles and *Summa Theologica*, 349
Sun: astronomical views, 17, 225, 240, 255-60; worship of (Egypt), 143-4, 184, 189
Sundial, *diagram*, 223
Sun-dried bricks, 121
Sunspots discovered, 406
Suppiluyuma, 197
Surgery. *See* Medicine and Surgery
Surplus, progress depends upon, 168, 418-19, 456
"Survival of the fittest," biology, 25, economic theory, 448
Susa, 193, *map*, 106
Swanscombe man, 53, 78, 88
Sword, 495
Syene, 260
Sylvester II, Pope, 325
Symbolization, 100, 145, painted pebbles, *picture*, 96
Synapse, of nerve, *diagram*, 31
Synodic month, 482
Synthesis, 347
Syracuse, Sicily, 219, 244
Syria, 108, 110, 142, 194-5, 197, 200

Tabenna, monastery, 309
Tabula rasa, 416
Tabun, et, 90
Taine, *L'Ancien Régime*, quoted, 317
Tardenoisian culture, 98
Tarsier, brain, *diagram*, 34
Tasian culture, 140, 485
Taurodonty, *diagram*, 50
Taxation, 275-6, 279, 304, 316, 340-42, 365
Tax farmers, 275
Tayacian culture, 90

Taylor, H. O., 369
Taylor, W. G., 470
Teeth, 44, 46, 51
Telescope, 406, 410, 415, 265
Tell, 115
Tell el-Amarna letters, 190, 200, 210, 203
Tell Halaf, 116, 174, *map*, 106
Temperament: early development, 70-72, 113, 123, 138-9; "*types*," 132-5, exploitive, 163-4, peasant, 113-14, 163
Temperate zone, 74, *diagrams*, 75
Templars, Knights, 334
Temporal region, brain, *diagram*, 34
Ten tribes of Israel, 204
Terracotta, 373
Terremare dwellings, 271
Terre pisée, 120
Tertiary Era (geol.), 28
Tetzel, John, 392
Teuton (Nordics), 89, 115, 166, 471, 475; invasions of Rome, 297-300; language, 162, 496; law, 305, 327
Textile industry, 426
Thales of Miletus, 220-22, 262
Thames River human fossils, 52
Theater, Athenian, 231-2, 242
Thebes, Egypt, *map*, 106
Thebes (Greece), 245, 488
Themistocles, 233
Theodosius I, 298
Theodosius II, 327
Thera, script, 488
Thermocoagulation of brain, 39
Thespis, 231-2
Thessalonica, 288
"Thinker type" of mentality, 133, 134-5
Third Dynasty (Egypt), 179-80, 181, 485, plow, *picture*, 180
Thomas Aquinas, 349-50
Thomas à Becket, 341
Thomism, 349
Thompson, B., 443-4
Thompson, J. W., 303
Thomson, Sir J. A., 24
Thomson, J. J., 446
Thomson, W., 450
Thorndike, L., 270, 368-9
Thorne, Robert, letter, 386, 389
Thoth, Egyptian month, 483
Thucydides, 229, 253
Thutmose I, II, III, of Egypt, 197
Tiberius, 285, 287, 486
Tidal, King of Goiim, 203
Tidal hypothesis of earth's origin, 17

Tigris River, 108, *map*, 106
Timaeus, 250
Time and timekeeping, 14, 405, 410, 411, *picture*, 266, *diagram*, 398. *See also* Chronology
Timocharis, 257
Tin, 150, 174, 175, 495
Tiryns, 208, 209, *map*, 106
Tobacco, in Virginia, 423
Tobacco mosaic virus, 23
Todd, T. Wingate, 469
Toledo, Moslem learning, 338
Toleration Act, 436
Tombs, 141, 176, 179, *diagram*, 180, 181, 493–4
Tools: beginnings, 47, 55, 64, 69, 78–9; early stone, *picture*, 78, 93, 98, 109, 111; metal, 121, 122, 174, 495; wheel (cart and potter's), 174
Tordesillas, treaty, 387
Toricelli, E., 407
Torquemada, 393
Tortems, 100, 141
Torture, 367
Torus, of primitive skulls, 51, 52
Touch, brain center, *diagram*, 34
Tournette, in pottery, 174
Tours, battle, 314
Tower of Babel, 123
Traction plow, 179, *picture*, 180
Trade. *See* Commerce
Trade guilds, 358
Trade winds, 107, 381, *diagrams*, 75, *map*, 362
Trajan, quoted on Christians, 291
Transylvanian Alps, 167
Tree life, 36, 42
Tree shrew, brain, *diagram*, 34
"Tribute Money," fresco, 372
Trigonometry, 261
Trinil fossil hominids, 46
Trinitarianism, 295, 307
Triticum (wheat), 110, 126
Trivium, 338
Troad, 153
Tronder race, 475
Tropical year, 483
Troubadours, 339
Trouvères, 339
Troy, 150, 209, 495, *map*, 106
Truce of God, 331
"True to type," in biology, 22
Truth, scientific test, 130, 153
Tumilat, Egypt, 195
Tundra, in Europe, 76

Tupaia, 37
Turkestan, 49, 57, 148–50
Turkish, language, 495
Tuscany, medieval, 360
Tutenkhamon, 197
Twelfth Dynasty in Egypt, 177, 185, 484
Tycho Brahe, 401–2
Tylor, Sir E. B., 80
Type, metal, 132
Type, printing, 378
Tyranny, 218–20, 230
Tyre, 211, 254
Tyrrhenian sea, 272
Tyrsenians, 272

'Ubaid, al, culture, 116, 117–22
Ucello, Paolo, 372
Ugarit, 487
Ukraine, 166
Ulotrichous race, 471
Ultima Thule, 219
Ultraviolet radiation, 446
Unicellular animals, 22, 27
United States: exploration and colonization, 388–9, 421–4; independence, 438–9; progress, 440, 453–4
Universe, theories of, 225, 227, 240, 250, 452, 455, 465–6
Universities and schools, 250, 252, 324, 338, 365, 411
Ur, 118, *map*, 106
Ural race, 471
Uralic, language, 495
Uranium as key to geologic age, 18
Urban II, Pope, 332

Vacuum, in physics, 407
Valens, 297
Vandals, 300
Van Eyck, 371, 372
Vanity, 131
Variations, in heredity, 24–5
Varro, chronology, 486
Varve dating, 478–80
Vassals, 305
Vaviloff, 110
Veneziano, Domenico, 372
Venice, 331, 359–60, 373–4, 378, 379, 397
"Venuses" in primitive art, 97, *picture*, 96
Verde, Cape, 387, 380
Verdun, Treaty and Partition, 316
Vergil, 280
Vertebrate structure, 27

Vesalius, Andreas, 402
Vespucci, Amerigo, 388
Vikings, 319–20
Villanovan culture, 271
Vincent of Beauvais, 351
Vinci, Leonardo da, 464
Vinegar fly, 19
Virginia, first ship built in North America, 422
Virginia, settlement, 422
Virus, 27, 22
Visigoths, 297, 313
"Vital air," 442
Vitalist theory of life, 23–4
"Vital spirit," 24, 414
Vivaldi, of Genoa, 374
Volta, A., 445
Voltaire, 432
Vowels, in alphabet, 488, 490
Vulgar chronology, 486

Wadi Hammamet, 146, map, 106
Wages, 217, 420, 448, 452
Waldseemüller, 388
Walking, specialization for, 42
Walter the Penniless, 332
Warfare: land, armies, 125, 195–6, 198, 275, 288, 293, horses and chariots, 164, 195, longbow and gunpower, 376, siegecraft, 199; naval, 233, 393–4, 396, 440
Warrior-religious states, 171–3
Washington, George, 439, birth date, 485
Waste, as social distinction, 426
Watches, for time, 411
Water, 18, 221, 443
Watling Street, 321
Watson, J. B., 37
Watt, James, 427
Wattle-and-daub houses, 111
Wavy-haired race, 471
Wealth of Nations (Adam Smith), 427, 438
Weather, science of, 408
Weaving, 112
Wedmore, Treaty, 321
Weidenreich, F., 44, 469
Welsh, language, 162
Weltmacht, 458
Westerly winds, 76, 107, 164, diagrams, 75
Westermann, W. L., 219

Western Roman Empire, formation and fall, 292, 300
Wheat, 110, 126
Wheel, 173, 165
White, John, of Carolina, 422
White race, 5, 6, 88, 89, 468, 469, 475
William of Champeaux, 344
William, of England: I (the Conqueror), 340; III, 425, 436
William of Orange, 395
Winckler, H., 194
Winged bull, 235
Wireless telegraphy, 446
Wisby, 360
Wishful thinking, 130, 133–4
Witch, 81, 366
Witch doctors, 81
Wöhler, F., 447
Wood tools, 77
Wool, 112, 162, 334, 358
Woolly-haired race, 471
Woolley, L., 118, 120, 176
Words, brain center for, 44
Working week, 454
World War of 1914–18, social and economic upheavals, 454
Worms, 27
Worms, Germany, 363, 392
Writing, 100, 144, 145; alphabetic, 185–8, 487 92; cuneiform method, picture, 127; Indus pictographs, 128; region for in brain, diagram, 34
Wundt, W., 449
Würmian glaciation, 73, 92, 480
Wycliffe, John, 377, 378

X rays, 24–5, 446

Yahveh (Jehovah), 203
Year, in chronology, 481
Yellow race, 88, 468
Yerkes, R. M., 14
Yoldia Sea, 481, map, 479

Zacharias, Pope, 314
Zenophanes, 226, 227
Zero, as number, 336–7
Ziggurat, 123, 125, picture, 127
Zoroastrianism, 205–6
Zoser, of Egypt, 179, 485
Zwingli, Ulrich, 392